T0192026

Lecture Notes in Computer Science 13107

More information about this subseries at https://link.springer.com/bookseries/7410

Robert Deng · Feng Bao · Guilin Wang ·
Jian Shen · Mark Ryan · Weizhi Meng ·
Ding Wang (Eds.)

Information Security Practice and Experience

16th International Conference, ISPEC 2021
Nanjing, China, December 17–19, 2021
Proceedings

 Springer

Editors
Robert Deng 🆔
Singapore Management University
Singapore, Singapore

Guilin Wang
School of Computer Science
University of Wollongong
Wollongong, NSW, Australia

Mark Ryan
School of Computer Science
University of Birmingham
Birmingham, UK

Ding Wang
Nankai University
Tianjin, China

Feng Bao
Huawei International
Singapore, Singapore

Jian Shen
Nanjing University of Information Science
and Technology
Nanjing, China

Weizhi Meng
Danmarks Tekniske Universitet
Kongens Lyngby, Denmark

ISSN 0302-9743 ISSN 1611-3349 (electronic)
Lecture Notes in Computer Science
ISBN 978-3-030-93205-3 ISBN 978-3-030-93206-0 (eBook)
https://doi.org/10.1007/978-3-030-93206-0

LNCS Sublibrary: SL4 – Security and Cryptology

This Springer imprint is published by the registered company Springer Nature Switzerland AG
The registered company address is: Gewerbestrasse 11, 6330 Cham, Switzerland

Preface

The 16th International Conference on Information Security Practice and Experience (ISPEC 2021) was held in Nanjing, China, during December 17–19, 2021, and hosted by the Nanjing University of Information Science and Technology (NUIST), China.

ISPEC is an annual conference that brings together researchers, scholars, and practitioners to provide a confluence of new information security technologies, including their applications and their integration with IT systems in various vertical sectors. In previous years, ISPEC has taken place in Singapore (2005), Hangzhou, China (2006), Hong Kong, China (2007), Sydney, Australia (2008), Xi'an, China (2009), Seoul, South Korea (2010), Guangzhou, China (2011), Hangzhou, China (2012), Lanzhou, China (2013), Fuzhou, China (2014), Beijing, China (2015), Zhangjiajie, China (2016), Melbourne, Australia (2017), Tokyo, Japan (2018), and Kuala Lumpur, Malaysia (2019).

The competition for acceptance in the conference proceedings is very fierce. This year, the conference received 94 submissions from authors in 14 countries/regions. At least three reviewers were assigned to each submission. Each reviewer carefully reviewed and discussed the submissions' novelty, practical application, and technical quality to reach a common conclusion. Finally, 24 of the papers were accepted and are included in this Springer volume, giving an acceptance rate of 26%. The topics of the accepted papers cover multiple aspects of information security, from technologies to systems and applications. Nowadays, information security technology has penetrated all walks of life, the importance and actual impact have been reflected in different industries and businesses. However, there is still a broad space for innovative applications and development. Therefore, ISPEC seeks to bring together researchers, scholars, and participators in the area of information security to address challenges and present effective solutions in practice.

ISPEC 2021 was organized through the joint efforts of numerous people around the world, and we would like to thank them for their continual dedication and support. First of all, we want to extend our sincere thanks to all the Program Committee members for their hard work of reading, reviewing, commenting on, and debating the submitted papers; we are deeply grateful for their contribution of time, energy, and wisdom in this process. There is no doubt that this was highly beneficial for. The committee also invited external reviewers to review papers, which helped expand the professional knowledge, and we thank them for providing more diverse comments and insights.

Last but not least, we would like to express our gratitude to the authors and attendees for their support, and we thank all of our generous sponsors.

November 2021

Guilin Wang
Jian Shen
Mark Ryan

Preface

Organization

Steering Committee

Feng Bao   Huawei Shield Lab, Singapore
Robert H. Deng   Singapore Management University, Singapore

General Chair

Guilin Wang   Huawei Shield Lab, Singapore

Program Chairs

Jian Shen   Nanjing University of Information Science and Technology, China
Mark Ryan   University of Birmingham, UK

Web Chairs

Leiming Yan   Nanjing University of Information Science and Technology, China
Yongjun Ren   Nanjing University of Information Science and Technology, China

Publicity Chairs

Ding Wang   Nankai University, China
Weizhi Meng   Technical University of Denmark, Denmark

Technical Program Committee

Man Ho Au   Hong Kong Polytechnic University, Hong Kong
Joonsang Baek   University of Wollongong, Australia
Pascal Berrang   University of Birmingham, UK
Aniello Castiglione   University of Salerno, Italy
Jiageng Chen   Central China Normal University, China
Xiaofeng Chen   Xidian University, China
Yueqiang Cheng   Baidu, USA
Kim-Kwang Raymond Choo   University of Texas at San Antonio, USA
Sherman S. M. Chow   Chinese University of Hong Kong, Hong Kong

Josep Domingo-Ferrer	Universitat Rovira i Virgili, Spain
Jose Maria de Fuentes	Universidad Carlos III de Madrid, Spain
Carmen Fernández-Gago	University of Malaga, Spain
José M. Fernandez	Ecole Polytechnique de Montreal, Canada
Dieter Gollmann	Hamburg University of Technology, Germany, and National University of Singapore, Singapore
Dimitris Gritzalis	Athens University of Economics and Business, Greece
Stefanos Gritzalis	University of the Aegean, Greece
Gerhard Hancke	City University of Hong Kong, Hong Kong
Debiao He	Wuhan University, China
Shoichi Hirose	University of Fukui, Japan
Xinyi Huang	Fujian Normal University, China
Julian Jang-Jaccard	Massey University, New Zealand
Hiroaki Kikuchi	Meiji University, Japan
Kwangjo Kim	Korea Advanced Institute of Science and Technology, South Korea
Noboru Kunihiro	University of Tsukuba, Japan
Miroslaw Kutylowski	Wroclaw University of Science and Technology, Poland
Dengzhi Liu	Jiangsu Ocean University, China
Costas Lambrinoudakis	University of Piraeus, Greece
Albert Levi	Sabanci University, Turkey
Shujun Li	University of Kent, UK
Tieyan Li	Huawei International Pte Ltd, Singapore
Wenting Li	Peking University, China
Yingjiu Li	Singapore Management University, Singapore
Kaitai Liang	University of Surrey, UK
Joseph Liu	Monash University, Australia
Zhe Liu	Nanjing University of Aeronautics and Astronautics, China
Giovanni Livraga	University of Milan, Italy
Jiqiang Lu	Beihang University, China
Rongxing Lu	University of New Brunswick, Canada
Tzu-Chuen Lu	Chaoyang University of Technology, Taiwan
Min Luo	Wuhan University, China
Di Ma	University of Michigan, USA
Weizhi Meng	Technical University of Denmark, Denmark
Chris Mitchell	Royal Holloway, University of London, UK
David Naccache	École Normale Supérieure, France
Takeshi Okamoto	Tsukuba University of Technology, Japan
Kazumasa Omote	University of Tsukuba, Japan
Pedro Peris-Lopez	Carlos III University of Madrid, Spain
Günther Pernul	Universität Regensburg, Germany
Josef Pieprzyk	Queensland University of Technology, Australia
Geong Sen Poh	Singtel, Singapore
C. Pandu Rangan	Indian Institute of Technology, Madras, India

Indrajit Ray	Colorado State University, USA
Na Ruan	Shanghai Jiao Tong University, China
Sushmita Ruj	Indian Statistical Institute, India
Pierangela Samarati	University of Milan, Italy
Jun Shao	Zhejiang Gongshang University, China
Jian Shen	Nanjing University of Information Science and Technology, China
Miguel Soriano	Universitat Politècnica de Catalunya, Spain
Chunhua Su	University of Aizu, Japan
Willy Susilo	University of Wollongong, Australia
Haowen Tan	Chosun University, South Korea
Syh-Yuan Tan	Newcastle University, UK
Jaideep Vaidya	Rutgers University, USA
Chen Wang	University of Aizu, Japan
Cong Wang	City University of Hong Kong, Hong Kong
Ding Wang	Peking University, China
Guilin Wang	Huawei International Pte Ltd, Singapore
Chris Williamson	the SW7 group, UK
Qianhong Wu	Beihang University, China
Shouhuai Xu	University of Texas at San Antonio, USA
Huijie Yang	Nanjing University of Information Science & Technology, China
Toshihiro Yamauchi	Okayama University, Japan
Kuo-Hui Yeh	National Dong Hwa University, Taiwan
Xun Yi	RMIT University, Australia
Yong Yu	Shaanxi Normal University, China
Tsz Hon Yuen	The University of Hong Kong, Hong Kong
Tianqi Zhou	Nanjing University of Information Science & Technology, China
Yuexin Zhang	Swinburne University of Technology, Australia
Yongjun Zhao	Nanyang Technological University, Singapore
Sencun Zhu	The Pennsylvania State University, USA

Additional Reviewers

Takahiro Baba	Partha Sarathi Roy
John Heaps	Minxin Du
Xiuhua Wang	Wenjuan Li
Chengjun Lin	S. J. Yang
Zhi Hu	Wenchang Zhou
Zengpeng Li	Zhuotao Lian
Shenqing Wang	Cheng-Kang Chu
Xiaochao Wei	Yasmin Rehana
Xiao Zhang	Peizhao Hu
Shimin Pan	Handong Cui

Andrei Kelarev

Haiguang Wang

Yuexin Zhang

Xin Kang

Hong Qin

Zhiyan Xu

Junbin Shi

Przemyslaw Blaskiewicz

Fei Zhu

Xianrui Qin

Cailing Cai

Wenjie Yang

Yang Liu

Xuechao Yang

Lukasz Krzywiecki

Haoyang An

Mingli Wu

Krzysztof Majcher

Junwei Luo

Anna Lauks-Dutka

Contents

Efficient Construction of Public-Key Matrices in Lattice-Based Cryptography: Chaos Strikes Again

Zhang Kaiwei[1], Ailun Ma[1], Lyu Shanxiang[1(✉)], Wang Jiabo[2(✉)], and Lou Shuting[1]

[1] College of Cyber Security, Jinan University, Guangzhou 510632, China
lsx07@jnu.edu.cn
[2] Beijing National Research Center for Information Science and Technology, Tsinghua University, Beijing 100084, China
wangjiabo@mail.tsinghua.edu.cn

Abstract. In order to solve the problem of excessive communication overhead in the public-key encryption scheme based on the Learning With Error (LWE) problem, this paper proposes to construct the public-key matrices based on chaotic systems. Specifically, by taking advantages of Logistic mapping, a long pseudo-random sequence is generated from the initial state and the bifurcation parameter. The non-uniform chaotic sequence is further tweaked towards a pseudo-random sequence admitting uniform distributions. The public-key matrix of LWE is therefore constructed efficiently. Simulations confirm the correctness and efficiency of our scheme.

Keywords: Chaotic sequence · Lattice-based cryptography · LWE · Uniform distribution

1 Introduction

The averaged-case lattice problem Learning With Errors (LWE) introduced by Regev is ubiquitous [1], as its computational hardness can be reduced to the worst-case problem of lattices. Given its great potential to cryptographic applications, LWE has attracted a significant amount of research interest from both academia and industry.

In LWE, the public matrix $\mathbf{A} \in \mathbb{Z}_q^{m \times n}$ consists of uniformly distributed random numbers with large dimensions, *i.e.* m, n are both in the order of hundreds or thousands. This poses a great challenge for the transmission of the excessively large amount of public information. The obvious simplification is to resort to the "seeding" method, where only a small amount of seeds are employed to represent the total randomness, which greatly reduces the communication overhead. Therefore, we focus on the seeding-based generation of random numbers in this work.

© Springer Nature Switzerland AG 2021
R. Deng et al. (Eds.): ISPEC 2021, LNCS 13107, pp. 1–10, 2021.
https://doi.org/10.1007/978-3-030-93206-0_1

Recall that random numbers are divided into two classes: true random number (TRN) and pseudo random number (PRN). While TRN has the characteristics of aperiodicity, unpredictability and admitting uniform distributions [2], it often fails to meet the requirements of high-speed computer calculation. Therefore, in order to improve the efficiency of data generation, we investigate the efficient generation of PRN in this work. PRN is generated by a deterministic algorithm which expand a short true random sequence (called seed) into a long pseudo random sequence.

A plenty of research has been carried out in the construction of pseudo-random number generators, including the linear congruence generator [3], the non-linear congruence generator [4] and the class of pseudo-random number generators based on carried addition and borrowed subtraction [5]. Another avenue to construct PRN is based on chaos theory [6–9]. Due to its good pseudo-randomness, unpredictability of orbit and extreme sensitivity to initial state and bifurcation parameters, chaos systems are attractive candidates for PRN generators [10]. This line of works include PRNs based on the one-dimensional Logistic mapping [11], the two-dimensional discrete chaotic mapping [12], and the three-dimensional discrete hyper-chaotic folded-towel mapping [13]. Nevertheless, the above PRN generators are either too complicated or too simple to guarantee sufficient randomness. Moreover, these methods are generated for different purposes in specific scenarios and are not the ideal candidates for public key encryption schemes based on the LWE problem.

Addressing the above issues, the contributions of this paper are two-fold. Firstly, we present a simple improvement over Logistic sequence to derive a uniform distributions. To be specific, a long pseudo-random sequence is generated from the initial state z_1 and bifurcation parameter r based on the Logistic mapping. Using the partition parameter q, the sequence is mapped to the finite field $\mathbb{Z}_q$. Secondly, we present a public-key encryption scheme where the uniform random matrix $\mathbf{A} \in \mathbb{Z}_q^{m \times n}$ is built from our derived uniform sequences. In this way, one can greatly reduce the communication overhead required by public key storage. Moreover, the randomness consumption is also saved because far less entropy is consumed to yield enough pseudo randomness which is computationally indistinguishable from the true randomness. The storage space of matrix $\mathbf{A}$ is also reduced from $m \times n$ dimension matrix to 7 parameters (initial state z_1, bifurcation parameter r, parameter q, sampling initial position i, sampling distance d and matrix size parameters m, n); thus the public key storage space is greatly reduced, making the lattice cipher scheme more efficient.

2   Preliminaries

2.1   The Chaotic System: Logistic Map

Chaos theory is about nonlinear systems exhibiting phenomenons of bifurcations, periodic motions, etc., leading to a certain non-periodic ordered motion. It originates from the "butterfly effect", which means that a subtle change may eventually lead to unpredictable results.

Among many chaotic sequences, the one-dimensional Logistic chaotic system has a wide range of applications due to its low complexity. Logistic chaotic system can be expressed by the following binary recursive equation

$$z'_{n+1} = rz'_n(1 - z'_n),\tag{1}$$

where r is the bifurcation parameter. For any $r \in (3.57, 4]$, the system drives into a chaotic state. As a nonlinear system, the sequence $\{z'_n\}$ has the characteristics of aperiodicity, initial value sensitivity and ergodicity. In addition, it is difficult to predict and analyze the output of chaotic systems.

Consider the Logistic map in the form of (1). If $r = 4$, the probability density function of Eq. (1) becomes [14]

$$\rho(y) = \begin{cases} \pi^{-1}/[y(1 - y)]^{1/2}, & 0 < y < 1, \\ 0, & \text{others.} \end{cases}\tag{2}$$

It can be seen from Eq. (2) that the sequence produced is non-uniformly distributed and does not meet the conditions for generating random sequence. Therefore, it is necessary to transform the non-uniformly distributed random variables to uniformly distributed random variables.

2.2   LWE and the Encryption Scheme

With $\mathbf{A} \in \mathbb{Z}_q^{m \times n}$ uniformly generated, $\mathbf{s} \in \mathbb{Z}_q^n$, and $\mathbf{e} \in \mathbb{Z}_q^m$ generated by the distribution χ, we construct an LWE instance of $\mathbf{b} = \mathbf{As} + \mathbf{e} \in \mathbb{Z}_q^m$. The search-version LWE refers to finding $\mathbf{s}$ given $\mathbf{b}$ and $\mathbf{A}$. The decision-version LWE refers to judging whether $\mathbf{b}$ is generated from a uniform distribution or the LWE distribution, given $\mathbf{b}$ and $\mathbf{A}$ [1]. The following is the lattice cipher scheme based on LWE [1] :

- $KeyGen(\lambda)$: Generate uniformly random $\mathbf{s} \in \mathbb{Z}_q^n$, output the private key as $sk = \mathbf{s}$. Uniformly and randomly generate $\mathbf{A} \in \mathbb{Z}_q^{m \times n}$, and let $\mathbf{b} = \mathbf{As} + \mathbf{e} \in \mathbb{Z}_q^m$. Output the public key as $pk = (\mathbf{A}, \mathbf{b})$.
- $Enc(pk, \mu \in \{0,1\})$: Randomly select $\mathbf{r} \in \mathbb{Z}_2^m$ and calculate $c_0 = r^T A$, $c_1 = r^T b + \lfloor \frac{q}{2} \rfloor x$. Output the cipher $c = (c_0, c_1)$.
- $Dec(sk, c)$: Output the plaintext

$$m = \begin{cases} 0, |c_1 - c_0 s| < \frac{q}{4}, \\ 1, |c_1 - c_0 s| \geq \frac{q}{4}. \end{cases}\tag{3}$$

In the above process, large the public key pk (represented by a uniform random matrix $\mathbf{A} \in \mathbb{Z}_q^{m \times n}$ and $\mathbf{b} = \mathbf{As} + \mathbf{e} \in \mathbb{Z}_q^m$, which is an $m \times (n + 1)-$ dimensional matrix) will increase the communication overhead. Besides, to generate such public key consumes a lot of randomness. In order to solve these problems, we introduce a chaotic system to construct matrix $\mathbf{A}$. Using chaotic systems, we can generate a long sequence with fewer parameters, and construct the matrix **A** with this long sequence. Therefore, the storage space of matrix **A** can be greatly reduced from $m \times n$ dimension to a small number of parameters, which greatly saves the communication overhead and is more convenient for the use of lattice cipher scheme based on LWE, e.g. key encapsulation scheme (KEM).

3   The Proposed Public-Key Construction

3.1   Generating Uniform Chaotic Sequences

Generating uniform distributions from chaotic systems is not new to the community of chaos theory. Hereby we present one of such constructions from the Logistic map [15]. Let $f(t)$, $g(t)$ be two probability density functions such that

$$\int_a^x f(t)\, dt = \int_c^y g(t)\, dt, \tag{4}$$

where $a \le x \le b$, $c \le y \le d$. According to the properties of probability density functions, it satisfies $f(x) > 0$ and $g(y) > 0$ for any x, y in the integral intervals. Further we define

$$p(x) \triangleq \int_a^x f(t)\, dt, \quad p(y) \triangleq \int_c^y g(t)\, dt. \tag{5}$$

Therefore, the functions $p(x)$, $p(y)$ on are monotonically increasing, and the probability cumulative functions $p(x)$, $p(y)$ admit one-to-one mapping in the intervals $[a, b]$, $[c, d]$.

Let $f(t)$ be admitting a uniform distribution in $[0, 1]$, i.e., $a = 0$, $b = 1$. Then we have

$$p(x) = x = \int_c^y g(t)\, dt, \tag{6}$$

where $x \in [0, 1]$. Regarding the *r.h.s.* of Eq. (4), we set the function $g(t)$ as the Logistic density function in Eq. (2), and let $[c, d] = [0, 1]$. Therefore, Eq. (6) can be reformulated as

$$x = \int_0^y \frac{1}{\pi \sqrt{t(1 - t)}}\, dt$$

$$= 1 - \frac{2}{\pi} \arccos(\sqrt{y}). \tag{7}$$

The implication of this equation is that, if we transform the samples $z'_1, \ldots, z'_n$ of Eq. (1) by using the function $\frac{2}{\pi} \arccos(\sqrt{z'_n})$, then the resulting sequence $\{z_n\}$ is

$$z_1 = \frac{2}{\pi} \arccos(\sqrt{z'_1}), \ldots, z_n = \frac{2}{\pi} \arccos(\sqrt{z'_n}), \tag{8}$$

admitting a uniform distribution.

We compare the Logistic sequence with the one derived by Eqs. (1) and (8) in Fig. 1. As shown in the figure, the improved sequences better obey the uniform distribution.

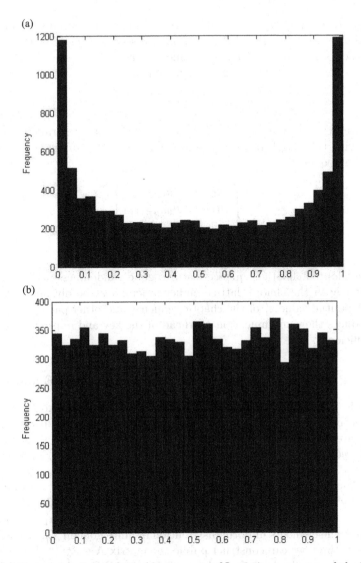

Fig. 1. (a) Comparing the statistical histograms of Logistic sequence and the improved sequence: Logistic sequence. (b) Comparing the statistical histograms of Logistic sequence and the improved sequence: Improved sequence.

3.2   Public Key Matrices Constructed from Chaotic Sequences

By using the improved sequence to construct the public key matrix $\mathbf{A}$, we argue that the constructed public key $\mathbf{A} \in \mathbb{Z}_q^{m \times n}$ not only satisfies the characteristic of uniform distributions, but also features low computational complexity.

The construction steps are as follows. According to the initial sampling position i and sampling distance d (the sampling distance d refers to the distance between each selected element), we define a chaotic sequence $Z(i, d, z_1, r) = \{z_i, z_{i+d}, \cdots, z_{i+kd}, \cdots\}$. Define $a_n \in A(i, d, a_0, r)$ as

$$a_n = \lfloor (q-1) \times z_{i+nd} \rfloor. \tag{9}$$

To construct the matrix $\mathbf{A} \in \mathbb{Z}_q^{m \times n}$, it is necessary to generate a sampling sequence with the length of $m \times n$, and then create the public key matrix $\mathbf{A}$ through this sequence as

$$\mathbf{A} = \left\{ \begin{array}{ccc} a_0 & \cdots & a_{m(n-1)} \\ a_1 & \cdots & a_{m(n-1)+1} \\ \vdots & \vdots & \vdots \\ a_{m-1} & \cdots & a_{mn-1} \end{array} \right\}. \tag{10}$$

As the adopted chaotic sequence features good randomness and uniformity, the public key in the chaotic lattice cipher scheme can be obtained by transmitting the initial value z_1' of the chaotic sequence and other parameters, which greatly reduces the communication overhead of the key and improves the transmission efficiency.

3.3 The Public-Key Encryption Scheme Based on LWE and Chaos

The chaotic encryption scheme based on the LWE problem proposed in this paper uses the chaotic mapping method mentioned above. The specific encryption steps are as follows:

(1). $KeyGen(\lambda)$

First, set the initial value of chaotic system as $z_1' \in [0, 1]$ (in Eq. (1)), then generate chaotic sequence; according to the initial sampling position i and sampling distance d, we can get sequence $Z(i, d, z_1')$, and the each value of the sequence $Z(i, d, z_1')$ is multiplied by the $q-1$ to get sequence $\{a_0, a_1, \cdots, a_{mn-1}\}$, which makes the elements uniform distribution in finite domain Z_q. According to the above method, we can construct public key matrix $\mathbf{A} \in \mathbb{Z}_q^{m \times n}$. We then randomly select the required $\mathbf{s} \in \mathbb{Z}_q^n$ and $\mathbf{e} \in \mathbb{Z}_B^m$ for the LWE problem and calculate $b = \mathbf{As} + \mathbf{e}$. Note the additional constraint that the value of B we select here must be $q/4 > mB$ so as to guarantee correct decoding of Regev's algorithm [1]. Finally, we get the private key $sk = s$ and the public key $pk = (b, z_1', i, d, q, m, n)$.

(2). $Encrypt(pk, M \in \{0, 1\})$

We encrypt each binary bit separately, and process one bit at a time. First of all, we randomly select a nonce vector $r \in \mathbb{Z}_2^m \in \{0, 1\}^m$, and then we calculate the matrix $\mathbf{A}$ based on the public key z_1', r, i, d, q, m, n, and then the first part of the calculation ciphertext $c_0 \leftarrow r^T A$. Then, we calculate the second part of the ciphertext $c_1 \leftarrow r^T b + \lfloor q/2 \rfloor M$. Finally, we output (c_0, c_1) as the final encrypted ciphertext.

(3). $Decrypt(sk, ct = (c_0, c_1))$

To recover the plaintext, we need to compute $\widehat{M} = c_1 - c_0 \cdot s$, then check whether the absolute value of the result is within decoding capability $\left|\widehat{M}\right| < \frac{q}{4}$. If it is, then it gives $M = 0$, otherwise it gives $M = 1$.

4   Tests

In this section, we adopt statistical tests and gap tests to verify whether the uniform distribution has been achieved. Moreover, we present a concrete example of constructing the public-key matrix **A**.

4.1   Chi-Square Tests and K-S Tests

We firstly use chi-square tests to verify whether the finite set S is uniformly distributed. It goes as follows:

(1). Partition interval

Partition S into r subsets $S = \bigcup_{j=1}^{r} S_j$, called bins.

(2). Statistics of the expected number of samples and the actual number of samples

Suppose there are samples $y_1, \cdots, y_M \in S$. For each $1 \leq j \leq r$, we compute the expected number of samples in the j-th subset: $c_j := \frac{|S_j|M}{|S|}$, and the actual number of samples: $t_j := |\{1 \leq i \leq r : y_i \in S_j\}|$.

(3). Calculate χ^2

$$\chi^2(S, y) = \sum_{j=1}^{r} \frac{(t_j - c_j)^2}{c_j}.$$

(4). Judge whether it is evenly distributed

Suppose the samples are drawn from the uniform distribution on S. Then the χ^2 value follows the chi-square distribution with $(r - 1)$ degrees of freedom, which we denote by χ_{r-1}^2.

Let $\mathscr{F}_{r-1}(x)$ denote its cumulative distribution function. That is, the sum of the probability of occurrence of all values less than or equal to x. Choose a confidence level parameter $\alpha \in (0, 1)$ and compute $\delta = \mathscr{F}_{r-1}^{-1}(\alpha)$.

If $\chi^2(S, y) \leq \delta$, then the hypothesis that the sample is extracted from the uniform distribution S is true; otherwise, the hypothesis is not true.

According to the above steps, we set the initial value z_1' of chaotic system (7) as 0:0.0001:1 (step size 0.001), and carried out chi-square tests (1000 times in total) for each chaotic sequence generated by (7). It is found that most of the chaotic sequences generated by (7) can pass the chi-square tests with the passing rate of more than 85% ($\alpha = 0.05$). Thus, the chaotic sequence generated by (7) has the uniform distribution characteristic with a high probability.

We further apply the Kolmogorov-Smirnov (K-S) test to judge whether the uniform distribution hypothesis is supported (*e.g.*, via the MATLAB function *kstest*). Results prove that the constructed sequence has the uniform distribution characteristic.

4.2 Gap Tests

Define interval $(\alpha, \beta) \subset (0,1)$. Let T_n be the number of times that the random number is in the interval (α, β); let G_n be the spacing between these degrees, such as $G_n = T_n - T_{n-1}$ (when $T_0 = 0$). If the random sequence is uniformly distributed, then G_n should be geometrically distributed with parameter $p = \beta - \alpha$. We can verify it with the χ^2 test.

A special case $(\alpha, \beta) \subset (0, 1/2)$ is called above average detection; when $(\alpha, \beta) \subset (1/2, 1)$, it is called sub-mean detection.

Based on previous research and experience, we define the interval $(\alpha, \beta) = (1/3, 2/3)$ and follow the steps above to calculate the G_n. Results show that G_n is geometrically distributed and passes the χ^2 test.

4.3 Construction of Keys

We select the secret initial value as $z_1' = 0.1$, set the initial sampling position as $i = 3$, and the sampling distance as $d = 100$. After 10^6 iterations, the chaotic matrix generated over the finite field $\mathbb{Z}_{2^{15}}^{640 \times 8}$ is as follows:

$$\begin{pmatrix} 5920 & 26257 & \cdots & 1047 & 27498 & 25010 \\ 22005 & 30692 & \cdots & 12247 & 17329 & 32411 \\ 7729 & 2102 & \cdots & 32734 & 10028 & 2659 \\ \vdots & \vdots & \vdots & \vdots & \vdots & \vdots \\ 32312 & 8762 & \cdots & 21933 & 13129 & 12563 \\ 12924 & 962 & \cdots & 960 & 552 & 11223 \\ 2024 & 20286 & \cdots & 26702 & 21399 & 10353 \end{pmatrix}.$$

The experimental results show that the matrix constructed by formula (7) features good pseudo randomness and passes the χ^2 test. We also plot Fig. 2(a) to show the frequency histogram of the matrix elements and Fig. 2(b) to show the scatter diagram of the matrix elements. They indicate that the matrix constructed by uniform chaotic sequence gives a distribution with good randomness and stability.

(a)

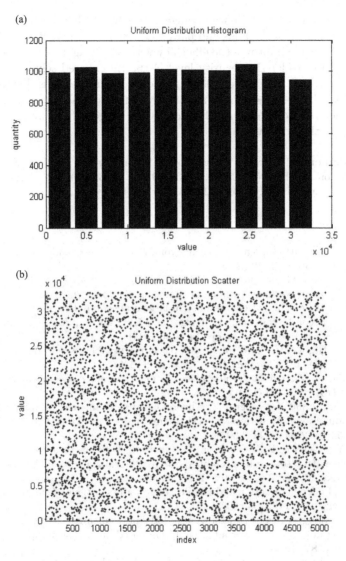

Fig. 2. (a) The statistical characteristics of the constructed matrix: frequency histogram. (b) The statistical characteristics of the constructed matrix: frequency scatter.

5   Conclusion

In this paper we proposed an efficient public key encryption scheme by judiciously leveraging the advantages of chaotic systems. Through the experimental results we have shown that the constructed sequences enjoy good randomness and uniformity. The public key size is significantly reduced. Instead of transmitting the whole public key matrix, it suffices to the transmit the initial value of chaotic sequence only, which can effectively reduce the transmission overhead.

Simultaneously, there is a wide range of cryptographic schemes based on LWE, and the choice of methods and parameters is quite different. To make sure the proposed scheme improves the efficiency while ensuring a certain security. It is necessary to consider the security level of the LWE-based scheme under the current parameter setting. The scheme proposed in this paper is devised based on a standard LWE-based cipher scheme by employing a chaotic system. No other parameters associated with the security is changed. Therefore it preserves the security of the original scheme.

Acknowledgment. This work was supported in part by the National Natural Science Foundation of China (61902149, 61932010 and 62032009), the Natural Science Foundation of Guangdong Province (2020A1515010393).

References

1. Regev, O.: On lattices, learning with errors, random linear codes, and cryptography. J. ACM **56**(6), 1–40 (2009)
2. Wang, F.: Key Generation and Verification Scheme Based on Blockchain and Pseudo Random Number Technology. Lanzhou Jiaotong University (2020)
3. Lehmer, D.H.: Mathematical methods in large-scale computing units. In: Proceedings of the Second Symposium on Large Scale Digital Computing Machinery, Harvard University Press, vol. 26, pp. 141–146 (1951)
4. Blum, L., Blum, M., Shub, M.: A simple unpredictable pseudo-random number generator. SIAM J. Comput. **16**(2), 364–393 (1986)
5. Marsaglia, G., Zaman, A.: A new class of random number generators. Ann. Appl. Probab. **1**(3), 462–480 (1991)
6. Simin, Yu., Jinhu, L., Chen, G.: Theoretical design and circuit implementation of multidirectional multi-torus chaotic attractors. IEEE Trans. Circ. Syst. Regul. Papers **54**(9), 2087–2098 (2007)
7. Simin, Y., Wallace, K.S., Tang, J.L., Guanrong, C.: Generation of $n \times m$-Wing Lorenz-like attractors from a modified Shimizu-Morioka model. IEEE Trans. Circ. Syst. II Exp. Briefs **55**(11), 1168–1172 (2008)
8. Chen, H., Li, Y.: Bifurcation and stability of periodic solutions of Duffing equations. Nonlinearity **21**(11), 2485 (2008)
9. Zhao, Y., Jiang, Y., Feng, J., Lifu, W.: Modeling of memristor-based chaotic systems using nonlinear Wiener adaptive filters based on backslash operator. Chaos Solit. Fract. **87**, 12–16 (2016)
10. Zheng, F., Tian, X., Fan, W., Li, X., Gao, B.: Digital image encryption based on Henon map. J. Beijing Univ. Posts Telecommun. **31**(1), 66–70 (2008)
11. Dabal, P., Pelka, R.: A study on fast pipelined pseudo-random number generator based on chaotic Logistic map. In: 17th International Symposium on Design and Diagnostics of Electronic Circuits & Systems, pp. 195–200. IEEE, Warsaw (2014)
12. Zhang, L., Min, L., Han, S.: Design of two-dimensional new chaotic system and pseudo-random number generator. Comput. Eng. Des. **35**(4), 1178–1182 (2014)
13. Qi, Y., Sun, K., Wang, H., He, S.: Design and performance analysis of hyperchaotic pseudorandom sequence generator. Comput. Eng. Appl. **53**(4), 135–139 (2017)
14. Cao, G., Kai, H., Tong, W.: Image scrambling based on logistic uniform distribution. Acta Phys. Sin. **60**(11), 133–140 (2011)
15. Gan, Y., Qinwei Ye, Yu., Zhou, Z.L.: Multi-channel parallel compression sampling based on uniform chaotic sequence. Data Commun. **2020**(006), 26–31 (2017)

Explore Capabilities and Effectiveness of Reverse Engineering Tools to Provide Memory Safety for Binary Programs

Ruturaj Vaidya[1], Prasad A. Kulkarni[1(✉)], and Michael R. Jantz[2]

[1] University of Kansas, Lawrence, USA
{ruturajkvaidya,prasadk}@ku.edu
[2] University of Tennessee, Knoxville, USA
mjantz@utk.edu

Abstract. Any technique to ensure memory safety requires knowledge of (a) precise array bounds and (b) the data types accessed by memory load/store and pointer move instructions (called, *owners*) in the program. While this information can be effectively derived by compiler-level approaches much of this information may be lost during the compilation process and become unavailable to binary-level tools. In this work we conduct the first detailed study on how accurately can this information be extracted or reconstructed by current state-of-the-art static reverse engineering (RE) platforms for binaries compiled with and without debug symbol information. Furthermore, it is also unclear how the imprecision in array bounds and instruction owner information that is obtained by the RE tools impacts the ability of techniques to detect illegal memory accesses at run-time. We study this issue by designing, building, and deploying a novel binary-level technique to assess the properties and effectiveness of the information provided by the static RE algorithms in the first stage to guide the run-time instrumentation to detect illegal memory accesses in the decoupled second stage. Our work explores the limitations and challenges for static binary analysis tools to develop accurate binary-level techniques to detect memory errors.

1 Introduction

Buffer overflow attacks rely on exploiting illegal memory accesses by referencing a buffer outside its legal array bounds. These attacks are mostly caused by bugs in software written in low-level memory unsafe languages, like C or C++ [37]. Such memory errors present an old security issue that persists in spite of advanced exploit mitigation mechanisms and can lead to silent data corruption, security vulnerabilities, and program crashes. In spite of solutions proposed through techniques at the programmer/source-level [16,24], compiler-level [2,4,7,9,14,27,29], and binary-level [33,36,38], the problem of memory safety persists especially in embedded, low-level, performance critical, and legacy software systems.

We thank the anonymous reviewers and the paper shepherd. This work is sponsored in part by the National Security Agency (NSA) Science of Security Initiative.

© Springer Nature Switzerland AG 2021
R. Deng et al. (Eds.): ISPEC 2021, LNCS 13107, pp. 11–31, 2021.
https://doi.org/10.1007/978-3-030-93206-0_2

Techniques to detect memory errors require the ability to determine accurate buffer bounds along with the data type referenced (called the *owner* in this work) by each memory access (read/write) and pointer assignment/move instruction. This information is largely available to the source-code and compiler-level techniques, and enables more precise memory error detection at run-time. Unfortunately, techniques at this level require access to the source code and may not be applicable to legacy software where source code may not be available. Such techniques also involve reprogramming and/or re-compiling the code. The *single* binary executable generated/deployed using these techniques cannot be easily adapted to different risk averseness and performance overhead tolerances of end-users. Such approaches also leaves the task of memory safety solely in the hands of the software developer (rather than the end-user).

Binary-level techniques can overcome these challenges of source-level approaches. However, much of the program syntax and semantic information needed by techniques to resolve memory errors may be lost during the compilation process, especially when the generated binary is *stripped* of debug symbols. To overcome this limitation for binary-level techniques, researchers have developed advanced reverse engineering (RE) frameworks with sophisticated disassemblers, decompilers, and binary type and symbol inference algorithms that attempt to reconstruct information lost during the source to binary translation process.

In this work we study how much of the array bounds and instruction owner information is preserved by the compilation process (for binaries generated with *debug* information and those *stripped* of debug symbols) and can be retrieved by traditional *disassemblers* provided with contemporary RE tools. We also conduct the first detailed study on how accurately can this information that is needed to detect/prevent memory errors be reconstructed by the advanced *decompilers* and type inference algorithms provided with modern RE frameworks for *stripped* binaries. Our work explores the capabilities of two state-of-the-art RE tools, specifically NSA's Ghidra [28] and Hex-Ray's IDA Pro [1], and assesses the accuracy of the information they derive from program binaries.

Imprecision in array bounds detection and instruction owner information obtained by static RE tools can affect the ability to detect and prevent buffer overflows at run-time. In this work, we design and build a new binary-level run-time tool to evaluate, for the first time, the effectiveness of the program information gathered by the RE frameworks (in different configurations) to detect and prevent memory errors. The tool uses the obtained static analysis information to keep track of owners as pointers are assigned, and check relevant buffer reads/writes to assess the ability to ensure fine-grained memory safety at run-time.

Thus, we claim two major contributions in this work.

1. We conduct the first detailed study to determine the ability of static RE tools, specifically Ghidra and IDA Pro, to derive precise array bounds and instruction *owner* information from binary programs, which is required to detect and prevent memory errors.
2. We design, build and employ a new decoupled binary-level execution-time tool with the goal to assess the efficacy of the statically derived program information to provide memory safety for binary programs.

2 Related Works

In this section we compare our work with studies that evaluate the capabilities and precision of reverse engineering frameworks to reconstruct program information lost during the translation process. We also discuss past research in binary-level techniques to detect and prevent memory errors.

Several prior research works have evaluated the accuracy of binary code disassemblers and decompilers. Meng and Miller identify challenging code constructs that make it hard for RE tools to accurately disassemble binary code and construct a correct control flow graph (CFG) [25]. Andriesse et al. compare 9 popular disassemblers and find that complex code constructs are rare in real-world programs [3]. Inaccuracy in function start/boundary detection by current RE tools was reported by some works [3,5]. Pang et al. analyze 9 open-source disassemblers to compare the algorithms and heuristics used for instruction recovery, symbolization, function detection and CFG construction and assess their precision [31]. They find that different tools use distinct algorithms and heuristics that complement each other, but also introduce coverage-correctness trade-offs. Another study explores the usability and effectiveness of decompilers to recover C output from binary code [21]. They find that while modern decompilers are getting increasingly powerful and accurate, issues such as type recovery and optimization still impede decompilers from generating accurate and presentable outputs. None of these works assess the efficacy of array bounds and instruction owner detection in RE tools.

A plethora of research has been conducted on type inference from program binaries [6,13,17,19,20,23,30,35,39]. Most of these research efforts are focused on prediction of basic or preliminary type information. Although some of these approaches claim to be able to detect higher order structures or aggregate types likes arrays, none of the approaches we know assess the accuracy of array bound detection, or evaluate the precision of instruction owner detection for binaries.

Past researchers have developed many techniques to detect and prevent memory errors. Many past approaches rely on the source-code with access to rich semantic program information [2,8,10,27,29,32,34].

Binary-level tools to locate fine-grained buffer overflows in memory at runtime have also been developed. The BinArmor technique [36] to detect memory errors relies on a tool called *Howard* [35] that uses past program execution traces to extract data structures and their memory bounds. BinArmor uses information from Howard to statically instrument the binary with checks to detect unsafe memory accesses during later program executions. Another technique develops a memory layout recovery algorithm to locate memory access vulnerabilities in the program *after* execution of the failed run [38]. This approach requires traces from a set of correct program executions to recover fine-grained memory layouts of variables. The recovered memory layouts from the passed program executions are then used to determine if the failed run exceeded any valid variable boundaries.

Both these past techniques employ a dynamic approach that relies on traces from multiple correct prior program executions to determine or predict relevant properties about the program, including buffer bounds. All dynamic analysis

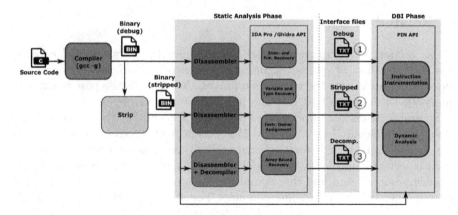

Fig. 1. Schematic of experimental framework setup

techniques require representative program inputs and are incomplete by design since they cannot guaranty complete code coverage and can only protect code and buffers that were seen by the analyzed program execution traces. Instead, our work is the first to explore the potential, capabilities and trade offs of using a static analysis and static type inference based approach to resolve this problem. Similar to BinArmor, but unlike the approach by Wang et al., our technique is designed to detect memory errors before they are triggered during program execution. Most importantly, none of these tools are available for use by researchers in the open-source domain and none have attempted to employ these tools to assess the *extent* and *impact* of inaccuracies in array bounds and instruction owner detection to locate and prevent buffer overflows at run-time.

3   Benchmarks and Frameworks

In this section we describe the experimental setup, benchmarks, and tools and frameworks used for this study.

3.1   Experimental Framework

A schematic of the overall framework is illustrated in Fig. 1. A C/C++ program is compiled with the standard gcc compiler with the "-g" flag to generate a binary with embedded debug symbol information. This binary is used by our ① **Debug** configuration. Later, the strip --strip-all Linux command is used to generate another binary executable that is *stripped* of all symbol information. This binary is used by our ② **Stripped** and ③ **Decomp.** configurations.

Our experiments employ two stages: (a) *static analysis* to assess the ability of our RE tools to derive precise array bounds and instruction owner information from binary programs, followed by (b) *dynamic binary instrumentation* (DBI) to assess the efficacy of the statically derived program information to provide memory safety for binary programs. We employ Ghidra version 9.1.2 (with Ghidra decompiler) [28] and IDA Pro version 7.5 (with Hex-Rays decompiler) [1] to conduct static analysis in the first stage. We use the PIN (version pin-3.15) [22] dynamic instrumentation engine in the second stage. All experiments are performed on a cluster of x86-64 Intel Xeon processors with the Fedora 28 OS.

The static RE tools we employ work independently of the program input(s). They include a *disassembler* to convert machine code to assembly code. They also provide a *decompiler* that employs sophisticated type inference and code reconstruction algorithms to raise the low-level assembly code into a higher-level language representation (commonly, C). Our ① Debug and ② Stripped configurations only use the *disassembler*. The ③ Decomp. configuration also uses the *decompiler*, which enables this configuration to recover higher-order program structures like arrays and pointers along with their associated sizes and assists with instruction owner detection from the *stripped* binary. Each configuration in the static analysis phase outputs a distinct *interface file* with the array bounds and instruction owner information that it can recover from the binary.

The stripped binary program and the statically generated interface file are provided to Pin. Pin adds instrumentation based on previously determined instruction owner mapping and array bounds information, tracks dynamically allocated buffers and relevant register and memory values, and inserts security checks to detect buffer overflows at run-time.

3.2 Benchmarks

In this work we use benchmarks from three different benchmark suites, SARD-89 [18,26], SARD-88 [26,40], and SPEC cpu2006 [15]. The SARD-89 suite contains 291 small programs that implement a taxonomy of diverse C buffer overflows (1164 total programs). Each test case has three versions with memory accesses that overflow *just outside*, *moderately outside*, and *far outside* the buffer, respectively. The fourth version for each test case is a patched version without any buffer overflow. 18 of the 291 test subjects in SARD-89 benchmark suite contain overflows that leverage library functions to succeed. Although not a fundamental limitation of our technique or tools, we currently do not analyze library functions, and so leave out these programs. Additionally, 152 test subjects in SARD-89 overflow the buffer with an index that is a *constant* integer, for example buf[2048]. We discuss these cases in more detail in Sect. 4.2. We use the remaining 121 test programs for all experiments in this work, unless mentioned otherwise.

The SARD-88 benchmark suite contains 14 "real-world" programs from various internet applications (BIND, Sendmail, WU-FTP) with known buffer overflows. Two versions are provided for each test case, one with and the other without a buffer overflow (28 programs in total). We statically link library functions like strcpy, strcmp, that can overflow in some of the SARD-88 programs. We also employ all the SPEC cpu2006 integer benchmarks to study the scalability and efficacy of the static tools on large programs. All benchmarks are compiled using GCC version 9.3.1; optimized benchmarks use -O3.

4   Static Reverse Engineering

Techniques to detect and prevent memory errors need precise information regarding buffer data types, their base address and size/bound, and the data type referenced (*owner*) by each memory access (read/write) and pointer assignment/-move instruction. Much of this information is lost during the compilation process. RE frameworks employ complex algorithms and heuristics to reconstruct lost program information from binaries. We explored the abilities of several RE tools to identify and reconstruct program information that is required to detect and prevent memory-related attacks in binaries, including Angr, Radare/r2, Debin, Ghidra, and IDA Pro. We found that only Ghidra and IDA Pro provide the capability and API for this task. In this section we present our results and observations. To our knowledge, this is the first work that evaluates and reports the efficacy of RE tools to extract or reconstruct the buffer/pointer bound and instruction owner information required to detect/prevent memory errors.

4.1   Setup and Implementation Details

In this section we describe the algorithms and extensions we develop to explore the capabilities of Ghidra and IDA Pro. Our scripts extract information relating to the statically known object bounds (local/global variables) and *instruction-owner* mappings. We use the term *owner* for program variables of type array or pointer that constitute the memory operand for the memory access instructions (of the kind MOV for the x86-64). Additionally, we have also extended the tools with block-level data-flow algorithms to track the instructions that propagate the *pointer* variables from memory to registers before they are used.

Figure 2 illustrates the information we gather from our RE tools. The figure shows the source code, the compiler generated binary code and corresponding IDA Pro output for a simple C program. This program has a single integer buffer, 'b', an integer pointer, 'ptr', and an integer scalar 'n'. The variable 'ptr' is the "*owner*" of the assembly instructions at offsets '8', '20' and '27'. 'ptr' is mapped to the corresponding addresses. The pointer access on line #6 overflows the array 'b' - corresponding to assembly instruction at offset '27'. Comparably, the direct array access on line #7 overflows the array 'b' - corresponding to assembly instruction at offset '32'. Memory safety algorithms need to check such accesses to determine the invalid access at run-time.

We found that the *owners* of direct variable access instructions (that employ $\{rbp, rsp, rip\}$ based relative addressing, like the instructions at address '8', '20' and '32' in Fig. 2) are determined automatically by the reverse engineering frameworks we study. However, the *owners* of pointer dereference instructions (for example, the instruction at address '27' in Fig. 2) are not detected automatically by our advanced tools. To analyze such memory accesses, we implement a simple data-flow algorithm that keeps track of the variables and owners as they move between the memory stack and registers.

Figure 2(c) shows the output of our RE scripts after analysing the binary generated using the example program shown in Fig. 2(a). This output file contains

```
                    1   0: push rbp                                1  1           # num. functions
                    2   1: mov rbp,rsp                             2  foo         # fn name
                    3   4: lea rax,[rbp-0x20]                      3  0           # fn start
                    4   8: mov QWORD PTR [rbp-0x8],rax             4  40          # fn end
                    5   c: mov DWORD PTR [rbp-0xc],0xa             5
                    6  13: mov eax,DWORD PTR [rbp-0xc]             6  32          # stack size
                    7  16: cdqe                                    7  addresses   # owner-ins mapping
                    8  18: lea rdx,[rax*4+0x0]                     8  8 foo_ptr
                    9  1f:                                         9  20 foo_ptr
                   10  20: mov rax,QWORD PTR [rbp-0x8]            10  27 foo_ptr
 1  int foo()      11  24: add rax,rdx                           11  32 foo_b
 2  {              12  27: mov DWORD PTR [rax],0x4               12
 3     int b[5], n;13  2d: mov eax,DWORD PTR [rbp-0xc]           13  locals      # locals info.
 4     int *ptr = b;14 30: cdqe                                  14  -32 ARRAY foo_b 20
 5     n = 10;     15  32: mov DWORD PTR [rbp+rax*4-0x20],0x9    15  -12 scalar foo_n 4
 6     *(ptr+n) = 4;16 39:                                       16  -8 PTR foo_ptr 8
 7     b[n] = 9;   17  3a: mov eax,0x0                           17
 8     return 0;   18  3f: pop rbp                               18  .global     # globals info.
 9  }              19  40: ret
```

Fig. 2. Example showing an invalid array access: (a) C source code (b) Assembly output (c) Output text file (interface file) after static analysis by IDA Pro

function related metadata such as *owner*-instruction address mapping I (listed under *addresses*), function variable metadata f_v - local variables along with their position (offset) on the stack relative to the stack pointer, their size and type (listed under *locals*), function boundary ($f_s \cup f_e$), and additional metadata f_m such as number of functions, stack size, base pointer relative addressing information, etc. This file also contains global variable metadata G_v - Variables defined in the *data* or *bss* sections and associated with their static address; the rest of the metadata is similar to local variables (listed under *.global*). This output of the static analysis $G_v \cup \sum f_i \{(f_s \cup f_e), f_v, f_m, I\}$ is fed to the Pin tool.

4.2   Efficacy of Reverse Engineering Tools

In this section we study the efficacy of existing reverse engineering tools to determine buffer bound and instruction owner information for programs compiled by standard compilers with and without debug symbols and compiler optimizations.

Failures Even with Debug Symbol Information. Building a binary with debug symbols retains useful information from the source program regarding the function *stack* and the global *data/bss* section layout, variable types, and buffer bounds. However, the owner information is not captured by the debug symbols and may become hard to infer from the static binary. An example of this challenging scenario is encountered for many SARD-89 benchmarks that overflow the buffer *with an index that is a constant integer*. An example of this case is illustrated in Fig. 3. The left-hand side of the figure shows the source code and the right-hand side shows the corresponding assembly code. This program declares two arrays, 'b1[5]' and 'b2[10]'. The write to 'b2[15]' corresponds to assembly instruction at location '40112e' and the read from 'b1[3]' corresponds to the assembly instruction at location '401135'. In the assembly code these buffer accesses that are *indexed by a constant* use a displacement relative to the stack frame pointer, rbp, rather than the base array pointer. Thus, although these two instructions reference different buffers (and one, b2[15] is an overflow),

```
1  #include <stdio.h>
2  int main()
3  {
4      int b1[5];
5      int b2[10];
6      b2[15] = 1;
7      printf("%i\n", b1[3]);
8      return 0;
9  }
```

```
1  0000000000401126 <main>:
2  401126: push rbp
3  401127: mov rbp,rsp
4  40112a: sub rsp,0x50
5  40112e: mov DWORD PTR [rbp-0x14],0x1
6  401135: mov eax,DWORD PTR [rbp-0x14]
7  401138: mov esi,eax
8  40113a: mov edi,0x402010
9  40113f: mov eax,0x0
10 401144: call 401030 <printf@plt>
11 401149: mov eax,0x0
12 40114e: leave
13 40114f: ret
```

Fig. 3. Ambiguous array access: (a) C source code (b) Assembly output

if these accesses are within the stack frame, then it is hard for the RE tools to infer or predict from the assembly code if they refer to the array 'b1' or 'b2' or neither. In such cases, we found that the reverse engineering tools cannot determine the correct instruction *owner* even in the presence of debug symbols.

Such failures caused due to buffer accesses by a constant numeral may be an *intrinsic* limitation of binary-level techniques. Fortunately, arrays dereferenced by a constant numeral may be a less critical hazard or attack vector in security threat models, as many real-world buffer-overflow and stack-smashing attacks are triggered by a malicious external input specifically devised to overflow the buffer bound. Lack of high-level program information also prevents our RE tools from associating the correct *owner* with instructions accessing individual members of a structure. We found that there are 152 test cases in the SARD-89 benchmark suite that our RE tools fail to analyze due to these *intrinsic* reasons. We leave out these programs from the remaining experiments in this paper.

Accuracy of Type and Owner Detection for Arrays and Pointers. Figures 4 and 6 (in Appendix A for optimized benchmarks) display the efficacy of array and pointer type detection for programs in the SARD-89, SARD-88, and SPEC suites. Each figure shows three configurations for each of our static RE tools, ① **Debug**, ② **Stripped** and ③ **Decomp**. We leverage the *pyelftools* [12] module to design and build a new tool to extract variable information directly from the "dwarf" [11] section of binaries[1]. The data from this tool is used as a baseline to compare the results obtained in the other RE-based configurations.

Figures in the first row (4(a), 4(e), 4(i)) display array bound detection accuracy for corresponding benchmarks. *#TP Arrays* show the (*True Positive*, TP) arrays detected at correct offsets regardless of their size/bound, while *#FP Arrays* show the (*False Positive*, FP) arrays that are detected at incorrect offsets compared to our baseline. Figures in the second row (4(b), 4(f), 4(j)) display the accuracy of pointer detection. The first set of bars in each of these figures show the number of TP and FP pointers as detected *directly* by the reverse engineering tools. The set of bars labeled "*with Pred.*" use a simple pointer prediction algorithm we employed that marks every variable with "undefined type"

---

[1] DWARF is a debugging file format used by many compilers, including the GCC compiler used in this work, to support source level debugging.

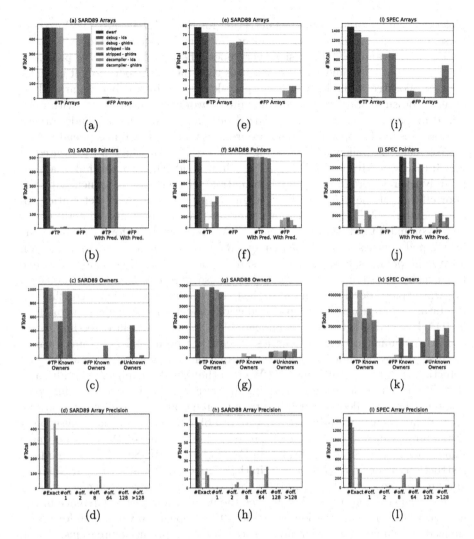

Fig. 4. Accuracy of array, pointers, and owner detection for SARD-89, SARD-88, SPEC-cpu2006 benchmarks, generated without compiler optimizations

(or undetermined type) and with a size of 8 bytes as a pointer. Figures in the third row (4(c), 4(g), 4(k)) display the accuracy of mapping the move and memory dereference instructions to array/pointer owners. The *known owners* are associated with instructions by our analysis algorithm. Static instructions mapped to owners that are scalar variables are ignored. Instructions are assigned *unknown owners* when relevant owners cannot be predicted. The *stripped* and *decompiler* results in these figures are compared against those when debug symbols are available with each respective RE tool. Finally, figures in the last row (4(d), 4(h), 4(l)) plot the accuracy of array bounds detection for the #*TP Arrays*. The Y-axis in these figures indicates the error magnitude in array bound detection.

Both Ghidra and IDA Pro show very poor efficacy with *optimized* programs for most of our experiments. One reason is that these RE tools do not consider register allocated variables which are prevalent in optimized benchmarks. This observation suggests a critical area for future work. Given this state with optimized binaries, we focus on unoptimized benchmarks for the remainder of this section. Results for optimized binaries are presented in Fig. 6 in Appendix A.

We make the following interesting observations from the data presented in Fig. 4: (1) Even advanced RE tools, like Ghidra and IDA Pro, can fail to appropriately leverage program symbol information, as seen most prominently by the poor efficacy of the *debug-ghidra* configuration to accurately detect static program pointers. (2) The *debug-ghidra* configuration misrepresents pointer types as int_64 or undefined_64 in many cases. (3) With no symbol information available in stripped binaries, *disassemblers* in our RE tools are unable to detect most/all arrays and pointers. Surprisingly, our simple pointer prediction algorithm is able to correctly detect most *true* pointers but also produces many false positives. We will explore developing more sophisticated pointer detection algorithms in the future to improve this simple prediction model. (4) *Decompiler* algorithms in IDA Pro and Ghidra do a commendable job, especially in detecting arrays and array bounds in stripped binaries. Interesting, even small programs seem to be able to provide sufficient context information to enable effective array type detection with these algorithms. (5) We find that the decompilers in Ghidra and IDA Pro are more accurate in inferring arrays and array bounds than inferring pointers. However, decompiler-based type inference algorithms often split arrays or combine them with adjacent arrays/variables resulting in many false positives and at times large inaccuracies in bound detection. (6) We can also make some more specific observations, like in Fig. 4(c) for SARD-89 benchmarks, many instructions associated with a scalar in the stripped-IDA case (which are ignored and are not plotted in the figure) are not assigned any owner (*unknown* owner) in the stripped-Ghidra case. We will see the implication of this difference in the next section. While instruction owner detection appears to works well for unoptimized benchmarks, it is largely unsuccessful for optimized programs. These observations reveal both the current capabilities of the static RE tools, Ghidra and IDA Pro, and open areas for research to more accurately derive program information that is necessary to detect memory errors at run-time.

5   Run-Time Framework to Detect Memory Errors

In this section we describe the implementation details of our run-time framework that employs the static program information gathered from the RE tools to detect spatial memory errors. We also assess the efficacy of the complete framework to effectively use the program information extracted by the static RE tools to detect memory errors in programs during execution. This approach does not require access to source code or hardware support.

Algorithm 1: Run-time Object overflow detection

Input: Function Metadata $F \rightarrow \sum f_i\{(f_s \cup f_e), f_v, f_m, I\}$
Input: Global Metadata $G \rightarrow G_v$

1   *ReadInput(Input)*;
2   *InstrumentMallocFree()*;
3   $F_d \longrightarrow$ Set of functions reached during execution;
4   $I_d \longrightarrow$ Instructions mapping per function reached during execution;
5   **foreach** $f \in F_d$ **do**
6   **foreach** $i \in I_d$ **do**
7   **if** $i.Address == f_s$ **then** InitializeStack() ;
8   **if** $i.Address == f_e$ **then** UnInitializeStack() ;
9   **if** $i.Owner \in Unknown$ **then** UnknownBoundCheck(); continue ;
10   **if** *IsInsMemStore()* **then**
11   **if** $i.Owner \in Pointer$ **then**
12   **if** $i.BaseReg \subseteq \{rbp, rsp, rip\}$ **then** BoundPropogationCheck();
13   **else** PtrBoundCheck();
14   **end**
15   **else** ObjBoundCheck();
16   **end**
17   **else if** *IsInsMemLoad()* **then**
18   **if** $i.Owner \in Pointer$ **then** PtrBoundCheck();
19   **else** ObjBoundCheck();
20   **end**
21   **end**
22 **end**

5.1 Dynamic Tracking and Instrumentation Using Pin

Pin [22] employs information supplied by the our static RE tools in the *interface file* to detect memory safety violations at run-time. We build scripts, called *Pintools*, that use the Pin API to insert dynamic checks in the executed code. Algorithm 1 explains our dynamic buffer overflow detection algorithm. Our Pintool will add instrumentation code at run-time for pointer/array memory move/dereference instructions that are mapped with corresponding instruction owners from the interface file. Run-time instrumentation is added for the *static* instruction categories mentioned below. We employ the example program in Fig. 2 to explain the run-time algorithm and illustrate the instrumentation categories.[2]

I. Function Start: The `InitializeStack()` function in Algorithm 1 will add instrumentation code at each function prologue to mark the locations of local variables w.r.t. the actual value of the stack pointer in memory. Function start (f_s) address obtained from the interface file (Fig. 2(c) - line #3) determines the instrumentation point. The dynamic array/pointer variable locations and available bounds get stored in a global metadata structure in this phase. Arguments passed to the program are also detected in this phase by adding a special check for function 'main'.

II. Function End/Return: The `UnInitializeStack()` function in Algorithm 1 will fetch the function end (f_e) address from the interface file (Fig. 2(c) - line #4) to add instrumentation at every function end. This type of instrumentation is required to roll-back the allocated stack and remove corresponding meta-data when the function returns.

---

[2] Our code can be accessed here: https://github.com/Ruturaj4/vulcan_prototype.

III. Pointer Move/Propagate: This type of instrumentation is used to transfer and assign the address/bound of the buffer to any associated pointer. The pointer can then be used to indirectly access the buffer. Similarly, bounds can also be transferred between two pointers. Instructions at offsets '4'–'8' (from Fig. 2(b)) give an example instruction pattern that represents pointer propagation.

```
lea rax,[rbp−0x20]
mov QWORD PTR [rbp−0x8],rax
```

Here, the `lea` (load effective address) instruction computes the address of buffer 'b' into a register (`rax`), and then assigns it to the pointer 'ptr' (at offset '(rbp-0x8)' on the stack). Thus, the static analysis tools mark the owner of instruction at offset '8' as pointer 'ptr' (line #8 in Fig. 2(c)).

At run-time, the `BoundPropogationCheck()` function in our Pintool will add instrumentation code (to the store instruction at offset '8' in Fig. 2(b)) to check the contents of the `rax` register to determine the location of object 'b' in memory. Note that the address and bounds of 'b' get stored in a global map structure during stack initialization at function start. It will then transfer these bounds to the pointer 'ptr'.

IV. Pointer Dereference: The following instruction triplet (instructions at offset '20'–'27' from Fig. 2(b)) shows an example pattern for pointer dereference.

```
mov rax,QWORD PTR [rbp−0x8]
add rax,rdx
mov DWORD PTR [rax],0x4
```

The buffer 'b' is accessed through pointer 'ptr'. Here, the `PtrBoundCheck()` function from Algorithm 1 will add instrumentation code (just before the store instruction at offset '27') to check whether the access is within the associated bounds, as follows:

```
if (access < low_bound || access >= up_bound)
    abort;
```

V. Array/Object Bound Check: Similar to `PtrBoundCheck()`, the `ObjBoundCheck()` function adds code to verify that a direct array access is within the associated bounds. An example pattern (instruction at offset '32' in Fig. 2(b)) is:

```
mov DWORD PTR [rbp+rax*4−0x20],0x9
```

VI. Memory Accesses with Unknown Instruction Owner: In some cases our static RE tools are unable to determine the instruction owners for the memory access instructions in the binary. In such cases, the `UnknownBoundCheck()` function will add instruction code to check that the access is within the bounds of the current function stack.

Apart from the above instrumentation categories, we instrument dynamic memory allocation functions like `malloc`, `calloc`, etc. We use Pin's *routine instrumentation support* to instrument these dynamic allocation functions. Our implementation also supports pointer metadata propagation through function calls, i.e. it propagates the pointer bounds information whenever pointers are passed between different functions.

5.2 Buffer Overflow Detection Accuracy

The efficacy of this framework to accurately detect memory errors is influenced by two factors: (a) the ability of the employed static RE tools in the first stage to correctly discover the necessary program information, and (b) the ability of the dynamic Pin-based run-time framework to correctly detect the program patterns that constitute valid instrumentation points. The run-time framework should also maintain and correctly propagate the desired program state at the relevant instrumentation points.[3]

We check the effectiveness of our prototype framework to detect memory overflows using two benchmark suites – SARD-89 and SARD-88. Table 1 presents the efficacy of the framework with the SARD-89 benchmarks. Each SARD-89 benchmark consists of four programs, one that is categorized as *benign* (no overflow), and three categorized as *Malicious* with a memory reference that overflows some buffer with a *Minimum*, *Medium*, or *Large* amount, respectively.

Tables 1(a) and 1(b) show the efficacy results for the 121 SARD benchmarks that overflow for an instruction with a *non-constant array access*, with static analysis conducted by IDA Pro and Ghidra, respectively. For each configuration and benchmark, the column labeled *Basic* lists the number of programs that behave correctly or as expected (no-overflow or overflow detected at correct location) with our mechanism that does not add any instrumentation for instructions associated with *unknown* owners. The columns labeled *Ext.* display the results with the small extension to our run-time algorithm to add instrumentation for instructions with *unknown* owners to detect an overflow *if the access is outside the bounds of the current stack*.

Thus, we can see that, (a) All *Benign* cases are correctly handled. (b) All cases with the *Debug* configuration are correctly detected. (c) Most *Malicious* cases with the *Stripped* configuration cannot be detected due to missing information from the static analysis phase. The run-time Pin extension enables the detection of overflows outside the stack bounds for binaries analysed by Ghidra (that contain instructions with unknown owners). This extension does not help binaries analyzed by IDA Pro as it assigns *some* owner (a scalar in many cases) to all such relevant instructions. (d) Interestingly, advanced type and bounds detection conducted by the static tools enables the *Decomp.* configuration to correctly detect a large majority of overflows for the *Malicious* programs.

Table 2 presents the efficacy results for the 14 SARD-88 benchmark programs with the IDA Pro RE tool used in the first stage.[4] For each SARD-88 benchmark, the program with the odd number is *malicious* and contains a buffer overflow and

---

[3] The implementation of our run-time framework can correctly process all programs in the SARD-88 and SARD-89 suites, as well as most of the SPEC cpu2006 integer benchmarks. However, our implementation currently encounters memory/performance issues with some larger SPEC benchmarks. We will address these implementation issues and improve tool robustness in our ongoing work.

[4] The results with Ghidra in the first stage are similar, and are included in the Appendix in Table 3 to conserve space. There are more failures in the Ghidra-based configuration primarily due to poorer analysis of global strings and buffers by Ghidra.

Table 1. SARD-89 run-time results for three experimental configurations: ① Debug, ② Stripped ③ Decomp. (Stripped + decompiler)

	Benign			Malicious								
				Minimum			Medium			Large		
	#Total	Basic	Ext.	#Total	Basic	Ext.	#Total	Basic	Ext.	#Total	Basic	Ext.
Debug	121	121	121	121	121	121	121	121	121	121	121	121
Stripped	121	121	121	121	1	1	121	1	1	121	1	1
Decomp.	121	121	121	121	110	110	121	110	110	121	110	110

(a) Benchmarks with non-constant array accesses (IDA Pro)

	Benign			Malicious								
				Minimum			Medium			Large		
	#Total	Basic	Ext.	#Total	Basic	Ext.	#Total	Basic	Ext.	#Total	Basic	Ext.
Debug	121	121	121	121	121	121	121	121	121	121	121	121
Stripped	121	121	121	121	1	29	121	1	42	121	1	118
Decomp.	121	121	121	121	95	95	121	110	115	121	110	118

(b) Benchmarks with non-constant array accesses (Ghidra)

the program with the even number is *benign*. All results displayed here include the Pin extension to detect memory access beyond the current function stack.

We find that while most cases with the *Debug* configuration are detected correctly, there are a few notable failures. Most of these failures are due to incorrect static bound detection for *global* read/write buffers. We did not encounter this case in SARD-89 benchmarks; most overflows there were in *local* buffers.

Programs analyzed by Ghidra encounter additional failures, even in the *Debug* case, because, unlike IDA Pro, Ghidra does not detect global strings that are usually defined in the binary's read-only (`.rodata`) section. For instance, benchmarks II, IX, XI and XIV fail when analyzed by Ghidra due to this issue. We also observed that global read-only strings with lengths less than 4 bytes are not detected by IDA Pro; for Ghidra this length is 5 bytes. This issue is a basic limitation for reverse engineering tools, as reducing this lower bound can lead to type detection conflicts with other types that may appear to be strings.[5].

As expected, malicious programs in the *Stripped* configuration fail due to incorrect static analysis. However, in contrast to our observation that the *benign* cases with the *Stripped* configuration in SARD-89 are successful (no overflow detected), we find that most *benign-Stripped* cases in SARD-88 fail (false positive overflow is detected). This difference in behavior is because our RE tools make no owner association (or *unknown* owner with Ghidra) for the SARD-89 programs in this configuration; so, no check is added for programs analyzed by IDA Pro, and the only check added is to detect out-of-stack overflows for binaries analyzed by Ghidra. In contrast our RE tools associate an owner (global variables in many cases) with incorrect bounds (1 in many cases) for many SARD-88 programs in this configuration; hence, they encounter a false positive overflow.

---

[5] https://github.com/NationalSecurityAgency/ghidra/issues/2274.

Table 2. SARD-88 test Results (IDA Pro) for our three experimental configurations: ① Debug, ② Stripped, and ③ Decomp. (Stripped + Decompiler)

Bechmarks		Debug	Stripped	Decomp.	Benchmarks		Debug	Stripped	Decomp.
I	283	✓	✗	✗	VIII	297	✗	✗	✗
	284	✓	✗	✓		298	✗	✗	✗
II	285	✓	✗	✓	IX	299	✓	✗	✓
	286	✓	✗	✗		300	✓	✗	✓
III	287	✓	✗	✗	X	301	✗	✗	✗
	288	✓	✗	✗		302	✓	✗	✓
IV	289	✓	✗	✗	XI	303	✓	✗	✗
	290	✓	✗	✗		304	✓	✗	✗
V	291	✓	✗	✓	XII	305	✗	✗	✗
	292	✓	✗	✓		306	✓	✓	✓
VI	293	✓	✗	✓	XIII	307	✗	✗	✗
	294	✓	✗	✓		308	✓	✓	✓
VII	295	✓	✗	✓	XIV	309	✓	✗	✓
	296	✓	✓	✓		310	✓	✗	✓

Again, we notice that advanced array bound and type inference enables several programs to be correctly handled in the *Decomp.* configuration. Of the 23 programs that are correctly detected in the *Debug* case, 15 are also correctly handled in the *Decomp.* configuration.

5.3 Performance Overhead

Figure 7 uses different metrics to estimate the performance overhead of the run-time framework.[6] Apart from the slowdown introduced by the Pin framework itself, the instrumentation added by our run-time algorithm is the primary source of performance overhead. Figures 5(a) and 5(b) plot the total number of instrumentation points encountered by all the SARD-89 and SARD-88 programs at run-time, respectively. The figures also highlight some interesting observations, including, (a) the number of *Stack sets* is less than the number of *Stack unsets* due to many programs exiting abruptly after an overflow is detected, (b) while SARD-89 programs are dominated by array dereferences, the SARD-88 programs encounter many more pointer dereferences, (c) the Ghidra-stripped configuration

---

[6] In theory, the performance of our run-time framework should be comparable with a compiler-based approach, like SoftBound [27]. Our run-time implementation is currently in the prototype stage and was designed to primarily explore the properties and potential of the static RE tools to detect memory errors in program binaries. As such, we have not yet explored performance optimizations and associated trade offs with memory error detection accuracy for the run-time framework.

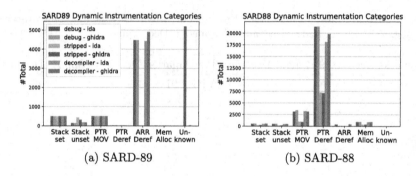

Fig. 5. Dynamic instrumentation points (subfigures (a) and (b))

assigns an *unknown owner* to several instruction in SARD-89, which enables the detection of *large* buffer overflows that exceed the current stack bounds.

We also compare the execution time of the benchmark in three settings, (a) native run, (b) using a minimal pintool that does not add any instrumentation, and (c) the pintool implementing our run-time algorithm (plots are available in Figs. 7(a) and 7(b) in Appendix C). Each program is run for 15 times and the average execution time is plotted. Most programs in the SARD-89 and SARD-88 suites run quickly, with an average execution time of 0.99 ms and 1.17 ms for the native run, respectively. The startup overhead of the minimal Pin framework increases the average run-time to 213.71 ms for SARD-89 and 417.99 ms for SARD-88 programs, respectively. Finally, our run-time framework increases the overhead to 227.85 ms for SARD-89 programs and 450.62 ms for the SARD-88 programs.

6   Conclusions and Future Work

Our goal in this work is to analyze and evaluate the ability of current state-of-art static reverse engineering tools, especially Ghidra and IDA, to accurately determine the required program information from binary programs to enable the effective detection of memory errors during program execution. We find that both Ghidra and IDA include advanced algorithms for array bound and instruction owner identification as part of their decompiler framework. However, more advanced techniques and algorithms are needed to further improve their capabilities and precision, especially for optimized binaries. We built a Pin-based run-time tool that can use the information from the static RE tools to detect buffer overflows during execution. We found that while our run-time tool can detect a large fraction of memory errors in our benchmarks, the accuracy of the tool is directly proportional to the limitations in the available static program information.

The practicality of this approach to detect memory errors is limited by the accuracy and completeness of the static tools and the efficiency of the run-time framework. In the future we will explore the potential of different approaches, including other dedicated type inference mechanisms, new static algorithms, and combining static and dynamic analysis, to improve array bound and owner detection, especially for optimized binaries. We will also study techniques to improve the efficiency of our prototype run-time framework, including using a static binary rewriting system. Finally, we will experiment with a larger benchmark set to more comprehensively study the properties of this approach.

Appendix A   Optimized Benchmarks

Figure 6 shows the results from the static analysis phase and compares the accuracy of array bounds detection, pointer identification, and instruction owner detection for *optimized* binaries.

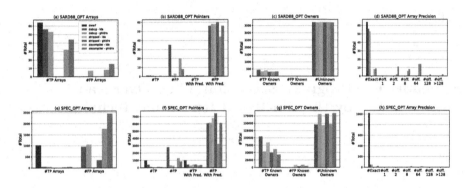

Fig. 6. Accuracy of array, pointers, and owner detection for SARD-88 (Optimized), SPEC-cpu2006 (Optimized)

Appendix B   Detection Accuracy Using Ghidra

Table 3 shows the detection accuracy of Ghidra for SARD-88 benchmarks.

Table 3. SARD-88 Test Results (Ghidra) for our three experimental configurations: ① Debug, ② Stripped, and ③ Decomp. (Stripped + Decompiler)

Benchmarks		Debug	Stripped	Decomp.	Benchmarks		Debug	Stripped	Decomp.
I	283	✓	✗	✗	VIII	297	✗	✗	✗
	284	✓	✗	✓		298	✗	✗	✗
II	285	✗	✗	✗	IX	299	✗	✗	✗
	286	✗	✗	✗		300	✗	✗	✗
III	287	✓	✗	✗	X	301	✗	✗	✗
	288	✓	✗	✗		302	✗	✗	✗
IV	289	✓	✗	✓	XI	303	✗	✗	✗
	290	✓	✗	✓		304	✗	✗	✗
V	291	✓	✗	✓	XII	305	✗	✗	✗
	292	✓	✗	✓		306	✓	✗	✗
VI	293	✓	✗	✗	XIII	307	✗	✗	✗
	294	✓	✗	✓		308	✓	✓	✓
VII	295	✓	✗	✓	XIV	309	✗	✗	✗
	296	✓	✓	✓		310	✗	✗	✗

Appendix C   Program Execution Time Overhead by the Pin-Based Run-Time Technique

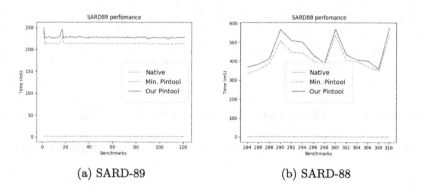

(a) SARD-89   (b) SARD-88

Fig. 7. Program execution time in msec

References

1. Hex-rays decompiler (2020). https://www.hex-rays.com/products/decompiler/
2. Akritidis, P., Costa, M., Castro, M., Hand, S.: Baggy Bounds checking: an efficient and backwards-compatible defense against out-of-bounds errors. In: USENIX Security Symposium, pp. 51–66 (2009)
3. Andriesse, D., Chen, X., van der Veen, V., Slowinska, A., Bos, H.: An in-depth analysis of disassembly on full-scale x86/x64 binaries. In: 25th USENIX Security Symposium (USENIX Security 16), pp. 583–600. Austin, August 2016
4. Austin, T.M., Breach, S.E., Sohi, G.S.: Efficient detection of all pointer and array access errors. In: Proceedings of the ACM SIGPLAN 1994 Conference on Programming Language Design and Implementation, PLDI 1994, pp. 290–301 (1994)
5. Bao, T., Burket, J., Woo, M., Turner, R., Brumley, D.: BYTEWEIGHT: learning to recognize functions in binary code. In: 23rd USENIX Security Symposium (USENIX Security 14), pp. 845–860. San Diego, August 2014
6. Caballero, J., Grieco, G., Marron, M., Lin, Z., Urbina, D.: ARTISTE: automatic generation of hybrid data structure signatures from binary code executions (2010)
7. Cowan, C., et al.: StackGuard: automatic adaptive detection and prevention of buffer-overflow attacks. In: Proceedings of the 7th Conference on USENIX Security Symposium - Volume 7. SSYM 1998, p. 5. (1998)
8. Dhumbumroong, S., Piromsopa, K.: BoundWarden: Thread-enforced spatial memory safety through compile-time transformations. Science of Computer Programming 198, 102519 (2020)
9. Dhurjati, D., Adve, V.: Backwards-compatible array bounds checking for c with very low overhead. In: Proceedings of the 28th International Conference on Software Engineering, pp. 162–171. ACM (2006)
10. Dhurjati, D., Kowshik, S., Adve, V.: SAFECode: enforcing alias analysis for weakly typed languages. In: ACM SIGPLAN Notices, vol. 41, pp. 144–157. ACM (2006)
11. dwarfstd.org: Dwarf debugging information format (2021). http://www.dwarfstd.org/doc/DWARF4.pdf
12. Eliben, p.: pyelftools (2021). https://github.com/eliben/pyelftools
13. ElWazeer, K., Anand, K., Kotha, A., Smithson, M., Barua, R.: Scalable variable and data type detection in a binary rewriter. SIGPLAN Not. 48(6), 51–60 (2013)
14. Hasabnis, N., Misra, A., Sekar, R.: Light-weight bounds checking. In: Proceedings of the Tenth International Symposium on Code Generation and Optimization, CGO 2012, pp. 135–144. ACM, New York (2012)
15. Henning, J.L.: Spec cpu2006 benchmark descriptions. SIGARCH Comput. Archit. News 34(4), 1–17 (2006)
16. Jim, T., Morrisett, J.G., Grossman, D., Hicks, M.W., Cheney, J., Wang, Y.: Cyclone: a safe dialect of c. In: Proceedings of the General Track of the Annual Conference on USENIX Annual Technical Conference, ATEC 2002, pp. 275–288 (2002)
17. Katz, O., El-Yaniv, R., Yahav, E.: Estimating types in binaries using predictive modeling. In: Proceedings of the 43rd Annual ACM SIGPLAN-SIGACT Symposium on Principles of Programming Languages. POPL 2016 .pp. 313–326 (2016)
18. Kratkiewicz, K.: A taxonomy of buffer overflow for evaluating static and dynamic software testing tools. In: In Proceedings of Workshop on Software Security Assurance Tools, Techniques and Metrics, NIST (2006)
19. Lee, J., Avgerinos, T., Brumley, D.: TIE: principled reverse engineering of types in binary programs. In: Proceedings of the Network and Distributed System Security Symposium, NDSS 2011, San Diego, California, USA, 6–9 February 2011 (2011)

20. Lin, Z., Zhang, X., Xu, D.: Automatic Reverse Engineering of Data Structures from Binary Execution. CERIAS - Purdue University, West Lafayette (2010)
21. Liu, Z., Wang, S.: How far we have come: testing decompilation correctness of C decompilers. In: Proceedings of the 29th ACM SIGSOFT International Symposium on Software Testing and Analysis, ISSTA 2020, pp. 475–487 (2020)
22. Luk, C.K., et al.: Pin: building customized program analysis tools with dynamic instrumentation. In: ACM Sigplan notices. vol. 40, pp. 190–200 (2005)
23. Maier, A., Gascon, H., Wressnegger, C., Rieck, K.: TypeMiner: recovering types in binary programs using machine learning. In: Perdisci, R., Maurice, C., Giacinto, G., Almgren, M. (eds.) DIMVA 2019. LNCS, vol. 11543, pp. 288–308. Springer, Cham (2019). https://doi.org/10.1007/978-3-030-22038-9_14
24. Matsakis, N.D., Klock, F.S.: The rust language. In: Proceedings of the 2014 ACM SIGAda Annual Conference on High Integrity Language Technology, HILT 2014, pp. 103–104 (2014)
25. Meng, X., Miller, B.: Binary code is not easy. In: Proceedings of the 25th International Symposium on Software Testing and Analysis (2016)
26. Metrics, S.S.A., Evaluation, T.: Nist Juliet test suite for c/c++ (2010). https://samate.nist.gov/SRD/testsuite.php
27. Nagarakatte, S., Zhao, J., Martin, M.M., Zdancewic, S.: Softbound: highly compatible and complete spatial memory safety for c. In: Proceedings of the 30th ACM SIGPLAN Conference on Programming Language Design and Implementation, pp. 245–258 (2009)
28. National Security Agency Ghidra, N.: Ghidra (2019). https://www.nsa.gov/resources/everyone/ghidra/
29. Necula, G.C., McPeak, S., Weimer, W.: Ccured: type-safe retrofitting of legacy code. SIGPLAN Not. **37**(1), 128–139 (2002)
30. Noonan, M., Loginov, A., Cok, D.: Polymorphic type inference for machine code. In: Proceedings of the 37th ACM SIGPLAN Conference on Programming Language Design and Implementation, PLDI 2016, pp. 27–41 (2016)
31. Pang, C., et al.: SoK: all you ever wanted to know about x86/x64 binary disassembly but were afraid to ask (2020)
32. Serebryany, K., Bruening, D., Potapenko, A., Vyukov, D.: Addresssanitizer: a fast address sanity checker. In: Presented as part of the 2012 {USENIX} Annual Technical Conference ({USENIX}{ATC} 12), pp. 309–318 (2012)
33. Seward, J., Nethercote, N.: Using valgrind to detect undefined value errors with bit-precision. In: Proceedings of the Annual Conference on USENIX Annual Technical Conference, ATEC 2005, p. 2 (2005)
34. Simpson, M.S., Barua, R.K.: Memsafe: ensuring the spatial and temporal memory safety of c at runtime. Software: Practice and Experience 43(1), 93–128 (2013)
35. Slowinska, A., Stancescu, T., Bos, H.: Howard: a dynamic excavator for reverse engineering data structures. In: Proceedings of the Network and Distributed System Security Symposium, NDSS 2011, San Diego, California, USA, 6th February - 9th February 2011. The Internet Society (2011)
36. Slowinska, A., Stancescu, T., Bos, H.: Body armor for binaries: preventing buffer overflows without recompilation. In: Proceedings of the 2012 USENIX Conference on Annual Technical Conference, . USENIX ATC 2012, p. 11 (2012)
37. Szekeres, L., Payer, M., Wei, T., Song, D.: SoK: eternal war in memory. In: Proceedings of the 2013 IEEE Symposium on Security and Privacy, SP 2013, pp. 48–62 (2013)

38. Wang, H., et al.: Locating vulnerabilities in binaries via memory layout recovering. In: Proceedings of the 2019 27th ACM Joint Meeting on European Software Engineering Conference and Symposium on the Foundations of Software Engineering, ESEC/FSE 2019, pp. 718–728 (2019)
39. Xu, Z., Wen, C., Qin, S.: Learning types for binaries. In: Duan, Z., Ong, L. (eds.) ICFEM 2017. LNCS, vol. 10610, pp. 430–446. Springer, Cham (2017). https://doi.org/10.1007/978-3-319-68690-5_26
40. Zitser, M., Lippmann, R., Leek, T.: Testing static analysis tools using exploitable buffer overflows from open source code. In: Proceedings of the 12th ACM SIGSOFT Twelfth International Symposium on Foundations of Software Engineering, SIGSOFT 2004/FSE-12, pp. 97–106 (2004)

Enhanced Mixup Training: a Defense Method Against Membership Inference Attack

Zongqi Chen[1], Hongwei Li[1]([✉]), Meng Hao[1], and Guowen Xu[2]

[1] School of Computer Science and Engineering, University of Electronic Science and Technology of China, Chengdu, China
hongweili@uestc.edu.cn
[2] Nanyang Technological University, Singapore, Singapore
guowen.xu@ntu.edu.sg

Abstract. Membership inference attacks (MIAs) have powerful attack ability to threaten the privacy of users. In general, it mainly utilizes model-based or metric-based inference methods to infer whether a particular data sample is in the training dataset of the target model. While several defenses have been proposed to mitigate privacy risks, they still suffer from some limitations: 1) Current defenses are limited to defend model-based attack and are still vulnerable to other types of attacks. 2) They make the impractical assumption that the defender already knows adversaries' attack strategies. In this paper, we present Enhanced Mixup Training (EMT) as a defense against MIAs. Specifically, EMT benefits from recursive mixup training, which mixes training data by using devised *Enhanced Mix Item* during the training process. Compared with existing defenses, EMT fundamentally improves the accuracy and generalization of the target model, and hence effectively reduces the risk of MIAs. We prove theoretically that EMT corresponds to a specific type of data-adaptive regularization which leads to better generalization. Moreover, our defense is adaptive and does not require knowing how adversaries launch attacks. Our experimental results on Location30, Purchase100 and Texas100 datasets show that our EMT successfully mitigates both model-based and metric-based attacks without the accuracy loss.

Keywords: Membership inference attack · Machine learning security · Privacy · Privacy-enhancing technologies

1 Introduction

1.1 A Subsection Sample

Machine learning (ML) has achieved state-of-the-art performance in many real-world tasks, such as autonomous driving [12], medical diagnosis [13] and speech recognition [14]. However, recent studies [4,6,15,17,18] have shown that ML

© Springer Nature Switzerland AG 2021
R. Deng et al. (Eds.): ISPEC 2021, LNCS 13107, pp. 32–45, 2021.
https://doi.org/10.1007/978-3-030-93206-0_3

models suffer from membership inference attacks (MIAs) due to their ability to over-remember sensitive training data, where adversaries can infer whether a particular data sample is used for training the target model. It has serious privacy risks in privacy-critical applications, since large amounts of individual's sensitive information (such as personal photos, medical and clinical records, and financial portfolios) are potentially included in the training dataset of the target model. Roughly speaking, existing MIAs can be divided into two categories: model-based attack [4] and metric-based attack [2]. Shokri et al. [4] constructed the first model-based MIA against black-box ML models by training multiple shadow models (similar to the target model). Specifically, an adversary takes a sample's probability vector predicted by shadow models as an input to train whether it is in the training dataset of the target model. Recently, Song et al. [2] proposed a metric-based attack, where adversaries use a sample's probability vector to compute specific function values and train thresholds. It will be inferred as member samples if its function values are higher than thresholds. Song et al. [2] experimentally showed that the metric-based attack achieve comparable success as model-based attacks.

To mitigate the privacy risks, several defenses [4,8,11] against MIAs have been proposed by utilizing diverse technologies, such as prediction truncation [6], L2-norm regularizer [4], dropout [6] and differential privacy [7]. For example, Jia et al. [1] put forward Memguard to defense against model-based attack. Inspired by the idea of adversarial example, Memguard crafts some perturbations and add them to the output feature vectors of the target model. Moreover, Nasr et al. [5] proposed adversarial regularization method, called AdvReg, which trains the target model and the attack model simultaneously. It uses the information of the attack model to improve the generalization ability of the target model to defend against model-based attack. Unfortunately, these defenses mainly focused on model-based attack. Recently, the metric-based attack proposed by Song et al. [2] can easily break the above defenses. Their experimental results [2] show that the attack accuracy is still high although the target model has been protected by state-of-the-art defenses such as Memguard [1] and AdvReg [5]. In fact, the metric-based attack is more attractive since it doesn't require training shadow models and the attack model, while achieving comparable attack performance to model-based attack. Moreover, prior defense methods responded to model-based attack have poor adaptability. They are difficult to transform into defending metric-based attack. On the other hand, existing defense methods make the impractical assumption that the defender already knows adversaries' attack strategies. However, in real situations, this is impractical because the adversary may adaptively choose distinct strategies to launch attacks, which always tend to be concealed. Therefore, it is urgent to propose an effective and general defense that can resist both model-based and metric-based attacks and even unknown attacks, while maintaining the target model's performance.

In this paper, we develop Enhanced Mixup Training (EMT), a general, effective and low-cost defense method. Inspired by the success of Mixup [3] in improving the generalization of ML models, we apply and improve existing Mixup methods to resist MIAs. The original mixup training that mixes two samples are still vulnerable to MIAs, because of retaining the linear relationship of samples. Therefore, we improve it by recursively mixing training data during the training process. Specifically, we define *Enhanced Mix Item* to effectively mix training samples and scale it to enhance our defense against MIAs. It corresponds to adding a data-adaptive regularization to the loss function. Based on the regularization-like method, we reduce the generalization differences between member (training) samples and non-member (test) samples, prevent the classifier from over-remembering the knowledge of member samples and hence effectively resist MIAs. The contributions of our proposed scheme can be summarized as follows:

- 1) We propose a general method (called EMT) against model-based and metric-based attacks in black-box setting *without sacrificing the accuracy.*
- 2) Our EMT is practical and adaptive, since it completes the defense deployment *without any prior assumption of adversaries' attack strategies.*
- 3) We prove theoretically that EMT corresponds to a specific type of data-adaptive regularization. Besides, we experimentally compare with Memguard and AdvReg on Location30, Purchase100 and Texas100 datasets. Evaluation results show EMT *successfully defenses model-based and metric-based attacks,* while Memguard and AdvReg fails in defending metric-based attack well.

The remainder of this paper is organized as follows. In Sect. 2, we will introduce some preliminaries of MIAs and our method. Our EMT method will be introduced in detail in Sect. 3, and compared with previous researchers' defense methods in Sect. 4. Finally, we analyze and summarize them in Sect. 5.

2 Preliminary

In this section, we will introduce the preliminaries about prior MIAs and Mixup training technology.

2.1 Membership Inference Attack

The first Membership inference attack (MIA) is proposed by shokri et al. [4], and it is a classic model-based attack. We will introduce both model-based attack and metric-based attack simply. Assume that all training samples $x_{privacy}$ are intended to be protected and the training classifier is denoted by F. Defenders do not want to leak them to malignant adversaries. Under the target model's parameter θ, the training process has an output precision vector: $f_{output} = F(x_{privacy}, \theta)$.

Model-Based Attack: In the model-based attack setting, users (including malicious users) can acquire the prediction vector f_{output} that represents output features after or before the softmax layer. Adversaries can utilize f_{output} to train an attack model H to attack the target model F, which can be denoted as:

$$h = H_{attack}(f_{output}, \theta), h \in 0, 1 \tag{1}$$

where H is a binary classifiers. When H outputs 1, it represents that adversaries guess right on member input sample while 0 is a wrong judgment. Defense goal is to make the outputs h close to 0.5.

$$\min \| h_0 - h_1 \| \Rightarrow \frac{h_{1,0}}{all\_sample} = 0.5 \qquad (2)$$

Metric-Based Attack: In the metric-based attack setting, adversaries do not need train an attack model. Adversaries can just use the performance metrics of target model's predictions to attack. They compare the metrics with the pre-setted certain threshold values to infer whether the input sample is member or a non-member. Song et al. [2] uses four threshold tactics. The first three are proposed by previous works. Attackers utilize the intuition that the target model tends to predict correctly or lower entropy of prediction confidence on member data. They used *entropy* or the entropy-like function *mentr* proposed by Song et al. [2] to set a threshold. I_{corr} represents whether the data sample is predicted correctly. I_{conf} utilizes the prediction confidence results to simply set a threshold. Adversaries use these statisticses to compare with the set threshold. If a single data sample satisfies the inequality or equality, it will be judged as a member sample by the attacker, or otherwise. The followings are the four different threshold inequality selection methods.

$$I_{corr}(F(x,y)) = \mathbf{1}\{arg\max_i(F(x)_i = y)\}$$

$$I_{conf}(F,(x,y)) = \mathbf{1}\{F(x)_y \geq t_y\}$$

$$I_{entropy}(F,(x,y)) = \mathbf{1}\{-\sum_i F(x)_i log(F(x)_i) \leq t_y\}$$

$$I_{mentr}(F,(x,y)) = \mathbf{1}\{mentr(F(x),y) \leq t_y\}$$

2.2   Recent Defense Against Membership Inference Attack

Previous defense methods mainly focus on defending against model. Memguard [1] and AdvReg [5] are reported to have highest defense ability. We will explain their details below and compare our methods with them in Sect. 4.

Memguard. [1] is proposed by Jia et al. to defense against MIA. For given a trained model F, they crafted noise vectors to obfuscate the output features to mitigate MIA. The attack classifier H utilizes the model prediction $F(x)$ and sample label y, to output a score $H(F(x),y)$ in the range $[0,1]$ for inferring: if the score is larger than 0.5, the data sample will be inferred as member data. The key question of adding noise $\mathbf{n}$ to $F(x)$ can be formulated as the following optimization problem:

$$\min_{n_i} d(F(x_i), F(x_i) + \mathbf{n}_i)$$

$$subject\ to : arg\max_i(F(x)_i + \mathbf{n})) = arg\max_i F(x)_i$$

$$H(F(x_i) + \mathbf{n}) = 0.5$$

$$F(x)_i + \mathbf{n}_i \geq \mathbf{0}, \, for \, any \, i$$

$$\sum_i \mathbf{n}_i = \mathbf{0}$$

Memguard [1] should be subject to two constraints. One is that the classification result does not change after adding noise $\mathbf{n}$. Another one is that the noise can indeed confuse the predictions made by attack classifier which is trained by defender in advance.

Adversarial Regularization. [5] is proposed to defense MIA with a Min-Max game. Defense classifier and attack classifier will be simultaneously trained and target to defense MIA. It uses a regularization called adversarial regularization to punish the loss of target model. For given classifier F with parameters θ, and attack classifier I with parameters v, attacker uses the output $F(x)$ and label y of F to conduct $I(F(x), y)$ for inference attack. The range of I is in [0,1], when the value is larger, the input prefers to be inferred as a member data sample. At every training epoch, defender updates F and I by minimizing the MIA accuracy and maximizing the MIA ability over the training set D_{tr} and validation set D_{val}. l is the loss function of target classifier, and λ is a hypermeter to control penalty.

$$\underset{v}{arg\max} \frac{\sum_{D_{tr}} log(I(F(x), y))}{2|D_{tr}|} + \frac{\sum_{D_{val}} log(1 - I(F(x), y))}{2|D_{val}|}$$

$$\underset{\theta}{arg\min} \frac{1}{|D_{tr}|} \sum_{D_{tr}} l(F(x), y) + \lambda log(I(F(x), y))$$

2.3   Definition of Mixup

Mixup is the building block of our EMT, which constructs virtual training examples by mixing samples and labels. The simple definition is denoted in Zhang et al. [3] as:

$$\tilde{x} = \lambda x_i + (1 - \lambda)x_j \tag{3}$$

$$\tilde{y} = \lambda y_i + (1 - \lambda)y_j \tag{4}$$

where $\lambda \sim BETA(\alpha, \beta)$ and $\lambda \in [0, 1]$, for $\alpha, \beta \in (0, \infty)$. (x_i, y_i) and (x_j, y_j) are two private samples randomly selected from the training dataset. Mixup extends training distribution by fusing linear prior knowledge. The interpolation of output feature vectors should lead to linear interpolation of related objects. In a conclusion, sampling from the Mixup vicinal distribution produces virtual feature-target vectors. Mixup can be implemented in short codes with minimal computation overhead. The Mixup hyper-parameter α controls the strength of interpolation between feature-target pairs. However, applying Mixup directly does not achieve the desired defense effect, and hence we will introduce Enhanced Mixup Training next section.

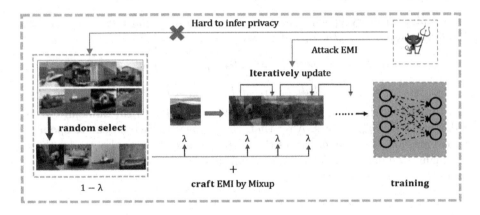

Fig. 1. High-level of enhanced mixup training.

3 Enhanced Mixup Training Against Membership Inference Attack

As shown in Fig. 1, we provide the high-level description of EMT. We use Mixup to mix the training samples in a variety of randomized operations, and propose the concept of **Enhanced Mix Items (EMI)**. It saves a part of the training data during each epoch and continues to mix in the next iteration process to make the EMI continue to contain more sample information. We use the mixed data samples to train the model instead of original samples. Research shows that this is a data argument method, but it can also be regarded as a way of regularization. We will show from the perspective of regularization that EMI punishes the model by using the samples of the training set itself, in order to avoid the model over-remembering the information of the training data. In this section, we will introduce the details of EMT.

3.1 Enhanced Mixup Training

We find out that the accuracy of H will be greatly reduced due to the influence of $f_{defense}$. We construct EMI iteratively to make the final training samples as far away from the original private samples as possible without at the cost of accuracy loss. The details are as follows:

Enhanced Mixup Training: We construct EMI among input samples. First, for training dataset D, we use mini-batch to train the model during every epoch. Assuming the amount of mini-batch is m, we have batches:

$$B_{ori} \to \{batch_1, batch_2, batch_3......, batch_m\}. \tag{5}$$

We craft EMI to train for model F, for epoch i, and copy and shuffle $batch_i$ p times to generate new items $e_p(batch_{copyij}, \lambda)$ to get EMI b_{mixi}. b_{mixi} is used for training in every epoch. The p is the iterations number per B_{mixup}, and $batch_{copyij}$ represents jth copy of $batch_i$:

$$batch_{copy} \rightarrow \{batch_{copyi0}, batch_{copyi1}......, batch_{copyip}\} \tag{6}$$

$$B_{mixup} \rightarrow \{batch_{mix1}, batch_{mix2}, ..., batch_{mixm}\} \tag{7}$$

For a mixed batch, we shuffle the samples in the original $batch_i$ randomly to get p different $batch_{copyi}$ copies. After that, the samples in each batch are operated by (3) and (4). It partly enhances the degree of mixing. Note the greater the p, the higher the degree of defense. We use m batches to iteratively construct mix items:

$$e_0(batch_{copyi0}, \lambda) = batch_i \tag{8}$$
$$e_1(batch_{copyi1}, \lambda) = \lambda \cdot e_0 + (1 - \lambda) \cdot batch_{copyi1}/1\ !$$

$$......$$

$$e_p(batch_{copyip}, \lambda) = \lambda \cdot e_{p-1} + (1 - \lambda) \cdot batch_{copyip}/p\ !$$
$$e_p(batch_{copyi}, \lambda) = (1 - \lambda) \sum_{j=0}^{p} \frac{batch_{copyij}}{j\ !} \lambda^{p-j} \tag{9}$$

$$batch_{mixi} = e_p(batch_{copyi}, \lambda) \tag{10}$$
$$z_{mixi} = e_p(z_{copyi}, \lambda)$$

Where z is one of the samples of $batch_{mixi}$, which can be any sample in a batch. j is an adaptive decay factor of iteratively updating. We train model with z_{mixi} instead of originally private samples x_i. In fact, this kind of mixing method is to mix data in a skillful regularization way. In next section, we will give a simple proof that the iterative method to construct the mixed term is to construct the penalty term on the loss function. This regularization method improves the generalization ability of the model, improves the robustness of the model, and reduces the risk of MIAs.

3.2   Regularization Proof of EMI

Recently, Zhang et al. [16] studied how Mixup can help improve the generalization of the model. They deduce that Mixup is essentially a regularization term constructed with the help of the second-order derivative information of Taylor expansion based on the sample distribution. Inspired by their method, we extend it to p-th order derivatives and deduce that our EMI is a regularization method.

We denote a general parameterized loss as $l(B, \theta)$ with considering a training dataset in every mini-batch $B = \{(x_1, y_1), (x_2, y_2), ..., (x_n, y_n)\}$, where n is the batchsize. θ is model's parameter. B is one of B_{mixup}, where $\theta \subseteq \mathbb{R}^d$, $x_i \subseteq \mathbb{R}^k$, $y_i \subseteq \mathbb{R}^r$. Let $L(f_\theta(x), y) = \sum_{i=1}^{n} l(Batch_{mixi}, \theta)/mn$, where m is the number of $batch_{mix}$. Then for the prediction function $f_\theta(x)$ and target y, we get:

$$L(f_\theta(x), y) = function(Y, p(y|x)) \tag{11}$$

$$= h(f_\theta(x)) - y f_\theta(x)$$

h can be any loss functions. If $h = 1$, L $\approx$ hinge-loss. Common loss functions can be used as L, such as CE (Cross-Entropy), LR (Linear regression) and so on. The form of loss function does not affect our conclusion in the definition field. We study the case of a single batch in each epoch. After randomly shuffle with (6), the $batch_{mixi}$ in current epoch has been determined, let $\phi(\lambda) = \frac{1}{n} \mathbb{E}_{batch_{mixi} \sim \chi} l(batch_{mixi}, \theta) = L(f_\theta(z_{xi}), z_{yi}), z \subseteq batch_{mixi}$. We let $1 - \lambda$ to substitute λ without changing the result, and we expand $\phi(\lambda)$ to p-th by Taylor expansion:

$$\phi(\lambda) = \sum_{i=0}^{p} \frac{\phi^{(i)}(0)}{i!} \lambda^i + o(\lambda) = h(f_\theta(z_{xi})) - z_{yi} f_\theta(z_{xi})$$

$$\phi'(\lambda) = h'(f_\theta(z_{xi})) \cdot \nabla f_\theta(z_{xi}) \cdot \frac{\partial z_{xi}}{\partial \lambda}$$

$$- z_{yi} \cdot \nabla f_\theta(z_{xi}) \cdot \frac{\partial z_{xi}}{\partial \lambda} - \frac{\partial z_{yi}}{\partial \lambda} \cdot \nabla f_\theta(z_{xi}) \tag{12}$$

To simplify it, we take $f = f_\theta(z_{xi}), f' = \nabla f_\theta(z_{xi}) \cdot \frac{\partial z_{xi}}{\partial \lambda}$, into (12). h' and ϕ' are the first derivative of their independent variables. Similarly, $h^{(k)}$ and $\phi^{(k)}$ are the k-th derivative of their independent variables.

$$\phi'(0) = [h' - z_{yi}] \cdot f' + (-\frac{\partial z_{yi}}{\partial \lambda}) \cdot f$$

$$\phi^{(2)}(0) = [h^{(2)} - 2\frac{\partial z_{yi}}{\partial \lambda}] \cdot f' + [h' - z_{yi}] \cdot f'$$

$$+ (-\frac{\partial z_{yi}}{\partial \lambda}) \cdot f^{(2)} + (-\frac{\partial^2 z_{yi}}{\partial^2 \lambda}) f$$

$$\phi^{(3)}(0) = [h^{(3)} f' - 3z_{yi}^{(2)}] \cdot f' + [h^{(2)}(1 + f') - 3\frac{\partial z_{yi}}{\partial \lambda}] \cdot f^{(2)}$$

$$+ [h'(f) - z_{yi}] \cdot f^{(3)} + (-\frac{\partial^3 z_{yi}}{\partial^3 \lambda}) \cdot f \tag{13}$$

According to the above equation, we can get the recursion. $\phi^{(k)}(0)$ consists $k+1$ items, and we denote it as $\phi^{(k)}(0) = \sum_{i=0,k=1}^{p} R_{i,k}$, where k is kth differentiability and $k \leq p$:

$$R_{0,k} = (-\frac{\partial^k z_{yi}}{\partial^k \lambda}) \cdot f$$

$$R_{1,k} = [h' - z_{yi}] \cdot f^{(k)}$$

$$R_{2,k} = [h^{(2)}(1 + (k-2)f') - k\frac{\partial z_{yi}}{\partial \lambda}] \cdot f^{(k-1)} \tag{14}$$

$$......$$

Since the e_p can be expanded to p-th order, we can substitute (14) into equations (13):

$$\phi'(0) = R_{0,1} + R_{1,1}$$

$$\phi^{(2)}(0) = R_{0,2} + R_{1,2} + R_{2,2}$$

$$\cdots\cdots$$

$$\phi^{(p)}(0) = \sum_{i=0,k=1}^{p} R_{i,k} \tag{15}$$

Finally, we denoted $L_i = \phi^{(i)} \cdot \lambda^i$, then we obtain the statement:

$$\phi(\lambda) = \phi(0) + \sum_{i=1}^{p} L_i + o(\lambda) \tag{16}$$

$$L(f_\theta(z_{xi}), z_{yi}) = L(f_\theta(x_i), y_i) + \sum_{i=1}^{p} L_i(x_i, y_i) + o(\lambda)$$

Since $lim_{a\to0,0<a<1} a = 0$, Peano remainder $o(\lambda) = 0$. So $\sum_{i=1}^{p} L_i(x_i, y_i)$ are the final regularization items. It avoids model over-remembering originally private samples. We further denote as:

$$\widetilde{L}(f_\theta(z_{xi}), z_{yi}) = L(f_\theta(x_i), y_i) + \sum_{i=1}^{p} L_i(x_i, y_i) \tag{17}$$

We make different hypermeter selects for the parameters of Beta distribution for different datasets. We find that the ratio $\dfrac{\alpha}{\beta}$ in good experimental results tends to be 1 when dataset is simple.

4   Experiment Results

4.1   Dataset

Texas 100: This dataset consists of real patients' information released by the Texas Department of State Health Services. We use the preprocessed and simplified Texas dataset provided by Shokri et al. [4]. The dataset has 67,330 samples

---

Algorithm 1. Enhanced Mixup Training

Input:
1: F:model need to be defending
2: *batch of training*: $batch_i$
3: *hypermeter*: α, β, n, m
Output: F
4: get $\lambda = BETA(\alpha, \beta)$
5: **repeat**
6:      generate n shuffled batch: $batch_{copyi1}..., batch_{copyip}$;
7:      $batch_{mixi} = e_p(Batch_{copyi}, \lambda)$;
8:      Train($batch_{mixi}$, F);
9:      Optimizer(F);
10: **until** $i < m$;

Algorithm 2. Enhanced Mix Item

Input:
1: $batch_i, \lambda, p$
Output: $EMI = batch_{mixi} = e_p$
2: initial $j = 1$;
3: let $e_0 = batch_i$;
4: **repeat**
5:     $e_i = \lambda \cdot e_{i-1} + (1 - \lambda) \cdot batch_{copyil}/j \,!$;
6:     $j = j + 1$;
7: **until** $j < p$;
8: return e_p

---

each with 6,170 features including the external causes of injury, the diagnosis, the procedures the patient underwent, and so on. We use 10,000 samples to train a model and 10,000 samples to test the model.

Purchase 100: This dataset contains shopping records of several thousand individuals. We use a simplified and preprocessed purchase dataset from previous work [4]. The dataset with 197,324 samples has 600 binary features which represents whether the individual has purchased it or not. Following Nasr et al. [5], 10% samples (19,732) are used to train the target model.

Location 30: This dataset is based on Foursquare dataset, which contains location *check-in* records of thousand individuals. This dataset is a simplified and preprocessed Location dataset provided by Shokri et al. [4]. The dataset contains 5,010 samples with 446 binary features. Each of the features contains a certain region or location type which represents whether the user has visited the location or not. We will utilize 1,000 samples to train the model and other 1,000 samples to test.

4.2   Experimental Setup

We will compare our EMT with both Memguard [1] and AdvReg [5] under two attack methods using the same experimental setting as them. Note that Texas100 and Purchase100 are trained in different network setting in their experiments, so we will revaluate them in their respective setting. We use a simple fully-connected neural network to follow them. We follow Jia et al. [1] to use 4 hidden layers as the target model, and the number of neurons for the four layers are respectively set as [1024, 512, 256, 128]. Besides, cross-entropy loss function and stochastic gradient descent are adopted to update the model parameters.

In the first evaluation, we use classic model-based attack proposed by Shokri et al. [4] to train an attack model. The number of neurons for three hidden layers of the attack model is [512, 256, 128]. We assume that the attacker has the same data distribution as the member data, and even knows the target model architecture such that can train a shadow model with the same architecture as the target model.

In the second evaluation, we set metric-based attack [2]. We use four different metrics to attack, including the prediction correctness based attack (I_{corr}), prediction confidence based attack (I_{conf}), conventional entropy based attack (I_{entr}), modified entropy attack (I_{mentr}) [2,9,10] (details can be refered to Sect. 2).

Table 1. Defend capability comparison

Defense	Model-based	Metric-based	No accuracy-loss
Memguard	✔	✗	✔
AdvReg	✔	✔	✗
EMT	✔	✔	✔

Table 2. Defense performance under model-based attacks

Dataset	Defense	Train Acc	Test Acc	Attack Acc
L30	no	100%	60.1%	77.1%
	Mem	100%	60.1%	50.1%
	EMT	81%	**61.1%**	**50.0%**
P100	no	99.8%	79.4%	67.7%
	Mem	99.8%	79.4%	51.3%
	AdvReg	93.1%	76.5%	51.6%
	EMT	80.3%	**80.3%**	**51.3%**
T100	no	99.95%	51.3%	72.1%
	Mem	99.95%	51.3%	**50.8%**
	AdvReg	56.5%	46.5%	51.1%
	EMT	81.9%	**57.3%**	52.9%

4.3 Experimental Results

We summarise the differences between the three defense methods in Table 1. As shown in Table 1, compared with existing defenses, EMT can defend against model-based and metric-based attacks, without sacrificing the prediction accuracy and any prior knowledge of attackers. Next, we will evaluate the ability of three defense models against two attacks in details. MIA has two main evaluation indexes: the attack accuracy and the prediction accuracy. (1) The model can successfully resist MIA so as to maintain the accuracy of MIA down to about 50%. (2) A good defense model can reduce the attack accuracy of MIA while making the loss of model accuracy as small as possible. Table 2 and Table 3 list the prediction accuracy and attack accuracy on all defended models against model-based and metric based attacks.

Defense Against Model-Based Attack. From Table 2, compared with the benchmark without defense, all three methods achieve low attack accuracy (e.g., about 50%), and hence all can defend model-based attack successfully. However, we find the prediction accuracy of AdvReg [5] based defense model has a huge loss. For examples, the accuracy downs to 76.5% from benchmark 79.4% on Purchase100, 46.5% from benchmark 51.3% on Texas100. While Memguard [1] maintains the prediction accuracy intact, our EMT method improves the accuracy of Texas100 dataset by nearly 6%.

Table 3. Defense performance under metric-based attacks

Data set	Defense	Train Acc	Test Acc	Attack (I_{corr})	Attack (I_{conf})	Attack (I_{entr})	Attack (I_{mentr})
L30	no	100%	60.1%	68.7%	76.3%	61.6%	78.1%
	Mem	100%	60.1%	68.7%	69.1%	**52.1%**	68.8%
	EMT	81.0%	**61.1%**	**67.4%**	**53.7%**	53.2%	**53.8%**
P100	no	99.8%	79.4%	59.6%	67.1%	65.6%	67.4%
	Mem	99.8%	79.4%	59.0%	61.1%	57.6%	60.1%
	AdvReg	93.1%	76.5%	58.2%	59.4%	55.8%	59.5%
	EMT	80.3%	**80.3%**	**56.0%**	**57.4%**	**55.5%**	**57.4%**
T100	no	99.95%	51.3%	74.2%	79.5%	70.1%	79.5%
	Mem	99.95%	51.3%	74.2%	74.1%	54.6%	74.0%
	AdvReg	56.5%	46.5%	**55.1%**	58.6%	53.6%	58.6%
	EMT	81.0%	**57.3%**	57.3%	**53.9%**	**51.3%**	**54.1%**

Defense Against Metric-Based Attack. Next, we evaluate the defense ability and prediction accuracy of the three defense methods against the metric-based attack [2]. Table 3 points out that Memguard [1] and AdvReg [5] are still vulnerable to metric-based attack. The attack accuracy against the model defended by memguard [1] is about 68% on L30, which indicates that Memguard [1] is still vulnerable to MIAs. In addition, the model defended by AdvReg [5] suffers attacks, e.g., it maintains the attack accuracy at 55%–58%. And we can see that EMT achieves the best defense performance and least accuracy loss on three datasets. EMT has the least attack accuracy all about 51%–57%, and reduces 2%–4% and 2%–20% compared with AdvReg [5] and Memguard [1], respectively. In conclusion, our method can effectively resist model-based and metric-based attacks and maintain or even improve the prediction accuracy. The main reason is that our iterative EMT does improve the generalization of the model. In other words, it essentially reduces the risk of privacy leakage, rather than designing defense strategies against specific MIA methods.

5   Conclusion and Future Work

In this work, we proposed EMT method to defend the black-box membership inference attack. EMT crafts EMI to make regularization on loss function to avoid over-remembering member samples. EMT has achieved good defense performance against both model-based attack and metric-based attack without the prior knowledge of attackers. Furthermore, its excellent performance makes us believe that EMT has the potential to resist unknown attack methods. From Table 1, our experimental result shows that EMT reduces the risks of MIAs, and even the generalization of the model is improved. But in some specific experimental results, EMT showed a little flaw which need to be made better. One of our interesting future works is to use the idea of gene mutation to make more fine-grained mix operations on samples randomly to improve performance.

Acknowledgment. This work is supported by the National Natural Science Foundation of China under Grants 62020106013, 61972454, 61802051, 61772121, and 61728102, Sichuan Science and Technology Program under Grants 2020JDTD0007 and 2020YFG0298, the Fundamental Research Funds for Chinese Central Universities under Grant ZYGX2020ZB027.

References

1. Jia, J., Salem, A., Backes, M., Zhang, Y., Gong, N.Z.: MemGuard. In: Proceedings of the 2019 ACM SIGSAC Conference on Computer and Communications Security (2019). https://doi.org/10.1145/3319535.3363201
2. Song, L., Mittal, P.: Systematic evaluation of privacy risks of machine learning models. In 30th USENIX Security Symposium (USENIX Security 21) (2021)
3. Zhang, H., Cisse, M., Dauphin, Y.N., Lopez-Paz, D.: mixup: beyond empirical risk minimization. Proc. ICLR **2018**, 1–13 (2017)
4. Shokri, R., Stronati, M., Song, C., Shmatikov, V.: Membership inference attacks against machine learning models. In: 2017 IEEE Symposium on Security and Privacy (SP) (2017). https://doi.org/10.1109/sp.2017.41
5. Nasr, M., Shokri, R., Houmansadr, A.: Machine learning with membership privacy using adversarial regularization. In: Proceedings of the 2018 ACM SIGSAC Conference on Computer and Communications Security (2018). https://doi.org/10.1145/3243734.3243855
6. Salem, A., Zhang, Y., Humbert, M., Berrang, P., Fritz, M., Backes, M.: ML-Leaks: model and data independent membership inference attacks and defenses on machine learning models. In: Proceedings 2019 Network and Distributed System Security Symposium (2019). https://doi.org/10.14722/ndss.2019.23119
7. Shokri, R., Shmatikov, V.: Privacy-preserving deep learning. In: Proceedings of the 22nd ACM SIGSAC Conference on Computer and Communications Security (2015). https://doi.org/10.1145/2810103.2813687
8. Abadi, M., et al.: Deep learning with differential privacy. In: Proceedings of the 2016 ACM SIGSAC Conference on Computer and Communications Security (2016). https://doi.org/10.1145/2976749.2978318
9. Yeom, S., Giacomelli, I., Fredrikson, M., Jha, S.: Privacy risk in machine learning: analyzing the connection to overfitting (2018). In: 2018 IEEE 31st Computer Security Foundations Symposium (CSF) (2018). https://doi.org/10.1109/csf.2018.00027
10. Leino, K., Fredrikson, M.: Stolen memories: leveraging model memorization for calibrated white-box membership inference. In: 29th USENIX Security Symposium (USENIX Security 20), pp. 1605–1622 (2020)

11. Bassily, R., Smith, A., Thakurta, A.: Private empirical risk minimization: efficient algorithms and tight error bounds. In: 2014 IEEE 55th Annual Symposium on Foundations of Computer Science (2014). https://doi.org/10.1109/focs.2014.56

12. Geiger, A., Lenz, P., Urtasun, R.: Are we ready for autonomous driving? the KITTI vision benchmark suite. In: 2012 IEEE Conference on Computer Vision and Pattern Recognition (2012). https://doi.org/10.1109/cvpr.2012.6248074

13. Kononenko, I.: Machine learning for medical diagnosis: history, state of the art and perspective. Artif. Intell. Medl. **23**(1), 89–109 (2001). https://doi.org/10.1016/s0933-3657(01)00077-x

14. Amodei, D., et al.: Deep speech 2: end-to-end speech recognition in English and mandarin. In: International Conference on Machine Learning, pp. 173–182. PMLR, June 2016

15. Hayes, J., Melis, L., Danezis, G., De Cristofaro, E.: LOGAN: membership inference attacks against generative models. Proc. Privacy Enhan. Technol. **2019**(1), 133–152 (2018). https://doi.org/10.2478/popets-2019-0008

16. Zhang, L., Deng, Z., Kawaguchi, K., Ghorbani, A., Zou, J.: How does mixup help with robustness and generalization. In: Proceedings of ICLR (2021)

17. Guowen, X., Li, H., Liu, S., Yang, K., Lin, X.: VerifyNet: secure and verifiable federated learning. IEEE Trans. Inf. Forens. Secur. **15**, 911–926 (2019)

18. Guowen, X., Li, H., Zhang, Y., Shengmin, X., Ning, J., Deng, R.H.: Priva-cy-preserving federated deep learning with irregular users. IEEE Trans. Depend. Secur. Comput. (2020). https://doi.org/10.1109/TDSC.2020.3005909

Isogeny Computation on Twisted Jacobi Intersections

Zhi Hu[1], Lin Wang[2], and Zijian Zhou[3,4(⊠)]

[1] School of Mathematics and Statistics, Central South University, Changsha, China
huzhi_math@csu.edu.cn
[2] Science and Technology on Communication Security Laboratory, Chengdu, China
[3] College of Liberal Arts and Sciences, National University of Defense Technology, Changsha, China
[4] Hunan Engineering Research Center of Commercial Cryptography Theory and Technology Innovation, Changsha, China

Abstract. Isogenies between elliptic curves act as a key role in isogeny-based cryptography. Formulas for isogenies on different elliptic curve models such as Weierstrass, Edwards, Huff and Hessian have been proposed. In this paper, we construct isogenies on twisted Jacobi intersections for the first time including a 2-isogeny and a generalized ℓ-isogeny for any odd ℓ. We also introduces ω-coordinate systems for twisted Jacobi intersections which provides biquadratic relations like the Montgomery model. As a result, such ω-coordinate systems would significantly simplify the computation of isogenies on twisted Jacobi intersections.

Keywords: Isogenies · Post-quantum cryptography · Twisted Jacobi intersection · ω-coordinate

1 Introduction

The supersingular isogeny-based cryptography is the most recent suggestion for post quantum cryptosystem and is founded on the hardness of finding an isogeny between two given supersingular elliptic curves over a finite field. It is drawing increased attention due to its relative small key sizes and messages compared to other post-quantum candidates. One of the instantiations is the key exchange protocol SIDH (Supersingular Isogeny Diffie-Hellman) proposed by De Feo and Jao [9]. Its secure key encapsulation mechanism version, named SIKE [10], was submitted to NIST's post-quantum cryptography standardization process and has been selected as an alternative candidate of PKE&KE in Round 3. There are also many other instantiations due to different choices of supersingular elliptic curves and isogenies. For example, the CSIDH [2] proposed by Castryck et al. in ASIACRYPT 2018 with supersingular elliptic curves over $\mathbb{F}_p$, the BSIDH [4] offered by Costello and the SiGamal [12] by Moriya et al. in ASIACRYPT 2020.

© Springer Nature Switzerland AG 2021
R. Deng et al. (Eds.): ISPEC 2021, LNCS 13107, pp. 46–56, 2021.
https://doi.org/10.1007/978-3-030-93206-0_4

As such, isogenies are a topic of interest in the isogeny-based cryptography as well as in elliptic curve cryptography. However, the bottleneck of isogeny-based cryptography is that its implementation efficiency does not meet the requirement of real-world application. The main contributor of this is that the isogeny computation is much more complicated than the traditional operations like scalar multiplications in elliptic curve cryptography.

It is well known that the existence of isogenies between two elliptic curves is independent of curve models. However, similar to the algebraic group arithmetic in traditional elliptic curve cryptography, the complexity of computing isogenies varies greatly from one model to another. The most famous method for efficiently presenting explicit isogeny with Weierstrass model is given by Vélu's formulas [16], which is based on point addition formulas. Moody and Shumow [13] presented formulas similar to Vélu's for isogenies on Edwards and Huff models of elliptic curves with efficient isogeny computation. Xu et al. [17] also gave explicit formulas for isogenies on Jacobi quartic curves.

Using the results above, cryptographers could choose corresponding curve models to accelerate the isogeny computation in the implementation of isogeny-based cryptography, for instants see the adaption of Montgomery model in SIDH [9]. Hence it is motivated to study the explicit and fast formulas for isogenies between other curve models such as the so-called twisted Jacobi intersection.

The twisted Jacobi intersections is the intersection of two quadratic surfaces in the three dimensional space such that they are birational equivalent to elliptic curves. It is a generalization of Jacobi intersections and was first introduced by Feng et al. [7]. Compared to Jacobi intersections, the twisted version has faster addition and doubling formulas. Furthermore, it was shown that every elliptic curve in positive characteristic with three points of order 2 is isomorphic to a twisted Jacobi intersection [7]. In [14], Silva et al. gave the explicit formula for odd isogeny of Jacobi intersections.

In this work, we study the fast isogeny computation between twisted Jacobi intersections model of elliptic curves. The following demonstrates the main contributions of this work:

- *Explicit Isogeny Formulas on Twisted Jacobi Intersections.* We present the explicit formulas for 2-isogeny and odd isogenies between twisted Jacobi intersections, extending Silva et al.'s results [14]. Our formula for computing the coefficients of curves of odd isogenies has a simple expression.
- *Differential Arithmetic on Twisted Jacobi Intersections.* Similar to the ω-coordinate system on Edwards model [6] and Huff Model [8], we construct a ω-coordinate system on twisted Jacobi intersections and prove a Montgomery-like group law formulas on these curves. Such ω-coordinate system also induces simple isogeny formulas for twisted Jacobi intersections, which share the same form as those on Montgomery curves with only x-coordinate.

Our work is organized as follows. Section 2 reviews basic facts about isogenies and twisted Jacobi intersections. Section 3 presents formulas for 2-isogenies and odd isogenies between twisted Jacobi intersections. In Sect. 4, we construct a new ω-coordinate system on twisted Jacobi intersections and give simplified isogeny formulas with this system. Finally, Sect. 5 concludes with a discussion about further study.

2 Preliminaries

An isogeny between two elliptic curves E_1 and E_2 is a dense morphism $\phi :$ $E_1 \to E_2$ preserves the basepoints, i.e. ϕ preserves the identity element with $\phi(E_1) = E_2$. Note that ϕ is also an endomorphism if $E_1 = E_2$. Two elliptic curves E_1, E_2 are said to be isogenous if there is an isogeny $\phi : E_1 \to E_2$. The degree of an isogeny is its degree as a rational map. In particular, a separable isogeny ϕ of degree ℓ has a kernel of size ℓ.

Recall that given an elliptic curve E and a subgroup G of E, there is a unique isogeny $E \to E'$ with kernel G up to isomorphism [15, III.4.12]. Hence one can identify an isogeny by specifying its kernel. Vélu's formula and its analogues shed a light on computing the isogeny that corresponds to a given subgroup. This correspondence may allow for compact representation and efficient computation of isogeny, especially for kernels generated by points of prime order.

Let K be a finite field with $\mathrm{char}(K) = p > 3$. A twisted Jacobi intersection model of elliptic curve over K is given by

$$J_{a,b} : \begin{cases} au^2 + v^2 = 1 \\ bu^2 + w^2 = 1 \end{cases} \tag{1}$$

where $a, b \in K$ and $ab(a - b) \neq 0$. Note that a Jacobi intersection is a twisted Jacobi intersection with $a = 1$. The j-invariant of $J_{a,b}$ is

$$j(J_{a,b}) = \frac{256(a^2 - ab + b^2)^3}{a^2 b^2 (a - b)^2}.$$

Note that $(0, 1, 1)$ is the identity point in the group $J_{a,b}(K)$, and the negative point of (u, v, w) is $(-u, v, w)$.

A twisted Jacobi intersection $J_{a,b} : au^2 + v^2 = 1, bu^2 + w^2 = 1$ is birationally equivalent to an elliptic curve $E_W : y^2 = x^3 - (a + b)x^2 + abx$, via the transformations [7]:

$$\sigma : J_{a,b} \longrightarrow E_W,$$
$$(0, 1, 1) \longmapsto \infty,$$
$$(0, 1, -1) \longmapsto (b, 0),$$
$$(u, v, w) \longmapsto (-\frac{a(w + 1)}{v - 1}, -\frac{au}{v - 1}(\frac{a(w + 1)}{v - 1} + b)).$$
$$\sigma^{-1} : E_W \longrightarrow J_{a,b},$$
$$\infty \longmapsto (0, 1, 1),$$
$$(b, 0) \longmapsto (0, 1, -1),$$
$$(x, y) \longmapsto (-\frac{2y}{x^2 - ab}, \frac{x^2 - 2ax + ab}{x^2 - ab}, \frac{x^2 - 2bx + ab}{x^2 - ab}).$$

$$\tag{2}$$

The group law on $J_{a,b}$ in affine coordinates is presented as follows [7]: given two points (u_1, v_1, w_1) and (u_2, v_2, w_2), the sum $(u_3, v_3, w_3) = (u_1, v_1, w_1) + (u_2, v_2, w_2)$ is

$$u_3 = \frac{u_1 v_2 w_2 + u_2 v_1 w_1}{v_2^2 + a u_2^2 w_1^2},$$

$$v_3 = \frac{v_1 v_2 - a u_1 w_1 u_2 w_2}{v_2^2 + a u_2^2 w_1^2}, \tag{3}$$

$$w_3 = \frac{w_1 w_2 - b u_1 v_1 u_2 v_2}{v_2^2 + a u_2^2 w_1^2}.$$

The above formulas are complete (i.e., defined for all inputs).

3   Isogenies on Twisted Jacobi Intersections

In this section we show how to present explicit (and simplified) formulas for isogenies on twisted Jacobi intersections. For a twisted Jacobi intersection $J_{a,b}$ over K with coefficient a, b, we denote by $\sqrt{a}$ (resp. $\sqrt{b}$) a square root of a (resp. b) and write simply $\sqrt{ab}$ for $\sqrt{a} \cdot \sqrt{b}$.

3.1   2-Isogeny

Theorem 1. *Let $J_{a,b}$ be a twisted Jacobi intersection over K, then there is a 2-isogeny from the curve $J_{a,b}$ as*

$$\phi_2(u, v, w) = (\frac{-u}{vw}, \frac{-\sqrt{ab}u^2 + 1}{vw}, \frac{\sqrt{ab}u^2 + 1}{vw}), \tag{4}$$

the image of ϕ_2 is the curve $J_{\hat{a},\hat{b}}$, where $\hat{a} = -(\sqrt{a} - \sqrt{b})^2$ and $\hat{b} = -(\sqrt{a} + \sqrt{b})^2$.

Proof. The desired 2-isogeny ϕ_2 can be derived as

$$\phi : J_{a,b} \xrightarrow{\sigma} E_1 \xrightarrow{\psi} E_2 \xrightarrow{\sigma'} J_{\hat{a},\hat{b}}.$$

Here $\sigma : J_{a,b} \to E_1$ is given as $(u, v, w) \longmapsto (-\frac{a(w+1)}{v-1}, -\frac{au}{v-1}(\frac{a(w+1)}{v-1} + b))$, with $E_1 : y^2 = x^3 - (a+b)x^2 + abx$.

The kernel of the desired isogeny is the set $\{(0, -1, -1), (0, 1, 1)\}$. For this kernel, it suffices to explicitly find the maps ψ, σ'. Formulas for 2-isogenies on Weierstrass curves are well known, see Example 4.5 of [15] for the 2-isogeny $\psi : E_1 \to E_2$ as

$$\psi(x, y) = (\frac{y^2}{x^2}, \frac{y(ab - x^2)}{x^2}),$$

where $E_2 : y^2 = x^3 + 2(a+b)x^2 + (a-b)^2 x$.

Therefore, we can get the corresponding map $\sigma' : E_2 \to J_{\hat{a}_i, \hat{b}_i}$ by pulling Weierstrass model back to a desired Jacobi intersection using the maps in Eq. (2).

Composing the maps as $\sigma' \circ \psi \circ \sigma$ leads to the stated formulas for ϕ_2. Since the arithmetic details are straightforward and thus we omitted them for brevity.

3.2   Odd Degree Isogenies

Let F be a subgroup of E of odd order ℓ, the well known Vélu formulas [16] on a Weierstrass elliptic curve for an isogeny $\phi : E \to E'$ with kernel F are presented here. Given a point $P = (x_P, y_P) \in E$, define

$$\phi(P) = \begin{cases} (x_P + \sum_{Q \in F - \{\infty\}} (x_{P+Q} - x_Q), y_P + \sum_{Q \in F - \{\infty\}} (y_{P+Q} - y_Q), & P \notin F, \\ \infty, & P \in F. \end{cases}$$

Silva et al. in [14] gave a formula for odd degree isogeny ϕ on the Jacobi intersection as

$$\phi(P) = \begin{cases} \infty, & P \in F, \\ (u_P \prod_{Q \in F - \{\infty\}} \frac{u_{P+Q}}{u_Q}, v_P \prod_{Q \in F - \{\infty\}} \frac{v_{P+Q}}{v_Q}, w_P \prod_{Q \in F - \{\infty\}} \frac{w_{P+Q}}{w_Q}), & P \notin F, \end{cases}$$

based on which they also gave an explicit formula for isogeies of degree ℓ.

In this work, we imitate the above work and present a new formula for the degree ℓ-isogeny, which yields the following result:

Theorem 2. *Let* $F = \{(0, 1, 1), (\pm\alpha_1, \beta_1, \gamma_1), ..., (\pm\alpha_s, \beta_s, \gamma_s)\}$ *be a subgroup of the twisted Jacobi intersection* $J_{a,b}$ *with odd order* $\ell = 2s + 1$. *Define*

$$\phi_\ell(P) = (\prod_{Q \in F} \frac{u_{P+Q} w_Q}{v_Q}, \prod_{Q \in F} \frac{v_{P+Q}}{v_Q}, \prod_{Q \in F} \frac{w_{P+Q}}{w_Q}). \tag{5}$$

Then ϕ_ℓ *is an* ℓ*-isogeny with kernel* F, *from* $J_{a,b}$ *to* $J_{\hat{a},\hat{b}}$ *where* $\hat{a} = a^\ell$ *and* $\hat{b} = b^\ell \prod_{i=1}^{s} \frac{(1-a\alpha_i^2)^4}{(1-b\alpha_i^2)^4}$. *The coordinate maps are given by*

$$\phi_\ell(u, v, w) = (u \prod_{i=1}^{s} \frac{(u^2 - \alpha_i^2)\gamma_i^2}{(1 - ab\alpha_i^2 u^2)\beta_i^2}, v \prod_{i=1}^{s} \frac{1 + ab\alpha_i^2 u^2 - a(u^2 + \alpha_i^2)}{(1 - ab\alpha_i^2 u^2)\beta_i^2},$$
$$w \prod_{i=1}^{s} \frac{1 + ab\alpha_i^2 u^2 - b(u^2 + \alpha_i^2)}{(1 - ab\alpha_i^2 u^2)\gamma_i^2}). \tag{6}$$

Proof. We have $\phi_\ell((0, 1, 1)) = (0, 1, 1)$ and ϕ_ℓ is invariant under the translation by elements of F, thus $F \subseteq \ker(\phi_\ell)$. Conversely, if $P \in \ker(\phi_\ell)$, then there exists some $Q \in F$ such that $P + Q = (0, 1, 1)$, which implies that $P = -Q \in F$, and hence $F = \ker(\phi_\ell)$. Moreover, suppose $P = (u, v, w)$, and $Q = (\alpha_i, \beta_i, \gamma_i) \neq (0, 1, 1)$, then we have

$$u_{P+Q} u_{P-Q} = \frac{(\beta_i^2 \gamma_i^2 u^2 - \alpha_i^2 v^2 w^2)}{(\beta_i^2 + a\alpha_i^2 w^2)^2} = \frac{u^2 - \alpha_i^2}{1 - ab\alpha_i^2 u^2},$$

$$v_{P+Q} v_{P-Q} = \frac{a^2 u^2 w^2 \alpha_i^2 \gamma_i^2 - v^2 \beta_i^2}{(\beta_i^2 + a\alpha_i^2 w^2)^2} = \frac{1 - a(\alpha_i^2 + u^2) + abu^2 \alpha_i^2}{1 - ab\alpha_i^2 u^2},$$

$$w_{P+Q} w_{P-Q} = \frac{b^2 u^2 v^2 \alpha_i^2 \beta_i^2 - \gamma_i^2 w^2}{(\beta_i^2 + a\alpha_i^2 w^2)^2} = \frac{1 - b(u^2 + \alpha_i^2) + abu^2 \alpha_i^2}{1 - ab\alpha_i^2 u^2}.$$

Thus it is straightforward to derive the above coordinate maps by the twisted Jacobi intersection addition law.

It remains to derive the formulas for $\hat{a}$ and $\hat{b}$ on the image curve

$$J_{\hat{a},\hat{b}} : \begin{cases} \hat{a}U^2 + V^2 = 1 \\ \hat{b}U^2 + W^2 = 1 \end{cases}, \tag{7}$$

where $U(P), V(P), W(P)$ are the coordinate maps of ϕ_ℓ. Consider the function

$$G_1(u,v,w) = (\hat{a}U^2 + V^2 - 1)(\prod_{i=1}^{s}(1 - ab\alpha_i^2 u^2)^2 \beta_i^4)$$

$$= \hat{a}(u^2 \prod_{i=1}^{s}((u^2 - \alpha_i^2)^2 \gamma_i^4)) + (1 - au^2) \prod_{i=1}^{s}(1 - a(\alpha_i^2 + u^2) + ab\alpha_i^2 u^2)^2 - \prod_{i=1}^{s}(1 - ab\alpha_i^2 u^2)^2 \beta_i^4$$

$$= (\hat{a} - a^\ell) \prod_{i=1}^{s} \gamma_i^4 u^{2\ell} + \text{lower terms with respect to } u.$$

Setting the coeffcients of $u^{2\ell}$ to zero and thus we obtain $\hat{a} = a^\ell$. Similarly we consider

$$G_2(u,v,w) = (\hat{b}U^2 + W^2 - 1)(\prod_{i=1}^{s}(1 - ab\alpha_i^2 u^2)^2 \beta_i^4 \gamma_i^4)$$

$$= \hat{b}(u^2 \prod_{i=1}^{s}((u^2 - \alpha_i^2)^2 \gamma_i^8)) + (1 - bu^2) \prod_{i=1}^{s}(1 - b(\alpha_i^2 + u^2) + ab\alpha_i^2 u^2)^2 \beta_i^4 - \prod_{i=1}^{s}(1 - ab\alpha_i^2 u^2)^2 \beta_i^4 \gamma_i^4$$

$$= (\hat{b}\prod_{i=1}^{s} \gamma_i^8 - b^\ell \prod_{i=1}^{s} \beta_i^8)u^{2\ell} + \text{lower terms with respect to } u.$$

By using the fact that $\beta_i^2 = 1 - a\alpha_i^2$, $\gamma_i^2 = 1 - b\alpha_i^2$ and by setting the coeffcients of $u^{2\ell}$ to zero, we obtain that

$$\hat{b} = b^\ell \prod_{i=1}^{s} \frac{\beta_i^8}{\gamma_i^8} = b^\ell \prod_{i=1}^{s} \frac{(1 - a\alpha_i^2)^4}{(1 - b\alpha_i^2)^4}.$$

Remark 1. While Silva et al. in [14] also gave similar formulas for odd isogeny on Jacobi intersections, we proved it in a different way for the twisted Jacobi intersections. Moreover, our formulas for the curve coefficients are easily transformed into inversion-free version, which are expected to provide performance advantage in isogeny computation.

4 ω-Coordinate on Twisted Jacobi Intersections

To evaluate the elliptic curve arithmetic efficiently, Farashahi and Hosseini proposed ω-coordinate system on Edwards curves [6], which was also applied to isogeny computation by Kim et al. [11]. Huang et al. [8] and Drylo et al. in [5] presented similar ω-coordinate systems on Huff curves which provide faster formulas for point addition and isogeny computation. In fact, such ω-coordinate systems could be generalized to other elliptic curve models, and induce analogous Montgomery-like formulas for group and isogeny arithmetic.

4.1 ω-Coordinate System for Differential Addition

In this work, we introduce such kind ω-coordinate system on twisted Jacobi intersections. We define a rational function ω by $\omega(u, v, w) = \sqrt{ab}u^2$, which is well computed for all affine points on a twisted Jacobi intersection. Let $P = (u, v, w)$ be a point on the curve, one can easily deduce that $\omega(P) = \omega(-P)$. Moreover, $\omega((0, 1, 1)) = 0$. Denote by $c = \frac{\sqrt{b}}{\sqrt{a}}$, then the equation of the twisted Jacobi intersection can be written as:

$$J_c : \begin{cases} \omega + cv^2 = c \\ c\omega + w^2 = 1 \end{cases} \tag{8}$$

Theorem 3. Let $\omega_i = \omega(P_i)$ with $P_i \in J_{a,b}$ for $i = 1, 2$, and let $\omega_0 = \omega(P_1 - P_2)$, $\omega_3 = \omega(P_1 + P_2)$ and $\omega_4 = \omega(2P_1)$. We have the following differential addition formulas

$$\omega_3\omega_0 = \frac{(\omega_1 - \omega_2)^2}{(\omega_1\omega_2 - 1)^2}, \quad \omega_4 = \frac{4\omega_1(\omega_1^2 + (c + \frac{1}{c})\omega_1 + 1)}{(1 - \omega_1^2)^2}.$$

Proof. This can be derived from the addition formula give by Eq. (3) and hence we omit the detail.

4.2 ω-Coordinate for Isogenies

Based on the above, we present the isogeny formulas using the ω-coordinate on twisted Jacobi intersection J_c as Eq. (8). Note that the j-invariant

$$j(J_c) = j(J_{a,b}) = \frac{256(1 - c^2 + c^4)^3}{c^4(1 - c^2)^2}.$$

We can use the parameter c to represent the isogenous curve instead of parameters (a, b) in $J_{a,b}$.

Recall that $\omega(u, v, w) = \sqrt{ab}u^2$ for $J_{a,b}$ and write $c = \frac{\sqrt{b}}{\sqrt{a}}$.

Theorem 4. Let ϕ_2 be the 2-isogeny from $J_{a,b}$ to $J_{\hat{a},\hat{b}}$ defined as in Theorem 1. Then the evaluation of $\omega = \omega(P), P = (u, v, w) \in J_{a,b}(K)$ under ϕ_2 is given by

$$\phi_2(\omega) = \frac{(\frac{1}{c} - c)\omega}{(1 - c\omega)(1 - \frac{\omega}{c})}, \tag{9}$$

where the parameter for the image curve is $\hat{c} = \frac{1+c}{1-c}$.

Proof. Suppose $P = (u, v, w)$ and denote by $\phi(u, v, w) = (U, V, W)$ the image point. Then the ω-coordinate in $J_{\hat{a},\hat{b}}$ is given by $\omega(\phi(u, v, w)) = \sqrt{\hat{a}\hat{b}}U^2$.

By Theorem 1, one has

$$\sqrt{\hat{a}\hat{b}}U^2 = \sqrt{(\sqrt{a} - \sqrt{b})^2(\sqrt{a} + \sqrt{b})^2}\frac{u^2}{v^2w^2}$$
$$= \frac{(a - b)u^2}{(1 - au^2)(1 - bu^2)}$$
$$= \frac{(\frac{1}{c} - c)\omega}{(1 - c\omega)(1 - \frac{\omega}{c})}.$$

Moreover, we have

$$\hat{c} = \sqrt{\frac{\hat{b}}{\hat{a}}} = \frac{(\sqrt{a} + \sqrt{b})}{(\sqrt{a} - \sqrt{b})} = \frac{1 + c}{1 - c}.$$

We have the following odd isogeny formula using the $\omega-$coordinate:

Theorem 5. *Let* $F = \{(0, 1, 1), (\pm\alpha_1, \beta_1, \gamma_1), ..., (\pm\alpha_s, \beta_s, \gamma_s)\}$ *be a subgroup of the twisted Jacobi intersection* $J_{a,b}$ *with odd order* $\ell = 2s + 1$. *Write* $\omega_i = \omega(\alpha_i, \beta_i, \gamma_i)$ *for* $i = 1, .., s$ *and let* ϕ_ℓ *be the* ℓ-*isogeny from* $J_{a,b}$ *to* $J_{\hat{a},\hat{b}}$ *with kernel* F. *Then the evaluation of* $\omega = \omega(P), P = (u, v, w) \in J_{a,b}(K)$ *under* ϕ_ℓ *is given by*

$$\phi_\ell(\omega) = \omega \prod_{i=1}^{s} (\frac{\omega - \omega_i}{1 - \omega\omega_i})^2, \tag{10}$$

with the codomain curve coefficient

$$\hat{c} = c \prod_{i=1}^{s} \frac{(c - \omega_i)^2}{(1 - c\omega_i)^2}. \tag{11}$$

Proof. Note that $c = \sqrt{b/a}$ and $\omega = \sqrt{ab}w^2$, which implies $bu^2 = c\omega, au^2 = \omega/c$. Let $P = (u, v, w)$ and write $U(P)$ the coordinate maps of ϕ_ℓ give in Theorem 2. Recall that by Theorem 2, we have $\hat{a} = a^\ell$ and

$$\hat{b} = b^\ell \prod_{i=1}^{s} \frac{(1 - a\alpha_i^2)^4}{(1 - b\alpha_i^2)^4} = b^\ell \prod_{i=1}^{s} \frac{\beta_i^8}{\gamma_i^8}.$$

Then

$$\hat{\omega} = \sqrt{\hat{a}\hat{b}}U(P)^2 = \sqrt{a^l b^l}u^2 \prod_{i=1}^{s} (\frac{\beta_i^4}{\alpha_i^4}\frac{(u^2 - \alpha_i^2)\gamma_i^2}{(1 - ab\alpha_i^2u^2)\beta_i^2})^2$$
$$= \sqrt{a^l b^l}u^2 \prod_{i=1}^{s} \frac{(\sqrt{ab}u^2 - \sqrt{ab}\alpha_i^2)^2}{(1 - ab\alpha_i^2u^2)^2}$$
$$= \omega \prod_{i=1}^{s} \frac{(\omega - \omega_i)^2}{(1 - \omega\omega_i)^2}.$$

Furthermore, one has

$$\hat{c} = \sqrt{\frac{\hat{b}}{\hat{a}}} = \sqrt{\frac{b}{a}} \prod_{i=1}^{s} \frac{(1 - a\alpha_i^2)^2}{(1 - b\alpha_i^2)^2} = c \prod_{i=1}^{s} \frac{(c - \omega_i)^2}{(1 - c\omega_i)^2}.$$

4.3 Computational Cost

Let $\mathbf{M}$ stand for a field multiplication, $\mathbf{S}$ for a field squaring, $\mathbf{C}$ for a multiplication by a curve constant, and $\mathbf{I}$ for a field inversion. In the following table we list the costs of our odd isogenies compared with those proposed by Silva et al. in [14].

Table 1. The computational costs of $\ell = 2s + 1$ isogeny evaluation on (twisted) Jacobi intersections

Work	Operation cost (affine)	Operation cost (projective)
Silva et al. [14]	$(4s + 2)\mathbf{M} + 3\mathbf{S} + (5s + 1)\mathbf{C} + \mathbf{I}$	$(4s + 7)\mathbf{M} + 5\mathbf{S} + (6s + 2)\mathbf{C}$
This work (ω-coordinate)	$3s\mathbf{M} + 1\mathbf{S} + \mathbf{I}$	$4s\mathbf{M} + 2\mathbf{S}$

It should be noted that Silva et al. in [14, Theorem 4.1] proposed the codomain curve parameter for Jacobi intersection (setting $b = 1$ in the twisted case) as $\hat{a} = a - 2a \sum_{i=1}^{s} (\frac{-\alpha_i^2 \beta_i^2}{\gamma_i^2} + 2\alpha_i^2 - 1)$, the evaluation of which costs much more than that of our $\hat{c}$ in Eq. (11).

Remark 2. The above result implies an interesting result that, the formulas of odd ℓ isogeny with ω-coordinate system on twisted Jacobi intersections share the same form with those on Montgomery model in [3]. Thus we would gain comparable cost for the isogeny computation by adopting the above formulas for twisted Jacobi intersections. Furthermore, due to the well form of the formulas in Eqs. (10) and (11), we can adapt the fast isogeny computation technique proposed by Bernstein et al. in [1] to twisted Jacobi intersections, and thus the ℓ-isogeny mapping and its codomain curve coefficient could be evaluated in $\tilde{O}(\sqrt{\ell})$ finite field operations.

5   Conclusion

In this work, we exploit the ω-coordinates to optimize the elliptic curve group arithmetic formulas as well as the isogenous formulas on twisted Jacobi intersections. Our results implies that the twisted Jacobi intersections also serve as an ideal model for isogeny-based cryptography. It was also noticed that the formulas of odd ℓ isogeny with w-coodinate system on twisted Jacobi intersections have the same expression as the Kummer line in Montgomery model. We hope that further research could find the connection between the w-coordinate systems (resp. Kummer line) on different curve models.

Acknowledgements. We would like to thank the reviewers for their helpful comments. Zhi Hu was supported by the National Natural Science Foundation of China (61972420, 61602526) and the Natural Science Foundation of Hunan Province (2020JJ3050, 2019JJ50827). Zijian Zhou (corresponding author of this paper) was supported by the Natural Science Foundation of Hunan Province (2021JJ40701) and The Research Fund of National University of Defense Technology (ZK20-42).

References

1. Bernstein, D., De Feo, L., Leroux, A., Smith, B.: Faster computation of isogenies of large prime degree. Cryptology ePrint Archive 2020/341 (2020)
2. Castryck, W., Lange, T., Martindale, C., Panny, L., Renes, J.: CSIDH: an efficient post-quantum commutative group action. In: Peyrin, T., Galbraith, S. (eds.) ASIACRYPT 2018. LNCS, vol. 11274, pp. 395–427. Springer, Cham (2018). https://doi.org/10.1007/978-3-030-03332-3_15
3. Costello, C., Hisil, H.: A simple and compact algorithm for SIDH with arbitrary degree isogenies. In: Takagi, T., Peyrin, T. (eds.) ASIACRYPT 2017. LNCS, vol. 10625, pp. 303–329. Springer, Cham (2017). https://doi.org/10.1007/978-3-319-70697-9_11
4. Costello, C.: B-SIDH: supersingular isogeny Diffie-Hellman using twisted torsion. Cryptology ePrint Archive 2019/1145 (2019)
5. Drylo, R., Kijko, T., Wronski, M.: Efficient montgomery-like formulas for general Huff's and Huff's elliptic curves and their applications to the isogeny-based cryptography. Cryptology ePrint Archive 2020/526 (2020)
6. Farashahi, R.R., Hosseini, S.G.: Differential addition on twisted Edwards curves. In: Pieprzyk, J., Suriadi, S. (eds.) ACISP 2017. LNCS, vol. 10343, pp. 366–378. Springer, Cham (2017). https://doi.org/10.1007/978-3-319-59870-3_21
7. Feng, R., Nie, M., Wu, H.: Twisted Jacobi intersections curves. In: Kratochvíl, J., Li, A., Fiala, J., Kolman, P. (eds.) TAMC 2010. LNCS, vol. 6108, pp. 199–210. Springer, Heidelberg (2010). https://doi.org/10.1007/978-3-642-13562-0_19
8. Huang, Y., Zhang, F., Hu, Z., Liu, Z.: Optimized arithmetic operations for isogeny-based cryptography on Huff curves. In: Liu, J.K., Cui, H. (eds.) ACISP 2020. LNCS, vol. 12248, pp. 23–40. Springer, Cham (2020). https://doi.org/10.1007/978-3-030-55304-3_2
9. Jao, D., De Feo, L.: Towards quantum-resistant cryptosystems from supersingular elliptic curve isogenies. In: Yang, B.-Y. (ed.) PQCrypto 2011. LNCS, vol. 7071, pp. 19–34. Springer, Heidelberg (2011). https://doi.org/10.1007/978-3-642-25405-5_2
10. Jao, D., et al.: Supersingular isogeny key encapsulation. In: NIST Post-Quantum Cryptography Standardization Round 2 Submission. 16 April 2020. http://www.sike.org/
11. Kim, S., Yoon, K., Park, Y.-H., Hong, S.: Optimized method for computing odd-degree isogenies on Edwards curves. In: Galbraith, S.D., Moriai, S. (eds.) ASIACRYPT 2019. LNCS, vol. 11922, pp. 273–292. Springer, Cham (2019). https://doi.org/10.1007/978-3-030-34621-8_10
12. Moriya, T., Onuki, H., Takagi, T.: SiGamal: a supersingular isogeny-based PKE and its application to a PRF. In: Moriai, S., Wang, H. (eds.) ASIACRYPT 2020. LNCS, vol. 12492, pp. 551–580. Springer, Cham (2020). https://doi.org/10.1007/978-3-030-64834-3_19
13. Moody, D., Shumow, D.: Analogues of Velu's formulas for isogenies on alternate models of elliptic curves. Math. Comput. **85**(300), 1929–1951 (2016)

14. Silva, J., Lopez, J., Dahab, R.: Isogeny formulas for Jacobi intersection and twisted hessian curves. Adv. Math. Commun. **14**(3), 507–523 (2020)
15. Silverman, J.H.: The Arithmetic of Elliptic Curves, 2nd edn. Springer-Verlag, New York (2009)
16. Isogenies entre courbes elliptiques: Vélu. J. CR Acad. Sci. Paris Ser. AB **273**, A238–241 (1971)
17. Xu, X., Yu, W., Wang, K., He, X.: Constructing isogenies on extended Jacobi quartic curves. In: Chen, K., Lin, D., Yung, M. (eds.) Inscrypt 2016. LNCS, vol. 10143, pp. 416–427. Springer, Cham (2017). https://doi.org/10.1007/978-3-319-54705-3_26

EPFSTO-ARIMA: Electric Power Forced Stochastic Optimization Predicting Based on ARIMA

Guangxia Xu$^{(\boxtimes)}$ (ID) and Yuqing Xu (ID)

School of Computer Science and Technology, Chongqing University of Posts
and Telecommunications, Chongqing 400065, China
xugx@cqupt.edu.cn
http://faculty.cqupt.edu.cn

Abstract. With the advance of new technology and management
reforms, data sharing has unleashed the full potential for social production during the past decade, especially for enterprise survival. Data poisoning attack is a typical attack faced by data sharing, EPSTO-ARIMA
(Electric Power Stochastic Optimization Predicting Based on Autoregressive Integrated Moving Average model) would increase prediction
error by generating adversarial shared data, which leads to the failure of
the prediction. In response to the EPSTO-ARIMA attack, this paper proposes EPFSTO-ARIMA (Electric Power Forced Stochastic Optimization
Predicting Based on Autoregressive Integrated Moving Average model)
combined with data sanitization and data grouping. The model was validated by seven sets of data from three datasets. Experimental results
indicate that EPFSTO-ARIMA can remedy the flaws of excessive accuracy error caused by the EPSTO-ARIMA. For publicly dataset "Col-
umn2", the proposed EPFSTO-ARIMA achieves 30.44% lower prediction error than EPSTO-ARIMA, respectively. Simultaneously, the ter-
rific results in other datasets have also been ascertained the viability
and generalization ability of our proposed EPFSTO-ARIMA.

Keywords: Stochastic sampling · Stochastic optimization ·
Adversarial examples · Inference attack · Data poisoning · Electric
power forced stochastic optimization predicting

1 Introduction

Data, as the source of all walks of life and an essential element for critical infrastructures, has been extremely successful used in the last decade, especially in

Supported by the National Natural Science Foundation (Grant No. 61772099,
61772098); the Science and Technology Innovation Leadership Support Program of
Chongqing (Grant No. CSTCCXLJRC201917); the Innovation and Entrepreneur-
ship Demonstration Team Cultivation Plan of Chongqing (Grant No. CSTC2017kjrc-
cxcytd0063); the National Key Research and Development Program of China (Grant
No. 2018YFB0904900, 2018YFB0904905).

R. Deng et al. (Eds.): ISPEC 2021, LNCS 13107, pp. 57–68, 2021.
https://doi.org/10.1007/978-3-030-93206-0_5

energy. Among data value extraction, data sharing technology plays a pivotal role in the whole life cycle of data. The maximization of data value has been achieved by data sharing in multi-field applications. As a promising application of data sharing, electricity data prediction, the amount of electricity used by different consumers can be predicted, which can assist the government in optimizing the planning of electricity infrastructure construction. In a nutshell, data prediction can help countries and enterprises put the resource to good use, improve social planning, optimize social management, and defend against cyber-attacks.

With the continuous evolution of LSTM (Long Short-Term Memory) [1], Bi-LSTM (Bi-directional Long Short-Term Memory) [2], ARIMA (Autoregressive Integrated Moving Average model) [3,4], the capability of data prediction has made great progress and gradually become maturity. However, existing studies have shown that data poisoning is widely concerned [5] in machine learning and data poisoning attacks have gradually eroded the power sector [6,7].

EPSTO-ARIMA (Electric Power Stochastic Optimization Predicting Based on Autoregressive Integrated Moving Average model) was proposed to increase error of prediction by using the concept of dropout and stochastic sampling to generate adversarial samples. The prediction error of EPSTO-ARIMA is higher than ARIMA. Motivated by this, this paper proposed a new prediction model, called EPFSTO-ARIMA (Electric Power Forced Stochastic Optimization Predicting Based on Autoregressive Integrated Moving Average model), which can deal with excessive accuracy error caused by EPSTO-ARIMA with data sanitization and data grouping.

Our main contributions in this paper include:

1) Reduce the prediction error caused by EPSTO-ARIMA. Data sanitization and data grouping are used to defend EPSTO-ARIMA attack.
2) Ensure the availability of data. The EPFSTO-ARIMA prediction results are in line with the original law of the data.
3) Explore data discipline. Utilizing EPFSTO-ARIMA, the influence of data inference prediction results is discussed according to data grouping.
4) The results of EPFSTO-ARIMA have an enlightening influence on the defense of poisoning attack and contribute to the defense of time series data poisoning research.

This paper proceeds as follows. The second section reviews adversarial examples, data poisoning attack defense in literature. The third section describes our response method. The fourth section presents the experimental conditions of models and measures indicators of models, describes and discusses the experimental results. The fifth section makes conclusions and describes future work.

2 Related Work

2.1 Data Poisoning and Adversarial Examples

The concept of adversarial example was proposed in [8], namely adding small perturbations to the original training data. Adversarial examples have been extensively studied [9,10]. The process of model training of adversarial examples is called data poisoning, adversarial examples are difficult to be perceived but become malicious for the trained model to incur erroneous results. To name a few, Papernot et al. [11] found that the adversarial examples generated by one model can cheat another model.

2.2   ARIMA

ARIMA is one of the most important and widely used models in time series data prediction, which has used in energy [3], transportation [4]. Besides these, ARIMA can be used in combination with other models [12]. But the topic of predicting angle of attack defense is rarely considered.

2.3   Dropout

In 2012, Hinton [13] proposed dropout, which can effectively prevent over-fitting in the training of complex feedforward neural network.

By randomly deleting some neurons on the network, dropout reduces the complex co-adaptive relationship between neurons. Through research, Jagielski et al. [5] found that dropping some contaminated data in training samples will increase the error of some models. Drawing on the above ideas, EPSTO-ARIMA was proposed to implement data poisoning.

2.4   Data Poisoning Attack Defense

In general, robustness improvement [14] and data sanitization [15] are used to defend against data poisoning. In this paper, we use data grouping based on data sanitization to counter data poisoning to improve the loss of prediction.

3   Our Approach

By referring to adversarial examples rapid generation method in [16] and the automatic modulation classification based on deep learning in [17], reversing use of the concept of data protection based on disturbance [18], following the intuition discussed in [19] for sub-Nyquist sampling and the working principle of Dropout [13], this paper proposed EPFSTO-ARIMA, which can realize data disturbance as presented in the later sections. The algorithm of EPFSTO-ARIMA is shown in Table 1 and Fig. 1.

We consider data poisoning and prediction scenario as shown in Fig. 1. In Part 1, the input of the original data is illustrated. In Part 2, data were grouped, stochastic sampling and optimized (Dropout) to generate and publish adversarial examples. In Part 3, adversarial examples and original data were used to train predictive models. In Part 4, the test data are used to verify the trained models and get the predicted results.

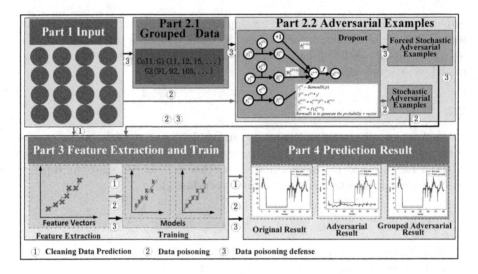

Fig. 1. Generation of adversarial examples vs. prediction.

3.1   Similarity Calculation

We utilize the idea of DTW (Dynamic Time Warping), a commonly used similarity calculation algorithm to calculate the similarity distance between each data and the average. According to similarity, the data is grouped to realize the implementation of the forced stochastic optimization prediction.

Suppose two standard reference templates $R = \{R(1), ...R(m), ...R(M)\}$ and $T = \{T(1), ...T(n), ...T(N)\}$, among them, R is an M-dimensional vector, T is an N-dimensional vector. The distance between R and T is shown as

$$D = \min_{c}(\sum_{n=1}^{N} [d(x_{i(n)}, y_{j(n)}) \bullet W_n] / \sum_{n=1}^{N} W_n) \tag{1}$$

where W_n is a weighting function, which is affected by the similarity distance of the previous data or the weight of the data. In this paper, we calculate the similarity distance between the average and the data.

From Eq. 1, we can calculate the similarity as

$$S_i = 1/(1 + D_i) \tag{2}$$

where D_i represents the similarity distance between the average value and the data, and it is default value is positive. Otherwise, its absolute value is taken. S_i represents the similarity. The larger the S, the higher the similarity.

3.2   Data Stochastic Sampling and Data Optimization

We utilize the idea of data sampling, Bayesian theory, and optimizing (Dropout) to generate adversarial examples. Sampling data are stochastic selected from the

Table 1. Algorithm of EPFSTO-ARIMA.

Algorithm 1:EPFSTO-ARIMA
Input:
1) Datasets;
2) The preprocessed data;
3) The start time(T_1).
Initialize:
1) i=0;
2) ARIMA model.
Generate adversarial examples:
1) Calculate the DP with Eq. 4;
2) Calculate the similarity with Eq. 1, Eq. 2;
3) Grouped data according Eq. 13;
4) Stochastic sampling with Eq. 3, Eq. 5 and Eq. 13;
5) Data optimize with Eq. 4 and the Dropout algorithm [13].
Verify data and determine parameters:
1) Determine d,p,q;
2) Determine G with Eq. 13.
Import and train models:
1) Import ARIMA(p,d,q);
2) Import EPSTO-ARIMA(p,d,q,DP);
3) Import EPFSTO-ARIMA(p,d,q,G,DP);
4) Train ARIMA(p,d,q) with original data;
5) Train EPSTO-ARIMA(p,d,q,DP) with adversarial examples;
6) Train EPFSTO-ARIMA(p,d,q,G,DP) with adversarial examples.
Predict:
1) Compute y_{DP} use Eq. 6, Eq. 7, Eq. 8, Eq. 9, Eq. 10;
2) Compute RMSE use Eq. 12;
3) Record the end time(T_2) and compute $TIME = T_2 - T_1$.
Output:
1) Output P_{DP} use Eq. 11;
2) Output RMSE;
3) Output TIME.

data sets according to the poisoning ratio. Each data point has the same probability of being selected, and the selected data is the optimized data (poisoned data), which can be expressed as

$$y^k = \{x_{1+ki}\}, 0 \le i \le [(n-1)/k] \tag{3}$$

$$DP = n_o/n_t \tag{4}$$

$$P\left(\bigcap_{i=1}^{n} S_i\right) = \prod_{i=1}^{n} P(S_i) \tag{5}$$

where y^k refers to the sampling data, k represents the sampling interval, DP represents the proportion of optimized data to total data, also known as the data poisoning ratio, n_o refers to the poisoned data, n_t refers to the total data, S_i is the $i - th$ data sampling, $P(S_i)$ is the generation probability of S_i and $P\left(\bigcap_{i=1}^{n} S_i\right)$ is the probability that independent events S_i occur simultaneously.

3.3   EPFSTO-ARIMA

The data are grouped according to their similarity, and each group is stochastically optimized in proportion. Suppose we divide the data into two groups of G_1 and G_2. When performing data optimization with the optimized ratio DP, the forced stochastic optimization includes two steps: i) optimizing DP in G_1 or G_2; ii) optimizing DP in the specific group according to actual needs. Compared with the stochastic optimization, the forced stochastic optimization is specific and can optimize data according to actual needs. We use adversarial examples and original data to train the models.

When original data was used, the predicted results can be expressed as

$$y_t = \theta_0 + \phi_1 y_{t-1} + \phi_2 y_{t-2} + \cdots + \phi_p y_{t-p} + \theta_2 e_{t-2} + \cdots + \theta_q e_{t-q} \qquad (6)$$

When using adversarial examples, the predicted results can be expressed as

$$y_{DP1} = u + \phi_2 y_{t-2} + \cdots + \phi_p y_{t-p} + \theta_1 e_{t-1} + \theta_2 e_{t-2} + \cdots + \theta_q e_{t-q} \qquad (7)$$

$$y_{DP2} = u + \phi_1 y_{t-1} + \cdots + \phi_p y_{t-p} + \theta_1 e_{t-1} + \theta_2 e_{t-2} + \cdots + \theta_q e_{t-q} \qquad (8)$$

$$y_{DP3} = u + \phi_1 y_{t-1} + \phi_2 y_{t-2} + \cdots + \phi_p y_{t-p} + \theta_2 e_{t-2} + \cdots + \theta_q e_{t-q} \qquad (9)$$

$$y_{DPn} = u + \phi_1 y_{t-1} + \phi_2 y_{t-2} + \cdots + \phi_p y_{t-p} + \theta_1 e_{t-1} + \cdots + \theta_q e_{t-q} \qquad (10)$$

where y_{DP} denotes the value of prediction results under DP parameters, u is estimated constant term, θ is an autoregressive coefficient, ϕ is moving average coefficient.

To exclude extreme values from the prediction process, each parameter is calculated n times, a maximum value and a minimum value are removed, respectively. Then the average value is calculated, which conduces to measure the effect of the model. The predicted value equals

$$P_{DP} = \left(\sum_{m=1}^{n} y_{DPn} - y_{DP\,\max} - y_{DP\,\min}\right)/(n-2) \qquad (11)$$

where P_{DP} denotes the mean value of prediction results, $\sum_{m=1}^{n} y_{DPn}$ is the sum of all prediction results under DP parameters. Variables $y_{DP\,\max}$ and $y_{DP\,\min}$ indicate the maximum value and the minimum value of the prediction results, respectively. Lastly, $n-2$ represents the number of prediction results involved in the final calculation.

4   Experiments and Results

4.1   Experimental Data and Parameter Description

The data sets used in this paper include ElectricityLoadDiagrams20112014 [20], Individual household electric power consumption [21] and the Solar power [22]. The Column2, Column257, Column277 and Column314 are selected from ElectricityLoadDiagrams20112014.

The parameters used in the experiments are shown in Table 2, the experimental environment is shown in Table 3. In EPSTO-ARIMA and EPFSTO-ARIMA experiments, DP values are the same. In addition, G refers to the grouping of data based on similarity calculation. The data is divided into two groups, as shown in Table 4.

Table 2. Experiments parameters.

Model	Column2,257,277,314	Household	Solar
Parameters	(p,d,q) or (p,d,q,DP) or (p,d,G,DP)		
ARIMA	(9,0,8)	(9,0,2)	(9,0,8)
EPSTO -ARIMA	(9,0,8,DP)	(9,0,2,DP)	(9,0,0,DP) (6,0,0,DP)
EPFSTO -ARIMA	(1,0,0,2,DP) (3,0,5,2,DP)	(1,0,3,2,DP) (1,0,2,2,DP)	(2,0,9,2,DP) (2,0,2,2,DP)
DP	0.001,0.002,0.003,0.004,0.005,0.006,0.007,0.008 0.009,0.01,0.02,0.03,0.04,0.05,0.06,0.07,0.08,0.09,0.1		

Table 3. Experimental environment.

Environment	Parameter
Operating system	Windows 10, 64bit
Processor	Intel(R) Core (TM) i7-9700 CPU @ 3.00 GHz
Internal storage	8.00 GB
Pycharm	Professional Edition 11.0.3
Tensorflow	2.3.0

4.2   Adopted Metrics

We measure the prediction effect of EPFSTO-ARIMA in terms of RMSE (Root Mean Squared Error). RMSE defines the deviation between the predicted value and the real value, which can be calculated as

Table 4. Grouping of data.

Item	Column2	Column257	Column277	Column314	Household	Solar
G_1	[0,0.053]	[0,0.0094]	[0,0.0006]	[0,0.00001]	[0,0.002066]	[0,0.1427]
G_2	(0.053,1]	(0.0094,1]	(0.0006,1]	(0.00001,1]	(0.002066,1]	(0.1427,1]

$$RMSE\,(X, P) = \sqrt{(1/m) \sum_{i=1}^{m} (p\,(x_i) - y_i)^2} \tag{12}$$

where $p\,(x_i)$ and y_i denote the predicted and the real values, respectively.

4.3   Experiments Results

In this section, ARIMA, EPSTO-ARIMA and EPFSTO-ARIMA experiments are carried out. In the experiments, we first check whether the data are flat and stable. After the ACF (Auto Correlation Function) test, the method of censoring and PACF (Partial Auto Correlation Function) diagram with the method of tailing, the value of d, p and q is determined. The value of G can be determined by

$$
\begin{aligned}
S_{(i,j)} &= 1/(1 + D_{(i,j)}) \\
&= 1/(1 + \min_{c}(\sum_{i=1}^{n} [d(y_i, V) \cdot W_n] / \sum_{i=1}^{n} W_n)) \\
&= 1/\left(1 + d(y_i, V) + \min \left\{ \begin{array}{l} D(i-1, j) \\ D(i, j-1) \\ D(i-1, j-1) \end{array} \right\} \right) \\
&= 1/\left(1 + d(y_i, (\sum_{i=1}^{n} y_i)/n) + \min \left\{ \begin{array}{l} D(i-1, j) \\ D(i, j-1) \\ D(i-1, j-1) \end{array} \right\} \right)
\end{aligned}
\tag{13}
$$

where V represents the average of the data, y_i represents the value of the $i-th$ data.

The results presented in this section are optimal solutions under the following two constraints. RMSE and TIME both take the minimum values. The models use the same environment to make prediction. From the Table 5, we can observe:

1) For EPFSTO-ARIMA, we perform forced optimization on the data according to Table 4. The RMSE is lower than that of EPSTO-ARIMA, but higher than that of ARIMA.
2) Take Column2 as an example. The RMSE of EPFSTO-ARIMA is 30.44% lower than that of EPSTO-ARIMA and 12.22% higher than that of ARIMA. For the rest of the clients, similar results can be obtained.

ARIMA is optimal for resource consumption in the existing data set. In EPFSTO-ARIMA, we optimize different amounts of data to analyze how they affect the results. Because EPFSTO-ARIMA has certain randomness, we carry out many experiments for each DP and take the mean value. The results of EPFSTO-ARIMA are shown in Fig. 2.

Table 5. RMSE of EPSTO-ARIMA (EPSTO) and EPFSTO-ARIMA (EPFSTO).

Item	Column2	Column257	Column277	Column314	Household	Solar
ARIMA	6.819	53.240	863.190	14105.370	412.520	0.570
EPSTO	11.000	79.604	1194.183	18190.421	418.333	1.027
EPFSTO	7.652	65.382	946.181	15345.276	414.574	0.588

Table 6. Maximum, minimum and increase rate of EPSTO-ARIMA and EPFSTO-ARIMA RMSE.

Item	Column2	Column257	Column277	Column314	Household	Solar
Min1	7.124	56.36	871.369	13898.56	412.994	0.617
Max1	16.957	113.083	1726.456	24181.739	430.323	1.633
Rate1	138.03%	100.64%	98.13%	73.99%	4.20%	164.67%
Min2	7.597	65.305	931.742	15115.735	412.642	0.583
Max2	7.682	65.562	971.298	16118.49	416.001	0.600
Rate2	1.12%	0.39%	4.25%	6.63%	0.81%	2.92%

For EPFSTO-ARIMA, the data used in the experiment is divided into two groups based on the similarity results, as shown in Table 4. According to DP, optimization is carried out in two groups. From Fig. 2, we can observe that:

1) The RMSE of EPSTO-ARIMA and EPFSTO-ARIMA increase with the increase of DP. However, the increase in EPSTO-ARIMA is more prominent.
2) For EPFSTO-ARIMA, with the continuous increase of DP, RMSE shows a slower upward trend than that of EPSTO-ARIMA. It means that EPFSTO-ARIMA is effective in solving the problem of prediction accuracy degradation as in EPSTO-ARIMA. According to the results, the ratio of the optimized data in the two groups can also be calculated.
3) Take Column2 as an example. In EPSTO-ARIMA, the RMSE increases gradually to about 138.03% with the increase of DP as shown in Table 6 (in Table 6, Min1 and Min2 are the min RMSE of EPSTO-ARIMA and EPFSTO-ARIMA, respectively. Max1 and Max2 are the max RMSE of EPSTO-ARIMA and EPFSTO-ARIMA, respectively. Rate1 and Rate2 are the increase rate of EPSTO-ARIMA and EPFSTO-ARIMA RMSE, respectively.). In EPFSTO-ARIMA, RMSE also increases gradually with the increase of DP, but by only about 1.12%. Other results are shown in Table 6.

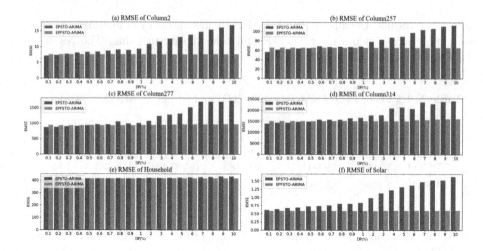

Fig. 2. The RMSE of EPFSTO-ARIMA and EPSTO-ARIMA.

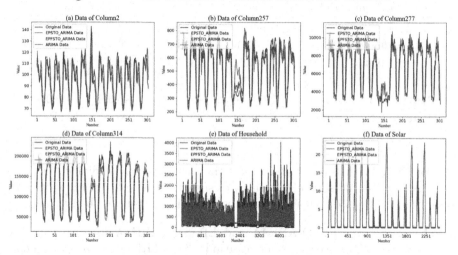

Fig. 3. The original data vs. Prediction data.

Meanwhile, the prediction data of EPFSTO-ARIMA basically conform to the data discipline of the original data as shown in Fig. 3.

In summary,

1) EPFSTO-ARIMA can effectively counter the excessive prediction loss caused by EPSTO-ARIMA.
2) In the aspect of data availability, EPFSTO-ARIMA basically conform to the data discipline of the original data.
3) In addition to the above conclusions, we also found that the time resources used are also saved (as shown in Fig. 4), which will not be discussed in detail in this paper.

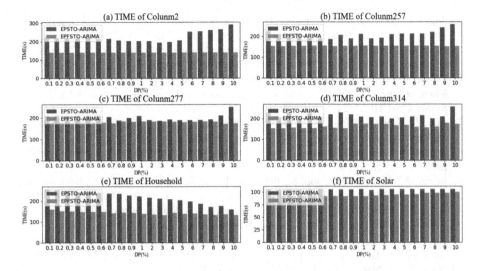

Fig. 4. The TIME of EPFSTO-ARIMA and EPSTO-ARIMA.

5   Conclusions and Future Work

Electricity data prediction is important for the national economy and the lives of people. However, EPSTO-ARIMA will causes serious degradation of electricity prediction service. To deal with the above challenge, we propose EPFSTO-ARIMA, which can reduce prediction error caused by EPSTO-ARIMA. In the meantime, the prediction result can help us to explore the discipline of data. Through experiments, proposed EPFSTO-ARIMA outperforms in reducing prediction error. In the future, the following aspects can be further analyzed:

1) EPFSTO will be tested and demonstrated in other models.
2) EPFSTO will be tested and verified under more detailed data grouping.
3) Exploring the specific effects of EPFSTO-ARIMA on model training time and prediction time.

References

1. Wang, Q., Guo, Y., Yu, L., Li, P.: Earthquake prediction based on spatio-temporal data mining: an LSTM network approach. IEEE Trans. Emerg. Top. Comput. **8**(1), 148–158 (2020)
2. Zhang, B., Zhang, H., Zhao, G., Lian, J.: Constructing a PM2.5 concentration prediction model by combining auto-encoder with Bi-LSTM neural networks. Environ. Model. Softw/ **124**,104600 (2020)
3. Erdogdu, E.: Electricity demand analysis using cointegration and ARIMA modelling: a case study of Turkey. Environ. Model. Softw. **35**, 1129–1146 (2007)
4. Guo, J., He, H., Sun, C.: ARIMA-based road gradient and vehicle velocity prediction for hybrid electric vehicle energy management. IEEE Trans. Veh. Technol. **68**(6), 5309–5320 (2019)

5. Jagielski, M., Oprea, A., Biggio, B., Liu, C., Nita-Rotaru, C., Li, B.: Manipulating machine learning: poisoning attacks and countermeasures for regression learning. In: 2018 IEEE Symposium on Security and Privacy (SP), pp. 19–35. IEEE, San Francisco (2018). https://doi.org/10.1109/SP.2018.00057
6. Chen, Y., Huang, S., Liu, F., Wang, Z., Sun, X.: Evaluation of reinforcement learning-based false data injection attack to automatic voltage control. IEEE Trans. Smart Grid **10**(2), 2158–2169 (2019)
7. Luo, J., Hong, T., Fang, S.C.: Benchmarking robustness of load forecasting models under data integrity attacks. Int. J. Forecast. **34**(1), 89–104 (2018)
8. Szegedy, C., et al.: Intriguing properties of neural networks. Computer Science (2013)
9. Fawzi, A., Moosavi-Dezfooli, S., Frossard, P.: Robustness of classifiers: from adversarial to random noise. In: Lee, D.D., Luxburg, U., Garnett, R., Sugiyama, M., Guyon, I. (eds.) 2016 Conference and Workshop on Neural Information Processing Systems (NIPS), pp. 1632–1640. ACM, Barcelona (2016)
10. Carlini, N., Wagner, D.A.: Towards evaluating the robustness of neural networks. In: 2017 IEEE Symposium on Security and Privacy (SP), pp. 39–57. IEEE, San Jose (2017). https://doi.org/10.1109/SP.2017.49
11. Papernot, N., McDaniel, P., Goodfellow, I.: Transferability in machine learning: from phenomena to black-box attacks using adversarial samples. Preprint, arXiv:1605.07277, (2016)
12. Zhang, G.P.: Time series predicting using a hybrid ARIMA and neural network model. Neurocomputing **50**, 159–175 (2003)
13. Hinton, G.E., Srivastava, N., Krizhevsky, A., Sutskever, I., Salakhutdinov, R.R.: Improving neural networks by preventing co-adaptation of feature detectors. Computer Science (2012)
14. Xu, H., Caramanis, C., Mannor, S.: Robust regression and lasso. IEEE Trans. Inf. Theory **56**(7), 3561–3574 (2010)
15. Cretu, G.F., Stavrou, A., Locasto, M.E., Stolfo, S.J., Keromytis, A.D.: Casting out demons: sanitizing training data for anomaly sensors. In: 2008 IEEE Symposium on Security and Privacy (2008), pp. 81–95. IEEE, Oakland, CA (2008). https://doi.org/10.1109/SP.2008.11
16. Goodfellow, I.J., Shlens, J., Szegedy, C.: Explaining and harnessing adversarial examples. Computer Science (2015)
17. Ramjee, S., Ju, S., Yang, D., Liu, X., Gamal, A.E., Eldar, Y.C.: Fast deep learning for automatic modulation classification (2019)
18. Lim, H.W., Poh, G.S., Xu, J., Chittawar, V.: PrivateLink: Privacy-preserving integration and sharing of datasets. IEEE Trans. Inf. Forensics Secur. **15**, 564–577 (2020)
19. Eldar, Y.C.: Sampling Theory: Beyond Bandlimited Systems. Cambridge University Press, Cambridge (2015)
20. Lichman, M.: Electricity load diagrams 20112014 data set. UCI machine learning repository (2013)
21. Hébrail, G., Bérard, A.: Individual household electric power consumption data set. UCI Machine Learning Repository (2012)
22. Lew, D.: The western wind and solar integration study phase 2. National Renewable Energy Laboratory (2013)

Out of Non-linearity: Search Impossible Differentials by the Bitwise Characteristic Matrix

Yunxiao Yang[1], Xuan Shen[2(✉)], and Bing Sun[1,3]

[1] College of Liberal Arts and Sciences, National University of Defense Technology, Changsha, China
yyx23@live.com, happy_come@163.com
[2] College of Information and Communication, National University of Defense Technology, Wuhan, China
shenxuan_08@163.com
[3] Hunan Engineering Research Center of Commercial Cryptography Theory and Technology Innovation, Changsha, China

Abstract. In this paper, we propose the $\mathcal{M}$-method which uses the bitwise characteristic matrix to search impossible differentials. $\mathcal{M}$-method exploits not only the linear components but also partial information of non-linear components. According to the principle of miss-in-the-middle, we construct two different types of contradiction to search the impossible differentials with limited time and memory complexity by calculating $\mathcal{M}_{en}^{r_1}$ and $\mathcal{M}_{de}^{r_2}$ which represent r_1 rounds encryption and r_2 rounds decryption, respectively. Compared with the previous methods, our technique is comprehensible and fast especially for large block size.

As a result, we find the 7-round impossible differentials of GIFT-128, the 5-round impossible differentials of PRIDE, and the 4-round impossible differentials of Pyjamask-96. For GIFT-64, PRESENT, RECTANGLE which are well-analyzed by MILP-method or SAT-method, we construct new impossible differentials. Moreover, the efficiency of our method will not be influenced by the block size, which makes us find the new 5-round impossible differentials of the 320-bit permutation of ASCON.

Keywords: Block cipher · Characteristic matrix · Impossible differential cryptanalysis

1 Introduction

The block cipher is of great importance in the field of cryptology. When designing a block cipher, designers always obey the *diffusion and confusion* principle

This study was funded by the National Natural Science Foundation of China (Grant Nos. 61772545 and 62002370), Scientific Research Plan of National University of Defense Technology (No. ZK21-36).

The original version of this chapter was revised: this chapter contained mistakes. This has been corrected. The correction to this chapter is available at
https://doi.org/10.1007/978-3-030-93206-0_24

R. Deng et al. (Eds.): ISPEC 2021, LNCS 13107, pp. 69–89, 2021.
https://doi.org/10.1007/978-3-030-93206-0_6

and guarantee them by iterating the round function which contains linear and non-linear layers. The SPN structure and Feistel structure with SP-type round functions are examples of the design principle. When it comes to lightweight block ciphers, such as PRESENT [4], GIFT [2], and PRIDE [1], the designers tend to use bitwise operations like bit permutation or cyclic shift rather than multiplication with the matrix over the finite field and to use 4-bit S-boxes rather than 8-bit S-boxes for efficient implementation. The diffusion of a bitwise permutation is much slower than the matrix multiplication such as the MDS matrix used in AES, and the confusion is weaker when the size of the S-box is smaller. Moreover, in some S-boxes such as the S-box of PRESENT and GIFT, certain bits of the output difference are determinate if the input difference is fixed with specific bits. In [20], Tezcan named the bits as undisturbed points which can simplify the differential cryptanalysis and the impossible differential cryptanalysis.

As one of the most powerful cryptanalysis techniques, impossible differential cryptanalysis was independently proposed by Knudsen [12] and Biham et al. [3]. Unlike the differential cryptanalysis aiming at finding high-probability differentials, the impossible differential cryptanalysis is to find the differential $(\Delta_{in}, \Delta_{out})$, where the input difference Δ_{in} can never propagate to Δ_{out}. Impossible differential cryptanalysis usually has two phases, the first one is to find the impossible differentials covering as many rounds as possible; the second one is to filter the wrong keys by extending the distinguisher several rounds. Therefore, constructing the impossible differentials is the key step that determines the number of attacking rounds.

To search longer impossible differentials efficiently, the automatic searching tools have been developed rapidly in the last decades. In 2003, Kim et al. [11] published the first automatic searching tool named $\mathcal{U}$-method for impossible differentials. The $\mathcal{U}$-method classifies every byte of a block into the $\mathcal{U}$-set and constructs contradictions in the middle state. In 2009, Luo et al. [14] improved the $\mathcal{U}$-method and proposed the UID-method. In 2012, Wu et al. [21] further exploited the properties of linear operations by solving the system of linear equations. Although the searching ability is improved rapidly compared with manual derivation, the above automatic tools cannot make use of the details of S-boxes and they can only cover the word-oriented block ciphers. To alleviate the above limitations, researchers have turned their attention to modeling the impossible differential searching into Mixed Integer Linear Programming (MILP) problem or Boolean Satisfiability Problem (SAT), which have been used maturely for optimization problems. In 2016, Cui et al. [5] extended the applications of MILP-method on searching impossible differentials. At EUROCRYPT 2017, Sasaki et al. [15] presented another MILP-based automatic tool for impossible differentials searching which can cover more structures. At ASIACRYPT 2020, Hu et al. [10] proposed a new automatic search tool based on SAT-method to model the impossible polytopic transitions and key dependent transitions which were not considered by the previous automatic tools. In summary, the more information of a block cipher that the automatic search tools can absorb, the more impossible differentials can be found and in some cases the more rounds can be covered.

In general, the methods based on MILP or SAT can cover more structures and find longer distinguishers, but there are also limitations. One of them is that the computation complexity will increase rapidly while the block size is large. In [15], the authors claimed that even if the size of the S-box is small, it is computationally hard to evaluate a large block size of more than 256 bits. And the automatic tools cannot tell why the differentials are impossible. Because of the heuristic algorithms used in MILP/SAT-solvers, the process of solving is nearly a black box. Therefore, the authors of the automatic tools always manually verify some of the results.

While the above research found impossible differentials by automatic tools, there is another line of research that determines the impossible differentials by theoretical proof. At CRYPTO 2015, Sun et al. [19] proved that without considering the details of S-boxes, the $\mathcal{WW}$-method [21] can find all word-oriented impossible differentials of both Feistel structure with SP-type round functions and SPN structure. Moreover, at EUROCRYPT 2016, Sun et al. [18] utilized the characteristic matrix to prove the upper bound of truncated impossible differentials for SPN structure. Following the line of research, Shen et al. [17] considered the details of the S-boxes and found longer impossible differentials for Russian standard block cipher Kuznyechik [8] and the permutation of PHOTON [9]. After that, at ISPEC 2017, Shen et al. [16] further studied the matrix representation of a block cipher and proposed a more precise matrix representation named diffusion matrix. By utilizing the diffusion matrix, they constructed impossible differentials of SIMON-like block ciphers.

Our Contributions. Along the research line of Sun et al. [18] and Shen et al. [16], we propose the $\mathcal{M}$-method which uses the bitwise characteristic matrix to search impossible differentials for more block ciphers while Shen et al. [16] only considered the SIMON-like block ciphers.

We first calculate the matrix representation of one round encryption which is denoted as $\mathcal{M}_{en}$. The matrix $\mathcal{M}_{en}$ contains not only the information of linear components but also some information of the S-box. After iterating the $\mathcal{M}_{en}$ for r times, i.e. $\mathcal{M}_{en}^r$, we get the matrix representation of the r-round encryption. By multiplying the difference with the corresponding matrix, we get the middle state of the block cipher. The decryption is the same. Then we can construct impossible differentials according to the principle of miss-in-the-middle. Moreover, we propose the indirect contradiction where we extend the rounds of impossible differentials by looking up the Difference Distribution Table (DDT) of the S-box. The main results of our technique for searching impossible differentials are listed in Table 1.

Compared with the MILP-based and SAT-based tools, our technique has the following advantages:

(1) Model Large States: Our method models an n-bit block cipher by an $n \times n$ matrix and the only computation is matrix multiplication, which is easy for a laptop. Therefore, our method can function with nearly no compromises no matter how large the block size is. We apply our method to the 320-bit

Table 1. Main results

Block ciphers	Search tool	Rounds	Ref.
GIFT-64	SAT	6	[2]
	MILP	6	[10]
	$\mathcal{M}$-method	6	Ours
GIFT-128	$\mathcal{M}$-method	**7**	Ours
PRIDE	$\mathcal{M}$-method	**5**	Ours
Pyjamask-96	Previous	3	[13]
	$\mathcal{M}$-method	**4**	Ours
Pyjamask-128	$\mathcal{M}$-method	3	Ours
PRESENT	MILP	6	[5]
	$\mathcal{M}$-method	6	Ours
ASCON	Previous	5	[7]
	$\mathcal{M}$-method	5	Ours
RECTANGLE	MILP	8	[15]
	$\mathcal{M}$-method	8	Ours

permutation of ASCON and find new impossible differentials. We also find the 7-round impossible differentials of GIFT-128.

(2) Comprehensible Contradictions: We construct contradictions by determining the middle states with the characteristic matrices. So we are clear about the type and the position of every contradiction. Utilizing the linear correlations between different contradictions, the $\mathcal{M}$-method can construct new impossible differentials for GIFT-64, PRESENT, ASCON, RECTANGLE.

(3) Negligible time and memory complexity: After the bitwise characteristic matrix is determinate, we can construct contradictions by combining the column vectors in the matrix. And we only consider specific columns with determinate entries, which is much less than the search range. During the computation, the only thing we have to store in the memory is several $n \times n$ matrices.

Paper Outline. In Sect. 2, we introduce necessary preliminaries. In Sect. 3, we introduce the bitwise characteristic matrix and demonstrate the mechanism of our searching tool for impossible differentials. In Sect. 4, we apply our technique to some block ciphers. In Sect. 5, we conclude this paper and put forward some future works. And the necessary supplemental material is given in the Appendixes.

2 Preliminaries

2.1 Notation

The notation in this paper is listed in Table 2.

Table 2. Notation

$\mathbb{F}_{2^n}^*$	All non-zero elements in $\mathbb{F}_{2^n}$
e_i	A vector with only the i-th bit being 1, others being 0
$\#(I)$	The number of elements in set I
$\oplus$	Bitwise XOR
$\bigoplus_{i \in \{0,1,2\}} x_i$	$x_0 \oplus x_1 \oplus x_2$
$\alpha[i]$	The i-th bit of α
$f^n(x)$	$\underbrace{f \circ f \circ \cdots \circ f(x)}_{n}$
$\mathcal{M}_F$	The bitwise characteristic matrix of $F(x)$
$\mathcal{M}_{ij}$	The element of $\mathcal{M}$ located at the i-row and the j-th column
$\alpha \xrightarrow{F_1 F_2} \beta$	$\beta = F_2 \circ F_1(\alpha)$
$\alpha \xleftarrow{F_1 F_2} \beta$	$\alpha = F_1 \circ F_2(\beta)$

2.2 The Boolean Function

The n-variable boolean function is a function maps $\mathbb{F}_2^n$ to $\mathbb{F}_2$. Let $f_0, f_1, \ldots f_{m-1}$ be n-variable boolean functions, so the vectorial boolean function maps $\mathbb{F}_2^n$ to $\mathbb{F}_2^m$ is defined as:

$$F(x) = (f_0(x), f_1(x), \ldots, f_{m-1}(x)).$$

For any block cipher with a block size of n bits, we can treat it as a vectorial boolean function that maps $\mathbb{F}_2^n$ into $\mathbb{F}_2^n$. ANF (Algebraic Normal Form) is one of the representations for a boolean function.

Let $x \in \mathbb{F}_2^n$, the ANF of a n-variable boolean function is as follows:

$$f(x) = \bigoplus_{I \in \mathcal{P}(N)} a_I (\prod_{i \in I} x_i),$$

$\mathcal{P}(N)$ is the power set of $N = \{0, 1, \ldots, n-1\}$, $a_I \in \mathbb{F}_2$. Note that all vectors in this paper are column vectors if not specified.

3 Searching the Impossible Differentials by Bitwise Characteristic Matrix

3.1 Description of Bitwise Characteristic Matrix

The definition of bitwise characteristic matrix can be obtained from the aspect of boolean function. Let E be an n-bit block cipher, the input and output of one round function are denoted as $x = (x_0, x_1, \ldots, x_{n-1})$ and $y = (y_0, y_1, \ldots, y_{n-1})$ respectively. The bitwise characteristic matrix is defined as follows:

Definition 1. *For a given block cipher E, the ANF of y_i is*

$$y_i = \bigoplus_{I \in \mathcal{P}(N)} a_I(\prod_{k \in I} x_k).$$

Concerning the correlation between the x_j and y_i, the above ANF can be expanded to

$$y_i = p(x_0, \ldots, x_{j-1}, x_{j+1}, \ldots, x_{n-1})x_j \oplus q(x_0, \ldots, x_{j-1}, x_{j+1}, \ldots, x_{n-1}),$$

$p(\cdot)$ and $q(\cdot)$ are $(n-1)$-variable boolean functions independent of x_j.
The bitwise characteristic matrix of E is denoted as $\mathcal{M}$, $\mathcal{M}_{ij}$ is defined as:

$$\mathcal{M}_{ij} = \begin{cases} 0, & p(x_0, \ldots, x_{j-1}, x_{j+1}, \ldots, x_{n-1}) = 0 \\ 1, & p(x_0, \ldots, x_{j-1}, x_{j+1}, \ldots, x_{n-1}) = 1 \\ ?, & p(x_0, \ldots, x_{j-1}, x_{j+1}, \ldots, x_{n-1}) \neq 0, 1 \end{cases}$$

the 0 and 1 of $\mathcal{M}$ are defined over $\mathbb{F}_2$ which are called determined points. $\mathcal{M}_{ij} = 0$ means x_j is independent of y_i; $\mathcal{M}_{ij} = 1$ means when x_j changes, y_i must change; $\mathcal{M}_{ij} =?$ means when x_j changes, we can not tell whether y_i changes. When all x_j and y_i are analyzed according to the above process, the bitwise characteristic matrix $\mathcal{M}$ of E can be obtained.

To explain the operation between the bitwise characteristic matrices, a 4-bit S-box is constructed, and the ANF is as follows

$$\begin{cases} y_0 = x_0, \\ y_1 = x_0 \oplus x_1, \\ y_2 = x_0 \oplus x_1 x_2, \\ y_3 = 1 \oplus x_2 \oplus x_3. \end{cases}$$

The bitwise characteristic matrix of the S-box is:

$$\mathcal{M}_S = \begin{pmatrix} 1 & 0 & 0 & 0 \\ 1 & 1 & 0 & 0 \\ 1 & ? & ? & 0 \\ 0 & 0 & 1 & 1 \end{pmatrix}.$$

Let $x, y, z \in \mathbb{F}_2^4$, and $x \xrightarrow{S} y \xrightarrow{S} z$. Easy to know the ANF of z is as follows:

$$\begin{cases} z_0 = y_0 = x_0, \\ z_1 = y_0 \oplus y_1 = x_1, \\ z_2 = y_0 \oplus y_1 y_2 = x_0 \oplus (x_0 \oplus x_1)(x_0 \oplus x_1 x_2) = x_0 x_1 \oplus x_1 x_2 \oplus x_0 x_1 x_2, \\ z_3 = 1 \oplus y_2 \oplus y_3 = x_0 \oplus x_2 \oplus x_3 \oplus x_1 x_2. \end{cases}$$

Then the bitwise characteristic matrix of two rounds S-box is:

$$\mathcal{M}_{S \circ S} = \begin{pmatrix} 1\ 0\ 0\ 0 \\ 0\ 1\ 0\ 0 \\ ?\ ?\ ?\ 0 \\ 1\ ?\ ?\ 1 \end{pmatrix}.$$

The addition and multiplication between two characteristic matrices is defined as the following tables.

Table 3. Addition

+	0	1	?
0	0	1	?
1	1	0	?
?	?	?	?

Table 4. Multiplication

×	0	1	?
0	0	0	0
1	0	1	?
?	0	?	?

According to the above calculation rules, it is easy to verify that $\mathcal{M}_{S \circ S} = \mathcal{M}_S \mathcal{M}_S$. For any two n-variable vectorial boolean functions F_1 and F_2, it can be deduced that

$$\mathcal{M}_{F_2 \circ F_1} = \mathcal{M}_{F_2} \mathcal{M}_{F_1},$$

note that the order of matrix multiplication needs to be consistent with the order of function composition.

For the above 4-bit S-box, when some bits of the input difference are fixed to be 0, some bits of the output difference can be linear combinations of the input bits. For example, let the input difference be $\alpha = (\alpha_0, 0, 0, ?)$, the output difference is $\beta = (\alpha_0, \alpha_0, \alpha_0, ?)$. These linearized bits are also called undisturbed points in [20]. The undisturbed points correspond to the determined points in the matrix, which is similar to the idea of Cube attack [6] where the attacker linearizes the nonlinear function by fixing some variables in the boolean function.

For a block cipher, it is difficult to find the undisturbed points, but for the S-box, the undisturbed points can be found easily by enumerating all input differences of the S-box. We find that most 4-bit S-boxes of lightweight block ciphers containing undisturbed points, such as GIFT, PRESENT, PRIDE. And some S-boxes with sizes more than 4 bits also have undisturbed points, such as the 8-bit S-boxes of Skinny-128 and Midori-128, the 5-bit S-box of ASCON.

Since the elements of a bitwise characteristic matrix represent the correlation between the input and output bits, the matrix and the input difference can be multiplied to get the output difference. In order to explain the usage of the bitwise characteristic matrix, this section we construct a simplified 8-bit Feistel block cipher (Fig. 1), and the function F is the 4-bit S-box constructed above.

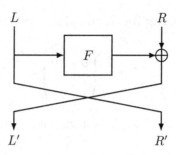

Fig. 1. A toy cipher

$$
\mathcal{M}_{en} = \begin{pmatrix} 1\,0\,0\,0\,1\,0\,0\,0 \\ 1\,1\,0\,0\,0\,1\,0\,0 \\ 1\,?\,?\,0\,0\,0\,1\,0 \\ 0\,0\,1\,1\,0\,0\,0\,1 \\ 1\,0\,0\,0\,0\,0\,0\,0 \\ 0\,1\,0\,0\,0\,0\,0\,0 \\ 0\,0\,1\,0\,0\,0\,0\,0 \\ 0\,0\,0\,1\,0\,0\,0\,0 \end{pmatrix}, \quad \mathcal{M}_{en}^2 = \begin{pmatrix} 1\,0\,0\,0\,1\,0\,0\,0 \\ 0\,1\,0\,0\,1\,1\,0\,0 \\ ?\,?\,?\,0\,1\,?\,?\,0 \\ 1\,?\,?\,1\,0\,0\,1\,1 \\ 1\,0\,0\,0\,1\,0\,0\,0 \\ 1\,1\,0\,0\,0\,1\,0\,0 \\ 1\,?\,?\,0\,0\,0\,1\,0 \\ 0\,0\,1\,1\,0\,0\,0\,1 \end{pmatrix}.
$$

According to the determined points of $\mathcal{M}_{en}^2$, some bits of the output difference can be quickly calculated. For example, let the input difference be $\alpha = (1,1,0,0,0,0,0,0)$, then the output difference β after two rounds of encryption is

$$
\beta = \mathcal{M}_{en}^2 \alpha = \begin{pmatrix} 1\,0\,0\,0\,1\,0\,0\,0 \\ 0\,1\,0\,0\,1\,1\,0\,0 \\ ?\,?\,?\,0\,1\,?\,?\,0 \\ 1\,?\,?\,1\,0\,0\,1\,1 \\ 1\,0\,0\,0\,1\,0\,0\,0 \\ 1\,1\,0\,0\,0\,1\,0\,0 \\ 1\,?\,?\,0\,0\,0\,1\,0 \\ 0\,0\,1\,1\,0\,0\,0\,1 \end{pmatrix} \begin{pmatrix} 1 \\ 1 \\ 0 \\ 0 \\ 0 \\ 0 \\ 0 \\ 0 \end{pmatrix} = \begin{pmatrix} 1 \\ 1 \\ ? \\ ? \\ 1 \\ 0 \\ ? \\ 0 \end{pmatrix}.
$$

For an SPN cipher, the linear layer can be represented by a $\mathbb{F}_2$ matrix and the S-box layer can be represented by a block diagonal matrix. So the matrix representation of a one round SPN cipher can be denoted as $\mathcal{M}_{P \circ S} = \mathcal{M}_P \mathcal{M}_S$.

3.2 Description of the Contradictions

After defining the bitwise characteristic matrix, we can construct contradictions in the middle state by exploiting the properties of the matrix representation. We introduce two different types of contradiction: direct contradiction and indirect contradiction.

Direct Contradiction: This type of contradiction happens when the middle states after encryption and decryption are obtained by directly multiplying the input and output differences with the corresponding matrix. Let the middle state after r_0-round encryption be α_1 and after r_1-round decryption be β_1, the corresponding matrix representations be $\mathcal{M}_{en}^{r_0}$ and $\mathcal{M}_{de}^{r_1}$, the input difference be α and the corresponding $(r_0 + r_1)$ rounds output difference be β, we have:

$$\alpha_1 = \mathcal{M}_{en}^{r_0} \ \alpha, \quad \beta_1 = \mathcal{M}_{de}^{r_1} \ \beta.$$

If specific bits of α_1 must be 1 and the same bits of β_1 must be 0, or vice versa, we can construct the direct contradiction. For convenience, we also denote the direct contradiction as follows:

$$\alpha \xrightarrow{encryption} \alpha_1 \neq \beta_1 \xleftarrow{decryption} \beta.$$

Indirect Contradiction: This type of contradiction happens when the middle states after encryption and decryption are obtained by multiplying the differences with the corresponding matrix and looking up the DDT of S-box before or after the matrix multiplication. If we look up the DDT only once, there are 3 different cases:

$$S(\alpha) \xrightarrow{encryption} \alpha_1 \neq \beta_1 \xleftarrow{decryption} \beta,$$
$$\alpha \xrightarrow{encryption} \alpha_1 \neq \beta_1 \xleftarrow{decryption} S^{-1}(\beta),$$
$$\alpha \xrightarrow{encryption} \alpha_1 \xcancel{\xrightarrow{S}} \beta_1 \xleftarrow{decryption} \beta.$$

Take the first case for example. We look up the DDT of a S-box at input layer, we should calculate $\mathcal{M}_{encryption}$ and the input of $\mathcal{M}_{encryption}$ enumerates all possible differences after the S-box. To simplify the enumeration of DDT, we can also choose the undisturbed points and directly sum up the corresponding columns of the bitwise characteristic matrix. Take the S-box of GIFT for example, since the output difference must be $(?, ?, 0, ?)$ when the input difference is $(1, 1, 1, 0)$, we can make the input difference be $(1, 1, 1, 0)$ and sum up the first, second and fourth columns in the r-round matrix representation to get the middle state of $(r + 1)$-round encryption.

By indirect contradiction, we always find new and even longer impossible differentials than direct contradiction as we can utilize all undisturbed points of the S-box. Therefore we can easily deduce that if there is an r-round direct contradiction, there must be an r-round indirect contradiction. But the efficiency of constructing direct contradiction is usually higher than constructing the indirect contraction. Thus we first determine the longest direct contradiction and then search for the longer indirect contradiction. Algorithm 1 shows the processing of searching impossible differentials with the $\mathcal{M}$-method.

In the following section, we will apply our method to several block ciphers and detail the process of finding the impossible differentials of GIFT.

Algorithm 1. Search the impossible differential

Input: $\mathcal{M}_{en}$, $\mathcal{M}_{de}$, DDT of the S-box
Output: the longest impossible differential
1: $r_1 = r_2 = 1$
2: **while** There is $(r_1 + r_2)$-round direct contradiction **do**
3:     $r_1 = r_1 + 1$
4:     Calculate $\mathcal{M}_{en}^{r_1}$
5:     **while** There is $(r_1 + r_2)$-round direct contradiction **do**
6:         $r_2 = r_2 + 1$
7:         Calculate $\mathcal{M}_{de}^{r_2}$
8:     **end while**
9: **end while**   //the longest direct contradiction is $r_1 + r_2$
10: Looking up the DDT, check if there is indirect contradiction
11: **if** There is indirect contradiction **then**
12:     Output the $(r_1 + r_2 + 1)$-round impossible differential
13: **end if**
14: **if** There is no indirect contradiction **then**
15:     Output the $(r_1 + r_2)$-round impossible differential
16: **end if**

---

4 Applications from Cryptanalysis Aspects and Main Results

4.1 GIFT-64 and GIFT-128

GIFT [2] is an SPN lightweight block cipher proposed at CHES 2017. It is composed of 4-bit S-boxes and bit-wiring. The designers of GIFT revisit the design rationale of PRESENT and improve both security and efficiency. According to different block sizes, GIFT can be denoted as GIFT-64 and GIFT-128. Both of them adopt the same 4-bit S-box, the specification of the S-box in hexadecimal notation is given in Table 5.

Table 5. 4-bit S-box of GIFT

x	0	1	2	3	4	5	6	7	8	9	a	b	c	d	e	f
$S(x)$	1	a	4	c	6	f	3	9	2	d	b	7	5	0	8	e

Firstly, we calculate the bitwise characteristic matrices of the S-box and the results are as follows:

$$\mathcal{M}_S = \begin{pmatrix} ? & ? & ? & ? \\ ? & ? & ? & ? \\ 1 & ? & ? & ? \\ 1 & 1 & ? & ? \end{pmatrix}, \quad \mathcal{M}_{S^{-1}} = \begin{pmatrix} ? & 1 & ? & 1 \\ ? & 1 & 1 & ? \\ ? & ? & ? & ? \\ ? & ? & ? & ? \end{pmatrix}.$$

Moreover, there are 2 other differentials of an S-box that contain undisturbed points which can not be modelled by bitwise characteristic matrix, they are: $(0,1,1,0) \xrightarrow{S} (?,?,1,?)$ and $(1,1,1,0) \xrightarrow{S} (?,?,0,?)$.

Then We apply the $\mathcal{M}$-method to evaluate both GIFT-64 and GIFT-128.

For GIFT-64, the designers of GIFT applied the MILP-method and found 6-round impossible differentials for GIFT-64. In our method, we construct indirect contradictions for 6 rounds by looking up the DDT for the first S-box layer, the contradiction is described as follows:

$$S(\alpha) \xrightarrow{PSPS} \alpha_1 \neq \beta_1 \xleftarrow{P^{-1}S^{-1}P^{-1}S^{-1}P^{-1}S^{-1}} \beta.$$

Firstly, we determine the matrix representation of 2-round encryption and 2.5-round decryption i.e. $\mathcal{M}_{S \circ P \circ S \circ P}$ and $\mathcal{M}_{S^{-1} \circ P^{-1} \circ S^{-1} \circ P^{-1} \circ S^{-1}}$, respectively.

The matrix representation of a single S-box layer is a diagonal block matrix with every sub-block on the main diagonal is the bitwise characteristic matrix of a single S-box. Therefore, the matrix representation of a single S-box layer can be denoted as:

$$\mathcal{M}_S = \begin{pmatrix} M & 0 & 0 & 0 \\ 0 & M & 0 & 0 \\ 0 & 0 & M & 0 \\ 0 & 0 & 0 & M \end{pmatrix}, \quad M \triangleq \begin{pmatrix} \mathcal{M}_S & 0 & 0 & 0 \\ 0 & \mathcal{M}_S & 0 & 0 \\ 0 & 0 & \mathcal{M}_S & 0 \\ 0 & 0 & 0 & \mathcal{M}_S \end{pmatrix}.$$

The bit permutation can be easily transferred into a permutation matrix, which has exactly one non-zero entry in each column and each row. So the matrix representation of single round encryption starting at P-layer is $\mathcal{M}_{en} \triangleq \mathcal{M}_{S \circ P} = \mathcal{M}_S \mathcal{M}_P$. Therefore, we can calculate the matrix representation of 2-round encryption i.e. $\mathcal{M}_{en}^2$, and the matrix representation of 3-round decryption i.e. $\mathcal{M}_{de}^3$. The specification of $\mathcal{M}_{en}$, $\mathcal{M}_{en}^2$ and $\mathcal{M}_{de}^3$ are given in Appendix A.

According to $\mathcal{M}_{en}$ and $\mathcal{M}_{en}^2$, there is no 1-entry after 2-round encryption. Since the matrix representations of 3-round encryption and 4-round decryption are all ?-entries, so we can only construct 5-round direct contradiction by $\mathcal{M}_{en}^2$ and $\mathcal{M}_{de}^3$ at most. But we can utilize the undisturbed points which are not contained in the matrix representation to construct an insufficient diffusion state after 2.5-round encryption i.e. $S \circ P \circ S \circ P \circ S(x)$.

Let the input difference only active the first S-box in the first S-box layer. According to the undisturbed points of the S-box, let the non-zero nibble of the input difference be $(1,1,1,0)$ i.e. the e in hexadecimal notation, the corresponding output difference must be $(?,?,0,?)$, which is exactly the non-zero nibble of the input difference of $S \circ P \circ S \circ P(x)$. Hence the output difference of 2.5-round encryption can be obtained by multiply the output difference of the first S-box layer with the $\mathcal{M}_{en}^2$. Since there is only one non-zero column in each C_i ($i = 0,1,2,3$), when the input difference of $\mathcal{M}_{en}^2$ contains 0-entry, the output difference must have zero nibbles. Take an example, $C_3 \cdot (?,?,?,0) = (0,0,0,0)$ and $C_2 \cdot (?,?,0,?) = (0,0,0,0)$.

Let the input difference be $\alpha = (e,0,\ldots,0)$ in hexadecimal notation, so the corresponding difference after 2.5-round encryption is $\alpha_1 =$

$\mathcal{M}_{en}^2 \cdot S(\alpha) = (?,0,?,?,?,0,?,?,?,0,?,?,?,0,?,?)$ which means there are 4 nibbles in α_1 that must be zero. Let the output difference β be $(0,0,0,0,4,0,0,0,0,0,0,0,0,0,0,0)$, according to $\mathcal{M}_{de}^3$, the corresponding difference after 3-round decryption must be $\beta_1 = \mathcal{M}_{de}^3\beta = (\beta_{10},\beta_{11},?,?,?,?,?,?,?,?,?,?,?,?,?,?)$ and the nibble $\beta_{10} = (1,?,?,?)$ and $\beta_{11} = (?,1,?,?)$ which means $\beta_1[0] = \beta_1[5] = 1$. Since the $\beta_1[5] = 1$ and $\alpha_1[5] = 0$ are the same bit in the same sate, we construct a 6-round impossible differential for GIFT-64 as follows:

$$(\mathsf{e},0,\ldots,0) \overset{6R}{\nrightarrow} (0,0,0,0,4,0,\ldots,0).$$

Moreover, since the matrix representation can reveal the linear correlations between every bit, we can construct impossible differentials activating more S-boxes. Besides looking up the DDT of the first S-box layer, we can also look up the DDT of the last S-box layer, which can provide more impossible differentials by utilizing more undisturbed points. The contradictions can be denoted as:

$$S(\alpha) \xrightarrow{PSPS} \alpha_1 \neq \beta_1 \xleftarrow{P^{-1}S^{-1}P^{-1}S^{-1}P^{-1}} S^{-1}(\beta).$$

In Appendix B, we present the difference propagation of one impossible differential which activates 8 S-boxes in the first layer and 8 S-boxes in the last layer. The 6-round impossible differential in hexadecimal notation is

$$(\mathsf{e},\mathsf{c},0,0,\mathsf{e},\mathsf{c},0,0,\mathsf{e},\mathsf{c},0,0,\mathsf{e},\mathsf{c},0,0) \overset{6R}{\nrightarrow} (9,9,9,9,4,6,6,6,0,0,0,0,0,0,0,0).$$

For GIFT-128, the designers only claim that GIFT-128 can achieve full diffusion after 4 rounds. According to the full diffusion state, GIFT-128 has no 8-round truncated impossible differentials. But the impossible differentials which consider the information of the S-box are missing in the document. At ASIACRYPT 2020, the SAT-method only considered GIFT-64, and there is no impossible differential cryptanalysis of GIFT-128 in other public documents.

Utilizing the indirect contradiction, we construct 7-round impossible differentials for GIFT-128. The contradiction can be denoted as:

$$\alpha \xrightarrow{SPSPSP} \alpha_1 \overset{S}{\nrightarrow} \beta_1 \xleftarrow{P^{-1}S^{-1}P^{-1}S^{-1}P^{-1}S^{-1}} \beta,$$

hence we need to calculate the matrix representation of 3-round encryption and 3-round decryption denoted as $\mathcal{M}_{en}^3$ and $\mathcal{M}_{de}^3$ respectively. And $\mathcal{M}_{en}^3 \cdot \alpha = \alpha_1$, $\mathcal{M}_{de}^3 \cdot \beta = \beta_1$.

Firstly, we calculate the matrix representation of 3-round encryption and the result is as follows:

$$\mathcal{M}_{en}^3 = \begin{pmatrix} D_0 & D_0 & D_1 & D_1 \\ D_1 & D_1 & D_0 & D_0 \\ D_0 & D_0 & D_1 & D_1 \\ D_1 & D_1 & D_0 & D_0 \end{pmatrix},$$

D_0 and D_1 represent two different 32×32 matrices, which can be denoted as two 8×8 block matrices:

$$D_0 = \left(\begin{array}{cccc:cccc} B_0 & B_0 & B_0 & B_0 & B_0 & B_0 & B_0 & B_0 \\ B_0 & B_0 & B_0 & B_0 & B_0 & B_0 & B_0 & B_0 \\ B_0 & B_0 & B_0 & B_0 & B_0 & B_0 & B_0 & B_0 \\ B_0 & B_0 & B_0 & B_0 & B_0 & B_0 & B_0 & B_0 \\ \hdashline B_0 & B_0 & B_0 & B_0 & B_0 & B_0 & B_0 & B_0 \\ B_0 & B_0 & B_0 & B_0 & B_0 & B_0 & B_0 & B_0 \\ B_0 & B_0 & B_0 & B_0 & B_0 & B_0 & B_0 & B_0 \\ B_0 & B_0 & B_0 & B_0 & B_0 & B_0 & B_0 & B_0 \end{array} \right), D_1 = \left(\begin{array}{cccc:cccc} B_1 & B_1 & B_1 & B_1 & B_1 & B_1 & B_1 & B_1 \\ B_1 & B_1 & B_1 & B_1 & B_1 & B_1 & B_1 & B_1 \\ B_1 & B_1 & B_1 & B_1 & B_1 & B_1 & B_1 & B_1 \\ B_1 & B_1 & B_1 & B_1 & B_1 & B_1 & B_1 & B_1 \\ \hdashline B_1 & B_1 & B_1 & B_1 & B_1 & B_1 & B_1 & B_1 \\ B_1 & B_1 & B_1 & B_1 & B_1 & B_1 & B_1 & B_1 \\ B_1 & B_1 & B_1 & B_1 & B_1 & B_1 & B_1 & B_1 \\ B_1 & B_1 & B_1 & B_1 & B_1 & B_1 & B_1 & B_1 \end{array} \right).$$

The definitions of B_0 and B_1 are as follows:

$$B_0 = \begin{pmatrix} 0 & 0 & 0 & 0 \\ ? & ? & ? & ? \\ 0 & 0 & 0 & 0 \\ ? & ? & ? & ? \end{pmatrix}, \quad B_1 = \begin{pmatrix} ? & ? & ? & ? \\ 0 & 0 & 0 & 0 \\ ? & ? & ? & ? \\ 0 & 0 & 0 & 0 \end{pmatrix}.$$

When we focus on the difference propagation through B_1, the output difference can be denoted as $(?, 0, ?, 0)$ which might be one of $\{0, 2, 8, \mathsf{a}\}$ in hexadecimal notation. According to the DDT of S-box, differences in $\{0, 2, 8, \mathsf{a}\}$ can **never** propagate to $\{2, 4, 8, \mathsf{c}\}$. Hence we can deduce two bit-level truncated impossible differentials for B_1, which are $(?, 0, ?, 0) \xrightarrow{\mathsf{S}}\hspace{-0.9em}/\hspace{0.4em} (1, ?, 0, 0)$ and $(?, 0, ?, 0) \xrightarrow{\mathsf{S}}\hspace{-0.9em}/\hspace{0.4em} (?, 1, 0, 0)$. From the matrix representation of 3-round encryption, it is clear that if the input difference $\alpha = e_0 \triangleq (1, 0, \ldots, 0)$, every nibble of the corresponding output difference is one column of B_0 or B_1, take a example, the 15th nibble of α_1 in binary notation is $\alpha_1[60 \cdots 63] = (?, 0, ?, 0)$.

Secondly, we calculate the matrix representation of 3-round decryption $\mathcal{M}_{de}^3$. Since the 128×128 matrix $\mathcal{M}_{de}^3$ is too large to present even by block matrix representation, we only depict 4 columns of the matrix. Let the output difference after 7-round encryption active the first S-box in the last layer, so we only need to present the first 4 columns of $\mathcal{M}_{de}^3$.

$$Row[0 \cdots 31] = (B_6, B_4, B_5, B_7, B_6, B_4, B_5, B_7),$$
$$Row[32 \cdots 63] = (B_6, B_4, B_5, B_7, B_3, B_4, B_5, B_2),$$
$$Row[64 \cdots 95] = (B_6, B_4, B_5, B_7, B_6, B_4, B_5, B_7),$$
$$Row[96 \cdots 127] = (B_6, B_4, B_5, B_7, B_6, B_4, B_5, B_7).$$

The definitions of B_i ($i = 2, 3, 4, 5, 6, 7$) are as follows:

$$B_2 = \begin{pmatrix} ? & 1 & 1 & ? \\ ? & ? & ? & ? \\ 0 & 0 & 0 & 0 \\ 0 & 0 & 0 & 0 \end{pmatrix}, B_3 = \begin{pmatrix} 0 & 0 & 0 & 0 \\ ? & 1 & 1 & ? \\ ? & ? & ? & ? \\ 0 & 0 & 0 & 0 \end{pmatrix}, B_4 = \begin{pmatrix} 0 & 0 & 0 & 0 \\ 0 & 0 & 0 & 0 \\ ? & ? & ? & ? \\ ? & ? & ? & ? \end{pmatrix},$$

$$B_5 = \begin{pmatrix} ? & ? & ? & ? \\ 0 & 0 & 0 & 0 \\ 0 & 0 & 0 & 0 \\ ? & ? & ? & ? \end{pmatrix}, B_6 = \begin{pmatrix} 0 & 0 & 0 & 0 \\ ? & ? & ? & ? \\ ? & ? & ? & ? \\ 0 & 0 & 0 & 0 \end{pmatrix}, B_7 = \begin{pmatrix} ? & ? & ? & ? \\ ? & ? & ? & ? \\ 0 & 0 & 0 & 0 \\ 0 & 0 & 0 & 0 \end{pmatrix}.$$

When the output difference $\beta = e_1 \triangleq (0,1,0,\ldots,0)$ or $\beta = e_2 \triangleq (0,0,1,\ldots,0)$, the corresponding difference $\beta_1[60\cdots 63] = (1,?,0,0)$.

Let $\alpha = e_0$ and $\beta = e_1$, $\alpha_1[60\cdots 63] = (?,0,?,0)$ is exactly the input difference of the 15th S-box in the fourth round and $\beta_1[60\cdots 63] = (1,?,0,0)$ is the output difference of the same S-box, therefore $\alpha_1 \overset{S}{\nrightarrow} \beta_1$ and $(\alpha,\beta) \triangleq (e_0,e_1)$ is an impossible differential.

According to the matrix representation of 3-round encryption, the 3-round GIFT-128 dose not achieve full diffusion and the first 16 nibbles cannot influence the 61st bit and the 63rd bit of α_1. Therefore, the input difference α can at most activate 16 S-boxes. And by looking up the DDT of the S-box in the last round, we can investigate more linear properties which make the output difference can at most activate 8 S-boxes and we present one of them in Appendix C.

4.2   Other Block Ciphers

By Algorithm 1, we also make applications to many other block ciphers. Due to the limitation of the page size, we only present the new impossible differentials found by $\mathcal{M}$-method.

For PRIDE, an 64-bit block cipher proposed at CRYPTO 2014, we find the first 5-round impossible differentials and there are only indirect contradictions for 5-round PRIDE, one of which is as follows:

$$S(\alpha) \xrightarrow{PSPS} \alpha_1 \neq \beta_1 \xleftarrow{P^{-1}S^{-1}P^{-1}} S^{-1}(\beta).$$

One of the impossible differentials is as follows:

$$(0,0,8,0,0,1,0,0,8,0,8,0,7,0,0,0) \overset{5R}{\nrightarrow} (0,0,0,\beta_0,0,0,0,\beta_1,0,0,\beta_2,0,0,0,\beta_3,0).$$

$\beta_i \in \mathbb{F}_{2^4}^*$ $(i = 0,1,2,3)$, therefore the input difference activates 5 S-boxes and the output difference activates 4 S-boxes.

For Pyjamask, one of the 2nd round candidates of the NIST lightweight cryptography project, the block size has two different versions i.e. 96-bit and 128-bit. As Pyjamask adopts complex binary matrices to be the linear component and LS-design, it can achieve full diffusion in 2 rounds which means there is no 4-round truncated impossible differentials. For Pyjamask-96, taking into consideration the information of the S-box, we construct 4-round impossible differentials by indirect contradiction. And our impossible differentials surpass the previous results which cover only 3 rounds. The contradiction for Pyjamask-96 is as follows:

$$S(\alpha) \xrightarrow{PSP} \alpha_1 \neq \beta_1 \xleftarrow{S^{-1}P^{-1}} S^{-1}(\beta).$$

One of the impossible differentials in Octal notation is as follows:

$$(6,0,0,0,0,0,0,0,0,0,0,0,0,0,0,0,0,0,0,0,0,0,0,0,0,0,0,0,0,0,0,0,0) \xrightarrow{4R}$$
$$(0,0,0,0,0,0,0,0,0,0,0,0,0,0,0,0,0,0,0,0,0,0,0,\beta_0,0,2,0,0,0,\beta_1,0,0,0),$$

$\beta_i \in \mathbb{F}_{2^3}^*$ $(i = 0, 1)$, therefore the input difference activates 1 S-boxes and the output difference activates 3 S-boxes. For Pyjamask-128, we can only find 3-round impossible differentials by direct contradictions and we construct an impossible differential which activate 13 input S-boxes and 21 output S-boxes. And the impossible differential is as follows:

$$(9,0,0,9,\alpha_0,0,0,\alpha_1,0,\alpha_2,2,\alpha_3,0,0,0,0,2,0,1,0,2,\alpha_4,0,0,0,0,0,\alpha_5,0,\alpha_6,0,0)$$
$$\xrightarrow{4R} (\beta_0,0,\beta_1,\beta_2,\beta_3,\beta_4,0,\beta_5,\beta_6,0,\beta_7,\beta_8,0,0,0,0,\beta_9,0,0,\beta_{10},\beta_{11},0,0,\beta_{12},\beta_{13},$$
$$\beta_{14},\beta_{15},\beta_{16},\beta_{17},\beta_{18},0,\beta_{19}) \quad \alpha_i,\beta_i \in \mathbb{F}_{2^4}^*.$$

For ASCON, one of the finalists of the NIST lightweight cryptography project, the block size is 320 bits and the S-box size is 5 bits, we construct new 5-round impossible differentials by indirect contradictions. One of the contradictions is as follows:

$$S(\alpha) \xrightarrow{PSPSP} \alpha_1 \neq \beta_1 \xleftarrow{S^{-1}P^{-1}S^{-1}} \beta.$$

And one of the 5-round impossible differentials in hexadecimal notation is as follows:

$$(0,0,0,0,0,0,0,0,0,10,0,0,4,0,0,0,0,7,0,0,0,0,\alpha_0,\mathtt{f},0,0,0,0,0,0,0,0,\mathtt{c},0,0,$$
$$13,0,0,\mathtt{c},0,0,0,8,0,0,\mathtt{c},0,0,0,0,0,0,0,\mathtt{c},0,0,0,0,0,0,0,0,13,0,0,\alpha_1,\mathtt{1c}) \xrightarrow{5R} (0,0,$$
$$0,0,0,0,0,0,0,0,0,0,0,0,0,\beta_0,0,\cdots,0) \quad \alpha_i,\beta_i \in \mathbb{F}_{2^5}^*.$$

For RECTANGLE, a 64-bit lightweight block cipher, we construct new 8-round impossible differentials by indirect contradictions. One of the contradictions is as follows:

$$S(\alpha) \xrightarrow{PSPSPSP} \alpha_1 \neq \beta_1 \xleftarrow{S^{-1}P^{-1}S^{-1}P^{-1}S^{-1}P^{-1}} S^{-1}(\beta).$$

And one of the 8-round impossible differentials in hexadecimal notation is as follows:

$$(0,0,0,0,5,0,0,\mathtt{c},0,0,0,0,0,0,0,0) \xrightarrow{8R} (0,0,0,0,0,0,0,0,0,0,0,0,2,6,0,0,0).$$

For PRESENT, a 64-bit block cipher proposed at CHES 2007, we construct new 6-round impossible differentials by indirect contradictions. One of the impossible differentials is as follows:

$$(9,9,9,9,9,9,9,9,9,9,9,9,9,9,9,9) \xrightarrow{6R} (5,5,5,5,5,1,5,5,5,5,5,5,5,5,5,5).$$

5   Conclusion

In this paper, we defined the bitwise characteristic matrix and applied it to search for impossible differentials. By iterating the matrix to represent r-round block ciphers, we improve the efficiency of searching. Moreover, the $\mathcal{M}$-method can easily model block ciphers with block sizes more than 256 bits and reveal the positions of the contradictions. And the matrix multiplication defined in this paper can function with low time and memory complexity. As a result, we find new impossible differentials for some block ciphers including the 7-round impossible differentials for GIFT-128, the 5-round impossible differentials for PRIDE, and the 4-round impossible differentials for Pyjamask-96.

Although $\mathcal{M}$-method has some advantages, there are still some limitations which are also the targets of our future works. The first one is to make our method cover more cryptanalysis techniques such as linear cryptanalysis and more block cipher structures such as ARX. The second one is to make our method containing more details of the block ciphers including the key schedule. The last but not least is to apply our method to optimize the key recovery phases.

A   The Matrix Representations of GIFT-64

Because of the page size, we can only represent each bitwise matrix as a block matrix and the dimension of each sub-block is equal to the size of the S-box, and the sub-block 0 in the matrix denotes a 4×4 matrix with all 16 entries are 0, the sub-block ? denotes a sub-block with all entries are ?.

$$
\mathcal{M}_{en} = \begin{pmatrix}
A_1 & A_2 & A_3 & A_0 & 0 & 0 & 0 & 0 & 0 & 0 & 0 & 0 & 0 & 0 & 0 & 0 \\
0 & 0 & 0 & 0 & A_1 & A_2 & A_3 & A_0 & 0 & 0 & 0 & 0 & 0 & 0 & 0 & 0 \\
0 & 0 & 0 & 0 & 0 & 0 & 0 & 0 & A_1 & A_2 & A_3 & A_0 & 0 & 0 & 0 & 0 \\
0 & 0 & 0 & 0 & 0 & 0 & 0 & 0 & 0 & 0 & 0 & 0 & A_1 & A_2 & A_3 & A_0 \\
A_2 & A_3 & A_0 & A_1 & 0 & 0 & 0 & 0 & 0 & 0 & 0 & 0 & 0 & 0 & 0 & 0 \\
0 & 0 & 0 & 0 & A_2 & A_3 & A_0 & A_1 & 0 & 0 & 0 & 0 & 0 & 0 & 0 & 0 \\
0 & 0 & 0 & 0 & 0 & 0 & 0 & 0 & A_2 & A_3 & A_0 & A_1 & 0 & 0 & 0 & 0 \\
0 & 0 & 0 & 0 & 0 & 0 & 0 & 0 & 0 & 0 & 0 & 0 & A_2 & A_3 & A_0 & A_1 \\
A_3 & A_0 & A_1 & A_2 & 0 & 0 & 0 & 0 & 0 & 0 & 0 & 0 & 0 & 0 & 0 & 0 \\
0 & 0 & 0 & 0 & A_3 & A_0 & A_1 & A_2 & 0 & 0 & 0 & 0 & 0 & 0 & 0 & 0 \\
0 & 0 & 0 & 0 & 0 & 0 & 0 & 0 & A_3 & A_0 & A_1 & A_2 & 0 & 0 & 0 & 0 \\
0 & 0 & 0 & 0 & 0 & 0 & 0 & 0 & 0 & 0 & 0 & 0 & A_3 & A_0 & A_1 & A_2 \\
A_0 & A_1 & A_2 & A_3 & 0 & 0 & 0 & 0 & 0 & 0 & 0 & 0 & 0 & 0 & 0 & 0 \\
0 & 0 & 0 & 0 & A_0 & A_1 & A_2 & A_3 & 0 & 0 & 0 & 0 & 0 & 0 & 0 & 0 \\
0 & 0 & 0 & 0 & 0 & 0 & 0 & 0 & A_0 & A_1 & A_2 & A_3 & 0 & 0 & 0 & 0 \\
0 & 0 & 0 & 0 & 0 & 0 & 0 & 0 & 0 & 0 & 0 & 0 & A_0 & A_1 & A_2 & A_3
\end{pmatrix},
$$

$$\mathcal{M}_{en}^2 = \left(\begin{array}{cccc|cccc|cccc|cccc}
C_1 & C_2 & C_3 & C_0 & C_1 & C_2 & C_3 & C_0 & C_1 & C_2 & C_3 & C_0 & C_1 & C_2 & C_3 & C_0 \\
C_2 & C_3 & C_0 & C_1 & C_2 & C_3 & C_0 & C_1 & C_2 & C_3 & C_0 & C_1 & C_2 & C_3 & C_0 & C_1 \\
C_3 & C_0 & C_1 & C_2 & C_3 & C_0 & C_1 & C_2 & C_3 & C_0 & C_1 & C_2 & C_3 & C_0 & C_1 & C_2 \\
C_0 & C_1 & C_2 & C_3 & C_0 & C_1 & C_2 & C_3 & C_0 & C_1 & C_2 & C_3 & C_0 & C_1 & C_2 & C_3 \\
\hline
\bar{C}_1 & \bar{C}_2 & \bar{C}_3 & \bar{C}_0 & \bar{C}_1 & \bar{C}_2 & \bar{C}_3 & \bar{C}_0 & \bar{C}_1 & \bar{C}_2 & \bar{C}_3 & \bar{C}_0 & \bar{C}_1 & \bar{C}_2 & \bar{C}_3 & \bar{C}_0 \\
C_2 & C_3 & C_0 & C_1 & C_2 & C_3 & C_0 & C_1 & C_2 & C_3 & C_0 & C_1 & C_2 & C_3 & C_0 & C_1 \\
C_3 & C_0 & C_1 & C_2 & C_3 & C_0 & C_1 & C_2 & C_3 & C_0 & C_1 & C_2 & C_3 & C_0 & C_1 & C_2 \\
C_0 & C_1 & C_2 & C_3 & C_0 & C_1 & C_2 & C_3 & C_0 & C_1 & C_2 & C_3 & C_0 & C_1 & C_2 & C_3 \\
\hline
\bar{C}_1 & \bar{C}_2 & \bar{C}_3 & \bar{C}_0 & \bar{C}_1 & \bar{C}_2 & \bar{C}_3 & \bar{C}_0 & \bar{C}_1 & \bar{C}_2 & \bar{C}_3 & \bar{C}_0 & \bar{C}_1 & \bar{C}_2 & \bar{C}_3 & \bar{C}_0 \\
C_2 & C_3 & C_0 & C_1 & C_2 & C_3 & C_0 & C_1 & C_2 & C_3 & C_0 & C_1 & C_2 & C_3 & C_0 & C_1 \\
C_3 & C_0 & C_1 & C_2 & C_3 & C_0 & C_1 & C_2 & C_3 & C_0 & C_1 & C_2 & C_3 & C_0 & C_1 & C_2 \\
C_0 & C_1 & C_2 & C_3 & C_0 & C_1 & C_2 & C_3 & C_0 & C_1 & C_2 & C_3 & C_0 & C_1 & C_2 & C_3 \\
\hline
\bar{C}_1 & \bar{C}_2 & \bar{C}_3 & \bar{C}_0 & \bar{C}_1 & \bar{C}_2 & \bar{C}_3 & \bar{C}_0 & \bar{C}_1 & \bar{C}_2 & \bar{C}_3 & \bar{C}_0 & \bar{C}_1 & \bar{C}_2 & \bar{C}_3 & \bar{C}_0 \\
C_2 & C_3 & C_0 & C_1 & C_2 & C_3 & C_0 & C_1 & C_2 & C_3 & C_0 & C_1 & C_2 & C_3 & C_0 & C_1 \\
C_3 & C_0 & C_1 & C_2 & C_3 & C_0 & C_1 & C_2 & C_3 & C_0 & C_1 & C_2 & C_3 & C_0 & C_1 & C_2 \\
C_0 & C_1 & C_2 & C_3 & C_0 & C_1 & C_2 & C_3 & C_0 & C_1 & C_2 & C_3 & C_0 & C_1 & C_2 & C_3
\end{array}\right),$$

$$\mathcal{M}_{de}^3 = \left(\begin{array}{cccc|cccc|cccc|cccc}
R_1 & ? & ? & ? & R_0 & ? & ? & ? & ? & ? & ? & ? & ? & ? & ? & ? \\
? & ? & ? & ? & R_1 & ? & ? & ? & R_0 & ? & ? & ? & ? & ? & ? & ? \\
? & ? & ? & ? & ? & ? & ? & ? & R_1 & ? & ? & ? & R_0 & ? & ? & ? \\
R_0 & ? & ? & ? & ? & ? & ? & ? & ? & ? & ? & ? & R_1 & ? & ? & ? \\
\hline
? & ? & ? & R_1 & ? & ? & ? & R_0 & ? & ? & ? & ? & ? & ? & ? & ? \\
? & ? & ? & ? & ? & ? & ? & R_1 & ? & ? & ? & R_0 & ? & ? & ? & ? \\
? & ? & ? & ? & ? & ? & ? & ? & ? & ? & ? & R_1 & ? & ? & ? & R_0 \\
? & ? & ? & R_0 & ? & ? & ? & ? & ? & ? & ? & ? & ? & ? & ? & R_1 \\
\hline
? & ? & R_1 & ? & ? & ? & R_0 & ? & ? & ? & ? & ? & ? & ? & ? & ? \\
? & ? & ? & ? & ? & ? & R_1 & ? & ? & ? & R_0 & ? & ? & ? & ? & ? \\
? & ? & ? & ? & ? & ? & ? & ? & ? & ? & R_1 & ? & ? & ? & R_0 & ? \\
? & ? & R_0 & ? & ? & ? & ? & ? & ? & ? & ? & ? & ? & ? & R_1 & ? \\
\hline
? & R_1 & ? & ? & ? & R_0 & ? & ? & ? & ? & ? & ? & ? & ? & ? & ? \\
? & ? & ? & ? & ? & R_1 & ? & ? & ? & R_0 & ? & ? & ? & ? & ? & ? \\
? & ? & ? & ? & ? & ? & ? & ? & ? & R_1 & ? & ? & ? & R_0 & ? & ? \\
? & R_0 & ? & ? & ? & ? & ? & ? & ? & R_1 & ? & ? & ? & R_1 & ? & ?
\end{array}\right).$$

$$A_0 \triangleq \begin{pmatrix} ? & 0 & 0 & 0 \\ ? & 0 & 0 & 0 \\ 1 & 0 & 0 & 0 \\ 1 & 0 & 0 & 0 \end{pmatrix},\ A_1 \triangleq \begin{pmatrix} 0 & ? & 0 & 0 \\ 0 & ? & 0 & 0 \\ 0 & ? & 0 & 0 \\ 0 & ? & 0 & 0 \end{pmatrix},\ A_2 \triangleq \begin{pmatrix} 0 & 0 & ? & 0 \\ 0 & 0 & ? & 0 \\ 0 & 0 & ? & 0 \\ 0 & 0 & 1 & 0 \end{pmatrix},\ A_3 \triangleq \begin{pmatrix} 0 & 0 & 0 & ? \\ 0 & 0 & 0 & ? \\ 0 & 0 & 0 & ? \\ 0 & 0 & 0 & ? \end{pmatrix},\ R_1 \triangleq \begin{pmatrix} ? & ? & ? & ? \\ ? & 1 & 1 & ? \\ ? & ? & ? & ? \\ ? & ? & ? & ? \end{pmatrix},$$

$$C_0 \triangleq \begin{pmatrix} ? & 0 & 0 & 0 \\ ? & 0 & 0 & 0 \\ ? & 0 & 0 & 0 \\ ? & 0 & 0 & 0 \end{pmatrix},\ C_1 \triangleq \begin{pmatrix} 0 & ? & 0 & 0 \\ 0 & ? & 0 & 0 \\ 0 & ? & 0 & 0 \\ 0 & ? & 0 & 0 \end{pmatrix},\ C_2 \triangleq \begin{pmatrix} 0 & 0 & ? & 0 \\ 0 & 0 & ? & 0 \\ 0 & 0 & ? & 0 \\ 0 & 0 & ? & 0 \end{pmatrix},\ C_3 \triangleq \begin{pmatrix} 0 & 0 & 0 & ? \\ 0 & 0 & 0 & ? \\ 0 & 0 & 0 & ? \\ 0 & 0 & 0 & ? \end{pmatrix},\ R_0 \triangleq \begin{pmatrix} ? & 1 & 1 & ? \\ ? & ? & ? & ? \\ ? & ? & ? & ? \\ ? & ? & ? & ? \end{pmatrix}.$$

B New 6-Round Impossible Differential for GIFT-64

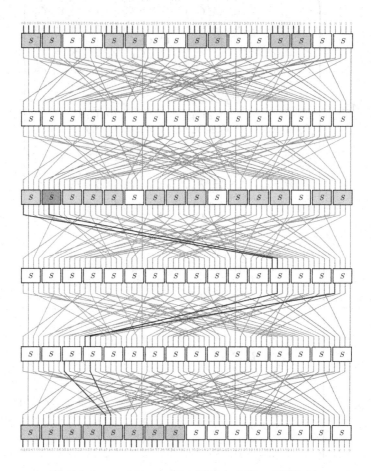

Fig. 2. 6-round impossible differential for GIFT-64

$$(e, c, 0, 0, e, c, 0, 0, e, c, 0, 0, e, c, 0, 0) \overset{6R}{\nrightarrow} (9, 9, 9, 9, 4, 6, 6, 6, 0, 0, 0, 0, 0, 0, 0, 0)$$

The blue lines mean the bit must be 1 according to DDT of the S-box, the orange lines mean the value of the bit cannot be determined. And the following figures adopt the same notation.

C 7-Round Truncated Impossible Differential for GIFT-128

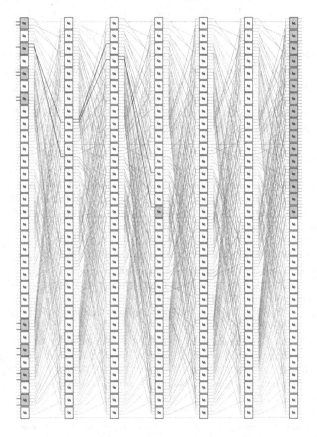

Fig. 3. 7-round truncated impossible differential

$$(\alpha[0\cdots 64]\|0_{64}) \overset{7R}{\not\to} (6,0,4,0,6,0,6,\underbrace{0,\ldots,0}_{17},5,0,5,0,5,0,5,0)$$

In Fig. 3, the left side denotes the 128-bit output difference and the right side denotes the 128-bit input difference. The difference propagation in the yellow S-box is a contradiction and the specification is given in Fig. 4.

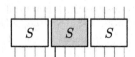

Fig. 4. Specification of the contradiction

References

1. Albrecht, M.R., Driessen, B., Kavun, E.B., Leander, G., Paar, C., Yalçın, T.: Block ciphers – focus on the linear layer (feat. PRIDE). In: Garay, J.A., Gennaro, R. (eds.) CRYPTO 2014. LNCS, vol. 8616, pp. 57–76. Springer, Heidelberg (2014). https://doi.org/10.1007/978-3-662-44371-2_4
2. Banik, S., Pandey, S.K., Peyrin, T., Sasaki, Y., Sim, S.M., Todo, Y.: Gift: a small present. In: Fischer, W., Homma, N. (eds.) Cryptographic Hardware and Embedded Systems – CHES 2017, pp. 321–345. Springer Cham (2017)
3. Biham, E., Biryukov, A., Shamir, A.: Cryptanalysis of skipjack reduced to 31 rounds using impossible differentials. In: Stern, J. (ed.) EUROCRYPT 1999. LNCS, vol. 1592, pp. 12–23. Springer, Heidelberg (1999). https://doi.org/10.1007/3-540-48910-X_2
4. Bogdanov, A., et al.: PRESENT: an ultra-lightweight block cipher. In: Paillier, P., Verbauwhede, I. (eds.) CHES 2007. LNCS, vol. 4727, pp. 450–466. Springer, Heidelberg (2007). https://doi.org/10.1007/978-3-540-74735-2_31
5. Cui, T., Jia, K., Fu, K., Chen, S., Wang, M.: New automatic search tool for impossible differentials and zero-correlation linear approximations. IACR Cryptol. ePrint Arch. p. 689 (2016). http://eprint.iacr.org/2016/689
6. Dinur, I., Shamir, A.: Cube attacks on tweakable black box polynomials. In: Joux, A. (ed.) EUROCRYPT 2009. LNCS, vol. 5479, pp. 278–299. Springer, Heidelberg (2009). https://doi.org/10.1007/978-3-642-01001-9_16
7. Dobraunig, C., Eichlseder, M., Mendel, F., Schlffer, M.: Ascon - submission to the CASEAR competition (2016)
8. Dolmatov, V.: GOST R 34.12-2015: Block cipher "kuznyechik". In: RFC, pp. 1–14 (2016)
9. Guo, J., Peyrin, T., Poschmann, A.: The PHOTON family of lightweight hash functions. In: Rogaway, P. (ed.) CRYPTO 2011. LNCS, vol. 6841, pp. 222–239. Springer, Heidelberg (2011). https://doi.org/10.1007/978-3-642-22792-9_13
10. Hu, X., Li, Y., Jiao, L., Tian, S., Wang, M.: Mind the propagation of states. In: Moriai, S., Wang, H. (eds.) Advances in Cryptology – ASIACRYPT 2020, pp. 415–445. Springer, Cham (2020)
11. Kim, J., Hong, S., Sung, J., Lee, S., Lim, J., Sung, S.: Impossible differential cryptanalysis for block cipher structures. In: Johansson, T., Maitra, S. (eds.) INDOCRYPT 2003. LNCS, vol. 2904, pp. 82–96. Springer, Heidelberg (2003). https://doi.org/10.1007/978-3-540-24582-7_6
12. Knudsen, L.: Deal - a 128-bit block cipher. In: NIST AES Proposal (1998)
13. Liu, Y., Weiming T., Shen, Z.: H.L.L.W.: Impossible differential cryptanalysis of lightweight block cipher pyjamask. Appl. Res. Comput. (2021). https://doi.org/10.19734/j.issn.1001-3695.2021.03.0063
14. Luo, Y., Wu, Z., Lai, X., Gong, G.: A unified method for finding impossible differentials of block cipher structures. IACR Cryptol. ePrint Arch. p. 627 (2009). http://eprint.iacr.org/2009/627
15. Sasaki, Yu., Todo, Y.: New impossible differential search tool from design and cryptanalysis aspects. In: Coron, J.-S., Nielsen, J.B. (eds.) EUROCRYPT 2017. LNCS, vol. 10212, pp. 185–215. Springer, Cham (2017). https://doi.org/10.1007/978-3-319-56617-7_7
16. Shen, X., Li, R., Sun, B., Cheng, L., Li, C., Liao, M.: Dual relationship between impossible differentials and zero correlation linear hulls of simon-like ciphers. In: Liu, J.K., Samarati, P. (eds.) Information Security Practice and Experience, pp. 237–255. Springer International Publishing, Cham (2017)

17. Shen, X., Liu, G., Sun, B., Li, C.: Impossible differentials of SPN ciphers. In: Chen, K., Lin, D., Yung, M. (eds.) Information Security and Cryptology, pp. 47–63. Springer, Cham (2017)

18. Sun, B., Liu, M., Guo, J., Rijmen, V., Li, R.: Provable security evaluation of structures against impossible differential and zero correlation linear cryptanalysis. In: Fischlin, M., Coron, J.-S. (eds.) EUROCRYPT 2016. LNCS, vol. 9665, pp. 196–213. Springer, Heidelberg (2016). https://doi.org/10.1007/978-3-662-49890-3_8

19. Sun, B., et al.: Links among impossible differential, integral and zero correlation linear cryptanalysis. In: Gennaro, R., Robshaw, M. (eds.) CRYPTO 2015. LNCS, vol. 9215, pp. 95–115. Springer, Heidelberg (2015). https://doi.org/10.1007/978-3-662-47989-6_5

20. Tezcan, C.: Improbable differential attacks on PRESENT using undisturbed bits. J. Comput. Appl. Math. **259**, 503–511 (2014)

21. Wu, S., Wang, M.: Automatic search of truncated impossible differentials for word-oriented block ciphers. In: Galbraith, S., Nandi, M. (eds.) INDOCRYPT 2012. LNCS, vol. 7668, pp. 283–302. Springer, Heidelberg (2012). https://doi.org/10.1007/978-3-642-34931-7_17

Message-Restriction-Free Commitment Scheme Based on Lattice Assumption

Hideaki Miyaji[1], Yuntao Wang[2(✉)], and Atsuko Miyaji[1,2]

[1] Graduate School of Engineering, Osaka University, Suita, Japan
hideaki@cy2sec.comm.eng.osaka-u.ac.jp, miyaji@comm.eng.osaka-u.ac.jp
[2] School of Information Science, Japan Advanced Institute of Science and
Technology, Nomi, Japan
y-wang@jaist.ac.jp

Abstract. A commitment scheme is a fundamental protocol and an essential component of basic cryptographic tasks, such as zero-knowledge identification. In recent years, lattice-based cryptography has been intensively studied owing to its potential to be promising post-quantum cryptography. Therefore, the commitment schemes based on lattice assumption have been studied for practical applications. Typically, many applications require to commit arbitrary vectors rather than only short ones. In order to send such large messages, one of a crucial challenges of commitment schemes is to increase the size of a message string. Various existing studies have been done to enlarge the size of a message string so far. Baum et al. constructed the commitment scheme, which can allow sending large message size in 2018. However, the domain available for message string is still being used for non-message purposes.

In this paper, by improving Baum et al.'s commitment scheme, we propose a commitment scheme that can send a larger message size than Baum et al.'s message string size. Furthermore, we prove that the hiding property of our commitment scheme is based on the hardness of the decisional knapsack problem, and the binding property is based on the hardness of the module small-integer solution problem. We also show how to achieve a statistically hiding commitment scheme by setting appropriate parameters.

Keywords: Commitment scheme · Hash function · Lattice-based protocol

1 Introduction

Commitment scheme, such as zero-knowledge proofs [6], which is executed between two parties (i.e., a sender and a receiver) through commitment and decommitment phases, is an essential component of the cryptographic scheme. In the commitment phase, the sender changes a message string into a commitment string and sends it to the receiver. Then, in the decommitment phase, the sender sends decommitment string, where the message is included; this allows

© Springer Nature Switzerland AG 2021
R. Deng et al. (Eds.): ISPEC 2021, LNCS 13107, pp. 90–105, 2021.
https://doi.org/10.1007/978-3-030-93206-0_7

the receiver to verify whether the commitment string was, in fact, generated from the message or not. The security of a commitment scheme is formalized based on the following two properties: hiding property and binding property [9,11]. The hiding property guarantees that no receiver can receive partial information of the messages before the decommitment phase. Simultaneously, the binding property ensures that no sender can make more than two decommitment strings for one commitment string.

1.1 History of Commitment Scheme

The notion of a commitment scheme with a one-way function was constructed by Blum in 1982 [3]. However, Blum did not present a concrete design to achieve the commitment scheme. Whereas, a concrete design was proposed later on [3]. A commitment scheme based on the hardness of factoring was introduced by Goldwasser et al. [10] in 1988. Pedersen introduced a commitment scheme based on discrete logarithm problem in 1991; further, a commitment scheme based on collision resistance hash function (Message Digest) was introduced by Halevi et al. in 1996. The study on commitment schemes has received considerable attention from the research community because the commitment scheme is a key tool for designing cryptographic protocols; they also have numerous applications (e.g. threshold encryption [8], and electronic voting [4]). In particular, when combined with zero-knowledge proofs, they can enforce "good" behavior by adversarial parties and enhance the security of design protocols against malicious attacks [1].

1.2 Lattice-Based Commitment Schemes

On the contrary, lattice-based cryptography has been extensively studied over the past several years since the quantum computer is believed to break the discrete logarithm and factoring problems in polynomial time. In 2008, Kawachi et al. constructed the first lattice-based commitment scheme [12]. This commitment scheme is based on the short integer solution (SIS) problem where one commits to vectors over $\mathbb{Z}_2$. However, the message space is restricted to vectors of the small norm; otherwise, the binding property is lost, such as restriction is not observed in the standard cryptographic commitment scheme based on discrete logarithm or factoring problems, where the message space means a domain of messages that can be committed. Consequently, several studies have attempted to remove the restriction of the message space in the lattice-based commitment scheme.

In 2015, Benhamouda et al. constructed a commitment scheme based on a ring-learning with errors (LWEs) problem [2]. This commitment scheme removes some restrictions in the message space. However, the available size of the message string is only one bit. Thus, a 1-bit message string is expected to be extended to a large size of a commitment string.

In 2018, Baum et al. constructed a commitment scheme based on the knapsack problem [1]. They constructed a commitment scheme with the message space R_q^l, (where R_q is a residue ring of a polynomial ring $R_q = \mathbb{Z}_q[X]/\langle X^N + 1 \rangle$). Thus, their commitment scheme can commit an arbitrary vector over R_q^l which is bigger than one bit [2]. However, their commitment scheme requires n zeroes to be appended to the message string in order to reduce the security to $SKS_{n,k,\beta}^2$. Thus, the size of a commitment string is exactly extended from that of a message string.

We define a new notion of extension ratio in a commitment scheme as

"(size of commitment string)/(size of message string)".

Then, in other words, the "optimal for message string size" commitment scheme satisfies the extension ratio of

(size of commitment string)/(size of message string) $= 1$

Based on this new notion, Baum et al.'s commitment scheme is not "optimal for message space". We call an optimal message space commitment scheme as *message-restriction-free* commitment scheme.

1.3 Our Contribution

In this paper, we propose a message-restriction-free commitment scheme by improving the lattice-based commitment scheme in [1].

In [1], a message vector $\mathbf{x} \in R_q^{m-n}$ is committed to a commitment string $\mathbf{c}_{m-n,m}^{\mathsf{BDLOP}}(\mathbf{x}, \mathbf{r})$ for a public parameter $A \in R_q^{m \times k}$, random vector $\mathbf{r} \in S_\beta^k$, and a positive integer n. Their scheme is expressed as follows, specifying the domain of message string and that of commitment string:

$$\mathbf{c}_{m-n,m}^{\mathsf{BDLOP}}(\mathbf{x}, \mathbf{r}) = A \cdot \mathbf{r} + \begin{bmatrix} 0^n \\ \mathbf{x} \end{bmatrix}.$$

Note that their protocol satisfies the binding property under $SKS_{n,k,\beta}^2$ and that the hiding property under $DKS_{m,k,\beta}^\infty$.

On the other hand, in our commitment scheme, a message vector $\mathbf{x} \in R_q^m$ is committed to a commitment string $\mathbf{c}_{m,m}(\mathbf{x}, \mathbf{r}) \in R_q^m$ for a public parameter $A \in R_q^{m \times k}$, random vector $\mathbf{r} \in S_\beta^k$, and a positive integer n. Our scheme is expressed as follows, specifying the domain of message string and that of commitment string:

$$\mathbf{c}_{m,m}(\mathbf{x}, \mathbf{r}) = A \cdot \mathbf{r} + \mathbf{x}.$$

As a result, our commitment scheme is optimal for a message space since it satisfies that the expansion ratio equals 1. Note that our protocol satisfies the binding property under Module Small Integer Solution($M - SIS_{q,m,m+k,\gamma}$) and that the hiding property under Decisional Knapsack Problem($DKS_{m,k,\beta}^\infty$). We also show how to achieve a statistically hiding commitment scheme by using our proposed commitment scheme.

The remainder of this paper is organized as follows. Section 2 summarizes commitment scheme and lattice-based problem. Section 3 describes building blocks of our construction. Then, we present our commitment scheme in Sect. 4. We also make comparison between our commitment scheme and other related commitment schemes in Sect. 5. Finally, we conclude our work in Sect. 6.

2 Preliminaries

In this section, we explain definitions of commitment scheme, hash functions, etc., after summarizing notations used in this paper.

- 1^k : security parameter
- Sender : sender
- Receiver : receiver
- com : commitment string
- dec : decommitment string
- message space : a domain of messages that can be committed
- m : security parameter used in the proposed commitment scheme
- $\varepsilon(k)$: negligible function in k
- PP : public parameter
- PPT : probabilistic polynomial time
- $\bot$: rejection output by R for invalid inputs
- $\mathrm{Hw}(x)$: Hamming weight of x and called Hamming weight
- $\Delta(x)$: The ratio of "1"s in x and called relative Hamming weight
- Com : commitment scheme
- $\mathbb{N}$: set of natural numbers
- q : prime number
- $N(= 2^r)$: degree of polynomial rings
- $\mathbb{F}_2$: prime field with characteristic 2
- In each $f \in R$, let $f = \Sigma_i f_i X^i$ and
  - $l_1 : ||f||_1 = \Sigma_i |f_i|$
  - $l_2 : ||f||_2 = \left(\Sigma_i |f_i|^2\right)^{1/2}$
  - $l_\infty : ||f||_\infty = \max_i |f_i|$
- ζ_n : primitive n-th root of unity
- I_n : Identity matrix with $n \times n$
- $R = \mathbb{Z}[X]/\langle X^N + 1\rangle$
- $R_q = \mathbb{Z}_q[X]/\langle X^N + 1\rangle$
- S_β : Set of all elements $x \in R$ with l_∞-norm at most β
- C : A subset of S_1 from which challenges come from
- κ : The maximum l_1 norm of any element in C
- $C = \{c \in R_q \ s.t. \ ||c||_\infty = 1, ||c||_1 = \kappa\}$
- $\sigma = 11 \cdot \kappa \cdot \beta \cdot \sqrt{k \cdot N}$: Standard deviation used in the zero-knowledge proof

We define a commitment scheme, which follows [5].

Definition 1 (Commitment Scheme).
A commitment scheme, Com(Sender, Receiver), *is a two-phase protocol between two probabilistic polynomial-time parties* Sender *and* Receiver, *which are called the sender and receiver, respectively.*

During the first phase (commitment phase), Sender *commits to a message string* **a** *to a pair of keys* (com, dec), *by executing* (com, dec) ⟵ Sender($1^k, PP$). *Then,* Sender *sends* com *(commitment string) to* Receiver.

During the second phase (decommitment phase), Sender *sends the keys* dec *(decommitment string) with* **a** *to* Receiver. *Then,* Receiver *verifies whether the decommitment string is valid by executing* Receiver(com, dec). *If invalid,* Receiver(com, dec) *outputs a special string,* ⊥, *meaning that* Receiver *rejects the decommitment of* Sender. *Otherwise,* Receiver(com, dec) *can efficiently compute the string* **a** *revealed by* Sender, *and verifies whether* **a** *was indeed chosen by* Sender *during the first phase.*
Consider the following three algorithms KeyGen, Commit, Decommit, which have 1^λ *as implicit input:*

- *Keygen: A PPT algorithm that outputs the public parameters* $PP \in \{0,1\}^{poly(\lambda)}$ *containing a definition of the message space* $\mathcal{M}$
- *Commit: A PPT algorithm that, on input the public parameters PP and a message* $x \in \mathcal{M}$ *outputs values* $c, r \in \{0,1\}^{poly(\lambda)}$
- *Decommit: A deterministic polynomial-time algorithm that, on input the public parameters PP, a message* $x \in \mathcal{M}$ *and values* $c, r \in \{0,1\}^{poly(\lambda)}$ *outputs a bit* $b \in \{0,1\}$

The following provides security notions of the commitment scheme Com(S, R).

Definition 2 (Computational Binding Property [1]**).** *Let* $a \in \mathcal{M}$ *as message string,* c *as a commitment string and Adv as a PPT adversary. The commitment scheme satisfies binding property if the following equation satisfies.*

$$\Pr \left[\begin{array}{ccc} Adv(PP) \to (a, a', c): & & \\ s.t. & a \neq a' \land & keygen \to PP \\ Decommit(PP, a, c) & = Decommit(PP, a, c) = 1 & \end{array} \right] < \varepsilon(k)$$

Next, we define the computational hiding property of a commitment scheme.

Definition 3 (Computational Hiding Property [11]**).** *Let PPT receiver* Receiver *and* Receiver *is given* $a_1, a_2 \in \mathcal{M}$. *We say the commitment scheme satisfies computational hiding property if the following satisfies*

$$|\Pr[\text{Receiver}(a_1) = 1] - \Pr[\text{Receiver}(a_2) = 1]| < \varepsilon(k)$$

Next, we define the security assumption which we rely on. We define the collision-resistance of a hash function in Definition 4.

Definition 4 (Collision-Resistance). *We have an arbitrary probabilistic polynomial algorithm, Adv, given a description of the hash function and length parameter as inputs. If the probability of Adv that outputs $x, x' \in \{0,1\}^k$ satisfying $x \neq x'$ and $f(x) = f(x')$ is negligible, the function is a collision-resistant hash function.*

$$\Pr[Adv(f, 1^k) \rightarrow (x, x') \ s.t. \ x \neq x', f(x) = f(x')] < \varepsilon(k).$$

From now on, we will define the security assumption which we use to prove hiding property or binding property. We define the Ring-SIS problem ($M - SIS_{q,m,m+k,\gamma}$) in Definition 5

Definition 5 ($M - SIS_{q,m,m+k,\gamma}$(Module Small Integer Solution Problem) [7]). *The $M - SIS_{q,m,m+k,\gamma}$ problem (over an implicit ring R) is defined as follows. Given $A' \in R_q^{m \times (m+k)}$ sampled uniformly at random, find $z \in R^{m+k}$ such that $A'\mathbf{z} = 0$ and $0 < ||\mathbf{z}||_2 \leq \gamma$.*

Next we define the Search Knapsack Problem in Definition 6

Definition 6 ($SKS^2_{n,k,\beta}$(Search Knapsack Problem))[1]). *The $SKS^2_{n,k,\beta}$ problem is to find a short vector $\mathbf{y} \in S_\beta^k$ satisfying $[I_n \ A'] \cdot \mathbf{y} = 0^n$ when given a random $A' \in R_q^{n \times (k-n)}$. $SKS^2_{n,k,\beta}$ problem asserts that for every efficient algorithm Adv, the probability given by*

$$\Pr\left[||y_i||_2 \leq \beta \wedge [I_n \ A'] \cdot \mathbf{y} = 0^n | A' \leftarrow R_q^{n \times (k-n)};\right.$$

$$0 \neq \mathbf{y} = \begin{bmatrix} y_1 \\ \vdots \\ y_2 \end{bmatrix} \leftarrow Adv(A')\right] \leq \varepsilon$$

Next, we define Decisional Knapsack Problem in Definition 7.

Definition 7 ($DKS^\infty_{m,k,\beta}$(Decisional Knapsack Problem) [1]). *The $DKS^\infty_{m,k,\beta}$ problem is to distinguish whether the distribution $[I_m \ A'] \cdot \mathbf{y}$ from the uniform distribution, for a short $\mathbf{y} = (y_1, \ldots, y_k) \in S_\beta^k$, $A' \in R_q^{m \times (k-m)}$ and identity matrix I_m. $DKS^\infty_{m,k,\beta}$ problem asserts that for every efficient algorithm Adv, the probability given by*

$$|\Pr\left[b = 1 \, A' \leftarrow R_q^{m \times (k-m)}; \mathbf{y} \leftarrow S_\beta^k; b \leftarrow Adv(A', [I_m \ A'] \cdot \mathbf{y})\right]$$

$$-\Pr\left[b = 1 \, A' \leftarrow R_q^{m \times (k-m)}; \mathbf{u} \leftarrow R_q^m; b \leftarrow Adv(A', \mathbf{u})\right]| < \varepsilon(n).$$

3 Related Works

In this section, we explain a commitment scheme used in [1] which we call $\mathsf{Com_{BDLOP}}$. We also explain how to achieve a statistically hiding commitment scheme by using $DKS^\infty_{m,k,\beta}$.

3.1   Commitment Scheme with Lattice Based Structure

The commitment scheme is constructed using algorithms of *Keygen, Commit, Decommit.*
$\mathsf{Com_{BDLOP}}(\mathsf{S}, \mathsf{R})$:
Keygen
Public parameter $A_1 \in R_q^{n \times k}$ and $A_2 \in R_q^{l \times k}$ from Eq. (1) and (2).

$$A_1 = [I_n \; A_1'], \text{ where } A_1' \leftarrow R_q^{n \times (k-n)} \tag{1}$$

$$A_2 = [0^{l \times n} \; I_\ell \; A_2'], \text{ where } A_2' \leftarrow R_q^{l \times (k-n-l)} \tag{2}$$

Commitment Phase by Sender
For a message string $\mathbf{x} \in R_q^l$, choose a random string $\mathbf{r} \in S_\beta^k$, and construct the commitment string from $(\mathbf{x}, \mathbf{r})$ as

$$\mathbf{c}_{m-n,m}^{\mathsf{BDLOP}}(\mathbf{x}, \mathbf{r}) = \begin{bmatrix} A_1 \\ A_2 \end{bmatrix} \cdot \mathbf{r} + \begin{bmatrix} 0^n \\ \mathbf{x} \end{bmatrix}.$$

Decommitment Phase from Sender **to** Receiver

1. Sender sends a decommit string $(\mathbf{x}', \mathbf{r}') \in R_q^l \times S_\beta^k$ as dec to Receiver.
2. Receiver computes

$$\mathbf{c}_{m-n,m}^{\mathsf{BDLOP}}(\mathbf{x}', \mathbf{r}') = \begin{bmatrix} A_1 \\ A_2 \end{bmatrix} \cdot \mathbf{r} + \begin{bmatrix} 0^n \\ \mathbf{x} \end{bmatrix}$$

from dec $= (\mathbf{x}', \mathbf{r}')$ and verify $\mathbf{c}_{m-n,m}^{\mathsf{BDLOP}}(\mathbf{x}, \mathbf{r}) = \mathbf{c}_{m-n,m}^{\mathsf{BDLOP}}(\mathbf{x}', \mathbf{r}')$.
3. Receiver outputs $\mathbf{x}$ if it satisfies $\mathbf{c}_{m-n,m}^{\mathsf{BDLOP}}(\mathbf{x}, \mathbf{r}) = \mathbf{c}_{m-n,m}^{\mathsf{BDLOP}}(\mathbf{x}', \mathbf{r}')$ and that for all i, $||r_i||_2 \leq 4 \cdot \sigma \cdot \sqrt{N}$. Otherwise, Receiver outputs $\perp$.

The computational binding property and computational hiding property in $\mathsf{Com_{BDLOP}}$ follow from Lemmas 1 and 2. We only describe their lemmas without proof.

Lemma 1 ([1]). *If there is an algorithm Adv who can break the hiding of* $\mathsf{Com_{BDLOP}}$ *with probability ε, then there is an algorithm Adv' who can solve the $DKS_{m,k,\beta}$ problem where $m = n + l$ with an advantage ε.*

Lemma 2 ([1]). *If there is an algorithm Adv who can break the binding of* $\mathsf{Com_{BDLOP}}$ *with probability ε, then there is an algorithm Adv' who can solve the $SKS_{n,k,\beta}^2$ problem where $m = n + l$ with an advantage ε.*

They also pose very interesting conditions, where $DKS_{m,k,\beta}^\infty$ and $SKS_{n,k,\beta}^2$ problems can be transformed into unconditionally hard. Since our method uses $DKS_{m,k,\beta}^\infty$, we can also use the conditions of $DKS_{m,k,\beta}^\infty$ posed by them, which is shown in the following Lemma 3.

Lemma 3 ([1]). *Let* $1 < d < N$ *be a power of* 2. *If* q *is a prime congruent to* $2d + 1 \pmod{4d}$ *and*

$$q^{n/k} \cdot 2^{256/(k \cdot N)} \le 2\beta < \frac{1}{\sqrt{d}} \cdot q^{1/d}$$

then any (all-powerful) algorithm A *has advantage at most* 2^{-128} *in solving* $DKS_{m,k,\beta}^{\infty}$.

4 Proposed Commitment Scheme

In this section, we propose a message-restriction-free commitment scheme Com and prove its computational hiding property and computational binding property by $DKS_{m,k,\beta}^{\infty}$ and $M - SIS_{q,m,m+k,\gamma}$, respectively. We also show how to achieve a statistically hiding scheme by using Lemma 3.

We first revisit the commitment scheme Com$_{\mathsf{BDLOP}}$ in Subsect. 4.1. We then show our proposed commitment scheme Com in Subsect. 4.2 and prove its computational binding property and computational hiding property in Subsect. 4.3. Finally, we propose a commitment scheme Com based on unconditionally hard $DKS_{m,k,\beta}^{\infty}$ problem in Subsect. 4.4 and prove our proposed commitment scheme Com also satisfies statistical hiding property.

4.1 (Optimal) Extension Ratio

We define properties of *message-restriction-free* rigorously to be considered in a commitment scheme, and then discuss how Com$_{\mathsf{BDLOP}}$is far from the property.

Definition 8 (*Message-Restriction-Free* Commitment Scheme). *For a commitment scheme,* Com(Sender, Receiver), *the extension ratio* ER *of commitment string to message string is defined as*

$$\mathsf{ER} = \frac{|size\ of\ commitment\ string|}{|size\ of\ message\ string|}.$$

If Com(Sender, Receiver) *satisfies* ER $= 1$, *we call* Com(Sender, Receiver) *as* message-restriction-free *commitment scheme.*

Now we revisit Com$_{\mathsf{BDLOP}}$ in Sect. 3, in which ℓ message string x is embedded into $\mathbf{L} = \begin{bmatrix} 0^n \\ \mathbf{x} \end{bmatrix}$, and the size of commitment string becomes $n + \ell$. Thus, Com$_{\mathsf{BDLOP}}$ satisfies

$$\mathsf{ER} = \frac{n + \ell}{\ell} > 1.$$

Unfortunately, the size of n, independent to a message $\mathbf{x}$, cannot be reduced because its security relies on $SKS_{m,k,\beta}^2$. In other words, the size of the commitment string is exactly expanded than that of the message string in Com$_{\mathsf{BDLOP}}$.

Our target commitment scheme which satisfies ER $= 1$.

4.2 Proposed commitment scheme

We present our *message-restriction-free* commitment scheme, which consists of three algorithm, *Keygen*, *Commit*, and *Decommit* as follows.
Com(S, R):
Keygen
Construct the public parameter $A_1 \in R_q^{n \times k}$ and $A_2 \in R_q^{\ell \times k}$ from the following Eqs. (3) and (4).

$$A_1 = [I_n \ A_1'], \text{ where } A_1' \leftarrow R_q^{n \times (k-n)}, \tag{3}$$

$$A_2 = [0^{l \times n} \ I_\ell \ A_2'], \text{ where } A_2' \leftarrow R_q^{\ell \times (k-n-\ell)}. \tag{4}$$

We denote the pubic parameter $PP = A$ where $A = \begin{bmatrix} A_1 \\ A_2 \end{bmatrix} \in R_q^{m \times k}$.

Commitment Phase by Sender

1. Choose a message string $\mathbf{x} \in S_\beta^m$ and a random string $\mathbf{r} \in S_\beta^k$ where $m = n + \ell$.
2. Set $\mathbf{z} = \begin{pmatrix} \mathbf{r} \\ \mathbf{x} \end{pmatrix}$ where a message string $\mathbf{x} \in S_\beta^m$ and a random string $\mathbf{r} \in S_\beta^k$
   which satisfies $||r_i||_2 \le 4 \cdot \sigma \cdot \sqrt{N}$.
3. Construct a commitment string from $(\mathbf{x}, \mathbf{r})$ as

$$\mathbf{c}_{m,m}(\mathbf{x}, \mathbf{r}) = \begin{bmatrix} A_1 \\ A_2 \end{bmatrix} \cdot \mathbf{r} + \mathbf{x}.$$

Decommitment Phase from Sender to Receiver

1. Sender sends decommit string $(\mathbf{x}', \mathbf{r}') \in S_\beta^m \times S_\beta^k$ as dec to Receiver.
2. Receiver Computes

$$\mathbf{c}_{m,m}(\mathbf{x}', \mathbf{r}') = A \cdot \mathbf{r}' + \mathbf{x}'$$

from dec $= (\mathbf{x}', \mathbf{r}')$ and verify $\mathbf{c}_{m,m}(\mathbf{x}, \mathbf{r}) = \mathbf{c}_{m,m}(\mathbf{x}', \mathbf{r}')$.
3. If it satisfies $\mathbf{c}_{m,m}(\mathbf{x}, \mathbf{r}) = \mathbf{c}_{m,m}(\mathbf{x}', \mathbf{r}')$ and $||r_i||_2 \le 4 \cdot \sigma \cdot \sqrt{N}$, Receiver outputs $\mathbf{x}$. Otherwise, Receiver outputs $\perp$.

In our protocol, the following ratio holds.

$$\text{ER} = \frac{|\text{size of commitment string}|}{|\text{size of message string}|} = \frac{m}{m} = 1.$$

In the following Subsection, we prove the computational binding and hiding properties of the proposed commitment scheme.

4.3   Binding and Hiding Properties of Proposed Commitment Scheme

We prove the computational hiding property in Theorem 1 and its computational binding property in Theorem 2.

Theorem 1. *For any* $\mathbf{x}, \mathbf{x}' \in S_\beta^m$, *let* k *be the length of a random number* $\mathbf{r} \in S_\beta^k$, *let* $A \cdot \mathbf{r} + \mathbf{x}$ *where* $m = n + l$. *If there exists an algorithm Adv that has an advantage* ε *in breaking the hiding property of the commitment scheme* Com, *then there exists another algorithm Adv', that runs in the same time and has advantage* ε *in solving the* $DKS_{m,k,\beta}^\infty$.

Proof: We first assume that an Adv exists, which breaks the computationally hiding property of the proposed commitment scheme. Then we show how the other Adv' tries to break $DKS_{m,k,\beta}^\infty$ problem.

The Adv' get the value $(B, \mathbf{t}) = R_q^n \times S_\beta^k$ from the $DKS_{m,k,\beta}^\infty$ Challenge. If Adv' can identify whether $\mathbf{t}$ is distributed from uniform distribution or the $DKS_{m,k,\beta}^\infty$ distribution in polynomial time, Adv' can break $DKS_{m,k,\beta}^\infty$ problem in polynomial time. In here, B can be express as

$$[I_{n+\ell} \ B']$$

where B' constructed from $B' \in R_q^{m \times (k-n-l)}$. Next, Adv' computes the matrix $A \in R_q^{m \times k}$ which is a public parameter. The matrix $A \in R_q^{m \times k}$ is composed by a matrix $R \in R_q^{n \times l}$, identity matrices I_n and I_ℓ, and a matrix B in Eq. (5).

$$A = \begin{bmatrix} I_n & R \\ 0^{l \times n} & I_\ell \end{bmatrix} \cdot B \tag{5}$$

Next, we denote how Adv' computes the commitment string. Adv' receive $\mathbf{x}_0, \mathbf{x}_1 \in S_\beta^m$ and choose either one and let $\mathbf{x}_b$. Then, computes $\mathbf{c}$ from Eq. (6).

$$\mathbf{c} = \begin{bmatrix} I_n & R \\ 0^{l \times n} & I_\ell \end{bmatrix} \cdot \mathbf{t} + \mathbf{x}_b^m \tag{6}$$

Adv' sends $\mathbf{c}$ to Adv. After Adv get the value $\mathbf{c}$, he tries to guess $\mathbf{x}_b$ and choose $b' \in [0, 1]$. If the probability of guessing b' is larger than ε, then Adv can identify the value $\mathbf{c}$ as a commitment string since we assume that Adv can break the hiding property of the commitment scheme.

If $\mathbf{t} = B \cdot \mathbf{r}$, then $\mathbf{c}$ can be express as follow.

$$\begin{aligned} \mathbf{c} &= \begin{bmatrix} I_n & R \\ 0^{\ell \times n} & I_\ell \end{bmatrix} \cdot [I_{n+\ell} \ B'] \cdot \mathbf{r} + \mathbf{x}_b^m \\ &= A \cdot \mathbf{r} + \mathbf{x}_b^m \end{aligned} \tag{7}$$

Consequently, Adv can distinguish $\mathbf{c}$ as commitment string in probability ε. The probability to identify $b = b'$ is

$$\Pr[b = b'] = \frac{1}{2} + \varepsilon.$$

On the other hand, when $\mathbf{t} \neq B \cdot \mathbf{r}$, the value $\mathbf{c}$ cannot be expressed as Eq. 7. Consequently, the probability to identify b' can be express as

$$\Pr[b = b'] = \frac{1}{2}$$

because $\mathbf{c}$ distinguish as a random value by Adv. In other words, the probability that Adv outputs b' can be arranged as follows.

- $\Pr[b = b'] = 1/2 + \varepsilon$ s.t. $\mathbf{t} \neq U$
- $\Pr[b = b'] = 1/2$ s.t. $\mathbf{t} = U$

Therefore, Adv' can distinguish whether $\mathbf{t}$ is distributed from uniform distribution or $DKS^\infty_{m,k,\beta}$ distribution in advantage ε when Adv can break the hiding property in Com. $\square$

From Theorem 1, our proposed commitment scheme Com satisfy the computationally hiding property under the $DKS^\infty_{m,k,\beta}$ problem.

Next, we prove the computational binding property of the proposed commitment scheme in Theorem 2.

Theorem 2. *For any* $\mathbf{x}, \mathbf{x}' \in S^m_\beta$, *let* k *be the length of a random number* $\mathbf{r} \in S^k_\beta$, *let* $A \in R^{m \times k}_q$ *as a public parameter, and* m *be the output length of* $A \cdot \mathbf{r} + \mathbf{x}$ *where* $m = n + l$. *If there exists an algorithm Adv that has an advantage* ε *in breaking the binding property of the commitment scheme which satisfies* $\gamma = \sqrt{(m+k)} \cdot \beta$. *Then there exists another algorithm Adv', that runs in the same time and has an advantage* ε *in solving the* $M - SIS_{q,m,m+k,\gamma}$.

Proof: We assume that an Adv exists that can break the computational biding property of the proposed commitment scheme. Then, another adversary Adv', tries to break the $M - SIS_{q,m,m+k,\gamma}$ problem.

Adv' get the value $A = \begin{bmatrix} A_1 \\ A_2 \end{bmatrix} \in R^{m \times k}_q$ from the $M - SIS_{q,m,m+k,\gamma}$ challenge. If the Adv' can find the value $\mathbf{z}$ which satisfy $A \cdot \mathbf{z} = 0$ and $||\mathbf{z}||_2 \leq \sqrt{(m+k)} \cdot \beta$ in polynomial time, then Adv' can break the $M - SIS_{q,m,m+k,\gamma}$ problem in polynomial time.

Adv' sends A to Adv which is the public parameter in binding property of the commitment scheme. Adv outputs

$$(\mathbf{x}, \mathbf{r}) \in S^m_\beta \times S^k_\beta$$

which satisfy $A \cdot \mathbf{r} + \mathbf{x} = 0$. Let I_m as identity matrix with $m \times m$. Then, Adv can gain the below equation

$$A \cdot \mathbf{r} + \mathbf{x} = 0$$

$$[A \ I_m] \cdot \begin{bmatrix} \mathbf{r} \\ \mathbf{x} \end{bmatrix} = 0.$$

Set A' and $\mathbf{z}$ as $A' = [A \; I_m]$ and $\mathbf{z} = \begin{bmatrix} \mathbf{r} \\ \mathbf{x} \end{bmatrix}$. Adv' can find $A' \cdot \mathbf{z} = 0$ since the matrix satisfies $A' \in R_q^{m \times (m+k)}$ and $\mathbf{z}$ satisfies $||\mathbf{z}||_2 \leq \sqrt{(m+k)} \cdot \beta$. Therefore, Adv' can break the $M - SIS_{q,m,m+k,\gamma}$ problem if another adversary can break the binding property of the commitment scheme. $\square$

From Theorem 2, our proposed commitment scheme satisfy the computationally binding property under the $M - SIS_{q,m,m+k,\gamma}$ problem.

4.4 Unconditional Hardness of the $DKS_{m,k,\beta}^{\infty}$ Problem

In this subsection, we propose our commitment scheme satisfies statistical hiding property when some ranges of parameters in $DKS_{m,k,\beta}^{\infty}$ problem becomes unconditionally hard. Before showing the conditions on the parameters of the $DKS_{m,k,\beta}^{\infty}$ problem for which the proposed commitment scheme Com is statistically hiding, we need to explain how to parse the statistical distance. We use the modified version of the leftover hash lemma, proved by Regev in 2009. We explain a modified version of the leftover hash lemma in Lemma 4.

Lemma 4 (Special version of the leftover hash lemma [13]). *Let G be a finite Abelian group and let ℓ be a positive integer. For any ℓ elements, $g_1, ..., g_\ell \in G$, consider the statistical distance between the uniform distribution on G and the distribution given by the sum of a random subset of $g_1, ..., g_\ell$. Then, the expectation of this statistical distance over a uniform choice of $g_1, ..., g_\ell \in G$ is at most $\sqrt{|G|/2^\ell}$. In particular, the probability that this statistical distance is more than $\sqrt[4]{|G|/2^\ell}$ is at most $\sqrt[4]{|G|/2^\ell}$.*

By using Lemma 4 and Lemma 3, the statistical hiding property of the proposed commitment scheme Com can be shown in Theorem 3.

Theorem 3. *Let $1 < d < N$ be a power of 2, let k be the length of a random number $\mathbf{r} \in S_\beta^k$, and m be the output length of Com, and let G as $G = R_q^m$. If q is a prime congruent to $2d + 1 \pmod{4d}$ and satisfies*

$$q^{m/k} \cdot 2^{2m/(k \cdot N)} \leq \beta < \frac{1}{\sqrt{d}} \cdot q^{1/d},$$

then any (all-powerful) algorithm A has advantage at most 2^{-m} in solving $DKS_{m,k,\beta}^{\infty}$.

Proof: Let Com as the commitment scheme

$$\mathsf{Com} = \{h_{A'} : S_\beta^k \to R_q^m\} \text{ where}$$
$$h_{A'}(\mathbf{y}) = [I_n \; A'] \cdot \mathbf{y}.$$

Let $\mathbf{g} = (g_1, \ldots, g_k)$. For $\mathbf{h} \in G$, we define

$$P_{\mathbf{g}}(\mathbf{h}) = \frac{1}{\beta^{kN}} \left| \left\{ \mathbf{y} \in S_\beta^k \mid \sum_{i=1}^{k} y_i g_i = \mathbf{h} \right\} \right|.$$

The statistical distance between the distribution $(A', h_{A'}(\mathbf{y}))$ and the uniform distribution can be express as

$$\operatorname{Exp}_{\mathbf{g}} \left[\sum_{\mathbf{h} \in R_q^n} |P_{\mathbf{g}}(\mathbf{h}) - |1/G|| \right]. \tag{8}$$

Then, the Eq. (8) can be parsed as

$$\operatorname{Exp}_{\mathbf{g}} \left[\sum_{\mathbf{h} \in R_q^m} |P_{\mathbf{g}}(\mathbf{h}) - 1/q^{mN}| \right] \leq \sqrt{\frac{q^{mN}}{\beta^{kN}}} \tag{9}$$

from Lemma 4 and $|G| = q^{mN}$. We parse the Eq. (9) as

$$\log \sqrt{\frac{q^{mN}}{\beta^{kN}}} = \frac{1}{2} \log \left(\frac{q^{mN}}{\beta^{kN}} \right) = \frac{1}{2} \left\{ \log q^{mN} - \log \beta^{kN} \right\}$$

$$= \frac{1}{2} \left\{ m \cdot N \cdot \log q - k \cdot N \cdot \log \beta \right\} \tag{10}$$

On the other hand, the condition $q^{m/k} \cdot 2^{2m/(k \cdot N)} \leq \beta$ can be parsed as Eq. (11)

$$k \cdot N \cdot \log \beta > m \cdot N \cdot \log q + 2m$$
$$-k \cdot N \cdot \log \beta < -m \cdot N \cdot \log q - 2m. \tag{11}$$

Equation (10) can be parsed as Equation (12) from Eq. (11).

$$\frac{1}{2} \left\{ m \cdot N \cdot \log q - k \cdot N \cdot \log \beta \right\} < \frac{1}{2} \left\{ m \cdot N \cdot \log q - m \cdot N \cdot \log q - 2m \right\}$$

$$= \frac{1}{2} \left\{ -2m \right\} = -m. \tag{12}$$

Therefore, the statistical distance between the distribution $(A', h_{A'}(\mathbf{y}))$ and the uniform distribution can be parsed as

$$\operatorname{Exp}_{\mathbf{g}} \left[\sum_{\mathbf{h} \in R_q^m} |P_{\mathbf{g}}(\mathbf{h}) - 1/q^{mN}| \right] \leq \sqrt{\frac{q^{mN}}{\beta^{kN}}} < 2^{-m}.$$

□

From Theorem 3, we can prove that our commitment scheme satisfies statistical hiding property under $DKS_{m,k,\beta}^{\infty}$ problem.

Theorem 4. *Our proposed commitment scheme* Com *is statistically hiding under*

$$q^{m/k} \cdot 2^{2m/(k \cdot N)} \leq \beta < \frac{1}{\sqrt{d}} \cdot q^{1/d},$$

based on the $DKS_{m,k,\beta}^{\infty}$ problem, and computationally binding based on the $M - SIS_{q,m,m+k,\gamma}$ problem.

5   Comparison of the Commitment Schemes

In this section, we compare the commitment schemes. We define commitment scheme $\mathsf{Com}_{\mathsf{BKLP}}$ which we introduced in Subsect. 1.2, where proposed by Benhamouda et al. in 2015 [2]. In $\mathsf{Com}_{\mathsf{BKLP}}$, a message vector $\mathbf{x} \in R_q$ is committed to a commitment string $\mathbf{c}_{1,k}^{\mathsf{BKLP}}(\mathbf{x}, \mathbf{r})$ for a public parameter $(\mathbf{a}, \mathbf{b}) \in R_q^k \times R_q^k$, random vector $\mathbf{r} \in R_q$ and some errors $e \in D^k$, (where D means density function), l is a security parameter, and k bounds in $1 < k \leq \frac{l}{\|e\|_\infty}$. The commitment scheme $\mathsf{Com}_{\mathsf{BKLP}}$ can be proved its hiding property by Decision-RLWE(D-RLWE) and proved its binding property by Information-theoretic security. However, the parameter of ER becomes

$$\mathrm{ER} = \frac{|\text{size of commitment string}|}{|\text{size of message string}|} = \frac{k}{1} > 1.$$

Table 1. Comparison of the commitment schemes

Commitment schemes	Hiding property	Binding property	ER
$\mathsf{Com}_{\mathsf{BKLP}}$ [2]	D-RLWE (computational)	Information-theoretic security (statistical)	>1
$\mathsf{Com}_{\mathsf{BDLOP}}$ [1]	$DKS_{m,k,\beta}^\infty$ (statistical)	$SKS_{n,k,\beta}^2$ (statistical)	>1
Our scheme	$DKS_{m,k,\beta}^\infty$ (statistical)	$M - SIS_{q,m,m+k,\gamma}$ (computational)	=1

The commitment scheme $\mathsf{Com}_{\mathsf{BDLOP}}$ can be proved its hiding property and binding property by $DKS_{m,k,\beta}^\infty$ and $SKS_{n,k,\beta}^2$, respectively. They also prove how to achieve a statistically binding scheme, a statistically hiding scheme, and a more efficient scheme that is only computationally hiding and binding. However, the parameter of ER becomes

$$\mathrm{ER} = \frac{m}{m - n} > 1.$$

On the other hand, our proposed commitment scheme Com can be proved its hiding property and binding property by $DKS_{m,k,\beta}^\infty$ and $M - SIS_{q,m,m+k,\gamma}$, respectively. We also proved that the commitment scheme Com satisfies the statistical hiding property based on Theorem 4. Also. the parameter of ER becomes

$$\mathrm{ER} = \frac{m}{m} = 1.$$

Therefore, ours is the only commitment scheme that satisfies the condition $\mathrm{ER} = 1$.

6   Conclusion

In this paper, we have proposed a commitment scheme that satisfies $\mathrm{ER} = 1$. Then, we proved that its computational hiding property and computational binding property from $DKS_{m,k,\beta}^\infty$ problem and $M - SIS_{q,m,m+k,\gamma}$ problem, respectively. We have also proved that our proposed commitment scheme Com satisfies statistical hiding property based on $DKS^{\infty}_{m,k,\beta}$ problem, and satisfies computationally binding property based on the $M - SIS_{q,m,m+k,\gamma}$ problem.

Our proposed commitment scheme solved the problem of the relation between the size of the commitment string and the size of the message string. This result will become more and more important since it can use all message space available to construct a commitment scheme.

Acknowledgement. This work is partially supported by enPiT (Education Network for Practical Information Technologies) at MEXT, JSPS KAKENHI Grant Number JP21H03443, and Innovation Platform for Society 5.0 at MEXT. This work is also supported by JSPS KAKENHI Grant Number JP21K11751, Japan.

References

1. Baum, C., Damgård, I., Lyubashevsky, V., Oechsner, S., Peikert, C.: More efficient commitments from structured lattice assumptions. In: Catalano, D., Prisco, R.D. (eds.) Security and Cryptography for Networks - 11th International Conference, SCN 2018, Amalfi, Italy, 5–7 September 2018, vol. 11035, LNCS, pp. 368–385. Springer, Cham (2018). https://doi.org/10.1007/978-3-319-98113-0

2. Benhamouda, F., Krenn, S., Lyubashevsky, V., Pietrzak, K.: Efficient zero-knowledge proofs for commitments from learning with errors over rings. In: Pernul, G., Ryan, P.Y.A., Weippl, E. (eds.) ESORICS 2015. LNCS, vol. 9326, pp. 305–325. Springer, Cham (2015). https://doi.org/10.1007/978-3-319-24174-6_16

3. Blum, M.: Coin flipping by telephone - a protocol for solving impossible problems. In: COMPCON 1982, Digest of Papers, Twenty-Fourth IEEE Computer Society International Conference, San Francisco, CA, USA, 22–25 February 1982, pp. 133–137. IEEE Computer Society (1982)

4. Cramer, R., Franklin, M., Schoenmakers, B., Yung, M.: Multi-Authority secret-ballot elections with linear work. In: Maurer, U. (ed.) EUROCRYPT 1996. LNCS, vol. 1070, pp. 72–83. Springer, Heidelberg (1996). https://doi.org/10.1007/3-540-68339-9_7

5. Crescenzo, G.D., Katz, J., Ostrovsky, R., Smith, A.D.: Efficient and non-interactive non-malleable commitment. In: Advances in Cryptology - EUROCRYPT 2001, Proceeding of the International Conference on the Theory and Application of Cryptographic Techniques, Innsbruck, Austria, May 6–10, 2001, pp. 40–59 (2001)

6. Damgård, I.: Commitment schemes and zero-knowledge protocols. In: Damgård, I.B. (ed.) EEF School 1998. LNCS, vol. 1561, pp. 63–86. Springer, Heidelberg (1999). https://doi.org/10.1007/3-540-48969-X_3

7. del Pino, R., Lyubashevsky, V., Seiler, G.: Lattice-based group signatures and zero-knowledge proofs of automorphism stability. In: Lie, D., Mannan, M., Backes, M., Wang, X. (eds.) Proceedings of the 2018 ACM SIGSAC Conference on Computer and Communications Security, CCS 2018, Toronto, ON, Canada, 15–19 October 2018, pp. 574–591. ACM (2018)

8. Desmedt, Y., Frankel, Y.: Threshold cryptosystems. In: Brassard, G. (ed.) CRYPTO 1989. LNCS, vol. 435, pp. 307–315. Springer, New York (1990). https://doi.org/10.1007/0-387-34805-0_28

9. Gentry, C.: Fully homomorphic encryption using ideal lattices. In: Proceedings of the 41st Annual ACM Symposium on Theory of Computing, STOC 2009, Bethesda, MD, USA, 31 June February 2009, pp. 169–178 (2009)

10. Goldwasser, S., Micali, S., Rivest, R.L.: A digital signature scheme secure against adaptive chosen-message attacks. SIAM J. Comput. **17**(2), 281–308 (1988)
11. Haitner, I., Nguyen, M., Ong, S.J., Reingold, O., Vadhan, S.P.: Statistically hiding commitments and statistical zero-knowledge arguments from any one-way function. SIAM J. Comput. **39**(3), 1153–1218 (2009)
12. Kawachi, A., Tanaka, K., Xagawa, K.: Concurrently secure identification schemes based on the worst-case hardness of lattice problems. In: Advances in Cryptology - ASIACRYPT 2008, Proceedings of the 14th International Conference on the Theory and Application of Cryptology and Information Security, Melbourne, Australia, December 7–11, 2008, pp. 372–389 (2008)
13. Regev, O.: On lattices, learning with errors, random linear codes, and cryptography. J. ACM, **56**(6), 34:1–34:40 (2009)

PUOKMS: Password-Protected Updatable Oblivious Key Management System for Cloud Storage

Shanshan Li[1] and Chunxiang Xu[1,2(✉)]

[1] School of Computer Science and Engineering, University of Electronic Science and Technology of China, Chengdu 611731, China
chxxu@uestc.edu.cn
[2] Yangtze Delta Region Institute (Huzhou), University of Electronic Science and Technology of China, Huzhou 313001, China

Abstract. Updatable oblivious key management system (UOKMS) has been widely applied in reality to protect outsourced data confidentiality. We demonstrate that existing UOKMS fails to prevent users' private information from being leaked. We show that an adversary can impersonate any user to access her/his sensitive data in existing UOKMS, and this problem is further exacerbated by the collusion between two entities (i.e., a key server and a cloud server). In this paper, we propose a secure two-layered encryption mechanism to resist impersonation and collusion attacks. Specifically, the first layer public/secret key is generated by a user's password via an oblivious way, where the user's password is hardened by a set of dedicated identity servers to thwart password guessing attacks; besides, multiple key servers secretly share a user-specific server-side key for each user to assist the user in generating the second layer symmetric key. We also utilize a key renewal mechanism that periodically updates the secret on each key server to resist perpetual leakage of the secret. With these two mechanisms, we develop a password-protected updatable oblivious key management system for cloud storage, dubbed PUOKMS. We evaluate PUOKMS in terms of security and efficiency, which demonstrates that PUOKMS achieves a strong security guarantee with high efficiency.

Keywords: Password-protected encryption · Oblivious PRF · Secret renewal · Key management · Cloud storage

1 Introduction

With the rapid growth of the total amount of data, outsourcing data to cloud storage has been a prevalent trend for users, which would save the local storage space, facilitate users' multi-terminal access, centralize data management, and so on [1,5–7]. Currently, many cloud storage providers (e.g., Google, Amazon, Microsoft) have provided specialized services satisfying the requirements of users. Therefore, these cloud service providers have access to any information stored on

© Springer Nature Switzerland AG 2021
R. Deng et al. (Eds.): ISPEC 2021, LNCS 13107, pp. 106–125, 2021.
https://doi.org/10.1007/978-3-030-93206-0_8

their infrastructure including the outsourced data of users, which raises concerns on data security. Particularly, once the cloud service provider is compromised, the content of outsourced data would be leaked, such that the users' privacy could be violated. As such, users always encrypt their data before data outsourcing, which is the most effective method to ensure data confidentiality and thereby becomes the most widely-used paradigm in the current cloud storage system [2].

In practice, to avoid all outsourced data ciphertexts of a target user are compromised due to the leakage of her/his encryption key, the user, prefers to encrypt different messages with different keys. To ensure these ciphertexts can still be decrypted by the user, she/he needs to store all encryption keys secretly. In such a case, the user bears additional storage overhead, which is intolerable for resource-constrained users. Additionally, when a key is utilized to decrypt some ciphertext, since the user stores multiple keys and does not know which one to use, she/he needs constant trial and error, which brings in time costs.

A feasible approach is to centralize key management by introducing an independent third party (e.g., the key server), which has been a prevalent paradigm for provisioning cryptographic keys in the current cryptosystem (e.g., key generation, exchange, storage, destruction). The typical deployment of key management system (KMS) (including large cloud service provider such as AWS[1], Microsoft[2], IBM[3], Google[4]) is constructed on a traditional wrap-unwrap approach for managing data encryption keys: a user encrypts her/his outsourced data by randomly choosing a symmetric key; a key server (KS) wraps the symmetric key with a user-specific key (chosen and kept by KS); the user outsources the wrapped result and the encrypted data to the cloud server; the user retrieves a specific object from the cloud server; KS unwraps the attached wrap using the user-specific key to get the symmetric key; the user retrieves the outsourced data with the symmetric key. Such a key encapsulation mechanism has present significant potential vulnerabilities [8]. One of the most severe problems is the security of the encryption keys. Since users would expose encryption keys in the form of plaintext to KS, they are anxious about the security of their keys. The security of these keys is being put at risk due to both internal and external threats in reality. For example, a misbehaved KS may intentionally wrap the symmetric key of one user with a user-specific key of others to tease users. Worse still, an adversary may compromise KS to steal users' encryption keys. Furthermore, such the mechanism increases the cost of rotating the user-specific key.

Oblivious key management system (OKMS) [8], a cryptographic primitive, addresses partial vulnerabilities above and offers additional features absent in traditional systems. In OKMS, a key server, secretly keeping a user-specific key for each user, assists users in generating a symmetric encryption key via an oblivious way (e.g., an oblivious pseudorandom function) [3,4]. Different from the traditional wrap-unwrap mechanism, the symmetric encryption key is blind

---

[1] Aws key management service cryptographic details.

[2] Key storage and azure key vault.

[3] https://console.bluemix.net/catalog/services/keyprotect.

[4] https://cloud.google.com/kms/.

to the key server and does not require to be stored in OKMS. Furthermore, to avoid the various attacks raised by the user-specific key leakage, OKMS is extended to updatable OKMS (UOKMS) that supports the periodic rotation of the user-specific key. Existing UOKMS schemes (e.g., [8]) require users to publish a certified public key (also referred to as a user-specific public key) generated by the user-specific secret key. In an interactive scenario, Bob first chooses a randomness, with the randomness and Alice's certified public key, Bob generates a symmetric encryption key, encrypts a message, and sends the wrapped message (including *a public value for the randomness*) to the cloud server without interacting with Alice before. Any time Alice wants to decrypt the message, she/he uses the public value for the randomness to retrieve the symmetric decryption key by interacting with the key server.

Despite the great benefits brought by the UOKMS, it still suffers from critical threats. Specifically, in existing UOKMS, due to lack of identity authentication, an adversary could impersonate a user to interact with the cloud server to retrieve the wrapped messages (including the public value for the randomness) and then impersonate the target user to interact with the key server to obtain the encryption key via an oblivious way. Worse still, a cloud server is a rational entity and it may curious about the outsourced data. The honest-but-curious cloud server may collude with the key server to unwrap the wrapped message. Such two attacks (impersonation and collusion attacks) would extremely undermine the confidentiality of outsourced messages and have been a severe challenge in existing UOKMS.

Furthermore, existing UOKMS [8] has pointed out that, UOKMS may suffer from a single-point-of-failure problem. Such a system bears a strong assumption that the key server is fully trusted and reliable. However, once an adversary compromises the key server, he can recover the decryption keys and decrypt the wrapped messages. A straightforward way is to utilize threshold cryptography, where a group of key servers is employed to share a secret and only a threshold number of key servers can recover the secret. Furthermore, in a long period of time, an adversary may collect more than the threshold number of shares from different epochs to retrieve the secret, which is called perpetual leakage attacks and has brought in critical threats.

In this paper, we propose a password-protected updatable oblivious key management system for cloud storage to thwart these problems. Specifically, the contributions of this paper are summarized as follows:

We analyze existing UOKMS and point out that they suffer from various attacks. To resist these attacks, we propose a password-protected updatable oblivious key management system for cloud storage, dubbed PUOKMS. PUOKMS actually is a message forwarding system, where each user only needs to keep her/his password, can she/he decrypt all messages sent to her/his.

In PUOKMS, we design a two-layered encryption mechanism. Specifically, the first layer is password-based encryption for securing the public value for the randomness, where the user's password is hardened by a set of dedicated identity servers to thwart password guessing attacks. With the public value for the randomness, the user is able to interact with multiple key servers to generate the second layer symmetric encryption key. Such a two-layered encryption mechanism guarantees that only a user possesses her/his password, can she/he decrypt the wrapped messages sent to her/him. Additionally, we utilize a key renewal mechanism that periodically updates the secret on each key server and guarantees high efficiency under strong security. Compared with existing UOKMS, the key renewal mechanism cancels the participation of cloud servers and reduces communication costs.

We define a formal security model and provide formal security proof based on the model. We also conduct a comprehensive performance analysis to show the efficiency of PUOKMS in terms of communication and computation.

2 Preliminaries

2.1 Technical Background

Oblivious Pseudorandom Functions. Oblivious pseudorandom function (OPRF), firstly proposed by Freedman et al. [3], is an oblivious pseudorandom function between a sender and a receiver, in which the receiver holds a key, but does not learn about the sender' input and the oblivious PRF outputs. OPRF has been widely used in numerous applications and there are very efficient OPRF implementations [5,6,8].

Threshold Cryptography. Threshold cryptography was proposed by Desmedt in [12], which is used to perform some highly sensitive operations (i.e., encryption/decryption, signing). In the (t, n)-threshold cryptosystem, the message is split into n pieces, which can be recovered by using any t pieces and are unrevealed even fully grasp $t - 1$ pieces.

Bilinear Maps. Let G be an additive group with a generator P, and G_T is a multiplicative cycle group. G and G_T have the same prime order p. A bilinear map is that $e : G \times G \to G_T$ with the following properties. Linearity: for all points in G then $e(P_1 + P_2, Q_1) = e(P_1, Q_1) \cdot e(P_2, Q_1), e(P_1, Q_1 + Q_2) = e(P_1, Q_1) \cdot e(P_1, Q_2)$, where $P_1, P_2, Q_1, Q_2 \in G$; Nondegeneracy: $e(P, P) \neq 1$, where P is the generator of G; Bilinearity: for $P_3, Q_3 \in G$ and $a, b \in Z_p^*$: $e(aP_3, bQ_3) = e(P_3, Q_3)^{ab}$; Computability: there exists an efficiently computable algorithm for computing e.

Hash Functions. The hash function is a simple function that takes the input of some length and compresses them into short, fixed-length output. A hash function H is collision-resistant, namely that it is infeasible for many probabilistic polynomial-time algorithms to find a collision in H.

A hash function $\Pi = (Gen, H)$ is collision resistant [15] if for all probabilistic polynomial-time adversaries $\mathcal{A}$ there is a negligible function $negl$ such that $Pr[Coll_{\mathcal{A},\Pi}(n) = 1] \leq negl(n)$, where $Coll_{\mathcal{A},\Pi}(n)$ is a collision-finding experiment performed by $\mathcal{A}$.

2.2   System Model

The system is depicted in Fig. 1. There are four entities in our scheme: users, a group of identity servers, multiple key servers, the cloud server.

Users: multiple users are involved in the scheme. Each user randomly chooses a master key, splits it into n' shares, and distributes them to identity servers. Meanwhile, each user also randomly chooses a user-specific secret key, splits it into n shares, and distributes them to key servers. In addition, each user can send a wrapped message to a target user and the target one can recover the message by entering her/his correct password subsequently.

Identity servers: a group of identity servers is involved in the scheme. Each identity server keeps a master secret share for each user and assists users in generating secret and public hardened passwords. All identity servers periodically renew their master secret shares to thwart an adversary who performs perpetual leakage attacks.

Key servers: a set of key servers is employed to keep a user-specific secret key for each user, which also assists the user in generating a certified public key. All key servers periodically renew their user-specific secret shares so as to thwart adversaries who can perpetually compromise secret shares.

Cloud server: the cloud server provides a cloud storage service, which stores the wrapped messages for users.

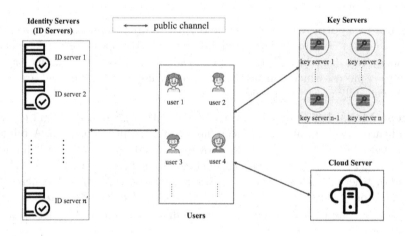

Fig. 1. System model

2.3   Adversarial Model

In the adversarial model, we consider the threats from two different angles: external adversaries and internal adversaries.

External Adversaries. An external adversary can perform the attacks as follows to break the system security.

Impersonation attacks. An external adversary may intercept wrapped messages, impersonate a target user to generate encryption keys, and recover her/his message.

Collusion attacks. An external adversary may intercept wrapped messages and collude with other entities to retrieve encryption keys.

Password guessing attacks. An external adversary may exhaust all password candidates, impersonate a target user, and compute all secret hardened password candidates by interacting with identity servers. As such, once he intercepts a wrapped message about the target user, he can decrypt the ciphertext and get the message by colluding with other entities. Such an attack is called the online password guessing attack.

Internal Adversaries. All internal adversaries can perform the attacks as follows to break the system security:

The malicious users. A malicious user may impersonate other valid users to retrieve the encryption keys that are used to decrypt the wrapped messages of other users.

Malicious identity servers. A malicious identity server may use its local stored secrets and perform offline password guessing attacks to retrieve users' passwords. Furthermore, in a long period of time, he may collect more than $t' - 1$ secret shares to retrieve the master secret key of a user from different epochs.

Malicious key servers. In a long period of time, a malicious key server may collect more than $t - 1$ secret shares to retrieve the user-specific secret key of a user from different epochs.

Honest-but-curious cloud server. The cloud server keeps all wrapped messages and it is curious about the ciphertexts. The cloud server is a rational entity and it may collude with other entities to recover the messages.

2.4   Design Goals

In this paper, we aim to present a password-protected updatable oblivious key management scheme, in which several challenging problems exist.

How to prevent impersonation attacks and collusion attacks. An adversary may impersonate valid users to retrieve wrapped messages and even encryption keys. Furthermore, an adversary may collude with other entities to retrieve encryption keys. How to prevent impersonation and collusion attacks has been a severe challenge.

How to prevent password guessing attacks performed by an adversary (including the external and internal adversaries). Specifically, an adversary may exhaust all password candidates and collect all secret hardened password candidates by interacting with a group of identity servers. Once the adversary intercepts a wrapped message, he can keep trial and error to decrypt the first layer encryption and collude with other entities to recover the message. Furthermore, a malicious identity server may use its local stored secrets and perform offline password guessing attacks to retrieve users' passwords. How to prevent password guessing attacks is a challenging problem.

How to resist perpetual leakage attacks. In a long period of time, a malicious identity server may gain $t' - 1$ master secret shares from different epochs to retrieve the master secret key of a target user. A malicious key server attempts to get the user-specific secret key of a target user in the same way. How to resist the attack without introducing heavy costs is a severe matter.

To address the challenges under the aforementioned model, our scheme should achieve the following objectives.

Functionality. The identity servers should authenticate users. For a user, only if she/he possesses the password can she/he pass the identity servers' authentication. Then, the authorized user can retrieve encryption keys by interacting with key servers. With the encryption keys, the user can decrypt the ciphertext to retrieve the content of a message.

Security. The proposed scheme should resist impersonation attacks, collusion attacks, password guessing attacks, and perpetual leakage attacks performed by external and internal adversaries.

Efficiency. The communication and computation overhead on users should be as efficient as possible. The update for the master secret key and the user-specific server-side secret key should not introduce heavy communication costs and other security problems.

3   The Proposed Scheme

3.1   Description of PUOKMS

Our scheme consists of four entities: a set of users $\{\mathcal{U}_1, \mathcal{U}_2, \ldots\}$, multiple key servers $\{\mathcal{KS}_1, \mathcal{KS}_2, \ldots, \mathcal{KS}_n\}$, a group of identity servers $\{\mathcal{IS}_1, \mathcal{IS}_2, \ldots, \mathcal{IS}_{n'}\}$, and the cloud server $\mathcal{CS}$. There are four phases in our scheme: **Setting, Encryption, Decryption** and **KeyUpdate**.

Setting. In this phase, public parameters are generated. Each user randomly chooses a master secret key, splits it into n' shares, and distributes one share to one identity server. Meanwhile, each user randomly chooses a user-specific secret key, splits it into n shares, and distributes one share to one key server. Additionally, each user generates her/his public hardened password and certified public key.

- With the security parameter l, the public parameter $PP = \{p, P, G, G_T, e, h(\cdot),$ $H(\cdot), SKE.Enc, PKE.Enc, SKE.Dec, PKE.Dec, q_L, q_E\}$ is determined. G is an additive group with the prime order p and the generator P, G_T is a multiplicative group, $e : G \times G \rightarrow G_T$ is a bilinear map, $h(\cdot) : G \rightarrow Z_p^*$, $H(\cdot) : \{0,1\}^* \rightarrow G$, $SKE.Enc$ is a secure symmetric encryption algorithm (e.g., AES), $PKE.Enc$ is a secure public encryption algorithm (e.g., RSA), $SKE.Dec$ is a secure symmetric decryption algorithm, $PKE.Dec$ is a secure public decryption algorithm. Time is divided into multiple epochs, multiple identity servers keep a list to record the number of queries that each user has required, which is denoted by q_L and is initialized with 0 in a new epoch. Here, q_E is the limitation bound of each epoch.

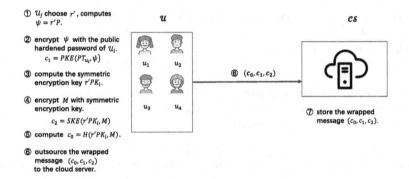

Fig. 2. Encryption process

- Each user $\mathcal{U}_i$ shares a master key msk_i for n' identity servers and publishes her/his public hardened password. The process is described as follows.
  - $\mathcal{U}_i$ randomly chooses $t' - 1$ independent coefficient $a_{i,1}, a_{i,2}, \ldots, a_{i,t'-1} \in Z_p^*$, and builds a polynomial $g(i,x) = a_{i,0} + a_{i,1}x + \ldots + a_{i,t'-1}x^{t'-1}$, here, $a_{i,0} = msk_i$.
  - For $\lambda = 1, 2, \ldots, n'$, $\mathcal{U}_i$ computes the master secret key share for $\mathcal{IS}_\lambda$ as $msk_{i,\lambda} = g(i,\lambda) \bmod p$.
  - $\mathcal{U}_i$ distributes $\{\lambda, msk_{i,\lambda}\}$ to each identity server $\mathcal{IS}_\lambda$. Here, $msk_{i,\lambda}$ is a secret share and secretly stored by $\mathcal{IS}_\lambda$. $Y_{i,\lambda} = msk_{i,\lambda}P$ is a public share and published.
  - After sharing, $\mathcal{U}_i$ deletes the secret key msk_i and publishes the public key $Y_i = msk_iP$.
  - $\mathcal{U}_i$ computes her/his public hardened password $PT_{\mathcal{U}_i} = h(msk_i \cdot H(pw_{\mathcal{U}_i})) \cdot P$ and publishes it, where $pw_{\mathcal{U}_i}$ is the password of $\mathcal{U}_i$. After publishing $PT_{\mathcal{U}_i}$, $\mathcal{U}_i$ deletes msk_i and only remembers $pw_{\mathcal{U}_i}$.
- Each user $\mathcal{U}_i$ shares a user-specific secret key s_i for n key servers and publishes her/his certified public key. The process is described as follows.
  - $\mathcal{U}_i$ randomly chooses $t - 1$ independent coefficient $b_{i,1}, b_{i,2}, \ldots, b_{i,t-1} \in Z_p^*$, and builds a polynomial $f(i,x) = b_{i,0} + b_{i,1}x + \ldots + b_{i,t-1}x^{t-1}$, here, $b_{i,0} = s_i$.
  - For $\gamma = 1, 2, \ldots, n$, $\mathcal{U}_i$ computes the secret share for $\mathcal{KS}_\gamma$ as $s_{i,\gamma} = f(i,\gamma) \bmod p$.
  - $\mathcal{U}_i$ distributes $\{\gamma, s_{i,\gamma}\}$ to each key server $\mathcal{KS}_\gamma$. Here, $s_{i,\gamma}$ is a secret share and secretly stored by $\mathcal{KS}_\gamma$. $PK_{i,\gamma} = s_{i,\gamma}P$ is a public share and published.
  - After sharing, $\mathcal{U}_i$ deletes the secret key s_i and publishes a certified public key $PK_i = s_iP$.

Encryption. A user $\mathcal{U}_j$ sends a message M to $\mathcal{U}_i$ via $\mathcal{CS}$. This process is depicted in Fig. 2 and is described as follows.

- $\mathcal{U}_j$ randomly chooses $r' \in Z_p^*$, computes $\psi = r'P$, encrypts ψ with the public hardened password of $\mathcal{U}_i$ as $c_1 = PKE.Enc(PT_{\mathcal{U}_i}, \psi)$.

- $\mathcal{U}_j$ computes a symmetric encryption key with $\mathcal{U}_i$'s certified public key PK_i. $\mathcal{U}_j$ encrypts the message M with the key as $c_2 = SKE.Enc(r'PK_i, M)$, and computes $c_0 = H(r'PK_i, M)$.
- $\mathcal{U}_j$ outsources the wrapped message (c_0, c_1, c_2) to $\mathcal{CS}$.

Decryption. $\mathcal{U}_i$ downloads a wrapped message from $\mathcal{CS}$, authenticates her/his identity by identity servers, and generates the decryption key by interacting with key servers. This process is depicted in Fig. 3 and is described as follows.

- $\mathcal{CS}$ sends the wrapped message $\{c_0, c_1, c_2\}$ to $\mathcal{U}_i$. Upon receiving the wrapped message, $\mathcal{U}_i$ inputs its password $pw_{\mathcal{U}_i}$, randomly chooses $\alpha \in Z_p^*$, and computes $pw_{\mathcal{U}_i}^* = \alpha H(pw_{\mathcal{U}_i})$. $\mathcal{U}_i$ sends $\{ID_{\mathcal{U}_i}, pw_{\mathcal{U}_i}^*\}$ to all identity servers.
- For $\lambda \in [1, n']$, $\mathcal{IS}_\lambda$ checks whether $ID_{\mathcal{U}_i}$ exists in its local storage and whether $q_L \leq q_E$ is satisfied, the query is rejected if one of the checking fails; otherwise, $\mathcal{IS}_\lambda$ updates $q_L = q_L + 1$, retrieves the corresponding master key share $msk_{i,\lambda}$, computes a blind signature $\sigma_\lambda = msk_{i,\lambda} \cdot pw_{\mathcal{U}_i}^*$ with its secret share $msk_{i,\lambda}$, and sends σ_λ to $\mathcal{U}_i$.
- Upon receiving σ_λ from $\mathcal{IS}_\lambda$, $\mathcal{U}_i$ verifies its validity by checking $e(\sigma_\lambda, P) \overset{?}{=} e(pw_{\mathcal{U}_i}^*, Y_{i,\lambda})$, if the checking fails, $\mathcal{U}_i$ rejects.
- After receiving t' valid signatures (for the sake of brevity, we denote these signatures by $\sigma_1, \sigma_2, \ldots, \sigma_{t'}$), $\mathcal{U}_i$ computes $\sigma = \alpha^{-1} \sum_{\lambda=1}^{t'} C_\lambda \sigma_\lambda$, where $C_\lambda = \prod_{\mu=1, \mu \neq \lambda}^{t'} \frac{\mu}{\mu - \lambda}$. $\mathcal{U}_i$ verifies the correctness of σ by checking $e(\sigma, P) \overset{?}{=} e(H(pw_{\mathcal{U}_i}), Y_i)$. If the verification passes, $\mathcal{U}_i$ computes the secret hardened password as $ST_{\mathcal{U}_i} = h(\sigma) = h(msk_i \cdot H(pw_{\mathcal{U}_i}))$.
- $\mathcal{U}_i$ decrypts c_1 with $ST_{\mathcal{U}_i}$ denoted as $\psi = PKE.Dec(ST_{\mathcal{U}_i}, c_1)$.
- $\mathcal{U}_i$ randomly chooses $\beta \in Z_p^*$, computes $\psi^* = \beta \cdot \psi$, and sends ψ^* to all key servers.
- For $\gamma = 1, 2, \ldots, n$, $\mathcal{KS}_\gamma$ computes a blind signature $\eta_\gamma = s_{i,\gamma} \cdot \psi^*$ with its secret share $s_{i,\gamma}$, and sends η_γ to $\mathcal{U}_i$.
- Upon receiving η_γ from $\mathcal{KS}_\gamma$, $\mathcal{U}_i$ verifies its validity by checking $e(\eta_\gamma, P) \overset{?}{=} e(\psi^*, PK_{i,\gamma})$, if the checking fails, $\mathcal{U}_i$ rejects.
- After receiving t valid blind signatures (for the sake of brevity, we denote these signatures by $\eta_1, \eta_2, \ldots, \eta_t$), $\mathcal{U}_i$ computes $\eta = \beta^{-1} \sum_{\gamma=1}^{t} \xi_\gamma \eta_\gamma$, where $\xi_\gamma = \prod_{\kappa=1, \kappa \neq \gamma}^{t} \frac{\kappa}{\kappa - \gamma}$.
- $\mathcal{U}_i$ verifies $e(\eta, P) \overset{?}{=} e(\psi, PK_i)$. If the verification passes, $\mathcal{U}_i$ computes $\eta = s_i \cdot \psi = s_i \cdot r'P = r'PK_i$ as the symmetric key. Otherwise, $\mathcal{U}_i$ rejects.
- $\mathcal{U}_i$ decrypts c_2 with the symmetric key η denoted as $M^* = SKE.Dec(r'PK_i, c_2)$.
- $\mathcal{U}_i$ verifies the integrity of the message by checking $H(\eta, M^*) \overset{?}{=} c_0$. If the verification passes, $\mathcal{U}_i$ accepts the wrapped message from $\mathcal{U}_j$; Otherwise, $\mathcal{U}_i$ rejects.

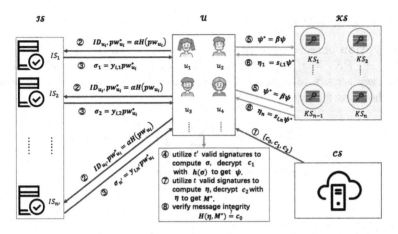

Fig. 3. Decryption process

KeyUpdate. All identity servers and key servers renew its share, which are described as follows.

For each key server $\mathcal{KS}_\gamma, (\gamma = 1, 2, \ldots, n)$, at the end of an epoch, it renews its user-specific secret share $s_{i,\gamma}$ for each user $\mathcal{U}_i, (i = 1, 2, \ldots)$ as follows.

- $\mathcal{KS}_\gamma$ randomly selects a polynomial $l_\gamma(x) = c_{\gamma,1}x + c_{\gamma,2}x^2 + \ldots + c_{\gamma,t-1}x^{t-1}$ over Z_p^* with degree at most $t - 1$.
- $\mathcal{KS}_\gamma$ sends $\{c_{\gamma,1}P, c_{\gamma,2}P, \ldots, c_{\gamma,t-1}P\}$ to all other key servers. $\mathcal{KS}_\gamma$ sends $l_\gamma(\omega)$ secretly to $\mathcal{KS}_\omega$, where $\omega = 1, 2, \ldots, n; \omega \neq \gamma$.
- After receiving $l_\omega(\gamma)$, $\mathcal{KS}_\gamma$ checks $l_\omega(\gamma)P \stackrel{?}{=} \sum_{\varepsilon=1}^{t-1} \gamma^\varepsilon \cdot c_{\omega,\varepsilon}P$. If the checking fails, it rejects.
- $\mathcal{KS}_\gamma$ computes a new secret key share $s_{i,\gamma}$ as $s_{i,\gamma}' = s_{i,\gamma} + \sum_{\omega=1}^{n} l_\omega(\gamma)$. The corresponding public secret share is denoted as $PK_{i,\gamma}' = s_{i,\gamma}'P$.
- $\mathcal{KS}_\gamma$ deletes $l_\gamma(x), \{c_{\gamma,1}, c_{\gamma,2}, \ldots, c_{\gamma,n}\}$, and $s_{i,\gamma}$.

For each identity server $\mathcal{IS}_\lambda, (\lambda = 1, 2, \ldots, n')$, at the end of an epoch, it renews its master secret share $msk_{i,\lambda}$ for each user $\mathcal{U}_i, (i = 1, 2, \ldots)$ as follows.

- $\mathcal{IS}_\lambda$ randomly selects a polynomial $v_\lambda(x) = d_{\lambda,1}x + d_{\lambda,2}x^2 + \ldots + d_{\lambda,t'-1}x^{t'-1}$ over Z_p^* with degree at most $t' - 1$.
- $\mathcal{IS}_\lambda$ sends $\{d_{\lambda,1}P, d_{\lambda,2}P, \ldots, d_{\lambda,t'-1}P\}$ to all other identity servers. $\mathcal{IS}_\lambda$ sends $v_\lambda(\mu)$ secretly to $\mathcal{IS}_\mu$, where $\mu = 1, 2, \ldots, n'; \mu \neq \lambda$.
- After receiving $v_\mu(\lambda)$, $\mathcal{IS}_\lambda$ checks $v_\mu(\lambda)P \stackrel{?}{=} \sum_{\varepsilon=1}^{t'-1} \lambda^\varepsilon \cdot d_{\mu,\varepsilon}P$. If the checking fails, it rejects.
- $\mathcal{IS}_\lambda$ computes a new secret key share $msk_{i,\lambda}$ as $msk_{i,\lambda}' = msk_{i,\lambda} + \sum_{\mu=1}^{n'} v_\mu(\lambda)$. The corresponding public secret share is denoted as $Y_{i,\lambda}' = msk_{i,\lambda}'P$.
- $\mathcal{IS}_\lambda$ deletes $v_\lambda(x), \{d_{\lambda,1}, d_{\lambda,2}, \ldots, d_{\lambda,n'}\}$, and $msk_{i,\lambda}$.

3.2   Correctness Proof

In **Encryption** phase, $\mathcal{U}_j$ encrypts the message M with the symmetric encryption key $r' \cdot PK_i = r' \cdot s_i \cdot P$. During **Decryption** phase, $\mathcal{U}_i$ interacts with multiple key servers to retrieve the symmetric decryption key η. The process can be shown as follows.

$$\eta = \beta^{-1} \sum_{\gamma=1}^{t} \xi_\gamma \eta_\gamma = \beta^{-1} \sum_{\gamma=1}^{t} \eta_\gamma \prod_{\kappa=1}^{t} \frac{\kappa}{\kappa - \gamma} (\kappa \neq \gamma),$$
$$= \beta^{-1} \cdot \beta \cdot \psi \cdot s_i = s_i \cdot \psi = s_i \cdot r' \cdot P = r' \cdot PK_i.$$

3.3   Further Discussion

In this section, we additionally discuss some problems ignored in PUOKMS. The key point of this paper is to secure the $w = g^r$. Actually, there are two types of methods to achieve this.

The first one is to directly add an authentication mechanism before performing the **Decryption** operation, which ensures only a valid user can perform the decryption operation. Specifically, a group of dedicated identity servers are employed. During the registration phase, a user $\mathcal{U}_i$ interacts with a group of dedicated identity servers to generate a servers-derived password $spu_i = F(msk_i \cdot H(pw_{\mathcal{U}_i}))$. For each $\lambda = \{1, 2, \cdots, n'\}$, $\mathcal{U}_i$ computes $sp_\lambda = h(spu_i, \lambda)$ and sends it to $\mathcal{IS}_\lambda$. Note that, sp_λ is the authentication token and is kept by each $\mathcal{IS}_i$. During the authentication phase, $\mathcal{U}_i$ inputs her/his password, interacts with identity servers, and computes spu_i. With spu_i, $\mathcal{U}_i$ can complete authentication. The details refer to Zhang et al.'s scheme [11]. If the authentication succeeds, $\mathcal{U}_i$ can get a token. With the token, she/he is able to access the cloud server and interact with the key servers to decrypt the wrapped messages. In such a method, w does not be encrypted. Such an authentication method is actually password-hardening service [13,14].

Another method is to just employ a group of key servers. Specifically, each key server keeps a master secret key share and a user-specific key share for each user $\mathcal{U}_i$. The master secret key is used to generate the public/secret hardened password; the user-specific key is used to assist users in generating the encryption/decryption key. To secure $w = g^r$, the two-layer encryption mechanism is used: first, $w = g^r$ is encrypted by a target user's public hardened password $PT_{\mathcal{U}_i}$ using the public encryption algorithm; second, the message M is encrypted by a secret key using the private encryption algorithm. To decrypt the wrapped message, $\mathcal{U}_i$ interacts with key servers to generate the secret hardened password $ST_{\mathcal{U}_i}$ by performing OPRF. With $ST_{\mathcal{U}_i}$, the first-layer ciphertext is decrypted to get $w = g^r$; Then, with w, $\mathcal{U}_i$ interacts with key servers to retrieve the symmetric key. Finally, $\mathcal{U}_i$ recovers the message M.

Note that, in this paper, we utilize the second method. To distinguish the master secret key and user-specific key, we employ two types of servers: the identity servers and the key servers. Although we introduce a group of dedicated identity servers, we do not adopt the authentication mechanism as described in the first method. Actually, in this paper, the identity servers and the key servers can be merged into one.

Since human-memorable passwords are inherently low-entropy, both the first method and the second method suffer from offline and online password guessing attacks. In Sect. 5, we will further analyze and provide formal security proofs.

In PUOKMS, we require users to randomly choose their passwords. However, such user-generated passwords suffer from critical problems as discussed in [18,19]. Specifically, for the sake of convenience, users prefer to choose simple passwords, such as popular passwords, reusing passwords, sister passwords. These passwords are called weak passwords that do not only compromise themselves, but the whole ecosystem. To prevent weak passwords, a promising approach is to blacklist any weak password. Such a method enables a server to identify popular passwords and publish a list of weak passwords that must be avoided. Some literature [20,21] has emerged to focus on this issue. In PUOKMS, we assume that users would prefer to choose strong passwords or we utilize the weak password detecting mechanism.

4 Security Analysis

4.1 Impersonation Attacks and Password Guessing Attacks

In existing updatable OKMS schemes (e.g., [8]), due to lack of user identity authentication, an adversary may intercept the interaction message between a valid user and the cloud server and impersonate the valid user to retrieve the wrapped message. In the following, we analyze PUOKMS can resist impersonation attacks.

In the **Encryption** phase, we note that $\mathcal{U}_j$ encrypts the message M with two layers. First, $\mathcal{U}_j$ encrypts $\psi = r'P$ with $\mathcal{U}_i$'s public hardened password $PT_{\mathcal{U}_i}$ in public encryption algorithm, where $PT_{\mathcal{U}_i} = ST_{\mathcal{U}_i}P = h(\sigma)P = h(msk_i \cdot H(pw_{\mathcal{U}_i}))P$. The security of first layer encryption relies on the security of master key msk_i and the password $pw_{\mathcal{U}_i}$. Second, $\mathcal{U}_j$ encrypts the message M with a symmetric encryption key $r'PK_i$, where $r'PK_i = r's_iP$. The security of second layer encryption relies on the security of secret key s_i and the randomly chosen value r'.

Assuming that an adversary $\mathcal{A}$ targets to retrieve a victim $\mathcal{U}_i$'s received message M. After intercepting the interaction wrapped message (c_0, c_1, c_2) between $\mathcal{U}_i$ and $\mathcal{CS}$, the first step for $\mathcal{A}$ to retrieve M is to decrypt the first layer by the secret hardened password $ST_{\mathcal{U}_i} = h(\sigma) = h(msk_i \cdot H(pw_{\mathcal{U}_i}))$. Here, if $\mathcal{A}$ wants to impersonates $\mathcal{U}_i$ to get $ST_{\mathcal{U}_i}$, he has to guess $\mathcal{U}_i$'s password.

Theorem 1. *In PUOKMS, if PUOKMS is secure against password guessing attacks, then it is secure against impersonation attacks.*

Proof. In PUOKMS, before decrypting wrapped messages, each user $\mathcal{U}_i$ has to interact with a group of identity servers to generate the asymmetric decryption key $ST_{\mathcal{U}_i}$. Only with $ST_{\mathcal{U}_i}$, can $\mathcal{U}_i$ decrypt the first layer ciphertext. $\mathcal{A}$ wants to impersonate a target user $\mathcal{U}_i$, he has to get $ST_{\mathcal{U}_i}$. $ST_{\mathcal{U}_i}$ is generated by the master key msk_i and the password $pw_{\mathcal{U}_i}$. Thus, the security of PUOKMS is transformed into the security of the secret hardened password key. To get the key, the only way is to guess passwords by performing password guessing attacks. Generally, resisting impersonation attacks is essentially resisting password guessing attacks.

Theorem 2. *PUOKMS is secure against offline password guessing attacks even if an adversary compromises up to $t' - 1$ identity servers.*

Proof. In our scheme, if any identity server is compromised, the security cannot be broken. For the sake of brevity, we assume the compromised identity server is $\mathcal{IS}_1$, then the adversary obtains a signature $\sigma_1 = y_{i,1}\alpha H(pw_{\mathcal{U}_i})$. However, it is computationally infeasible to compute σ from σ_1 due to the difference between signatures generated by different identity servers. Moreover, if more identity servers are compromised, PUOKMS still guarantees security. In our scheme, multiple identity servers are employed to execute (t', n')-threshold blind signature to generate σ, which can tolerate even $t' - 1$ of $n' > 2t' - 1$ identity servers are corrupted [9]. We prove it from two aspects.

– The secret hardened password $ST_{\mathcal{U}_i}$ is unpredictable. That is, given a user $\mathcal{U}_i$'s password $pw_{\mathcal{U}_i}$, an adversary $\mathcal{A}$ cannot predict the secret hardened password $ST_{\mathcal{U}_i}$, even if $\mathcal{A}$ compromises up to $t' - 1$ identity servers. To prove it, we define a game.
  - The environment $\mathcal{Z}$ initiates our scheme, generates a master secret key msk_i for $\mathcal{U}_i$, and splits msk_i into n' shares as $\{msk_{i,1}, msk_{i,2}, \ldots, msk_{i,n'}\}$ using the threshold secret sharing protocol, and produces the public parameter PP. $\mathcal{Z}$ sends PP to a simulator $\mathcal{S}$. And then, $\mathcal{S}$ forwards it to $\mathcal{A}$.
  - $\mathcal{A}$ randomly selects a index set $T' = \{1, 2, \ldots, t' - 1\}$ and sends it to $\mathcal{S}$. $\mathcal{S}$ forwards T' to $\mathcal{Z}$. And then, $\mathcal{Z}$ computes $\{msk_{i,1}, msk_{i,2}, \ldots, msk_{i,t'-1}\}$ and sends it to $\mathcal{S}$. $\mathcal{S}$ forwards it to $\mathcal{A}$.
  - $\mathcal{A}$ randomly chooses $\tilde{\beta}$ and $\tilde{\alpha}$, computes $\tilde{c}^* = \tilde{\beta} \cdot H(\tilde{\alpha})$.
  - For $\lambda \in [1, n']/T'$, $\mathcal{A}$ sends a query of $\sigma_\lambda = msk_{i,\lambda}\tilde{c}^*$ to $\mathcal{S}$. $\mathcal{S}$ forwards it to $\mathcal{Z}$ and sets $q_1, q_2, \cdots, q_{n'} = 0$.
  - $\mathcal{Z}$ computes σ_λ and sends it to $\mathcal{S}$. $\mathcal{S}$ forwards it to $\mathcal{A}$.
  - $\mathcal{A}$ repeats the above query on different λ. Finally, $\mathcal{A}$ outputs $\tilde{\sigma}$.

  - If $\tilde{\sigma}$ is a valid signature on $\tilde{c}^*$ and $\sum\limits_{\lambda=1}^{n'} q_\lambda < t'$ then $\mathcal{A}$ wins.

During the game, $\mathcal{S}$ collects up to $t' - 1$ pairs $\{msk_{i,\lambda}, \sigma_\lambda\}$ and $\tilde{\sigma}$. For $\mathcal{A}$, he can obtain $\{\sigma_1, \sigma_2, \sigma_{t'-1}\}$ and he outputs a signature $\tilde{\sigma}$. Assuming that $\mathcal{A}$ can forge t'-th signature on $\tilde{c}^*$, he outputs $\sigma_{t'} = (\tilde{\sigma} - \sum\limits_{\lambda=1}^{t'-1} C_\lambda \sigma_\lambda) \cdot \frac{1}{C_t'}$ as the forged BLS signature, where $C_\lambda = \prod\limits_{\mu=1, \mu\neq\lambda}^{t'} \frac{\mu}{\mu-\lambda}$ and $C_{t'} = \prod\limits_{\mu=1, \mu\neq t'}^{t'} \frac{\mu}{\mu-t'}$.

If $\mathcal{A}$ can forge the t'-th signature on $\tilde{c}^*$, $\mathcal{S}$ can use the result to break the

BLS signature. Actually, BLS can not be forged, thus, $\mathcal{A}$ cannot forge t'-th signature.

- The secret hardened password $ST_{\mathcal{U}_i}$ is oblivious. That is, given a user $\mathcal{U}_i$'s secret hardened password $ST_{\mathcal{U}_i}$, $\mathcal{A}$ cannot learn anything about the corresponding password $pw_{\mathcal{U}_i}$. To prove it, we define a game.
  - The environment $\mathcal{Z}$ initiates our scheme, generates a master secret key msk_i for $\mathcal{U}_i$, and splits msk_i into n' shares as $\{msk_{i,1}, msk_{i,2}, \ldots, msk_{i,n'}\}$ using the threshold secret sharing protocol, and produces the public parameter PP. $\mathcal{Z}$ sends PP to a simulator $\mathcal{S}$. And then, $\mathcal{S}$ forwards it to $\mathcal{A}$.
  - $\mathcal{A}$ randomly chooses $\tilde{\alpha}$ and sends it to $\mathcal{S}$. $\mathcal{S}$ then forwards it to $\mathcal{Z}$.
  - $\mathcal{Z}$ selects computes $\tilde{\beta}$, computes $\sigma_{\tilde{\alpha}} = \tilde{\beta} \cdot msk_{\mathcal{U}} \cdot H(\tilde{\alpha})$, and sends $ST_{\mathcal{U}_i} = F(h(\sigma_{\tilde{\alpha}}), \tilde{\alpha})$ to $\mathcal{S}$. $\mathcal{S}$ forwards $ST_{\mathcal{U}_i}$ to $\mathcal{A}$. $\mathcal{A}$ repeats the above operations at most $poly(l)$ times.
  - $\mathcal{A}$ chooses α_0 and α_1, and sends them to $\mathcal{S}$. $\mathcal{S}$ forwards them to $\mathcal{Z}$.
  - $\mathcal{Z}$ randomly selects $b \in [0,1]$ and β. If $b = 0$, $\mathcal{Z}$ computes $ST_{\mathcal{U}_i} = F(h(\beta \cdot msk_{\mathcal{U}} \cdot H(\alpha_b)), \alpha_b)$; otherwise, $\mathcal{Z}$ computes $ST_{\mathcal{U}_i} = \mathcal{F}(\alpha_b)$. F is a pseudorandom function, $\mathcal{F}$ is the set of all functions mapping Z_p^* to Z_p^*. $\mathcal{Z}$ sends $ST_{\mathcal{U}_i}$ to $\mathcal{S}$. $\mathcal{S}$ sends it to $\mathcal{A}$.
  - $\mathcal{A}$ returns b^*. If and only if $b^* = b$, $\mathcal{A}$ wins the game. In the above game, we construct two types of schemes that is Π and $\tilde{\Pi}$. In Π, $\mathcal{Z}$ uses F to compute the secret hardened password, the probability of winning can be denoted by $Pr[Pu_{\mathcal{A},\Pi} = 1]$. In $\tilde{\Pi}$, $\mathcal{Z}$ uses $\mathcal{F}$ to compute the secret hardened password, the probability of winning can be denoted by $Pr[Pu_{\mathcal{A},\tilde{\Pi}} = 1]$. The key point is to prove the following equation holds.

$$|Pr[Pu_{\mathcal{A},\Pi} = 1] - Pr[Pu_{\mathcal{A},\tilde{\Pi}} = 1| \le negl(l).$$

If $\mathcal{Z}$ uses F, then the view of $\mathcal{A}$ when runs as a subroutine by $\mathcal{S}$ is identically to the view of $\mathcal{A}$ in experiment $Pr[Pu_{\mathcal{A},\Pi}]$. Thus, $Pr[Pu_{\mathcal{A},\Pi}]$ can be transferred as follows:

$$Pr[S^F(1^l) = 1] = Pr[Pu_{\mathcal{A},\Pi} = 1].$$

If $\mathcal{Z}$ uses $\mathcal{F}$, then the view of $\mathcal{A}$ when runs as a subroutine by $\mathcal{S}$ is identically to the view of $\mathcal{A}$ in experiment $Pr[Pu_{\mathcal{A},\tilde{\Pi}}]$. Thus, $Pr[Pu_{\mathcal{A},\tilde{\Pi}}]$ can be transferred as follows:

$$Pr[S^{\mathcal{F}}(1^l) = 1] = Pr[Pu_{\mathcal{A},\tilde{\Pi}} = 1].$$

Thus, for $\mathcal{A}$, the key point to win the game is to distinguish F and $\mathcal{F}$. As discussed in [15], there exits an equation:

$$|Pr[S^{\mathcal{F}}(1^l) = 1] - Pr[S^F(1^l) = 1]| \le negl(l).$$

Therefore, by reduction, we prove that the probability of winning the game for $\mathcal{A}$ is negligible.

Theorem 3. *PUOKMS is secure against online password guessing attacks.*

Proof. We transform Theorem 3 to a claim:

Claim: For all polynomial-time adversary $\mathcal{A}$ who can launch at most $Q(l)$ online password guessing attacks, if the following equation holds,

$$Adv_{\mathcal{A}}(l) \leq Q(l)/|N| + \varepsilon(l),$$

then the scheme is secure against online password guessing attacks, where $|N|$ is the password space. Recently, Wang et al. have pointed out that the password distribution matches the Zipf-distribution [18]. Following the Zipf's law, $\mathcal{A}$'s advantage is

$$Adv_{\mathcal{A}}(l) \leq C' \cdot Q^{s'}(l) + \varepsilon(l),$$

where C' and s' are the Zipf parameters, and l is the system security parameter. In [16,17], the claim has been proved. Thus, in this paper, we omit the formal security proof. In PUOKMS, each user shares a master secret key in **Setting** phase and we predetermine the rate-limiting bound of each epoch as q_E in PUOKMS. Note that, $\mathcal{A}$ can impersonate a target user $\mathcal{U}_i$ to compute $ST_{\mathcal{U}_i}$ at most q_E that is much less than the space of passwords. Thus, it is infeasible to retrieve a target user's password in PUOKMS by performing password guessing attacks.

In Theorem 1, Theorem 2, and Theorem 3, we have prove that $\mathcal{A}$ cannot obtain the secret hardened password. Thus, even $\mathcal{A}$ intercepts wrapped message and impersonates a target user, it would not retrieve the plaintext message M.

4.2   Collusion Attacks

An adversary (including external and internal adversary) may perform collusion attack to break the security of PUOKMS: the adversary $\mathcal{A}$ may collude with other entities to retrieve the message plaintext M. In the following, we analyze PUOKMS can resist collusion attacks.

Theorem 4. *Users' wrapped messages in PUOKMS are secure against collusion attacks.*

Proof. In traditional updatable OKMS schemes (e.g., [8]), $\mathcal{A}$ may collude with the key server to retrieve the symmetric key. The main reason for the above vulnerability is that the public value ψ (respectively w in [8]) is stored in plaintext in cloud storage. In PUOKMS, we deploy the password-authentication protocol, where the public value is encrypted by valid user $\mathcal{U}_i$'s public hardened password with the public encryption algorithm. Only $\mathcal{U}_i$ can decrypt it with her/his secret hardened password $ST_{\mathcal{U}_i}$. The security of $ST_{\mathcal{U}_i}$ has been proved in Theorem 1, Theorem 2, and Theorem 3. Additionally, the symmetric decryption key η cannot be predicted, even if up to $\nu(\nu \leq t-1)$ key servers are compromised, which will be proved in Theorem 5.

4.3   Perpetual Leakage Attacks

In a long period of time, a malicious key server may collect more than $t-1$ secret shares to retrieve the user-specific key of $\mathcal{U}_i$. Thus, in PUOKMS, the shares of s_i are periodically updated. We prove that the malicious key server, who collects t shares of s_i generated in two different epochs which are denoted by $\{s_{i,1}, s_{i,2}, \ldots, s_{1,\nu}; s'_{i,\nu+1}, s'_{i,\nu+2}, \ldots, s'_{i,t}\}, (1 < \nu < t < n)$, cannot retrieve s_i. The secret key has the form as follows:

$$s_i = \sum_{\gamma=1}^{t} \xi_\gamma s_{i,\gamma} = \sum_{\gamma=1}^{t} (\prod_{1 \le \kappa \le t, \kappa \ne \gamma} \frac{\kappa}{\kappa - \gamma}) s_{i,\gamma} = \sum_{\gamma=1}^{t} (\prod_{1 \le \kappa \le t, \kappa \ne \gamma} \frac{\kappa}{\kappa - \gamma}) \sum_{\varepsilon=1}^{n} f'_\varepsilon(\gamma),$$

$$= \sum_{\gamma=1}^{t} (\prod_{1 \le \kappa \le t, \kappa \ne \gamma} \frac{\kappa}{\kappa - \gamma}) (\sum_{\varepsilon=1}^{n} f_\varepsilon(\gamma) + f_\varepsilon(\gamma)) = \sum_{\gamma=1}^{t} (\prod_{1 \le \kappa \le t, \kappa \ne \gamma} \frac{\kappa}{\kappa - \gamma}) \sum_{\varepsilon=1}^{n} f_\varepsilon(\gamma).$$

Here, the only way the malicious retrieves s_i is to compute

$$\sum_{\gamma=1}^{\nu} \xi_\gamma s_{i,\gamma} + \sum_{\gamma=\nu+1}^{t} \xi_\gamma s'_{i,\gamma} = s_i + \sum_{\gamma=\nu+1}^{t} (\prod_{\nu+1 \le \kappa \le t, \kappa \ne \gamma} \frac{\kappa}{\kappa - \gamma}) \sum_{\varepsilon=1}^{n} l_\varepsilon(\gamma).$$

Since $\mathcal{A}$ cannot collect $l_\varepsilon(\gamma)$ for $\varepsilon = 1, 2, \ldots, n$ and $\gamma = \nu+1, \nu+2, \ldots, t$, he cannot compute

$$s_i = \sum_{\gamma=1}^{\nu} \xi_\gamma s_{i,\gamma} + \sum_{\gamma=\nu+1}^{t} \xi_\gamma s'_{i,\gamma} - \sum_{\gamma=\nu+1}^{t} (\prod_{\nu+1 \le \kappa \le t, \kappa \ne \gamma} \frac{\kappa}{\kappa - \gamma}) \sum_{\varepsilon=1}^{n} l_\varepsilon(\gamma).$$

In Theorem 1, we have prove that $\mathcal{A}$ cannot impersonate the valid user $\mathcal{U}_i$ to pass the authentication of identity servers. In reality, once the secret token $ST_{\mathcal{U}_i}$ is obtained, $\mathcal{A}$ would collude with the malicious key server to retrieve the symmetric encryption key η. The security of the symmetric encryption η is captured by the Theorem 5, which ensures that our scheme can resist against the malicious key server and the adversary $\mathcal{A}$.

Theorem 5. *In our scheme, the symmetric encryption key η is unpredictable, which means that even $\mathcal{A}$ decrypts c_1 with the secret token $ST_{\mathcal{U}_i}$ to get ψ, he cannot predict the symmetric encryption key η, even if he compromises up to ν key servers.*

Proof. The game is the same with Theorem 2. If $\mathcal{A}$ can win the game with a non-negligible probability, $\mathcal{S}$ can break the BLS signature with the same probability [10]. The proof will be identical to the proofs of Theorem 2 above.

5   Performance Evaluation

We evaluate the performance of PUOKMS in terms of communication and computation overhead in different phases. We implement an experiment in JAVA with JPBC using a computer with a Window 10 system and a single Intel Core i7-9700 CPU running at 3.00 GHz CPU, 32 GB RAM (31). SHA-3 is implemented in the hash functions. We select 80 bits security level for analysis, the size of RSA modulus is selected as $|N| = 2048$, the length of the symmetric key of AES is 128 bits, and the curve of field size is 159 bits.

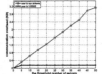 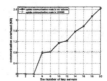 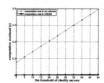 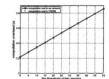

Fig. 4. Communication costs on user-side

Fig. 5. Communication costs on **KeyUpdate**

Fig. 6. Computation costs on user side (a)

Fig. 7. Computation costs on user side (b)

5.1   Communication Overhead

Compared with UOKMS scheme [8], PUOKMS brings in additional communication overhead due to the interaction between users and identity servers. However, such the communication in PUOKMS guarantees that only a valid user can obtain her/his secret hardened password from the identity servers, which enables PUOKMS to resist the impersonation attacks of the malicious user or an adversary.

In Fig. 4, we show the communication costs of the user in the **Decryption** phase of PUOKMS and UOKMS [8], where the number of identity servers and key servers are set 50, respectively. Compared with UOKMS, PUOKMS introduces more communication costs on the user side, the additional costs are caused by interacting with identity servers. To decrypt the wrapped messages, firstly, the user has to retrieve her/his secret hardened password to unwrap the first layer encryption by interacting with multiple identity servers, which ensures the authenticity of a user's identity. Secondly, the user communicates with a group of key servers to obtain the symmetric encryption/decryption key. By comparison, in UOKMS, users' identity authentication is not required and the user only needs to retrieve the symmetric key by interacting with key servers, which raises many serious security concerns as described in the adversary model (Sect. 2.3). With the development of mobile devices, the additional communication costs can be acceptable and would not be a bottleneck for users in practice. In the **Decryption** phase, all key servers and identity servers do not need to interact with each other. Thus, the communication costs on each key server and identity server are constant, here, we would not analyze the communication efficiency.

In Fig. 5, we show the communication costs in the **KeyUpdate** phase of PUOKMS and UOKMS. Both schemes do not introduce a trusted party to assist key servers in renewing the user-specific secret shares. In contrast, in UOKMS, the key servers not only update their secret shares but also update the user-specific secret key for each user. Furthermore, in UOKMS, the update token should be sent to the cloud server for update. Although the communication overhead of PUOKMS is only a little less than UOKMS, the security of PUOKMS is much stronger than it. Once the update token is stolen, the security of UOKMS would be broken.

5.2   Computation Overhead

We first estimate the computation overhead in terms of basic cryptographic operations. $Hash_{Z_p^*}$ is a hash function that maps a value into Z_p^*; $Hash_G$ is a hash function that maps a value into G; $Add_{Z_p^*}$ is an additive operation in group Z_p^*; $Mul_{Z_p^*}$ is a multiplicative operation in Z_p^*; Add_G is an additive operation in group G; Mul_G is a multiplicative operation in group G; $Pair_{G_T}$ denotes that computing pairing e; $T_{SKE.Enc/SKE.Dec}$ denotes the time of performing symmetric encryption algorithm; $T_{PKE.Enc/PKE.Dec}$ denotes the time of performing public encryption algorithm; T_{Sig} denotes the tine of performing a signature algorithm. We show the performance of PUOKMS from three aspects: the user side, identity server side, key server side.

In Fig. 6 and Fig. 7, we show the computation overhead between PUOKMS and UOKMS in the **Decryption** phase. In PUOKMS, each user computes her/his secret hardened password by communicating with multiple identity servers, and decrypts the first layer encryption. Then, the user computes the symmetric encryption/decryption key by interacting with multiple key servers, and decrypts the second layer encryption. The total computation overhead of user side is $2Hash_G + Hash_{Z_p^*} + (t' + t + 5)Mul_G + (t' + t - 2)Add_G + (t'^2 + t^2)Add_{Z_p^*} + (t'^2 + t^2 - t' - t)Mul_{Z_p^*} + (2t' + 2t + 4)Pair_{G_T} + T_{SKE.Enc/SKE.Dec} + T_{PKE.Enc/PKE.Dec}$, where t' is the threshold number of identity servers, t is the threshold number of key servers. In Fig. 6, we show the relationship between the computation costs on user-side and the threshold of identity servers, in which we set the threshold of key servers is $t = 10$. In Fig. 7, we show the relationship between the computation costs on user-side and the threshold of key servers, where the threshold of identity servers is set $t' = 15$. Compared with UOKMS, PUOKMS introduces more computation costs on the user side in the **Decryption** phase, the additional costs are caused by authentication with identity servers and interacting with multiple key servers. However, these servers ensure the security of PUOKMS, which can resist impersonation attacks and single-point-of-failure attacks. With the development of mobile devices, the additional communication costs can be acceptable and would not be a bottleneck for users in practice.

In the **Decryption** phase, the computation cost on the identity server side is Mul_G. Compared with UOKMS, PUOKMS additionally introduces a group of identity servers to ensure the authenticity of users' identities. In the **KeyUpdate** phase, each identity server needs to compute a new secret share to renew the master secret key. The corresponding computation costs of each identity server is $(t'n' - 1)Mul_G + (2t'n' - 2n' - 2t' + 2)Mul_{Z_p^*} + (t'n' - n' - t' + 2)Add_{Z_p^*} + (t'n' - 2n' - t' + 2)Add_G$, in which t' is the threshold of identity servers, n' is the total number of key servers.

The computation costs on the key servers side in the **Decryption** phase are constant (Mul_G). In the **KeyUpdate** phase, each key server needs to compute a new secret share to renew the user-specific secret key. The corresponding computation costs of each key server is $(tn - 1)Mul_G + (2tn - 2n - 2t + 2)Mul_{Z_p^*} + (tn - n - t + 2)Add_{Z_p^*} + (tn - 2n - t + 2)Add_G$, in which t is the threshold of key servers, n is the total number of key servers. Compared with UOKMS, PUOKMS introduces more computation costs on the key server side to prevent single-point-of-failure attacks.

In summary, according to the efficiency analysis and performance evaluation, we observe that PUOKMS introduces more communication and computation overhead. However, these additional costs are mainly for protecting PUOKMS from various attacks. Furthermore, with the development of mobile devices, these costs would not introduce a heavy burden for current mobile devices.

6   Conclusion

In this paper, we have proposed a two-layered encryption mechanism, where multiple identity servers are employed to assist users in generating the hardened password-based first layer encryption key. Such a key has been used to protect thee confidentiality of the public value. Then, a set of key servers, secretly sharing a user-specific server-side key for each user, assists users in generating the second layer encryption key that has been used to encrypt the messages. Furthermore, we have utilized a key renewal mechanism that periodically updates the secret on each key server. Finally, with these two mechanisms, we have developed a password-protected updatable oblivious key management system for cloud storage. The security analysis has shown that PUOKMS guarantees stronger security and the performance evaluation has indicated that the efficiency of PUOKMS would be acceptable and would not be a bottleneck for current mobile devices for application.

References

1. Li, S., et al.: Efficient data retrieval over encrypted attribute-value type databases in cloud-assisted ehealth systems. IEEE Syst. J., 1–12 (2021)
2. Kamara, S., Lauter, K.: Cryptographic cloud storage. In: Sion, R., et al. (eds.) FC 2010. LNCS, vol. 6054, pp. 136–149. Springer, Heidelberg (2010). https://doi.org/10.1007/978-3-642-14992-4_13
3. Freedman, M.J., Ishai, Y., Pinkas, B., Reingold, O.: Keyword search and oblivious pseudorandom functions. In: International Proceedings on TCC, Cambridge, MA, USA, pp. 303–324 (2005)

4. Naor, M., Reingold, O.: Number-theoretic constructions of efficient pseudo-random functions. J. ACM **51**(2), 231–262 (2004)
5. Zhang, Y., Xu, C., Li, H., Yang, K., Zhou, J., Lin, X.: Healthdep: an efficient and secure deduplication scheme for cloud-assisted ehealth systems. IEEE Trans. Industr. Inf. **14**(9), 4101–4112 (2018)
6. Li, S., Xu, C., Zhang, Y.: CSED: client-Side encrypted deduplication scheme based on proofs of ownership for cloud storage. J. Inf. Secur. Appl. **46**, 250–258 (2019)
7. Zhang, Y., Xu, C., Lin, X., Shen, X.S.: Blockchain-based public integrity verification for cloud storage against procrastinating auditors. IEEE Trans. Cloud Comput. **9**, 1–15 (2019)
8. Jarecki, S., Krawczyk, H., Resch, J.: Updatable oblivious key management for storage systems. In: International Proceedings of CCS, London, United Kingdom, pp. 379–393 (2019)
9. Vo, D.L., Zhang, F., Kim, K.: A new threshold blind signature scheme from pairings. In: Proceedings of SCIS, pp. 514–532 (2003)
10. Boneh, D., Lynn, B., Shacham, H.: Short signatures from the Weil pairing. In: Boyd, C. (ed.) ASIACRYPT 2001. LNCS, vol. 2248, pp. 514–532. Springer, Heidelberg (2001). https://doi.org/10.1007/3-540-45682-1_30
11. Zhang, Y., Xu, C., Li, H., Yang, K., Cheng, N., Shen, X.S.: PROTECT: efficient password-based threshold Single-sign-on authentication for mobile users against perpetual leakage. IEEE Trans. Mobile Comput. **20**, 1–16 (2020)
12. Desmedt, Y.G.: Threshold cryptography. Eur. Trans. Telecommun. **5**(4), 449–458 (1994)
13. Lai, R.W.F., Egger, C., Schröder, D., Chow, S.S.M.: Phoenix: rebirth of a cryptographic password-hardening service. In: International Proceedings of USENIX Security, Vancouver, BC, Canada, pp. 899–916 (2017)
14. Lai, R.W.F., Egger, C., Reinert, M., Chow, S.S.M., Maffei, M., Schröder, D.: Simple password-hardened encryption services. In: International Proceedings of USENIX Security, Santa Clara, CA, USA, pp. 1405–1421 (2018)
15. Katz, J., Lindell, Y.: Introduction to Modern Cryptography (2014)
16. Katz, J., Ostrovsky, R., Yung, M.: Efficient and secure authenticated key exchange using weak passwords. J. ACM **57**(1), 1–39 (2009)
17. Li, Z., Wang, D., Morais, E.: Quantum-safe round-optimal password authentication for mobile devices. IEEE Trans. Dependable Secure Comput., 1–16 (2020)
18. Ding, W., Gaopeng, J., Xinyi, H., Ping, W.: Zipf's law in passwords. IEEE Trans. Inf. Forensics Secur. **12**(11), 2776–2791 (2017)
19. Ding, W., Zijian, Z., Ping, W., Jeff, Y., Xinyi, H.: Targeted online password guessing: an underestimated threat. In: International Proceedings of CCS, Vienna, Austria, pp. 1–13 (2016)
20. Moni, N., Benny, P., Eyal, R.: How to (not) share a password: privacy preserving protocols for finding heavy hitters with adversarial behavior. In: International Proceedings of CCS, London, United Kingdom, pp. 1–18 (2019)
21. Jeremiah, B., Anupam, D., Joseph, B.: Differentially private password frequency lists. In: International Proceedings of NDSS, San Diego, CA, USA, pp. 1–15 (2016)

OblivShare: Towards Privacy-Preserving File Sharing with Oblivious Expiration Control

Yanjun Shen[1,2], Xingliang Yuan[1], Shi-Feng Sun[3], Joseph K. Liu[1(✉)], and Surya Nepal[2]

[1] Department of Software Systems and Cybersecurity, Faculty of Information Technology, Monash University, Melbourne, Australia
joseph.liu@monash.edu
[2] Data61, CSIRO, Canberra, Australia
[3] Shanghai Jiao Tong University, Shanghai, China

Abstract. People have personal and/or business need to share private and confidential documents; however, often at the expense of privacy. Privacy aware users demand that their data is secure during the entire life cycle, and not residing in clouds indefinitely. A trending feature in industry is to set download constraints of shared files - a file can be downloaded for a restricted number of times and/or within a limited time framework. Metadata privacy becomes concerning with web services and applications providing such additional level of security control but not hiding the metadata. There is no prior research focusing on privacy-preserving expiration control, hence we propose OblivShare, a privacy-preserving file sharing scheme to proactively fill the gap. The scheme is based on ORAM for secure computation that 1) supports file expiration at users' control, 2) hides expiration metadata from the server, 3) server is fully oblivious of file access pattern and expiration state of a file. We demonstrate that our protocol has a complexity poly-logarithmic to the number of files while achieving privacy of metadata.

Keywords: E2EE file sharing · Metadata privacy · ORAM · Secure computation

1 Introduction

Users sharing files with other users over the Internet are common practices today. However, data leakages and mass surveillance projects [16,27] have drawn public attention of the vulnerability and sensitivity of personal data, and in turn promoted privacy awareness of users. Further, existing regulations and acts to protect personal data [19,31], also impose on service providers to grant individuals control over their private information. Therefore, sharing files securely and privately is becoming a fundamental requirement.

In order to achieve secure file sharing, systems and services have been developed to support end-to-end encryption (E2EE) [29], using which, a user encrypts file content before it leaves their device and only authorised users are able to

© Springer Nature Switzerland AG 2021
R. Deng et al. (Eds.): ISPEC 2021, LNCS 13107, pp. 126–146, 2021.
https://doi.org/10.1007/978-3-030-93206-0_9

decrypt the file. However, E2EE does not appear to fully protect the privacy of user or file metadata, and a file can stay in servers indefinitely. Recent innovative services [7,17] provide impermanence of data store on top of E2EE, which offers extra security control to users over the files they share: setting files to expire after a certain amount of time or number of downloads. On the one hand, such services incorporate two most desired features, **E2EE** and **ephemeral**, which meets personal needs of more secure connections and intimate sharing; on the other hand, limitations are also apparent: 1) Users send expiration control metadata (expiration metadata for short in the rest of the paper), i.e. download number and time limits to check if a file has expired, to servers in plaintext, which can be used to deduce the popularity and sensitivity of specific file(s). 2) Expiration control is at servers' hand and users have to fully trust a service to honestly check if a file has expired.

Inadequate discussion has since occurred to understand the privacy of expiration metadata. Therefore, we aim to propose a new protocol to solve this emerging problem with practical values. This is a first attempt to focus on secure file expiration control, and the proposed protocol has not yet been implemented in real cloud environment. Security and performance analysis are provided in the paper, and we consider real experimental evaluation to illustrate the performance in the future.

1.1   Motivation

"If you have enough metadata, you don't really need content", "we kill people based on metadata" [22,23]. Sharing a file resembles calling or messaging someone from the perspective of metadata exposure, hence metadata privacy in file sharing is also concerning. While increasing service providers provide expiration control on top of E2EE, a gap exists in both industry and academia. To illustrate the motivation of hiding expiration metadata and oblivious file sharing, we present some privacy issues even with E2EE file sharing systems.

Sensitivity Derived from Expiration Metadata. Alice is an oncologist, and shares files with patients and other contacts in an E2EE system. Alice shares medical records with her patients and sets each to expire after 1 download, and other files without expiration conditions. With knowledge of the expiration metadata, a curious server learns that Alice shares some files with strict access, hence deduces they are sensitive. Bob is a patient of Alice and downloads his report from the system. With Alice's identity and the sensitivity of the file, the server thus infers Bob is suspected to have cancer without decrypting the report.

1.2   Summary of Contributions

We now propose OblivShare, a secure and ephemeral file-sharing system that for the first time provides users with advanced and oblivious expiration control. OblivShare puts forward a new framework of a file-sharing scheme that not only supports comprehensive file expiration control, but is also expiration-metadata-private and oblivious. This is a generic solution that can be integrated

Table 1. Overview of techniques to achieve the goals.

Goal	Technique
Expiration metadata privacy	Secret sharing
Oblivious expiration control	Secure two party computation
Oblivious file sharing	ORAM
User IP addresses	Anonymous network, e.g., Tor

into file sharing services to address metadata privacy issues. To understand our contributions, we now outline the main challenges OblivShare aims to address.

Challenge 1: how to achieve expiration control over protected expiration metadata? We define expiration metadata as: 1) User-set download constraints, i.e., download number and time limits to facilitate expiration control. 2) Internal download state, i.e., current download count used to compute expiration control outcome. Users are not able to download a file if it has expired. To the best of our knowledge, whereas many scholars focus on protection of general security control metadata in file sharing such as user identity and access pattern, there is no prior research aiming to prevent leakage of expiration metadata, hence a gap exists to address such expiration-metadata-privacy.

Challenge 2: how to make download requests of a specific file indistinguishable from servers? Only hiding the expiration control process, outcome and metadata is not sufficient, as a server can still infer that a file has expired if the specific file has not been accessed for a long time. A server not fully oblivious of the file sharing process learns which file is accessed for each download and can reasonably deduce the expiration metadata.

Contribution. OblivShare supports E2EE meanwhile protects the expiration metadata through the entire course with oblivious file access and expiration control. Our goals and techniques are summarized in Table 1. Overall, our contributions are:

1. We are the first to address metadata privacy issues in file sharing systems that support expiration control. User-defined download constraints are hidden from servers through the entire course of file upload, sharing and download. Internal download state is also protected by secret sharing between servers, therefore the servers cannot directly learn file expiration status.
2. We use synchronised tree-based ORAMs to store both file content and metadata, which hides file access patterns from servers, hence the servers cannot distinguish which file and how many times is requested so as to deduce file expiration status and further expiration metadata.
3. We are the first to use secure computation for oblivious expiration control, which not only guarantees that a single server cannot manipulate the expiration control result, but is also efficient to implement using garbled circuits.
4. We also approve that our scheme has negligible extra computation and communication overhead on top of a primitive ORAM file sharing system, which requires one interaction with users hence not sacrifices user experience.

Table 2. Secure file sharing services.

Product	E2EE	Time limit	Number limit	Hide expiration metadata	Oblivious server
OblivShare	✓	✓	✓	✓	✓
Firefox Send [17]	✓	✓	✓	✗	✗
DropSecure [7]	✓	✓	Future	✗	✗
SendSafely [24]	✓	✓	✗	✗	✗
WhatsApp [34]	✓	Future	✗	✗	✗
Digify [8]	✗	✓	✗	✗	✗
Dropbox [6]	✗	✗	✗	NA	✗

2 Related Work

2.1 Existing Secure File Sharing

Ephemeral content sharing is a highly pursued feature in industry [7,12,17,24, 29,34,37]. With certain expiration control, users are confident that what they share is only accessible to dedicated users for limited time or number of times, and never stay in a server for longer than necessary and become a vulnerability later.

Table 2 compares several existing secure file sharing applications or web services. We organise the comparison by the following properties: 1) Does it support E2EE? 2) Does it support file expiration? 3) Does it hide expiration metadata? 4) Is the server oblivious of file access and expiration control if applicable?

[7,17] and [24] claim to offer zero-knowledge E2EE. [7] (premium) provides client-side encryption that keeps a public key protected encryption key in a key sever (isolated from the file storage server), and only a recipient's private key can decrypt the encryption key. [24] uses OpenPGP encryption and the file encryption key consists of a server secret (generated by the server) and a client secret (generated by the sender). Services such as [6] and [8], though do not support E2EE, but provide an addition layer of password security on top of server-side encryption. A user can double encrypt files or folders by setting a password, and share it to recipients outside the service. [34] also offers E2EE for file attachments and has been developing its "Expiring Messages" feature.

Our solution is aiming to address the security weakness of existing systems mentioned in Sect. 1 with a good balance of desired features and cost.

2.2 ORAM for File Storage

Oblivious RAM (ORAM) [10] is an attempt to hide a user's access pattern from service providers meanwhile supporting extra operations. Traditional ORAM schemes usually have worst-case communication complexity linear to their capacity and block size even with amortized communication cost [18], and their single client setting [10,18,25] is not suitable for file sharing. Multi-user ORAM

Table 3. Notation

Notation	Description
λ	ORAM's statistical security parameters
ts_U	A timestamp that denotes the upload time
ts_D	A timestamp that denotes the download time
ts_{Exp}	A timestamp that denotes the expiration time, that is $ts_U + t$
D	An array of data content stored in ORAM
x	An positive integer that denotes a file index in ORAM, up to the ORAM file number bound, and $D[x]$ is the data stored in ORAM
Exp	An expiration policy that stores download constraints and state indexed by x
$[s]$	A secret share of s
N	The number of real data blocks in ORAM
h	The height of the ORAM tree, that is $\lceil log_2 N \rceil$
θ	A threshold of timestamp difference that is accepted by OblivShare

schemes are promising designs that can be applied in file sharing, but unfortunately, very few of such works exist. Among those that support file sharing, GORAM [14] is a system that guarantees anonymity of users and obliviousness of data access; but it does not protect the owner of a file. PIR-MCORAM [15] is a multi-user ORAM-based file sharing system, but has a very high overhead hence liner worst-case complexity. There are other ORAM schemes that focus on malicious users but do not readily support file sharing [1,11].

At the best of our knowledge, none of the existing ORAM schemes, either hide access patterns and/or user identities or not, with linear or poly-logarithm complexity, has addressed expiration control. With OblivShare, we propose an efficient secure file sharing scheme that not only achieves lightweight system design on top of ORAM (we present performance analysis in Sect. 5 that proves OblivShare has poly-logarithmic complexity), but also enables expiration control while hiding expiration metadata.

3   Preliminaries

OblivShare makes black box use of secure two party computation, and also follows ORAM paradigm for metadata and file storage.

Notation. We define parameters, entities, denotations in OblivShare in Table 3.

3.1   Secure Computation

The Millionaires' Problem first described by Yao [35] enables to solve the following problem: Alice and Bob have their own secret inputs, which are their wealth x^A and x^B million, respectively. Yao's protocol enables that Alice and Bob can compute a function $f(x^A, x^B) \longrightarrow (y^A, y^B)$ such that Alice learns only its function output y^A while Bob knows only y^B, i.e., who is richer, and nothing else about the other party's wealth.

Since Yao's secure computation protocol was proposed, researchers have advanced a number of variations and extensions to address different scenarios. Recent secure multiparty computation (MPC) solutions includes private sorting [13], private computational geometry [26], private voting [30], and private data mining [2,9] etc.

3.2 ORAM

OblivShare deploys ORAM for oblivious data storage and retrieval. More specifically, we use ORAM for secure computation [5,32,36], so as to ensure oblivious data access in MPC applications. There is a class of tree-based ORAM schemes [25,28,32] that are efficient for practical implementations especially in MPC, among which, we consider Circuit ORAM [32] as an appropriate scheme for our setting because of its competitive performance. Comparing to schemes like SqrtORAM [36] and Floram [5], Circuit ORAM client has complexity that is poly-logarithmic to the number of files, and also reduces the circuit size comparing to Path ORAM [28] and SCORAM [33]. Circuit ORAM is a tree-based ORAM. To store N files, Circuit ORAM constructs a binary tree with height $h = \lceil log_2 N \rceil$. The tree is composed of tree nodes, each of which has three blocks with fixed block size; apart from that, it also has a stash (up to the stash size bound) that temporarily stores blocks that will be later evicted to the tree. Each block either stores the data of a file or is left empty. To store a file $D[x]$ in a file array D, a block contains the file index x, the file data $D[x]$, and its position that is the path from leaf to root. If a block is cached in the stash, the block stores the corresponding path that the block will be evicted onto. The file index x and its corresponding path p constitute a position map. We adapt Metal's protocol [3] as a underlying primitive for efficient and oblivious data access in S2PC.

Read from ORAM. To read a file, the two servers first check the file's leaf label (hence corresponding path) in the position map, then search for the block with the file index via a linear scan over both the stash and path. The servers then read the file block stored in the block. After reading the file, they randomly assign a new path to this block, put it back into the stash, and update the position map accordingly.

Write to ORAM. To write a file, the steps are similar until when the two servers add the block into the stash, and they replace it with the data to write provided by the user.

Stash Eviction. Circuit ORAM performs a stash eviction for each read and write operation, at which stage, blocks cached in the stash are evicted to the ORAM tree to prevent stash overflowing. We do not elaborate the eviction algorithms of Circuit ORAM in detail here, but will illustrate rearrangement steps that are relevant to OblivShare. A generic Circuit ORAM data access operation is provided in Algorithm 1.

Algorithm 1: ORAMAccess

---

1 **Input** $op, idx, data$
2 **Output** $returnData$
   1. $label \leftarrow PositionMap[idx]$
   2. $\{idx\|label\|returnData\} \leftarrow ReadnRemove(idx, label)$
   3. $PositionMap[idx] \leftarrow UniformRandom(0, ..., N-1)$ //update position map
   4. **if** $op = "read"$ **then**
      (a) $data \leftarrow retrunData$
   5. $stash.add(\{idx\|PositionMap[idx]\|data\})$
   6. Evict()
   7. Outputs $returnData$

3.3 Synchronised Inside-Outside ORAM Trees

We identify that the **synchronising inside-outside ORAM trees** technique used by METAL [3] is suitable for OblivShare. As has been introduced in Sect. 3.2, taking Circuit ORAM as an instance, each block in an ORAM tree contains the file index x, the file data $D[x]$, and its position. METAL, however, splits position map (i.e. index and path position) and actual file data, and stores them in two ORAM trees separately: one tree contains files' indices and positions stays inside S2PC procedures because it is small while the other tree that stores actual file contents stays outside S2PC. The two trees are maintained synchronised during initialisation and after each data access so that the file identifier and content can be found at the same position in the two trees. By doing so, the position of a file can be processed and revealed securely and efficiently in S2PC without loading large file data, and the block fetching and eviction of the actual file data are achieved by two protocols to keep the trees re-synchronised. METAL uses a secret-shared doubly oblivious transfer protocol to ensure that servers fetch the actual file data after revealing the position (in secret shares), and a distributed permutation protocol to track the movement of blocks after eviction and apply the rearrangement to according positions, without any servers learning the actual file's position.

In what follows, we provide some background knowledge of METAL's techniques relevant to our setting and describe more details in Appendix A.

Secret-Shared Doubly Oblivious Transfer. In order to get the actual file block outside S2PC, the two servers first process and reveal the file position inside S2PC, which means that the i-th block on the path p stores the position map and file data respectively in two ORAM trees. The S2PC then generates a list of keys for all the blocks on the path and outputs all these keys to Server 1 that stores the ORAM of actual file data, and Server 2 receives only one key corresponding to the actual file location i. Server 1 then needs to encrypt all the file blocks on the path p using the corresponding keys in order and re-randomise the encrypted blocks before sending them to Server 2. Server 2 uses its key received from the S2PC and decrypt blocks received from Server 1 to obtain the i-th block without either server getting the actual file location.

Distributed Permutation. As has been mentioned in Sect. 3.2, stash eviction is called after every read or write after fetching a data block in ORAM. *Distributed permutation* [3,36] captures the rearrangement of blocks, which is used when putting the read block into stash before eviction and later evicting stash blocks to selected paths. The two servers in S2PC generate a permutation of an array of blocks, including the blocks in the stash, the block read and the block to write; then secret shares the permutation; and apply permutation shares accordingly. The result of the protocol is that the two ORAMs store the permuted blocks in the same location as per the updated file position map. By following this protocol, neither server learns the new position of the file after eviction, and neither server knows which permutation, read or write, is performed.

4   System Overview

In OblivShare, a data owner encrypts a file and sets the file to expire at certain conditions before uploading. OblivShare stores both the cipher file and expiration policy in a secure manner. When a recipient makes a download request to OblivShare, OblivShare first performs expiration control over download constraints and download state, then sends the cipher file to the recipient if the file has not expired. To understand how OblivShare fulfils these operations securely, we present an overview of OblivShare's design, threats and security goals.

4.1   System Architecture

A high-level framework of OblivShare is illustrated in Fig. 1, which consists of two servers, a data owner and multiple clients (in this paper, client is used interchangeably with recipient):

- **Owner** sends upload requests to OblivShare, and shares the file index and file encryption key embedded in a URL to recipients via secure channels.
- **Recipient(s)** sends download requests to the servers, and receives results from OblivShare as per expiration check.
- **Servers** each takes its share of the requests as inputs to the S2PC, and together run S2PC procedures and send the outputs from S2PC to the recipients. The servers also keep updated ExpCtrlORAM and DataORAM, which is explained in detail in Sect. 5.1.

OblivShare incorporates two major components: **OblivExp** for expiration Control and **OblivData** for file access. **OblivExp** is placed in front of **OblivData** to conduct expiration control. A client's request first arrives at **OblivExp**, which checks whether the requested file has expired or not inside the S2PC by the two servers. If no, the request is sent to **OblivData** for a file access. If yes, the request is also dispatched to make the expiration control result indistinguishable to the servers, but in a manner to access dummy data instead. This is a loose description, and detailed construction is elaborated in Sect. 5.

OblivExp updates ExpCtrlORAM after each access and the changes to blocks as a result of stash eviction are applied to DataORAM during **OblivData** via synchronisation between ExpCtrlORAM and DataORAM.

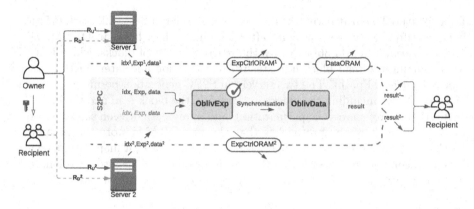

Fig. 1. High level framework. A client sends its secret-shared request of file access to the two servers. The request is reconstructed and executed in S2PC.

4.2   Threat Model

Assumptions. OblivShare makes the following assumptions:

At Least One Server is Honest. An attacker can compromise one of the servers in the two party secure computation while the other is not.

Key Secrecy. A client does not reveal the URL with the key to adversaries.

Out-of-Band Communication. A data owner in OblivShare shares a URL with recipient(s) through third party secured channels of their own control, such as *Telegram* [29] and *Signal* [21]. OblivShare only uses such out-of-band communication once at the sharing stage, which is a common practice of other secure file sharing systems [6,17], keeping all other activities within OblivShare.

Anonymous Network. In order to hide other metadata during file sharing, OblivShare assumes the clients communicate with servers in an anonymous manner that does not reveal network information via existing tools such as Tor [4] or secure messaging [29] based on decentralised trust.

Secure Communication. Each client establishes secure connections with each server, e.g., Transport Layer Security, so that data in transition are secured.
    OblivShare does not address denial-of-service attacks.

Threats. OblivShare considers the following threats:

1. A server can see the expiration metadata of a file. It enables the server to learn data sensitivity and popularity of the file, also deduces other valuable information of encrypted data, which has been explained in Sect. 1.
2. A server on its own has control over its internal download state metadata, hence can forge the state, e.g. a small download count or an expiration timestamp that never expire.

3. A server can observe the file access pattern, hence the server is able to learn which specific file is accessed and the number of times the file has been accessed. If a file no longer receives download request, the server can deduce that the file has expired hence infer the user-set expiration metadata.
4. An attacker controlling a client tries to compromise the security of a file that has expired.
5. A recipient can forge its download timestamp so as to make an invalid download pass the expiration control check.

Security Goals. We now present security goals of OblivShare with respect to the threats given in Sect. 4.2.

1. **Expiration metadata privacy.** OblivShare ensures expiration metadata is totally at a data owner's control, and not visible in transit or at rest on either server.
2. **File confidentiality.** OblivShare ensures that neither server learns the actual file content; further, a compromised client cannot access the encrypted file and decrypt the content after the file has expired.
3. **Oblivious expiration control.** OblivShare ensures both servers are oblivious of the expiration control process. Though OblivShare does not prevent a server from manipulating its download state or a client forging its timestamp, the S2PC procedure for expiration control will fail if it detects compromised inputs to the S2PC. Hence such attack gains no information and little value.
4. **Oblivious file sharing.** OblivShare ensures neither server learns access patterns so that the servers are not able to infer if a specific file has expired hence expiration metadata.
5. **Download timestamp integrity.** OblivShare ensures that the download timestamp is independent of a recipient's input, but is controlled in S2PC.
6. **General metadata protection.** Recall the anonymous network assumptions OblivShare makes in Sect. 4.2, users' IP addresses are garbled when communicating with a server, and OblivShare addresses general metadata privacy in file sharing.

OblivShare guarantees the goals above based on common cryptographic assumptions. However, OblivShare does not address denial-of-service (DoS) attacks, which means OblivShare does not prevent a dishonest server from denying a valid download request even if the time has not expired or the number of downloads permissible has not been exceeded.

5   Detailed Construction

Note that in Circuit ORAM, the linear search of the file index happens within the S2PC, the real data is too large to process. We identify that METAL's synchronised ORAM trees [3] benefits our design to reduce the data accessed inside the S2PC. Below we introduce building blocks of OblivShare. In the following, we present our protocol assuming each file is an single file block for simplicity, but in practice, an uploaded file consists of multiple file blocks and is padded to have the same size.

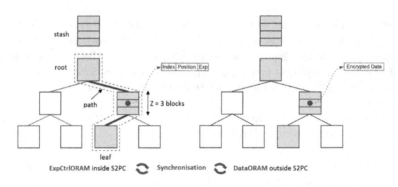

Fig. 2. OblivShare has two tree ORAMs that store small metadata and large real data respectively and synchronised in ExpCtrlORAM and DataORAM.

5.1 Synchronised ORAM Trees

OblivShare has two ORAM trees, an ExpCtrlORAM tree to store the metadata in a recursive manner and a DataORAM tree to store the actual file data. The two trees are synchronised so that the content and the metadata of a file are at the same location in DataORAM and ExpCtrlORAM.

ExpCtrlORAM is a set of trees that recursively stores small metadata, including: 1) the position map; 2) the expiration metadata, i.e. download constraints set by the data owner and the current download state. The ExpCtrlORAM is secret shared with two servers, and will be completed loaded and accessed inside the S2PC. OblivShare uses the standard recursive technique [3,32] to store the metadata in ExpCtrlORAM, and for simplicity purpose, we refer to the last tree when using ExpCtrlORAM in the rest of the paper.

DataORAM resembles ExpCtrlORAM's last tree but only stores the data (encrypted file). The DataORAM tree is stored on Server 1, and only relevant portion of the data structure will be loaded into the S2PC.

Figure 2 shows the ORAM structure in OblivShare and how two ORAMs are synchronised by storing corresponding metadata and data at the same location.

The read and write operations of Circuit ORAM still suffice data retrieval and update in ExpCtrlORAM but no longer fulfil fetching data from and putting data into DataORAM. OblivShare follows MTEAL's *secret-shared doubly oblivious transfer* (SS-DOT) [3] protocol to fetch the i-th block on path p from DataORAM. At the end of SS-DOT, Server 2 obtains the fetched block, i.e. the i-th block (encrypted under ElGamal) in the array, without either server learning i. We describe the details relevant to OblivShare in Appendix A.1. OblivShare also follows *distributed permutation* to make sure ExpCtrlORAM and DataORAM are re-synchronised after each eviction by tracking and permuting block movements. At the end of *distributed permutation*, Server 1 stores the permuted file blocks in DataORAM in the same location as metadata blocks in ExpCtrlORAM. By following this protocol, neither server learns the new location of the evicted block. We give more details of how permutation is created, shared and applied in Appendix A.2.

Algorithm 2: OblivExp.Upload

---

1 **Input of S1:** $[x]^1, [Exp]^1, [ExpCtrlORAM]^1$
2 **Input of S2:** $[x]^2, [Exp]^2, [ExpCtrlORAM]^2$
3 **Output:** $[ExpCtrlORAM]^1, [ExpCtrlORAM]^2$

    1. $x \leftarrow [x]^1 \oplus [x]^2, Exp \leftarrow [Exp]^1 \oplus [Exp]^2, ExpCtrlORAM \leftarrow$
       $[ExpCtrlORAM]^1 \oplus [ExpCtrlORAM]^2; //\text{reconstruct}$

    2. $p \leftarrow PositionMap[x]; //\text{select a path}$

    3. $(ExpCtrlORAM', \bot) \leftarrow ORAMAccess(ExpCtrlORAM, x, Exp)$,
       $ExpCtrlORAM \leftarrow ExpCtrlORAM'; //\text{the distribute permutation protocol will be}$
       invoked before and after ExpCtrlORAM's stash eviction

    4. $[ExpCtrlORAM]^1 \leftarrow \$, [ExpCtrlORAM]^2 \leftarrow ExpCtrlORAM \oplus [ExpCtrlORAM]^1;$
       $//\text{secret share ExpCtrlORAM}$

    5. Output to $[ExpCtrlORAM]^1$ to S1 and $[ExpCtrlORAM]^2$ to S2 respectively.

5.2   OblivExp for Expiration Control

Upload a File. During the initialisation stage at the Data Owner's end, it generates an expiration policy Exp locally, which is a description of file download constraints and download state that is shared among the two servers. For example, a policy of a file that expires after 10 downloads and on "21 June 2021 21:21:21" has a policy "File Index x : 10, 21-06-2021T21:21:21, 0" where x is the file index, 10 is the download count (e.g. expire after 10 downloads) chosen by the Data Owner, t_{Exp} is the expiration timestamp derived based on upload timestamp (e.g. 18 June 2021 21:21:21) and download time setting (e.g. expire after 3 days) chosen by the Data Owner, and 0 is the initial download count. The Data Owner also encrypts a file using a secret key before the file is sent to Server 1. Algorithm 2 shows the secure computation during Upload.

Remark. After ExpCtrlORAM's stash eviction, evicted blocks are at new locations but the blocks in DataORAM are not rearranged. To synchronise DataORAM, we use *distributed permutation protocol* by applying the same rearrangement to data blocks in DataORAM. We will elaborate how OblivData ensures the data blocks in DataORAM is still synchronisation in Sect. 5.3.

Download a File. When a client requests a file download by a file index, the two servers search the file index in ExpCtrlORAM, then retrieve the path p and the expiration policy Exp of the file following primitive ORAM read process. The two servers then access DataORAM on the client's behalf and return the file block back to the client via secret shares if the expiration control check passes; otherwise a dummy instead. Note that the S2PC locates the i-th block on the path p in ExpCtrlORAM is the block for file x by a linear search, hence can access the encrypted data of file x in the i-th block of the same path p in DataORAM due to the synchrony between two ORAMs.

During the expiration control check, the two servers inside the S2PC determine a mutually agreed download timestamp (e.g. agree on a deviation threshold θ and then take a mean of the two timestamps from each server), and run the S2PC to compare download constraints to internal download state.

Algorithm 3: OblivExp.Download
---

1 **Input of S1:** $[x]^1, [ts_D]^1, [ExpCtrlORAM]^1$
2 **Input of S2:** $[x]^2, [ts_D]^2, [ExpCtrlORAM]^2$
3 **Public Input:** θ
4 **Output:** $[ExpCtrlORAM]^1, [ExpCtrlORAM]^2, [i]^1, [i]^2$

    1. $ts_D \leftarrow agree(ts_D^1, ts_D^2, \theta)$; //agree on a download timestamp
    2. **if** $ts_D = \perp$ **then stop.** //the procedure stops if the agreement fails
    3. $x \leftarrow [x]^1 \oplus [x]^2, ExpCtrlORAM \leftarrow [ExpCtrlORAM]^1 \oplus [ExpCtrlORAM]^2$;
    4. $locked \leftarrow Exp(status)$; //check the current lock status
    5. **if** $locked = TRUE$ **then stop.**
    6. **else** $locked \leftarrow TRUE$; //change the lock status to locked
    7. $(ExpCtrlORAM', \{p, Exp\}) \leftarrow$
       $ORAMAccess(ExpCtrlORAM, x, \perp), ExpCtrlORAM \leftarrow ExpCtrlORAM'$;
       //run an ORAM read operation to get the expiration policy
    8. $i = search(x, p)$; //determine the i-th location on path p that stores Exp
    9. $r = isValid(Exp(count), Exp(number), Exp(ts_{Exp}), ts_D)$; //expiration check
  10. **if** $r = TRUE$ **then** $Exp(count)+ = 1$; //increments the current download count
  11. **else** $i \leftarrow |stash| + 3h + 1$; //add a dummy at the end of the array and point i to it
  12. $locked \leftarrow FALSE$ and $Exp(status) \leftarrow locked$; //reset the lock status
  13. Generate $[ExpCtrlORAM]^1$,
     $[ExpCtrlORAM]^2 \leftarrow ExpCtrlORAM \oplus [ExpCtrlORAM]^1$
  14. Generate $[i]^1, [i]^2 \leftarrow i \oplus [i]^1$
  15. Output $[ExpCtrlORAM]^1, [i]^1$ to S1 and $[ExpCtrlORAM]^2, [i]^2$ to S2 respectively.

The two servers in the S2PC also update lock status of a file requested on the fly to indicate if the file is being accessed. The file is locked until the data, either the encrypted file or a dummy, has been successfully returned to the client.

To ensure the servers do not know if a file has expired, the S2PC appends a dummy block, and secret share the location i related to this dummy block instead of the actual block if a file has expired (step 11 in Algorithm 3).

Remark. Note that the two servers cannot simply fetch the i-th block in DataO-RAM, after revealing i in ExpCtrlORAM as the location i is related to the block history, i.e. a location i that is closer to the root level of the ORAM is more likely to have been accessed and evicted recently, and vice versa [20].

To make Upload and Download indistinguishable, expiration policy is constructed as {File Index: download number, expiration timestamp, download count, download timestamp, lock status}, hence {File Index: download number, expiration timestamp, 0, $\perp$, FALSE} for Upload and {File Index: $\perp$, $\perp$, $\perp$, download timestamp, $\perp$} for Download.

5.3 OblivData for File Access

In what follows, we show how the two servers in combination fetch and put a file, which is the same for each ORAM Upload and Download.

Fetch Data from DataORAM. In Sect. 5.2, we already provide a solution of indistinguishable file fetch regardless of expiration status by appending a dummy block. After OblivExp completes the expiration control, either passed or failed, it proceeds the request to OblivData that fetches a block, either a real data block or a dummy depending on the expiration control result, in the form of different values of the location i. As has been briefed in Sect. 5.1, at the end of *SS-DOT*, Server 2 received ElGamal cipher-texts of the data block at the i-th location on path p in DataORAM, with neither server aware of i. Upon ElGamal decipher, the result is either the actual file content or the dummy encrypted under a file encryption key (shared by a data owner to dedicated recipients during the share stage), which is finally returned to the recipient who can further decrypt the result. Algorithm 4 in Appendix A.1 shows how the *SS-DOT* protocol works in OblivData.

Remark. Note that in Algorithm 4, j is independent of i as a result of shuffle, hence Server 2 is not aware of i all through the course.

Evict Data to DataORAM. After ExpCtrlORAM's stash eviction, positions of blocks are updated in ExpCtrlORAM, hence OblivData needs to ensure the corresponding real data blocks in DataORAM are rearranged in the same manner. To guarantee that the two ORAMs are still synchronised, OblivShare tracks the block movements in ExpCtrlORAM and apply the same changes to DataORAM. We use *Distributed Permutation* again during this stage following a similar manner of METAL to re-synchronising trees after each eviction.

Algorithm 5 in Appendix A.2 demonstrates how the re-synchronisation is achieved by tracking the movement of blocks in ExpCtrlORAM and applying the same permutation to DataORAM, hence Server 1 stores the blocks in the corresponding locations.

5.4 Security Guarantees

We now present security guarantees of OblivShare with respect to the goals given in Sect. 4.2.

1. **Expiration metadata privacy.** OblivShare hides expiration metadata from both servers yet is able to enforce the expiration control by using secret sharing. The standard secret sharing technique ensures the shares of the expiration metadata are of the same length hence indistinguishable, and each share reveals no information about the secret (line 1 in Algorithm 2). Also, OblivShare uses ElGamal encryption for data blocks stored in ORAM, which prevents the leakage of sensitive expiration metadata from the servers during the entire course.
2. **File confidentiality.** Data owner of OblivShare encrypts a file before uploading the file to servers and only shares the private key to authorised clients. In addition, all data blocks in ORAM are ElGamal encrypted hence the servers cannot decrypt the actual file content without non-trivial computation. OblivShare also prevents invalid access to expired file by returning a

dummy instead of the encrypted file (ensured by line 11 in Algorithm 3) so that a compromised client cannot retrieve a file that has expired even with the private key.

3. **Oblivious expiration control.** During OblivExp and OblivData, OblivShare uses S2PC protocols to perform expiration control (line 7–11 in Algorithm 3 and the first stage of SS-DOT that samples random keys in line 2(a)–2(d) in Algorithm 4). The security of S2PC guarantees neither server learns or tampers the expiration control result.

4. **Oblivious file sharing.** The obliviousness of ORAM guarantees that file access patterns are hidden from the servers.

5. **Download timestamp integrity.** (line 1–2 in Algorithm 3) The security of S2PC guarantees neither server learns the input timestamp of the other hence cannot modify the actual timestamp or fabricate a new timestamp that is used in the following expiration control operation (line 9 in Algorithm 3).

6. **General metadata protection.** OblivShare makes the anonymous network assumptions in Sect. 4.2 that users' identities and their online activity are encrypted during client-server communications through existing secure tools [4,29]. OblivShare also encrypts metadata such as file name, size, type in the same way as it does for a file hence addresses general metadata privacy in file sharing.

Non-guarantees. As stated in Sect. 4.2, OblivShare does not address DoS attacks by a server, neither protects from malicious server(s), which means OblivShare does not guarantee the availability of a file if a dishonest server denies a valid download request.

5.5 Performance

We consider the system supports N files in total (for simplicity, each file is a single block hence N data blocks) with block size S in DataORAM. As a result of METAL's synchronised inside-outside ORAM trees, the cost for accessing small metadata blocks in ExpORAM is negligible and considered as constant comparing to accessing large data blocks in DataORAM [3]. We use $\mathcal{O}_\lambda(\cdot)$ to present the complexity, while N_{block} is polynomially bounded by λ. We parameterise to have $\frac{1}{N^{\omega(1)}}$ failure probability that is the same as Circuit ORAM [32].

The amortised computational cost of Circuit ORAM is $\mathcal{O}_\lambda((S+\log_N^2)\log N)\cdot \omega(1)$, and OblivShare has minimal additional cost on top of Circuit ORAM. The file access, i.e., read and write operations in OblivShare's Upload and Download are indistinguishable and have the same cost that includes the cost of Circuit ORAM, SS-DOT and distributed permutation. During Download, OblivShare's expiration control incurs additional cost.

The cost for creating download timestamp (line 1–2 in Algorithm 3) is $\mathcal{O}_\lambda(1)$. Expiration control is independent of data blocks in DataORAM and has constant cost $\mathcal{O}_\lambda(1)$ (line 3–12 in Algorithm 3). The total cost of SS-DOT, including Server 1 fetching blocks (line 1(a) in Algorithm 4), the S2PC generating keys (line 2(d)

Table 4. Total computational complexity for `Upload` and `Download` stages.

Stage	Computational complexity
`Upload`	$\mathcal{O}_\lambda((S + \log_N^2) \log N + \log N) \cdot \omega(1) = \mathcal{O}_\lambda((S + \log_N^2) \log N) \cdot \omega(1)$
`Download`	$\mathcal{O}_\lambda((S + \log_N^2) \log N + \log N + 1) \cdot \omega(1) = \mathcal{O}_\lambda((S + \log_N^2) \log N) \cdot \omega(1)$

in Algorithm 4), Server 1 encrypting blocks (line 3(b) in Algorithm 4), and the maximum cost of Server 2 decrypting blocks (line 4(b) in Algorithm 4), is linear to the number of blocks fetched on the path and in the stash (with constant size) hence is $\mathcal{O}_\lambda(\log N)$. Distributed permutation also has total cost linear to the blocks on the paths and in the stash (line 1 in Algorithm 5), therefore $\mathcal{O}_\lambda(\log N)$.

Table 4 summaries the above cost and the total computational complexity of OblivShare for both `Upload` and `Download` is $\mathcal{O}_\lambda((S + \log_N^2) \log N) \cdot \omega(1)$. `Upload` and `Download` have the same computational complexity and communication complexity following Metal's protocol [3], which is linear to the file size S and poly-logarithmic to the number of files N.

6   Conclusion

We propose OblivShare, a lightweight privacy-preserving file sharing scheme that for the first time protects expiration metadata together with file access patterns from servers meanwhile ensures oblivious expiration control by adopting cryptography protocols like secure computation and ORAM. We prove that our protocol can achieve its security goals without additional cost that the computation and communication complexity is poly-logarithmic to the number of files. The current framework focuses on semi-honest thread models and we consider malicious security setting as future work. Corresponding prototype implementation and evaluation will also be part of the future work to prove practicality of the proposed protocol.

A   METAL's Synchronised Inside-Outside ORAM Trees

A.1   Secret-Shared Doubly Oblivious Transfer

Let N be an array of the blocks in the stash and the $3h$ blocks on path p:

1. The two servers inside S2PC, generate n keys $k_1, \ldots, k_n$ such that S1 receives as output all these keys, and S2 receives only k_i. $n = |stash| + 3h + 1$.
2. For each $j \in 1, \ldots, n$, S1 uses k_j to encrypt 0 and m_j to obtain cipher-texts z_j and c_j respectively. S1 shuffles all the (z_j, c_j) pairs and sends them to S2.
3. S2 uses k_i to decrypt the first cipher-text of each pair: only one z_j, will decrypt to 0. It then decrypts the corresponding c_j and hence obtain m_i.

Algorithm 4: OblivData.Fetch

---

1 **Input of S1:** $[i]^1, p, DataORAM$
2 **Input of S2:** $[i]^2$
3 **Output:** m_i

    1. S1:
        (a) $blocks \leftarrow Fetch(DataORAM, p)$. //fetch all blocks in stash and on path p
    2. S2PC:
        (a) $i \leftarrow [i]^1 \oplus [i]^2$
        (b) $blocks.Append(\bot)$; //add a dummy block at the end of the array
        (c) $n \leftarrow |blocks| + 1$; //so that $n = |stash| + 3h + 1$
        (d) **for** $j = 1$ **to** n **do** $k_j \xleftarrow{\$} (0, 1)^l$; //generate n keys
        (e) Outputs $k_1, \ldots, k_n$ to S1 and k_i to S2.
    3. S1:
        (a) $M \leftarrow \{\}[n]$ //initialise an array to store the encrypted pairs
        (b) **for** $j = 1$ **to** n **do** $(z_j, c_j) \leftarrow Enc_{k_j}(0, m_j))$; $M.add((z_j, c_j))$;
        (c) $M.Shuffle()$;
        (d) Sends M to S2.
    4. S2:
        (a) $found \leftarrow FALSE$;
        (b) $p \leftarrow 1$ **while** $p \leq n$ and $!found$ **do**
            i. $(z_p, c_p) \leftarrow M[p - 1]$; $z'_p \leftarrow Dec_{k_i}(z_p)$;
            ii. **if** $z'_p = 0$ **then** $found \leftarrow TRUE$; $m_p \leftarrow Dec_{k_i}(c_p) = m_i$; //$m_i$ is the i-th block on path p in DataORAM
            iii. $p + +$;
        (c) Outputs m_i.

A.2   Distributed Permutation

Recall that Circuit ORAM selects two paths during eviction, hence we need to track the movement of blocks in the stash and on the two paths, which has $|stash| = 6h - 3$ blocks.

Before each eviction, OblivShare appends a number tracker from 1 to $|stash| = 6h - 3$ to each block on the stash and two paths in ExpCtrlORAM inside S2PC. After the ExpCtrlORAM's stash eviction, the protocol extracts the trackers and construct an array of the numbers. Note that some numbers no longer exist as the attaching blocks are removed during the eviction. In order to generate a permeation of the same $|stash| = 6h - 3$ elements, OblivShare searches for the missing trackers using a linear scan and fill in the empty slots with unused numbers.

Below, we present how the two servers in secure computation put a block into the DataORAM's stash before eviction:

1. The S2PC places the following in an array: the blocks in the stash, the block read, and the block to write, which has $(|stash| + 2)$ blocks.
2. The S2PC finds that the k-th block of the stash is vacant, then generates a permutation σ^{read} or σ^{write}, which exchanges the k-th block with the read block for σ^{read} or the block to write for σ^{write}. As a result, the correct block is inserted into the stash (i.e. the first $|stash|$ blocks of the permuted array).

Algorithm 5: OblivData.Sync

---

1 **Input of S2PC:** M

2 **Output:** M'

   1. **for** $i = 0$ **to** $|stash| + 6h - 4$ **do** $M[i].Append(i + 1)$; //attach a tracker to each block before ExpCtrlORAM's stash eviction

   2. $M' \leftarrow ExpCtrlORAM.Evict()$; //extract trackers after stash eviction

   3. $trackers \leftarrow \{\}$; //initialise an array to store the missing trackers
      //do a linear scan to find numbers in $\{1, 2, \ldots, |stash| + 6h - 3\}$ that are missing

   4. **for** $t = 1$ **to** $|stash| + 6h - 3$ **do**
      (a) $found \leftarrow FALSE$;
      (b) $k \leftarrow 0$ **while** $k \leq 18$ and $!found$ **do**
          i. **if** $M'[k] = t$ **then** $found = TRUE$;
          ii. **else** $k + +$;
      (c) **if** $!found$ **then**
          i. $trackers.add(i)$;
      (d) $t + +$
      //do a linear scan to fill missing trackers into the empty slots

   5. $r \leftarrow 0$

   6. **for** $j = 0$ **to** $|stash| + 6h - 4$ **do**
      (a) **if** $M'[j] = \bot$ **then** $M'[j] = trackers[r]$; $r + +$; //locate the empty slots and fill in missing trackers
      (b) $j + +$

   7. $\sigma \leftarrow Permutation.Gen(M, M')$ //generate a permutation σ so that $M' = M \circ \sigma$

   8. $\sigma^1 \leftarrow \$$ //sample a random permutation

   9. $\sigma^2 \leftarrow \sigma \circ (\sigma^1)^{-1}$ //composition of σ and inversion of σ^1

  10. Outputs σ^1 to S1 and σ^2 to S2;

  11. S1:
      (a) Re-randomise the cipher-texts of $blocks$;
      (b) $M^1 = M \circ \sigma^1$; //apply σ^1 to M
      (c) Sends M^1 to S2.

  12. S2:
      (a) Re-randomize the cipher-texts of the blocks in M^1;
      (b) $M^2 = M^1 \circ \sigma^2 = M'$; //apply σ^2 to M^1
      (c) Sends M' to S1.

---

3. The S2PC secret shares the permutation (σ^{read} or σ^{write}) into two permutations σ^1 and σ^2, when $\sigma^2 = \sigma \circ (\sigma^1)^{-1}$. $\circ$ denotes composition of permutation and $\sigma \circ (\sigma)^{-1}$ is the identity permutation.

4. S1 re-randomise the blocks, apply the permutations σ^1, and sends the permuted blocks to S2.

5. S2 re-randomise the blocks received, apply the permutations σ^2, and sends the permuted blocks back to S1.

6. S1 stores the permuted blocks in the corresponding location in DataORAM.

References

1. Backes, M., Herzberg, A., Kate, A., Pryvalov, I.: Anonymous RAM. In: Askoxylakis, I., Ioannidis, S., Katsikas, S., Meadows, C. (eds.) ESORICS 2016. LNCS, vol. 9878, pp. 344–362. Springer, Cham (2016). https://doi.org/10.1007/978-3-319-45744-4_17
2. Bogdanov, D., Niitsoo, M., Toft, T., Willemson, J.: High-performance secure multiparty computation for data mining applications. Int. J. Inf. Secur. 11(6), 403–418 (2012). https://doi.org/10.1007/s10207-012-0177-2
3. Chen, W., Popa, R.A.: Metal: a metadata-hiding file-sharing system. IACR Cryptology ePrint Archive 2020/83 (2020)
4. Dingledine, R., Mathewson, N., Syverson, P.: Tor: the second-generation onion router. Technical report, Naval Research Lab Washington DC (2004)
5. Doerner, J., Shelat, A.: Scaling ORAM for secure computation. In: Proceedings of the 2017 ACM SIGSAC Conference on Computer and Communications Security, pp. 523–535 (2017)
6. Dropbox: Dropbox Business Security: A Dropbox whitepaper. Technical report, Dropbox (2019)
7. DropSecure: Enabling True File Transfer Security: How DropSecure safeguards your confidential data. Technical report, DropSecure (2019)
8. Fitzpatrick, K.: Password protect files with Digify passkey encryption (2019). https://help.digify.com/en/articles/747136-password-protect-files-with-digify-passkey-encryption
9. Fu, Z., Ren, K., Shu, J., Sun, X., Huang, F.: Enabling personalized search over encrypted outsourced data with efficiency improvement. IEEE Trans. Parallel Distrib. Syst. 27(9), 2546–2559 (2015)
10. Goldreich, O.: Towards a theory of software protection and simulation by oblivious RAMs. In: Proceedings of the Nineteenth Annual ACM Symposium on Theory of Computing, pp. 182–194 (1987)
11. Hamlin, A., Ostrovsky, R., Weiss, M., Wichs, D.: Private anonymous data access. In: Ishai, Y., Rijmen, V. (eds.) EUROCRYPT 2019. LNCS, vol. 11477, pp. 244–273. Springer, Cham (2019). https://doi.org/10.1007/978-3-030-17656-3_9
12. Liang, K., Liu, J.K., Lu, R., Wong, D.S.: Privacy concerns for photo sharing in online social networks. IEEE Internet Comput. 19(2), 58–63 (2015)
13. Liu, W., Wang, Y.B., Jiang, Z.T., Cao, Y.Z.: A protocol for the quantum private comparison of equality with χ-type state. Int. J. Theor. Phys. 51(1), 69–77 (2012). https://doi.org/10.1007/s10773-011-0878-8
14. Maffei, M., Malavolta, G., Reinert, M., Schröder, D.: Privacy and access control for outsourced personal records. In: 2015 IEEE Symposium on Security and Privacy, pp. 341–358. IEEE (2015)
15. Maffei, M., Malavolta, G., Reinert, M., Schröder, D.: Maliciously secure multi-client ORAM. In: Gollmann, D., Miyaji, A., Kikuchi, H. (eds.) ACNS 2017. LNCS, vol. 10355, pp. 645–664. Springer, Cham (2017). https://doi.org/10.1007/978-3-319-61204-1_32
16. McMillan, R., Knutson, R.: Yahoo triples estimate of breached accounts to 3 billion (2017). https://www.wsj.com/articles/yahoo-triples-estimate-of-breached-accounts-to-3-billion-1507062804
17. Nguyen, N.: Introducing Firefox send, providing free file transfers while keeping your personal information private (2019). https://blog.mozilla.org/blog/2019/03/12/introducing-firefox-send-providing-free-file-transfers-while-keeping-your-personal-information-private/

18. Pinkas, B., Reinman, T.: Oblivious RAM revisited. In: Rabin, T. (ed.) CRYPTO 2010. LNCS, vol. 6223, pp. 502–519. Springer, Heidelberg (2010). https://doi.org/10.1007/978-3-642-14623-7_27

19. Regulation, G.D.P.: Regulation (EU) 2016/679 of the European parliament and of the council of 27 April 2016 on the protection of natural persons with regard to the processing of personal data and on the free movement of such data, and repealing directive 95/46. Off. J. Eur. Union (OJ) **59**(1–88), 294 (2016)

20. Roche, D.S., Aviv, A., Choi, S.G.: A practical oblivious map data structure with secure deletion and history independence. In: 2016 IEEE Symposium on Security and Privacy (SP), pp. 178–197. IEEE (2016)

21. Rösler, P., Mainka, C., Schwenk, J.: More is less: on the end-to-end security of group chats in Signal, WhatsApp, and Threema. In: 2018 IEEE European Symposium on Security and Privacy (EuroS&P), pp. 415–429. IEEE (2018)

22. Rusbridger, A.: The Snowden leaks and the public (2013)

23. Schneier, B.: Data and Goliath: The Hidden Battles to Collect Your Data and Control Your World. WW Norton & Company, New York (2015)

24. SendSafely: Powerful security that's simple to use (2019). https://www.sendsafely.com/howitworks/

25. Shi, E., Chan, T.-H.H., Stefanov, E., Li, M.: Oblivious RAM with $O((\log N)^3)$ worst-case cost. In: Lee, D.H., Wang, X. (eds.) ASIACRYPT 2011. LNCS, vol. 7073, pp. 197–214. Springer, Heidelberg (2011). https://doi.org/10.1007/978-3-642-25385-0_11

26. Shundong, L., Chunying, W., Daoshun, W., Yiqi, D.: Secure multiparty computation of solid geometric problems and their applications. Inf. Sci. **282**, 401–413 (2014)

27. Silverstein, J.: Hundreds of millions of Facebook user records were exposed on amazon cloud server (2019). https://www.cbsnews.com/news/millions-facebook-user-records-exposed-amazon-cloud-server/

28. Stefanov, E., et al.: Path ORAM: an extremely simple oblivious RAM protocol. In: Proceedings of the 2013 ACM SIGSAC Conference on Computer & Communications Security, pp. 299–310 (2013)

29. Telegram: What is a secret chat in Telegram (2019). https://telegramguide.com/secret-chat-telegram/

30. Toft, T.: Secure data structures based on multi-party computation. In: Proceedings of the 30th Annual ACM SIGACT-SIGOPS Symposium on Principles of Distributed Computing, pp. 291–292 (2011)

31. de la Torre, L.: A guide to the California consumer privacy act of 2018. SSRN 3275571 (2018)

32. Wang, X., Chan, H., Shi, E.: Circuit ORAM: on tightness of the Goldreich-Ostrovsky lower bound. In: Proceedings of the 22nd ACM SIGSAC Conference on Computer and Communications Security, pp. 850–861 (2015)

33. Wang, X.S., Huang, Y., Chan, T.H., Shelat, A., Shi, E.: SCORAM: oblivious RAM for secure computation. In: Proceedings of the 2014 ACM SIGSAC Conference on Computer and Communications Security, pp. 191–202 (2014)

34. WhatsApp: WhatsApp encryption overview: technical white paper. Technical report, WhatsApp (2017)

35. Yao, A.C.C.: How to generate and exchange secrets. In: 27th Annual Symposium on Foundations of Computer Science (SFCS 1986), pp. 162–167. IEEE (1986)

36. Zahur, S., et al.: Revisiting square-root ORAM: efficient random access in multi-party computation. In: 2016 IEEE Symposium on Security and Privacy (SP), pp. 218–234. IEEE (2016)

37. Zuo, C., Shao, J., Liu, J.K., Wei, G., Ling, Y.: Fine-grained two-factor protection mechanism for data sharing in cloud storage. IEEE Trans. Inf. Forensics Secur. **13**(1), 186–196 (2018)

Automatic Key Recovery of Feistel Ciphers: Application to SIMON and SIMECK

Yingjie Zhang[1,2]([✉]), Lijun Lyu[3,4], Kexin Qiao[5], Zhiyu Zhang[3,4], Siwei Sun[6,7], and Lei Hu[3,4]

[1] Ding Lab, Yanqi Lake Beijing Institute of Mathematical Sciences and Applications, Beijing 101408, China
zhangyingjie161@mails.ucas.ac.cn

[2] Yau Mathematical Sciences Center, Tsinghua University, Beijing 100084, China

[3] School of Cyber Security, University of Chinese Academy of Sciences, Beijing 100049, China
{lvlijun,zhangzhiyu,hulei}@iie.ac.cn

[4] SKLOIS, Institute of Information Engineering, CAS, Beijing 100093, China

[5] School of Cyberspace Science and Technology, Beijing Institute of Technology, Beijing 100081, China
qiao.kexin@bit.edu.cn

[6] School of Cryptology, University of Chinese Academy of Sciences, Beijing 100049, China

[7] State Key Laboratory of Cryptology, P.O. Box 5159, Beijing 100878, China

Abstract. Linear cryptanalysis is one of the most effective statistical analysis methods on symmetric-key ciphers. It has benefited from many improvements since being proposed. Among these works, Antonio *et al.* proposed a fast arbitrary-round key recovery method based on Fast Walsh-Hadamard Transform (FWHT) in EUROCRYPT 2020. However, they did not promote their method on the Feistel structure, which is used widely. In addition, there are very few automatic methods for the key recovery phase.

This paper extends Antonio *et al.*'s method to the Feistel structure and builds a Mixed-Integer Linear Programming (MILP) model to determine the guessed subkeys automatically. Due to this, we can automatically optimize the time complexity of linear cryptanalysis. Afterward, we apply our method to SIMON and SIMECK and increase the attackable rounds of SIMON64/96, SIMON64/128, SIMON96/96, SIMON96/144, SIMECK48/96, and SIMECK64/128 by one round to 31, 32, 38, 39, 31, and 38, respectively.

Keywords: Linear cryptanalysis · Matsui's Algorithm 2 · FWHT · MILP · Feistel structure · SIMON · SIMECK

The original version of this chapter was revised: this chapter contained one mistake. This has been corrected. The correction to this chapter is available at https://doi.org/10.1007/978-3-030-93206-0_24

1   Introduction

Linear cryptanalysis was proposed by Matsui in 1993 [17], and it is one of the most effective statistical analysis methods on symmetric-key ciphers. Its main idea is to search for linear correlations between some bits of plaintext, key, and ciphertext and use this specific property to recover some key bits. Since being proposed, linear cryptanalysis has benefited from many improvements. For example, linear hull cryptanalysis [21] deepens the understanding of the underlying principles of linear attacks; multiple linear attacks [4,14], multidimensional linear attacks [12] and multivariate linear attacks [5] reduce the complexity by exploiting several linear approximations at the same time.

For the key recovery phase of linear cryptanalysis, Matsui proposed the partial key recovery attack known as Matsui's Algorithm 2 in the form of the last round attack [17], the data complexity is $N = \mathcal{O}(1/c^2)$, and the time complexity is $\mathcal{O}(N2^{|k_r|})$, where c is the correlation of distinguisher and k_r is the round key of the last round. Then, Matsui pointed out that the time complexity could be reduced to $\mathcal{O}(N + 2^{2|k_r|})$ by a distillation phase when $2^{k_r} < N$ [18]. Furthermore, Collard *et al.* used FWHT to reduce the time complexity to $\mathcal{O}(N + |k_r|2^{|k_r|})$ [7]. Subsequently, Nguyen *et al.* extended the FWHT-based Matsui Algorithm 2 to multidimensional linear cryptanalysis [20]. However, the FWHT-based key recovery has not been generalized to arbitrary-round key recovery until Eurocrypt 2020 [9]. Antonio *et al.* proposed a fast arbitrary-round key recovery method based on FWHT and extended it to multiple and multidimensional linear cryptanalysis. Nevertheless, they did not promote their method to Feistel structure. There are many ciphers based on Feistel structure, so it is significant to capture the influence of FWHT-based key recovery method on Feistel structure.

Recently, the MILP-based method is getting more and more popular in the field of cryptanalysis [8,10,19,23,25–28]. However, the MILP-based linear cryptanalysis [25,26] mainly focuses on the distinguisher searching phase rather than the key recovery phase. To the best of our knowledge, only Zong *et al.* addressed the automatic method for key recovery phase in FSE 2021 [31]. They proposed a two-step strategy to search for key-recovery-attack friendly distinguishers and applied it to GIFT-128. As they only modeled SBox and bit-wise permutation but not COPY, AND, and XOR, we cannot directly apply their method to the Feistel structure.

The best linear cryptanalysis on SIMON and SIMECK are derived from dynamic key-guessing attacks [1,6,22][1]. Also, there are some better linear hulls of SIMON and SIMECK in [13,16,25,26]. However, [13,16] do not utilise the linear hulls to carry out key recovery attack. As mentioned in [13], *the process of dynamic key-guessing attack is too cumbersome*. Since each step of the attack requires carefully manual derivation of the algorithm details, it is not easy to quickly find the best key recovery. On the other hand, the results of Matsui Algorithm 2 based key recovery attack in [25,26] are not as good as the results of dynamic key-guessing attack in [6]. So, it is urgent to develop automatic tools to calculate key recovery complexity with given linear distinguishers, such as the FWHT-based key recovery method procedure.

---

[1] After submitting this paper, Gaëtan *et al.* give better linear cryptanalysis on SIMON and SIMECK by exploring the clustering effect [15], and they also generalize the FWHT-based arbitrary-round key recovery method to Feistel structure.

Our Contribution. First, we generalize the FWHT-based arbitrary-round key recovery method proposed by Antonio *et al.* to Feistel structure. Furthermore, we propose a MILP modeling strategy to automatically determine the guessed subkeys whose size determines the time complexity of the whole linear cryptanalysis. Thus the complexity can also be given automatically. Finally, using known linear hulls, we increase the attackable rounds of SIMON64/96, SIMON64/128, SIMON96/96, SIMON96/144, SIMECK48/96, and SIMECK64/128 by one round to 31, 32, 38, 39, 31, and 38, respectively. The results are listed in Table 4.

Organization. In Sect. 2, we present the notations and preliminaries that will be used throughout the paper. In Sect. 3, we generalize the FWHT-based arbitrary-round key recovery method proposed by Antonio *et al.* to Feistel structure. In Sect. 4, we implement a MILP-based automatic tool to find guessed subkeys and introduce some strategies to search for relationship between these subkeys. In Sect. 5, we give efficient key recovery attacks on SIMON and SIMECK using the tool proposed in Sect. 4. The conclusion of this paper is in Sect. 6.

2   Preliminaries

2.1   Notations

- P/C : plaintext/ciphertext
- k_i : subkey used in round i; i begins with 1 in this paper
- $x[j]$: j-th bit of x; the leftmost bit of x is denoted as $x[0]$
- $x \lll l$: x rotates left by l bits
- $\oplus$: bitwise XOR
- $\&$: bitwise AND
- F_{k_i} : the round function with subkey k_i
- $E_\kappa(P)$: encrypt plaintext P with master key κ.

Following are some notations only used for Feistel ciphers.

- P_L/P_R, C_L/C_R : left/right half of P and C
- L_i/R_i : left/right half output of i-th round
- F : non-linear function whose input is the left half of round function input.

2.2   Linear Cryptanalysis

Linear cryptanalysis [17] was used initially to attack DES. It is a known-plaintext attack, which assumes that the attacker knows some plaintext-ciphertext pairs. Its main idea is to search for linear approximation functions about some bits of the plaintext, key, and ciphertext and use this specific property to perform a distinguishing attack or recover some bits of the key.

Matsui's last round key recovery attack [17] separates the last round of the cipher as follow

$$E_\kappa(P) = (\bar{F} \circ E'_\kappa)(P) \oplus k_r,$$

where E'_κ is the composition of the first $(R-1)$ round functions and $\bar{F}$ is the last round function without key addition. To carry out linear attack, the attacker tries to find a correlated linear approximation $\alpha \cdot P \oplus \beta \cdot y \oplus \gamma \cdot K$ of E'_κ whose correlation is c, where $y = F^{-1}_{k_r}(C)$ is the output of E'_κ and $K = k_1 || \cdots || k_{r-1}$. Let

$$f(C|_\chi \oplus \bar{k}_r) = \beta \cdot \bar{F}^{-1}(C \oplus k_r),$$

where $C|_\chi$ and $\bar{k}_r$ denotes the relevant bits of C and k_r to decrypt part of the last round, we call $\bar{k}_r$ **guessed subkeys**. Then, given a plaintext-ciphertext data set $\mathcal{D}$ of size N, the attacker can recover $\bar{k}_r$ with Algorithm 1 based on the assumption that for any wrong guess of $\bar{k}_r$, the linear approximation will have value 0 with probability $1/2$.

Algorithm 1: Matsui's Algorithm 2 [17]

Input: A set $\mathcal{D} = \{(P, C = E_\kappa(P))\}$ of N plaintext-ciphertext pairs.
Output: A probable guess for $\bar{k}_r$.

1 **begin**
2    $\mathbf{T} \leftarrow 0$
3   // Compute $\mathbf{T}_i = \#\{(P, C) \in \mathcal{D} : \alpha \cdot P \oplus f(C|_\chi \oplus i) = 0\}$
4   **forall** $(P, C) \in \mathcal{D}$ **do**
5   **for** $i \leftarrow 0$ **to** $2^{|\bar{k}_r|} - 1$ **do**
6   **if** $\alpha \cdot P \oplus f(C|_\chi \oplus i) = 0$ **then** $\mathbf{T}_i \leftarrow \mathbf{T}_i + 1$;
7   **end**
8   **end**
9   **return** $argmax_i(|T_i - N/2|)$;   // Find the T_i most different to $N/2$
10 **end**

Selçuk introduced advantage to measure the effectiveness of Algorithm 1 based attack [24], and we use the same description as Antonio *et al.* in [9].

Definition 1 (Attack Advantage [24]). *An Algorithm 1 based attack achieveves an advantage of a bits if the right key ranks among the best $2^{\kappa-a}$ key candidates.*

Theorem 1 (Success Probability [24]). *The success probability is the probability that the actual advantage surpasses a, where a is the desired advantage. Assume the key-ranking statistical data q_k has the cumulative distribution function F_R for the right key guess and F_W for any wrong guess, then the success probability of the associated statistical attack for a given desired advantage a is*

$$P_S = 1 - F_R(F_W^{-1}(1 - 2^{-a})).$$

The successful probability of Algorithm 1 is reasonable when $N = \mathcal{O}(1/c^2)$. In 1994, Nyberg improved the successful probability by introduced the definition of linear hull [21]. A **linear hull** is the set of linear approximations sharing the same input-output masks. A linear hull with input mask α and output mask β is denoted as (α, β). The **potential** of (α, β) is defined as follow, where $c(\alpha, \beta, \gamma)$ is the correlation of a linear approximation.

$$ALH(\alpha, \beta) = \text{Exp}_\kappa(c(\alpha, \beta)^2) = \sum_\gamma c(\alpha, \beta, \gamma)^2.$$

For a linear approximation with correlation c or a linear hull with potential c^2, the relationship between a and P_S is shown in Table 1.

Table 1. Probability of achieving an a-bit advantage with $N = 4C_N|c|^{-2}$ plaintext-ciphertext pairs [24].

P_S \ C_N a	2^{-2}	2^{-1}	1	2	4	8	16	32	64
1	0.628	0.770	0.908	0.984	1.000	1.000	1.000	1.000	1.000
2	0.440	0.604	0.802	0.953	0.998	1.000	1.000	1.000	1.000
4	0.194	0.327	0.555	0.833	0.984	1.000	1.000	1.000	1.000
8	0.030	0.071	0.188	0.477	0.867	0.997	1.000	1.000	1.000
12	0.004	0.012	0.048	0.200	0.630	0.977	1.000	1.000	1.000
16	0.000	0.002	0.010	0.067	0.373	0.909	1.000	1.000	1.000
32	0.000	0.000	0.000	0.000	0.010	0.248	0.952	1.000	1.000

The time complexity of Algorithm 1 is $\mathcal{O}(N2^{|\bar{k}_r|})$ one-round decryptions with an additional $2^{|\kappa|-|\bar{k}_r|}$ full encryptions if attacker searches the rest of the key exhaustively. The memory requirement is $2^{|\bar{k}_r|} \cdot |\log N|$ bits. In [18], Matsui noted that the time complexity could be reduced to $\mathcal{O}(N + 2^{2|\bar{k}_r|})$ by distillation when $2^{|\bar{k}_r|} < N$, which is often the case.

In addition, Algorithm 1 can also be used in multiple-round key recovery, which covers an arbitrary number of rounds at both the beginning and the end of the cipher. The time complexity increases with the number of guessed subkeys.

2.3 Description of SIMON and SIMECK

SIMON is a family of lightweight block ciphers with Feistel structure published by the NSA in 2013 [3]. It aims to achieve optimal performance in hardware environment. SIMON with block size $2n$-bit is denoted by SIMON$2n$ and SIMON$2n$ with mn-bit key is represented by SIMON$2n/mn$. The parameters of different SIMON instances are summarized in Table 2. The i-th round function $F_{k_i} : \mathbb{F}_2^n \times \mathbb{F}_2^n \to \mathbb{F}_2^n \times \mathbb{F}_2^n$ of SIMON$2n$ is defined as

$$(L_i, R_i) = F_{k_i}((L_{i-1}, R_{i-1})) = (F(L_{i-1}) \oplus R_{i-1} \oplus k_i, L_{i-1}).$$

$F : \mathbb{F}_2^n \to \mathbb{F}_2^n$ is defined as follow, where $(a, b, c) = (1, 8, 2)$.

$$F(L_i) = (L_i \lll a)\&(L_i \lll b) \oplus (L_i \lll c).$$

SIMECK family of lightweight block ciphers were proposed by Yang $et\ al.$ at CHES 2015 [29]. It aims to get a more efficient hardware implementation by combining the good components of SIMON and SPECK. SIMECK with block size $2n$-bit and key size mn-bit is represented by SIMECK$2n/mn$. There are three variants of SIMECK family: SIMECK32/64 (32 rounds), SIMECK48/96

Table 2. Parameters for SIMON2n/mn

2n/mn	32/64	48/72	48/96	64/96	64/128	96/96	96/144	128/128	128/192	128/256
Rounds	32	36	36	42	44	52	54	68	69	72

(36 rounds), SIMECK64/128 (44 rounds). The round function of SIMECK is the same as SIMON's except that $(a, b, c) = (0, 5, 1)$ in SIMECK.

SIMON has linear key schedule while SIMECK reuses the nonlinear function F in key schedule. Please refer to [3,29] for more details.

3   Efficient Key Recovery with FWHT

Collard *et al.* reduced the time complexity of Algorithm 1 to $\mathcal{O}(|\bar{k}_r|2^{|\bar{k}_r|})$ by FWHT [7], and Antonio *et al.* generalized Collard *et al.*'s method to an arbitrary number of key recovery rounds and multiple linear cryptanalysis [9]. We will introduce Antonio *et al.*'s method and then generalize it to Feistel structure.

We first review the following two propositions.

Proposition 1 (Matrix Diagonalization [11]). *Let* $f : \mathbb{F}_2^m \to \mathbb{F}_2$ *be a boolean function. We consider a matrix* $M \in \mathbb{Z}^{2^m \times 2^m}$ *whose entries are of the form*

$$m_{ij} = (-1)^{f(i \oplus j)}, \quad 0 \le i, j \le 2^m - 1.$$

This matrix diagonalizes as $2^m M = H_{2^m} \triangle H_{2^m}$*, where* H_{2^m} *is the Hadamard-Sylvester matrix of size* 2^m *whose entries are* $h_{ij} = (-1)^{i \cdot j}$*, and* $\triangle = diag(\boldsymbol{\lambda})$ *is a diagonal matrix,* $\boldsymbol{\lambda} = H_{2^m} M_{\cdot 1} \in \mathbb{Z}^{2^m}$*.*

Hadamard-Sylvester matrices are symmetric orthogonal matrices. Proposition 1 shows that when entries in matrix M are of the form $m_{ij} = (-1)^{f(i \oplus j)}$, the first column of M contains the information of the entire M.

Proposition 2 (Acceleration with FWHT [30]). $H_{2^m}\mathbf{v}$ *can be evaluated efficiently with the Fast Walsh-Hadamard Transform (sometimes called Fast Walsh Transform or simply FWHT or FWT) with* $|\mathbf{v}|2^{|\mathbf{v}|}$ *additions/substractions, where* $\mathbf{v}$ *is a* 2^m*-dimensional column vector whose entries are integers.*

See [9,30] for more details of FWHT.

3.1   Efficient Arbitrary-Round Key Recovery

The FWHT-based arbitrary-round key recovery method proposed by Antonio *et al.* [9] applies to block ciphers that can be separated into

$$E_\kappa(X) = E_2 \circ E_M \circ E_1(X \oplus K_0) \oplus K_3.$$

Note that plaintext-ciphertext is represented as (X, Y) instead of (P, C) in this subsection to avoid symbol confusion in Sect. 4. As shown in Fig. 1, $\hat{X}$ and $\hat{Y}$

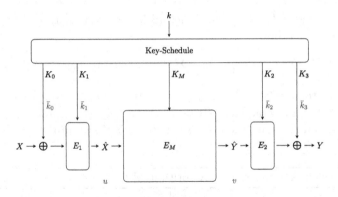

Fig. 1. The decomposition of E_κ.

are input and output of E_M. Assume the attacker knows a correlated linear approximation (α, β) of E_M. Let

$$
\begin{aligned}
f_1(X|_{\chi_0} \oplus \bar{k}_0, \bar{k}_1) &= \alpha \cdot E_1(X \oplus K_0, K_1), \\
f_2(Y|_{\chi_3} \oplus \bar{k}_3, \bar{k}_2) &= \beta \cdot E_2^{-1}(Y \oplus K_3, K_2),
\end{aligned}
\tag{1}
$$

where $X|_{\chi_0}$, $Y|_{\chi_3}$, $\bar{k}_0$, $\bar{k}_1$, $\bar{k}_2$ and $\bar{k}_3$ denote the relevant bits of X, Y, K_0, K_1, K_2 and K_3 to compute $\alpha \cdot \hat{X} \oplus \beta \cdot \hat{Y}$. Given a plaintext-ciphertext data set $\mathcal{D}$ of size N, for each possible guess of subkeys, the attacker need to compute

$$
\begin{aligned}
q(\bar{k}_0, \bar{k}_1, \bar{k}_2, \bar{k}_3) &= \#\{(X,Y) \in \mathcal{D} : f_1(X|_{\chi_0} \oplus \bar{k}_0, \bar{k}_1) \oplus f_2(Y|_{\chi_3} \oplus \bar{k}_3, \bar{k}_2) = 0\} \\
&\quad - \#\{(X,Y) \in \mathcal{D} : f_1(X|_{\chi_0} \oplus \bar{k}_0, \bar{k}_1) \oplus f_2(Y|_{\chi_3} \oplus \bar{k}_3, \bar{k}_2) = 1\} \\
&= \sum_{i=0}^{2^{|\bar{k}_0|-1}} \sum_{j=0}^{2^{|\bar{k}_3|-1}} \left(\sum_{\substack{(X,Y) \in \mathcal{D} \\ X|_{\chi_0}=i, Y|_{\chi_3}=j}} 1 \right) (-1)^{f_1(i \oplus \bar{k}_0, \bar{k}_1)} (-1)^{f_2(j \oplus \bar{k}_3, \bar{k}_2)}.
\end{aligned}
$$

When $\bar{k}_1$ and $\bar{k}_2$ are fixed, we can define $Q^{\bar{k}_1, \bar{k}_2} \in \mathbb{Z}^{2^{|\bar{k}_0|} \times 2^{|\bar{k}_3|}}$ with entries $q_{\bar{k}_0, \bar{k}_3}^{\bar{k}_1, \bar{k}_2} = q(\bar{k}_0, \bar{k}_1, \bar{k}_2, \bar{k}_3)$. The whole linear attack turns to calculating $Q^{\bar{k}_1, \bar{k}_2}$ under all possible values of k_1, k_2. The top maximum arguments in $Q^{\bar{k}_1, \bar{k}_2}$ indicate the candidates of right guesses of K_1, K_2, K_3, K_4. We can decompose $Q^{\bar{k}_1, \bar{k}_2}$ into $B^{\bar{k}_1} A M^{\bar{k}_2}$, where $A \in \mathbb{Z}^{2^{|\bar{k}_0|} \times 2^{|\bar{k}_3|}}$, $B^{\bar{k}_1} \in \mathbb{Z}^{2^{|\bar{k}_0|} \times 2^{|\bar{k}_0|}}$ and $M^{\bar{k}_2} \in \mathbb{Z}^{2^{|\bar{k}_3|} \times 2^{|\bar{k}_3|}}$. The entries of these matrices are

$$
\begin{aligned}
a_{ij} &= \#\{(X,Y) \in \mathcal{D} : X|_{\chi_0} = i, Y|_{\chi_3} = j\}, \\
b_{\bar{k}_0, i}^{\bar{k}_1} &= (-1)^{f_1(i \oplus \bar{k}_0, \bar{k}_1)}, \quad m_{j, \bar{k}_3}^{\bar{k}_2} = (-1)^{f_2(j \oplus \bar{k}_3, \bar{k}_2)}.
\end{aligned}
$$

Matrices $B^{\bar{k}_1}$ and $M^{\bar{k}_2}$ obey the structure in Proposition 1, so $Q^{\bar{k}_1,\bar{k}_2}$ can be further decomposed into

$$2^{|\bar{k}_0|+|\bar{k}_3|}Q^{\bar{k}_1,\bar{k}_2} = H_{2^{|\bar{k}_0|}}\mathrm{diag}(\boldsymbol{\lambda}_1^{\bar{k}_1})H_{2^{|\bar{k}_0|}}AH_{2^{|\bar{k}_3|}}\mathrm{diag}(\boldsymbol{\lambda}_2^{\bar{k}_2})H_{2^{|\bar{k}_3|}},$$

where $\boldsymbol{\lambda}_1^{\bar{k}_1} = H_{2^{|\bar{k}_0|}}B_{\cdot 1}^{\bar{k}_1}$, $\boldsymbol{\lambda}_2^{\bar{k}_2} = H_{2^{|\bar{k}_3|}}M_{\cdot 1}^{\bar{k}_2}$. According to Proposition 2, calculation of $Q^{\bar{k}_1,\bar{k}_2}$ can be accelerated by FWHT. The attack process is shown in Algorithm 2 and the complexity of Algorithm 2 is shown in Proposition 3.

Algorithm 2: Antonio *et al.*'s Algorithm [9] (without final phase)

Input: A set $\mathcal{D} = \{(P, C = E_\kappa(P))\}$ of N plaintext-ciphertext pairs.
Output: Some probable guesses for $(\bar{k}_0, \bar{k}_1, \bar{k}_2, \bar{k}_3)$.

1 begin
2   // DISTILLATION PHASE
3    $A \leftarrow \mathbf{0}$
4   **forall** $(X, Y) \in \mathcal{D}$ **do** $a_{X|_{x_0}, Y|_{x_3}} \leftarrow a_{X|_{x_0}, Y|_{x_3}} + 1$;
5   // ANALYSIS PHASE
6   **for** $i \leftarrow 0$ **to** $2^{|\bar{k}_0|} - 1$ **do** $A_{i\cdot} \leftarrow \mathrm{FWHT}(A_{i\cdot})$;   // FWHT on rows of A
7   **for** $j \leftarrow 0$ **to** $2^{|\bar{k}_3|} - 1$ **do** $A_{\cdot j} \leftarrow \mathrm{FWHT}(A_{\cdot j})$;   // FWHT on columns of A
8   **for** $\bar{k}_1 \leftarrow 0$ **to** $2^{|\bar{k}_1|} - 1$ **do**
9   **for** $i \leftarrow 0$ **to** $2^{|\bar{k}_0|} - 1$ **do** $(\lambda_1^{\bar{k}_1})_i \leftarrow (-1)^{f_1(i, \bar{k}_1)}$;   // $B_{\cdot 1}^{\bar{k}_1}$
10      $\boldsymbol{\lambda}_1^{\bar{k}_1} \leftarrow \mathrm{FWHT}(\boldsymbol{\lambda}_1^{\bar{k}_1})$;   // Eigenvalue vector of $H_{2^{|\bar{k}_0|}}B^{\bar{k}_1}$
11   **end**
12   **for** $\bar{k}_2 \leftarrow 0$ **to** $2^{|\bar{k}_2|} - 1$ **do**
13   **for** $j \leftarrow 0$ **to** $2^{|\bar{k}_3|} - 1$ **do** $(\lambda_2^{\bar{k}_2})_j \leftarrow (-1)^{f_2(j, \bar{k}_2)}$;   // $M_{\cdot 1}^{\bar{k}_2}$
14      $\boldsymbol{\lambda}_2^{\bar{k}_2} \leftarrow \mathrm{FWHT}(\boldsymbol{\lambda}_2^{\bar{k}_2})$;   // Eigenvalue vector of $H_{2^{|\bar{k}_3|}}M_{\cdot 1}^{\bar{k}_2}$
15   **end**
16   **for** $\bar{k}_1 \leftarrow 0$ **to** $2^{|\bar{k}_1|} - 1; \bar{k}_2 \leftarrow 0$ **to** $2^{|\bar{k}_2|} - 1$ // Compute $Q^{\bar{k}_1,\bar{k}_2}$
17   **do**
18   **for** $\bar{k}_0 \leftarrow 0$ **to** $2^{|\bar{k}_0|} - 1; \bar{k}_3 \leftarrow 0$ **to** $2^{|\bar{k}_3|} - 1$ **do**
19       $q_{\bar{k}_0, \bar{k}_3}^{\bar{k}_1, \bar{k}_2} = a_{\bar{k}_0, \bar{k}_3} \cdot (\lambda_1^{\bar{k}_1})_{\bar{k}_0} \cdot (\lambda_2^{\bar{k}_2})_{\bar{k}_3}$;
20   **end**
21   **for** $\bar{k}_0 \leftarrow 0$ **to** $2^{|\bar{k}_0|} - 1$ **do**
22       $Q_{\bar{k}_0 \cdot}^{\bar{k}_1, \bar{k}_2} \leftarrow \mathrm{FWHT}(Q_{\bar{k}_0 \cdot}^{\bar{k}_1, \bar{k}_2})$;   // FWHT on rows of $Q^{\bar{k}_1,\bar{k}_2}$
23   **end**
24   **for** $\bar{k}_3 \leftarrow 0$ **to** $2^{|\bar{k}_3|} - 1$ **do**
25       $Q_{\cdot \bar{k}_3}^{\bar{k}_1, \bar{k}_2} \leftarrow \mathrm{FWHT}(Q_{\cdot \bar{k}_3}^{\bar{k}_1, \bar{k}_2})$;   // FWHT on columns of $Q^{\bar{k}_1,\bar{k}_2}$
26   **end**
27   **end**
28   **return** $argmax_{(\bar{k}_0, \bar{k}_1, \bar{k}_2, \bar{k}_3)}(|q_{\bar{k}_0, \bar{k}_3}^{\bar{k}_1, \bar{k}_2}|)$;   // $(\bar{k}_0, \bar{k}_1, \bar{k}_2, \bar{k}_3)$ with max $|q_{\bar{k}_0, \bar{k}_3}^{\bar{k}_1, \bar{k}_2}|$
29 end

Proposition 3 (Complexity of Algorithm 2 [9]). *The time complexity is*

$$\underbrace{\rho_D N}_{\text{distillation phase}} + \underbrace{\rho_A(|\bar{k}_0| + |\bar{k}_3|)2^{|\bar{k}_0| + |\bar{k}_3|}}_{\text{analysis phase 1: FWHT on } A}$$

$$+ \underbrace{\rho_{f_1}2^{|\bar{k}_0| + |\bar{k}_1|} + \rho_{f_2}2^{|\bar{k}_2| + |\bar{k}_3|} + \rho_A\left(|\bar{k}_0|2^{|\bar{k}_0| + |\bar{k}_1|} + |\bar{k}_3|2^{|\bar{k}_2| + |\bar{k}_3|}\right)}_{\text{analysis phase 2: compute eigenvalue vectors}}$$

$$+ \underbrace{2\rho_M 2^{|\bar{k}_0| + |\bar{k}_1| + |\bar{k}_2| + |\bar{k}_3|} + \rho_A(|\bar{k}_0| + |\bar{k}_3|)2^{|\bar{k}_0| + |\bar{k}_1| + |\bar{k}_2| + |\bar{k}_3|}}_{\text{analysis phase 3: compute } Q^{\bar{k}_1, \bar{k}_2} \text{ for all the values of } \bar{k}_1 \text{ and } \bar{k}_2}$$

$$+ \underbrace{\rho_C 2^{|\bar{k}_0| + |\bar{k}_1| + |\bar{k}_2| + |\bar{k}_3|}}_{\text{analysis phase 4: find probable subkeys}} + \underbrace{\rho_E 2^{\kappa - a}}_{\text{exhaustive search phase}}.$$

Where ρ_D is the cost of checking a plaintext-ciphertext pair in distillation phase; ρ_{f_1} and ρ_{f_2} are the costs of computing $(\lambda_1^{\bar{k}_1})_i$ and $(\lambda_2^{\bar{k}_2})_j$, respectively, which are usually less than one-round encryption; ρ_A, ρ_M, ρ_C are the costs of adding, multiplying and comparing two integers, respectively; ρ_E is the cost of full encryption; a is the attack advantage[2]. The memory requirement is

$$\underbrace{2^{|\bar{k}_0| + |\bar{k}_3|} \cdot n}_{A} + \underbrace{(2^{|\bar{k}_0| + |\bar{k}_1|} + 2^{|\bar{k}_2| + |\bar{k}_3|}) \cdot \max\{|\bar{k}_0|, |\bar{k}_3|\}}_{\text{eigenvalue vectors}} + \underbrace{2^{|\bar{k}_0| + |\bar{k}_3|} \cdot (n + |\bar{k}_0| + |\bar{k}_3|)}_{Q^{\bar{k}_1, \bar{k}_2}}$$

bits, where n is block size. When $Q^{\bar{k}_1, \bar{k}_2}$ needs to be stored in full, the last term of memory requirement becomes $2^{|\bar{k}_0| + |\bar{k}_1| + |\bar{k}_2| + |\bar{k}_3|} \cdot n$.

Furthermore, the dependencies between $\bar{k}_0$, $\bar{k}_1$, $\bar{k}_2$ and $\bar{k}_3$ help to reduce the cost of computing $Q^{\bar{k}_1, \bar{k}_2}$. When $(\bar{k}_1, \bar{k}_2)$ can only take $2^{|\bar{k}_1| + |\bar{k}_2| - l_{12}}$ different values, l_0 bits of $\bar{k}_0$ can be computed from $(\bar{k}_1, \bar{k}_2)$ and l_3 bits of $\bar{k}_3$ can be computed from $(\bar{k}_0, \bar{k}_1, \bar{k}_2)$, then the time cost of evaluating $Q^{\bar{k}_1, \bar{k}_2}$ becomes

$$2\rho_M 2^{|\bar{k}_0| + |\bar{k}_1| + |\bar{k}_2| + |\bar{k}_3| - l_{12}} + \rho_A 2^{|\bar{k}_1| + |\bar{k}_2| + |\bar{k}_3| - l_{12}}\left(2^{|\bar{k}_0|} + (|\bar{k}_0| - l_0 - 1)2^{|\bar{k}_0| - l_0}\right)$$

$$+ \rho_A 2^{|\bar{k}_0| - l_0 + |\bar{k}_1| + |\bar{k}_2| - l_{12}}\left(2^{|\bar{k}_3|} + (|\bar{k}_3| - l_3 - 1)2^{|\bar{k}_3| - l_3}\right),$$

and the memory becomes $2^{|\bar{k}_0| + |\bar{k}_1| + |\bar{k}_2| + |\bar{k}_3| - l_{12} - l_0 - l_3} \cdot n$ bits.

3.2 Extended Algorithm – Efficient Arbitrary-Round Key Recovery of Feistel Ciphers

As the precondition of FWHT-based acceleration is the diagonalization of the matrix whose elements are of the form $(-1)^{f(i \oplus j)}$, which is derived from definition of f_1 and f_2 in Eq. (1) in the linear attack. Algorithm 2 is only applicable

---

[2] When blocksize is n, ρ_D is less than $2n$. For two m-bit integers, $\rho_A \approx 2m$ binary operations, $\rho_M \approx 3 \cdot m^{\log_2(3)}$ binary operations, $\rho_C \approx m$ binary operations [9].

to ciphers XORing the whole state with subkeys at the beginning and end of the encryption algorithm. Since Feistel ciphers only inject the subkey into half of the state by XOR, we cannot directly apply Algorithm 2 to Feistel ciphers.

However, we can adjust the order of key addition of second and penulti-mate round as in Fig. 2. By setting $X = (F(P_L) \oplus P_R, P_L)$, $K_0 = (k_1, k_2)$, $Y = (C_R, F(C_R) \oplus C_L)$, $K_3 = (k_{r-1}, k_r)$, we can tweak the Feistel network to the framework in Fig. 1 without changing the encryption and decryption results. Then, given a suitable linear distinguisher, we can get a probable guess for sub-keys by Algorithm 3 with additional time complexity of N one-round encryption and decryption. There is no additional cost of memory complexity.

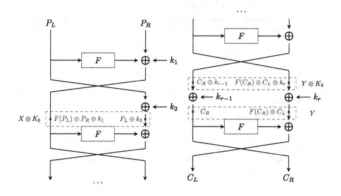

Fig. 2. R-round Feistel structure.

Algorithm 3: Key Recovery of Feistel Ciphers (without final phase)

Input: A set $\mathcal{D} = \{(P, C = E_\kappa(P))\}$ of N plaintext-ciphertext pairs.
Output: Some probable guesses for $(\bar{k}_0, \bar{k}_1, \bar{k}_2, \bar{k}_3)$.

1 **begin**
2   // PRETREATMENT PHASE
3   **foreach** $(P, C) \in \mathcal{D}$ **do**
4         $X = (F(P_L) \oplus P_R, P_L)$; $Y = (C_R, F(C_R) \oplus C_L)$;
5         $\mathcal{D}.replace((P, C), (X, Y))$;   // Replace (P, C) with (X, Y)
6   **end**
7     $K_0 = (k_1, k_2)$; $K_3 = (k_{r-1}, k_r)$;
8   Call Algorithm 2;
9 **end**

---

4 Getting Attack Complexity Automatically

4.1 The Automatic Model of Detecting Guessed Subkeys

Partial K_0, K_1, K_2, and K_3 should be guessed as the linear distinguisher is only related to partial bits of $\hat{X}$ and $\hat{Y}$. These subkeys are denoted as $\bar{k}_0$, $\bar{k}_1$, $\bar{k}_2$ and $\bar{k}_3$. The size of guessed subkeys and the correlation of linear distinguisher are two decisive factors of attack complexity. Thus, it is essential to determine the size of guessed subkeys and the relationship between them. We implement a MILP-based automatic tool to find $\bar{k}_0$, $\bar{k}_1$, $\bar{k}_2$ and $\bar{k}_3$ for a given approximation. The high level modeling strategy is shown in Fig. 3.

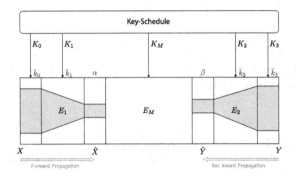

Fig. 3. The high level modeling strategy of key recovery phase. The coloring part represents the value propagation of V-type variables.

Binary Variables for Activeness Propagation. To define whether each subkey and state bit will affect the value of $\hat{X} \cdot \alpha \oplus \hat{Y} \cdot \beta$ or not, we assign a binary variable for each subkey and state bit. Namely,

$$v = \begin{cases} 1, & \text{if the subkey/state bit influences the value of } \hat{X} \cdot \alpha \oplus \hat{Y} \cdot \beta; \\ 0, & \text{otherwise.} \end{cases}$$

If $v = 1$, it is active; otherwise, it is inactive. We call these binary variables V-type variables.

Objective Function. The complexity is positively correlated with the number of subkeys that need to be guessed, so an objective function needs to be selected to make sure the smallest size of guessed subkeys.

$$\text{Minimize} \sum_{i=1}^{R_1} \sum_{j=1}^{n} V_k[i,j] + \sum_{i=R_2}^{R} \sum_{j=1}^{n} V_k[i,j].$$

where $V_k[i, j](j \in \{1, \cdots, n\})$ are V-type variables corresponding to k_i, R_1 and $(R - R_2 + 1)$ are the number of rounds included in E_1 and E_2, respectively.

Constraints for Forward Propagation

– **Initial Constraints.** Let α be the mask of $\hat{X}$ and the V-type variables corresponding to $\hat{X}$ be $\hat{X}_V$, then

$$\hat{X}_V[i] \geq \alpha[i], \quad i \in \{0, 1, \cdots, n-1\}.$$

– **Modeling XOR.** Let $(a_1, \cdots, a_t) \xrightarrow{\text{XOR}} b$, where $a_1, \cdots, a_t, b \in \mathbb{F}_2$ are bit-level input and output V-type variables of the XOR operation. Then $a_1 = \cdots = a_t = 1$ if $b = 1$. That is

$$a_i \geq b, \quad i \in \{1, \cdots, t\}.$$

– **Modeling COPY.** Let $a \xrightarrow{\text{COPY}} (a_1, \cdots, a_t)$, where $a, a_1, \cdots, a_t \in \mathbb{F}_2$ are bit-level input and output V-type variables of the COPY operation. Then $a \geq \max\{a_1, \cdots, a_t\}$. That is

$$a \geq a_i, \quad i \in \{1, \cdots, t\}.$$

– **Modeling AND.** Let $(a_1, \cdots, a_t) \xrightarrow{\text{AND}} b$, where $a_1, \cdots, a_t, b \in \mathbb{F}_2$ are bit-level input and output V-type variables of the AND operation. Then $a_1 = \cdots = a_t = 1$ if $b = 1$. That is

$$a_i \geq b, \quad i \in \{1, \cdots, t\}.$$

– **Modeling SBox.**[3] Let $(a_0, a_1, \cdots, a_{\omega-1}) \xrightarrow{\text{SBox}} (b_0, b_1, \cdots, b_{\nu-1})$, where $a_0, a_1, \cdots, a_{\omega-1}, b_0, b_1, \cdots, b_{\nu-1} \in \mathbb{F}_2$ are bit-level input and output V-type variables of the $\omega \times \nu$ SBox operation. Then $a_0 = a_1 = \cdots = a_{\omega-1} = 1$, if $\exists\, b_j = 1$ for $j \in \{0, 1, \cdots \nu - 1\}$. That is

$$a_i \geq b_j, \quad i \in \{0, \cdots \omega - 1\}, \ j \in \{0, \cdots \nu - 1\}.$$

Constraints for Backward Propagation

– **Initial Constraints.** Let β be the mask of $\hat{Y}$ and $\hat{Y}_V$ be the V-type variables corresponding to $\hat{Y}$, then

$$\hat{Y}_V[i] \geq \beta[i] \,, \quad i \in \{0, 1, \cdots, n-1\}.$$

– **Modeling Round Function.** Constraints for backward and forward propagation are the same, except that modeling is performed according to the decryption and encryption process respectively. Due to the consistency of encryption and decryption of Feistel structure, constraints for XOR, COPY, AND, and SBox are the same for both-ward.

---

[3] Our method to model SBox is similar to Zong *et al.*'s method in [31].

Modeling Key Addition. Let $(a, c) \xrightarrow{\oplus} b$, where $a, b \in \mathbb{F}_2$ are bit-level input and output V-type variables of key addition, $c \in \mathbb{F}_2$ is V-type variable of round key bit, then $c = b$.

Additional Constraints of Feistel Structure. Let $(V_{L^{i-1}}, V_{R^{i-1}})$ and (V_{L^i}, V_{R^i}) be input and output V-type variables of one-round Feistel structure, then

$$\begin{cases} V_{R^{i-1}} = V_{L^i} & \text{for forward propagation,} \\ V_{R^i} = V_{L^{i-1}} & \text{for backward propagation.} \end{cases}$$

where $V_{L^{i-1}}, V_{L^{i-1}}, V_{L^{i-1}}, V_{R^i} \in \mathbb{F}_2^n$, $2n$ is block size.

4.2   The Strategy of Reducing Guessed Subkeys' Size

In this subsection, we introduce some strategies to search for the relationships between $\bar{k}_0$, $\bar{k}_1$, $\bar{k}_2$ and $\bar{k}_3$. Further, we can reduce the attack complexity or increase the number of rounds attacked.

Assume there exits an active subkey k_a such that

$$\alpha \cdot \hat{X} \oplus \beta \cdot \hat{Y} = k_a \oplus \text{Items without } k_a.$$

Then k_a is an unknown but constant bit in the algebraic normal form (ANF) of $\alpha \cdot \hat{X} \oplus \beta \cdot \hat{Y}$, its value will not affect the value of $|q(\bar{k}_0, \bar{k}_1, \bar{k}_2, \bar{k}_3)|$. Although k_a is active, we do not need to guess its value during the key recovery period. As Feistel structure injects subkeys by XOR at the end of round function, there are many such subkeys. We can recursively extract them by tracing linear patterns.

Moreover, as suggested in [9], the dependency between $\bar{k}_0$, $\bar{k}_1$, $\bar{k}_2$ and $\bar{k}_3$ helps to reduce the cost of key recovery phase. Particularly, for ciphers with linear key schedules, every bit of subkeys is a linear combination of the master key bits. And the expressions of all active subkeys form a system of linear equations, which is denoted by $A \cdot \kappa = \mathbf{k}$, where κ and $\mathbf{k} = (\bar{k}_0, \bar{k}_1, \bar{k}_2, \bar{k}_3)^T$ are binary column vectors of master key and active subkeys, A is a matrix of size $|\mathbf{k}| \times |\kappa|$ and the inner product of i-th row of A and κ represents the i-th bit of $\mathbf{k}$. When A is full-rank, we need to guess all $\mathbf{k}$; when A is not full-rank, we just need to guess $rank(A)$ bits of $\mathbf{k}$ and the remaining active subkeys can be derived from the guessed subkeys. We can use this method to investigate the relationship between any subset of subkeys of ciphers with a linear key schedule.

For ciphers with nonlinear key schedules, it is more difficult to detect relationships between active subkeys. It may be helpful to investigate master key bits to which each subkey bit is related and guess these master key bits.

5   Application

In this section, we give efficient key recovery attacks on SIMON and SIMECK using the semi-automatic tool proposed in Sect. 3 and Sect. 4. The linear hulls used in our attack are summarized in Table 3.

Table 3. Linear hulls for SIMON and SIMECK

	Input-output masks	Round	ALH^{a}	Ref.
SIMON32	0x00200000 0x00002000	13	$2^{-26.99}$	[25]
SIMON48	0x200022800000 0x000022800000	16	$2^{-42.92}$	[26]
SIMON64	0x4000000400000001 0x1000000044000004	23	$2^{-60.84}$	[16]
SIMON96	0x400000004044000000000001 0x000000001010000000004044	31	$2^{-91.80}$	[16]
SIMON128	0x40000000000000440000000000000001 0x00000000000000014000000000000044	41	$2^{-121.15}$	[16]
SIMECK48	0x800000000001 0x200000500001	22	$2^{-45.68}$	[13]
SIMECK64	0x8000000100000005 0x0000000040000004	28	$2^{-61.67}$	[13]

^{a}The definition of ALH in [13, 16, 25, 26] is $\frac{1}{4}$ of the definition in this paper.

For every linear hull in Table 3, we build a MILP model to search for active $\bar{k}_0$, $\bar{k}_1$, $\bar{k}_2$ and $\bar{k}_3$, and minimize the size of guessed subkeys with the method proposed in Sect. 4. The results for SIMON and SIMECK are listed in Table 4. For SIMON32, SIMON48, and SIMECK32/64, we get no better result; for all versions of SIMON64 and SIMON96, SIMECK48/96 and SIMECK64/128, we improve previous results by one round; for SIMON128, we reduce the time complexity and increase the success probability of the attack on SIMON128/192 and SIMON128/256. Note that the time complexities in Table 4 are converted into ρ_E by method in [9]. Since the relationship between ρ_A and ρ_E in [6, 22] is uncertain, we keep time complexities in [6, 22] as they are.

We take SIMON64/96 as an example to show the details. Knowing the 23-round liner hull, we add four rounds to the beginning and the end of the linear hull respectively by guessing some subkeys, as shown in Table 5. As the underlined bits have no effect on the value of $|q(\bar{k}_0, \bar{k}_1, \bar{k}_2, \bar{k}_3)|$, we do not need to guess their values. Using method in Sect. 4.2, we find that all active subkeys are independent. $|\bar{k}_0| = 29$, $|\bar{k}_1| = 4$, $|\bar{k}_2| = 6$, $|\bar{k}_3| = 39$. When $N = 2^{63.84}$, we can recover 8 bit subkey with success probability 18.8%. The time complexity is $2^{63.84}\rho_D + 2^{84.09}\rho_A + 2^{79.00}\rho_M + 2^{78.00}\rho_C + \frac{2^{65.84}}{31}\rho_E + 2^{88}\rho_E$. As $\rho_E \approx 32 \cdot 4 \cdot 31 = 3968$, $\rho_A \approx 78$, $\rho_M \approx 3 \cdot 64^{\log_2(3)} \approx 2187$ binary operations, $\rho_C \approx \rho_A$, $\rho_D \ll \rho_E$, the time complexity is about $2^{88.00}$ full encryptions. The memory requirement is at most 2^{78} state size. Active subkeys of other versions of SIMON and SIMECK are shown in Appendix A.

To compare the time complexity of our method with known Matsui Algorithm 2 based method, for SIMON32, we use the same linear hull as [25]. It shows that our method increases the attackable rounds and decreases the time complexity.

To compare the time complexity of our method with the dynamic key-guessing attack, for SIMON32 and SIMON48, we use the same linear hull as [6]. It shows that attackable rounds of each method are the same. For SIMON32, the time complexities of each method are close. However, for SIMON48, our complexity is higher. The main reason is that the method in Sect. 4.2 cannot find all the correlations between the active subkeys.

Table 4. Summary of linear key recovery attacks on SIMON and SIMECK

Cipher	$2n$	mn	Rounds	Data	Time	Memory	P_S	Ref.
SIMON	32	64	21	$2^{31.19}$	$2^{63.19}$	–	·	57.1%	[25]
			23	$2^{31.19}$	$2^{61.84}\rho_A + 2^{56.3}\rho_E$	–		57.1%	[6]
			23	$2^{31.19}$	$2^{59.59}$	2^{58}	57.1%	This paper
			24	$2^{30.59}$	$2^{63.9}$	–	3%	[1]
				$2^{31.57}$	$2^{63.57}$	–	–	[2]
	48	72	24	$2^{47.92}$	$2^{68.56}$	2^{67}	90.9%	This paper
				$2^{47.92}$	$2^{67.89}\rho_A + 2^{65.34}\rho_E$	–	90.9%	[6]
		96	25	$2^{47.92}$	$2^{90.96}$	2^{89}	90.9%	This paper
				$2^{47.92}$	$2^{89.89}\rho_A + 2^{88.28}\rho_E$	–	90.9%	[6]
	64	96	30	$2^{63.53}$	$2^{93.62}\rho_A + 2^{88.13}\rho_E$	–	7.1%	[6]
			31	$2^{63.84}$	$2^{88.00}$	2^{78}	18.8%	This paper
		128	31	$2^{63.53}$	$2^{119.62}\rho_A + 2^{120.00}\rho_E$	–	7.1%	[6]
			32	$2^{63.84}$	$2^{120.00}$	2^{109}	18.8%	This paper
	96	96	37	$2^{95.20}$	$2^{67.94}\rho_A + 2^{88}\rho_E$	–	7.1%	[6]
			38	$2^{95.80}$	$2^{92.61}$	2^{71}	86.7%	This paper
		144	38	$2^{95.20}$	$2^{98.94}\rho_A + 2^{136.00}\rho_E$	–	7.1%	[6]
			39	$2^{95.80}$	$2^{128.00}$	2^{102}	37.3%	This paper
	128	128	49	$2^{127.60}$	$2^{87.77}\rho_A + 2^{120.00}\rho_E$	–	7.1%	[6]
			49	$2^{126.15}$	$2^{122.54}$	2^{90}	90.9%	This paper
		192	51	$2^{127.60}$	$2^{155.77}\rho_A + 2^{184.00}\rho_E$	–	7.1%	[6]
			51	$2^{127.15}$	$2^{160.69}$	2^{158}	95.2%	This paper
		256	53	$2^{127.60}$	$2^{239.77}\rho_A + 2^{248.01}\rho_E$	–	7.1%	[6]
			53	$2^{126.15}$	$2^{243.98}$	2^{242}	90.9%	This paper
SIMECK	32	64	23	$2^{31.91}$	$2^{61.78}\rho_A + 2^{56.41}\rho_E$	–	47.7%	[22]
	48	96	30	$2^{47.66}$	$2^{92.2}\rho_A + 2^{88.04}\rho_E$	–	86.7%	[22]
			31	$2^{47.92}$	$2^{91.13}$	2^{89}	86.7%	This paper
	64	128	37	$2^{63.09}$	$2^{111.44}\rho_A + 2^{121.25}\rho_E$	–	47.7%	[22]
			38	$2^{63.67}$	$2^{120.00}$	2^{104}	86.7%	This paper

Table 5. Active subkeys of 31-round SIMON64/96.

	Round	Active subkeys
$\bar{k}_0$	1	$k_1[0,1,2,\underline{3},4,5,6,7,8,9,11,12,13,14,15,18,19,21,25,30,\underline{31}]$
	2	$k_2[0,\underline{1},3,4,\underline{5},6,7,10,11,13,17,\underline{29},31]$
$\bar{k}_1$	3	$k_3[2,\underline{3},5,9,30,\underline{31}]$
	4	$k_4[\underline{1},\underline{29}]$
		$0x4000000400000001 \xrightarrow{23\ round} 0x1000000044000004$
$\bar{k}_2$	28	$k_{28}[\underline{1},\underline{5},\underline{29}]$
	29	$k_{29}[2,\underline{3},5,6,\underline{7},9,13,30,\underline{31}]$
$\bar{k}_3$	30	$k_{30}[0,\underline{1},3,4,\underline{5},6,7,8,\underline{9},10,11,13,14,15,17,21,29,31]$
	31	$k_{31}[0,1,2,\underline{3},4,5,6,7,8,9,10,11,12,13,14,15,16,17,18,$ $19,21,22,23,25,29,30,31]$

6   Conclusion

We extend the FWHT-based arbitrary-round key recovery method to Feistel structure and build a MILP model to determine the guessed subkeys automatically. Due to this, we can optimize the time complexity of linear cryptanalysis. Then, using linear hulls in the existing literature, we increase the numbers of rounds of linear cryptanalysis on some versions of SIMON and SIMECK. Compared with dynamic key-guessing techniques, our method is more straightforward, easier to understand and implement. When the linear distinguisher is known, our method avoids tedious manual derivation and automatically determines linear attacks' complexity. Therefore, we can widely use it in the design and analysis of cryptographic algorithms.

In the future, we will apply our method to other Feistel ciphers. Furthermore, we expect to automatically search linear distinguishers of Feistel ciphers that optimize the time complexity of the resulting attack.

Acknowledgment. We would like to thank the anonymous reviewers for their valuable comments and suggestions. This work is sponsored by the research funding of BIMSA, the National Key Research and Development Program of China (Grant No. 2018YFA0704704), the National Natural Science Foundation of China (Grant No. 62102025, 61772519, 62032014), the Chinese Major Program of National Cryptography Development Foundation (Grant No. MMJJ20180102), and Beijing Institute of Technology Research Fund Program for Young Scholars.

A   Active Subkeys of SIMON and SIMECK

See Tables 6, 7, 8, 9, 10, 11, 12 and 13.

Table 6. Active subkeys of 32-round SIMON64/128

	Round	Active subkeys
$\bar{k}_0$	1	$k_1[0, 1, 2, \underline{3}, 4, 5, 6, 7, 8, 9, 11, 12, 13, 14, 15, 18, 19, 21, 25, 30, \underline{31}]$
	2	$k_2[0, \underline{1}, 3, 4, \underline{5}, 6, 7, 10, 11, 13, 17, \underline{29}, 31]$
$\bar{k}_1$	3	$k_3[2, \underline{3}, 5, 9, 30, \underline{31}]$
	4	$k_4[\underline{1}, \underline{29}]$
$0x4000000400000001 \xrightarrow{23\ round} 0x1000000044000004$		
$\bar{k}_2$	28	$k_{28}[\underline{1}, \underline{5}, \underline{29}]$
	29	$k_{29}[2, \underline{3}, 5, 6, \underline{7}, 9, 13, 30, \underline{31}]$
	30	$k_{30}[0, \underline{1}, 3, 4, \underline{5}, 6, 7, 8, \underline{9}, 10, 11, 13, 14, 15, 17, 21, \underline{29}, 31]$
$\bar{k}_3$	31	$k_{31}[0, 1, 2, \underline{3}, 4, 5, 6, 7, 8, 9, 10, 11, 12, 13, 14, 15, 16, 17, 18, 19, 21, 22, 23, 25, 29, 30, \underline{31}]$
	32	$k_{32}[0, 1, 2, 3, 4, 5, 6, 7, 8, 9, 10, 11, 12, 13, 14, 15, 16, 17, 18, 19,$ $20, 21, 22, 23, 24, 25, 26, 27, 29, 30, 31]$

Table 7. Active subkeys of 38-round SIMON96/96

	Round	Active subkeys
$\bar{k}_0$	1	$k_1[0, 1, 2, 3, 4, \underline{5}, 6, 7, 9, 10, 11, 13, 17, \underline{33}, 35, 36, \underline{37}, \underline{41}, 42, 43, 44, \underline{45}, 47]$
	2	$k_2[1, 2, \underline{3}, 5, 9, 34, \underline{35}, 41, 42, \underline{43}, 46, \underline{47}]$
$\bar{k}_1$	3	$k_3[\underline{1}, \underline{33}, \underline{41}, \underline{45}]$

$0x4000000040440000000000001 \xrightarrow{31\ round} 0x0000000001010000000004044$

	Round	Active subkeys
$\bar{k}_2$	35	$k_{35}[\underline{33}, \underline{41}, \underline{45}]$
	36	$k_{36}[1, 5, 34, \underline{35}, 41, 42, \underline{43}, 46, \underline{47}]$
$\bar{k}_3$	37	$k_{37}[0, 1, 2, 3, 6, 7, 9, 13, \underline{33}, 35, 36, \underline{37}, \underline{41}, 42, 43, 44, \underline{45}, 47]$
	38	$k_{38}[0, 1, 2, 3, 4, 5, 7, 8, 9, 10, 11, 14, 15, 17, 21, 34, \underline{35}, 36, 37, 38, \underline{39}, 41, 42, 43, 44, 45, 46, \underline{47}]$

Table 8. Active subkeys of 39-round SIMON96/144

	Round	Active subkeys
$\bar{k}_0$	1	$k_1[0, 1, 2, 3, 4, 5, 6, 7, 8, 9, 10, 11, 12, 13, 14, 15, 17, 18, 19, 21, 25,$ $34, \underline{35}, 36, 37, 38, \underline{39}, 41, 42, 43, 44, 45, 46, \underline{47}]$
	2	$k_2[0, 1, 2, 3, 4, \underline{5}, 6, 7, 9, 10, 11, 13, 17, \underline{33}, 35, 36, \underline{37}, \underline{41}, 42, 43, 44, \underline{45}, 47]$
$\bar{k}_1$	3	$k_3[1, 2, \underline{3}, 5, 9, 34, \underline{35}, 41, 42, \underline{43}, 46, \underline{47}]$
	4	$k_4[\underline{1}, \underline{33}, \underline{41}, \underline{45}]$

$0x4000000040440000000000001 \xrightarrow{31\ round} 0x0000000001010000000004044$

	Round	Active subkeys
$\bar{k}_2$	36	$k_{36}[\underline{33}, \underline{41}, \underline{45}]$
	37	$k_{37}[1, 5, 34, \underline{35}, 41, 42, \underline{43}, 46, \underline{47}]$
$\bar{k}_3$	38	$k_{38}[0, 1, 2, 3, 6, 7, 9, 13, \underline{33}, 35, 36, \underline{37}, \underline{41}, 42, 43, 44, \underline{45}, 47]$
	39	$k_{39}[0, 1, 2, 3, 4, 5, 7, 8, 9, 10, 11, 14, 15, 17, 21, 34, \underline{35}, 36, 37,$ $38, \underline{39}, 41, 42, 43, 44, 45, 46, \underline{47}]$

Table 9. Active subkeys of 49-round SIMON128/128

	Round	Active subkeys
$\bar{k}_0$	1	$k_1[0, 1, 2, 3, 4, 5, 6, 7, 8, 9, 10, 11, 12, 13, 14, 15, 17, 18, 19, 21, 25, 58, \underline{59}, 60, 61, 62, \underline{63}]$
	2	$k_2[0, \underline{1}, 2, 3, 4, \underline{5}, 6, 7, 9, 10, 11, 13, 17, \underline{57}, 59, 60, \underline{61}, 63]$
$\bar{k}_1$	3	$k_3[1, 2, \underline{3}, 5, 9, 58, \underline{59}, 62, \underline{63}]$
	4	$k_4[\underline{1}, \underline{57}, \underline{61}]$

$0x40000000000000044000000000000000001 \xrightarrow{41\ round} 0x000000000000000014000000000000044$

	Round	Active subkeys
$\bar{k}_2$	46	$k_{46}[\underline{1}, \underline{57}, \underline{61}]$
	47	$k_{47}[1, 2, \underline{3}, 5, 9, 58, \underline{59}, 62, \underline{63}]$
$\bar{k}_3$	48	$k_{48}[0, \underline{1}, 2, 3, 4, \underline{5}, 6, 7, 9, 10, 11, 13, 17, \underline{57}, 59, 60, \underline{61}, 63]$
	49	$k_{49}[0, 1, 2, 3, 4, 5, 6, 7, 8, 9, 10, 11, 12, 13, 14, 15, 17, 18, 19, 21, 25, 58, \underline{59}, 60, 61, 62, \underline{63}]$

Table 10. Active subkeys of 51-round SIMON128/192

	Round	Active subkeys
$\bar{k}_0$	1	$k_1[0,1,2,3,4,5,6,7,8,9,10,11,12,13,14,15,16,17,18,19,$ $20,21,22,23,25,26,27,29,33,\underline{57},59,60,61,62,63]$
	2	$k_2[0,1,2,3,4,5,6,7,8,9,10,11,12,13,14,15,17,18,19,21,25,58,\underline{59},60,61,62,\underline{63}]$
$\bar{k}_1$	3	$k_3[0,\underline{1},2,3,4,\underline{5},6,7,9,10,11,13,17,\underline{57},59,60,\underline{61},63]$
	4	$k_4[1,2,\underline{3},5,9,58,\underline{59},62,\underline{63}]$
	5	$k_5[\underline{1},\underline{57},\underline{61}]$

$0x40000000000000044000000000000001 \xrightarrow{41\ round} 0x00000000000000014000000000000044$

	Round	Active subkeys
$\bar{k}_2$	47	$k_{47}[\underline{1},\underline{57},\underline{61}]$
	48	$k_{48}[1,2,\underline{3},5,9,58,\underline{59},62,\underline{63}]$
	49	$k_{49}[0,\underline{1},2,3,4,\underline{5},6,7,9,10,11,13,17,\underline{57},59,60,\underline{61},63]$
$\bar{k}_3$	50	$k_{50}[0,1,2,3,4,5,6,7,8,9,10,11,12,13,14,15,17,18,19,21,25,58,\underline{59},60,61,62,\underline{63}]$
	51	$k_{51}[0,1,2,3,4,5,6,7,8,9,10,11,12,13,14,15,16,17,18,19,$ $20,21,22,23,25,26,27,29,33,\underline{57},59,60,61,62,63]$

Table 11. Active subkeys of 53-round SIMON128/256

	Round	Active subkeys
$\bar{k}_0$	1	$k_1[0,1,2,3,4,5,6,7,8,9,10,11,12,13,14,15,16,17,18,19,20,21,22,$ $23,24,25,26,27,28,29,30,31,33,34,35,37,41,58,\underline{59},60,61,62,63]$
	2	$k_2[0,1,2,3,4,5,6,7,8,9,10,11,12,13,14,15,16,17,18,19,$ $20,21,22,23,25,26,27,29,33,\underline{57},59,60,61,62,63]$
$\bar{k}_1$	3	$k_3[0,1,2,3,4,5,6,7,8,9,10,11,12,13,14,15,17,18,19,21,25,58,\underline{59},60,61,62,\underline{63}]$
	4	$k_4[0,\underline{1},2,3,4,\underline{5},6,7,9,10,11,13,17,\underline{57},59,60,\underline{61},63]$
	5	$k_5[1,2,\underline{3},5,9,58,\underline{59},62,\underline{63}]$
	6	$k_6[\underline{1},\underline{57},\underline{61}]$

$0x40000000000000044000000000000001 \xrightarrow{41\ round} 0x00000000000000014000000000000044$

	Round	Active subkeys
$\bar{k}_2$	48	$k_{48}[\underline{1},\underline{57},\underline{61}]$
	49	$k_{49}[1,2,\underline{3},5,9,58,\underline{59},62,\underline{63}]$
	50	$k_{50}[0,\underline{1},2,3,4,\underline{5},6,7,9,10,11,13,17,\underline{57},59,60,\underline{61},63]$
	51	$k_{51}[0,1,2,3,4,5,6,7,8,9,10,11,12,13,14,15,17,18,19,21,25,58,\underline{59},60,61,62,\underline{63}]$
$\bar{k}_3$	52	$k_{52}[0,1,2,3,4,5,6,7,8,9,10,11,12,13,14,15,16,17,18,$ $19,20,21,22,23,25,26,27,29,33,\underline{57},59,60,61,62,63]$
	53	$k_{53}[0,1,2,3,4,5,6,7,8,9,10,11,12,13,14,15,16,17,18,19,20,21,22,$ $23,24,25,26,27,28,29,30,31,33,34,35,37,41,58,\underline{59},60,61,62,63]$

Table 12. Active subkeys of 31-round SIMECK48/96

	Round	Active subkeys
$\bar{k}_0$	1	$k_1[0, 1, 2, 3, 4, 5, 6, 7, 8, 9, 10, 11, 12, 14, 15, 16, 20, 23]$
	2	$k_2[0, 1, 2, \underline{3}, 4, 5, 6, 7, 9, 10, 11, 15, 23]$
$\bar{k}_1$	3	$k_3[0, 1, \underline{2}, 4, 5, 6, 10, 23]$
	4	$k_4[0, \underline{1}, 5, \underline{23}]$
	5	$k_5[\underline{0}]$
$0x800000000001 \xrightarrow{22\ round} 0x200000500001$		
$\bar{k}_2$	28	$k_{28}[\underline{1}, \underline{3}, \underline{23}]$
	29	$k_{29}[\underline{0}, 1, \underline{2}, 3, 4, 6, 8, 23]$
$\bar{k}_3$	30	$k_{30}[0, 1, 2, 3, 4, 5, 6, 7, 8, 9, 11, 13, 23]$
	31	$k_{31}[0, 1, 2, 3, 4, 5, 6, 7, 8, 9, 10, 11, 12, 13, 14, 16, 18, 23]$

Table 13. Active subkeys of 38-round SIMECK64/128

	Round	Active subkeys
$\bar{k}_0$	1	$k_1[0, 1, 2, 3, 4, 5, 6, 7, 8, 9, 10, 11, 12, 14, 15, 16, 19, 20, 29, 30, 31]$
	2	$k_2[0, 1, 2, 3, 4, 5, 6, 7, 9, 10, 11, 14, 15, 29, 30, 31]$
$\bar{k}_1$	3	$k_3[0, 1, 2, 4, 5, 6, 9, 10, 29, \underline{30}, 31]$
	4	$k_4[0, \underline{1}, 4, 5, \underline{29}, 31]$
	5	$k_5[\underline{0}, \underline{31}]$
$0x8000000100000005 \xrightarrow{28\ round} 0x0000000040000004$		
$\bar{k}_2$	34	$k_{34}[\underline{1}, \underline{29}]$
	35	$k_{35}[1, 2, 6, 29, \underline{30}]$
	36	$k_{36}[1, 2, 3, 6, 7, 11, 29, 30, \underline{31}]$
$\bar{k}_3$	37	$k_{37}[\underline{0}, 1, 2, 3, 4, 6, 7, 8, 11, 12, 16, 29, 30, 31]$
	38	$k_{38}[0, 1, 2, 3, 4, 5, 6, 7, 8, 9, 11, 12, 13, 16, 17, 21, 29, 30, 31]$

References

1. Abdelraheem, M.A., et al.: Improved linear cryptanalysis of reduced-round SIMON-32 and SIMON-48. In: Biryukov, A., Goyal, V. (eds.) INDOCRYPT 2015. LNCS, vol. 9462, pp. 153–179. Springer, Cham (2015). https://doi.org/10.1007/978-3-319-26617-6_9

2. Ashur, T.: Improved linear trails for the block cipher Simon. IACR Cryptol. ePrint Arch. 2015:285 (2015)

3. Beaulieu, R., Shors, D., Smith, J., Treatman-Clark, S., Weeks, B., Wingers, L.: The SIMON and SPECK families of lightweight block ciphers. IACR Cryptol. ePrint Arch. 2013:404 (2013)

4. Biryukov, A., De Cannière, C., Quisquater, M.: On multiple linear approximations. In: Franklin, M. (ed.) CRYPTO 2004. LNCS, vol. 3152, pp. 1–22. Springer, Heidelberg (2004). https://doi.org/10.1007/978-3-540-28628-8_1

5. Bogdanov, A., Tischhauser, E., Vejre, P.S.: Multivariate profiling of hulls for linear cryptanalysis. IACR Trans. Symmetric Cryptol. **2018**(1), 101–125 (2018)

6. Chen, H., Wang, X.: Improved linear hull attack on round-reduced SIMON with dynamic key-guessing techniques. In: Peyrin, T. (ed.) FSE 2016. LNCS, vol. 9783, pp. 428–449. Springer, Heidelberg (2016). https://doi.org/10.1007/978-3-662-52993-5_22

7. Collard, B., Standaert, F.-X., Quisquater, J.-J.: Improving the time complexity of Matsui's linear cryptanalysis. In: Nam, K.-H., Rhee, G. (eds.) ICISC 2007. LNCS, vol. 4817, pp. 77–88. Springer, Heidelberg (2007). https://doi.org/10.1007/978-3-540-76788-6_7

8. Cui, T., Jia, K., Kai, F., Chen, S., Wang, M.: New automatic search tool for impossible differentials and zero-correlation linear approximations. IACR Cryptol. ePrint Arch. 2016:689 (2016)

9. Flórez-Gutiérrez, A., Naya-Plasencia, M.: Improving key-recovery in linear attacks: application to 28-round PRESENT. In: Canteaut, A., Ishai, Y. (eds.) EUROCRYPT 2020. LNCS, vol. 12105, pp. 221–249. Springer, Cham (2020). https://doi.org/10.1007/978-3-030-45721-1_9

10. Fu, K., Wang, M., Guo, Y., Sun, S., Hu, L.: MILP-based automatic search algorithms for differential and linear trails for speck. In: Peyrin, T. (ed.) FSE 2016. LNCS, vol. 9783, pp. 268–288. Springer, Heidelberg (2016). https://doi.org/10.1007/978-3-662-52993-5_14

11. Gray, R.M.: Toeplitz and circulant matrices: a review. Found. Trends Commun. Inf. Theory **2**(3), 155–239 (2005)

12. Hermelin, M., Cho, J.Y., Nyberg, K.: Multidimensional extension of Matsui's algorithm 2. In: Dunkelman, O. (ed.) FSE 2009. LNCS, vol. 5665, pp. 209–227. Springer, Heidelberg (2009). https://doi.org/10.1007/978-3-642-03317-9_13

13. Huang, M., Wang, L., Zhang, Y.: Improved automatic search algorithm for differential and linear cryptanalysis on SIMECK and the applications. In: Naccache, D., et al. (eds.) ICICS 2018. LNCS, vol. 11149, pp. 664–681. Springer, Cham (2018). https://doi.org/10.1007/978-3-030-01950-1_39

14. Kaliski, B.S., Robshaw, M.J.B.: Linear cryptanalysis using multiple approximations. In: Desmedt, Y.G. (ed.) CRYPTO 1994. LNCS, vol. 839, pp. 26–39. Springer, Heidelberg (1994). https://doi.org/10.1007/3-540-48658-5_4

15. Leurent, G., Pernot, C., Schrottenloher, A.: Clustering effect in Simon and Simeck. In: Tibouchi, M., Wang, H. (eds.) ASIACRYPT 2021. LNCS, vol. 13090, pp. 272–302. Springer, Cham (2021). https://doi.org/10.1007/978-3-030-92062-3_10

16. Liu, Z., Li, Y., Wang, M.: The security of SIMON-like ciphers against linear cryptanalysis. IACR Cryptol. ePrint Arch. 2017:576 (2017)

17. Matsui, M.: Linear cryptanalysis method for DES cipher. In: Helleseth, T. (ed.) EUROCRYPT 1993. LNCS, vol. 765, pp. 386–397. Springer, Heidelberg (1994). https://doi.org/10.1007/3-540-48285-7_33

18. Matsui, M.: The first experimental cryptanalysis of the data encryption standard. In: Desmedt, Y.G. (ed.) CRYPTO 1994. LNCS, vol. 839, pp. 1–11. Springer, Heidelberg (1994). https://doi.org/10.1007/3-540-48658-5_1

19. Mouha, N., Wang, Q., Gu, D., Preneel, B.: Differential and linear cryptanalysis using mixed-integer linear programming. In: Wu, C.-K., Yung, M., Lin, D. (eds.) Inscrypt 2011. LNCS, vol. 7537, pp. 57–76. Springer, Heidelberg (2012). https://doi.org/10.1007/978-3-642-34704-7_5

20. Nguyen, P.H., Wu, H., Wang, H.: Improving the algorithm 2 in multidimensional linear cryptanalysis. In: Parampalli, U., Hawkes, P. (eds.) ACISP 2011. LNCS, vol. 6812, pp. 61–74. Springer, Heidelberg (2011). https://doi.org/10.1007/978-3-642-22497-3_5

21. Nyberg, K.: Linear approximation of block ciphers. In: De Santis, A. (ed.) EUROCRYPT 1994. LNCS, vol. 950, pp. 439–444. Springer, Heidelberg (1995). https://doi.org/10.1007/BFb0053460

22. Qin, L., Chen, H., Wang, X.: Linear hull attack on round-reduced Simeck with dynamic key-guessing techniques. In: Liu, J.K., Steinfeld, R. (eds.) ACISP 2016. LNCS, vol. 9723, pp. 409–424. Springer, Cham (2016). https://doi.org/10.1007/978-3-319-40367-0_26

23. Sasaki, Y., Todo, Y.: New impossible differential search tool from design and cryptanalysis aspects - revealing structural properties of several ciphers. In: EUROCRYPT 2017, pp. 185–215 (2017)

24. Selçuk, A.A.: On probability of success in linear and differential cryptanalysis. J. Cryptol. **21**, 131–147 (2008)

25. Shi, D., Lei, H., Sun, S., Song, L., Qiao, K., Ma, X.: Improved linear (hull) cryptanalysis of round-reduced versions of SIMON. IACR Cryptol. ePrint Arch. 2014:973 (2014)

26. Sun, S., et al.: Towards finding the best characteristics of some bit-oriented block ciphers and automatic enumeration of (related-key) differential and linear characteristics with predefined properties. Cryptology ePrint Archive, Report 2014/747 (2014)

27. Sun, S., Hu, L., Wang, P., Qiao, K., Ma, X., Song, L.: Automatic security evaluation and (related-key) differential characteristic search: application to SIMON, PRESENT, LBlock, DES(L) and other bit-oriented block ciphers. In: Sarkar, P., Iwata, T. (eds.) ASIACRYPT 2014. LNCS, vol. 8873, pp. 158–178. Springer, Heidelberg (2014). https://doi.org/10.1007/978-3-662-45611-8_9

28. Xiang, Z., Zhang, W., Bao, Z., Lin, D.: Applying MILP method to searching integral distinguishers based on division property for 6 lightweight block ciphers. In: Cheon, J.H., Takagi, T. (eds.) ASIACRYPT 2016. LNCS, vol. 10031, pp. 648–678. Springer, Heidelberg (2016). https://doi.org/10.1007/978-3-662-53887-6_24

29. Yang, G., Zhu, B., Suder, V., Aagaard, M.D., Gong, G.: The Simeck family of lightweight block ciphers. IACR Cryptol. ePrint Arch. 2015:612 (2015)

30. Yarlagadda, R.K., Hershey, J.E.: Hadamard Matrix Analysis and Synthesis. Springer, Boston (1997). https://doi.org/10.1007/978-1-4615-6313-6

31. Zong, R., Dong, X., Chen, H., Luo, Y., Wang, S., Li, Z.: Towards key-recovery-attack friendly distinguishers: application to GIFT-128. IACR Trans. Symmetric Cryptol. **2021**(1), 156–184 (2021)

Efficient Fully Anonymous Public-Key Trace and Revoke with Adaptive **IND-CCA** Security

Mriganka Mandal[1]($\boxtimes$), Ramprasad Sarkar[2], Junbeom Hur[3], and Koji Nuida[1,4]

[1] Institute of Mathematics for Industry, Kyushu University, Fukuoka, Japan
{m-mriganka,nuida}@imi.kyushu-u.ac.jp
[2] Department of Mathematics, Indian Institute of Technology Kharagpur,
Kharagpur, India
rpsarkar@iitkgp.ac.in
[3] Department of Computer Science and Engineering, Korea University, Seoul, Korea
jbhur@korea.ac.kr
[4] National Institute of Advanced Industrial Science and Technology, Tokyo, Japan

Abstract. We aim to efficiently design a unified, cost-effective primitive exhibiting two mutually orthogonal functionalities, namely *subscribed users anonymity* and *public-key traitor traceability* in the context of **B**roadcast **E**ncryption (BE), and propose an explicit construction of identity-based **F**ully **Ano**nymous Public-**K**ey **T**race and **R**evoke (FAnoPKTR) scheme that is obtained by coupling the **I**dentity-**B**ased **E**ncryption (IBE) framework with the collusion-secure *optimal probabilistic fingerprinting codes*. In addition to being *adaptively* secure, our design is proven to be **IND**istinguishable **C**hosen-**C**iphertext **A**ttack (IND-CCA) secure under asymmetric **D**ecisional **B**ilinear **D**iffie-**H**ellman **T**ype-**3** (DBDH-3) assumption in standard security model without random oracles. Our asymmetric Type-3 bilinear pairing-based scheme has communication bandwidth that grows with the size of a subscriber set for any encryption, and the user secret-key size is constant. Moreover, our decryption algorithm is faster, which requires only three asymmetric pairings to recover the encrypted broadcast message.

Keywords: Broadcast encryption · Identity-based encryption · Collusion-secure codes · Anonymity and privacy · Fraud detection and revocation · Type-3 bilinear map · Adaptive IND-CCA security

1 Introduction

Broadcast **E**ncryption (BE) [15] authorizes subscribers to listen broadcast encrypted channels after paying a one-time amount for a single or time-limited viewing. A unique device, known as "set-top decoder box", is given to each subscriber to register the network. The **I**dentity-**B**ased **B**roadcast **E**ncryption (IBBE) [8,9,11] is an advanced form of BE in which the **P**ublic-**K**ey **I**nfrastructure (PKI) is not needed. In an IBBE, the public-key of each user

© Springer Nature Switzerland AG 2021
R. Deng et al. (Eds.): ISPEC 2021, LNCS 13107, pp. 168–189, 2021.
https://doi.org/10.1007/978-3-030-93206-0_11

is described utilizing a unique identifier linked with the user index (e.g., a user's IP, phone number or email). A **G**roup **M**anager (**GM**), also identified as **P**rivate-**K**ey **G**eneration **C**enter (**PKGC**), produces corresponding secret-key of each user employing the associated public identifier of the user. To encrypt a message, a set of receiver's identities along with the public parameters are used by any broadcaster. Nonetheless, an authorized user can retrieve the correct message utilizing its secret decryption key.

Recently, numerous privacy-preserving BE is constructed in different flavors [1,5,11,18] in which the anonymity of the subscribed users from any outside attackers is at primary concern. These systems are known as the **O**utsider **A**nonymous **B**roadcast **E**ncryption (**OAnoBE**), where any subscriber, i.e., an insider, knows the information of all other subscribers of the system. From the real-life application point of view, a subscribed user usually expects that others not to identify his personal information. Consequently, it is also expected that the BE system should also protect each subscriber's insider anonymity. The OAnoBE system with the insider anonymity is called **F**ully **A**nonymous **B**roadcast **E**ncryption (**FAnoBE**) system [8,9,12,15,17].

On the other hand, aid with the full anonymity, a subscriber might make a reprint of its secret-key to resell or even publish it on the Internet without being bothered to be caught. Besides, such traitors' alliance might make collusion to build a pirate decoder bearing an obfuscated malicious program capable of decrypting the encrypted database. Since the system is fully anonymous, the traitors might fuse their original decoder box so that the pirate decoder box cannot be directly connected with their own identities. In this situation, the network system must have the capability to run an efficient tracing mechanism that interacts polynomially many times with the pirate decoder to trace the traitors. Tracing mechanism falls into two categories: *public-key tracing* [10,13] and *secret-key tracing* [3,14]. In a public-key tracing, anyone can execute the tracing algorithm using only the public parameters, whereas secret-key tracing requires a personal input and runs only by the GM. An identity-based FAnoBE with public-key traceability is termed identity-based **F**ully **A**nonymous **P**ublic-**K**ey **T**race and **R**evoke (**FAnoPKTR**) system.

Our Contribution. Full anonymity and public-key traceability are mutually orthogonal functionalities that repudiate each other regarding the recipients' privacy. It is non-trivial to realize a secure identity-based FAnoPKTR by simply coupling identity-based FAnoBE [8,9,15] with tracing [3,4,6,7,10,13,14], leading to efficiency and security degradation [2]. The communication bandwidth grows linearly with the size of maximal subscribers in FAnoBE schemes. Consequently, if we concatenate a FAnoBE with a tracing system, the tracing algorithm runs linearly with the size of maximal subscribers [3,4]. In this work, we have alleviated this inefficiency to achieve significantly low tracing time instead of similar results. Furthermore, the user's storage overhead grows sub-linearly with the maximal number of system users or polynomially with security parameter in tracing schemes. So that if we simply combine such a scheme with a FAnoBE, the size of user's secret-keys also grows likewise [2]. We emphasize that in our identity-based FAnoPKTR, the user's storage overhead is constant, which is a plausible achievement. Most importantly, all the existing FAnoBE and tracing schemes are only able to achieve adaptive **IND**istinguishable **C**hosen-**P**laintext **A**ttack (IND-CPA) security. If we directly merge these two frameworks, it also outputs an adaptive IND-CPA secure FAnoPKTR. Our work is the first that shows a technique to achieve the most robust adaptive **IND**istinguishable **C**hosen-**C**iphertext **A**ttack (IND-CCA) security while combining both these orthogonal functionalities. Although the identity-based FAnoBE and the tracing have been investigated separately, so far, there does not exist any identity-based BE that accomplishes public-key traceability with the receiver's full anonymity and *adaptive IND-CCA security*. In light of the above, we initiate the study to resolve this difficulty and develop a construction of an identity-based FAnoPKTR with order-of-magnitude improvements in computation, communication, and storage without any security breach. More specifically, we summarize below our main findings.

Table 1. Comparison among existing outsider anonymous BE schemes

Scheme	Commu	Storage			ROM	Group Type	Security		DecTm	IBE
	|CT|	|PP|	|SK|				Model	Assumption		
Acharya et al. [1]	$O(N)$	poly($\ln_3 N$)	$O(\ln_{3^2} N)$		✗	ComO, T1	SEL-IND-CPA	q-wDBDHI, q-cDDH	$O(N^2)$	✗
Fazio et al. [5]	$O(r \ln \frac{N}{r})$	$O(N)$	$O(\ln N)$		✓	PriO, T1	ADAP-IND-CPA	GDH, DDH	$O(r \ln N)$	✗
Li et al. [11]	$O(1)$	$O(N)$	$O(N)$		✗	PriO, T3	ADAP-IND-CPA	BDHE	$O(L)$	✓
Zhang et al. [18]	$O(N)$	$O(1)$	$O(1)$		✓	PriO, T1	ADAP-IND-CPA	BDH, eBDH	$O(N)$	✗
Ours	$O(L)$	$O(N)$	$O(1)$		✗	PriO, T3	ADAP-IND-CCA	DBDH-3	$O(L)$	✓

Table 2. Comparison among existing fully anonymous BE schemes

Scheme	Commu	Storage		ROM	Group Type	Security		DecTm	IBE
	|CT|	|PP|	|SK|			Model	Assumption		
He et al. [8]	$O(N)$	$O(1)$	$O(1)$	✓	PriO,T1	ADAP-IND-CPA	DBDH	$O(1)$	✓
Lai et al. [9]	$O(N)$	$O(1)$	$O(1)$	✓	PriO,T1	ADAP-IND-CPA	DBDH	$O(N)$	✓
Libert et al. [12]	$O(N)$	$O(N)$	$O(1)$	✗	PriO,T1	ADAP-IND-CPA	DDH	$O(N)$	✗
Ren et al. [15]	$O(L)$	$O(l)$	$O(l)$	✗	PriO,T3	ADAP-IND-CPA	DBDH	$O(L)$	✓
Tseng et al. [17]	$O(L)$	$O(1)$	$O(1)$	✓	PriO,T1	SEL-IND-CPA	gBDH	$O(L)$	✓
Ours	$O(L)$	$O(N)$	$O(1)$	✗	PriO,T3	ADAP-IND-CCA	DBDH-3	$O(L)$	✓

N = total number of users of the system, r = total number of revoked users, L = number of subscribers for an encryption, l = length of the user identity, η = security parameter, ROM = random oracle model, Commu = communication bandwidth, DecTm = decryption time, IBE = identity-based encryption, \|CT\| = ciphertext size, \|PP\| = public parameter size, \|SK\| = user secret key size, ADAP = adaptive, SEL = selective, IND-CPA = indistinguishable chosen-plaintext attack, IND-CCA = indistinguishable chosen-ciphertext attack, ComO = composite order, PriO = prime order, poly = polynomial, T1 = Type-1 pairing, T3 = Type-3 pairing, GDH = gap diffie-Hellman, DDH = decisional Diffie-Hellman, BDH = bilinear Diffie-Hellman, eBDH = extended bilinear Diffie-Hellman, BDHE = bilinear Diffie-Hellman exponent, wDBDHI = weak decisional bilinear Diffie-Hellman inversion, cDDH = composite decisional Diffie-Hellman, gBDH = gap bilinear Diffie-Hellman, DBDH-3 = decisional bilinear Diffie-Hellman type-3

- The security against adaptive **IND**istinguishable **C**hosen-**C**iphertext **A**ttacks (IND-CCA) is the strongest and very useful notion of security, which is not easily accomplishable for the **P**ublic-**K**ey **E**ncryption (PKE) schemes.

As compared to all the existing outsider anonymous **BE** [1,5,11,18] (cf. Table 1), fully anonymous BE [8,9,12,15,17] (cf. Table 2) and traceable BE [3,4,6,7,10,13,14] (cf. Table 3), our main contribution in this paper is that we are the *first* to achieve the adaptive IND-CCA security.

- As exhibited in Table 1, our construction is fully anonymous, whereas the works [1,5,11,18] are OAnoBE without having traitor traceability. Instead of having constant storage, the DecTm and the |CT| of [18] is linear to the total users N, which is significantly high as compared to ours. Besides, the user's storage size of our design is significantly less as opposed to [1,5,11], although the |CT| and DecTm of ours are significantly less as compared to [5] (where the number of revoked users is higher compared to the number of subscribers). However, the security proof of [5,18] is in the ROM and [1] is selectively secure under the non-standard q-type security assumptions over composite order groups. In contrast, our construction is proven to be adaptively secure under the standard DBDH-3 assumption without the ROM.

- More interestingly, compared to the existing FAnoBE [8,9,12,15,17], our identity-based FAnoPKTR is the first to achieve the public-key traceability against arbitrary collusion. Table 2 shows that the DecTm of [8] and the storage size of [8,9,17] are constant, whereas ours is slightly high. However, we note that the |CT| of [8,9,12], the DecTm of [9,12] is linear to N, which are significantly high as opposed to ours. Moreover, the work of [17] is selectively secure and [8,9,17] are proven to be secured under ROM. Although the design of [12] and ours have the same parameter sizes, we emphasize that if we transform [12] into an identity-based FAnoPKTR using the (only known) generic transformation of Murat et al. [2], then the storage overhead grows linearly in the square of N, which is highly inefficient.

Table 3. Comparison among existing trace and revoke schemes

Scheme	Commu	Storage			ROM	Group Type	Security		DecTm	IBE
	|CT|	|PP|	|SK|				Model	Assumption		
Boneh et al. [3]	$O(\sqrt{N})$	$O(\sqrt{N})$	$O(\sqrt{N})$		✗	ComO, T1	ADAP-IND-CPA	D3DH, BSD	$O(1)$	✗
Boneh et al. [4]	poly$(\ln N, \eta)$	poly$(\ln N, \eta)$	poly(η)		✗	–	ADAP-IND-CPA	FE, iO	–	✗
Garg et al. [6]	poly$(\ln N)$	poly$(\ln N)$	poly$(\ln N)$		✗	ComO, ML	ADAP-IND-CPA	FE	–	✗
Garg et al. [7]	$O(\sqrt{N})$	$O(\sqrt{N})$	$O(\sqrt{N})$		✓	PriO, T1	ADAP-IND-CPA	D3DH, XDH	$O(1)$	✗
Lee et al. [10]	$O(r)$	$O(\eta)$	$O(\ln^{1.5} N)$		✓	PriO, T1	ADAP-IND-CPA	q-SMEBDH	$O(1)$	✗
Mandal et al. [13]	poly$(\ln N, \eta)$	poly$(\ln N, \eta)$	$O(1)$		✗	PriO, ML	ADAP-IND-CPA	DHDHE, iO	$O(N)$	✗
Nishimaki et al. [14]	poly$(l, |m|)$	poly(η)	poly(l)		✗	–	ADAP-IND-CPA	FE, iO	–	✗
Ours	$O(L)$	$O(N)$	$O(1)$		✗	PriO, T3	ADAP-IND-CCA	DBDH-3	$O(L)$	✓

$|m|$ = length of the message, poly = polynomial, SMEBDH = simplified multi-exponent bilinear Diffie-Hellman, D3DH = decisional (modified) 3-party Diffie-Hellman, BSD = bilinear subgroup decision, XDH = external Diffie-Hellman, DHDHE = decisional hybrid Diffie-Hellman exponent, FE = functional encryption, iO = indistinguishability obfuscation, ML = multilinear maps

- Table 3 shows the comparison of our scheme with the existing tracing systems [3,4,6,7,10,13,14] none of which preserves receiver's full anonymity. All the works [3,7,10], except the design of [13], have constant DecTm which is slightly less than ours. The DecTm in [13] is linear to N. In contrast to [3,4,6,7,10,14], our construction has less communication bandwidth and user's storage overhead (i.e., user secret-key size) as $L < \sqrt{N}$, where L denotes a very small number of subscribers for an encryption and N stands for the total number of system users. Moreover, the construction of [3] uses composite order group, and [10] is secure in ROM under the non-standard q-SMEBDH with ciphertext size linear to revoked users r. However, the ciphertext size in our construction is linear to L and our construction is proven to be secure under the standard DBDH-3 assumption without ROM. The designs in [4,6,13,14] require less storage for public parameters than ours. However, these schemes utilize heavy duty cryptographic machinery such as multilinear maps, indistinguishability obfuscation, constrained pseudorandom functions, functional encryption, etc., secure and efficient realization of which are still to be instantiated. Moreover, the DecTm of [4,6,14] depends on a suitable FE scheme, which is highly inefficient.

2   Preliminaries

Proposition 1 (Chernoff Bound [2]). *Let $\mathcal{X}_i$ be independent random variables with $Pr[\mathcal{X}_i = 1] = p_i$, $Pr[\mathcal{X}_i = 0] = 1 - p_i$ for $i \in [1, n]$ and $\mathcal{X} = \sum_{i=1}^{n} \mathcal{X}_i$. Let $\mu = E(\mathcal{X}) = \sum_{i=1}^{n} p_i$ be the expectation. Then, the inequality $Pr\left[|\mathcal{X} - \mu| \geq a\right] \leq 2e^{\frac{-2a^2}{n}}$ holds, where $a = \mu\delta$ represents an arbitrary constant and $\delta \in (0, 1)$.*

2.1   Asymmetric Bilinear Pairings and Hardness Assumption [9,15]

Definition 1 (Asymmetric Bilinear Map). *Let $\mathbb{G}^+$ and $\widetilde{\mathbb{G}}^+$ be two additive source groups with no efficient computable isomorphism from $\mathbb{G}^+$ to $\widetilde{\mathbb{G}}^+$, and $\mathbb{G}_T^\times$ be a multiplicative target group. The groups $\mathbb{G}^+$ and $\mathbb{G}_T^\times$ have the same large prime order p ($> 2^\eta$), and the order of $\widetilde{\mathbb{G}}^+$ is some power of p. Let P, $\widetilde{P}$ be two generators of $\mathbb{G}^+$ and $\widetilde{\mathbb{G}}^+$ respectively. A function $e : \mathbb{G}^+ \times \widetilde{\mathbb{G}}^+ \to \mathbb{G}_T^\times$ is said to be asymmetric bilinear mapping if it has the following three properties.*

1. **Bilinearity:** $e(aU, b\widetilde{V}) = e(U, \widetilde{V})^{ab}$, $\forall\ U \in \mathbb{G}^+$, $\widetilde{V} \in \widetilde{\mathbb{G}}^+$ and $\forall\ a, b \in \mathbb{Z}_p$.
2. **Non-degeneracy:** *The function is non-degenerate, i.e., $e(P, \widetilde{P})$ is a generator of $\mathbb{G}_T^\times$.*
3. **Computability:** *The function e is efficiently computable.*

The tuple $\mathbb{BG} = (p, \mathbb{G}^+, \widetilde{\mathbb{G}}^+, \mathbb{G}_T^\times, e)$ is known as Type-3 asymmetric bilinear system.

Decisional Bilinear Diffie-Hellman Type-3 (DBDH-3) Assumption

- **Input:** The instance $\langle Z, K \rangle$, where $Z = \left[\mathbb{BG}, P, bP, cP, \widetilde{P}, a\widetilde{P}, b\widetilde{P}, c\widetilde{P} \right]$ for some $a, b, c \in \mathbb{Z}_p^*$ and either $K = e(P, \widetilde{P})^{abc}$ or $K = X \in_R \mathbb{G}_T^\times$.
- **Output:** 0 if $K = e(P, \widetilde{P})^{abc}$; 1 otherwise.

Definition 2 (DBDH-3 Assumption). *The asymmetric DBDH-3 assumption holds with* (t', ϵ') *if for every* PPT *adversary* $\mathcal{B}$ *with running time at most* t', *the advantage of solving the above problem is at most* $\epsilon' = \epsilon'(\eta)$, *i.e.,*

$$Adv_{\mathcal{B}}^{DBDH\text{-}3}(\eta) = \left| Pr[\mathcal{B}(Z, K = e(P, \widetilde{P})^{abc}) = 0] - Pr[\mathcal{B}(Z, K = X) = 0] \right| \leq \epsilon'$$

2.2 Tardos Codes [16]

An optimal probabilistic collusion-secure code known as *Tardos codes* $\mathsf{TC} = (\mathsf{CodeGen}, \mathsf{Identify})$, introduced by Gábor Tardos [16], consists of two randomized algorithms, which are described below.

- $(\Gamma, \mathsf{WatMTK}) \leftarrow \mathsf{CodeGen}(1^\eta, N)$: The tracer executes this code generation algorithm by taking as input η along with a positive integer $N = \mathsf{poly}(\eta)$. It first chooses an error bound $\epsilon \in (0, 1)$ together with a maximal collusion bound $L = \mathsf{poly}(\eta) \leq N$ to set $k = \lceil \log\left(\frac{1}{\epsilon}\right) \rceil$ and code length $l = 100L^2 k$. Then, it chooses independent and identically distributed random variables $X_i \in [t, 1-t]$ with $t = \frac{1}{300L}$ and $X_i = \sin^2 r_i$, where $i = 1, 2, \ldots, l$, r_i is selected uniformly at random from $[t', \frac{\pi}{2} - t']$ with $0 < t' < \frac{\pi}{4}$, and $\sin^2 t' = t$. It generates a code matrix $C_{N \times l}$ by selecting each entry c_{ji} independently from $\{0, 1\}$ with probability $Pr[c_{ji} = 1] = X_i$ for $j = 1, 2, \ldots, N$ and $i = 1, 2, \ldots, l$. Note that the random variables c_{ji} and $c_{j'i}$ (with $j \neq j'$) are positively correlated as both of them tend to be 1 if X_i is very large. It constructs the code book $\Gamma = \{w_j\}_{j=1}^N$, where $w_j \in \{0, 1\}^l$ is the j-th row of code matrix $C_{N \times l}$. It computes a threshold parameter $Z = 20Lk$ to set the watermarking master tracing key $\mathsf{WatMTK} = (Z, \{X_i\}_{i=1}^l)$. Finally, the algorithm outputs the pair $(\Gamma, \mathsf{WatMTK})$.
- $(\mathbb{T}) \leftarrow \mathsf{Identify}(\mathsf{WatMTK}, w)$: The traitor identification algorithm is run by the tracer taking $\mathsf{WatMTK} = (Z, \{X_i\}_{i=1}^l)$ and a l-length pirate code word w as inputs. Suppose that $\mathcal{S} = \{w_j\}_{j=1}^L (\subseteq \Gamma)$ be a coalition of traitors, and let $F(\mathcal{S})$ denotes the feasible set of $\mathcal{S}$ containing w. Then $F(\mathcal{S})$ satisfies the marking condition: if $w_j[i] = b \in \{0, 1\}$ for all positions $1 \leq i \leq l$, then $w[i] = b$, where $w_j[i]$ is the i-th bit of $w_j \in \mathcal{S}$ and $w[i]$ represents the i-th bit of $w \in \{0, 1\}^l$. It extracts $\{X_i\}_{i=1}^l$ from WatMTK, and generates a matrix $M_{N \times l}$ with the following entries.

$$m_{ji} = \begin{cases} \sqrt{\frac{1 - X_i}{X_i}}, & \text{if } w_j[i] = 1 \\ -\sqrt{\frac{X_i}{1 - X_i}}, & \text{if } w_j[i] = 0 \end{cases}$$

Note that the random variables m_{ji} are independent and each has expected value 0 and variance 1. It extracts Z from WatMTK, checks whether $\sum_{i=1}^{l} w[i] \cdot m_{ji} > Z$ and if so, then it accuses the code word $w_j \in S$ as a fraud code word used in creating the pirate code word $w \in F(S)$. Finally, it outputs a set $\mathbb{T}(\subseteq S)$ such that the members in $\mathbb{T}$ are accused in creating w.

Correctness: The correctness of TC follows from the following theorems.

Theorem 1 ([16]). *Assume that $j \in \{1, 2, \ldots, N\}$ be an arbitrary user index. Let $S \subseteq \Gamma \backslash \{w_j\}$ be a coalition of size $L \leq N$, and $F(S)$ be the feasible set of S. Then, $Pr[w_j \in \mathbb{T}] < \epsilon$.*

Theorem 2 ([16]). *Let $S \subseteq \Gamma$ be a coalition of size $|S| \leq L$, and $F(S)$ be the feasible set of S. Then, $Pr[(S \cap \mathbb{T}) = \emptyset] < (\epsilon)^{\frac{L}{4}}$.*

2.3   Identity-Based Fully Anonymous Public-Key Trace and Revoke

Syntax: An identity-based *fully anonymous public-key trace and revoke* scheme, denoted by FAnoPKTR, is a tuple of three **P**robabilistic **P**olynomial **T**ime (PPT) algorithms-(Setup, KeyGen, Enc), one deterministic polynomial time algorithm Dec and a probabilistic tracing algorithm Trace$^{\mathcal{D}}$, which are described below.

- $(MPK, MSK) \leftarrow Setup(1^{\eta}, l)$: Taking a security parameter η along with the length l of the user identities as input, this algorithm outputs a master public-key MPK and a master secret-key MSK.
- $(SK_{ID_i}) \leftarrow KeyGen(MPK, MSK, ID_i)$: On receiving (MPK, MSK) and an identity $ID_i \in \{0, 1\}^l$, the algorithm outputs the secret-key $SK_{ID_i} = (d_i)$.
- $(CT) \leftarrow Enc(MPK, S, M)$: On input MPK, a set S of subscribed users and a message M, the encryption algorithm outputs the ciphertext CT corresponding to M.
- $(M \vee \perp) \leftarrow Dec(MPK, SK_{ID_i}, CT)$: Getting MPK, SK_{ID_i} and CT as inputs, it either recovers the correct message M or gets a designated symbol $\perp$ indicating decryption failure.
- $(\mathbb{T}) \leftarrow Trace^{\mathcal{D}}(MPK)$: Taking MPK as input, the tracing algorithm interacts polynomially many times with the decoder $\mathcal{D}$ and outputs a set of users $\mathbb{T}(\subseteq S)$, who are accused as traitors.

Correctness: We say that the scheme is correct if for all η, M and $ID_i \in S$

$$
Pr \left[M \leftarrow Dec(MPK, SK_{ID_i}, CT) : \begin{array}{l} (MPK, MSK) \leftarrow Setup(1^{\eta}, l) \\ SK_{ID_i} \leftarrow KeyGen(MPK, MSK, ID_i) \\ CT \leftarrow Enc(MPK, S, M) \end{array} \right] = 1
$$

Security: The security against message indistinguishability, receivers anonymity and traceability are the three security attributes of a identity-based FAnoPKTR scheme. The following three games model these security attributes.

(i) Ciphertext indistinguishability [12,15]: This game, under the adaptive IND-CCA security, is played between a PPT adversary $\mathcal{A}$ and a challenger $\mathcal{C}$. The advantage of $\mathcal{A}$ in winning the game is defined as $\mathsf{Adv}^{\mathsf{IND\text{-}CCA}}_{\mathcal{A},\mathsf{FAnoPKTR}}(\eta) = |\mathsf{MIAdvc}(\eta) - \frac{1}{2}|$, where $\mathsf{MIAdvc}(\eta)$ is given by the following quantity.

$$\Pr \left[(\zeta = \zeta') : \begin{array}{l} (\mathsf{MPK}, \mathsf{MSK}) \leftarrow \mathsf{Setup}(1^\eta, l) \\ ((M_0^*, M_1^*), \mathcal{S}^*) \leftarrow [\mathcal{A}(1^\eta)]^{\mathcal{O}_1(\mathsf{MPK},\mathsf{MSK},\cdot),\mathcal{O}_2(\mathsf{MPK},\cdot,\cdot)} \\ \zeta \in_R \{0,1\} \\ (\mathsf{CT}^*) \leftarrow \mathsf{Enc}(\mathsf{MPK}, \mathcal{S}^*, M_\zeta^*) \\ (\zeta') \leftarrow \mathcal{A}(\mathsf{CT}^*, \{\mathsf{SK}_{ID_u} : ID_u \notin \mathcal{S}^*\}_{u=1}^q) \end{array} \right]$$

Here, $\mathcal{O}_1(\mathsf{MPK}, \mathsf{MSK}, \cdot)$ denotes the key generation oracle access that allows $\mathcal{A}$ to adaptively query on identities ID_{u_i} such that $i \in \mathbb{I} \subseteq [N]$ with $|\mathbb{I}| \leq q = \mathsf{poly}(\eta) \leq N$, and it returns $(\mathsf{SK}_{ID_{u_i}}) \leftarrow \mathsf{KeyGen}(\mathsf{MPK}, \mathsf{MSK}, ID_{u_i})$ for all $i \in \mathbb{I}$. Also, $\mathcal{O}_2(\mathsf{MPK}, \cdot, \cdot)$ denotes the decryption oracle access that allows $\mathcal{A}$ to query on a ciphertext CT and an identity ID_{u_i}, and it returns $\mathsf{Dec}(\mathsf{MPK}, \mathsf{SK}_{ID_{u_i}}, \mathsf{CT})$.

Definition 3 (Security of Ciphertext Indistinguishability). *We say that FAnoPKTR scheme is (t, ϵ, q) IND-CCA secure if $\mathsf{Adv}^{\mathsf{IND\text{-}CCA}}_{\mathcal{A},\mathsf{FAnoPKTR}}(\eta)$ is negligible function of η for all PPT adversary $\mathcal{A}$ with runtime at most t and making at most q secret key queries.*

(ii) Anonymity [12,15]: This game is also played between a PPT adversary $\mathcal{A}$ and a challenger $\mathcal{C}$. The advantage of $\mathcal{A}$ in winning the game is defined as $\mathsf{Adv}^{\mathsf{IND\text{-}ANO\text{-}CCA}}_{\mathcal{A},\mathsf{FAnoPKTR}}(\eta) = |\mathsf{AAdvc}(\eta) - \frac{1}{2}|$, where $\mathsf{AAdvc}(\eta)$ is given by

$$\Pr \left[(\varkappa' = \varkappa) : \begin{array}{l} (\mathsf{MPK}, \mathsf{MSK}) \leftarrow \mathsf{Setup}(1^\eta, l) \\ (M^*, (\mathcal{S}_0^*, \mathcal{S}_1^*)) \leftarrow [\mathcal{A}(1^\eta)]^{\mathcal{O}_1(\mathsf{MPK},\mathsf{MSK},\cdot),\mathcal{O}_2(\mathsf{MPK},\cdot,\cdot)} \\ \varkappa \in_R \{0,1\} \\ (\mathsf{CT}^*) \leftarrow \mathsf{Enc}(\mathsf{MPK}, \mathcal{S}_\varkappa^*, M^*) \\ (\varkappa') \leftarrow \mathcal{A}(\mathsf{CT}^*, \{\mathsf{SK}_{ID_u} : ID_u \notin \mathcal{S}_0^* \triangle \mathcal{S}_1^*\}_{u=1}^q) \end{array} \right]$$

Here, $\mathcal{O}_1(\mathsf{MPK}, \mathsf{MSK}, \cdot)$ and $\mathcal{O}_2(\mathsf{MPK}, \cdot, \cdot)$ can be defined as before.

Definition 4 (Security of Anonymity). *We say that the FAnoPKTR is* (t, ϵ, q) **IND***istinguishable* **ANO***nymous* **C***hosen-Ciphertext* **A***ttack (IND-ANO-CCA)-secure if* $\mathsf{Adv}^{IND\text{-}ANO\text{-}CCA}_{\mathcal{A},\mathsf{FAnoPKTR}}(\eta)$ *is negligible function of* η *for all PPT adversary* $\mathcal{A}$ *with runtime at most* t *and making at most* q *secret key queries.*

(iii) Traceability [2]: This game is played between an adversary $\mathcal{A}$ and a tracer $\mathcal{C}$. The advantage of $\mathcal{A}$ in winning the game is defined as

$$\mathsf{Adv}^{\mathsf{TT}}_{\mathcal{A},\mathsf{FAnoPKTR}}(\eta) = \left|\mathsf{TAdvc}(\eta)\right|,$$

where $\mathsf{TAdvc}(\eta)$ is given by the following quantity.

$$\Pr\left[\begin{array}{l}(\mathsf{MPK}, \mathsf{MSK}) \leftarrow \mathsf{Setup}(1^\eta, l) \\[2pt] (\zeta = 1) : (\mathcal{D}) \leftarrow [\mathcal{A}(1^\eta, \mathsf{MPK}, L)]^{\mathcal{O}_1(\mathsf{MPK},\mathsf{MSK},\cdot),\mathcal{O}_2(\mathsf{MPK},\cdot,\cdot)} \\[2pt] (\mathbb{T}) \leftarrow \mathsf{Trace}^{\mathcal{D}}(\mathsf{MPK}) \\[2pt] \text{If } (X_1 \wedge X_2) \text{ holds, set } \zeta = 1; \text{ Else, set } \zeta = 0\end{array}\right]$$

Here, X_1 is the event that $\mathcal{D}$ is an ϵ-useful decoder and X_2 is the event that $\mathbb{T}$ is either empty or not a subset of $\mathcal{E} = \{ID_{u_i} : i \in \mathbb{I}\}$ such that all ID_{u_i} queried to $\mathcal{O}_1(\mathsf{MPK}, \mathsf{MSK}, \cdot)$. For a randomly chosen message M_i, we say that $\mathcal{D}$ is ϵ-useful decoder if $\Pr[\mathcal{D}(\mathsf{Enc}(\mathsf{MPK}, \mathcal{S}, M_i)) = M_i] \geq \epsilon$. Here, $\mathcal{O}_1(\mathsf{MPK}, \mathsf{MSK}, \cdot)$ and $\mathcal{O}_2(\mathsf{MPK}, \cdot, \cdot)$ can be defined as before.

Definition 5 (Security of Traceability). *We say that the scheme FAnoPKTR is* (t, ϵ) *traceable if* $\mathsf{Adv}^{\mathsf{TT}}_{\mathcal{A},\mathsf{FAnoPKTR}}(\eta)$ *is negligible function of* η *for all decoder, corresponding to some polynomial-sized set of identities, provided by all PPT adversary* $\mathcal{A}$ *with run-time at most* t.

3   Our Construction

The communication model of our identity-based $\mathsf{FAnoPKTR} = (\mathsf{Setup}, \mathsf{KeyGen}, \mathsf{Enc}, \mathsf{Dec}, \mathsf{Trace}^{\mathcal{D}})$ scheme involves a GM, a broadcaster, several users and a tracer. The algorithms are detailed below.

- $(\mathsf{MPK}, \mathsf{MSK}) \leftarrow \mathsf{Setup}(1^\eta, l)$: The GM, on input the security parameter η along with the length l of user identities, proceeds as follows. Here, the set of all user's identities is given by $\mathcal{ID} = \{ID_1, ID_2, \ldots, ID_N\}$, where $N = 2^l$.

  (i) It first generates an asymmetric bilinear group system $\mathbb{BG} = (p, \mathbb{G}^+, \widetilde{\mathbb{G}}^+, \mathbb{G}^\times_T, e)$ (cf. Sect. 2.1). Let P, $\widetilde{P}$ be two random generators of $\mathbb{G}^+$ and $\widetilde{\mathbb{G}}^+$ respectively. It chooses random exponents $\alpha, \beta, \gamma, \{\gamma_j, \lambda_j\}^l_{j=1}, x, y \in \mathbb{Z}^*_p$ and computes the following.

$$\{U_j = \gamma_j P, \widetilde{U}_j = \gamma_j \widetilde{P}\}^l_{j=1}, U^{'} = \gamma P, \widetilde{U}^{'} = \gamma \widetilde{P}, \widetilde{B} = \beta \widetilde{P}, \widetilde{X} = x\widetilde{P}, \widetilde{Y} = y\widetilde{P},$$

$$\left\{Q_i = \sum_{ID_i[k]=1} \lambda_k \cdot \sum_{ID_i[k]=1} U_k, \widetilde{Q}_i = \sum_{ID_i[k]=1} \lambda_k \cdot \sum_{ID_i[k]=1} \widetilde{U}_k\right\}^N_{i=1}, \Omega = e(P, \widetilde{P})^{\alpha\beta}$$

Here, $ID_i[k] \in \{0, 1\}$ denotes the k-th bit of $ID_i \in \{0, 1\}^l$.

(ii) It selects a collision resistant cryptographic hash function H : $\{0,1\}^* \rightarrow \mathbb{Z}_p^*$ to set the master public key as $\mathsf{MPK} = (\mathbb{BG}, P, \tilde{P}, \Omega, U', \{Q_i\}_{i=1}^N, \tilde{X}, \tilde{Y}, H)$ and the master secret key $\mathsf{MSK} = (\alpha \tilde{B}, \tilde{U}', \{\tilde{Q}_i\}_{i=1}^N)$. Finally, the GM publishes MPK and keeps MSK secret to itself.

- $(\mathsf{SK}_{ID_i}) \leftarrow \mathsf{KeyGen}(\mathsf{MPK}, \mathsf{MSK}, ID_i)$: On receiving a user identity $ID_i = (ID_i[1] \, ID_i[2] \dots ID_i[l]) \in \{0,1\}^l$ from a user i, the GM selects $r \in_R \mathbb{Z}_p^*$ and generates a secret key $\mathsf{SK}_{ID_i} = (d_{i,1}, d_{i,2})$, using the MSK and extracting $\tilde{P}$ from the MPK, as follows.

$$d_{i,1} = \alpha \tilde{B} + r(\tilde{U}' + \tilde{Q}_i) \text{ and } d_{i,2} = r\tilde{P}$$

Finally, the GM sends SK_{ID_i} to user i through a secure communication channel between them.

- $(\mathsf{CT}) \leftarrow \mathsf{Enc}(\mathsf{MPK}, \mathcal{S}, M)$: The broadcaster takes as input MPK, a polynomial sized set $\mathcal{S} = \{ID_i : i \in I_{\mathcal{S}}\}$ of subscribed users, and a message $M \in \mathbb{G}_T^\times$. Here, $I_{\mathcal{S}}$ is the index set of $\mathcal{S}$ with $|I_{\mathcal{S}}| \leq L = \mathsf{poly}(\eta) \leq N$. It performs the following steps to produce a ciphertext corresponding to M.

(i) The encryptor first chooses a random partition $(\mathcal{S}_0, \mathcal{S}_1)$ of the set $\mathcal{S}$, where $\mathcal{S}_0 = \{ID_{0,i}\}_{i=1}^\xi$ and $\mathcal{S}_1 = \{ID_{1,i}\}_{i=1}^\delta$ are disjoint sets with $\mathcal{S} = \mathcal{S}_0 \cup \mathcal{S}_1$, $\xi + \delta = L \leq N$. It then executes the following steps for the set $\mathcal{S}_b = \{ID_{b,i}\}_{i=1}^m$, where either $m = \xi$ if $b = 0$ or $m = \delta$ if $b = 1$.

(a) It extracts H from MPK to compute $x_{b,1} = H(ID_{b,1})$, $x_{b,2} = H(ID_{b,2})$, $\dots$, $x_{b,m} = H(ID_{b,m})$. For $i = 1, 2 \dots, m$ sets the following polynomials

$$f_{b,i}(x) = \prod_{\substack{j=1 \\ j \neq i}}^m \frac{(x - x_{b,j})}{(x_{b,i} - x_{b,j})} = a_{b,i,1} + \dots + a_{b,i,m} \, (x)^{m-1} \pmod p.$$

Here, either $f_{b,i}(x) = 1$ if $x = x_{b,i}$ or $f_{b,i}(x) = 0$ if $x = x_{b,j}$ for all $i \neq j$.

(b) It randomly chooses $s \in \mathbb{Z}_p^*$. For $i = 1, 2 \dots, m$, it computes

$$\mathcal{R}_{b,i} = \sum_{j=1}^m a_{b,j,i} \, s(U' + Q_{b,j}),$$

and sets $\mathcal{V} = sP$, $\mathcal{W} = M \cdot \Omega^s$. It generates the ciphertext components $\mathsf{CT}_b = (\{\mathcal{R}_{b,i}\}_{i=1}^m, \mathcal{V}, \mathcal{W})$ corresponding to $\mathcal{S}_b$ for $b = 0, 1$.

(c) It also computes $\theta_b = H\left(\{\mathcal{R}_{b,i}\}_{i=1}^m, \mathcal{V}, \mathcal{W}, M\right)$ and $\tilde{\Gamma}_b = s\left(\tilde{X} + (\theta_b \tilde{Y})\right)$.

(ii) Finally, the broadcaster publishes $\mathsf{CT} = \left(\mathsf{CT}_0, \mathsf{CT}_1, \tilde{\Gamma}_0, \tilde{\Gamma}_1\right)$ as the ciphertext.

- $(M \vee \perp) \leftarrow \mathsf{Dec}(\mathsf{MPK}, \mathsf{SK}_{ID_i}, \mathsf{CT})$: A subscribed user i, belonging to $\mathcal{S} = \mathcal{S}_0 \cup \mathcal{S}_1$, with SK_{ID_i} and MPK can recover the correct message M from the ciphertext CT by trying to decrypt both the ciphertext components CT_0 and CT_1. One of them, say CT_b for $b \in \{0,1\}$, leads the decryptor i to a valid decryption when executes the following steps.

  (i) Since CT_b leads to a valid decryption, therefore, $ID_i \in \mathcal{S}_b$ for $b \in \{0,1\}$. Consequently, the identity is of the form $ID_i = ID_{b,i} = (ID_{b,i}[1]\, ID_{b,i}[2] \ldots ID_{b,i}[l])$ for i belonging to either $[\xi]$ or $[\delta]$ depending on whether $ID_i = ID_{0,i} \in \mathcal{S}_0$ or $ID_i = ID_{1,i} \in \mathcal{S}_1$ respectively. Decryptor extracts H from MPK, and computes the followings.

$$x_{b,i} = H(ID_{b,i}),$$
$$\Lambda_{b,i} = \mathcal{R}_{b,1} + \ldots + \mathcal{R}_{b,i}(x_{b,i})^{i-1} + \ldots + \mathcal{R}_{b,m}(x_{b,i})^{m-1} \ (\mathrm{mod}\, p),$$

  where $\{\mathcal{R}_{b,i}\}_{i=1}^{m}$ are separated from CT_b, and $ID_{b,i}$ is the identity of i. Note that if $b = 0$, then $m = \xi$ and if $b = 1$, then $m = \delta$.

  (ii) It also recovers computes $M' = \mathcal{W} \times \frac{e(\Lambda_{b,i}, d_{i,2})}{e(\mathcal{V}, d_{i,1})}$ and $\theta'_b = H\Big(\{\mathcal{R}_{b,i}\}_{i=1}^{m}, \mathcal{V}, \mathcal{W}, M'\Big).$

  (iii) Finally, it retrieves the correct message as follows.

$$M = \begin{cases} M' & \text{if } e\Big(\mathcal{V}, \widetilde{X} + (\theta'_b \widetilde{Y})\Big) = e\Big(P, \widetilde{\Gamma}_b\Big) \\ \perp & \text{Otherwise} \end{cases}$$

- $(\mathbb{T}) \leftarrow \mathsf{Trace}^{\mathcal{D}}(\mathsf{MPK})$: To execute the tracing algorithm, the tracer, who knows the set $\mathcal{S}$, takes MPK as input and proceeds as follows.

  (i) It first runs $\mathsf{TC.CodeGen}(1^\eta, N)$ algorithm to generate the watermarking master tracing key $\mathsf{WatMTK} = (Z, \{X_i\}_{i=1}^{l})$ and the code book $\Gamma = \{w_i\}_{i=1}^{N}$ (cf. Sect. 2.2). It assigns code word $w_i \in \Gamma$ to each user $i \in [N]$ and constructs the set $\widetilde{S} = \{w_i : i \in I_S\} \subset \Gamma$ that corresponds to the subscribed users set $\mathcal{S}$. It chooses a random permutation $\pi : [N] \to [N]$ and shuffles the indices of all the code words in the subset $\widetilde{S}$ by employing π. It initially sets a code word $w = 0^l$ as a pirate code word.

  (ii) The tracer executes the following steps to construct a l-length pirate code word w belonging to the feasible set $F(\widetilde{S})$ of $\widetilde{S}$. For each index $j = 1, 2, \ldots, l$, the tracer repeatedly performs the following steps.

    – A partition of $\mathcal{S}$, denoted by $\mathsf{RS}_\pi^{(j)} = (\mathcal{S}_0^{(j)}, \mathcal{S}_1^{(j)})$, is constructed by setting

$$\mathcal{S}_b^{(j)} = \begin{cases} \mathcal{S} \cap \{ID_v | w_{\pi(v)}[j] = 0, \forall w_v \in \widetilde{S}\}, & \text{if } b = 0 \\ \mathcal{S} \cap \{ID_v | w_{\pi(v)}[j] = 1, \forall w_v \in \widetilde{S}\}, & \text{if } b = 1 \end{cases}$$

Due to the random choice of π, the partition $\mathsf{RS}_\pi^{(j)}$ is indistinguishable from the original partition $(\mathcal{S}_0, \mathcal{S}_1)$ of $\mathcal{S}$ in the main encryption algorithm.

– A random message $M_{\mathsf{rand}} \in \mathbb{G}_T^\times$ is chosen to construct the tracing ciphertexts: $\mathsf{CT}[j] = [\mathsf{CT}_0[j] = (\{\mathcal{R}_{0,i}\}_{i=1}^{\xi'}, \mathcal{V}, \mathcal{W}_{\mathsf{rand}}), \mathsf{CT}_1[j] = (\{\mathcal{R}_{1,i}\}_{i=1}^{\delta'}, \mathcal{V}, \mathcal{W})]$ corresponding to the index j and $\mathsf{RS}_\pi^{(j)}$, where $\mathcal{W}_{\mathsf{rand}} = M_{\mathsf{rand}} \cdot \Omega^s$, $\mathcal{W} = M \cdot \Omega^s$ and rest of the ciphertext components are constructed in the similar manner as shown in the main encryption algorithm.

– It interacts with $\mathcal{D}$ by providing polynomially many tracing ciphertexts $\mathsf{CT}[j]$ for different choices of M, $M_{\mathsf{rand}} \in_R \mathbb{G}_T^\times$. Let $p_{1,j}$ be the success probability of $\mathcal{D}$ in decrypting the ciphertext corresponding to the j-th bit. The tracer will replace the j-th bit $w[j]$ of the pirate code word w with 1 if $p_{1,j} \geq \frac{1}{2}$.

– It outputs the pirate code cord $w \in \{0,1\}^l$. Note that we can estimate w in a similar manner by considering $p_{0,j}$ instead of $p_{1,j}$, by setting $\mathsf{CT}_1[j]$ to be the encryption of random message.

(iii) Finally, the tracer runs $\mathsf{TC.Identify}(\mathsf{WatMTK}, w)$ algorithm of Sect. 2.2 to get a subset $\mathbb{T}_\pi (\subseteq \widetilde{\mathcal{S}})$ such that the elements of the set are accused in creating the pirate code word w. Hence, the set $\mathbb{T} = \{ID_{\pi^{-1}(t)} : w_t \in \mathbb{T}_\pi\}$ $(\subseteq \mathcal{S})$ is the set of all traitors involved in the production of the pirate decoder $\mathcal{D}$.

Approximation of the success probability $p_{1,j}$ of $\mathcal{D}$ for each index j and the correctness of tracing algorithm are shown in Theorem 5. Here, we assume that at the beginning $\mathcal{S}$ is given to tracer by the broadcaster and it is entirely outside the control of adversary. Consequently, any broadcaster, who has the knowledge of $\mathcal{S}$, plays the role of tracer.

Correctness: Assume that a subscribed user i, having its identity string ID_i belonging to $\mathcal{S}_0$ and valid ciphertext components, is running the decryption algorithm. Therefore, the identity ID_i will be of the form $ID_i = ID_{0,i} = (ID_{0,i}[1] \ldots ID_{0,i}[l]) \in \{0,1\}^l$. The first component of the secret-key SK_{ID_i} is given by $d_{i,1} = \alpha \widetilde{B} + r(\widetilde{U}' + \widetilde{Q}_{0,i})$. The decryptor i will try to decrypt both CT_0 and CT_1. Since CT_1 corresponds to $\mathcal{S}_1$ and $ID_i \notin \mathcal{S}_1$, therefore, decryption on CT_1 will output $\bot$. However, user i recovers M from CT_0 by the following computations.

$$\mathcal{R}_{0,1} + \cdots + \mathcal{R}_{0,i}\left(x_{0,i}\right)^{i-1} + \cdots + \mathcal{R}_{0,\xi}\left(x_{0,i}\right)^{\xi-1}$$

$$= \sum_{j=1}^{\xi} a_{0,j,1}\; s(U' + \sum_{ID_{0,j}[k]=1} \lambda_k \cdot \sum_{ID_{0,j}[k]=1} U_k) + \cdots + \sum_{j=1}^{\xi} a_{0,j,i}\; s(U' +$$

$$\sum_{ID_{0,j}[k]=1} \lambda_k \cdot \sum_{ID_{0,j}[k]=1} U_k)(x_{0,i})^{i-1} + \cdots + \sum_{j=1}^{\xi} a_{0,j,\xi}\; s(U' + \sum_{ID_{0,j}[k]=1} \lambda_k \cdot \sum_{ID_{0,j}[k]=1} U_k)(x_{0,i})^{\xi-1}$$

$$= [a_{0,1,1}\; s(U' + \sum_{ID_{0,1}[k]=1} \lambda_k \cdot \sum_{ID_{0,1}[k]=1} U_k) +$$

$$\cdots + a_{0,\xi,1}\; s(U' + \sum_{ID_{0,\xi}[k]=1} \lambda_k \cdot \sum_{ID_{0,\xi}[k]=1} U_k)] + \cdots + [a_{0,1,i}\; s(U' + \sum_{ID_{0,1}[k]=1} \lambda_k \cdot \sum_{ID_{0,1}[k]=1} U_k) +$$

$$\cdots + a_{0,\xi,i}\; s(U' + \sum_{ID_{0,\xi}[k]=1} \lambda_k \cdot \sum_{ID_{0,\xi}[k]=1} U_k)](x_{0,i})^{i-1} + \cdots + [a_{0,1,\xi}\; s(U' +$$

$$\sum_{ID_{0,1}[k]=1} \lambda_k \cdot \sum_{ID_{0,1}[k]=1} U_k) + \cdots + a_{0,\xi,\xi}\; s(U' + \sum_{ID_{0,\xi}[k]=1} \lambda_k \cdot \sum_{ID_{0,\xi}[k]=1} U_k)](x_{0,i})^{\xi-1}$$

$$= s(\sum_{j=1}^{\xi} a_{0,1,j} x_{0,i}^{j-1})(U' + \sum_{ID_{0,1}[k]=1} \lambda_k \cdot \sum_{ID_{0,1}[k]=1} U_k) + \cdots + s(\sum_{j=1}^{\xi} a_{0,i,j} x_{0,i}^{j-1})(U' +$$

$$\sum_{ID_{0,i}[k]=1} \lambda_k \cdot \sum_{ID_{0,i}[k]=1} U_k) + \cdots + s(\sum_{j=1}^{\xi} a_{0,\xi,j} x_{0,i}^{j-1})(U' + \sum_{ID_{0,\xi}[k]=1} \lambda_k \cdot \sum_{ID_{0,\xi}[k]=1} U_k)$$

$$= s f_{0,1}(x_{0,i})(U' + \sum_{ID_{0,1}[k]=1} \lambda_k \cdot \sum_{ID_{0,1}[k]=1} U_k) + \cdots + s f_{0,i}(x_{0,i})(U' + \sum_{ID_{0,i}[k]=1} \lambda_k \cdot \sum_{ID_{0,i}[k]=1} U_k) +$$

$$\cdots + s f_{0,\xi}(x_{0,i})(U' + \sum_{ID_{0,\xi}[k]=1} \lambda_k \cdot \sum_{ID_{0,\xi}[k]=1} U_k) = s(U' + \sum_{ID_{0,i}[k]=1} \lambda_k \cdot \sum_{ID_{0,i}[k]=1} U_k)$$

Therefore, $\Lambda_{0,i} = s\left(U' + \sum_{ID_{0,i}[k]=1} \lambda_k \cdot \sum_{ID_{0,i}[k]=1} U_k\right)$, since $f_{0,i}(x_{0,i}) = 1$ and $f_{0,j}(x_{0,i}) = 0$ for all $j \neq i$ as described before.

$$e(\mathcal{V}, d_{i,1}) = e\left(sP, \alpha\widetilde{B} + r(\widetilde{U}' + \widetilde{Q}_{0,i})\right)$$

$$= e\left(sP, \alpha\widetilde{B} + r(\widetilde{U}' + \sum_{ID_{0,i}[k]=1} \lambda_k \cdot \sum_{ID_{0,i}[k]=1} \widetilde{U}_k)\right)$$

$$= e(sP, \alpha\widetilde{B})e\left(sP, r(\gamma + \sum_{ID_{0,i}[k]=1} \lambda_k \cdot \sum_{ID_{0,i}[k]=1} \gamma_k)\widetilde{P}\right)$$

$$= \Omega^s \cdot e\left(s(\gamma + \sum_{ID_{0,i}[k]=1} \lambda_k \cdot \sum_{ID_{0,i}[k]=1} \gamma_k)P, r\widetilde{P}\right) = \Omega^s \cdot e(\Lambda_{0,i}, d_{i,2})$$

The decryptor recovers the correct message by the following computation.

$$\mathcal{W} \times \frac{e(\Lambda_{0,i}, d_{i,2})}{e(\mathcal{V}, d_{i,1})} = M \cdot \Omega^s \times \frac{e(\Lambda_{0,i}, d_{i,2})}{e(\Lambda_{0,i}, d_{i,2}) \cdot \Omega^s} = M$$

Finally, we can show that for a valid message $M' = M$ and valid ciphertext components $\mathsf{CT}_0 = \left(\{\mathcal{R}_{0,i}\}_{i=1}^m, \mathcal{V}, \mathcal{W}\right)$ the following holds.

$$\theta_0' = H\left(\{\mathcal{R}_{0,i}\}_{i=1}^m, \mathcal{V}, \mathcal{W}, M = M'\right) = \theta_0$$

$$e\left(\mathcal{V}, \widetilde{X} + (\theta_0'\widetilde{Y})\right) = e\left(sP, \widetilde{X} + (\theta_0\widetilde{Y})\right) = e\left(P, s\left(\widetilde{X} + (\theta_0\widetilde{Y})\right)\right) = e\left(P, \widetilde{\Gamma}_0\right)$$

Similarly, if the user identity $ID_i \in S_1$, then it can recover the correct message M from CT_1 by accomplishing the similar computations.

4   Security Analysis

Theorem 3 (Ciphertext Indistinguishability). *Our proposed identity-based FAnoPKTR scheme, presented in Sect. 3, accomplishes adaptive IND-CCA security as per the $(t, \epsilon, poly(\eta))$ message indistinguishability security under the standard asymmetric (t', ϵ') DBDH-3 assumption, where η is the security parameter and $poly(\eta)$ represents a polynomial in η.*

Proof. Assume that there exists a PPT adversary $\mathcal{A}$ that breaks the adaptive IND-CCA security of our identity-based FAnoPKTR with a non-negligible advantage, where $\mathcal{A}$ makes at most $q = poly(\eta)$ number of secret key queries. Then, we can construct a PPT simulator $\mathcal{B}$ that attempts to break the asymmetric DBDH-3 assumption of Sect. 2.1 using $\mathcal{A}$ as a subroutine. At the beginning, $\mathcal{B}$ obtains the DBDH-3 challenge instance $\langle Z = [\mathbb{BG}, P, bP, cP, \widetilde{P}, a\widetilde{P}, b\widetilde{P}, c\widetilde{P}], K \rangle$ to decide whether $K = e(P, \widetilde{P})^{abc}$ or a random element X from $\mathbb{G}_T^{\times}$, where $a, b, c \in \mathbb{Z}_p^*$, $\mathbb{BG} = (p, \mathbb{G}^+, \widetilde{\mathbb{G}}^+, \mathbb{G}_T^{\times}, e)$ and P, $\widetilde{P}$ are random generators of $\mathbb{G}^+$ and $\widetilde{\mathbb{G}}^+$ respectively. Then, $\mathcal{B}$ proceeds as follows.

Setup: Initially, $\mathcal{B}$ sets an integer $m = 4q$ and randomly chooses another integer $l' \in \{0, 1, \ldots, l\}$, where l is the length of the users' identity. It also randomly selects $x', y', \{w_i, x_i, y_i, z_i\}_{i=1}^{l}, \hat{x}, \hat{y} \in \{0, 1, \ldots, m - 1\}$. For a user i with the identity $ID_i \in \{0, 1\}^l$, $\mathcal{B}$ defines the functions:

$$\mathcal{F}(ID_i) = (p - l'm + x') + \sum_{ID_i[k]=1} w_k \cdot \sum_{ID_i[k]=1} x_k,$$

$$\mathcal{J}(ID_i) = y' + \sum_{ID_i[k]=1} z_k \cdot \sum_{ID_i[k]=1} y_k,$$

$$\mathcal{Q}(ID_i) = \left\{ \begin{array}{l} 0, \text{if } x' + \sum\limits_{ID_i[k]=1} w_k \cdot \sum\limits_{ID_i[k]=1} x_k \equiv 0 \ (\text{mod } m) \\ 1, \text{otherwise} \end{array} \right\}$$

To publish the master public key MPK, $\mathcal{B}$ chooses a collusion resistant cryptographic hash function $H : \{0, 1\}^l \longrightarrow \mathbb{Z}_p^*$. Utilizing $\langle Z = [\mathbb{BG}, P, bP, cP, \widetilde{P}, a\widetilde{P}, b\widetilde{P}, c\widetilde{P}], K \rangle$, it sets the elements $U' = (p - l'm + x')(bP) + y'P$, $\widetilde{U}' = (p - l'm + x')(b\widetilde{P}) + y'\widetilde{P}$, $\Omega = e(bP, a\widetilde{P})$, $\widetilde{B} = b\widetilde{P}$, $\widetilde{X} = \hat{x}\widetilde{P}$, $\widetilde{Y} = \hat{y}\widetilde{P}$ and $\{\widetilde{Q}_i = \sum\limits_{ID_i[k]=1} w_k \cdot \sum\limits_{ID_i[k]=1} x_k(b\widetilde{P}) + \sum\limits_{ID_i[k]=1} z_k \cdot \sum\limits_{ID_i[k]=1} y_k\widetilde{P},$

$Q_i = \sum\limits_{ID_i[k]=1} w_k \cdot \sum\limits_{ID_i[k]=1} x_k(bP) + \sum\limits_{ID_i[k]=1} z_k \cdot \sum\limits_{ID_i[k]=1} y_kP\}_{i=1}^{N}$. Finally, $\mathcal{B}$ sends MPK $= (\mathbb{BG}, P, \widetilde{P}, \Omega, U', \{Q_i\}_{i=1}^{N}, \widetilde{X}, \widetilde{Y}, H)$ to $\mathcal{A}$.

Phase 1: (a) The adversary $\mathcal{A}$ adaptively issues polynomially many user secret key queries. It sends an identity $ID_i \in \{0,1\}^l$ of user i to $\mathcal{B}$. To return a valid secret key corresponding to ID_i, $\mathcal{B}$ does the following.
 – If $\mathcal{Q}(ID_i) = 0$, $\mathcal{B}$ aborts the game and chooses a random bit from $\{0,1\}$ to solve the asymmetric DBDH-3 problem.
 – Otherwise, $\mathcal{B}$ chooses an exponent $r \in_R \mathbb{Z}_p^*$ to sets the secret-key components as: $d_{i,1} = -\frac{\mathcal{J}(ID_i)}{\mathcal{F}(ID_i)}(a\widetilde{P}) + r(\widetilde{U}' + \widetilde{Q}_i)$ and $d_{i,2} = -\frac{1}{\mathcal{F}(ID_i)}(a\widetilde{P}) + r\widetilde{P}$.
 – Finally, $\mathcal{B}$ returns $\mathcal{A}$ the secret-key $\mathsf{SK}_{ID_i} = (d_{i,1}, d_{i,2},)$ corresponding to the identity ID_i of the user i.

Observe that SK_{ID_i} components are valid secret-key components as that of in the original protocol. Assume that $\widehat{r} = r - \frac{a}{\mathcal{F}(ID_i)}$, then

$$
\begin{aligned}
d_{i,1} &= -\frac{\mathcal{J}(ID_i)}{\mathcal{F}(ID_i)}(a\widetilde{P}) + r(\widetilde{U}' + \widetilde{Q}_i) \\
&= -\frac{\mathcal{J}(ID_i)}{\mathcal{F}(ID_i)}(a\widetilde{P}) + r\Big[(p - l'm + x')(\widetilde{B}) + y'\widetilde{P} + \sum_{ID_i[k]=1} w_k \cdot \sum_{ID_i[k]=1} x_k(b\widetilde{P}) \\
&\quad + \sum_{ID_i[k]=1} z_k \cdot \sum_{ID_i[k]=1} y_k\widetilde{P}\Big] \\
&= -\frac{\mathcal{J}(ID_i)}{\mathcal{F}(ID_i)}(a\widetilde{P}) + r\Big[\big(y' + \sum_{ID_i[k]=1} z_k \cdot \sum_{ID_i[k]=1} y_k\big)\widetilde{P} \\
&\quad + (p - l'm + x' + \sum_{ID_i[k]=1} w_k \cdot \sum_{ID_i[k]=1} x_k)\widetilde{B}\Big] \\
&= -\frac{\mathcal{J}(ID_i)}{\mathcal{F}(ID_i)}(a\widetilde{P}) + r\big[\mathcal{F}(ID_i)\widetilde{B} + \mathcal{J}(ID_i)\widetilde{P}\big] \\
&= a\widetilde{B} + \big(-\frac{a}{\mathcal{F}(ID_i)}\big)\big[\mathcal{F}(ID_i)\widetilde{B} + \mathcal{J}(ID_i)\widetilde{P}\big] + r\big[\mathcal{F}(ID_i)\widetilde{B} + \mathcal{J}(ID_i)\widetilde{P}\big] \\
&= a\widetilde{B} + \big(r - \frac{a}{\mathcal{F}(ID_i)}\big)\big(\mathcal{F}(ID_i)\widetilde{B} + \mathcal{J}(ID_i)\widetilde{P}\big) \\
&= a\widetilde{B} + \widehat{r}\big(\mathcal{F}(ID_i)\widetilde{B} + \mathcal{J}(ID_i)\widetilde{P}\big) = a\widetilde{B} + \widehat{r}(\widetilde{U}' + \widetilde{Q}_i), \text{ and } d_{i,2} = \big(r - \frac{a}{\mathcal{F}(ID_i)}\widetilde{P}\big) = \widehat{r}\widetilde{P}
\end{aligned}
$$

To compute the above secret key components, $\mathcal{B}$ requires $\mathcal{F}(ID_i) \not\equiv 0 \pmod{p}$. (b) The adversary $\mathcal{A}$ also adaptively issues polynomially many decryption queries. For each query, $\mathcal{A}$ sends the ciphertext-user identity pair (CT, ID_u). The simulator $\mathcal{B}$ first generates the secret-key SK_{ID_u} by executing the aforementioned step (a). Finally, it returns to $\mathcal{A}$ the result $\mathsf{Dec}(\mathsf{MPK}, \mathsf{SK}_{ID_u}, CT)$ by executing the same decryption algorithm of the proposed scheme.

Challenge: The adversary $\mathcal{A}$ submits a challenge set $\mathcal{S}^*$ of size L and two equal length messages M_0^*, M_1^* subject to the restriction that for all ID_i of secret-key queries in Phase 1, $ID_i \notin \mathcal{S}^*$. Let the challenge set is of the form $\mathcal{S}^* = \{ID_i^*\}_{i=1}^L$. The simulator $\mathcal{B}$ aborts the game and chooses a random bit if for any identity $ID_i^* \in \mathcal{S}^*$, $(x' + \sum_{ID_i[k]=1} w_k \cdot \sum_{ID_i[k]=1} x_k) \neq l'm$. Observe that for ID_i^* if $(x' + \sum_{ID_i[k]=1} w_k \cdot \sum_{ID_i[k]=1} x_k) \neq l'm$ holds, then $\mathcal{F}(ID_i^*) \not\equiv 0 \pmod{p}$.

As a result, $\mathcal{A}$ can trivially compute $\mathsf{SK}_{ID_i^*}$. Now, $\mathcal{B}$ randomly chooses a bit $\zeta \in \{0,1\}$ and selects a random split $(\mathcal{S}_0^*, \mathcal{S}_1^*)$ of the set $\mathcal{S}^*$, where $\mathcal{S}_0^* = \{ID_{0,i}\}_{i=1}^{\xi}$, $\mathcal{S}_1^* = \{ID_{1,i}\}_{i=1}^{\delta}$ are disjoint sets and $\mathcal{S}^* = \mathcal{S}_0^* \cup \mathcal{S}_1^*$. Then, $\mathcal{B}$ executes the following steps for the set $\mathcal{S}_b^* = \{ID_{b,i}\}_{i=1}^{m}$, where either $m = \xi$ if $b = 0$ or $m = \delta$ if $b = 1$.

- Using H, it computes $x_{b,1} = H(ID_{b,1}), \ldots, x_{b,m} = H(ID_{b,m})$, and for $i = 1, \ldots, m$ sets the polynomial

$$f_{b,i}(x) = \prod_{\substack{j=1 \\ j \neq i}}^{m} \frac{(x - x_{b,j})}{(x_{b,i} - x_{b,j})} \quad = \quad a_{b,i,1} + \ldots + a_{b,i,m}\, x^{m-1} \pmod{p}.$$

Observe that either $f_{b,i}(x) = 1$ if $x = x_{b,i}$ or $f_{b,i}(x) = 0$ if $x = x_{b,j}$ for all $i \neq j$.

- It computes $\{\mathcal{R}_{b,i} = \sum_{j=1}^{m} a_{b,j,i}\, \mathcal{J}(ID_{b,j}) \cdot (cP)\}_{i=1}^{m}$, $\mathcal{V} = cP$, $\mathcal{W} = M_\zeta^* \cdot K$, and sets the challenge ciphertext component corresponding to $\mathcal{S}_b^*$ as $\mathsf{CT}_b^* = (\{\mathcal{R}_{b,i}\}_{i=1}^{m}, \mathcal{V}, \mathcal{W})$.

- It also computes $\theta_b = H\left(\{\mathcal{R}_{b,i}\}_{i=1}^{m}, \mathcal{V}, \mathcal{W}, M_\zeta^*\right)$ and $\widetilde{\varGamma}_b^* = \left(\hat{x} + \theta_b \hat{y}\right)\left(c\widetilde{P}\right)$.

Finally, $\mathcal{B}$ passes $\mathcal{A}$ the challenge ciphertext $\mathsf{CT}^* = (\mathsf{CT}_0^*, \mathsf{CT}_1^*, \widetilde{\varGamma}_0^*, \widetilde{\varGamma}_1^*)$, which is a valid ciphertext. For the first component CT_0^*, assume that $s^* = c$, $K = e(P, \widetilde{P})^{abc}$, then $\mathcal{V} = s^* P$, $\mathcal{W} = M_\zeta^* \cdot K = M_\zeta^* \cdot e(P, \widetilde{P})^{abc} = M_\zeta^* \cdot \Omega^{s^*}$ and for $i = 1, \ldots, \xi$

$$\mathcal{R}_{0,i} = \sum_{j=1}^{\xi} a_{0,j,i} \cdot \mathcal{J}(ID_{0,j}) \cdot (cP) = \sum_{j=1}^{\xi} a_{0,j,i} \cdot s^* \left[\mathcal{F}(ID_{0,j})(bP) + \mathcal{J}(ID_{0,j})P\right]$$

$$= \sum_{j=1}^{\xi} a_{0,j,i} \cdot s^* \left[(p - l'm + x')(bP) + y'P + \sum_{ID_{0,j}[k]=1} w_k \cdot \sum_{ID_{0,j}[k]=1} x_k(bP)\right.$$

$$\left. + \sum_{ID_{0,j}[k]=1} z_k \cdot \sum_{ID_{0,j}[k]=1} y_k P\right] = \sum_{j=1}^{\xi} a_{0,j,i} \cdot s^* (U' + Q_{0,j})$$

Since $c = s^*$ is uniformly random, CT_0^* is valid and uniformly distributed over the ciphertext space. Observe that for a valid message M_ζ^* and the valid ciphertext component CT_0^*, the component $\widetilde{\varGamma}_0^*$ is also valid by the following computations.

$$\widetilde{\varGamma}_0^* = \left(\hat{x} + \theta_0 \hat{y}\right)\left(c\widetilde{P}\right) = c\left(\hat{x}\widetilde{P} + (\theta_0(\hat{y}\widetilde{P}))\right) = s^*\left(\hat{x}\widetilde{P} + (\theta_0(\hat{y}\widetilde{P}))\right) = s^*\left(\widetilde{X} + (\theta_0\widetilde{Y})\right)$$

Similarly, we can show that CT_1^* is also a valid ciphertext component.

Phase 2: Same as the Phase 1.

Guess: At last, $\mathcal{A}$ returns a guess bit $\zeta' \in \{0,1\}$ of ζ to $\mathcal{B}$.

Probability Analysis

If $\zeta = \zeta'$, $\mathcal{B}$ outputs 0, indicating that $K = e(P, \widetilde{P})^{abc}$; otherwise, it outputs 1, indicating that K is a random element of $\mathbb{G}_T^\times$. The simulation of $\mathcal{B}$ is perfect when $K = e(P, \widetilde{P})^{abc}$. Therefore, we have

$$\Pr[\mathcal{B}(Z, K = e(P, \widetilde{P})^{abc}) = 0] = \frac{1}{2} + \mathsf{Adv}^{\mathsf{IND\text{-}CCA}}_{\mathcal{A},\mathsf{FAnoPKTR}}(\eta),$$

where $\mathsf{Adv}^{\mathsf{IND\text{-}CCA}}_{\mathcal{A},\mathsf{FAnoPKTR}}(\eta)$ is the advantage of $\mathcal{A}$ in the above game. However, M_ζ^* is completely hidden from $\mathcal{A}$ when $K = X$, a random element from $\mathbb{G}_T^\times$. Therefore, we have the following probability.

$$\Pr[\mathcal{B}(Z, K = X) = 0] = \frac{1}{2}$$

Hence, the advantage of $\mathcal{B}$ in breaking the DBDH-3 challenge is

$$Adv_{\mathcal{B}}^{\mathsf{DBDH\text{-}3}}(\eta) = |\Pr[\mathcal{B}(Z, K = e(P, \widetilde{P})^{abc}) = 0] - \Pr[\mathcal{B}(Z, K = X) = 0]|$$

$$= \frac{1}{2} + \mathsf{Adv}^{\mathsf{IND\text{-}CCA}}_{\mathcal{A},\mathsf{FAnoPKTR}}(\eta) - \frac{1}{2} = \mathsf{Adv}^{\mathsf{IND\text{-}CCA}}_{\mathcal{A},\mathsf{FAnoPKTR}}(\eta)$$

Therefore, if $\mathcal{A}$ has non-negligible advantage in correctly guessing ζ', then $\mathcal{B}$ predicts $K = e(P, \widetilde{P})^{abc}$ or random element of $\mathbb{G}_T^\times$ (i.e., breaks DBDH-3 challenge) with non-negligible advantage. Hence, the proof. □

Theorem 4 (Anonymity).   *Assuming the asymmetric* (t', ϵ') *DBDH-3 assumption, our proposed FAnoPKTR scheme of Sect. 3 is indistinguishable anonymous secure against all* $(t, \epsilon, poly(\eta))$ *IND-ANO-CCA adversaries, where* η *is the security parameter and* $poly(\eta)$ *represents a polynomial in* η.

Theorem 5 (Traceability). *Suppose that our proposed identity-based FAnoPKTR is adaptive IND-CCA secure against the message indistinguishability game proved in Theorem 3. Then, assuming the* (t, ϵ) *collusion-secure optimal probabilistic Tardos codes TC, detailed in Sect. 2.2, our tracing algorithm* $Trace^{\mathcal{D}}$ *of Sect. 3 outputs identity of at least one traitor user.*

The proof of the above Theorem 4 is similar as the Theorem 3. Due to the page restriction, the proof of the above Theorem 4 is given in the Appendix A and the proof of the above Theorem 5 is also given in the Appendix B.

5   Conclusion

We have constructed an identity-based FAnoPKTR scheme, which is proven to be adaptive IND-CCA secure under the asymmetric DBDH-3 assumption in the standard security model without ROM. By tweaking the T3 bilinear pairing over the Tardos codes TC, we have obtained constant size user secret-key. Moreover, computation cost and communication bandwidth grow with the size of the subscribed user's set for an encryption.

Acknowledgments. This work was supported by Institute of Information & Communications Technology Planning & Evaluation (IITP) grant funded by the Korea government (MSIT) (No. 2019-0-00533, IITP-2021-2020-0-01819).

A   Proof of the Theorem 4

Proof. **Setup, Phase 1:** Exactly same as the Theorem 3.

Challenge: The adversary $\mathcal{A}$ submits a challenge message M^* belongs to $\mathbb{G}_T^\times$ and two equal sized sets $\mathcal{S}_0^*, \mathcal{S}_1^*$ of size L with the restriction that for all ID_i of secret-key queries in Phase 1, $ID_i \notin \mathcal{S}_0^* \triangle \mathcal{S}_1^*$, i.e., the identities of $(\mathcal{S}_0^* \cup \mathcal{S}_1^*)$ excluding $(\mathcal{S}_0^* \cap \mathcal{S}_1^*)$ have not been executed the secret key query in Phase 1. The simulator $\mathcal{B}$ aborts the game and chooses a random bit for the asymmetric DBDH-3 problem if for any identity ID_i belongs to either $\mathcal{S}_0^*$ or $\mathcal{S}_0^*$, the condition $(x' + \sum_{ID_i[k]=1} w_k \cdot \sum_{ID_i[k]=1} x_k) \neq l'm$ holds. Since, $(x' + \sum_{ID_i[k]=1} w_k \cdot \sum_{ID_i[k]=1} x_k) \neq l'm$ implies that $\mathcal{F}(ID_i) \not\equiv 0 \pmod{p}$ and consequently, $\mathcal{A}$ can compute the secret-key SK_{ID_i} corresponding to ID_i. Now, $\mathcal{B}$ randomly chooses $\varkappa \in \{0,1\}$ and selects a random split $(\mathcal{S}_{\varkappa,0}^*, \mathcal{S}_{\varkappa,1}^*)$ of the set $\mathcal{S}_\varkappa^*$, where $\mathcal{S}_{\varkappa,0}^* = \{ID_{\varkappa,0,i}\}_{i=1}^\xi$ and $\mathcal{S}_{\varkappa,1}^* = \{ID_{\varkappa,1,i}\}_{i=1}^\delta$ are disjoint sets and $\mathcal{S}_\varkappa^* = \mathcal{S}_{\varkappa,0}^* \cup \mathcal{S}_{\varkappa,1}^*$. Then, $\mathcal{B}$ executes the following steps for the set $\mathcal{S}_{\varkappa,b}^* = \{ID_{\varkappa,b,i}\}_{i=1}^m$, where either $m = \xi$ if $b = 0$ or $m = \delta$ if $b = 1$.

- Using H, it computes $x_{\varkappa,b,1} = H(ID_{\varkappa,b,1}), \ldots, x_{\varkappa,b,m} = H(ID_{\varkappa,b,m})$, and for $i = 1, \ldots, m$ sets

$$f_{\varkappa,b,i}(x) = \prod_{\substack{j=1 \\ j \neq i}}^m \frac{(x - x_{\varkappa,b,j})}{(x_{\varkappa,b,i} - x_{\varkappa,b,j})} = a_{\varkappa,b,i,1} + \ldots + a_{\varkappa,b,i,m}\, x^{m-1} \pmod{p}$$

Observe that either $f_{\varkappa,b,i}(x) = 1$ if $x = x_{\varkappa,b,i}$ or $f_{\varkappa,b,i}(x) = 0$ if $x = x_{\varkappa,b,j}$ for all $i \neq j$.
- It computes $\{\mathcal{R}_{\varkappa,b,i} = \sum_{j=1}^m a_{\varkappa,b,j,i}\, \mathcal{J}(ID_{\varkappa,b,j}) \cdot (cP)\}_{i=1}^m$, $\mathcal{V} = cP$, $\mathcal{W} = M^* \cdot K$, and sets the challenge ciphertext component corresponding $\mathcal{S}_{\varkappa,b}^*$ as $\mathsf{CT}_{\varkappa,b}^* = (\{\mathcal{R}_{\varkappa,b,i}\}_{i=1}^m, \mathcal{V}, \mathcal{W})$.
- It also computes $\theta_b = H\left(\{\mathcal{R}_{\varkappa,b,i}\}_{i=1}^m, \mathcal{V}, \mathcal{W}, M^*\right)$ and $\widetilde{\Gamma}_{\varkappa,b}^* = \left(\hat{x} + \theta_b \hat{y}\right)\left(c\widetilde{P}\right)$.

Finally, $\mathcal{B}$ passes $\mathcal{A}$ the challenge ciphertext $\mathsf{CT}^* = \left(\mathsf{CT}_{\varkappa,0}^*, \mathsf{CT}_{\varkappa,1}^*\right)$. Observe that CT^* is a valid. For the first component $\mathsf{CT}_{\varkappa,0}^*$, assume that $s^* = c$, $K = e(P, \widetilde{P})^{abc}$, then $\mathcal{V} = s^* P$ and for $i = 1, \ldots, \xi$

$$R_{\varkappa,0,i} = \sum_{j=1}^{m} a_{\varkappa,0,j,i} \; \mathcal{J}(ID_{\varkappa,0,j}) \cdot (cP)$$

$$= \sum_{j=1}^{\xi} a_{\varkappa,0,j,i} \; \cdot s^* \big[\mathcal{F}(ID_{\varkappa,0,j})(bP) + \mathcal{J}(ID_{\varkappa,0,j})P \big]$$

$$= \sum_{j=1}^{\xi} a_{\varkappa,0,j,i} \; \cdot s^* \big[(p - l'm + x')(bP) + y'P$$

$$+ \sum_{ID_{\varkappa,0,j}[k]=1} w_k \cdot \sum_{ID_{\varkappa,0,j}[k]=1} x_k(bP) + \sum_{ID_{\varkappa,0,j}[k]=1} z_k \cdot \sum_{ID_{\varkappa,0,j}[k]=1} y_k P \big]$$

$$= \sum_{j=1}^{\xi} a_{\varkappa,0,j,i} \; \cdot s^* \big(U' + Q_{\varkappa,0,j} \big)$$

$$\mathcal{W} = M^* \cdot K = M^* \cdot e(P, \widetilde{P})^{abc} = M^* \cdot \Omega^{s^*}$$

Since $c = s^*$ is uniformly random, $\mathsf{CT}^*_{\varkappa,0}$ is valid and uniformly distributed over the ciphertext space. Observe that for a valid message M^*_ζ and the valid ciphertext component $\mathsf{CT}^*_{\varkappa,0}$, the component $\widetilde{\varGamma}^*_{\varkappa,0}$ is also valid by the following computations.

$$\widetilde{\varGamma}^*_{\varkappa,0} = \big(\hat{x} + \theta_0 \hat{y} \big) \big(c\widetilde{P} \big) = c \big(\hat{x}\widetilde{P} + (\theta_0(\hat{y}\widetilde{P})) \big) = s^* \big(\hat{x}\widetilde{P} + (\theta_0(\hat{y}\widetilde{P})) \big) = s^* \big(\widetilde{X} + (\theta_0 \widetilde{Y}) \big)$$

Similarly, we can show that $\mathsf{CT}^*_{\varkappa,1}$ is also the valid ciphertext component.

Phase 2: Similar to Phase 1.

Guess: Finally, $\mathcal{A}$ returns a guess bit $\varkappa' \in \{0,1\}$ of $\varkappa$ to $\mathcal{B}$.

Probability Analysis. Same as the Theorem 3. Hence, the proof.   □

B   Proof of the Theorem 5

Proof. The traceability of our identity-based AnoPKTR against arbitrary collusion is played between a PPT adversary $\mathcal{A}$ and a tracer $\mathcal{C}$. Here, broadcaster plays the role of the tracer. Initially, a polynomial-sized set $\mathcal{S}$ is chosen by $\mathcal{C}$ and interacts with the pirate decoder box $\mathcal{D}$ corresponding to the set $\mathcal{S}$. More precisely, the game is described as follows.

Setup: First, $\mathcal{C}$ runs Setup $(1^\eta, l)$ of the AnoPKTR and outputs the MPK and the MSK. Then, $\mathcal{C}$ sends MPK to $\mathcal{A}$ and keeps MSK secret to itself.

KeyGen: The adversary $\mathcal{A}$ has the access to the key generation oracle $\mathcal{O}$KeyGen (MPK, MSK, ·) that allows $\mathcal{A}$ to query on a set of indices $\mathbb{I} \subseteq [N]$ with $|\mathbb{I}| \leq L \leq$

N. The oracle returns $((\mathsf{SK}_{ID_i})) \leftarrow \mathsf{KeyGen}\,(\mathsf{MPK}, \mathsf{MSK}, ID_i)$ for all $i \in \mathbb{I}$, where $\mathcal{E} = \{ID_i : i \in \mathbb{I}\}$.

Trace$^{\mathcal{D}}$: The tracer uses the OAnoTPK, the decoder $\mathcal{D}$ to execute the algorithm Trace$^{\mathcal{D}}$ (OAnoTPK) which is shown in Sect. 3. Due to random choice of π, type (π, j) split $\mathsf{RP}_\pi^{(j)} = (S_0^{(j)}, S_1^{(j)})$ of $\mathcal{S}$ is indistinguishable from a random split $\mathsf{RP} = (\mathcal{S}_0, \mathcal{S}_1)$ of $\mathcal{S}$ in main encryption algorithm. Therefore, both RP and $\mathsf{RP}_\pi^{(j)}$ belong to the same distribution space. The tracing phase can be divided into two stages which are described below.

[a] Approximating success probability. Let $\mathcal{C}$ interacts $\Re$ many times with $\mathcal{D}$ by providing the tracing ciphertext corresponding to a particular split $\mathsf{RP}_\pi^{(j)} = (S_0^{(j)}, S_1^{(j)})$, where $S_0^{(j)} = \mathcal{S} \cap \{ID_v \mid w_{\pi(v)}[j] = 0, \ \forall \ w_v \in \widetilde{\mathcal{S}}\}$ and $S_1^{(j)} = \mathcal{S} \cap \{ID_v \mid w_{\pi(v)}[j] = 1, \ \forall \ w_v \in \widetilde{\mathcal{S}}\}$. For a bit $b \in \{0, 1\}$, we denote a tracing split of $\mathcal{S}_b$ by $(\mathsf{RP}_\pi^{(j)}, b)$. For $\Re$ trials, corresponding to $(\mathsf{RP}_\pi^{(j)}, b)$, the decoder $\mathcal{D}$ has the expected success probability $\mu_{b,j} = \Re \cdot \sigma_{b,j}$ and the observed success probability $\rho_{b,j} = \Re \cdot p_{b,j}$, where $\sigma_{b,j}$ and $p_{b,j}$ are respectively the expected success probability and the observed success probability of $\mathcal{D}$ in a single trial. Observe that throughout the entire Trace$^{\mathcal{D}}$ algorithm of Sect. 3, $b = 1$ and π is fixed as $\mathcal{D}$ is stateless and re-settable.

Using the two tailed Chernoff Bound (cf. Definition 1), we obtain the relation between the observed value and the expected value for $\Re$ trials, taking $\Re = 48 \ln\left(\frac{2}{\epsilon}\right)$ and setting $a = \frac{\Re}{4}$, as: $\Pr[|\rho_{1,j} - \mu_{1,j}| \geq a] \leq 2e^{-\frac{a^2}{3\mu_{1,j}}} \leq 2e^{-\frac{a^2}{3\Re}}$. Substituting $a = \frac{\Re}{4}$ and $\Re = 48 \ln\left(\frac{2}{\epsilon}\right)$, we obtain $2e^{-\frac{a^2}{3\Re}} = 2e^{-\frac{\Re^2}{3 \cdot 16 \cdot \Re}} = 2e^{-\ln\left(\frac{2}{\epsilon}\right)} = \epsilon$, where ϵ is a negligible quantity that can be decreased by increasing number of trials. Therefore, $|\rho_{1,j} - \mu_{1,j}| \leq \frac{\Re}{4}$ holds with probability at least $1 - \epsilon$. This condition is equivalent to $|p_{1,j} - \sigma_{1,j}| \leq \frac{1}{4}$. Hence, it holds with probability at least $1 - \epsilon$.

[b] Producing pirate code word. If the code word w, produced by Trace$^{\mathcal{D}}$ (see Sect. 3), be a pirate code word, then we can prove that the code words belongs to the set $\mathbb{T}_\pi \leftarrow \mathsf{TC.Identify}\,(\mathsf{WatMTK}, w)$, are accused in creating w with high probability. We show that for all $j \in [l]$, if $w[j] = b$, then $S_b^{(j)} \cap \mathbb{T}_\pi \neq \emptyset$ for $b \in \{0, 1\}$. We now consider the following two cases.

- **Case I ($w[j] = 0$):** Due to the tracing strategy of Trace$^{\mathcal{D}}$, $w[j] = 0$ only when $\mathcal{D}$ is unable to decrypt the ciphertext corresponding to $\mathsf{RP}_\pi^{(j)}$. Thus, $p_{1,j} < \frac{1}{2}$ holds. Assume by contradiction that $S_0^{(j)} \cap \mathbb{T}_\pi = \emptyset$. Therefore, there is no traitor in $S_0^{(j)}$ who is accused in creating w. Since $\mathcal{D}$ is a perfect decoder, therefore, the probabilities $p_{0,j} = \sigma_{0,j} = 1$. From the approximation phase, it also holds that $|\sigma_{1,j} - p_{1,j}| \leq \frac{1}{4}$ with probability at least $1 - \epsilon$. Substituting all the conditions into the triangle inequality $|\sigma_{0,j} - \sigma_{1,j}| + |\sigma_{1,j} - p_{1,j}| \geq |\sigma_{0,j} - p_{1,j}|$, we obtain $|\sigma_{0,j} - \sigma_{1,j}| \geq \frac{1}{4}$. Hence, we can conclude that $\mathcal{D}$ has a non-negligible advantage in distinguishing the tracing ciphertexts corresponding to $(\mathsf{RP}_\pi^{(j)}, 0)$ and $(\mathsf{RP}_\pi^{(j)}, 1)$. Therefore, with advantage at least $\frac{1}{4}$, the decoder can distinguish the two ciphertexts corresponding to the random message M_{rand} and the actual message M. Since we assume by contradiction that $\mathcal{S}_0^{(j)} \cap \mathbb{T}_\pi = \emptyset$, we can use the distinguishing capability of $\mathcal{D}$ to break the message indistinguishability with receivers anonymity security of our AnoPKTR. Thus, we arrive at a contradiction.

- **Case II** ($w[j] = 1$): Due to our tracing strategy, $w[j] = 1$ only when $p_{1,j} \geq \frac{1}{2}$. Following the Case I, we obtain $\sigma_{1,j} \geq \frac{1}{4}$ with probability at least $1-\epsilon$. Assuming the security of message indistinguishability with receivers anonymity of our OAnoPKTR, we can conclude that the traitor belongs to the set $\mathcal{S}_1^{(j)}$.

We repeat the above process for all $j = 1, \ldots, l$ and apply the union probability over all the choices of j. In sum, we can conclude that w is the pirate code word with probability at least $1 - \epsilon l$. Finally, the trace get a traitor user identity belonging to $\mathbb{T} = \left\{ ID_{\pi^{-1}(t)} : w_t \in \mathbb{T}_\pi \right\}$ with probability at least $1 - \epsilon$, where the overall failure probability of accusing an innocent user is bounded by $(l + 1)\epsilon$. Hence, the proof.   □

References

1. Acharya, K., Dutta, R.: Enhanced outsider-anonymous broadcast encryption with subset difference revocation. IACR Cryptology ePrint Archive 2017/265 (2017)
2. Ak, M., Pehlivanoğlu, S., Selçuk, A.A.: Anonymous trace and revoke. J. Comput. Appl. Math. **259**, 586–591 (2014)
3. Boneh, D., Waters, B.: A fully collusion resistant broadcast, trace, and revoke system. In: ACM CCS, pp. 211–220. ACM (2006)
4. Boneh, D., Zhandry, M.: Multiparty key exchange, efficient traitor tracing, and more from indistinguishability obfuscation. Algorithmica **79**(4), 1233–1285 (2017). https://doi.org/10.1007/s00453-016-0242-8
5. Fazio, N., Perera, I.M.: Outsider-anonymous broadcast encryption with sublinear ciphertexts. In: Fischlin, M., Buchmann, J., Manulis, M. (eds.) PKC 2012. LNCS, vol. 7293, pp. 225–242. Springer, Heidelberg (2012). https://doi.org/10.1007/978-3-642-30057-8_14
6. Garg, S., Gentry, C., Halevi, S., Zhandry, M.: Functional encryption without obfuscation. In: Kushilevitz, E., Malkin, T. (eds.) TCC 2016. LNCS, vol. 9563, pp. 480–511. Springer, Heidelberg (2016). https://doi.org/10.1007/978-3-662-49099-0_18
7. Garg, S., Kumarasubramanian, A., Sahai, A., Waters, B.: Building efficient fully collusion-resilient traitor tracing and revocation schemes. In: ACM CCS, pp. 121–130 (2010)
8. He, K., Weng, J., Liu, J.-N., Liu, J.K., Liu, W., Deng, R.H.: Anonymous identity-based broadcast encryption with chosen-ciphertext security. In: ACM ASIA CCS, pp. 247–255. ACM (2016)
9. Lai, J., Mu, Y., Guo, F., Susilo, W., Chen, R.: Anonymous identity-based broadcast encryption with revocation for file sharing. In: Liu, J.K., Steinfeld, R. (eds.) ACISP 2016. LNCS, vol. 9723, pp. 223–239. Springer, Cham (2016). https://doi.org/10.1007/978-3-319-40367-0_14
10. Lee, K., Koo, W.K., Lee, D.H., Park, J.H.: Public-key revocation and tracing schemes with subset difference methods revisited. In: Kutyłowski, M., Vaidya, J. (eds.) ESORICS 2014. LNCS, vol. 8713, pp. 1–18. Springer, Cham (2014). https://doi.org/10.1007/978-3-319-11212-1_1

11. Li, X., Yanli, R.: Efficient anonymous identity-based broadcast encryption without random oracles. Int. J. Digit. Crime Forensics **6**(2), 40–51 (2014)
12. Libert, B., Paterson, K.G., Quaglia, E.A.: Anonymous broadcast encryption: adaptive security and efficient constructions in the standard model. In: Fischlin, M., Buchmann, J., Manulis, M. (eds.) PKC 2012. LNCS, vol. 7293, pp. 206–224. Springer, Heidelberg (2012). https://doi.org/10.1007/978-3-642-30057-8_13
13. Mandal, M., Dutta, R.: Cost-effective private linear key agreement with adaptive CCA security from prime order multilinear maps and tracing traitors. In: SECRYPT, pp. 356–363. SciTePress (2018)
14. Nishimaki, R., Wichs, D., Zhandry, M.: Anonymous traitor tracing: how to embed arbitrary information in a key. In: Fischlin, M., Coron, J.-S. (eds.) EUROCRYPT 2016. LNCS, vol. 9666, pp. 388–419. Springer, Heidelberg (2016). https://doi.org/10.1007/978-3-662-49896-5_14
15. Ren, Y., Niu, Z., Zhang, X.: Fully anonymous identity-based broadcast encryption without random oracles. IJ Netw. Secur. **16**(4), 256–264 (2014)
16. Tardos, G.: Optimal probabilistic fingerprint codes. J. ACM (JACM) **55**(2), 10 (2008)
17. Tseng, Y.-M., Huang, Y.-H., Chang, H.-J.: CCA-secure anonymous multi-receiver ID-based encryption. In: Advanced Information Networking and Applications Workshops, pp. 177–182. IEEE (2012)
18. Zhang, M., Takagi, T.: Efficient constructions of anonymous multireceiver encryption protocol and their deployment in group e-mail systems with privacy preservation. IEEE Syst. J. **7**(3), 410–419 (2013)

Ring Trapdoor Redactable Signatures from Lattice

Shaojun Yang[1,2], Xinyi Huang[1(✉)], Mingmei Zheng[3], and Jinhua Ma[1]

[1] The Fujian Provincial Key Laboratory of Network Security and Cryptology,
College of Mathematics and Computer Science, Fujian Normal University,
Fuzhou 350108, People's Republic of China
xyhuang@fjnu.edu.cn

[2] State Key Laboratory of Cryptology, P. O. Box 5159, Beijing 100878, China

[3] Division of Electrical Engineering and Computer Science,
Graduate School of Natural Science and Technology, Kanazawa University,
Kanazawa, Ishikawa 920-1192, Japan

Abstract. Redactable signature plays a significant role in real-life applications such as electronic health records, and has been studied extensively. Nevertheless, how to construct a redactable signature scheme with designated redactors is still unknown. In this paper, we affirmatively answer this problem by presenting a notion of ring trapdoor redactable signature (RTRS). RTRS is a variant of redactable signature where the redactors are specified. We first introduce the concept of ring trapdoor preimage sampleable functions (RPSFs), which inherits the merit of preimage sampleable functions and ring trapdoor functions, and then show an instantiation of RPSFs under the assumption of inhomogeneous small integer solution problem. We then present two concrete constructions of RTRS (a simplified version and a full version) from a family of RPSFs and a common signature scheme. It is proved that the unforgeability, privacy and restriction of proposed schemes relies on the security of underlying common signature schemes and ring one-way property of the RPSFs. Besides, we also prove that our schemes satisfy the indistinguishability.

Keywords: Ring trapdoor preimage sampleable functions · Ring trapdoor redactable signature scheme · Inhomogeneous small integer solution problem

1 Introduction

To meet the requirements of authenticated data redaction, Johnson et al. presented the concept of redactable signatures in 2002 [11]. As an instance of editable homomorphic signatures, the redactor can revise a signed message and generates a valid signature for the new message without private key. That is to say, the generation of the redacted data-signature pair can be completed independently. Redactable signatures have found wide applications in scenarios such as electronic health records systems, social networks, and smart grids. Privacy is a concern on authenticated data publish [3,14,15,17,25,29].

© Springer Nature Switzerland AG 2021
R. Deng et al. (Eds.): ISPEC 2021, LNCS 13107, pp. 190–208, 2021.
https://doi.org/10.1007/978-3-030-93206-0_12

Unforgeability and privacy are the two basic security requirements of redactable signatures [30]. Different from the unforgeability definition of traditional digital signatures [9], the unforgeability of redactable signatures allow the redactor to delete some portions of the signed message. However, he cannot generate a valid signature for any new message except for the authentic remained message. It satisfies the requirement for the integrity and origin authentication of the redacted data. The privacy ensures that the redacted data-signature pair reveals no information about the deleted message. It satisfies the privacy protection requirement for the sensitive portions of the original signed data [4].

To meet different application requirements, there are other security demands for redactable signatures, including transparency, unlinkability and accountability. Transparency ensures that the third party cannot determine whether the received data-signature pair is redacted or not [5]. Unlinkability ensures that the third party cannot identify which is the original data by given the redacted data-signature pairs [6]. Transparency and unlinkability provide stronger privacy protection ability. Accountability demands that anyone can affirm which one generates the redacted data-signature pairs by using the evidence tags [16,27]. It supports auditing on controversial signatures.

With the rapid development of quantum computers and quantum algorithms, secure cryptographic algorithms against quantum computing have become the current consensus of researchers. Almost all of the existing redactable signature (RS) schemes to have been constructed on traditional complexity problems in number theory, such as large number decomposition and discrete logarithm problem (DLP). But the super computing power of quantum computers will make them totally insecure. However, to the best of our knowledge, there are few RS schemes against quantum computing are constructed.

Related Work. A number of RS schemes have been presented since the introduction of redactable signatures [11,30]. Most of the general constructions are based on traditional digital signature schemes [3–7,14–19,25–27,29]. Specifically, the constructions in [11,13,24,30] are based on RSA algorithms, and their security depends on the complexity of large number decomposition. The security of those designs using pairing in [10,12,15,22,23,28,31] depends on the complexity of DLP. However, all schemes suffer from potential security threats brought by the quantum information technologies. Furthermore, there are no quantum-secure RS schemes, to our knowledge.

Lattice-based cryptography is well known as the post-quantum cryptography. The notion of preimage sampleable functions (PSFs) is defined by Gentry et al. [8]. Indeed, a collection of functions is called a family of PSFs if it satisfies generating a function with trapdoor, domain sampling with uniform output, preimage sampling with trapdoor and one-wayness without trapdoor. Besides, by the sampling algorithm of discrete Gaussian probability distribution and the trapdoor of lattice, a construction of lattice-based PSFs is presented.

In 2010, Brakerski and Kalai [2] introduce the notion of ring trapdoor functions (RTFs) and it can be applied to building ring signature schemes. Ring trapdoor functions can be viewed as a generalization of PSFs in some sense.

In 2012, as an efficient method of trapdoor generation for lattices, the notion of **G**-trapdoor is presented [20]. By this trapdoor, we can sample from a discrete Gaussian over a desired coset of $\Lambda^\perp(\mathbf{A})$ by an efficient algorithm.

Our Contribution. We improve the notion of RTFs by present the concept of ring trapdoor preimage sampleable functions (RPSFs) in this paper. According to the construction of RTFs in [2] and the method of trapdoor in [20], we construct RPSFs under the assumption of ISIS in lattice.

In the framework of [7], anyone who receives the message-signature pair and modification instruction can redact the message. An intriguing question of great interest is the definition and construction of RS scheme when the redactors are appointed. Thus we introduce the formal definition of ring trapdoor redactable signature (RTRS), and by the notion of PRSFs, we construct a simplified version of RTRS scheme and a full version of RTRS scheme.

2   Preliminaries

For the sake of descriptive integrality, some related definitions and properties required by our paper are displayed in this section.

Firstly, the symbols used in our paper are listed in the following Table 1.

Table 1. Symbols used in our paper

Symbol	Meaning
$\mathbb{Z}$, $\mathbb{R}$	The families of integers and real numbers
O, ω	The standard notation of growth functions
$[t]$	$\{1, 2, \dots, t\}$
$g(n) = \widetilde{O}(f(n))$	$\exists c \in \mathbb{R}$ such that $g(n) = O(f(n) \cdot \log^c n)$
$g(n) = \mathsf{Poly}(n)$	$\exists c \in \mathbb{R}$ with $g(n) = O(n^c)$
$g(n) = \mathsf{negl}(n)$	Negligible function, i.e., $g(n) = O(n^{-c})$ $(\forall c > 0)$
Bold lowercase letters	Column vectors
Bold capital letters	Matrices
$\mathbf{I}$	Identity matrix
$\leftarrow_r$	Choosing elements from the uniform distribution
$(\mathbf{X}\|\mathbf{Y})$	The columns of $\mathbf{X}$ are followed by the columns of $\mathbf{Y}$

Besides, $s_1(\mathbf{X}) = \max_{\mathbf{t}} \|\mathbf{X}\mathbf{t}\|$ ($\mathbf{t} \in \mathbb{R}^m$ with $\|\mathbf{t}\| = 1$) is called the largest singular value of matrix $\mathbf{X} \in \mathbb{R}^{n \times m}$.

Let $\mathbf{b}_1, \mathbf{b}_2, \cdots, \mathbf{b}_m \in \mathbb{R}^{m \times m}$ be m linearly independent vectors and $\mathbf{B} = (\mathbf{b}_1, \mathbf{b}_2, \cdots, \mathbf{b}_m)$. Then the discrete additive subgroup

$$\Lambda = L(\mathbf{B}) = \left\{ \sum_{i=1}^{m} x_i \mathbf{b}_i : x_i \in \mathbb{Z} \right\}$$

is named a m-dimensional lattice generated by $\mathbf{B}$. For arbitrary matrix $\mathbf{A} \in \mathbb{Z}_q^{n \times m}$ where $n, m, q \in \mathbb{Z}^+$, we can verify that

$$\Lambda^\perp(\mathbf{A}) = \{\mathbf{x} \in \mathbb{Z}^m : \mathbf{A}\mathbf{x} = 0 \mod q\}$$

and

$$\Lambda(\mathbf{A}) = \left\{\mathbf{x} \in \mathbb{Z}^m : \mathbf{x} = \mathbf{A}^\top \mathbf{y} \mod q \text{ for some } \mathbf{y} \in \mathbb{Z}_q^n\right\}$$

form two lattices. In addition, we let $\Lambda_{\mathbf{u}}^\perp(\mathbf{A}) = \{\mathbf{z} \in \mathbb{Z}^m : \mathbf{A}\mathbf{z} = \mathbf{u} \mod q\}$ be the coset for arbitrary $\mathbf{u} \in \mathbb{Z}^n$.

The function $\rho_{s,\mathbf{c}} : \mathbb{R}^m \longrightarrow \mathbb{R}$ defined by $\rho_{s,\mathbf{c}}(\mathbf{x}) = \exp(-\pi \|(\mathbf{x} - \mathbf{c})/s\|^2)$ is called the Gaussian function, where $\mathbf{c} \in \mathbb{R}^m$ and $s > 0$. For any fixed countably subset $\Sigma \subseteq R^m$, we let $\rho_{s,\mathbf{c}}(\Sigma) = \sum_{\mathbf{x} \in \Sigma} \rho_{s,\mathbf{c}}(\mathbf{x})$. Then $D_{\Sigma,s,\mathbf{c}}$ defined by $D_{\Sigma,s,\mathbf{c}}(\mathbf{x}) = \rho_{s,\mathbf{c}}(\mathbf{x})/\rho_{s,\mathbf{c}}(\Sigma)$ for arbitrary $\mathbf{x} \in \Sigma$ is called the discrete Gaussian distribution.

Lemma 1 [21]. *Let Λ be a lattice with dimension n, $\mathbf{c} \in \mathrm{span}(\Lambda)$, $\varepsilon \in (0,1)$ and $s \geq \eta_\varepsilon(\Lambda)$. We have*

$$\frac{1-\varepsilon}{1+\varepsilon} \cdot \rho_s(\Lambda) \leq \rho_{s,\mathbf{c}}(\Lambda) \leq \rho_s(\Lambda)$$

and

$$\Pr_{\mathbf{x} \sim D_{\Lambda,s,\mathbf{c}}} \left[\|\mathbf{x} - \mathbf{c}\| \leq s\sqrt{n}\right] \geq 1 - \frac{1+\varepsilon}{1-\varepsilon} \cdot 2^{-n}.$$

For any $n \in \mathbb{Z}^+$ and odd prime number q, we denote $k = \lceil \log_2 q \rceil$ and $\mathbf{g} = (1, 2, 4, \cdots, 2^{k-1})^\top \in \mathbb{Z}_q^k$. Let $\mathbf{G} = \mathbf{I}_n \otimes \mathbf{g}^\top \in \mathbb{Z}_q^{n \times nk}$ be a public matrix, where "$\otimes$" is the tensor product. The notion of $\mathbf{G}$-trapdoor for the lattice $\Lambda^\perp(\mathbf{A})$, which can be viewed as a improvement of the trapdoor of Ajtai [1], is proposed in [20].

Definition 1 [20]. *Given a matrix $\mathbf{A} \in \mathbb{Z}_q^{n \times m}$ with $n, q, m \in \mathbb{Z}$ and $k = \lceil \log_2 q \rceil$, if there exists some invertible matrix $\mathbf{S} \in \mathbb{Z}_q^{n \times n}$ such that $\mathbf{A}(\mathbf{R}^\top \| \mathbf{I}_{nk})^\top = \mathbf{S}\mathbf{G}$, then $\mathbf{R} \in \mathbb{Z}_q^{(m-nk) \times nk}$ is named a $\mathbf{G}$-trapdoor for $\mathbf{A}$.*

In addition, the quality of any $\mathbf{G}$-trapdoor is measured by the largest singular value $s_1(\mathbf{R})$.

Theorem 1 [20]. *Let $n, q \in \mathbb{Z}^+$ and $\mathbf{S} \in \mathbb{Z}_q^{n \times n}$ be invertible matrix. For any sufficiently large $m = O(n \log q)$, $\mathsf{TrapGen}(1^n, 1^m, q, \mathbf{S})$ is a polynomial time algorithm which can output a matrix $\mathbf{A} \in \mathbb{Z}_q^{n \times m}$ and a $\mathbf{G}$-Trapdoor $\mathbf{R} \in \mathbb{Z}_q^{(m-nk) \times nk}$, where $k = \lceil \log_2 q \rceil$. Moreover, the distribution of $\mathbf{A}$ is within $\mathsf{negl}(n)$ statistical distance of uniform and $s_1(\mathbf{R}) \leq \sqrt{m} \cdot \omega(\sqrt{\log n})$.*

In addition, given any $\mathbf{u} \in \mathbb{Z}_q^n$ and sufficiently large $s \geq s_1(\mathbf{R}) \cdot \omega(\sqrt{\log n})$, $\mathsf{SampleD}(\mathbf{R}, \mathbf{A}, \mathbf{S}, \mathbf{u}, s)$ is a polynomial time algorithm which can sample from a distribution which is $\mathsf{negl}(n)$-far from $D_{\Lambda_{\mathbf{u}}^\perp(\mathbf{A}),s}$.

Theorem 2 [20]. *Let* $n, m, q \in \mathbb{Z}^+$ *such that* $q \geq 2$ *is a prime and* $m = O(n \log q)$ *is sufficiently large. Then for arbitrary real* $s \geq \omega(\log m)$ *and for all but at most negligible part* $\mathbf{A} \leftarrow_r \mathbb{Z}_q^{n \times m}$, *we have the following facts.*

- *If* $\mathbf{e}$ *samples from* $D_{\mathbb{Z}^m, s}$, *then the distribution of* $\mathbf{u} = \mathbf{Ae} \mod q$ *is* $\mathsf{negl}(n)$-*far from uniform over* $\mathbb{Z}_q^n$.
- *For a fixed* $\mathbf{u} \in \mathbb{Z}_q^n$, *let* $\mathbf{v}$ *be a vector such that* $\mathbf{Av} = \mathbf{u} \mod q$. *Then the distribution of* $\mathbf{x} \sim D_{\mathbb{Z}^m, s}$ *given the condition* $\mathbf{Ax} = \mathbf{u} \mod q$ *is* $\mathbf{v} + D_{\Lambda^\perp(\mathbf{A}), s, -\mathbf{v}}$.

3   Ring Trapdoor Preimage Sampleable Functions

In 2010, Brakerski and Kalai introduce the notation of ring trapdoor functions in [2]. Roughly, it can be viewed as a collection of functions which satisfies **Ring one-way** and **Ring Trapdoor**.

Now we perfect the definition of ring trapdoor functions and present the notion of ring trapdoor preimage sampleable functions (RPSFs). It can also be viewed as a ring trapdoor version of preimage sampleable functions [8]. By this notion, we construct two ring trapdoor redactable signature schemes in Sect. 4.

Definition 2 [2]. *For any* $n \in \mathbb{N}$, *let* X_n *and* $\mathbb{G}_n$ *be an efficiently recognizable set and a commutative group, respectively. We denote* $X = \{X_n\}_{n \in \mathbb{N}}$ *and* $\mathbb{G} = \{\mathbb{G}_n\}_{n \in \mathbb{N}}$. $\mathcal{T} = \{\mathcal{T}_n\}_{n \in \mathbb{N}}$, *where* $\mathcal{T}_n$ *is a set of functions* $f : X_n \longrightarrow \mathbb{G}_n$, *is called a family of ring trapdoor functions if it satisfies the following conditions.*

1. ***Sampling.*** *Given* 1^n, *one can efficiently sample* $f \in \mathcal{T}_n$ *according to some fixed distribution. For the sake of convenience, we reuse notation of* $\mathcal{T}_n$ *to denote this distribution.*
2. ***Zero.*** *For every integer* $n \in \mathbb{N}$, *there exists a fixed element in* X_n *such that the image of this element under any* $f \in \mathcal{T}_n$ *is* 0, *which is the identity element of* $\mathbb{G}_n$.
3. ***Verifiability.*** *For any* $n \in \mathbb{N}$ *and any polynomial* $t = t(n)$, *one can efficiently verify that* $\sum_{i \in [t]} f_i(x_i) = y$ *by given* $f_1, \cdots, f_t \in \mathcal{T}_n$, $x_1, \cdots, x_t \in X_n$ *and* $y \in \mathbb{G}_n$.
4. ***Ring one-way.*** *For every polynomial* $t = t(n)$, *it is hard to compute* $x_1, \cdots, x_t \in X_n$ *such that* $\sum_{i \in [t]} f_i(x_i) = y$ *by given* $y \leftarrow_r \mathbb{G}_n$ *and* $f_1, \cdots, f_t \leftarrow \mathcal{T}_n$. *Formally, let* $\mathcal{A}$ *be any polynomial time adversary and* $t = t(n)$. *Then the following condition holds.*

$$\text{RingInv}_{\mathcal{T}}^t \text{Adv}[\mathcal{A}] = \Pr\left[\sum_{i \in [t]} f_i(x_i) = y : \begin{array}{l} f_1, \cdots, f_t \leftarrow \mathcal{T}_n, y \leftarrow_r \mathbb{G}_n, \\ (x_1, \cdots, x_t) \leftarrow \mathcal{A}(1^n, f_1, \cdots, f_t, y) \end{array} \right]$$
$$= \mathsf{negl}(n).$$

5. ***Trapdoor.*** *Given* 1^n, *one can efficiently sample a function* f *from a distribution which is statistically indistinguishable from* $\mathcal{T}_n$ *and the corresponding trapdoor* td. *In addition, for arbitrary polynomial* $t = t(n)$, *let* $f_1, \cdots, f_t \in \mathcal{T}_n$,

and $y \in \mathbb{G}_n$. *Given any trapdoor td_i for f_i with some $i \in [t]$, one can efficiently obtain $x_1, \cdots, x_t \in X_n$ such that $\sum_{i \in [t]} f_i(x_i) = y$. Furthermore, let td_j be a trapdoor for f_j, using td_j instead of td_i will result in a statistically indistinguishable distribution of $(x_1, \cdots, x_t)$.*

Furthermore, we can present the notation of ring trapdoor preimage sampleable functions based on ring trapdoor functions.

Definition 3. *For any $n \in \mathbb{N}$, let X_n and $\mathbb{G}_n$ be an efficiently recognizable set and a commutative group, respectively. We denote $X = \{X_n\}_{n \in \mathbb{N}}$ and $\mathbb{G} = \{\mathbb{G}_n\}_{n \in \mathbb{N}}$. $\mathcal{T} = \{\mathcal{T}_n\}_{n \in \mathbb{N}}$, where $\mathcal{T}_n$ is a set of functions $f : X_n \longrightarrow \mathbb{G}_n$, is called a family of ring trapdoor functions if it satisfies **Sampling, Zero, Verifiability, Ring one-way** and the following conditions.*

1. **Domain sampling with uniform output.** *For any polynomial $t = t(n)$, let χ_t be a fixed distribution over $(X_n)^t$. Given any $f_1, \cdots, f_t \in \mathcal{T}_n$, there is a probabilistic polynomial-time algorithm $\mathsf{RSampleDom}(1^n, t)$ samples $(x_1, \cdots, x_t)$ according to the distribution χ_t such that $\sum_{i \in [t]} f_i(x_i)$ follows uniform distribution over $\mathbb{G}_n$.*
2. **Preimage sampling with trapdoor.** *Given 1^n, one can efficiently sample a function f from a distribution which is statistically indistinguishable from $\mathcal{T}_n$ and the corresponding trapdoor td. Besides, for arbitrary polynomial $t = t(n)$, any $f_1, \cdots, f_t \in \mathcal{T}_n$ with td_i for some fixed $i \in [t]$, and any $y \in \mathbb{G}_n$, there is a probabilistic efficient algorithm $\mathsf{RSamplePre}(t, td_i, y)$ can efficiently sample $(x_1, \cdots, x_t) \in (X_n)^t$ satisfying the following conditions.*
   (1) $\sum_{i \in [t]} f_i(x_i) = y$.
   (2) If y follows uniform distribution over $\mathbb{G}_n$, then $(x_1, \cdots, x_t)$ satisfies the distribution χ_t over $(X_n)^t$.

Combining the construction of ring trapdoor functions in [2] and **G**-trapdoor, we can now construct a collection of RPSFs based on ISIS.

- **Parameters.** Let n, m, q, s be the parameters satisfying Theorem 1. The domain is $X_n = \{\mathbf{x} \in \mathbb{Z}^m : \|\mathbf{x}\| \leq s\sqrt{m}\}$, while the co-domain $\mathbb{G}_n = \mathbb{Z}_q^n$.
- **Sampling.** Given 1^n, one can use the algorithm $\mathsf{TrapGen}(1^n, 1^m, q, \mathbf{S})$ in Theorem 1 to choose $(\mathbf{A}, \mathbf{R})$, where $\mathbf{A} \in \mathbb{Z}_q^{n \times m}$ and $\mathbf{R} \in \mathbb{Z}_q^{(m-nk) \times nk}$. The matrix $\mathbf{A}$ defines the function $f_{\mathbf{A}} : X_n \longrightarrow \mathbb{G}_n$ such that $f_{\mathbf{A}}(\mathbf{x}) = \mathbf{A}\mathbf{x} \mod q$. The matrix $\mathbf{R}$ is the corresponding trapdoor.
- **Ring one-way.** Let $f_{\mathbf{A}_1}, \cdots, f_{\mathbf{A}_t} \leftarrow \mathcal{T}_n$ and $\mathbf{y} \leftarrow_r \mathbb{Z}_q^n$. If there exists an adversary $\mathcal{A}$ can returns $(\mathbf{x}_1, \cdots, \mathbf{x}_t) \in (X_n)^t$ such that $\sum_{i \in [t]} f_{\mathbf{A}_i}(\mathbf{x}_i) = \sum_{i \in [t]} \mathbf{A}_i \mathbf{x}_i = \mathbf{y}$. We denote $\mathbf{A} = (\mathbf{A}_1 \| \mathbf{A}_1 \| \cdots \| \mathbf{A}_t)$ and $\mathbf{x} = (\mathbf{x}_1^T, \cdots, \mathbf{x}_t^T)^T$. Thus $\mathbf{A}\mathbf{x} = \mathbf{y}$ and $\|\mathbf{x}\| = \sqrt{\sum_{i \in [t]} \|\mathbf{x}_i\|} \leq s\sqrt{tm}$. That is, there exist some adversaries $\mathcal{B}$ which can solve the ISIS instance $(\mathbf{A}, \mathbf{y})$. Thus we have

$$\mathsf{RingInv}_{\mathcal{T}}^t \mathsf{Adv}[\mathcal{A}] \leq \mathsf{ISIS}_{q, tm, s\sqrt{tm}}[\mathcal{B}].$$

- **Domain sampling with uniform output.** By related conclusions in [20], we have $s \geq s_1(\mathbf{R}) \cdot \omega(\sqrt{\log n}) \geq \eta_\varepsilon(\Lambda^\perp)$ for some $\varepsilon(n) = \mathsf{negl}(n)$. For any polynomial $t = t(n)$, let χ_t be the $D_{\mathbb{Z}^{mt},s}$. With the standard basis of $\mathbb{Z}^{mt}$, we can sample $\mathbf{x} = (\mathbf{x}_1^T, \cdots, \mathbf{x}_t^T)^T$ from $D_{\mathbb{Z}^{mt},s}$ by the algorithm presented in [8]. According to Lemma 1, we have $\mathbf{x}_i$ follows $D_{\mathbb{Z}^m,s}$ for arbitrary $i \in [t]$ and $\mathbf{x}_i \in X_n$ except with exponentially small probability. In addition, the following holds: given any $f_{\mathbf{A}_1}, \cdots, f_{\mathbf{A}_t} \in \mathcal{T}_n$, $\sum_{i \in [t]} f_{\mathbf{A}_i}(\mathbf{x}_i)$ follows uniform distribution over $\mathbb{G}_n$.

- **Preimage sampling with trapdoor.** For any polynomial $t = t(n)$, given any $f_{\mathbf{A}_1}, \cdots, f_{\mathbf{A}_t} \in \mathcal{T}_n$ such that $\mathbf{R}_i$ is a trapdoor for $f_{\mathbf{A}_i}$ for some $i \in [t]$, and given any $\mathbf{y} \in \mathbb{G}_n$, the trapdoor inversion algorithm $\mathsf{RSamplePre}(t, \mathbf{R}_i, \mathbf{y})$ can be described as follows.

  Let $\mathbf{A} = (\mathbf{A}_1 \| \cdots \| \mathbf{A}_{i-1} \| \mathbf{A}_{i+1} \| \cdots \| \mathbf{A}_t)$. With the standard basis of $\mathbb{Z}^{m(t-1)}$, we can sample $(\mathbf{x}_1^T, \cdots, \mathbf{x}_{i-1}^T, \mathbf{x}_{i+1}^T, \cdots, \mathbf{x}_t^T)^T$ from $D_{\mathbb{Z}^{m(t-1)},s}$. If we denote $\mathbf{y}_i = \mathbf{y} - \sum_{j \neq i} f_{\mathbf{A}_j}(\mathbf{x}_j)$, then $\mathbf{x}_i$ can be sampled by $\mathsf{SampleD}(\mathbf{R}_i, \mathbf{A}_i, \mathbf{S}, \mathbf{y}_i, s)$. Let $\mathbf{x} = (\mathbf{x}_1^T, \cdots, \mathbf{x}_t^T)^T$. Thus we have:

  - $\sum_{j \in [t]} f_{\mathbf{A}_j}(\mathbf{x}_j) = \mathbf{y}$.
  - $\mathbf{x}_j \in X_n$ except with exponentially small probability for arbitrary $j \in [t]$.
  - It is clear that $\mathbf{x}_j$ satisfies the distribution $D_{\mathbb{Z}^m,s}$ over X_n for any $j \neq i$. If $\mathbf{y}$ follows uniform distribution over $\mathbb{G}_n$, then $\mathbf{y}_i$ also follows the uniform distribution over $\mathbb{G}_n$. Thus we deduce that $\mathbf{x}_i$ follows the distribution within $\mathsf{negl}(n)$ statistical distance of $D_{\mathbb{Z}^m,s}$. In addition, $\mathbf{x}_1, \cdots, \mathbf{x}_t$ are independent between them. Thus $\mathbf{x}$ follows $D_{\mathbb{Z}^{mt},s}$.

4   Ring Trapdoor Redactable Signatures

Let us consider the following application background. A message which is signed includes two parts. Some appointed redactors can redact the first part and return a new valid signature pair, while the second part can not be redacted. In addition, the second part determines who can redact the signature pair. In some sense, the second part can be viewed as the intrinsic content of this message. For this application, we introduce the formal definition of ring trapdoor redactable signature.

Definition 4. *A tuple of polynomial-time algorithms $\mathcal{R} = (\mathsf{R.Gen}, \mathsf{R.Gen}_{red},$ $\mathsf{R.Sign}, \mathsf{R.Ver}, \mathsf{R.Redact})$ is called a ring trapdoor redactable signature (RTRS) if $\mathcal{R}$ satisfies the following conditions.*

- **Parameters.** *Suppose that there are t redactors $\mathsf{R}_1, \cdots, \mathsf{R}_t$ in the system. Let $\mathcal{M} = \mathcal{M}_1 \times \mathcal{M}_2$ be the messages space and let $\mathcal{V} : \mathcal{M} \longrightarrow \{0,1\}^t$ be a function such that: for arbitrary $M = (M_1, M_2)$ and $M' = (M_1', M_2') \in \mathcal{M}$, $\mathcal{V}(M) = \mathcal{V}(M')$ if $M_2 = M_2'$. For convenience, we denote $\mathcal{V}(M) = (v_1, \cdots, v_t)$ and $\mathcal{I}_M = \{i \in [t] : v_i = 1\}$. Specifically, redactor R_i can revise M_1 by giving a valid signature pair (M, σ), and returns a new valid signature pair $(M' = (M_1', M_2), \sigma')$ if and only if $v_i = 1$.*

- R.Gen(1^κ) *takes the security parameter κ as the input, and it outputs a verification key R.pk and a signing key R.sk.*
- R.Gen$_{red}$(1^κ) *takes the security parameter κ as the input, and it outputs a public key and a private key for the redactor.*
  For any $i \in [t]$, let $(R.pk_{red_i}, R.sk_{red_i})$ be the pair of keys of redactor R_i. We denote $R.pk_{red} = (R.pk_{red_1}, \cdots, R.pk_{red_t})$.
- R.Sign($M, R.sk, R.pk_{red}$) *takes the verification key R.sk, $R.pk_{red}$ and a message $M = (M_1, M_2) \in \mathcal{M}$ as the input. It outputs a corresponding signature σ.*
- R.Ver($M, \sigma, R.vk, R.pk_{red}$) *takes a message $M = (M_1, M_2) \in \mathcal{M}$, $R.vk$, $R.pk_{red}$ and a signature σ as the inputs. It outputs $b \in \{0, 1\}$. Specifically, $b = 1$ signifies "accept" and $b = 0$ signifies "reject".*
- R.Redact($M, \sigma, R.pk_{red}, R.sk_{red_i}$) *takes the private key $R.sk_{red_i}$ for the ith redactor and a message $M = (M_1, M_2) \in \mathcal{M}$, $R.pk_{red}$ with the corresponding signature σ as the input. It output $M' = (M_1', M_2) \in \mathcal{M}$ and σ' as the new data-signature pair.*

The following essential requirements can be considered in RTRS scheme.

- **Correctness.**
  - R.Ver($M, $R.Sign$(M, R.sk, R.pk_{red}), R.vk, R.pk_{red}) = 1$.
  - If R.Ver($M, \sigma, R.vk, R.pk_{red}) = 1$ and $\mathcal{V}(M) = (v_1, \cdots, v_t)$ satisfying $v_i = 1$, then

$$\text{R.Ver}(\text{R.Redact}(M, \sigma, R.pk_{red}, R.sk_{red_i}), R.vk, R.pk_{red}) = 1.$$

- **Unforgeability.** (R.Gen, R.Sign, R.Ver) is existentially unforgeable under adaptive chosen-message attacks as a traditional signature scheme [9].
- **Privacy.** Privacy is defined by the following game $\mathcal{G}_1$ between adversary $\mathcal{A}$ and challenger $\mathcal{C}$.
  - $\mathcal{C}$ runs R.Gen(1^κ) and R.Gen$_{red}$(1^κ) respectively, and obtains $(R.pk, R.sk)$ and $(R.pk_{red_i}, R.sk_{red_i})$ for arbitrary $i \in [t]$. Then $\mathcal{A}$ is given $R.pk$ and $R.pk_{red_i}$ ($i \in [t]$).
  - $\mathcal{C}$ accepts signing queries of messages from $\mathcal{A}$.
  - $\mathcal{A}$ sends two messages $M^0 = (M_1^0, M_2^0)$ and $M^1 = (M_1^1, M_2^1)$ with $M_2^0 = M_2^1$ to $\mathcal{C}$.
  - $\mathcal{C}$ completes the following steps.
    * $b \leftarrow_r \{0, 1\}$.
    * $\sigma^b \leftarrow$ R.Sign($M^b, R.sk, R.pk_{red}$).
    * R.Redact($M^b, \sigma^b, R.pk_{red}, R.sk_{red_i}$) returns (M', σ') for some i satisfying $v_i = 1$, where $M' = (M_1', M_2^b)$.
    Finally, $\mathcal{C}$ sends (M', σ') to $\mathcal{A}$.
  - $\mathcal{C}$ accepts signing queries of messages (include M^0 and M^1) from $\mathcal{A}$.
  - $\mathcal{A}$ guesses the value of b and returns $b' \in \{0, 1\}$.

Definition 5. *A RTRS scheme has privacy if the probability $|\Pr[b = b'] - \frac{1}{2}|$ in $\mathcal{G}_1$ is negligible for arbitrary probabilistic polynomial time adversary $\mathcal{A}$.*

- **Restriction.** For any fixed $i \in [t]$, redactor R_i can redact a valid signature pair $(M = (M_1, M_2), \sigma)$ and returns a new valid signature pair $(M' = (M_1', M_2), \sigma')$ iff $\mathcal{V}(M) = (v_1, \cdots, v_t)$ satisfying $v_i = 1$. That is to say, R_i can not redact the valid signature pair $(M = (M_1, M_2), \sigma)$ if $v_i = 0$ or return a new valid signature pair $(M' = (M_1', M_2'), \sigma')$ with $M_2' \neq M_2$. More specifically, let us consider the following game $\mathcal{G}_2$ between challenger $\mathcal{C}$ and redactor R_i.

  1. **Setup.** $\mathcal{C}$ runs R.Gen(1^κ) and R.Gen$_{red}(1^\kappa)$ to obtain $(R.pk, R.sk)$ and $(R.pk_{red_j}, R.sk_{red_j})$ for arbitrary $j \neq i$. R_i gets $(R.pk_{red_i}, R.sk_{red_i})$ by R.Gen$_{red}(1^\kappa)$ and publishes $R.pk_{red_i}$. R_i is given $R.pk$ and $R.pk_{red_j}$ $(j \neq i)$.
  2. **Hash queries.** $\mathcal{C}$ accepts hash queries of message $M = (M_1, M_2)$ from redactor R_i. Let q_{h2} be the most number that R_i is allowed to do hash queries of M_2 such that $i \notin \mathcal{I}_M$ and let q_{h1} be the most number that R_i is allowed to do hash queries of massage M has the same second part such that $i \notin \mathcal{I}_M$. We denote $q_h = q_{h1} \cdot q_{h2}$.
  3. **Signature queries.** $\mathcal{C}$ accepts signing queries of message $M = (M_1, M_2)$ from redactor R_i. Let $q_s < q_h$ be the most number that R_i is allowed to do signature queries with the massage M such that $i \notin \mathcal{I}_M$.
  4. **Forge.** R_i outputs a new message M^* and a signature $\sigma^* = (\sigma_1^*, \{r_j^*\}_{j \in [t]})$.

Definition 6. *Let Q be the messages set required by R_i in the signature queries phase. A RTRS scheme has restriction if for arbitrary $i \in [t]$, the probability that redactor R_i forge a valid signature $(M^* = (M_1^*, M_2^*), \sigma^*)$ such that $M^* \notin Q$ satisfies one of the following conditions is negligible.*

- $i \notin \mathcal{I}_{M^*}$.
- *For any message $M = (M_1, M_2) \in Q$, we have $M_2 \neq M_2^*$.*

- **Indistinguishability.** Anyone is infeasible to distinguish in a statistical sense whether a signature is generated by the signer directly or it has been redacted by some redactor R_i, except the signer and redactor R_i.

From now on, we present two concrete constructions of RTRS by a family of RPSFs. Let (Gen, Sign, Ver) be a signature scheme satisfying existentially unforgeable under adaptive chosen-message attacks. $\mathcal{M}_S$ is the messages space of (Gen, Sign, Ver). Let $\mathcal{T} = \{\mathcal{T}_n\}_{n \in \mathbb{N}}$ be a collection of RPSFs, and let $h : \{0, 1\}^* \longrightarrow \mathbb{G}_n$ and $H : \{0, 1\}^* \longrightarrow \mathcal{M}_S$ be hash functions.

4.1 A Simplified Version of RTRS Scheme

For the simplified version of RTRS scheme, let $\mathcal{M} = \mathcal{M}_1$ and $\mathcal{V}(M) = (1, 1, \cdots, 1)$ for arbitrary $M \in \mathcal{M}$. Then a simplified version of RTRS scheme $\mathcal{R}_s = (\mathsf{R}_s.\mathsf{Gen}, \mathsf{R}_s.\mathsf{Gen}_{red}, \mathsf{R}_s.\mathsf{Sign}, \mathsf{R}_s.\mathsf{Ver}, \mathsf{R}_s.\mathsf{Redact})$ is constructed as follows.

- $\mathsf{R}_s.\mathsf{Gen}(1^\kappa)$: Given a security parameter κ, computer $(pk, sk) \leftarrow \mathsf{Gen}(1^\kappa)$. Then return $(R_s.pk, R_s.sk) = (pk, sk)$.

- $R_s.\mathsf{Gen}_{red}(1^\kappa)$: Given a security parameter κ, redactor R_i can efficiently sample a function-trapdoor pair (f_i, td_i) from $\mathcal{T}_n$ for arbitrary $i \in [t]$. Let $(R_s.pk_{red_i}, R_s.sk_{red_i}) = (f_i, td_i)$. For convenience, we denote $R_s.pk_{red} = (f_1, \cdots, f_t)$ and $R_s.sk_{red} = (td_1, \cdots, td_t)$.
- $R_s.\mathsf{Sign}(M, R_s.sk, R_s.pk_{red})$: Given $R_s.pk_{red}$, $R_s.sk = sk$, an message $M \in \mathcal{M}$, computer

$$\{r_i\}_{i\in[t]} \leftarrow \mathsf{RSampleDom}(1^n, t)$$

and

$$\sigma_1 \leftarrow \mathsf{Sign}(sk, H(h(M) + \sum_{i\in\mathcal{I}_M} f_i(r_i))).$$

Finally, return the signature $\sigma = (\sigma_1, \{r_i\}_{i\in[t]})$.
- $R_s.\mathsf{Ver}(M, \sigma, R_s.pk, R_s.pk_{red})$: Given $R_s.pk = pk$, $R_s.pk_{red}$, an message $M \in \mathcal{M}$ and a signature $\sigma = (\sigma_1, \{r_i\}_{i\in[t]})$. It outputs 1 iff all of the following accepted.
  - $r_i \in X_n$ for arbitrary $i \in [t]$.
  - $1 \leftarrow \mathsf{Ver}(H(h(M) + \sum_{i\in[t]} f_i(r_i)), \sigma_1, pk)$.
- $R_s.\mathsf{Redact}(M, \sigma, R_s.pk_{red}, R_s.sk_{red_i})$: Given $R_s.pk_{red}$, an message $M \in \mathcal{M}$, the private key $R_s.sk_{red_i} = td_i$ for the ith redactor R_i and a valid signature σ of M, R_i revises M to M'. Then computer $y = h(M) + \sum_{i\in[t]} f_i(r_i) - h(M')$ and $\{r'_i\}_{i\in[t]} \leftarrow \mathsf{RSamplePre}(t, td_i, y)$. R_i returns M' and $\sigma' = (\sigma_1, \{r'_i\}_{i\in[t]})$ as the new data-signature pair.

Theorem 3. *The scheme R_s defined above satisfies correctness, unforgeability, privacy and indistinguishability.*

Proof. – **Correctness.**
  - According to the correctness of Sign, we have that σ_1 is a valid signature of $H(h(M) + \sum_{i\in[t]} f_i(r_i))$. It follows that

$$1 \leftarrow \mathsf{Ver}(H(h(M) + \sum_{i\in[t]} f_i(r_i)), \sigma_1, pk).$$

  - According to the definition of $R_s.\mathsf{Redact}$, we have $h(M) + \sum_{i\in[t]} f_i(r_i) = h(M') + \sum_{i\in[t]} f_i(r'_i)$. Thus $1 \leftarrow \mathsf{Ver}(H(h(M') + \sum_{i\in[t]} f_i(r'_i)), \sigma_1, pk)$.
- **Unforgeability.** Let $\mathcal{H} = \emptyset$ be an empty set and $Q_1 = Q_2 = \emptyset$ be two message sets. When the challenger $\mathcal{C}$ is given $f_1, \cdots f_t \in \mathcal{T}_n$ and $y \leftarrow_r \mathbb{G}_n$, the game $\mathcal{G}_0$ between challenger $\mathcal{C}$ and adversary $\mathcal{A}$ is defined as follows.
  1. **Setup.** $\mathcal{C}$ receive the public key pk of signature scheme $(\mathsf{Gen}, \mathsf{Sign}, \mathsf{Ver})$. Then $\mathcal{C}$ sends $R_s.pk = pk$ and $R_s.pk_{red} = (f_1, \cdots, f_t)$ to $\mathcal{A}$. Let $\mathcal{O}$ be the signature oracle of $(\mathsf{Gen}, \mathsf{Sign}, \mathsf{Ver})$.
  2. **Hash queries.** Let q_h be the most number that $\mathcal{A}$ is allowed to do hash queries. For any $k \in [q_h - 1]$, $\mathcal{C}$ samples $y_k \leftarrow_r \mathbb{G}_n$ and $\{r_{ki}\}_{i\in[t]}$ by algorithm $\mathsf{RSampleDom}(1^n)$. Then $\mathcal{C}$ keeps $y_k, \{r_{ki}\}_{i\in[t]}$ and puts $y_k - \sum_{i\in[t]} f_i(r_{ki})$ to $\mathcal{H}$. The $\mathcal{C}$ picks $j \leftarrow_r [q_h - 1]$ and put $y_j - y$ to $\mathcal{H}$.
  When $\mathcal{C}$ receive the message M from $\mathcal{A}$, he randomly select a value as the hash value of M and remove it from $\mathcal{H}$. If this value is the first form, then he puts M to Q_1. Otherwise, M is put to Q_2.

3. **Signature queries.** Let $q_s < q_h$ be the most number that $\mathcal{A}$ is allowed to do signature queries.

   If $M \in Q_1$, then there exists $k \in [q_h - 1]$ such that $h(M) = y_k - \sum_{i \in [t]} f_i(r_{ki})$. So $\mathcal{C}$ queries the signature of $H(y_k)$ from oracle $\mathcal{O}$ and gets σ_1. Then he returns $\sigma = (\sigma_1, \{r_{ki}\}_{i \in [t]})$ to $\mathcal{A}$. If $M \in Q_2$, then $\mathcal{C}$ reports failure and terminates.

4. **Forge.** $\mathcal{A}$ outputs a new message M^* and a signature $\sigma^* = (\sigma_1^*, \{r_i^*\}_{i \in [t]})$. Let ε be the probability that $\sigma^* = (\sigma_1^*, \{r_i^*\}_{i \in [t]})$ is a valid signature of message M^*. If $M^* \in Q_1$, then $\mathcal{C}$ reports failure and terminates. If $M^* \in Q_2$, then $h(M^*) = y_j - y$. Thus there is a message $M' \in Q_1$ such that $\sigma' = (\sigma_1', \{r_i'\}_{i \in [t]})$ is given by $\mathcal{C}$ with

$$H(h(M^*) + \sum_{i \in [t]} f_i(r_i^*)) = H(h(M') + \sum_{i \in [t]} f_i(r_i')).$$

Otherwise, $\mathcal{C}$ can forge the signature of $H(h(M^*) + \sum_{i \in [t]} f_i(r_i^*))$ about scheme $(\mathsf{Gen}, \mathsf{Sign}, \mathsf{Ver})$. Hence we get $M^* \neq M'$ and

$$h(M^*) + \sum_{i \in [t]} f_i(r_i^*) = h(M') + \sum_{i \in [t]} f_i(r_i')$$

$$= y_k$$

for some $k \in [q_h - 1]$. If $k \neq j$, then $\mathcal{C}$ reports failure and terminates. Otherwise, $\mathcal{C}$ get $\sum_{i \in [t]} f_i(r_i^*) = y$ without trapdoor. The successful probability of $\mathcal{C}$ is

$$\frac{\binom{q_h - 1}{q_s}}{\binom{q_h}{q_s}} \cdot \frac{1}{q_h - q_s} \cdot \frac{1}{q_h - 1} \cdot \varepsilon \approx \frac{1}{q_h^2} \cdot \varepsilon.$$

This is a contradiction to the ring one-way of $\mathcal{T}$. Hence, $\mathcal{R}_s$ is existentially unforgeable under adaptive chosen-message attacks as a signature scheme.

– **Privacy.** Let us consider the following games between challenger $\mathcal{C}$ and adversary $\mathcal{A}$.

$\mathcal{G}_1$ is defined as follows.

- $\mathcal{C}$ run $\mathsf{R_s.Gen}(1^\kappa)$ and $\mathsf{R_s.Gen}_{red}(1^\kappa)$ respectively, and obtains the key pairs $(R_s.pk, R_s.sk) = (pk, sk)$ and (f_i, td_i) for arbitrary $i \in [t]$. Then $\mathcal{A}$ is given $R.pk$ and $R.pk_{red_i}$ $(i \in [t])$.
- $\mathcal{C}$ accepts signing queries of messages from $\mathcal{A}$.
- $\mathcal{A}$ sends two messages M^0 and M^1 to $\mathcal{C}$.
- $\mathcal{C}$ completes the following steps.
    * $b \leftarrow_r \{0, 1\}$.
    * $\sigma^b \leftarrow \mathsf{R_s.Sign}(M^b, R_s.sk, R_s.pk_{red})$, where $\sigma^b = (\sigma_1^b, \{r_i^b\}_{i \in [t]})$.
    * $(M', \sigma') \leftarrow \mathsf{R_s.Redact}(M^b, \sigma^b, R_s.pk_{red}, R_s.sk_{red_i})$, where $\sigma' = (\sigma_1^b, \{r_i'\}_{i \in [t]})$.
    Finally, $\mathcal{C}$ sends (M', σ') to $\mathcal{A}$.
- $\mathcal{C}$ accepts signing queries of messages from $\mathcal{A}$.
- $\mathcal{A}$ guesses the value of b and returns $b' \in \{0, 1\}$.

$\mathcal{G}_1'$ is the same as $\mathcal{G}_1$ except the step that $\mathcal{C}$ computes the signatures of M' after he receives the messages M^0 and M^1. $\mathcal{C}$ picks $y \leftarrow_r \mathbb{G}_n$. Then he samples $\{r_i'\}_{i \in [t]}$ such that $h(M') + \sum_{i \in [t]} f_i(r_i') = y$ and computes the signature of $H(y)$ by $\sigma_1' \leftarrow \mathsf{Sign}(sk, H(y))$. Finally, $\mathcal{C}$ get the signature $\sigma' = (\sigma_1', \{r_i'\}_{i \in [t]})$. According to the construction of $\mathcal{R}_s$, we know that $h(M^b) + \sum_{i \in [t]} f_i(r_i^b)$ in $\mathcal{G}_1$ follows the uniform distribution over $\mathbb{G}_n$. Thus it is statistically indistinguishable from the y in $\mathcal{G}_1'$ at the view of the adversary. Thus $\mathcal{A}$ can not distinguish between σ_1^b in $\mathcal{G}_1$ and σ_1' in $\mathcal{G}_1'$. In addition, $\mathsf{R}_s.\mathsf{Redact}$ is unrelated to $\{r_i^b\}_{i \in [t]}$ except the value of $h(M^b) + \sum_{i \in [t]} f_i(r_i^b)$. Thus $(r_i')_{i \in [t]}$ in $\mathcal{G}_1$ and $\mathcal{G}_1'$ follow the distribution χ_t over $(X_n)^t$. Hence, $\mathcal{G}_1$ is statistically indistinguishable with $\mathcal{G}_1'$ from the sense of $\mathcal{A}$.

According to the construction of $\mathcal{G}_1'$, $\sigma' = (\sigma_1', \{r_i'\}_{i \in [t]})$ is irrelevant to M^0 and M^1. It can deduce that $\Pr(b' = b) = \dfrac{1}{2}$.

– **Indistinguishability.**
  According to the property of preimage sampling with trapdoor, it is clear that signature of message M outputted by signer has the same distribution with the signature modified by R_i for arbitrary $i \in [t]$ such that $i \in [t]$.

Remark 1. In the simplified version, we have $\mathcal{M} = \mathcal{M}_1$, $\mathcal{M}_2 = \emptyset$ and $\mathcal{V}(M) = (1, 1, \cdots, 1)$ for arbitrary $M \in \mathcal{M}$. Thus any redactor R can revise the hole message M. So the scheme has restriction naturally according to the definition of restriction.

4.2 A Full Version of RTRS Scheme

A full version of RTRS scheme $\mathcal{R} = (\mathsf{R.Gen}, \mathsf{R.Gen}_{red}, \mathsf{R.Sign}, \mathsf{R.Ver}, \mathsf{R.Redact})$ is described as follows.

– $\mathsf{R.Gen}(1^\kappa)$: Given a security parameter κ, compute $(pk, sk) \leftarrow \mathsf{Gen}(1^\kappa)$. Then return $(R.pk, R.sk) = (pk, sk)$.
– $\mathsf{R.Gen}_{red}(1^\kappa)$: Given a security parameter κ, redactor R_i can efficiently sample a function-trapdoor pair (f_i, td_i) from $\mathcal{T}_n$ for arbitrary $i \in [t]$. Let $(R.pk_{red_i}, R.sk_{red_i}) = (f_i, td_i)$. For convenience, we denote $R.pk_{red} = (f_1, \cdots, f_t)$ and $R.sk_{red} = (td_1, \cdots, td_t)$.
– $\mathsf{R.Sign}(M, R.sk, R.pk_{red})$: Given $R.pk_{red}$, $R.sk = sk$ and an message $M = (M_1, M_2) \in \mathcal{M}$, compute $\mathcal{V}(M) = (v_1, \cdots, v_t)$ and $\mathcal{I}_M$. Then let $\{r_i\}_{i \in \mathcal{I}_M} \leftarrow \mathsf{RSampleDom}(1^n, |\mathcal{I}_M|)$ and $\sigma_1 \leftarrow \mathsf{Sign}(sk, H(h(M) + \sum_{i \in \mathcal{I}_M} f_i(r_i), M_2))$. Finally, return the signature $\sigma = (\sigma_1, \{r_i\}_{i \in \mathcal{I}_M})$.
– $\mathsf{R.Ver}(M, \sigma, R.pk, R.pk_{red})$: Given $R.pk = pk$, $R.pk_{red}$, an message $M = (M_1, M_2) \in \mathcal{M}$ and a (purported) signature $\sigma = (\sigma_1, \{r_i\}_{i \in \mathcal{I}_M})$. It outputs 1 if and only if all of the following accepted.
  - $r_i \in X_n$ for arbitrary $i \in \mathcal{I}_M$.
  - $\mathsf{Ver}(H(h(M) + \sum_{i \in \mathcal{I}_M} f_i(r_i), M_2), \sigma_1, pk)$ returns 1.

- R.Redact($M, \sigma, R.pk_{red}, R.sk_{red_i}$): Given $R.pk_{red}$, the private key $R.sk_{red_i} = td_i$ for the ith redactor R_i, an message $M = (M_1, M_2) \in \mathcal{M}$ such that $v_i = 1$ and a signature σ of M, R_i revises M to $M' = (M_1', M_2)$. Then compute $y = h(M) + \sum_{i \in \mathcal{I}_M} f_i(r_i) - h(M')$ and $\{r_i'\}_{i \in \mathcal{I}_{M'}} \leftarrow$ RSamplePre($|\mathcal{I}_M|, td_i, y$). R_i returns M' and $\sigma' = (\sigma_1, \{r_i'\}_{i \in \mathcal{I}_M})$ as the new data-signature pair.

Theorem 4. *The scheme $\mathcal{R}$ defined above satisfies correctness, unforgeability, privacy, restriction and indistinguishability.*

Proof. – **Correctness.**

- Let According to the correctness of Sign, we have that σ_1 is a valid signature of $H(h(M) + \sum_{i \in \mathcal{I}_M} f_i(r_i), M_2)$. It follows that $1 \leftarrow$ Ver($H(h(M) + \sum_{i \in \mathcal{I}_M} f_i(r_i), M_2), \sigma_1, pk$).
- According to the definition of R.Redact, we have $h(M) + \sum_{i \in \mathcal{I}_M} f_i(r_i) = h(M') + \sum_{i \in \mathcal{I}_{M'}} f_i(r_i')$. Thus we deduce that

$$1 \leftarrow \text{Ver}(H(h(M') + \sum_{i \in \mathcal{I}_{M'}} f_i(r_i')), M_2), \sigma_1, pk).$$

- **Unforgeability.** When the challenger $\mathcal{C}$ is given $\{f_j\}_{j \in [t]} \in \mathcal{T}_n$ and $y \leftarrow_r \mathbb{G}_n$, let us consider the following game $\mathcal{G}_0$ between the Challenger $\mathcal{C}$ and adversary $\mathcal{A}$.

  1. **Setup.** Let q_{h2} be the most number that $\mathcal{A}$ is allowed to do hash queries of M_2 and let q_{h1} be the most number that $\mathcal{A}$ is allowed to do hash queries of massage M has the same second part. We denote $q_h = q_{h1} \cdot q_{h2}$. Suppose $\mathcal{H}_k = \emptyset$ be a empty set for any $k \in [q_{h2}]$, $\mathfrak{M}_2 = \emptyset$ and $Q_1 = Q_2 = \emptyset$ be two message sets. $\mathcal{C}$ receives the public key pk of signature scheme (Gen, Sign, Ver). Then $\mathcal{C}$ sends $R_s.pk = pk$ and $R.pk_{red_j} = f_j$ to $\mathcal{A}$. Let $\mathcal{O}$ be the signature oracle of (Gen, Sign, Ver). In addition, $\mathcal{A}$ gets $(R.pk_{red_i}, R.sk_{red_i})$ by R.Gen$_{red}(1^\kappa)$ and publishes $R.pk_{red_i}$.
  2. **Hash queries.** $\mathcal{C}$ randomly select a value $k^* \leftarrow_r [q_{h2}]$. When $\mathcal{C}$ receive the message $M = (M_1, M_2)$ from $\mathcal{A}$, he responds to this query as follows:
     - If $M_2 \notin \mathfrak{M}_2$, then put M_2 to $\mathfrak{M}_2$ and let $k = |\mathfrak{M}_2|$. For any $s \in [q_{h1} - 1]$, $\mathcal{C}$ samples $y_{ks} \leftarrow_r \mathbb{G}_n$ and $\{r_{ksj}\}_{j \in \mathcal{I}_M}$ by algorithm RSampleDom. Then $\mathcal{C}$ keeps y_{ks}, $\{r_{ksj}\}_{j \in \mathcal{I}_M}$ and puts $y_{ks} - \sum_{j \in \mathcal{I}_M} f_j(r_{ksj})$ to $\mathcal{H}_k$. If $k = k^*$, then $\mathcal{C}$ picks $s_{k^*} \leftarrow_r [q_{h1} - 1]$ and puts $y_{k^* s_{k^*}} - y$ to $\mathcal{H}_{k^*}$. Else if $k \neq k^*$, $\mathcal{C}$ samples $y_{kq_{h1}} \leftarrow_r \mathbb{G}_n$ and $\{r_{kq_{h1}j}\}_{j \in \mathcal{I}_M}$ and puts $y_{kq_{h1}} - \sum_{j \in \mathcal{I}_M} f_j(r_{kq_{h1}j})$ to $\mathcal{H}_k$.
       Finally $\mathcal{C}$ randomly select a value from $\mathcal{H}_k$ as the hash value of M and remove it from $\mathcal{H}_k$. If this value is the form of $y_{ks} - \sum_{j \in \mathcal{I}_M} f_j(r_{ksj})$, then he puts M to Q_1. Otherwise, M is put to Q_2.
     - If $M_2 \in \mathfrak{M}_2$ is the k-th element in $\mathfrak{M}_2$, then $\mathcal{C}$ randomly select a value from $\mathcal{H}_k$ as the hash value of M and remove it from $\mathcal{H}_k$. If this value is the form of $y_{ks} - \sum_{j \in \mathcal{I}_M} f_j(r_{ksj})$, then he puts M to Q_1. Otherwise, M is put to Q_2.
  3. **Signature queries.** Let $q_s < q_h$ be the most number that $\mathcal{A}$ is allowed to do signature queries. $\mathcal{A}$ responds to the query of M as follows.

- If $M \in Q_1$, then there exists k and s such that $h(M) = y_{ks} - \sum_{j \in \mathcal{I}_M} f_j(r_{ksj})$. So $\mathcal{C}$ queries the signature of $H(y_{ks})$ from oracle $\mathcal{O}$ and receives σ_1. Finally he returns $\sigma = (\sigma_1, \{r_{ksj}\}_{j \in \mathcal{I}_M})$ to $\mathcal{A}$.
- If $M \in Q_2$, then $\mathcal{C}$ reports failure and terminates.

4. **Forge.** $\mathcal{A}$ outputs a new message M^* and a signature $\sigma^* = (\sigma_1^*, \{r_j^*\}_{j \in \mathcal{I}_{M^*}})$.

Let Q be the messages set required by $\mathcal{A}$ in the signature queries phase and ε be the probability that $\sigma^* = (\sigma_1^*, \{r_j^*\}_{j \in \mathcal{I}_{M^*}})$ is a valid signature of message M^*.

- If $M^* \in Q_1$, then $\mathcal{C}$ reports failure and terminates.
- If $M^* \in Q_2$, then $h(M^*) = y_{k^* s_{k^*}} - y$. Thus there is a message $M' \in Q_1$ such that $\sigma' = (\sigma_1', \{r_j'\}_{j \in \mathcal{I}_{M'}})$ is given by $\mathcal{C}$ with

$$H(h(M') + \sum_{j \in \mathcal{I}_{M'}} f_j(r_j'), M_2') = H(h(M^*) + \sum_{j \in \mathcal{I}_{M^*}} f_j(r_j^*), M_2^*).$$

Otherwise, $\mathcal{C}$ can forge the signature of $H(h(M^*) + \sum_{j \in \mathcal{I}_{M^*}} f_j(r_j^*), M_2^*)$ about scheme (Gen, Sign, Ver). Hence we get $M^* \neq M'$, $M_2^* = M_2'$ and

$$h(M^*) + \sum_{j \in \mathcal{I}_{M^*}} f_j(r_j^*) = h(M') + \sum_{j \in \mathcal{I}_{M'}} f_j(r_j')$$

$$= y_{k^* s}$$

for some $s \in [q_{h1} - 1]$. If $s \neq s_{k^*}$, then $\mathcal{C}$ reports failure and terminates. Otherwise, let

$$x_j = \begin{cases} r_j^*, & j \in \mathcal{I}_{M^*} \\ 0, & j \notin \mathcal{I}_{M^*}. \end{cases}$$

So $\mathcal{C}$ gets $\sum_{j \in [t]} f_j(x_j) = y$ without trapdoor. The successful probability of $\mathcal{C}$ is

$$\frac{\binom{q_h - 1}{q_s}}{\binom{q_h}{q_s}} \cdot \frac{1}{q_h - q_s} \cdot \frac{1}{q_{h1} - 1} \cdot \varepsilon = \frac{1}{q_h \cdot (q_{h1} - 1)} \cdot \varepsilon.$$

This is a contradiction to the ring one-way of $\mathcal{T}$. Hence, $\mathcal{R}$ has restriction.

- The proof of **Privacy** is similar to Theorem 3.
- **Restriction.** When the challenger $\mathcal{C}$ is given $f_1, \cdots f_{i-1}, f_{i+1} \cdots f_t \in \mathcal{T}_n$ and $y \leftarrow_r \mathbb{G}_n$, let us consider the following game $\mathcal{G}_2$ between the Challenger $\mathcal{C}$ and redactor R_i.

  1. **Setup.** Let $\mathcal{H}_k = \emptyset$ be a empty set for any $k \in [q_{h2}]$, $\mathfrak{M}_2 = \emptyset$ and $Q_1 = Q_2 = \emptyset$ be two message sets. $\mathcal{C}$ receives the public key pk of signature scheme (Gen, Sign, Ver). Then $\mathcal{C}$ sends $R_s.pk = pk$ and $R.pk_{red_j} = f_j$ ($j \neq i$) to R_i. Let $\mathcal{O}$ be the signature oracle of (Gen, Sign, Ver). In addition, R_i gets $(R.pk_{red_i}, R.sk_{red_i})$ by $R.\mathsf{Gen}_{red}(1^\kappa)$ and publishes $R.pk_{red_i}$.
  2. **Hash queries.** $\mathcal{C}$ randomly select a value $k^* \leftarrow_r [q_{h2}]$. When $\mathcal{C}$ receive the message $M = (M_1, M_2)$ from R_i, he responds to this query as follows:

- If M satisfies $i \in \mathcal{I}_M$, then $\mathcal{C}$ samples $y \leftarrow_r \mathbb{G}_n$ and $\{r_j\}_{j \in \mathcal{I}_M}$ by algorithm RSampleDom. Then he keeps y, $\{r_j\}_{j \in \mathcal{I}_M}$ and returns $y - \sum_{j \in \mathcal{I}_M} f_j(r_j)$ to R_i.
- If M satisfies $i \notin \mathcal{I}_M$, then $\mathcal{C}$ does the following steps.
  * If $M_2 \notin \mathfrak{M}_2$, then put M_2 to $\mathfrak{M}_2$ and let $k = |\mathfrak{M}_2|$. For any $s \in [q_{h1} - 1]$, $\mathcal{C}$ samples $y_{ks} \leftarrow_r \mathbb{G}_n$ and $\{r_{ksj}\}_{j \in \mathcal{I}_M}$ by algorithm RSampleDom. Then $\mathcal{C}$ keeps y_{ks}, $\{r_{ksj}\}_{j \in \mathcal{I}_M}$ and puts $y_{ks} - \sum_{j \in \mathcal{I}_M} f_j(r_{ksj})$ to $\mathcal{H}_k$. If $k = k^*$, then $\mathcal{C}$ picks $s_{k^*} \leftarrow_r [q_{h1} - 1]$ and puts $y_{k^* s_{k^*}} - y$ to $\mathcal{H}_{k^*}$. Else if $k \neq k^*$, $\mathcal{C}$ samples $y_{kq_{h1}} \leftarrow_r \mathbb{G}_n$ and $\{r_{kq_{h1}j}\}_{j \in \mathcal{I}_M}$ and puts $y_{kq_{h1}} - \sum_{j \in \mathcal{I}_M} f_j(r_{kq_{h1}j})$ to $\mathcal{H}_k$. Finally $\mathcal{C}$ randomly select a value from $\mathcal{H}_k$ as the hash value of M and remove it from $\mathcal{H}_k$. If this value is the form of $y_{ks} - \sum_{j \in \mathcal{I}_M} f_j(r_{ksj})$, then he puts M to Q_1. Otherwise, M is put to Q_2.
  * If $M_2 \in \mathfrak{M}_2$ is the k-th element in $\mathfrak{M}_2$, then $\mathcal{C}$ randomly select a value from $\mathcal{H}_k$ as the hash value of M and remove it from $\mathcal{H}_k$. If this value is the form of $y_{ks} - \sum_{j \in \mathcal{I}_M} f_j(r_{ksj})$, then he puts M to Q_1. Otherwise, M is put to Q_2.

3. **Signature queries.** Let $q_s < q_h$ be the most number that R_i is allowed to do signature queries. R_i responds to the query of M as follows.
   - If $i \in \mathcal{I}_M$, then $\mathcal{C}$ get the corresponding y and $\{r_j\}_{j \in \mathcal{I}_M}$. Thus he can queries the signature of $H(y)$ from oracle $\mathcal{O}$. After he $\mathcal{C}$ receives σ_1, he returns $\sigma = (\sigma_1, \{r_j\}_{j \in \mathcal{I}_M})$ to R_i.
   - If $i \notin \mathcal{I}_M$, then $M \in Q_1 \cup Q_2$. $\mathcal{C}$ does the following steps.
     * If $M \in Q_1$, then there exists k and s such that $h(M) = y_{ks} - \sum_{j \in \mathcal{I}_M} f_j(r_{ksj})$. So $\mathcal{C}$ queries the signature of $H(y_{ks})$ from oracle $\mathcal{O}$ and receives σ_1. Finally he returns $\sigma = (\sigma_1, \{r_{ksj}\}_{j \in \mathcal{I}_M})$ to R_i.
     * If $M \in Q_2$, then $\mathcal{C}$ reports failure and terminates.

4. **Forge.** R_i outputs a new message M^* and a signature $\sigma^* = (\sigma_1^*, \{r_j^*\}_{j \in \mathcal{I}_{M^*}})$.

Let Q be the messages set required by R_i in the signature queries phase and ε be the probability that $\sigma^* = (\sigma_1^*, \{r_j^*\}_{j \in \mathcal{I}_{M^*}})$ is a valid signature of message M^* satisfying one of the following conditions.
- $i \notin \mathcal{I}_{M^*}$.
- For any message $M = (M_1, M_2) \in Q$, we have $M_2 \neq M_2^*$.

If $M_2 \neq M_2^*$ for any message $M = (M_1, M_2) \in Q$, then $\mathcal{C}$ can forge the signature of $H(h(M^*) + \sum_{j \in \mathcal{I}_{M^*}} f_i(r_j^*), M_2^*)$ about scheme (Gen, Sign, Ver). Thus we have $i \notin \mathcal{I}_{M^*}$ and $M^* \in Q_1 \cup Q_2$.
- If $M^* \in Q_1$, then $\mathcal{C}$ reports failure and terminates.
- If $M^* \in Q_2$, then $h(M^*) = y_{k^* s_{k^*}} - y$. Thus there is a message $M' \in Q_1$ such that $\sigma' = (\sigma_1', \{r_j'\}_{j \in \mathcal{I}_{M'}})$ is given by $\mathcal{C}$ with

$$H(h(M') + \sum_{j \in \mathcal{I}_{M'}} f_j(r_j'), M_2') = H(h(M^*) + \sum_{j \in \mathcal{I}_{M^*}} f_j(r_j^*), M_2^*).$$

Otherwise, C can forge the signature of $H(h(M^*) + \sum_{j \in \mathcal{I}_{M^*}} f_j(r_j^*), M_2^*)$ about scheme $(\mathsf{Gen}, \mathsf{Sign}, \mathsf{Ver})$. Hence we get $M^* \neq M'$, $M_2^* = M_2'$ and

$$h(M^*) + \sum_{j \in \mathcal{I}_{M^*}} f_j(r_j^*) = h(M') + \sum_{j \in \mathcal{I}_{M'}} f_j(r_j')$$

$$= y_{k^* s}$$

for some $s \in [q_{h1} - 1]$. If $s \neq s_{k^*}$, then C reports failure and terminates. Otherwise, let

$$x_j = \begin{cases} r_j^*, & j \in \mathcal{I}_{M^*} \\ 0, & j \notin \mathcal{I}_{M^*}. \end{cases}$$

So C gets $\sum_{j \neq i} f_j(x_j) = y$ without trapdoor. The successful probability of C is

$$\frac{\binom{q_h - 1}{q_s}}{\binom{q_h}{q_s}} \cdot \frac{1}{q_h - q_s} \cdot \frac{1}{q_{h1} - 1} \cdot \varepsilon = \frac{1}{q_h \cdot (q_{h1} - 1)} \cdot \varepsilon.$$

This is a contradiction to the ring one-way of $\mathcal{T}$. Hence, $\mathcal{R}$ has restriction.

- **Indistinguishability.**
  According to the property of preimage sampling with trapdoor, it is clear that signature of message M outputted by signer has the same distribution with the signature modified by R_i for arbitrary $i \in \mathcal{I}_M$.

5 Conclusion

The notion of ring trapdoor preimage sampleable functions (RPSFs) is presented in this paper. According to the construction of ring trapdoor functions in [2] and the method of **G**-trapdoor in [20], we introduce a construction of RPSFs under the assumption of ISIS problem on lattice. According to some application backgrounds such that the redactors should be designated in a redactable signature scheme, we propose a formal definition of ring trapdoor redactable signature (RTRS). By a family of RPSFs and a traditional signature scheme, two generic constructions of RTRS are given, i.e., a simplified version and a full version. Given a valid signature pair $(M = (M_1, M_2), \sigma)$, the simplified version allows any redactor in the system to redact the message M and present a valid signature σ' for the new message $M' = (M_1', M_2')$. While in the full version, M_2 can be viewed as the essential attribute of M and can not be redacted. Besides, M_2 determines whether a redactor can redact the first part of the message and output a valid signature σ' for the new message $M' = (M_1', M_2)$.

Acknowledgements. This work is supported by National Natural Science Foundation of China (61822202, 61872089, 62172096), Science Foundation of Fujian Provincial Science and Technology Agency (2019J01428, 2020J02016), and State Key Laboratory of Cryptology Research Fund (MMKFKT202008).

References

1. Ajtai, M.: Generating hard instances of lattice problems (extended abstract). In: Proceedings of the Twenty-Eighth Annual ACM Symposium on the Theory of Computing, pp. 99–108. ACM (1996). https://doi.org/10.1145/237814.237838
2. Brakerski, Z., Kalai, Y.T.: A framework for efficient signatures, ring signatures and identity based encryption in the standard model. IACR Cryptology ePrint Archive 2010(086) (2010). http://eprint.iacr.org/2010/086
3. Brown, J., Blough, D.M.: Verifiable and redactable medical documents. In: AMIA Annual Symposium Proceedings, pp. 1148–1157 (2012). https://www.ncbi.nlm.nih.gov/pmc/articles/PMC3540582/
4. Brzuska, C., et al.: Redactable signatures for tree-structured data: definitions and constructions. In: Zhou, J., Yung, M. (eds.) ACNS 2010. LNCS, vol. 6123, pp. 87–104. Springer, Heidelberg (2010). https://doi.org/10.1007/978-3-642-13708-2_6
5. Brzuska, C., et al.: Security of sanitizable signatures revisited. In: Jarecki, S., Tsudik, G. (eds.) PKC 2009. LNCS, vol. 5443, pp. 317–336. Springer, Heidelberg (2009). https://doi.org/10.1007/978-3-642-00468-1_18
6. Brzuska, C., Fischlin, M., Lehmann, A., Schröder, D.: Unlinkability of sanitizable signatures. In: Nguyen, P.Q., Pointcheval, D. (eds.) PKC 2010. LNCS, vol. 6056, pp. 444–461. Springer, Heidelberg (2010). https://doi.org/10.1007/978-3-642-13013-7_26
7. Derler, D., Pöhls, H.C., Samelin, K., Slamanig, D.: A general framework for redactable signatures and new constructions. In: Kwon, S., Yun, A. (eds.) ICISC 2015. LNCS, vol. 9558, pp. 3–19. Springer, Cham (2016). https://doi.org/10.1007/978-3-319-30840-1_1
8. Gentry, C., Peikert, C., Vaikuntanathan, V.: Trapdoors for hard lattices and new cryptographic constructions. In: Proceedings of the Fortieth Annual ACM Symposium on Theory of Computing. STOC 2008, pp. 197–206. ACM, New York (2008). https://doi.org/10.1145/1374376.1374407
9. Goldwasser, S., Micali, S., Rivest, R.L.: A digital signature scheme secure against adaptive chosen-message attacks. SIAM J. Comput. **17**(2), 281–308 (1988)
10. Izu, T., Kunihiro, N., Ohta, K., Takenaka, M., Yoshioka, T.: A sanitizable signature scheme with aggregation. In: Dawson, E., Wong, D.S. (eds.) ISPEC 2007. LNCS, vol. 4464, pp. 51–64. Springer, Heidelberg (2007). https://doi.org/10.1007/978-3-540-72163-5_6
11. Johnson, R., Molnar, D., Song, D., Wagner, D.: Homomorphic signature schemes. In: Preneel, B. (ed.) Topics in Cryptology - CT-RSA 2002, pp. 244–262. Springer, Heidelberg (2002). https://doi.org/10.5555/646140.680938
12. Lim, S., Lee, E., Park, C.M.: A short redactable signature scheme using pairing. Secur. Commun. Netw. **5**(5), 523–534 (2012). https://doi.org/10.1002/sec.346
13. Lim, S., Lee, H.S.: A short and efficient redactable signature based on RSA **33**, 621–628 (2011). https://doi.org/10.4218/etrij.11.0110.0530
14. Liu, J., Ma, J., Xiang, Y., Zhou, W., Huang, X.: Authenticated medical documents releasing with privacy protection and release control. IEEE Trans. Dependable Secure Comput., 1 (2019). https://doi.org/10.1109/TDSC.2019.2892446
15. Liu, J., Ma, J., Zhou, W., Xiang, Y., Huang, X.: Dissemination of authenticated tree-structured data with privacy protection and fine-grained control in outsourced databases. In: Lopez, J., Zhou, J., Soriano, M. (eds.) ESORICS 2018. LNCS, vol. 11099, pp. 167–186. Springer, Cham (2018). https://doi.org/10.1007/978-3-319-98989-1_9

16. Ma, J., Huang, X., Mu, Y., Deng, R.H.: Authenticated data redaction with account-ability and transparency. IEEE Trans. Dependable Secure Comput., 1 (2020). https://doi.org/10.1109/TDSC.2020.2998135
17. Ma, J., Liu, J., Huang, X., Xiang, Y., Wu, W.: Authenticated data redaction with fine-grained control. IEEE Trans. Emerg. Top. Comput. 8(2), 291–302 (2020). https://doi.org/10.1109/TETC.2017.2754646
18. Ma, J., Liu, J., Wang, M., Wu, W.: An efficient and secure design of redactable signature scheme with redaction condition control. In: Au, M.H.A., Castiglione, A., Choo, K.-K.R., Palmieri, F., Li, K.-C. (eds.) GPC 2017. LNCS, vol. 10232, pp. 38–52. Springer, Cham (2017). https://doi.org/10.1007/978-3-319-57186-7_4
19. de Meer, H., Pöhls, H.C., Posegga, J., Samelin, K.: Redactable signature schemes for trees with signer-controlled non-leaf-redactions. In: Obaidat, M.S., Filipe, J. (eds.) ICETE 2012. CCIS, vol. 455, pp. 155–171. Springer, Heidelberg (2014). https://doi.org/10.1007/978-3-662-44791-8_10
20. Micciancio, D., Peikert, C.: Trapdoors for lattices: simpler, tighter, faster, smaller. In: Pointcheval, D., Johansson, T. (eds.) EUROCRYPT 2012. LNCS, vol. 7237, pp. 700–718. Springer, Heidelberg (2012). https://doi.org/10.1007/978-3-642-29011-4_41
21. Micciancio, D., Regev, O.: Worst-case to average-case reductions based on gaussian measures. SIAM J. Comput. 37(1), 267–302 (2007). https://doi.org/10.1137/S0097539705447360
22. Miyazaki, K., et al.: Digitally signed document sanitizing scheme with disclosure condition control. IEICE Trans. Fundam. Electron. Commun. Comput. Sci. 88-A, 239–246 (2005). https://doi.org/10.1093/ietfec/E88-A.1.239
23. Miyazaki, K., Hanaoka, G., Imai, H.: Digitally signed document sanitizing scheme based on bilinear maps. In: Proceedings of the 2006 ACM Symposium on Information, Computer and Communications Security, ASIACCS 2006, pp. 343–354, Association for Computing Machinery, New York (2006). https://doi.org/10.1145/1128817.1128868
24. Nojima, R., Tamura, J., Kadobayashi, Y., Kikuchi, H.: A storage efficient redactable signature in the standard model. In: Samarati, P., Yung, M., Martinelli, F., Ardagna, C.A. (eds.) ISC 2009. LNCS, vol. 5735, pp. 326–337. Springer, Heidelberg (2009). https://doi.org/10.1007/978-3-642-04474-8_26
25. Pöhls, H.C., Karwe, M.: Redactable signatures to control the maximum noise for differential privacy in the smart grid. In: Cuellar, J. (ed.) SmartGridSec 2014. LNCS, vol. 8448, pp. 79–93. Springer, Cham (2014). https://doi.org/10.1007/978-3-319-10329-7_6
26. Pöhls, H.C., Samelin, K., Posegga, J., De Meer, H.: Length-hiding redactable signatures from one-way accumulators in $O(n)$. Technical report MIP-1201, Faculty of Computer Science and Mathematics (FIM...) (2012)
27. Pöhls, H.C., Samelin, K.: Accountable redactable signatures. In: 2015 10th International Conference on Availability, Reliability and Security, pp. 60–69, August 2015. https://doi.org/10.1109/ARES.2015.10
28. Sanders, O.: Efficient redactable signature and application to anonymous credentials. In: Kiayias, A., Kohlweiss, M., Wallden, P., Zikas, V. (eds.) PKC 2020. LNCS, vol. 12111, pp. 628–656. Springer, Cham (2020). https://doi.org/10.1007/978-3-030-45388-6_22
29. Slamanig, D., Rass, S.: Generalizations and extensions of redactable signatures with applications to electronic healthcare. In: De Decker, B., Schaumüller-Bichl, I. (eds.) CMS 2010. LNCS, vol. 6109, pp. 201–213. Springer, Heidelberg (2010). https://doi.org/10.1007/978-3-642-13241-4_19

30. Steinfeld, R., Bull, L., Zheng, Y.: Content extraction signatures. In: Kim, K. (ed.) ICISC 2001. LNCS, vol. 2288, pp. 285–304. Springer, Heidelberg (2002). https://doi.org/10.1007/3-540-45861-1_22
31. Zuo, F., Wang, Q., Cheng, P.: Identity-based redactable Lamport signature scheme. J. Phys. Conf. Ser. **1314**, 012147 (2019). https://doi.org/10.1088/1742-6596/1314/1/012147

WADS: A Webshell Attack Defender Assisted by Software-Defined Networks

Beiyuan Yu[ORCID], JianWei Liu[✉], and Ziyu Zhou

School of Cyber Science and Technology, Beihang University, Beijing, China
{yumingyuan,liujianwei,zhouziyu}@buaa.edu.cn

Abstract. Webshell is a code execution environment with extensions like php, asp, and jsp, which essence is to help managers of the system manage the web application effortlessly. Therefore, an attacker can use weshell as a backdoor program to control the webserver similarly. Traditional webshell detection mechanisms like rule matching and feature code detection usually suffer from poor generalization capabilities, leading to a higher rate of false negatives. Based on the Machine Learning model N-Gram, TF-IDF to extract the webshell sample features, three Machine Learning algorithms Multilayer Perceptron, XGBoost, and Naive Bayesian, to train the model. Analysis through training and testing, detection accuracy is more than 99% under the experimental environment, which detectable scope includes php, jsp, asp, and others. By combing the Machine Learning webshell detection model with the Software-Defined Networks using the flow table operate method, we implement a dynamic defense solution against webshell attackers, leading attackers to disconnect with the target network.

Keywords: SDN · Webshell detection · Machine learning

1 Introduction

1.1 Basic Information

In recent years, with the gradual popularization of Internet technology, various web applications have emerged and served our daily life. Web applications are widely used in e-government, e-commerce, and other fields, considerably facilitating people's lives. However, with the evolution and development of various web application development frameworks, the security issues associated with web applications have gradually surfaced. Hackers with experience in offense and defense can often exploit flaws in the server and use attacks to invade the web server.

Due to the characteristic of the webshell, once it is uploaded to the server and parsed by the server, it will be difficult for traditional Web Application Firewalls (WAF) to avoid its traffic and behavior. Traditional webshell protection

This work is supported by the National Natural Science Foundation of China (Grant No. 61972018, 61932014 and U21B2021).

© Springer Nature Switzerland AG 2021
R. Deng et al. (Eds.): ISPEC 2021, LNCS 13107, pp. 209–222, 2021.
https://doi.org/10.1007/978-3-030-93206-0_13

schemes mainly consist of writing keyword regular expression matching methods to match key characters or strings with webshell characteristics. Some webshell detection schemes target the statistical differences between webshell and traditional server programs, combining the features of Entropy, LongestWord, and Index of Coincidence to detect webshell that are deformed and obfuscated. However, this method has poor generalization ability for webshell that have without obfuscation. Research on machine learning methods has risen in recent years, and solutions that use machine learning methods for webshell detection have gradually become mainstream [5]. This paper mainly focuses on PHP, JSP, ASP, and PYTHON because these languages are suitable for webshell development.

Software-Defined Network (SDN) [16] has become the fundamental infrastructure of the 5G communication technology. The Clean State research group from Stanford University propose SDN conception and implement the OpenFlow [10] framework for reference and simulation. The SDN facilitates a fine-grained network device management by introducing a centralized SDN controller, which decouples the control plane from the data plane. The features provided by SDN enable the developer to implement the real-world network devices programmatically. Based on this feature, developers can develop network devices that are more consistent with business logic. Previous studies have shown that using controller to dynamically adjust flow rules while ensuring the security of SDN controllers can provide reasonable protection against DoS or DDoS attacks [2]. In this research, the SDN controller plays a crucial role by combining machine learning algorithms to detect the requested data and reduce the threat posed by attackers to the server by modifying the flow table to block attacker traffic or forward it to the server honeypot.

Based on machine learning methods for webshell detection, using the SDN network can dynamically modify the network topology and flow rules. Our solution can effectively disconnect the attacker from the target servers to avoid further damage to the target servers. WADS runs on the SDN controller. When WADS's machine learning model inspects that the request packet contains the webshell, the SDN controller will supports WADS through flow update operation. By updating the flow table, the source of the attack that initiated the upload webshell will not access the target server.

1.2   Contribution

We proposed a model based on a combination of N-Gram [3], TF-IDF with Multilayer Perceptron (MLP), XGBoost algorithm. Our method uses source code of webshell gathered from the Github repository developed by the whitehat or the red team attacker, including PHP, JSP, JSPX, ASP, ASPX, etc. During the experiment, a dataset includes 11461 webshell files and 11518 benign files applied to the model. The experimental result shows that the detection accuracy reaches 99.75% with the recall of 99.55% and precision is 99.94%. This paper organizes as follows: Sect. 2 describes background of the problem. Section 3 presents machine learning methods and techniques that we used in this study. Section 4 proposes strategies and techniques that implement the SDN-assisted webshell attack defender. Section 5 presents the results, discussion that we obtained, and finally. Section 6 presents the conclusions of this paper.

2   Background

2.1   Webshells

The attacker usually designs a malicious script using the standard web application development language to obtain a webshell [19], which helps them achieve long-term control of servers; after finding the flaw on the web server, they will upload the webshell to the webserver. Once the webshell is infected, parsed by the web server, and execute properly, it will help the attacker build up an operating interface [21] with the server. An attacker will control the server by using the shell execution environment provided by the webshell using the connect tools. The webshell has enough function to help the attacker manage the database, execute as the system administrator, access the server's file system, and so on. We can divide webshell into three groups based on file size and functional complexity: one-sentence webshell, small version webshell, and full version webshell. One-sentence webshell is very distinctive in that they usually consist of a concise line of code. Despite the simplicity of the code writing, attackers can obtain the server's information by dynamically adjusting the content of the request parameter vector. Miniature version webshell has more features include file transfer, database operator, etc. Full version webshell usually has a much larger size, with an interface that can obtain the privilege permissions of the server's operating system.

2.2   Webshell Detection

Once the webshell has been successfully uploaded to the server and executed, its behavior will be challenging to capture and intercept by the web application firewall. Detection of webshell by keyword matching alone often results in a high rate of misses. Some researchers who combine lexical analysis techniques with webshell detection have been able to identify web shells more accurately when the webshell without any cryptographic scrambling [6]. Some researchers have proposed an information entropy-based webshell detection method based on PHP language features using the regular PHP file's information entropy as a threshold to identify the webshell [22]. However, this method only supports the detection of PHP files and cannot be helpful in multi-language webshell detection. With the development and large-scale application of machine learning algorithms, solutions that use machine learning algorithms to detect webshell are increasingly shifting to the mainstream. Researchers utilize packet tools to extract the data portion of the HTTP request body and use the word vector processing method to convert the string into a word vector that machine learning models accept. After research, word2vec, a word vector processing method, and machine learning techniques to design a webshell detection method can better achieve the detection of webshell. Researchers using the convolutional neural network model [18] as the detection model and achieve 98.6% precision. The webshell threat model shows in Fig. 1.

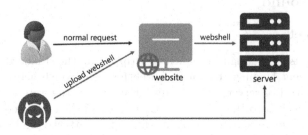

Fig. 1. Webshell threat model

2.3   Software-Defined Network

The Software-Defined Network helps the user define and build up a centralized point to control the data flow that routes the network devices. OpenFlow is an implementation version of software-defined networks. The SDN architecture consists of an application plane, a control plane, and a data plane. The application plane reflects user intent and allows developers to build the applications based on their purpose and actual needs. In the application plane, developers can accumulate network data such as topology and network statistics to develop network visualization applications and network automation-related applications that provide end-to-end solutions, which requirements were coming from the user. The control plane is primarily responsible for managing the underlying physical network, obtaining and maintaining the device's statistic information to help enhance the network's robustness. The data plane consists of various software/hardware-based infrastructure devices, which handle the packet follow the instruction from the upper plane. Researchers have done a lot of work on how to use SDN more securely as network infrastructure. By identifying and verifying the TCP handshake packet in the flow, AvantGuard [17] introduces a connection movement module to mitigate the attack on the SDN data plane. Also, there has been a lot of research on machine learning-based SDN protection mechanisms, mainly intrusion detection and DDoS attack elimination. Chen et al. focus on SDN in the cloud environment, starting from the perspective of SDN controllers, combining the classifier XGBoost with the collected stream packet dataset for DDoS detection [4]. Sanda et al. use machine learning algorithms to predict and define security rules for SDN controllers to prevent malicious users from accessing the network [11]. This paper primarily focuses on webshell detection by utilizing the machine learning method, which combines the SDN flow control mechanism to reduce the attacker's influence on the target network.

3   Machine Learning Method and Techniques

Machine learning algorithms can classify the legitimacy of network traffic (including the upload traffic of webshell) with a high degree of accuracy. Extract the feature from many webshell samples collected from the field using the N-gram method. The extracted features were processed using the TF-IDF method to achieve the goal of building the vectorized sample. This scheme uses a multilayer perceptron, XGBoost, and other models to train the data and obtain dependable webshell detection results. To lay the groundwork for the subsequent task of combining machine learning models with SDN controllers.

3.1   N-Gram Method

The N-Gram is the most frequently used text categorization method, which can help build up the statistical data on the frequency of occurrence of a gram in the NLP area. N-gram will split the text by parameter N and combine the split words into form multiple sample sets. The N-Gram is suitable for the data with noise [3], so we choose it as the first process method for our webshell sample. In this scheme, the researcher introduces the Markov Assumption [7] to the N-gram to help avoid the problem of redundant parameter spaces. The Markov Assumption showed as follows Eq. (1).

$$p(w_1 \cdots w_n) \approx \prod p(w_i \mid w_{i-1} \cdots w_{i-N+1}) \tag{1}$$

In our experiment, parameter N takes $2, 3$. When N takes 2, it is named Bi-gram. When N takes 3, it is called Tri-gram. The Bi-gram follows as Eq. (2), and Tri-gram follows as Eq. (3).

$$p(w_1 w_2 \cdots w_n) = p(w_1) p(w_2 \mid w_1) \cdots p(w_n \mid w_{n-1}) \tag{2}$$

$$p(w_1 w_2 \cdots w_n) = p(w_1) p(w_2 \mid w_1) \cdots p(w_n \mid w_{n-1} w_{n-2}) \tag{3}$$

3.2   TF-IDF Method

TF-IDF (Term Frequency Inverse Document Frequency) is a statistical analysis method for keywords to evaluate the significance of a word to a document set or a corpus. As the work implies [14], TF-IDF acts by determining the related frequency of words in a particular document compared to the inverse proportion of that word over the complete document corpus. The TF-IDF can reveal the importance of words to the corpus properly. The formula of TF-IDF can express following Eq. (4).

$$tfidf(t, d, D) = \frac{f_{t,d}}{\sum_{t' \in d} f_{t',d}} * \log \frac{N}{|\{d \in D : t \in d\}|} \tag{4}$$

As Eq. (4) shows, $f_{t,d}$ denotes the count of times that term t occurs in document d. The N indicates the count of documents in corpus and $N = |D|$. The $|\{d \in D : t \in d\}|$ means the number of documents in the corpus. Using the TF-IDF approach to webshell data, we can automatically and swiftly extract significant keywords [8] or syntax building for a webshell.

3.3 Model Training

We collected over 10,000 webshell samples from the wild using Github's open-source repository. We also manually extracted webshell samples generated by well-known tools such as Godzilla to build the training data. The model is trained and tested by splitting the dataset according to 7-3. For the raw data, the system will pre-process using N-gram and TF-IDF methods. The processed samples will be applied to different Machine Learning algorithms to train the model and adjust the hyper-parameter for better detection effects. We will compare and evaluate the detection result to reach the approximately optimal webshell detection model. Figure 2 shows the process imposed on the webshell sample.

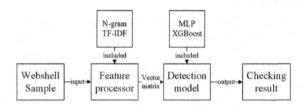

Fig. 2. Feature extraction and model training process

The original data need to treat utilizing N-Gram and TF-IDF. The XGBoost, MLP are the algorithms we practiced in training the detection model individually. Then the detection result will estimate based on the train test split's test samples.

We are seeking to apply more than four metrics to evaluate the model performance that we trained before, which include classification Accuracy rate, Precision rate, Recall rate, and F_1 score. Model training interval will additionally record as a metric.

3.4 Experimental and Analysis

We use Scikit-learn [12] as a framework to write training code to pre-process the data faster and train the machine learning model. In practice, Scikit-learn utilizes sklearn as a package name to be called by Python, which is suitable for developers to build up machine learning code systematically.

To obtain better model detection performance. Among them, we use $Ngram_{range}$ to denote the range of N value, Min_{df} called as the cut-off value, which acting as a threshold to help ignore some low-frequency words when constructing word lists, $Max_{feature} = n$ denote to extract the first n words from the frequency word lists. Finally, the $Test_{size}$ describes the percentage of the test data from the total volume.

XGBoost Algorithm. XGBoost algorithm builds up a Gradient Boosting Decision Tree group to make the residuals of prediction in a lower scope. XGBoost applies cache access patterns, data compression, and sharding process to build a better boosting system. The training situation and the information of selected hyperparameters are shown in Table 1; meanwhile, Table 2 shows us the XGBoost model evaluation metrics' results, where the unit of Table 2 is %. We use cases in the table to differentiate between different hyperparameters and evaluation results. As the table shows, hyperparameters in case 1 work better for the XGBoost algorithm. When $Ngram_{range}$ is same, much smaller Min_{df} will achieve a higher accuracy rate.

Table 1. XGBoost algorithm parameter

Case	$Ngram_{range}$	Min_{df}	$Max_{feature}$	$Test_{size}$
1	1,2	1	25000	0.3
2	2,2	1	25000	0.3
3	2,2	0.1	25000	0.3
4	2,2	0.01	25000	0.3
5	2,2	0.001	25000	0.3
6	2,4	1	25000	0.3
7	2,4	1	35000	0.3

Table 2. Evaluation metrics of XGBoost

Case	Accuracy rate	Precision rate	Recall rate	F_1 score
1	99.9138	99.8846	99.9422	99.9134
2	99.6983	99.5795	99.8314	99.7053
3	99.5115	99.1125	99.9134	99.5113
4	99.8276	99.6834	99.9711	99.8270
5	99.7845	99.5974	99.9711	99.7839
6	99.8276	99.6834	99.9711	99.8270
7	99.8563	99.7122	100.0	99.8559

MLP Algorithm. Multilayer perceptron (MLP) is a non-linear network that supports classification features [15]. The different layers of the multilayer perceptron are attached using the fully connected link. By introducing an activation function, the multilayer perceptron model can adequately solve the classification problem. The training situation and the information of selected hyperparameters are shown in Table 3; meanwhile, Table 4 shows us the MLP model evaluation metrics's results.

Table 3. MLP algorithm parameter

Case	$Ngram_{range}$	Min_{df}	$Max_{feature}$	$Test_{size}$
1	1,2	1	25000	0.3
2	2,2	1	25000	0.3
3	2,2	0.1	25000	0.3
4	2,2	0.01	25000	0.3
5	2,2	0.001	25000	0.3
6	2,4	1	25000	0.3
7	2,4	1	30000	0.3

Table 4. Evaluation metrics of MLP

Case	Accuracy rate	Precision rate	Recall rate	F_1 score
1	99.8132	99.8267	99.7979	99.8123
2	99.7414	99.6256	99.8556	99.7405
3	99.3248	98.7728	99.8845	99.3255
4	99.8276	99.7120	99.9422	99.8270
5	99.8132	99.7693	99.8556	99.8124
6	99.8563	99.7408	99.9711	99.8558
7	99.7701	99.6830	99.8556	99.7693

4 Design

To help mitigate the security problems mentioned before, we introduce the WADS, an efficient, lightweight, and user-friendly webshell defense framework based on the SDN networks.

4.1 System Architecture

The WADS Added two new functional modules based on the existing Openflow architecture: 1) a webshell detection module, which includes model training function and webshell detection function based on the network packet, and 2) a flow table modifying module, which assists the servers deployed in the SDN to disconnect from the attacker, with the ultimate goal of weakening or blocking the attacker's attack traffic. The webshell detection module supports training models dynamically and selecting the latest model to detect the traffic injected into the network. The flow table modifying module adjusts flow table rules to pass traffic sent by benign nodes and block traffic sent by nodes with malicious behavior. The SDN architecture provides high-frequency monitoring and emergency response features to improve the security of network assets.

Webshell Detection Module. The machine learning detection module will detect any messages passing through the SDN network infrastructure. The RYU SDN framework's packet manager will assist us in getting the critical portion of the packet (usually the HTTP data) to be the input data of the machine learning detection model. The data will experience a series of transformations, as in the model training process, and eventually, compute to produce a classification result. The system will not discard the data samples and their classification results. Still, they will store it in a collection (webshell/normal file) maintained by the system according to their classification result. The detection model parameters can train and adjust dynamically later through the scheduler of the model training module in our solution. Due to the features of various webshell types with high concealment, the traditional rule matching-based detection method is hard to detect. Our approach uses XGBoost, MLP to train the detection method in optimizing the detection model based on Machine Learning. Integrating the detection model with the webshell detection module helps the SDN controller mitigate the noise of the attacker to the service provider, which deploys the service based on the SDN architecture. The architecture of WADS show in Fig. 3.

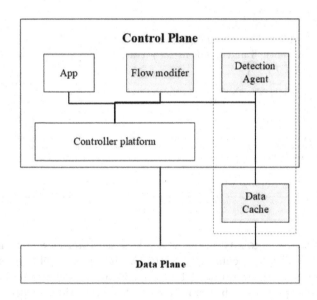

Fig. 3. WADS's conceptutal atchitecture

Model Scheduler. We have logically implemented a model scheduler based on the Python language to detect inbound traffic by the relatively freshest model. The scheduler will add labels to the relevant data from the classification results of the detection model. Also, dynamically store the data in the dataset to train. The corresponding data can be used as input to automatically train an updated detection model compared to the current state. The system is a new detection model for the next phase by applying this idea of training models with the latest and real-time data and using newer models for detection. It is possible to effectively improve the accuracy of detection models while taking into account the training and use of new models. When the current detection model detects more than 1000 webshell traffic, the cached traffic data will automatically feed into the training module as additional webshell samples and normal samples to train the updated detection model. The detection model schedule algorithm is shown in Algorithm 1, where T indicates the current batch and the $T+1$ shows the next batch. And $train(P_T, N_T)$ means use P_T and N_T as the data sample to train a new webshell detection model at T and make it effective at next phase.

Algorithm 1. Detection Model Schedule algorithm

Require:
  The set of positive samples for current batch, P_T;
  The set of negative samples for current batch, N_T;
  The set of detected positive samples for current batch, DP_T;
Ensure: webshell detection model $model_T$ exist;
  loop
    $model_{detect} \leftarrow model_T$
    if $len(DP_T) \neq 1000$ **then**
      Detect traffic t_r using $model_{detect}$
      if t_r is a webshell and t_r not in DP_T **then**
        $DP_T \leftarrow DP_T \cup \{t_r\}$
      else
        $DP_T \leftarrow DP_T$
      end if
    else
      $P_T \leftarrow P_T \cup DP_T$
      $model_T \leftarrow train(P_T, N_T)$
    end if
  end loop

Attack Source Mitigator. In the TCP/IP-based Internet environment, many attackers use multiple techniques to attack the target web system to show off their skills or damage the target system. Common defense mainly includes deploying Web application firewalls [13] on the server-side, security inspection of high-frequency request traffic, etc. By adding a series of security rules at the application layer, the WAF can help mitigate the frequency of attacks on Web application systems to a certain extent. Unlike traditional application layer-based security schemes, this paper provides attack source blocking features at the network layer by adding an attack source mitigator to the system and using the SDN controller's feature to manipulate flow table [9]. The detection model mitigation algorithm shows in Algorithm 2, which can help the controller block the attack source.

Algorithm 2. Attack source mitigate algorithm

Require:
  Inbound traffic t_r
  Flow table record the prohibit attack source $flow_{ban}$
Ensure: webshell detection model $model_T$ exist;
  repeat
    if $detect(model_T, t_r)$ is webshell **then**
      $Ban_{IP} = t_r.ipaddr$
      $flow_{ban} \leftarrow flow_{ban} \cup Ban_{IP}$
      apply($flow_{ban}$)
    else
      pass t_r
    end if
  until No inbound traffic

4.2 Machine Learning Framework

Scikit-learn is a general machine learning library built on top of SciPy and written with Python language. The Scikit-learn provides numerous statistical learning algorithms, including supervised and unsupervised algorithms [1]. Using the efficient statistical learning language interface provided by sci-kit-learn with the data processing framework NumPy, developers can easily use Python to quickly train models with datasets and test them according to their needs. Among them, NumPy provides the data type ndarray, which can store samples and their features very well. The NumPy also provides the dot product operation internally. The training code combine with the Scikit-learn's module includes CountVectorizer and TfidfTransformer to preprocess the data samples. The pseudo-code of the training logic is shown in Algorithm 3.

Algorithm 3. pseudo-code of the training logic

Input:
    The set of positive samples for current batch, P_{data};
    The set of negative samples , N_{data};
Output: trained model $Model_T$;
    $train_{data} \leftarrow P_{data} \cup N_{data}$
    $Ctrain_{data} \leftarrow CountVectorizer(train_{data})$
    $tfCtrain_{data} \leftarrow TfidfTransformer(Ctrain_{data})$
    if Use MLP model **then**
      $Model_T \leftarrow MLPClassifier(tfCtrain_{data})$
      Save $Model_T$
    else
      $Model_T \leftarrow XGBClassifier(tfCtrain_{data})$
      Save $Model_T$
    end if

4.3 SDN Controller Framework

Ryu is a component-based software-defined networking framework. Ryu provides a bunch of components that are useful for build up SDN applications. Ryu has implemented a well-defined API that makes it easy for developers to create new network management and control applications [20]. Ryu itself provides a Python-based development module, which can configure by installing it using the mininet virtual machine.

5 Experiment

We use the simple switching hub developed by Ryu as an experimental environment to verify the feasibility of our solution. The network structure shows in Fig. 4, and Port represents the switch port to which the net asset is connected. We have implemented the machine learning model training and detection code in Python (over 500 LoC). The model and detection code was introduced into the Ryu environment by writing an SDN application that suitable for the Ryu framework (over 200 LoC). Experiment using Mininet to construct a network topology that simulated an attacker uploading a webshell to a target server deployed within the SDN. Table 5 shows the flow table before webshell attack. The trained webshell model can be accessed and processed directly by the SDN controller by reading it in the SDN application. When webshell traffic is detected, the application will notify the controller to block the source of the attack by triggering a notification. And Table 6 shows the flow table after the WADS detect the webshell attack.

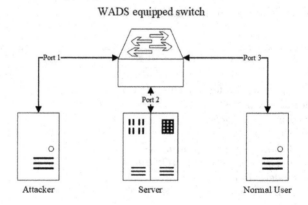

Fig. 4. Experimental network topology

Table 5. Flow table's item before webshell attack

Flow item	In port	eth destination	Output port
1	1	Server	2
2	1	Normal user	3
3	2	Attacker	1
4	2	Normal user	3
5	3	Attacker	1
6	3	Server	2

Table 6. Flow table's item after detect webshell attack

Flow item	In port	eth destination	Output port
1	2	Normal user	3
2	3	Server	2

6   Conclusion

Due to the feature of the web development language, the webshell contains various types and variants. This paper, based on the Machine Learning algorithm, discusses a webshell detection method to detect multiple types of webshell and their variants. With this work, we have implemented webshell detection model training to provide a module prototype for SDN applications capable of using machine learning models. By implementing the SDN application's webshell detection functionality and the flow table control features provided by the SDN controller, nodes in the SDN network will be protected by the SDN controller. In addition, by combining with the SDN, this solution reduces the burden on the WAF. WADS is not intended to replace WAF but rather reduce the risk posed to the entire network by the source of the attack from the network layer. We will continue to refine this solution and investigate its usability in complex network environments in subsequent work.

References

1. Abraham, A., et al.: Machine learning for neuroimaging with Scikit-learn. Front. Neuroinform. **8**, 14 (2014)
2. Bawany, N.Z., Shamsi, J.A., Salah, K.: DDoS attack detection and mitigation using SDN: methods, practices, and solutions. Arab. J. Sci. Eng. **42**(2), 425–441 (2017)
3. Cavnar, W.B., Trenkle, J.M., et al.: N-gram-based text categorization. In: Proceedings of SDAIR-94, 3rd Annual Symposium on Document Analysis and Information Retrieval, vol. 161175. Citeseer (1994)
4. Chen, Z., Jiang, F., Cheng, Y., Gu, X., Liu, W., Peng, J.: XGBoost classifier for DDoS attack detection and analysis in SDN-based cloud. In: 2018 IEEE International Conference on Big Data and Smart Computing (BigComp), pp. 251–256. IEEE (2018)

5. Cui, H., Huang, D., Fang, Y., Liu, L., Huang, C.: Webshell detection based on random forest-gradient boosting decision tree algorithm. In: 2018 IEEE Third International Conference on Data Science in Cyberspace (DSC), pp. 153–160. IEEE (2018)
6. Deng, L.Y., Lee, D.L., Chen, Y.H., Yann, L.X.: Lexical analysis for the webshell attacks. In: 2016 International Symposium on Computer, Consumer and Control (IS3C), pp. 579–582. IEEE (2016)
7. Jespersen, S., Pedersen, T.B., Thorhauge, J.: Evaluating the Markov assumption for web usage mining. In: Proceedings of the 5th ACM International Workshop on Web Information and Data Management, pp. 82–89 (2003)
8. Koloski, B., Pollak, S., Škrlj, B., Martinc, M.: Extending neural keyword extraction with TF-IDF tagset matching. arXiv preprint arXiv:2102.00472 (2021)
9. Kuźniar, M., Perešíni, P., Kostić, D.: What you need to know about SDN flow tables. In: Mirkovic, J., Liu, Y. (eds.) PAM 2015. LNCS, vol. 8995, pp. 347–359. Springer, Cham (2015). https://doi.org/10.1007/978-3-319-15509-8_26
10. McKeown, N., et al.: OpenFlow: enabling innovation in campus networks. ACM SIGCOMM Comput. Commun. Rev. **38**(2), 69–74 (2008)
11. Nanda, S., Zafari, F., DeCusatis, C., Wedaa, E., Yang, B.: Predicting network attack patterns in sdn using machine learning approach. In: 2016 IEEE Conference on Network Function Virtualization and Software Defined Networks (NFV-SDN), pp. 167–172. IEEE (2016)
12. Pedregosa, F., et al.: Scikit-learn: machine learning in python. J. Mach. Learn. Res. **12**, 2825–2830 (2011)
13. Prandl, S., Lazarescu, M., Pham, D.-S.: A study of web application firewall solutions. In: Jajodia, S., Mazumdar, C. (eds.) ICISS 2015. LNCS, vol. 9478, pp. 501–510. Springer, Cham (2015). https://doi.org/10.1007/978-3-319-26961-0_29
14. Ramos, J., et al.: Using TF-IDF to determine word relevance in document queries. In: Proceedings of the First Instructional Conference on Machine Learning, vol. 242, pp. 29–48. Citeseer (2003)
15. Ruck, D.W., Rogers, S.K., Kabrisky, M.: Feature selection using a multilayer perceptron. J. Neural Netw. Comput. **2**(2), 40–48 (1990)
16. Scott-Hayward, S., O'Callaghan, G., Sezer, S.: SDN security: a survey. In: 2013 IEEE SDN for Future Networks and Services (SDN4FNS), pp. 1–7. IEEE (2013)
17. Shin, S., Yegneswaran, V., Porras, P., Gu, G.: Avant-guard: scalable and vigilant switch flow management in software-defined networks. In: Proceedings of the 2013 ACM SIGSAC Conference on Computer & Communications Security, pp. 413–424 (2013)
18. Tian, Y., Wang, J., Zhou, Z., Zhou, S.: CNN-webshell: malicious web shell detection with convolutional neural network. In: Proceedings of the 2017 VI International Conference on Network, Communication and Computing, pp. 75–79 (2017)
19. Tianmin, G., Jiemin, Z., Jian, M.: Research on webshell detection method based on machine learning. In: 2019 3rd International Conference on Electronic Information Technology and Computer Engineering (EITCE), pp. 1391–1394. IEEE (2019)
20. Tomonori, F.: Introduction to RYU SDN framework. Open Networking Summit, pp. 1–14 (2013)
21. Tu, T.D., Guang, C., Xiaojun, G., Wubin, P.: Webshell detection techniques in web applications. In: Fifth International Conference on Computing, Communications and Networking Technologies (ICCCNT), pp. 1–7. IEEE (2014)
22. Wang, C., Yang, H., Zhao, Z., Gong, L., Li, Z.: The research and improvement in the detection of PHP variable webshell based on information entropy. J. Comput. **28**, 62–68 (2016)

Cloud-Assisted LLL: A Secure and Efficient Outsourcing Algorithm for Approximate Shortest Vector Problem

Xiulan Li[1,2], Yanbin Pan[1,2], and Chengliang Tian[3(✉)]

[1] Key Laboratory of Mathematics Mechanization, Academy of Mathematics and Systems Science, Chinese Academy of Sciences, Beijing 100190, China
{lixiulan,panyanbin}@amss.ac.cn
[2] School of Mathematical Sciences, University of Chinese Academy of Sciences, Beijing 100049, China
[3] College of Computer Science and Technology, Qingdao University, Qingdao 266071, China
tianchengliang@qdu.edu.cn

Abstract. Approximating the shortest vector of a given lattice is one of the most important computational problems in public-key cryptanalysis and lattice-based cryptography. However, existing LLL reduction algorithm and its variants for this problem are too time-consuming for resource-constrained clients. To handle this dilemma, in this paper, we propose an efficient and secure outsourcing algorithm under the cloud environment. Compared with the prior Liu et al.'s algorithm, besides realizing the privacy preservation of client's input/output information, satisfying verifiability and greatly reducing the local-client's computational overhead, our algorithm is superior in the following aspects. First, our algorithm is technically concise. The main technique ingredient involved in our algorithm is a skillful combination of the unimodular matrix transformation and the Gram matrix, which is concise and effective. Second, our algorithm does not reduce the quality of the reduced basis, that is, the vector finally obtained by the client is as short as that of the vector generated by the client directly performing the existing reduction algorithm. Last but not least, our algorithm not only works for the LLL reduction algorithm, but also for any other algorithms that solve (approximate-)SVP with Euclidean norm.

Keywords: Cloud computing · Outsourcing computation · Approximate SVP · Gram matrix · Unimodular transformation

This work is supported by National Key Research and Development Program of China (No. 2018YFA0704705, 2020YFA0712300), National Natural Science Foundation of China (No. 61702294, 62032009), National Development Foundation of Cryptography (MMJJ20170126).

© Springer Nature Switzerland AG 2021
R. Deng et al. (Eds.): ISPEC 2021, LNCS 13107, pp. 223–241, 2021.
https://doi.org/10.1007/978-3-030-93206-0_14

1   Introduction

A lattice is a discrete additive subgroup of $\mathbb{R}^m$, which is a classic research object in the geometry of numbers. One of the most important computational problems in lattice theory is the Shortest Vector Problem (SVP) which aims to find the shortest nonzero vector of arbitrary given lattice and is shown to be NP-hard under random reduction [1].

Lattice has been widely used in mathematics and computer science, especially in cryptography. Many different problems can be solved via solving SVP in some lattices, such as factoring polynomials with rational coefficients [15], finding integer relations among real numbers [11], factoring integers and computing discrete logarithms [22], and attacking RSA [7]. In addition, lattice-based cryptographic constructions [10] have been widely considered as one of the most promising post-quantum cryptosystems and the hardness of SVP directly determines their theoretical security.

Due to the hardness of SVP, various lattice basis reduction algorithms have been designed to approximate shortest vector as far as possible. The first lattice basis reduction algorithm proposed by Lagrange [14] in 1773 is a groundbreaking work, though it finds a minimal basis in two dimensions. Hermite's proposed second lattice basis reduction algorithm generalizes Lagrange's algorithm to n dimensions. After that, the first polynomial-time lattice basis reduction algorithm, the LLL algorithm, was proposed by Lenstra, Lenstra and Lovász in 1982. It achieves an approximation factor of $2^{O(n)}$ for the approximation variant of SVP with worst-case time complexity $O(n^5 m \log^3 B)$, and can be used to attack some cryptosystems, such as knapsack-based cryptosystems and special cases of RSA [7]. To get somewhat better approximation factor $(6k^2)^{nk/2}$ where k is some integer, Schnorr [21] extended the LLL algorithm by making block size larger at the price of an increased running time in 1987.

In the last two decades, many improvements for lattice basis reduction algorithm have been investigated [2,6,18,19]. In 2005, Nguyen and Stehlé [18] introduced L^2 algorithm, a floating-point variant of L^3, to make LLL reduction algorithm practical with computational complexity $O(n^4 m(n+\log B) \log B)$. Saruchi et al. [20] proposed an effective reduction algorithm, which is the expansion of the algorithm proposed by Bi et al. [4]. Although these algorithms can find a relatively short vector in polynomial time, they are still time-consuming in practice. Especially, in practical applications, the dimension of the lattice is usually very large and the user or the terminal device could be with limited computing and storage capability. It is unrealistic for these clients to perform these algorithms to approximate the shortest vector.

The emergence of cloud computing provides a new paradigm for resource-constrained clients to handle heavy computational tasks, in which scenario, these resource-constrained clients can outsource their overloaded computational task to the resource-abundant cloud server on a pay-as-you-use manner. However, this promising computing paradigm also brings new security concerns [13,25]. The remote cloud server is out of control, and for the sake of business interests, it could deviate the prescribed execution rules and collect valuable information.

Simultaneously, the outsourcing computational task may contain client's privacy and sensitive information. The exposure of this information may cause critical loss of lift and property. Therefore, a well-designed outsourcing algorithm, apart from ensuring the client to achieve the correct computation result at a greatly reduced time cost, should protect the client's privacy information and discern the cloud server's misbehaviors. Therefore, in-depth studies on the outsourcing computation of many aspects have been conducted in recent years, such as large-scale linear algebra operations [3,8], solving quadratic congruences [26,27], modular exponentiations [5,12,29] and modular inversion [24] in cryptography, heavy computations in artificial intelligence (AI) and Internet of Things (IoT) [16,28].

In 2019, Liu et al. [17] proposed the first outsourcing computation mechanism of lattice-reduction algorithm based on the work of Saruchi et al. [20]. They utilized rounding technique and unimodular transformation matrix to encrypt the original computation task by generating a outsourcing task $\mathbf{B} + \Delta\mathbf{B}$ for the lattice basis $\mathbf{B}$. The cloud server reduces it by LLL-reduction algorithm and returns the transformation matrix. After receiving the response of the cloud server, the client can obtain the LLL-reduced basis for the target lattice $\Lambda(\mathbf{B})$ finally, but with a bigger approximation factor. Their outsourcing algorithm has high-efficiency. However, the perturbation term $\Delta\mathbf{B}$ in their outsourcing algorithm has to satisfy some special properties, which makes the algorithm complex. Furthermore, their outsource algorithm yields a LLL-reduced basis with a bigger approximation factor than applying LLL-reduction algorithm directly on the original basis, which weakens the requirement of the outsourcing computation task.

Our Contribution. In this paper, we study the algorithm for approximate SVP under the cloud environment, and propose a secure outsourcing algorithm for this problem. In our design, the resource-constrained client can efficiently find a relatively short lattice vector by leveraging the powerful computing capacity of the cloud server.

The idea is quite simple. Roughly speaking, for any given lattice basis $\mathbf{B}$, consider the corresponding Gram matrix $\mathbf{G} = \mathbf{B}^{\mathrm{T}}\mathbf{B}$. Note that for any orthogonal matrix $\mathbf{O}$, the Gram matrix of $\mathbf{OB}$ is exactly $\mathbf{G}$, which means that $\mathbf{G}$ can protect $\mathbf{B}$ well. Moreover, the lattices generated by $\mathbf{OB}$ and $\mathbf{B}$ are different, but for any integer coefficient vector $\mathbf{z}$, the lattice vectors $\mathbf{OBz}$ and $\mathbf{Bz}$ has exactly the same length under the Euclidean norm. This inspires us to send the Gram matrix $\mathbf{G}$ to the cloud server, which can perform LLL algorithm on $\mathbf{G}$ (or some $\mathbf{C}$ such that $\mathbf{G} = \mathbf{C}^{\mathrm{T}}\mathbf{C}$, which can be obtained by Cholesky decomposition on $\mathbf{G}$ by the cloud server). The cloud server will send the transformation matrix to the client and the client can recover the LLL-reduced basis, since the orthogonal transformation does not affect that properties that an LLL-reduced basis should satisfy.

We can show that our design can protect the privacy of client's input/output information under CPA model, and make the client discern the cloud's fraud behavior with optimal probability 1. Hence, our design can be employed in the algorithms that involves with LLL algorithm, such as Coppersmith's attack [7].

Compared to Liu et al.'s work [17], our algorithm also has high-efficiency. Besides, our algorithm is technically concise, which just involves with a simple combination of unimodular matrix transformation and Gram matrix. Furthermore, our algorithm does not reduce the quality of the reduced basis, that is, the vector finally obtained by the client is as short as that of the vector generated by the client directly performing the existing reduction algorithm. Last but not least, it is obvious that our algorithm not only works for the LLL reduction algorithm, but also for any other algorithms that solve (approximate-)SVP with Euclidean norm, since we employ an isometry of the lattice essentially.

Roadmap. The paper is organized as follows: Sect. 2 introduces the system model and security definitions of the outsourcing computation. Section 3 reviews the main computational problems in lattices and presents some necessary preliminaries. In Sect. 4, we propose Gram matrix-based outsourcing algorithm for approximate SVP. In Sect. 5, we analyze the correctness, security and efficiency of our algorithm, followed by extensive experimental analysis to evaluate the practical performance of our design in Sect. 6. In Sect. 7, we give a simple application. Finally, we conclude this article in Sect. 8.

2 System Model and Security Definitions

2.1 System Model

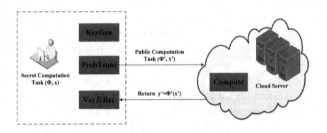

Fig. 1. The system model

Outsourcing computation is an interaction system between two entities with asymmetric computing capacities: the client and the cloud server, out of which, the client is with limited computational power and storage space, and the cloud server providing computing and storage service is resource-abundant yet maybe untrusted. Formally, as illustrated in Fig. 1, the light-weight client C (or customer, data user, etc.) wants to take advantage of the capacity of the cloud server to accomplish his overloaded calculation task $\Phi(\cdot)$ with an input x.

To protect the input information form being stolen, C transforms the original computation task $\Phi(\cdot)$ into another computation task $\Phi'(\cdot)$, which may be the same as Φ, with corresponding encrypted input x' by the previously generated secret key sk. Then, C sends $(\Phi(\cdot), x')$ to the cloud server S. Next, the cloud server S applies its resources to compute the specified task $y' = \Phi'(x')$ and returns y' to C. After that, C verifies the correctness of y' and recovers y' to the actual result $y = \Phi(x)$ if it passes the verification. Otherwise, C rejects. Precisely, the general framework of secure outsourcing computation can be formalized as a four-tuple $\text{OCAlg}_\Phi = (\textbf{KeyGen}, \textbf{ProbTrans}, \textbf{Compute}, \textbf{Ver\&Rec})$ with the following four probabilistic polynomial-time (PPT) sub-algorithms [9]:

1. $\textbf{KeyGen}(\Phi, x, 1^\kappa) \to \{sk\}$: Input a security parameter κ, the client C conducts the randomized algorithm $\textbf{KeyGen}$ to generate a secret key sk for any input computation task (Φ, x).
2. $\textbf{ProbTrans}(\Phi, x, sk) \to \{\Phi', x'\}$: The algorithm $\textbf{ProbTrans}$ utilizes the secret key sk to transform (Φ, x) into another computation task (Φ', x'). This algorithm is performed by the client C.
3. $\textbf{Compute}(\Phi', x') \to \{y'\}$: According to the computation task Φ' with the encoded input x', the cloud server S invokes the algorithm $\textbf{Compute}$ to compute $y' = \Phi'(x')$ and returns the encoded output y' to the client C.
4. $\textbf{Ver\&Rec}(\Phi, y', sk) \to \{y\}$: With the secret key sk, the algorithm $\textbf{Ver\&Rec}$ performs as follows. It firstly verifies the correctness of y'. Then, if y' passes the verification, the algorithm recovers y' to $y = \Phi(x)$. Else, the algorithm outputs $y = \perp$.

2.2   Threat Models

In an outsourcing system, the threats are mainly from the untrusted cloud server. The potential misbehaviors of the cloud can be included into two types:

- **Honest-and-curious (HC) Server.** In this case, the cloud server will honestly perform the assigned computation task and return the correct result to the client. However, for financial incentive, it may collect or even sell client's valuable information.
- **Fully-malicious (FM) Server.** In this case, the cloud server not only tries to capture client's valuable information, but also may deliberately forge a false result to fool the client.

Further, according to the attack abilities owned by the untrusted cloud server, there mainly exist three kinds of attack models:

- **Ciphertext-only attack (COA) Model.** In COA model, the cloud server is assumed to have only access to the computation tasks Φ, Φ' and the blinded input x', and tries to recover the actual input x and the actual output $y = \Phi(x)$.
- **Known-plaintext attack (KPA) Model.** In KPA model, the cloud server knows the computation tasks (Φ, Φ') and has the ability of collecting a polynomial number of plaintexts x_i $(1 \le i \le \ell)$ and the corresponding ciphertexts

x_i', y_i' and δ_i. Given challenge ciphertexts x' and $y' = \Phi'(x')$, the cloud server tries to recover the actual input x and the actual output $y = \Phi(x)$.

- **Chosen-plaintext attack (*CPA*) Model.** In *CPA* model, the cloud server knows the computation tasks (Φ, Φ') and is allowed to adaptively choose a polynomial number of inputs x_i ($1 \leq i \leq N$) and obtain the corresponding ciphertext x_i', y_i' and δ_i. Given challenge ciphertexts x' and $y' = \Phi'(x')$, the cloud server tries to recover the actual input x and the actual output $y = \Phi(x)$.

Overall, there exist 6 possible threat models: *HC+COA*, *HC+KPA*, *HC+CPA*, *FM+COA*, *FM+KPA*, *FM+CPA*. Clearly, in the above-mentioned threat models, the ability of the *FM+CPA* model is the most powerful. Therefore, an outsourcing algorithm that is secure under the *FM+CPA* model is certainly secure under the other models, and thus, it is more meaningful to design a secure outsourcing algorithm under the *FM+CPA* model.

2.3   Correctness and Security Definitions

Based on the above-mentioned system architecture and threat models, a secure outsourcing algorithm should at least meet four requirements: correctness, input/output privacy, verifiability and High efficiency. We now present their strictly formalized definitions.

Correctness is a basic requirements for an outsourcing algorithm. It means that, if the cloud server performed the specified computations in the algorithm honestly, the client can correctly achieve the result of the original computation task. Precisely,

Definition 1 (Correctness). *A secure outsourcing algorithm* $\mathrm{OCAlg}_\Phi(\cdot)$ *of some computation task* Φ *is correct if the key generation algorithm generates key* $\{sk\} \leftarrow \mathbf{KeyGen}(\Phi, x, 1^\kappa)$ *such that, for any valid input* x *of* Φ, *if* $\{\Phi', x'\} \leftarrow \mathbf{ProbTrans}(\Phi, x, sk)$ *and* $y' \leftarrow \mathbf{Compute}(\Phi', x')$, *where* $y' = \Phi'(x')$, *the algorithm* $\mathbf{Ver\&Rec}(\Phi, y', sk)$ *outputs* $y = \Phi(x)$.

Input/output privacy is a security requirement for an outsourcing algorithm. It asks the outsourcing algorithm to protect the input and output information of client's computation task from being disclosed to the cloud server. Here, we mainly discuss the input (resp. output) privacy with one-way notion under the *FM+CPA* model. To give the strict privacy definition, we first formalize the description of *CPA* model with the following experiments $\mathbf{Exp}_\mathcal{A}^{Ipriv}[\Phi, 1^\kappa]$ and $\mathbf{Exp}_\mathcal{A}^{Opriv}[\Phi, 1^\kappa]$.

Experiment $\mathbf{Exp}_\mathcal{A}^{Ipriv}[\Phi, 1^\kappa]$

Query and response:

$x_0 = \sigma_{x_0} = \perp$.

For $i = 1, \cdots, \ell = \mathrm{poly}(\kappa)$

$\quad x_i \leftarrow \mathcal{A}(\Phi, (x_j, \sigma_{x_j})_{0 \leq j \leq i-1})$.

$\quad sk_i \leftarrow \mathbf{KeyGen}(\Phi, x_i, 1^\kappa)$.

$\quad \sigma_{x_i} = (\Phi', x_i') \leftarrow \mathbf{ProbTrans}(\Phi, sk_i, x_i)$.

Challenge:
$\tilde{x} \leftarrow \text{Domain}(\Phi)$.
$\tilde{sk} \leftarrow \textbf{KeyGen}(\Phi, \tilde{x}, 1^\kappa)$.
$\sigma_{\tilde{x}} = (\Phi', \tilde{x}') \leftarrow \textbf{ProbTrans}(\Phi, \tilde{sk}, \tilde{x})$.
$\bar{x} \leftarrow \mathcal{A}(\Phi, (x_j, \sigma_{x_j})_{0 \le j \le \ell}, \sigma_{\tilde{x}})$.
if $\bar{x} = \tilde{x}$, output $'1'$;
else output $'0'$.

Experiment $\textbf{Exp}_{\mathcal{A}}^{Opriv}[\Phi, 1^\kappa]$
Query and response:
$x_0 = \sigma_{x_0} = y_0 = \perp$.
For $i = 1, \cdots, \ell = \text{poly}(\kappa)$
$\quad x_i \leftarrow \mathcal{A}(\Phi, (x_j, \sigma_{x_j}, y_j)_{0 \le j \le i-1})$.
$\quad sk_i \leftarrow \textbf{KeyGen}(\Phi, x_i, 1^\kappa)$.
$\quad \sigma_{x_i} = (\Phi', x') \leftarrow \textbf{ProbTrans}(\Phi, sk_i, x_i)$.
$\quad y_i' \leftarrow \mathcal{A}(\Phi, (x_j, \sigma_{x_j}, y_j)_{0 \le j \le i-1}, \sigma_{x_i})$.
$\quad y_i \leftarrow \textbf{Ver\&Rec}(\Phi, sk_i, y_i')$.

Challenge:
$\tilde{x} \leftarrow \text{Domain}(\Phi)$.
$\tilde{sk} \leftarrow \textbf{KeyGen}(\Phi, \tilde{x}, 1^\kappa)$.
$\sigma_{\tilde{x}} = (\Phi', \tilde{x}') \leftarrow \textbf{ProbTrans}(\Phi, \tilde{sk}, \tilde{x})$.
$\tilde{y}' \leftarrow \textbf{Compute}(\sigma_{\tilde{x}})$.
$\tilde{y} \leftarrow \mathcal{A}(\Phi, (x_j, \sigma_{x_j}, y_j)_{0 \le j \le \ell}, \sigma_{\tilde{x}}, \tilde{y}')$.
if $\tilde{y} = \Phi(\tilde{x})$, output $'1'$;
else output $'0'$.

Now, the input/output privacy can be exactly defined.

Definition 2 (Input/output privacy). *A secure outsourcing algorithm* $\text{OCAlg}_\Phi(\cdot)$ *of some computation task* Φ *is input-private (resp. output-private) if, for any PPT adversary* $\mathcal{A}$, *the probability of the experiment* $\textbf{Exp}_{\mathcal{A}}^{Ipriv}[\Phi, 1^\kappa]$ *(resp.* $\textbf{Exp}_{\mathcal{A}}^{Opriv}[\Phi, 1^\kappa]$*) outputting 1 is negligible, i.e.*

$$\Pr[\textbf{Exp}_{\mathcal{A}}^{Ipriv}[\Phi, 1^\kappa] = 1] \le \text{negli}(\kappa) \ (resp. \Pr[\textbf{Exp}_{\mathcal{A}}^{Opriv}[\Phi, 1^\kappa] = 1] \le \text{negli}(\kappa)),$$

where $\text{negli}(\kappa)$ *is a negligible function of the security parameter* κ.

Verifiability is another security requirement for an outsourcing algorithm. That is, the algorithm should guarantee that the client can not be cheated by an untrusted cloud server. Conversely, the client can verify the correctness of the results returned from the cloud with a non-negligible probability.

Definition 3 ($(1 - \beta)$-Verifiable). *A secure outsourcing algorithm* $\text{OCAlg}_\Phi(\cdot)$ *of some computation task* Φ *is* $(1 - \beta)$-*verifiable if, for any valid input* x, *the algorithm* **KeyGen** *outputs a secret key* sk *such that, if* $(\Phi', x') \leftarrow$ **ProbTrans**(Φ, x, sk) *and* $y' \leftarrow$ **Compute**(Φ', x'), *the probability of* **Ver\&Rec** (Φ, y', sk) *outputting* y *satisfies*

$$\Pr[y = \Phi(x) \leftarrow \textbf{Ver\&Rec}(\Phi, y', sk) \mid y' = \Phi'(x')] = 1,$$
$$\Pr[y = \Phi(x) \leftarrow \textbf{Ver\&Rec}(\Phi, y', sk) \mid y' \ne \Phi'(x')] \le \beta.$$

High efficiency is a necessary requirement for an outsourcing algorithm which refers to that the client's calculation amount in the outsourcing algorithm must be lower than the original computation task performed by the client itself.

Definition 4 (α-Efficient). *For some computation task Φ, a secure outsourcing algorithm $\mathrm{OCAlg}_\Phi(\cdot)$ is α-efficient if $\frac{t_c}{t_o} \leq \alpha$, out of which, t_o is the client's time cost of achieving the task without outsourcing, and t_c represents the local-client's time cost of achieving the task by employing the outsourcing algorithm $\mathrm{OCAlg}_\Phi(\cdot)$.*

3   Notations and Preliminaries

In the rest of our paper, we use bold upper-case letter to denote matrix and use bold lower-case letter to denote vector. The frequently used notations are described in Table 1. Next, we introduce some basic knowledge about lattices, and then review the famous LLL reduction algorithm for solving approximate SVP.

Table 1. Notations

Symbols	Descriptions
m, n	Positive integers
$\mathbb{R}^m$	m-dimensional Euclidean space
$\mathbf{v}$	A column vector in $\mathbb{Z}^m$
Λ	A lattice in $\mathbb{R}^m$ with rank n
$\mathbf{B}$	A basis matrix of the lattice
$\mathbf{U}$	An unimodular matrix in $\mathbb{Z}^{n \times n}$
$\lambda_i(\Lambda)$	The ith successive minimum of the lattice Λ
κ	Security parameter

3.1   Lattice

A lattice Λ is a discrete subgroup of $\mathbb{R}^m$, or equivalently,

Definition 5 (Lattice). *Given $n(\leq m)$ linearly independent vectors $\mathbf{b}_1, \mathbf{b}_2, \ldots,$ $\mathbf{b}_n \in \mathbb{R}^m$, the lattice Λ generated by them is the set of all integral linear combinations of $\mathbf{b}_i$, i.e.,*

$$\Lambda(\mathbf{b}_1, \ldots, \mathbf{b}_n) = \left\{ \sum_{i=1}^{n} x_i \mathbf{b}_i | x_i \in \mathbb{Z} \right\},$$

where the matrix $\mathbf{B} = [\mathbf{b}_1, \ldots, \mathbf{b}_n]$ is called a basis of the lattice Λ and n is the rank of the lattice. When $n = m$, the lattice is full-rank.

The lattice generated by the basis $\mathbf{B}$ is also denoted as

$$\Lambda(\mathbf{B}) = \Lambda(\mathbf{b}_1, \ldots, \mathbf{b}_n) = \{\mathbf{B}\mathbf{x} \mid \mathbf{x} \in \mathbb{Z}^n\}.$$

Since there are many bases for a lattice, a natural question is how to determine whether two bases $\mathbf{B}_1, \mathbf{B}_2$ generate the same lattice (*i.e.*, $\Lambda(\mathbf{B}_1) = \Lambda(\mathbf{B}_2)$). To illustrate this, we need to introduce the definition of unimodular matrix.

Definition 6 (Unimodular Matrix). *A matirx* $\mathbf{U} \in \mathbb{Z}^{n \times n}$ *is called unimodular if* $\det \mathbf{U} = \pm 1$.

Then, we have

Lemma 1. *Two bases* $\mathbf{B}_1, \mathbf{B}_2 \in \mathbb{R}^{m \times n}$ *are equivalent, i.e.,* $\Lambda(\mathbf{B}_1) = \Lambda(\mathbf{B}_2)$ *if and only if* $\mathbf{B}_2 = \mathbf{B}_1\mathbf{U}$, *for some unimodular matrix* $\mathbf{U}$.

Definition 7 (Determinant). *Let* $\Lambda = \Lambda(\mathbf{B})$ *be a lattice of rank* n. *The determinant of* Λ *is defined as* $vol(\Lambda) = \sqrt{\det(\mathbf{B}^T\mathbf{B})}$, *where* $\mathbf{B}^T$ *denotes the transpose of the basis* $\mathbf{B}$.

Besides, the length of the shortest nonzero vector in the lattice Λ is denoted as $\lambda_1(\Lambda)$, where the length refers to the Euclidean norm. That is, for any vector $\mathbf{x}$, $\|\mathbf{x}\|_2 = \sqrt{\sum x_i^2}$. The most important computational problem SVP is defined as follows:

Definition 8 (SVP). *Given a lattice basis* $\mathbf{B} \in \mathbb{Z}^{m \times n}$, *find a nonzero vector* $\mathbf{x} \in \Lambda(\mathbf{B})$ *such that* $\|\mathbf{x}\| = \lambda_1(\Lambda(\mathbf{B}))$.

So far, there is no known efficient algorithm to solve this problem. However, we are more interested in the approximation variant, which aims to find a relatively shorter lattice vector with length no bigger than $\gamma(n)\lambda_1(\Lambda)$. Here, n is the dimension of the lattice and the approximation factor $\gamma = \gamma(n) \geq 1$. Formally,

Definition 9 (SVP$_\gamma$). *Given a lattice basis* $\mathbf{B} \in \mathbb{Z}^{m \times n}$, *find a nonzero vector* $\mathbf{x} \in \Lambda(\mathbf{B})$ *such that* $\|\mathbf{x}\| \leq \gamma \cdot \lambda_1(\Lambda(B))$.

3.2   LLL Reduction Algorithm and Its Properties

This section describes the famous LLL reduction algorithm of solving SVP_γ. First, we recall what is an LLL-reduced basis.

Definition 10 [15]. *A basis* $\mathbf{B} = \{\mathbf{b}_1, \ldots, \mathbf{b}_n\}$ *is a* δ-*LLL reduced basis if the following two inequalities hold:*

1. $\forall 1 \leq i \leq n, j < i, |\mu_{i,j}| \leq \frac{1}{2}$.
2. $\forall 1 \leq i < n, \delta\|\tilde{\mathbf{b}}_i\|^2 \leq \|\mu_{i+1,i}\tilde{\mathbf{b}}_i + \tilde{\mathbf{b}}_{i+1}\|^2$.

Some useful properties are given as follows:

Proposition 1 [15]. *Let* $\mathbf{B} = \{\mathbf{b}_1, \ldots, \mathbf{b}_n\}$ *be an LLL reduced basis of a lattice* Λ, *then*

1. $vol(\Lambda) \leq \prod_{i=1}^{n} \|\mathbf{b}_i\| \leq 2^{\frac{n(n-1)}{4}} vol(\Lambda)$.
2. $\|\mathbf{b}_1\| \leq 2^{\frac{n-1}{4}} (vol(\Lambda))^{\frac{1}{n}}$.
3. $\forall 1 \leq i \leq n, \|\mathbf{b}_i\| \leq 2^{\frac{n-1}{2}} \lambda_i(\Lambda)$.

Lenstra et al. [15] presented an efficient algorithm (*i.e.*, the celebrated LLL algorithm) to output a LLL reduced basis. Precisely,

Proposition 2 [15]. *Let* $\Lambda = \Lambda(\mathbf{B})$ *be a rank-n lattice with* $\mathbf{B} \in \mathbb{Q}^{m \times n}$. *Then LLL reduction algorithm can find an LLL-reduce basis within time* $O(n^5 m B^3)$ *without fast multiplication techniques, where* $B = \max_{1 \leq i \leq n} \log \|\mathbf{b}_i\|$.

For a lattice basis $\mathbf{B}$, the corresponding Gram matrix is defined as $\mathbf{G} = \mathbf{B}^T \mathbf{B}$. Gram matrix has been used in LLL algorithm [2,18,19]. In practice, we can directly perform LLL reduction on it to get the transformation matrix $\mathbf{T}$ such that $\mathbf{BT}$ is LLL-reduced. Here, we summarize the result as the following Lemma 2.

Lemma 2. *Let* $\Lambda = \Lambda(\mathbf{B})$ *be a lattice of rank n. There exists a variant of LLL algorithm, with the input of the Gram matrix* $\mathbf{G} = \mathbf{B}^T \mathbf{B}$, *outputting a transformation matrix* $\mathbf{T}$ *such that* $\mathbf{BT}$ *is LLL-reduced.*

This algorithm has already been implemented in SageMath [23].

4   Our Outsourcing Algorithm for SVP$_\gamma$

In this section, we first overview the design rationale, and then present our algorithm in detail.

4.1   Design Rationale

Given some lattice basis $\mathbf{B} \in \mathbb{R}^{m \times n}$, a resource-limited client aims to leverage the computing resource of the cloud to find a non-zero shorter vector $\mathbf{x} \in \Lambda(\mathbf{B})$ such that $\|\mathbf{x}\| \leq 2^{\frac{n-1}{4}} \cdot (vol(\Lambda))^{\frac{1}{n}}$, where n is the dimension of the lattice. If the cloud server is honest, the client can directly rent the cloud server to perform the famous LLL algorithm with input $\mathbf{B}$. However, under the *FM+CPA* model, the client must figure out an effective method to protect the privacy of the input lattice basis $\mathbf{B}$ and the output lattice vector $\mathbf{x}$. By Lemma 1, a natural idea is to blind $\mathbf{B}$ with a random unimodular matrix $\mathbf{U}$. Namely, compute $\mathbf{B}' = \mathbf{BU}$ and let the cloud perform LLL algorithm on $\mathbf{B}'$. However, since $\Lambda(\mathbf{B}) = \Lambda(\mathbf{B}')$, this simple method can not ensure the privacy of the output vector $\mathbf{x}$. Enlightened by the property of the variant of LLL in Lemma 2, to protect the output information, we can send the Gram matrix $\mathbf{G} = (\mathbf{B}')^T \mathbf{B}'$ to the cloud and rent the cloud to perform the variant algorithm on $\mathbf{G}$ to get the transformation matrix $\mathbf{T}$ such that $\mathbf{B}'\mathbf{T}$ is LLL-reduced. After that, the cloud returns the first column vector $\mathbf{z}$ of $\mathbf{T}$. Finally, the client can obtain a shorter lattice vector by computing $\mathbf{x} = \mathbf{B}'\mathbf{z}$. Since $\mathbf{G} = (\mathbf{B}')^{\mathrm{T}}\mathbf{B}' = (\mathbf{OB}')^{\mathrm{T}}(\mathbf{OB}')$ for any orthogonal matrix $\mathbf{O}$, even if the cloud performs Cholesky decomposition on $\mathbf{G}$ and obtain $\mathbf{G} = \mathbf{C}^{\mathrm{T}}\mathbf{C}$, it can not distinguish $\mathbf{C} = \mathbf{B}'$ from $\mathbf{C} = \mathbf{OB}'$ for any orthogonal matrix $\mathbf{O}$. This ensures the input privacy. Meanwhile, the cloud only obtains vector $\mathbf{z}$, without knowing the lattice basis $\mathbf{B}'$, it can not recover the shorter lattice vector $\mathbf{x}$. This ensures the output privacy. Besides, the verifiability can be realized by checking $\|\mathbf{x}\| \le 2^{\frac{n-1}{4}} \cdot (\sqrt{\det(\mathbf{G})})^{\frac{1}{n}}$.

4.2 Detailed Algorithm

Note that we almost focus on the short vector in practice, such as in the lattice-based cryptanalysis, instead of the whole LLL-reduced basis, so below we don't take consideration into getting the whole LLL-reduced basis, but just aims to find a short lattice vector, and we would like to point out that it is very easy to extend the algorithm below to compute the whole LLL-reduced basis as discussed in Sect. 4.3.

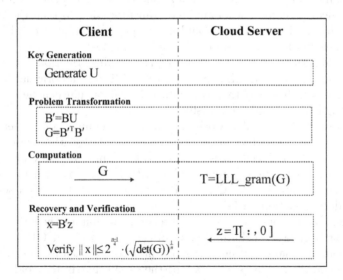

Fig. 2. The workflow of algorithm OCAlg_{SVP}.

Figure 2 shows the workflow of our outsourcing algorithm OCAlg_{SVP}, which is designed as follows:

1. **Key Generation**: With an inputted basis matrix $\mathbf{B} \in \mathbb{R}^{m \times n}$ of lattice Λ, the client picks a secret unimodular matrix $\mathbf{U} \in \mathbb{Z}^{n \times n}$ in a secret finite set consisting of unimodular matrices produced in advance.

2. **Problem Transformation**: With the secret key $\mathbf{U}$, the client first computes $\mathbf{B}' = \mathbf{B}\mathbf{U}$ and further calculates the Gram-matrix $\mathbf{G} = (\mathbf{B}')^{\mathrm{T}}\mathbf{B}'$. Finally, $\mathbf{G}$ is sent to the cloud server.
3. **Computation**: On receiving the matrix $\mathbf{G}$, the cloud server applies the variant algorithm of LLL to $\mathbf{G}$ and obtains a transformation matrix $\mathbf{T}$. Then, the cloud returns the first column vector $\mathbf{z} \in \mathbb{Z}^n$ of the matrix $\mathbf{T}$ to the client.
4. **Recovery and Verification**: After receiving the vector $\mathbf{z} \in \mathbb{Z}^n$, the client computes $\mathbf{x} = \mathbf{B}'\mathbf{z}$ and checks whether the inequality $\|\mathbf{x}\| \leq 2^{\frac{n-1}{4}} \cdot (\sqrt{\det(\mathbf{G})})^{\frac{1}{n}}$ holds. If it holds, the vector $\mathbf{x}$ is the desired result. Otherwise, the client rejects the result.

4.3 Some Remarks

Note that the secret unimodular transformation $\mathbf{U}$ is not necessary if no additional information about the private input $\mathbf{B}$ leaks to the adversary. However, we may know some additional information about $\mathbf{B}$ in some cases, such as for Coppersmith's algorithm [7], $\mathbf{B}$ must be an upper (or lower) triangular matrix, which means that the domain of the outsourcing task is not the whole $\mathbb{R}^{m \times n}$ any more and some secret information about $\mathbf{B}$ can be implied from the Gram matrix. Hence, we employ a unimodular transformation to keep the privacy of $\mathbf{B}$ further in our algorithm and would like to point out that it can be removed in some cases which depends on the domain of the task.

It is obvious that if the cloud server sends the transformation $\mathbf{T}$ to the client, the client can recover the LLL-reduced basis $\mathbf{B}'\mathbf{T}$ for the original lattice due to Lemma 2, which shows that the outsoucing algorithm can be extended to compute the LLL-reduced basis easily.

Compared to Liu et al.'s work [17], since we employ an isometry of the lattice essentially, the orthogonal transformation, our algorithm does not reduce the quality of the reduced basis, and our algorithm can work for any other algorithms that solve (approximate-)SVP with Euclidean norm (sometimes, a matrix $\mathbf{C}$ such that $\mathbf{G} = \mathbf{C}^{\mathrm{T}}\mathbf{C}$ should be computed by the cloud server with Cholesky decomposition on $\mathbf{G}$).

Another way to construct the outsourcing algorithm for the client is to generate the orthogonal transformation $\mathbf{O}$ directly and to send $\mathbf{O}\mathbf{B}$ to the cloud server. There are many efficient ways to construct $\mathbf{O}$, such as the Householder transformation. In this paper, we adopt the Gram matrix to avoid generating the orthogonal matrix.

5 Correctness, Security, Verifiability and Efficiency

In this section, we will present strict analysis on the correctness, input/output privacy, verifiability and efficiency of our proposed algorithm.

5.1   Correctness

Clearly, if the cloud server performs the assigned computation task honestly, the client definitely obtains a shorter vector. In fact, by Lemma 1, $\mathbf{B}$ and $\mathbf{B}' = \mathbf{B}\mathbf{U}$ are equivalent, *i.e.*, $\Lambda = \Lambda(\mathbf{B}) = \Lambda(\mathbf{B}')$. By Lemma 2, if the cloud is honest, we have $\mathbf{B}'\mathbf{T}$ is LLL-reduced. Then $\mathbf{x} = \mathbf{B}'\mathbf{z} \in \Lambda$ is the first vector of the LLL-reduced basis $\mathbf{B}'\mathbf{T}$. According to the properties (Proposition 1) of LLL-reduced basis, $\|\mathbf{x}\| \leq 2^{\frac{n-1}{4}} \cdot (\sqrt{\det(\mathbf{G})})^{\frac{1}{n}}$.

5.2   Input/Output Privacy

Here, we mainly argue the privacy of our algorithm with the one-way notation under *CPA* model.

Theorem 1. *For any input lattice basis $\mathbf{B}$, our proposed outsourcing algorithm* OCAlg_{SVP} *satisfies the input/output privacy according to Definition 2.*

Proof. We first argue the input privacy. Corresponding to our design, in the experiment $\mathbf{Exp}_{\mathcal{A}}^{Ipriv}[\Phi, 1^{\kappa}]$, the computation task Φ refers to finding a non-zero shorter vector $\mathbf{x}$ of some lattice Λ such that $\|\mathbf{x}\| \leq 2^{\frac{n-1}{4}} \cdot (vol(\Lambda))^{\frac{1}{n}}$, Φ' represents performing the variant algorithm of LLL on the Gram-matrix $\mathbf{G} = (\mathbf{B}')^{\mathrm{T}}\mathbf{B}'$, and $\kappa = mn \log\|\mathbf{B}\| = mn \log \max_{1 \leq i \leq m, 1 \leq j \leq n} |b_{ij}|$ denotes the bit-size of the input lattice basis $\mathbf{B}$. The adversary $\mathcal{A}$ can adaptively choose $x_i = \mathbf{B}_i$ and obtain corresponding Gram matrices $\mathbf{G}_i = (\mathbf{B}_i')^{\mathrm{T}}\mathbf{B}_i'$ for $1 \leq i \leq \ell$ in the *Query and response* phase. In the *Challenge* phase, given a challenge input lattice basis $\tilde{x} = \mathbf{B}$, the adversary tries to recover $\mathbf{B}$ based on the collected information $\mathbf{G}_i = (\mathbf{B}_i')^{\mathrm{T}}\mathbf{B}_i'(1 \leq i \leq \ell)$ and $\mathbf{G} = (\mathbf{B}')^{\mathrm{T}}\mathbf{B}'$. Since $\mathbf{G} = (\mathbf{B}')^{\mathrm{T}}\mathbf{B}' = (\mathbf{O}\mathbf{B}')^{\mathrm{T}}(\mathbf{O}\mathbf{B}')$ for any orthogonal matrix $\mathbf{O}$ and there exist at least exponentially many orthogonal matrices, the probability of the adversary recovering the correct $\mathbf{B}'$ is negligible. Due to the fact that $\mathbf{B}' = \mathbf{B}\mathbf{U}$ for some unimodular matrix $\mathbf{U}$ produced in advance, the probability of the adversary recovering the correct $\mathbf{B}$ is clearly negligible, *i.e.*,

$$\Pr[\mathbf{Exp}_{\mathcal{A}}^{Ipriv}[\Phi, 1^{\kappa}] = 1] \leq \mathrm{negli}(\kappa).$$

Now, we argue the output privacy. Similar to the above analysis, the adversary can adaptively choose and obtain $(x_i, \sigma_{x_i}, y_i) = (\mathbf{B}_i, \mathbf{G}_i, \mathbf{x}_i)$ (or $(\mathbf{B}_i, \mathbf{G}_i, \perp)$) for $1 \leq i \leq \ell$ in the *Query and response* phase. In the *Challenge* phase, given a challenge input lattice basis $\tilde{x} = \mathbf{B}$ of the lattice Λ, the adversary tries to recover a shorter vector $\tilde{y} = \mathbf{x} \in \Lambda(\mathbf{B})$ such that $\|\mathbf{x}\| \leq 2^{\frac{n-1}{4}} vol(\Lambda)^{\frac{1}{n}}$. Besides the collected information in the *Query and response* phase, the adversary also captures the Gram matrix $\tilde{x}' = \mathbf{G} = (\mathbf{B}')^{\mathrm{T}}\mathbf{B}' = (\mathbf{B}\mathbf{U})^{\mathrm{T}}(\mathbf{B}\mathbf{U})$ for some secret and random matrix $\mathbf{U}$, and an integer vector $\tilde{y}' = \mathbf{z}$, which is the first column of the transformation matrix $\mathbf{T}$. Since $\mathbf{G} = (\mathbf{B}')^{\mathrm{T}}\mathbf{B}' = (\mathbf{O}\mathbf{B}')^{\mathrm{T}}(\mathbf{O}\mathbf{B}')$ for any orthogonal matrix $\mathbf{O}$ and there exist infinitely many orthogonal matrices, the probability of the adversary recovering the correct $\mathbf{B}'$ is negligible. Due to

$\mathbf{x}' = \mathbf{B}'\mathbf{z}$, we have that, without knowing the correct $\mathbf{B}'$, the probability of the adversary recovering the correct $\mathbf{x}$ is clearly negligible, $i.e.$,

$$\Pr[\mathbf{Exp}_{\mathcal{A}}^{Opriv}[\Phi, 1^{\kappa}] = 1] \leq \text{negli}(\kappa).$$

5.3 Verifiability

Theorem 2. *Our proposed outsourcing algorithms* OCAlg$_{SVP}$ *is 100%-verifiable.*

Proof. Since $\Lambda(B) = \Lambda(\mathbf{B}')$, we have $\mathbf{x} = \mathbf{B}'\mathbf{z} \in \Lambda(\mathbf{B})$. According to Lemma 2 and the Proposition 1, $\mathbf{B}'\mathbf{T}$ is LLL-reduced and thus $\|\mathbf{x}\| = \|\mathbf{B}'\mathbf{z}\| \leq 2^{\frac{n-1}{4}} \cdot (\sqrt{\det(G)})^{\frac{1}{n}}$, Hence, $\Pr[y = \Phi(x) \leftarrow \mathbf{Ver\&Rec}(\Phi, y', sk) \mid y' = \Phi'(x')] = 1$. If the cloud server returns a forged integer vector $\mathbf{z}$, then the inequality $\|\mathbf{x}\| = \|\mathbf{B}'\mathbf{z}\| \leq 2^{\frac{n-1}{4}} \cdot (\sqrt{\det(G)})^{\frac{1}{n}}$ doesn't hold.

5.4 Efficiency

Theorem 3. *Our outsourcing algorithm* OCAlg$_{SVP}$ *is at least* $O(\frac{1}{n^2 \log B})$-*efficient.*

Proof. The original algorithm used to approximate the shortest nonzero lattice vector is the famous LLL-reduction algorithm with an asymptotic complexity of $O(n^5 m \log^3 B)$ [15], where $B = \max\limits_{1 \leq i \leq n} \log \|\mathbf{b}_i\|$. While the principal term of the computational complexity on the client side in our proposed algorithm is the time cost of matrix multiplication and determinant computation which takes time at most $O(n^3 m \log^2 B)$. Therefore, according to Definition 4, our algorithm is $O(\frac{n^3 m \log^2 B}{n^5 m \log^3 B}) = O(\frac{1}{n^2 \log B})$-efficient.

6   Practical Performance Evaluation

6.1   Evaluation Methodology

After analyzing the correctness, verifiability, efficiency and security of our proposed algorithm, we conclude that our proposed algorithm are beneficial to the client. We next evaluate the practical performance of our proposed algorithm by simulating both client and cloud on a Windows 10 machine with Intel(R) Core(TM) i7-7500U 2.70 GHz CPU and 12 GB RAM. We implemented our proposed algorithm in a free software SageMath [23] in which the function LLL_gram() adapted from Nguyen and Stehlé's algorithm [18] returns the LLL transformation matrix for this Gram matrix. Because this LLL reduction algorithm has default parameters $(0.51, 0.99)$ meaning that the Gram-Schmidt coefficients for the reduced basis satisfy $|\mu_{i,j}| \geq 0.51$, and the Lovász's constant is 0.99, thus we modified parameters of the function LLL() as $(0.51, 0.99)$ for better evaluation.

In each of the experimental instances, we first constructed basis matrix inputted by the client, whose entries were randomly chosen from interval $[-2^{20}, 2^{20}]$. For the sake of convenience, basis matrices were chosen in $\mathbb{Z}^{n \times n}$ and their dimensions varied from 100 to 600. Then we produced a sufficiently large and finite set consisting of unimodular matrices whose entries ranging from -100 to 100. Besides, we simulated all stages of our proposed algorithm in each of experiments to evaluate the performance more objectively. The client-side time "Client", which is also the time "Outsourcing", denotes the sum of time "Problem Transformation" and "Recovery and Verification". The time "Without Outsourcing" denotes the time for the client to solve the approximation of SVP without outsourcing. Theoretically, the value (Outsourcing/Without Outsourcing) is a positive number less than 1. The time "Cloud" refers to the time for the cloud server to compute the outsourced task.

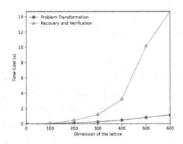 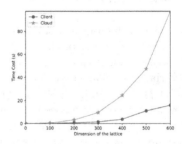

(a) Time comparison of different phases

(b) Time comparison between cloud server and client

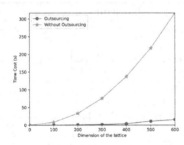

(c) Time comparison of outsourcing and without outsourcing

Fig. 3. Evaluation results for algorithm

6.2 Evaluation Results

Figure 3 shows the evaluation results of our proposed algorithm. In Fig. 3(a), we make time comparison among phases. From it, we can see that the time of "Problem Transformation" and "Recovery and Verification" increases with the dimension of the lattice and it is sound. Moreover, it is obvious that "Recovery and Verification" takes more time than "Problem Transformation". By rigorous analysis, we can come to the same conclusion. In the Problem Transformation phase, the main time-consuming operation is matrix multiplication, while there are operations for determinant and exponentiation besides matrix multiplication in the Recovery and Verification phase. Then the second result is also rational. After outsourcing process, the time taken by the client decreases dramatically in Fig. 3(b), where we make time comparison between cloud server and client. It means that our proposed algorithm works well. In Fig. 3(c), we show a visual efficiency comparison and compare it with theoretical analysis above. Clearly, the client takes less time in outsourcing process than implementing original algorithm itself, i.e., our proposed outsourcing algorithm is very efficient.

7   Applications

Next, we take the famous Copersmith's algorithm [7] as an example to show how to use our outsourcing algorithm.

Copersmith's algorithm, described in Algorithm 1, finds all small roots x_0 of a univariate modular equation $f(x) = 0 \bmod N$ with $|x_0| \leq N^{\frac{1}{\delta}}$, where the polynomial $f(x)$ is a monic polynomial of degree δ. It has many applications in the cryptanalysis. It can be seen that the most time-consuming step is Step 5, running the LLL algorithm to get a short lattice vector. Hence, our outsourcing algorithm can be used directly to obtain a short lattice vector while keeping the privacy of input and output.

Algorithm 1. Coppersmith's Algorithm

Require: A monic polynomial $f(x) \in \mathbb{Z}_N[x]$ of degree δ, where N is a modulus with unknown factorization.

Ensure: Set $R = \{x_0 \in \mathbb{Z} | f(x_0) = 0 \bmod N \text{ and } |x_0| \leq X\}$.

1: for $i \leftarrow 0$ to $h - 1$ do
2:     for $j \leftarrow 0$ to $\delta - 1$ do
3:         $g_{i,j}(x) = N^{h-i-1} f(x)^i x^j$.
4: Construct the lattice basis B, where the basis vectors are the coefficient vectors of $g_{i,j}(xX)$.
5: $v = LLL(B).get\_column(0)$.
6: Construct $g(x)$ from v.
7: Find the set R of all roots of $g(x)$ over the integers using standart techniques. For every root $x_0 \in R$ check wether or not $\gcd(N, f(x_0)) \geq N$. If it doesn't hold then remove x_0 from R.

---

8   Conclusion

In this paper, we present an efficient and secure outsourcing algorithm solving (approximate-)SVP for the client with limited computing and storage capability, which has many applications in computational number theory, cryptanalysis and some other related areas.

Acknowledgements. We thank the anonymous referees for their valuable suggestions on how to improve this paper.

References

1. Ajtai, M.: The shortest vector problem in L_2 is NP-hard for randomized reductions (extended abstract). In: Vitter, J.S. (ed.) Proceedings of the Thirtieth Annual ACM Symposium on the Theory of Computing, Dallas, Texas, USA, 23–26 May 1998, pp. 10–19. ACM (1998). https://doi.org/10.1145/276698.276705

2. Backes, W., Wetzel, S.: An efficient LLL gram using buffered transformations. In: Ganzha, V.G., Mayr, E.W., Vorozhtsov, E.V. (eds.) CASC 2007. LNCS, vol. 4770, pp. 31–44. Springer, Heidelberg (2007). https://doi.org/10.1007/978-3-540-75187-8_4

3. Benjamin, D., Atallah, M.J.: Private and cheating-free outsourcing of algebraic computations. In: Korba, L., Marsh, S., Safavi-Naini, R. (eds.) Sixth Annual Conference on Privacy, Security and Trust, PST 2008, Fredericton, New Brunswick, Canada, 1–3 October 2008, pp. 240–245. IEEE Computer Society (2008). https://doi.org/10.1109/PST.2008.12

4. Bi, J., Coron, J., Faugère, J., Nguyen, P.Q., Renault, G., Zeitoun, R.: Rounding and chaining LLL: finding faster small roots of univariate polynomial congruences. IACR Cryptol. ePrint Arch. **2014**, 437 (2014). http://eprint.iacr.org/2014/437

5. Chen, X., Li, J., Ma, J., Tang, Q., Lou, W.: New algorithms for secure outsourcing of modular exponentiations. IEEE Trans. Parallel Distributed Syst. **25**(9), 2386–2396 (2014). https://doi.org/10.1109/TPDS.2013.180

6. Cohen, H.: A Course in Computational Algebraic Number Theory, Graduate Texts in Mathematics, vol. 138. Springer, Heidelberg (1993). https://www.worldcat.org/oclc/27810276

7. Coppersmith, D.: Finding a small root of a univariate modular equation. In: Maurer, U. (ed.) EUROCRYPT 1996. LNCS, vol. 1070, pp. 155–165. Springer, Heidelberg (1996). https://doi.org/10.1007/3-540-68339-9_14

8. Fiore, D., Gennaro, R.: Publicly verifiable delegation of large polynomials and matrix computations, with applications. In: Yu, T., Danezis, G., Gligor, V.D. (eds.) The ACM Conference on Computer and Communications Security, CCS 2012, Raleigh, NC, USA, 16–18 October 2012, pp. 501–512. ACM (2012). https://doi.org/10.1145/2382196.2382250

9. Gennaro, R., Gentry, C., Parno, B.: Non-interactive verifiable computing: outsourcing computation to untrusted workers. In: Rabin, T. (ed.) CRYPTO 2010. LNCS, vol. 6223, pp. 465–482. Springer, Heidelberg (2010). https://doi.org/10.1007/978-3-642-14623-7_25

10. Gentry, C., Peikert, C., Vaikuntanathan, V.: Trapdoors for hard lattices and new cryptographic constructions. In: Dwork, C. (ed.) Proceedings of the 40th Annual ACM Symposium on Theory of Computing, Victoria, British Columbia, Canada, 17–20 May 2008, pp. 197–206. ACM (2008). https://doi.org/10.1145/1374376.1374407

11. Håstad, J., Just, B., Lagarias, J.C., Schnorr, C.: Polynomial time algorithms for finding integer relations among real numbers. SIAM J. Comput. **18**(5), 859–881 (1989). https://doi.org/10.1137/0218059

12. Hohenberger, S., Lysyanskaya, A.: How to securely outsource cryptographic computations. In: Kilian, J. (ed.) TCC 2005. LNCS, vol. 3378, pp. 264–282. Springer, Heidelberg (2005). https://doi.org/10.1007/978-3-540-30576-7_15
13. Hu, C., Alhothaily, A., Alrawais, A., Cheng, X., Sturtivant, C., Liu, H.: A secure and verifiable outsourcing scheme for matrix inverse computation. In: 2017 IEEE Conference on Computer Communications, INFOCOM 2017, Atlanta, GA, USA, 1–4 May 2017, pp. 1–9. IEEE (2017). https://doi.org/10.1109/INFOCOM.2017.8057199
14. Lagrange, J.L.: Recherches d'arithmétique. Proc. Nouv. Mém. Acad. (1773)
15. Lenstra, A.K., Lenstra, H.W., Lovász, L.: Factoring polynomials with rational coefficients. Math. Ann. **261**(4), 515–534 (1982)
16. Liu, D., Bertino, E., Yi, X.: Privacy of outsourced k-means clustering. In: Moriai, S., Jaeger, T., Sakurai, K. (eds.) 9th ACM Symposium on Information, Computer and Communications Security, ASIA CCS 2014, Kyoto, Japan, 03–06 June 2014, pp. 123–134. ACM (2014). https://doi.org/10.1145/2590296.2590332
17. Liu, J., Bi, J.: Secure outsourcing of lattice basis reduction. In: Gedeon, T., Wong, K.W., Lee, M. (eds.) ICONIP 2019, Part II. LNCS, vol. 11954, pp. 603–615. Springer, Cham (2019). https://doi.org/10.1007/978-3-030-36711-4_51
18. Nguên, P.Q., Stehlé, D.: Floating-point LLL revisited. In: Cramer, R. (ed.) EUROCRYPT 2005. LNCS, vol. 3494, pp. 215–233. Springer, Heidelberg (2005). https://doi.org/10.1007/11426639_13
19. Nguyen, P.Q., Stehlé, D.: LLL on the average. In: Hess, F., Pauli, S., Pohst, M. (eds.) ANTS 2006. LNCS, vol. 4076, pp. 238–256. Springer, Heidelberg (2006). https://doi.org/10.1007/11792086_18
20. Saruchi, Morel, I., Stehlé, D., Villard, G.: LLL reducing with the most significant bits. In: Nabeshima, K., Nagasaka, K., Winkler, F., Szántó, Á. (eds.) International Symposium on Symbolic and Algebraic Computation, ISSAC 20, Kobe, Japan, 23–25 July 2014, pp. 367–374. ACM (2014). https://doi.org/10.1145/2608628.2608645
21. Schnorr, C.: A hierarchy of polynomial time lattice basis reduction algorithms. Theor. Comput. Sci. **53**, 201–224 (1987). https://doi.org/10.1016/0304-3975(87)90064-8
22. Schnorr, C.P.: Factoring integers and computing discrete logarithms via diophantine approximation. In: Davies, D.W. (ed.) EUROCRYPT 1991. LNCS, vol. 547, pp. 281–293. Springer, Heidelberg (1991). https://doi.org/10.1007/3-540-46416-6_24
23. The Sage Developers: SageMath, the Sage Mathematics Software System (Version 9.2) (2020). https://www.sagemath.org
24. Tian, C., Yu, J., Zhang, H., Xue, H., Wang, C., Ren, K.: Novel secure outsourcing of modular inversion for arbitrary and variable modulus. IEEE Trans. Serv. Comput., 1 (2019). https://doi.org/10.1109/TSC.2019.2937486
25. Yang, Y., et al.: A comprehensive survey on secure outsourced computation and its applications. IEEE Access **7**, 159426–159465 (2019). https://doi.org/10.1109/ACCESS.2019.2949782
26. Zhang, F., Ma, X., Liu, S.: Efficient computation outsourcing for inverting a class of homomorphic functions. Inf. Sci. **286**, 19–28 (2014). https://doi.org/10.1016/j.ins.2014.07.017
27. Zhang, H., Yu, J., Tian, C., Xu, G., Gao, P., Lin, J.: Practical and secure outsourcing algorithms for solving quadratic congruences in internet of things. IEEE Internet Things J. **7**(4), 2968–2981 (2020). https://doi.org/10.1109/JIOT.2020.2964015

28. Zhang, L., Zhang, H., Yu, J., Xian, H.: Blockchain-based two-party fair contract signing scheme. Inf. Sci. **535**, 142–155 (2020). https://doi.org/10.1016/j.ins.2020. 05.054
29. Zheng, Y., Tian, C., Zhang, H., Yu, J., Li, F.: Lattice-based weak-key analysis on single-server outsourcing protocols of modular exponentiations and basic countermeasures. J. Comput. Syst. Sci. **121**, 18–33 (2021). https://doi.org/ 10.1016/j.jcss.2021.04.006. https://www.sciencedirect.com/science/article/pii/S00 22000021000441

Privacy-Preserving Support Vector Machines with Flexible Deployment and Error Correction

Weican Huang and Ning Ding[✉]

School of Electronic Information and Electrical Engineering,
Shanghai Jiao Tong University, 800 Dongchuan RD, Shanghai 200240, China
{hwc394519627,dingning}@sjtu.edu.cn

Abstract. Support vector machines (SVMs) are one of the most commonly used models for classification problems in machine learning. Nowadays there is an important scenario that many different parties jointly perform SVM training by integrating their individual data, while at the same time it is required that privacy of data can be preserved. At present there are three main routes to achieving privacy-preserving SVM. First, all parties jointly generate kernel matrices privately and then use them for remaining training (e.g. Yu et al. 2006). Second, based on the first route, an additional randomization is adopted to randomize kernel matrices in order to (heuristically) hide information exposed by kernel matrices (e.g. Mangasarian et al. 2008). Third, also the securest one, all parties run MPC protocols for computing whole optimization algorithms privately (not merely the generation of kernel matrices as the first two routes do) (e.g. Liu et al. 2018 and Wang et al. 2020).

In this paper we propose a new efficient privacy-preserving SVM protocol in the third route that privately realizes the gradient descent method to optimize SVM and its security is proven in the semi-honest model. Our protocol admits the following advantages.

- The protocol is of flexible deployment. It supports the deployment of arbitrarily multiple servers and multiple clients.
- The protocol can tolerate dropping-out of some servers.
- The protocol admits the ability of malicious-error-message correction (which is actually beyond the semi-honest security). If a small number of messages are corrupted, it can still recover correct messages as desired.

We remark that none of the above advantages can be obtained by some known work. Moreover, when compared to the privacy-preserving SVM by Liu et al. 2018 and Wang et al. 2020, our protocol achieves higher efficiency. We implement our protocol in Python and the experiments verify its efficiency.

Keywords: Privacy-preserving SVM · Multi-party computation · Shamir's secret sharing

© Springer Nature Switzerland AG 2021
R. Deng et al. (Eds.): ISPEC 2021, LNCS 13107, pp. 242–262, 2021.
https://doi.org/10.1007/978-3-030-93206-0_15

1   Introduction

Machine learning has been widely used in various fields, in which classification is one of the most commonly used functions and often applied in image recognition, data mining, text analysis, anomaly detection, recommendation systems and many other businesses. Usually sufficient perfect training data is always the premise to ensure the accuracy of trained models. But in reality complete data and sufficient computing power are not always held by one party, and the need for protecting privacy prevents arbitrary flow of data among different owners. Due to the increasing requirement of distributed machine learning and privacy preserving, privacy-preserving machine learning has attracted more and more attention recently.

Support vector machines (SVMs) are a widely used model in machine learning for classification problems. So there have been many achievements in the research line of privacy-preserving SVM. Basically there are three main routes to realizing it. The first route is that all parties jointly generate kernel matrices privately and then use them for remaining training [15,19,21]. When data is vertically partitioned and linearly separable, [21] asks each party computes its own kernel matrix and then lets a party/server integrate them to the whole kernel matrix. To prevent a party from obtaining the kernel matrix of someone else, this method requires data to be held by at least three parties. [19] uses homomorphic encryption to compute kernel matrices under arbitrary partition based on similar ideas. [15] also uses Paillier homomorphic encryption to calculate the kernel matrix under vertical partition.

The second route is that based on the first route an additional randomization is adopted to randomize kernel matrices in order to (heuristically) hide information exposed by kernel matrices [11,12,22]. Combining random kernel functions and matrix summation, [12] uses random linear transformations to avoid possible information leakage caused by publishing local kernel matrices. In [8] random linear transformations are also applied to one class SVM, and transformed data is used as a new input to calculate kernel matrices. [22] uses random kernel functions and integer vector encryption to encrypt data sets with horizontal or vertical partitions, allowing different parties to encrypt their data with different keys, and train them by a single server.

The third route is that all parties run MPC/2PC protocols for computing whole optimization algorithms privately (not merely the generation of kernel matrices as the first two routes do), which include SMO (Sequential Minimal Optimization), the kernel-adatron algorithm and gradient descent algorithm [7,9,20] etc. [7] proposes protocols to implement kernel-adatron and kernel perceptron learning algorithms, but without conducting experiments to verify efficiency. [9] implements a secure SMO protocol with the distributed two-trapdoor public-key cryptosystem (DT-PKC). [20] also designs GD (gradient descent) based secure SVM training using DT-PKC. These methods can protect all data throughout the whole training, but also at a cost of great time.

Besides the above works specializing in SVM, there are some works aiming at realizing privacy-preserving training for a variety of models. SecureML [14] applies the ABY framework with a new fixed-point multiplication protocol to linear regression, logistic regression and neural network. Chameleon [16] and ABY3 [13] change the setting from two servers to three servers, managing to simplify the protocols. FLASH [1] expands to four servers, allowing at most one malicious, proposing a framework with high robustness only by using symmetric-key primitives. These works have made great achievements in improving efficiency, but there are still some shortcomings and, for instance, the number of servers have to be fixed to constants, which is inflexible in deployment. (In practice each data owner is usually willing to participate joint training instead of just providing data to others. So an owner is not only a data provider, but also a server. The present works require the number of servers small (≤ 4), which thus limits their applications. Besides flexibility, another motivation to increase the number of servers is to enhance the resistance to collusive servers. Assuming the protocol has the (n, t)-threshold property, i.e. at least t corrupted servers of n ones together can recover data, which makes malicious recovery more difficult as n, t increases.)

Summary. We provide a summary to the current state of the art in privacy-preserving SVM. The first route is essentially private-preserving matrix summation which gains high efficiency, but kernel matrices are exposed and may leak information. The second route, adopting an additional randomization to kernel matrices, only provides a heuristic strategy to hide kernel matrices without a security proof. The third route is the securest, protecting all data throughout the training but at the cost of a large loss of efficiency. Moreover, all the works, including general privacy preserving machine learning for a variety of models, cannot be applied to scenarios of multiple servers and cannot handle the case that some messages are corrupted.

1.1 Our Contribution

In this paper we propose a new efficient privacy-preserving SVM protocol in the third route that privately realizes the SGD (stochastic gradient descent) method to optimize SVM. Our protocol admits the following advantages.

- The protocol is of flexible deployment. It supports the deployment of arbitrarily multiple servers and multiple clients.
- The protocol can tolerate dropping-out of some servers (up to some threshold value).
- The protocol admits the ability of malicious-error-message correction. Error messages caused by the adversary's malicious behaviors are not randomly distributed and will hinder secret reconstruction, or even lead to wrong results. If a small number of messages (up to some threshold value) are corrupted, it can still recover correct messages as desired.

We note that none of the above advantages can be obtained by some known work. The security of privacy preserving is established in the semi-honest adversarial model. Our protocol has the ability to deal with the collusion of servers less than the secret sharing threshold. We remark that the third advantage above shows that our protocol can resist some malicious-message attack, which is actually beyond the semi-honest adversarial model. For simplicity we just claim that our protocol is secure in the semi-honest adversarial model.

Thus our protocol can be flexibly used between n servers (calculators) and m clients (data holders), and tolerates some servers dropping out halfway. In the running of the protocol, all clients submit the sharing of their sample data to all servers, which then perform MPC to execute the SGD algorithm to optimize the parameters of SVM, and finally output the shares of the optimized parameters. We note that there is no significant difference in accuracy between the models trained by our protocol and those trained with plain data directly.

Compared with [9,20], our protocol achieves higher efficiency. [9,20] use a public key encryption system based on modular exponentiation, so 100 rounds of their training takes nearly 10 h on a 236 × 13 training set. Our protocol runs MPC based on shares, which only consists of addition and multiplication over finite fields, so 1000 rounds of our training takes about 48 s on the breast-cancer training set of 500 × 10 and 1000 rounds of training takes about 10 min on the diabetes training set of 500 × 10, and 30 min on the german.number training set of 800 × 24. The programming language used in our experiment code is Python.

Compared with [1,13,14] as well as [9,20], which should fix the number of servers to a value among 2 to 4, our protocol can be deployed among any number of servers (no less than 3). Also, by using Shamir's (n, t)-threshold secret sharing scheme, we can arbitrarily deploy n servers and tolerate dropping out of at most $n - 2t$ ones. Also, less than t colluding servers learn nothing in our protocol more than what they deserve. Moreover, by introducing the Berlekamp-Welch algorithm as an optional recovery algorithm, correct messages can be recovered even if less than t messages/shares are corrupted. The security parameter of the protocol is the bit length of the random number in the protocol.

Finally, we note that the SGD optimization algorithm we use (see Algorithm 1) is for linear kernel functions originally, it can be extended for nonlinear SVM training. To train nonlinear kernel function SVMs, the input feature $\mathbf{x}$ should be replaced by its mapping result $\phi(\mathbf{x})$ corresponding to nonlinear kernel functions, or apply the quadratic form (see [17]).

1.2 Our Techniques

Now we present a high-level description of our protocol and sketch main techniques. Assume there are m clients trying to cooperate on privacy-preserving SVM training, while n servers provide secure computation services. Basically, the protocol runs as follows. First the clients submit the shares of the sample data to the servers. Then the servers jointly compute the parameters of the SVM model using the SGD strategy. That is, the protocol consists of many repetitions, each of which computes an iteration of the SGD method. In each repetition, the servers have as input the shares of current values of the parameters and then perform some MPC protocols to compute gradient iteration and finally obtain the shares of the new values of the parameters. When the protocol halts, all servers output the shares of the optimized parameters of the model.

More concretely, in the SGD for SVM, the gradient and iteration of the parameters are given in the following formulas.

$$grad = \alpha \cdot \mathbf{w} - C \cdot \mathrm{I}(\mathbf{y}_i(\mathbf{x}_i \cdot \mathbf{w}^T) - 1)(\mathbf{y}_i\mathbf{x}_i) \tag{1}$$

$$\mathbf{w} = \mathbf{w} - l \cdot grad, \tag{2}$$

where $\mathbf{w}$ are the parameters to be optimized, $\mathbf{y}_i$ and $\mathbf{x}_i$ are the label and features of the ith sample, C is the penalty coefficient of the relaxation variable, and l is the learning rate and C, l are constants, and $\mathrm{I}(x)$ is the function such that if $x > 0, \mathrm{I}(x) = 0$, and if $x < 0, \mathrm{I}(x) = 1$.

According to the above formulas, each iteration of SGD only consists of addition, multiplication and comparison operations. Thus to realize the MPC for SGD, it suffices to show how to realize these operations privately.

Notice that the SGD algorithm is not over integers, while Shamir's secret sharing is built over finite fields like $\mathbb{Z}_p$. Recall that [3] presents secure fixed-point addition, multiplication and truncation with respect to Shamir's scheme. Thus we adopt [3] to realize the secure addition and multiplication.

We introduce the Berlekamp-Welch algorithm as an optional error correction algorithm. The algorithm takes the received codewords (i.e. shares of Shamir's secret sharing) as input, and recovers the correct values. In our protocol, all communication takes place within the reveal protocol. By replacing the calculation in the reveal protocol with the Berlekamp-Welch algorithm, we can get the correct result when there are a few errors in the received messages.

1.3 Organization

The rest of the paper is arranged as follows. In Sect. 2 we present a part of preliminaries and relegate the rest to Appendix A due to lack of space. In Sect. 3 we present the security model. In Sect. 4 we show the details of building blocks (i.e. secure addition, multiplication and comparison etc.). In Sect. 5, we present our privacy-preserving SVM protocol. In Sect. 6 we give performance evaluation of our protocol via theoretical analysis and experiments.

2 Preliminaries

We recall the notion of support vector machines and Shamir's secret sharing here, and relegate the Berlekamp-Welch algorithm to Appendix A.

2.1 Support Vector Machines

Support vector machines (SVM) are a classical machine learning model. The concept of SVM was proposed by Vladimir N. Vapnik and Alexey Ya Chervonenkis in 1963. The current version was proposed by Corinna Cortes and Vapnik in 1993 and published in 1995 [5]. As a supervised learning model, SVM is mainly used in regression and classification problems. The principle of SVM is to find a hyperplane to maximize the minimum distance between the hyperplane and the two kinds of sample points.

SVM can be optimized by the gradient descent method. We consider linear SVM which has a loss function, called hinge loss function, $\max(0, 1 - \mathbf{y}_i(\mathbf{x}_i\mathbf{w}^T))$, where the subscript i represents the ith sample, and $\mathbf{x}$ and $\mathbf{y}$ represent the feature data and labels. Considering slack variable ξ_i and regular term $\alpha\|\mathbf{w}\|$, the gradient of the objective function is $grad = \alpha \cdot \mathbf{w} - C(\mathbf{y}_i(\mathbf{x}_i \cdot \mathbf{w}^T) < 1)(\mathbf{y}_i\mathbf{x}_i)$. The gradient descent method of SVM uses the following algorithm to optimize $\mathbf{w}$. In the algorithm, the bias b can be optimized by directly adding an all 1 column to $\mathbf{x}$.

Algorithm 1. SVM – GD

Input: features $\mathbf{x} \in R^{t\times d}$, labels $\mathbf{y} \in \{\pm1\}^t$, batch-size k, learning rate l, α, C, T
Output: parameters $\mathbf{w} \in R^d$

1: Randomly initialize $\mathbf{w}$, set $t = 0$
2: **while** $t < T$ **do**
3:     Random sample batch B
4:     $grad = \alpha \cdot \mathbf{w}$
5:     $grad- = \frac{C}{k}\sum_{i\in B}(\mathbf{y}_i(\mathbf{x}_i \cdot \mathbf{w}^T) < 1)(\mathbf{y}_i\mathbf{x}_i)$
6:     $\mathbf{w}- = l \cdot grad$
7:     $t+ = 1$
8: return w

2.2 Shamir's Secret Sharing

The secret sharing decomposes a secret into several shares. It is required that no information about the secret can be extracted from the sets of shares that do not meet specific requirements, while the sets that do can restore the secret. Shamir's secret sharing [18] is a classic (n, t)-threshold secret sharing, that is, it decomposes a secret value into n shares, and only when the number of shares is greater than t can it be recovered the secret value. In Shamir's secret sharing scheme, the secret owner generates a $t-1$ degree polynomial $f(x) = s + a_1x + \cdots + a_{t-1}x^{t-1}$ over a finite field, where $s = f(0)$ is set as the secret value and the other parameters are random values. Then $(f(i), i), i \in [1, n]$ are distributed to party i as the secret shares. When parties need to reconstruct the secret, first collect enough secret shares (at least t), and then calculate the secret value $f(0) = \sum_{i\in A, |A|=t}(f(i)\prod_{j\in A, j\neq i}\frac{-j}{i-j})$ according to the Lagrange interpolation formula. We use $[\![x]\!]$ to denote the Shamir's secret shares of x, and $x \leftarrow \mathsf{Reveal}([\![x]\!])$ is the reconstruct protocol as described above.

Like some other secret sharing schemes, Shamir's secret-sharing also has the homomorphic property. The secret value can be calculated by calculating the shared value. When the shares corresponding to the two polynomials f_1, f_2 are added accordingly, the result is exactly the share corresponding to $f_3 = f_1 + f_2$. Therefore, Shamir's secret sharing has the property of additive homomorphism. When we want to calculate the addition of the secret values of two corresponding polynomials on the same finite field, we can simply add their shared values of the same independent variable without any communication. Similarly, Shamir's secret sharing has similar properties to multiplication, but it should be noted that the multiplication of two $t - 1$ degree polynomials will produce a $2(t - 1)$ degree polynomial, which will change the threshold structure, so the degree of the new polynomial needs to be reduced in time, which brings additional communication.

3 Security Definition for Privacy-Preserving SVM

In this section, we specify the security definition for privacy-preserving computing Algorithm 1. Assume there is a group of clients $C_1, \cdots, C_m$, which want to train a SVM model. Each client holds some data. Assume there are n servers $S_1, \cdots, S_n$ that provide secure computation services. Assume there is a semi-honest adversary A that can corrupt $t - 1$ servers and any proper subset of clients. Very informally, we say a protocol involving these roles secure, if the semi-honest adversary above cannot obtain more knowledge than what can be retrieved from outputs of the protocol.

Let x be the feature data of the samples, which is arbitrarily divided into m pieces $x_1, \cdots, x_m$ and held by m clients (i.e. data holders). Let y be the labels of the samples, and its partition also does not affect training. Let S_A denote the set of corrupted servers, C_A the set of corrupted clients. The view of the adversary, denoted $\text{view}_A(x_A)$, is defined as $(x_A, r_A, M, \text{output}_A)$, where x_A are the input held by the clients in C_A, r_A are the random numbers used by the servers in S_A in the protocols, M is the set of messages sent by honest participants in protocols, and output_A is the output of the protocol that A can get. We hope that our protocol can realize the function of Algorithm 1, denoted by f, which takes the sample data $x_1, \cdots, x_m$ of m clients and the labels y as inputs, and outputs the optimized model parameters w. Let f_A denote the subset of f's output that can be obtained by A. We have security definition as follows.

Definition 1. *Let $f : (x_1, \cdots, x_m, y) \to w$ be the ideal function of Algorithm 1 where $x_1, \cdots, x_m$ denote the sample data of m clients, y denotes the labels of the samples, w denote the optimized parameters. We use f_A to denote the subset of f's output that A can get. We say a protocol π privately–computes f against the semi-honest adversary A described above, if for any $(x_1, \cdots, x_m, y)$, the output of the protocol π $\text{output}^\pi(x_1, \cdots, x_m, y) = f(x_1, \cdots, x_m, y)$, and there exists a probabilistic poly-nomial-time algorithm S:*

$$\{S(x_A, f_A(x, y)), f(x, y)\} \equiv \{\text{view}_A(x_A), \text{output}^\pi(x_1, \cdots, x_m, y)\}$$

where $\equiv$ denotes that the distributions on both sides are statistical indistinguishable.

4   Building Blocks of Our Protocol

As sketched previously, our protocol consists of many repetitions, each of which computes an iteration of the SGD method. In each repetition, the servers have as input the shares of current values of the parameters and then perform some MPC protocol to compute gradient iteration and finally obtain the shares of the new values of the parameters. According to Formula 1 and 2, each iteration of SGD only consists of addition, multiplication and comparison operations. Thus to realize the MPC for SGD, it suffices to show how to realize these operations privately.

Notice that the SGD algorithm is not over integers, while Shamir's secret sharing is built over finite fields like $\mathbb{Z}_p$. Recall that [2] and [3] presents secure fixed-point addition, multiplication, truncation and less-then-zero (LTZ) protocol with respect to Shamir's scheme. Thus we adopt [2] and [3] to realize the secure addition and multiplication, which details are recalled in Sect. 4.1. Lastly in Sect. 4.2 we show the details of how to use the Berlekamp-Welch algorithm to correct wrong messages.

4.1   Secure Fixed-Point Calculation [2] and [3]

We now present a detailed overview of fixed-point calculations in [2] and [3], which also explains the notations to make it easier to read the following subsections. We will first introduce the representation of fixed-point numbers in Shamir's sharing and then recall the addition and multiplication with truncation, and finally introduce the less-than-zero protocol. More details of the protocols can be referred to [2] and [3] or Appendix B.

Data Type and Encoding. In this paper the target data is signed fixed-point numbers, denoted as $\mathbb{Q}_{\langle k,f\rangle} = \{\tilde{x} \in \mathbb{Q} | \tilde{x} = \bar{x} \cdot 2^{-f}, \bar{x} \in \mathbb{Z}_{\langle k\rangle}\}$, where $\mathbb{Z}_{\langle k\rangle} = \{\bar{x} \in \mathbb{Z}| -2^{k-1} \le \bar{x} \le 2^{k-1}-1\}$ denotes the signed integers. f is the number of decimal places, k is the number of significant digits, and $\tilde{x}$ and $\bar{x}$ indicate their types $\mathbb{Q}_{\langle k,f\rangle}$ and $\mathbb{Z}_{\langle k\rangle}$. We use the integer function $\mathsf{int}_f : \mathbb{Q}_{\langle k,f\rangle} \mapsto \mathbb{Z}_{\langle k\rangle}, \mathsf{int}_f(\tilde{x}) = \tilde{x} \cdot 2^f$ to realize the conversion of elements between these two types. We use the p's complement encoding system to encode elements on $\mathbb{Z}_{\langle k\rangle}$ onto $\mathbb{Z}_p$.

The p's complement encoding system uses a sufficiently large p to generate $\mathbb{Z}_p$, where $p > 2^{2k+\kappa}$, κ is the security parameter, and uses the function $\mathsf{fld}(\bar{x}) = \bar{x}$ (mod p) mapping the element $\bar{x}$ over $\mathbb{Z}_{\langle k\rangle}$ to the element over the finite field $\mathbb{Z}_p$. This mapping allows addition and multiplication of elements on $\mathbb{Z}_{\langle k\rangle}$ to be directly implemented through the corresponding calculations on $\mathbb{Z}_p$, and realizing of the calculation of fixed-point numbers by simpler conversion. In addition, choosing a large enough p can also ensure that the signed multiplication does not cross the bounds, and retains many related properties.

Fixed-Point Calculation. As we have already said in the previous paragraphs, we realize the calculation of the signed integer elements over $\mathbb{Z}_{\langle k\rangle}$ by directly calculating the elements over $\mathbb{Z}_p$, and further realizing the calculation of the signed fixed-point numbers over $\mathbb{Q}_{\langle k,f \rangle}$. Since f, the number of decimal places we set, is fixed and public, we can directly use the calculation over $\mathbb{Z}_{\langle k \rangle}$ of the signed integer element $\bar{x}$ to implement the addition and subtraction of $\tilde{x}$ and determine the sign, for $\mathsf{int}_f(\tilde{x}_1) + \mathsf{int}_f(\tilde{x}_2) = \mathsf{int}_f(\tilde{x}_1 + \tilde{x}_2)$. But the multiplication between $\tilde{x}$ will cause the expansion of digits. The key difference between fixed-point calculations and integer calculations is that in order to maintain the number of decimal places, we need to truncate the results after performing multiplication calculations. Next, we will introduce the truncation protocol in [3] that we will use in this paper.

Truncation. Div2mP [3] is the truncation protocol that we will use in this paper. It takes a secret integer value $\bar{a} \in \mathbb{Z}_{\langle k \rangle}$ and a public integer $m \in [1, k-1]$ as inputs, calculates the shares of $\bar{c} = \lfloor \bar{a}/2^m \rceil$ and rounds up or down with some probability. Details of the protocol are shown as Protocol 5.

Using the above truncation protocol, we get the multiplication of fixed-point numbers. As for $\tilde{x}_3 = \tilde{x}_1 \tilde{x}_2 = \bar{x}_1 \bar{x}_2 \cdot 2^{-2f} \in \mathbb{Q}_{\langle 2k, 2f \rangle}$, using Div2mP$(\llbracket \tilde{x}_3 \rrbracket, k+f, f)$ to do the truncation, $\tilde{x}_3$ will be turned to $\tilde{x}'_3 = \bar{x}_1 \bar{x}_2 \cdot 2^{-f} \in \mathbb{Q}_{\langle k,f \rangle}$. And this is how FXMul works.

The Less-Than-Zero Protocol. In this subsection we introduce the LTZ protocol from [2] based on bit comparison and precise truncation Div2m for secure comparison. According to Formula 1, we need to decide whether a number is greater than 0. The LTZ protocol obtains the sign of the secret value by truncating to only one bit remaining. Because Shamir's secret sharing works on $\mathbb{Z}_p$, we will map signed integers to $\mathbb{Z}_p$ by modulo p, and positive numbers will be mapped to $[0, p/2]$, while negative numbers will be mapped to $(p/2, p)$. Therefore, when guaranteed to be rounded down, the truncated result of a positive number is 0, and the result of a negative number is -1 (i.e. $p-1$ in $\mathbb{Z}_p$), so that the two can be distinguished. LTZ$(\llbracket a \rrbracket, k)$ outputs $s = (\bar{a} < 0)?1 : 0$ as $\llbracket s \rrbracket = -\mathsf{Div2m}(\llbracket a \rrbracket, k, k-1)$.

4.2 Error-Message Recovery via the Berlekamp-Welch Algorithm

Now we show the details of how to use the Berlekamp-Welch algorithm to correct wrong messages. Assume that there are wrong messages in communication and these error messages are corrupted shares. Notice that all the communications in our secure computation framework are in Reveal (see Sect. 2.2), except the initial share distribution of clients, and all situations only include the Reveal of random values or the Reveal hidden in the degree reduction protocol. Moreover, error correction algorithms such as Berlekamp–Welch algorithm can fully assume the role of recovering secret values from shares in the Reveal protocol, and have the ability of error correction (see Appendix A.1). Therefore, in our secure computation, participants can directly replace the Reveal with the Reveal$_{BW}$ of Berlekamp–Welch algorithm version, when they reveal the secrets after each

Protocol 2. Div2mP$_{BW}$($[\![a]\!]_p, k, m$)

Input: Secret share $[\![a]\!]_p$, digits length k, divisor length m, random number r
Output: Secret sharing modulus result $[\![c]\!]_p$, where $\bar{c} = \lfloor \bar{a}/2^m \rfloor + u$, and $u \leftarrow \{0,1\}$

1: $[\![r'']\!] \leftarrow$ PRandInt($k - m - 1$), $[\![r']\!] \leftarrow$ PRandInt(m)
2: $[\![r]\!] \leftarrow 2^m [\![r'']\!] + [\![r']\!]$
3: $[\![a']\!] \leftarrow 2^{k-1} + [\![a]\!] + [\![r]\!]$
4: $b \leftarrow$ Reveal$_{BW}(r[\![a']\!])$
5: $b' \leftarrow (r^{-1}b) \pmod{2^m}$
6: $[\![c]\!] \leftarrow ([\![a]\!] - (b' - [\![r']\!]))2^{-m}$
7: return $[\![c]\!]$

round of communication. In order to ensure correctness, we also need some other operations.

Since the Berlekamp-Welch algorithm is proposed as a decoding algorithm, the errors it deals with are considered as random noise. Similarly, there are some heuristic algorithms among the following multi-polynomial reconstruction algorithm, which clearly requires that the errors should be random. In secure computing, error messages may be actively tampered with by malicious adversaries to prevent the reconstruction of secrets or even lead to the wrong results. Such errors are obviously not random. To use these algorithms in our secure computation, we need to randomize the errors in different distributions.

Let the received shares be $[\![x]\!]$, some of which are corrupted to $[\![x]\!]_i + \Delta x_i$, where Δx_i is the malicious error. The participant can multiply all shares $[\![x]\!]$ by a same random number r, i.e. $[\![x']\!] = r[\![x]\!]$. So the error Δx_i is turned to $r\Delta x_i$, which is a uniformly distributed random number. Then the participant can apply Berlekamp-Welch algorithm to recover the secret $x' = rx \leftarrow$ Reveal$_{BW}([\![x']\!])$. In the end he multiplies the result x' by the inverse of the random number r^{-1} to obtain the secret value $x \leftarrow r^{-1}x'$. Taking Div2mP for example, (see Protocol 5 in Appendix B.1) after introducing BW algorithm, the protocol is modified as Protocol 2.

Finally, we summarize the error correction algorithm. We use noisy polynomial reconstruction algorithms such as Berlekamp-Welch to replace the original reveal algorithm in Shamir's secret sharing. Since there is no change in the interaction, the introduced algorithm will not reduce security. On the contrary, due to its error correction function, it can resist the dropping out and tampering of some messages, thereby obtaining stronger security than before. As these correction algorithms increase the computational cost compared to the original Reveal, it is sufficient to use the original Reveal under semi-honest security, so as in our experiments.

5   Privacy-Preserving SVM

After presenting the building blocks, this section will formally introduce our privacy-preserving SVM protocol. Section 5.1 will give an overview of the protocol. Section 5.2 will explain the details of the protocol and prove its security.

Protocol 3. PPSVM – GD

Input: Features $\mathbf{x} \in R^{t \times d}$, labels $\mathbf{y} \in \{\pm 1\}^t$, batch-size bs, learning rate r, PRG, α, k, f, C, T

Output: shares $[\![\mathbf{w}]\!]$ of parameters $\mathbf{w} \in R^d$

1: Clients generate the shares $[\![\mathbf{x}]\!]$, $[\![\mathbf{y}]\!]$, and send them to the servers
2: Servers randomly initialize $[\![\mathbf{w}]\!]$, set $t = 0$
3: calculate $\lambda = [\frac{C \cdot r}{bs} \times 2^f]$
4: **while** $t < T$ **do**
5:      Get batch index according to PRG
6:      $grad = \alpha \cdot [\![\mathbf{w}]\!]$
7:      $a_1 = [\![\mathbf{y}_i]\!][\![\mathbf{x}_i]\!]$ //need degree reduction
8:      $a_2 = a_1 \cdot [\![\mathbf{w}]\!]$ //need degree reduction
9:      $a_3 = \mathsf{LTZ}(a_2 - 2^f)$
10:     $a_4 = \lambda \sum_i a_3 a_1$ //need degree reduction
11:     $grad = \mathsf{Div2mP}(grad - a_4, k + f, f)$
12:     $[\![\mathbf{w}]\!]- = \mathsf{Div2mP}(r \cdot grad, k + f, f)$
13:     $t+ = 1$
14: Servers return $[\![\mathbf{w}]\!]$

5.1   Protocol Overview

We use the above protocols based on Shamir's secret sharing to realize the secure training of SVM. In the training protocol, the clients submit the shares of the sample data $[\![\mathbf{x}]\!]$ and labels $[\![\mathbf{y}]\!]$ to the servers. The servers use them to calculate the homomorphism of gradient descent according to Formula (1) and (2), so as to optimize the model parameters $\mathbf{w}$ in privacy, and finally output the shares of the optimized model parameters $[\![\mathbf{w}]\!]$.

Our secure training has no special requirements for the distribution of data, whether it is horizontal or vertical. As long as the data from different clients can form a complete training set, and this combination is public, then the servers can do the same operation to the shares of these data. However, in order to normalize the data before training, the horizontal distributed data may need other additional operations to get the maximum value per column, while the vertical distributed data can be calculated directly and locally.

5.2   Protocol Details

The following is the specific process of the protocol. Before the formal training, the data holders (the clients) and the calculators (the servers) need to agree on the number of fixed-point decimal places f, as well as the parameters related to the secure protocols, such as the modulus p of the finite field. The data holders owning vertical partitioned data need to align the data. During the training, the data holders submit the secret shares to the calculators. After coordination and sorting, the calculators hold the shares of the same and complete sample data matrix. The calculators use the shares to perform the secure computation of the iterations in the SGD method according to Formula (1) and (2), as shown in the Protocol 3, and finally get the shares of the optimized parameter $\mathbf{w}$. The shares can be given to the data holders to reveal $\mathbf{w}$, or can be left to the calculators for secure classification.

While compared with the other secure machine learning protocols like SecureML, our protocol works in the scenario of n servers and m clients, while theirs need two to four fixed servers. And because of the (n, t) threshold property of Shamir's scheme, our SGD protocol can tolerate dropping out of at most $n - 2t$ servers.

Security: The protocol can maintain privacy when facing semi-honest adversaries that corrupt at most $t - 1$ servers. Therefore, we have the ability to deal with the collusion of up to $t - 1$ servers. We believe that the protocol will not leakage any additional information except normal output. Since our protocol is implemented by the secure computing framework from [3] and [2], the security of the protocol can also be reduced to their security. More specifically, we make the following claim and proof.

Theorem 1. *Protocol 3 privately computes SVM training with respect to Definition 1.*

Proof. Our model should be able to deal with such an adversary $\mathcal{A}$: it can corrupt at most $t - 1$ out of the total number of n servers and a subset of clients, and executes the protocol semi-honestly. We believe that it cannot obtain any information other than its own input and output. We set the scenario where $\mathcal{A}$ corrupts $t-1$ servers $\mathcal{S}_1, \mathcal{S}_2, \cdots \mathcal{S}_{t-1}$ and $m-1$ clients $\mathcal{C}_1, \mathcal{C}_2, \cdots \mathcal{C}_{m-1}$. The above two sets of servers and clients are denoted by $\mathcal{S}_A$ and $\mathcal{C}_A$.

Next we start to construct a simulator $\mathcal{S}$ that runs algorithm S in Definition 1. The input of $\mathcal{S}$ is the sample data of $\mathcal{C}_A$ and the output of both $\mathcal{C}_A$ and $\mathcal{S}_A$, which is denoted by x_A and f_A.

Now we analyze the messages $\mathcal{A}$ gets in its view. Since all communications take place in Reveal, all the messages $\mathcal{A}$ receive are shares. All the results of Reveals contain two types of secret values. One is the random elements over the finite field, which $\mathcal{S}$ can directly simulate directly with random elements over the field, while the other is the random value generated by additive hiding. Given a shared variable $[\![x]\!]$ and an unknown shared random secret value $[\![r]\!]$ jointly generated by participants, calculate $[\![y]\!] = [\![x]\!] + [\![r]\!] \mod p$ and reveal $y = x + r \mod p$. For $x \in [0, 2^k - 1]$, $r \in [0, 2^{k+\kappa} - 1]$, $p > 2^{k+\kappa+1}$, the statistical distance between y and r $\Delta(y, r) = \frac{1}{2} \sum_{v \in [0, 2^{k+\kappa}+2^k-1]} |Pr(x = v) - Pr(r = v)| < 2^{-\kappa}$, leading to statistical privacy with security parameter κ. Therefore, as long as we ensure that the bit length involved in addition hiding in the protocol is κ bits longer than the actual digital range, we can also maintain the above statistical indistinguishability. Thus, the simulator can sample random number shares of the same bit length for simulation.

These two are statistically indistinguishable due to the security of Shamir's secret sharing that a group of less than t servers cannot obtain any information about the secret. Finally, also from the security of Shamir's secret sharing for homomorphic computation, the view of $\mathcal{A}$ and the overall output of f are also independent of each other. Therefore, we construct such $\mathcal{S}$, which outputs the same number of random field elements corresponding to the view of $\mathcal{A}$, so that

$$\{S(x_\mathcal{A}, f_\mathcal{A}(\mathbf{x}, \mathbf{y})), f(\mathbf{x}, \mathbf{y})\} \equiv \{\mathsf{view}_\mathcal{A}(\mathbf{x}_\mathcal{A}), \mathsf{output}^\pi(\mathbf{x}_1, \cdots, \mathbf{x}_m, \mathbf{y})\}$$

In summary, Protocol 3 privately computes SVM training for Definition 1.

6   Evaluation

In this section, we will evaluate the proposed privacy preserving support vector machine protocol. We will evaluate the efficiency and accuracy through theoretical analysis and experimental verification. Finally, we will compare our results with the existing works.

6.1   Theoretical Analysis

We first analyze the theoretical communication complexity of PPSVM. In each iteration, the participants perform Div2mP protocol twice, degree reduction protocol twice, and LTZ protocol once. They need 2 rounds, 3 rounds, 3 rounds of communication respectively, for a total of 8 rounds of communication. In these communications, they need to make $k + 6$ calls of Reveal, where the revealed original matrix size is one of $s \times d$ and $k + 2$ of $s \times 1$ size, 3 of $1 \times d$, so the total communication volume of each participant in one round of SVM training is $(s \times d + s \times (k+2) + d \times 3)(n-1)\log p$ bits. In the above, n represents the number of servers, s is the number of samples, d is the feature dimension of samples, and k represents the bit length of secrets.

Then we discuss the computational complexity. Each calculator's calculation includes four element-wise multiplications, one matrix multiplication and one comparison in each round of the original SVM training algorithm, and their extra computational complexity comes from the security protocols. Each degree reduction protocol needs at least 2 matrix multiplications, and for the truncation protocol, 1 additional matrix multiplication and 2 element-wise multiplications, while the LTZ protocol requires $k - 1$ matrix multiplications and $8k - 2$ element-wise multiplications. Therefore, each cycle introduces an additional $k + 7$ matrix multiplications and $8k + 4$ element-wise multiplications.

6.2   Experimental Analysis

Because the calculation of long integer matrix is involved, we use Python to program, and simulate the scene of secure multi-party SVM training on a single machine. The communication related time will not be included, which can be calculated by the previous section. We use native Python for programming, so the running speed of the experiment will be lower than the theoretical value, but our results are still much faster than the results of [9,20]. Another significance of the experiment is to verify that the errors brought by fixed-point number in SVM training can be ignored.

Settings. The parameters we use are as follows: the number of calculators $n = 3$, the threshold $t = 2$, the number of fixed-point digits $f = 20$, and the finite field prime p's length $\lceil \log p \rceil = 120$. Other parameters such as C are selected by grid search method. Before the experiment, the sample feature data is expanded and rounded according f, and then they are secret shared, which are used as inputs.

Table 1. Data set details

Dataset	Feature	Trainset	Testset
Breast-cancer	10	500	183
Diabetes	8	500	268
German.number	24	800	200

Dataset. The data sets used in the experiment are three binary-class data sets from libsvm: breast cancer, german.number and diabetes. All three datasets have linearly scaled each attribute to $[-1, 1]$ or $[0, 1]$. See Table 1 for details.

Result. We test the secure training protocol on the above three data sets and compare it with gradient descent training using plaintext directly. We repeat each experiment 10 times and take the average of 10 results as the final result. The results are shown in the Table 2.

Table 2. Accuracy of normal SVM and PPSVM among datasets

Dataset	T	SVM	PPSVM
Breast-cancer	100	98.56% (0.0210 s)	98.98% (47.98 s)
Diabetes	1000	68.28% (0.0822 s)	68.06% (677.78 s)
German.number	1000	69.90% (0.2588 s)	68.40% (1846.67 s)

Due to the different separability of the three data sets, we use different iteration numbers. Obviously, the total training time is directly proportional to the number of iterations, whether secure computation is used or not. At the same time, the rise of feature dimension and training set size will also increase the calculation time. Comparing the time of two models on the same data set, the training time of PPSVM is about 2000–8000 times that of ordinary SVM. Considering that we use a single machine to simulate three parties, this proportion needs to be reduced to about 1/3. However, this is still quite different from the previous theoretical analysis. We believe that the magnification outside the theory comes from the native Python language and numpy library. In the secure protocol, we use the native data type of Python to increase the number of data bits, which will greatly reduce the efficiency of numpy library.

For accuracy, the results of the two models on the breast-cancer dataset are the best, where the average accuracy of ordinary SVM and privacy-preserving SVM is 98.56% and 98.98%. The results on german.number and diabetes are not ideal, which are about 68%. This may be because the kernel function type or penalty coefficient is not appropriate. It can be seen that the average accuracy difference between PPSVM and ordinary SVM on the same data set is less than 1%. Considering the randomness of gradient descent algorithm, we believe that there is no significant difference between the results whether using secure calculation or not. That is, when the number of fixed-point digits is sufficient, the calculation using the number of fixed-point digits will not affect the optimization result of gradient descent.

Table 3. Comparison among normal SVM and PPSVMs of different thresholds on breast-cancer dataset

	Time/s	Single server time/s	Accuracy
SVM	0.0109		96.89%
(3, 2)	81.30	27.10	96.61%
(5, 3)	127.95	25.59	96.39%
(7, 4)	195.13	27.88	96.34%

We also conduct experiments on different server numbers and secret sharing thresholds to explore their impact on the efficiency of the protocol. Our experiment is a single machine simulation, so it does not include communication, but only the total computing cost. We use three different thresholds for experiments, each of which conduct 10 experiments and average their results, and further divide the average results by the number of simulated servers to obtain the approximate computing time of a single server. The results are shown in Table 3. The time of a single server on the three thresholds is 27.10 s, 25.59 s and 27.88 s, which are almost the same. This is consistent with our results in theoretical analysis, that is, the number of servers only affects a small number of matrix shapes in the matrix calculations, and has little impact on the calculation cost. When the threshold and the number of servers are small, their growth has almost no impact on the calculation. But on the other hand, according to the theoretical analysis above, the communication cost is linearly related to the threshold and the number of servers, so it is more affected.

6.3 Comparison

To conclude this section, we will compare our protocol with some previous works. Our work is closer to the methods of [9, 20]. Compared with them, our protocol achieves higher efficiency. They use a public key encryption system based on modular exponentiation, so their 100 rounds of training take nearly 10 h on a 236 × 13 training set. Our protocol runs MPC based on shares, which only contains addition and multiplication over the finite field. Therefore, our 100 rounds of training takes about 48s on the breast-cancer training set of 500 × 10, our 1000 rounds of training takes about 10 min on the diabetes training set of 500 × 8, and 30 min on the german.number training set of 800 × 24. For efficiency, our protocol is much faster than theirs. They need two semi-honest servers, while we need not less than three servers.

Compared with [1, 13, 14] as well as [9, 20], which have to fix the number of servers to a value among 2 to 4, our protocol can be deployed among any number of servers (no less than 3). Increased number of servers and flexible deployment also enhance the difficulty of server collusion and enhanced the security and generality of our protocol (for example, let some clients act as the calculators). Also, by using Shamir's (n, t)-threshold secret sharing scheme, we can arbitrarily deploy among n servers and tolerate dropping out of at most $n - 2t$ ones. Moreover, by introducing the Berlekamp-Welch algorithm as an optional recovery algorithm, correct messages can be recovered even if less than t messages/shares are corrupted (Table 4).

Table 4. Comparison in functionality

Functions	[9, 20]	SecureML	Ours
Efficiency	Low	High	Medium
Non fixed number of servers	✗	✗	✓
Error correction	✗	✗	✓

7 Conclusion

We propose a new privacy preserving support vector machine protocol, which enables no less than three servers to help several data holders train SVM models, where the data distribution can be can be arbitrary. We introduce Shamir's secret sharing scheme to perform secure computation and protect privacy. We verify the feasibility and effectiveness of the scheme through experiments.

Acknowledgements. This work was supported in part by the National Key Research and Development Project 2020YFA0712300.

A   Preliminaries

A.1   Error-Correcting Codes and Berlekamp-Welch Algorithm

Reed Solomon code is an error correction code, which can deal with damaged and lost symbols. Like Shamir's secret sharing, RS code is based on polynomial interpolation, that is, the codewords $\{f(x_1), f(x_2), \cdots, f(x_n)\}$ can be generated by polynomial $f(x) = s + a_1 x + \cdots + a_{t-1} x^{t-1}$ from source of $\{s, a_1, \cdots, a_{t-1}\}$, where n is the number of participants, t is the threshold. $\{s, a_1, \cdots, a_{t-1}\}$ is the input message for RS coding, also the secret and randomness for Shamir's secret sharing.

Berlekamp-Welch algorithm [10] is a decoding algorithm of RS code. The algorithm takes the received codewords (the share in Shamir's secret sharing) as input, and recovers the correct true values from by solving a system of equations and dividing between polynomials. It can deal with up to $v < (n - t + 1)/2$ errors in the received codewords. The principle of Berlekamp-Welch algorithm is based on error location polynomial. The error location polynomial is $E(x) = \prod_{i \in \mathbb{E}}(x - i) = e_0 + e_1 x + \cdots + e_{k-1} x^{k-1} + x^k$, where $\mathbb{E}$ represents the index set of error messages that need to be found. The received codewords are $S_1, S_2, \cdots, S_n$. Note that when $f(x) \neq S_x, E(x) = 0$, so there is the equation $f(x)E(x) = S_x E(x)$. Let the left side of the equation be $Q(x)$, and we get the equation system $\{Q(x) = S_x E(x)\}_{x=1}^n$. As long as $2k + t + 1 \leq n$ is satisfied, there are solutions of $Q(x)$ and $E(x)$. After the two polynomials are obtained by solving the linear equations, we can get $f(x)$ by calculating $Q(x)/E(x)$. In Shamir's secret sharing, Berlekamp–Welch algorithm has the same input and output as the Reveal function, and also has the ability of error correction, so it can directly replace the Reveal function.

Protocol 4. Reveal$_{BW}$

Input: codewords(shares) $S_1, S_2, \cdots, S_n \in \mathbb{Z}_p$
Output: secrets $s \in \mathbb{Z}_p$

1: Each participant gets $S_1, S_2, \cdots, S_n$ from others
2: Determine the number of items of $Q(x)$ and $E(x)$ according to the assumed number of error messages
3: Solve the equation system $\{Q(x) = S_x E(x)\}_{x=1}^n$
4: $f(x) = Q(x)/E(x)$
5: return s in $f(x)$

Berlekamp-Welch algorithm can only recover one secret in one calculation, while some other further algorithms [4, 6] can recover multiple polynomials at the same time in one calculation. This problem is also called noisy multi-polynomial reconstruction. These different algorithms have the same application in our framework. So in our framework, we only take Berlekamp-Welch algorithm as the representative.

B   Details of Protocols in [3] and [2]

Protocol 5. Div2mP($[\![a]\!]_p, k, m$) [3]

Input: Secret share $[\![a]\!]_p$, digits length k, divisor length m, security parameter κ
Output: Secret sharing modulus result $[\![c]\!]_p$, where $\bar{c} = \lfloor \bar{a}/2^m \rfloor + u$, and $u \leftarrow \{0, 1\}$

1: $[\![r'']\!] \leftarrow$ PRandInt($k + \kappa$), $[\![r']\!] \leftarrow$ PRandInt(m)
2: $[\![r]\!] \leftarrow 2^m [\![r'']\!] + [\![r']\!]$
3: $b \leftarrow$ Reveal($2^{k+\kappa-1} + [\![a]\!] + [\![r]\!]$)
4: $b' \leftarrow b \pmod{2^m}$
5: $[\![c]\!] \leftarrow ([\![a]\!] - (b' - [\![r']\!]))2^{-m}$
6: return $[\![c]\!]$

B.1   Truncation

Div2mP [3] is the truncation protocol that we will use in this paper. It takes a secret integer value $\bar{a} \in \mathbb{Z}_{\langle k \rangle}$ and a public integer $m \in [1, k-1]$ as inputs, calculates $\bar{a}/2^m$ and rounds up or down with some probability. Details of the protocol are shown as Protocol 5.

The protocol uses a truncated random number r to mask the secret value a to the garbled value b, reveals the garbled value b for truncation, and then removes the truncated result r' of r from the result b'. The actual output of the protocol is $\bar{c} = \lfloor \bar{a}/2^m \rfloor + u$, which contain an error $u = (b' < r')?1 : 0$. This error is acceptable in the truncation of fixed-point numbers. The PRandInt in the protocol is used by each participant to generate a share of an unknown random number of a specified length without communication.

B.2   Fixed-Point Multiplication

Using the above truncation protocol, we get the multiplication of fixed-point numbers. As for $\tilde{x}_3 = \tilde{x}_1 \tilde{x}_2 = \bar{x}_1 \bar{x}_2 \cdot 2^{-2f} \in \mathbb{Q}_{\langle 2k, 2f \rangle}$, using Div2mP($[\![\tilde{x}_3]\!], k + f, f$) to do the truncation, $\tilde{x}_3$ will be turned to $\tilde{x}'_3 = \bar{x}_1 \bar{x}_2 \cdot 2^{-f} \in \mathbb{Q}_{\langle k, f \rangle}$. And this is how FXMul works.

Protocol 6. FXMul($[\![a_1]\!], [\![a_2]\!], k + f, f$) [3]

Input: Secret share $[\![a_1]\!], [\![a_2]\!]$, digits length k, decimal digits length f
Output: Secret share $[\![a_3]\!]_p$, where $\bar{a}_3 = \bar{a}_1 \cdot \bar{a}_2$

1: $[\![a]\!] \leftarrow [\![a_1]\!] \cdot [\![a_2]\!]$
2: $[\![a_3]\!] \leftarrow$ Div2mP($[\![a]\!], k + f, f$)
3: return $[\![a_3]\!]$

The communication required for each multiplication is a large overhead, and the reason for communication is that the multiplication expands the degree of polynomials in Shamir's secret sharing. In order to ensure subsequent successful recovery, the number of polynomials needs to be maintained less than n through computation.

B.3   Batch Calculation

As mentioned earlier, the communication required for the degree reduction of each multiplication is a large overhead. Observing our goal, when calculating SGD, we will first use multiplication and addition to calculate the inner product. Each time the inner product is calculated, the multiplications do not interfere with each other, so we can communicate and reduce the degree after the complete inner product.

B.4   The Less-Than-Zero Protocol

The LTZ protocol in [2] is actually an application of the precise truncation protocol Div2m. The above Div2mP is a truncation protocol, but it has errors caused by random rounding. First, the protocol uses $\mathsf{PRandM}(k, m)$ to generate two shares of random numbers with specified lengths k and m, and the shares of each bit of the latter. Based on the Div2mP protocol, Div2m uses the bit comparison protocol BitLT from [2] to obtain an accurate result of truncating 2^{k-1} bits and keep rounding down, thereby revealing whether the secret is less than zero. BitLT takes a plaintext data and a set of random bit shares as input, and outputs whether this plaintext data is less than the binary random number represented by these bit shares. The BitLT requires 2 rounds and $k+1$ interactions of Reveal online, 3 rounds and $3k - 1$ interactions offline.

Using BitLT, Div2m can find out whether $2^{k-1} + [\![a]\!] + [\![r]\!]$ produces carry in the least significant m bits and remove it. So that Div2mP is turned to accurate Div2m. And finally, we have $\mathsf{LTZ}([\![a]\!], k)$ outputs $s = (\bar{a} < 0)?1 : 0$ as $[\![s]\!] = -\mathsf{Div2m}([\![a]\!], k, k - 1)$.

Protocol 7. $\mathsf{Div2m}([\![a]\!]_p, k, m)$ [2]

Input: Secret share $[\![a]\!]_p$, digits length k, divisor length m, security parameter κ
Output: Secret sharing modulus result $[\![c]\!]_p$, where $\bar{c} = \lfloor \bar{a}/2^m \rfloor + u$, and $u \leftarrow \{0, 1\}$

1: $([\![r'']\!], [\![r']\!], \{[\![r'_i]\!]\}_{i=1}^m) \leftarrow \mathsf{PRandM}(k + \kappa, m)$
2: $[\![r]\!] \leftarrow 2^m [\![r'']\!] + [\![r']\!]$
3: $b \leftarrow \mathsf{Reveal}(2^{k+\kappa-1} + [\![a]\!] + [\![r]\!])$
4: $b' \leftarrow b \pmod{2^m}$
5: $[\![u]\!] \leftarrow \mathsf{BitLT}(b', \{[\![r'_i]\!]\}_{i=1}^m)$
6: $[\![c]\!] \leftarrow ([\![a]\!] - (b' - [\![r']\!] + 2^m [\![u]\!]))2^{-m}$
7: return $[\![c]\!]$

Security: Since all the massages exchanged in protocols above are Shamir's secret shares, and values masked by uniformity random numbers (also resulting in uniformity random values or with only negligible differences), according to the security of secret sharing, this protocol is secure.

References

1. Byali, M., Chaudhari, H., Patra, A., Suresh, A.: FLASH: fast and robust framework for privacy-preserving machine learning. Proc. Priv. Enhancing Technol. **2020**(2), 459–480 (2020)
2. Catrina, O.: Round-efficient protocols for secure multiparty fixed-point arithmetic. In: 2018 International Conference on Communications (COMM), pp. 431–436. IEEE (2018)
3. Catrina, O., de Hoogh, S.: Improved primitives for secure multiparty integer computation. In: Garay, J.A., De Prisco, R. (eds.) SCN 2010. LNCS, vol. 6280, pp. 182–199. Springer, Heidelberg (2010). https://doi.org/10.1007/978-3-642-15317-4_13
4. Cohn, H., Heninger, N.: Approximate common divisors via lattices. In: The Open Book Series, vol. 1, no. 1, pp. 271–293 (2013)
5. Cortes, C., Vapnik, V.: Support-vector networks. Mach. Learn. **20**(3), 273–297 (1995). https://doi.org/10.1007/BF00994018
6. Guruswami, V., Rudra, A.: Explicit codes achieving list decoding capacity: error-correction with optimal redundancy. IEEE Trans. Inf. Theory **54**(1), 135–150 (2008)
7. Laur, S., Lipmaa, H., Mielikäinen, T.: Cryptographically private support vector machines. In: Proceedings of the 12th ACM SIGKDD International Conference on Knowledge Discovery and Data Mining, pp. 618–624 (2006)
8. Lin, Q., Pei, H., Wang, K., Zhong, P.: Privacy-preserving one-class support vector machine with vertically partitioned data. Int. J. Multimed. Ubiquit. Eng. **11**(5), 199–208 (2016)
9. Liu, X., Deng, R.H., Choo, K.K.R., Yang, Y.: Privacy-preserving outsourced support vector machine design for secure drug discovery. IEEE Trans. Cloud Comput. **8**(2), 610–622 (2018)
10. Lloyd, W., Elwyn, B.: Error correction for algebraic block codes, December 1986
11. Maekawa, T., Kawamura, A., Nakachi, T., Kiya, H.: Privacy-preserving support vector machine computing using random unitary transformation. IEICE Trans. Fundam. Electron. Commun. Comput. Sci. **102**(12), 1849–1855 (2019)
12. Mangasarian, O.L., Wild, E.W., Fung, G.M.: Privacy-preserving classification of vertically partitioned data via random kernels. ACM Trans. Knowl. Discov. Data (TKDD) **2**(3), 1–16 (2008)
13. Mohassel, P., Rindal, P.: ABY³: a mixed protocol framework for machine learning. In: Lie, D., Mannan, M., Backes, M., Wang, X. (eds.) Proceedings of the 2018 ACM SIGSAC Conference on Computer and Communications Security, CCS 2018, Toronto, ON, Canada, 15–19 October 2018, pp. 35–52. ACM (2018). https://doi.org/10.1145/3243734.3243760
14. Mohassel, P., Zhang, Y.: SecureML: a system for scalable privacy-preserving machine learning. In: 2017 IEEE Symposium on Security and Privacy, SP 2017, San Jose, CA, USA, 22–26 May 2017, pp. 19–38. IEEE Computer Society (2017). https://doi.org/10.1109/SP.2017.12
15. Omer, M.Z., Gao, H., Sayed, F.: Privacy preserving in distributed SVM data mining on vertical partitioned data. In: 2016 3rd International Conference on Soft Computing & Machine Intelligence (ISCMI), pp. 84–89. IEEE (2016)

16. Riazi, M.S., Weinert, C., Tkachenko, O., Songhori, E.M., Schneider, T., Koushan-far, F.: Chameleon: a hybrid secure computation framework for machine learning applications. In: Kim, J., Ahn, G., Kim, S., Kim, Y., López, J., Kim, T. (eds.) Proceedings of the 2018 on Asia Conference on Computer and Communications Security, AsiaCCS 2018, Incheon, Republic of Korea, 04–08 June 2018, pp. 707–721. ACM (2018). https://doi.org/10.1145/3196494.3196522
17. Sakr, C.: Analytical guarantees for reduced precision fixed-point margin hyperplane classifiers (2017)
18. Shamir, A.: How to share a secret. Commun. ACM **22**(11), 612–613 (1979)
19. Vaidya, J., Yu, H., Jiang, X.: Privacy-preserving SVM classification. Knowl. Inf. Syst. **14**(2), 161–178 (2008). https://doi.org/10.1007/s10115-007-0073-7
20. Wang, J., Wu, L., Wang, H., Choo, K.K.R., He, D.: An efficient and privacy-preserving outsourced support vector machine training for internet of medical things. IEEE Internet Things J. **8**(1), 458–473 (2020)
21. Yu, H., Vaidya, J., Jiang, X.: Privacy-preserving SVM classification on vertically partitioned data. In: Ng, W.-K., Kitsuregawa, M., Li, J., Chang, K. (eds.) PAKDD 2006. LNCS (LNAI), vol. 3918, pp. 647–656. Springer, Heidelberg (2006). https://doi.org/10.1007/11731139_74
22. Zhang, J., Yiu, S.M., Jiang, Z.L.: Outsourced privacy-preserving reduced SVM among multiple institutions. In: Qiu, M. (ed.) ICA3PP 2020. LNCS, vol. 12453, pp. 126–141. Springer, Cham (2020). https://doi.org/10.1007/978-3-030-60239-0_9

Lightweight EdDSA Signature Verification for the Ultra-Low-Power Internet of Things

Johann Großschädl[1(✉)], Christian Franck[1], and Zhe Liu[2]

[1] Department of Computer Science, University of Luxembourg,
6, Avenue de la Fonte, 4364 Esch-sur-Alzette, Luxembourg
{johann.groszschaedl,christian.franck}@uni.lu
[2] College of Computer Science and Technology, Nanjing University of Aeronautics
and Astronautics (NUAA), 29 Jiangjun Avenue, Nanjing 211106, Jiangsu, China
zhe.liu@nuaa.edu.cn

Abstract. EdDSA is a digital signature scheme based on elliptic curves
in Edwards form that is supported in the latest incarnation of the TLS
protocol (i.e. TLS version 1.3). The straightforward way of verifying an
EdDSA signature involves a costly double-scalar multiplication of the
form $kP - lQ$ where P is a "fixed" point (namely the generator of the
underlying elliptic-curve group) and Q is only known at run time. This
computation makes a verification not only much slower than a signature
generation, but also more memory demanding. In the present paper we
compare two implementations of EdDSA verification using Ed25519 as
case study; the first is speed-optimized, while the other aims to achieve
low RAM footprint. The speed-optimized variant performs the double-
scalar multiplication in a simultaneous fashion and uses a Joint-Sparse
Form (JSF) representation for the two scalars. On the other hand, the
memory-optimized variant splits the computation of $kP - lQ$ into two
separate parts, namely a fixed-base scalar multiplication that is carried
out using a standard comb method with eight pre-computed points, and
a variable-base scalar multiplication, which is executed by means of the
conventional Montgomery ladder on the birationally-equivalent Montgomery curve. Our experiments with a 16-bit ultra-low-power MSP430
microcontroller show that the separated method is 24% slower than the
simultaneous technique, but reduces the RAM footprint by 40%. This
makes the separated method attractive for "lightweight" cryptographic
libraries, in particular if both Ed25519 signature generation/verification
and X25519 key exchange need to be supported.

1 Introduction

Digital signature schemes can be used to provide entity and data-origin authentication, integrity protection, and non-repudiation services, which makes them
an essential tool for enabling secure communication over the Internet. Common
security protocols like TLS rely on these services to authenticate the server to

ⓒ Springer Nature Switzerland AG 2021
R. Deng et al. (Eds.): ISPEC 2021, LNCS 13107, pp. 263–282, 2021.
https://doi.org/10.1007/978-3-030-93206-0_16

the client (and optionally the client to the server) and to securely exchange the public keys needed for the establishment of a shared pre-master secret [34]. To date, the most widely used signature schemes are based on the RSA algorithm [35] and a variant of the ElGamal cryptosystem, which is standardized by the NIST [30]. However, signature schemes operating on elliptic curves, such as the Elliptic Curve Digital Signature Algorithm (ECDSA) from [30], have gained in acceptance over the past few years. What makes ECDSA attractive is that its security is based on the intractability of the Elliptic Curve Discrete Logarithm Problem (ECDLP), which allows one to use much smaller groups compared to its classical counterpart RSA, whose security rests on the Integer Factorization Problem (IFP). For example, it is generally accepted that ECDSA instantiated with a 160-bit elliptic-curve group provides about the same level of security as the RSA signature scheme using a 1024-bit modulus [19]. Smaller group sizes directly translate into shorter signatures, which is a crucial feature in settings where communication bandwidth is limited or data transfer consumes a large amount of energy (e.g. battery-powered devices [15]). Another major difference between RSA and ECDSA is the (relative) complexity of signature generation versus signature verification. While the verification of an RSA signature is less costly than the generation, exactly the opposite holds for ECDSA: verifying an ECDSA signature is more demanding than signature generation.

From an arithmetic point of view, the main operation of elliptic curve cryptosystems such as ECDSA is scalar multiplication, a computation of the form $R = kP$ where k is a positive integer and R, P are points on an elliptic curve E over a finite field $\mathbb{F}_q$. This computation can be decomposed into a sequence of point additions and point doublings, both of which, in turn, consist of arithmetic operations in the field $\mathbb{F}_q$ [12,19]. In the case of signature generation, the scalar multiplication is performed on a point P that is fixed and known a priori since it is part of the domain parameters (namely, it is generator of a subgroup of prime order). Therefore, it is possible to speed up the scalar multiplication through pre-computation of multiples of P following the comb approach or the windows method [19]. Both techniques are suitable for resource-limited devices with little RAM since, at any time, only one point from the table (but not the full table) is required as input for the computation, which means the table can actually be stored in non-volatile memory [26]. The verification of a signature is more costly and requires a double-scalar multiplication, which is a computation of the form $R = kP + lQ$ where P is fixed (it is actually the same point P as in the signature generation), while Q is the signer's public key and, thus, becomes only available at run time [19,30]. There exist different implementation options for a double-scalar multiplication, whereby the most widely-used approach is to compute the sum $kP + lQ$ in a simultaneous fashion with "joint" doublings as described in [19, Algorithm 3.48]. Assuming that each of the two scalars k and l has a length of b bits, the simultaneous double-scalar multiplication technique requires b point doublings, while the number of point additions depends on the joint Hamming weight of the two scalars.

The Edwards-curve Digital Signature Algorithm (EdDSA) is a state-of-the-art signature scheme using elliptic curves in (twisted) Edwards form that was developed with the intention of achieving both high performance (especially in software) and high security [8,9]. A variant of EdDSA as specified in RFC 8032 [21] is one of the digital signature systems supported in the most-recent version of the TLS protocol, i.e. TLS 1.3. EdDSA is a "Schnorr-like" signature scheme that combines the strong security and simplicity of classical Schnorr signatures [36] with the efficiency (and further positive implementation aspects) of twisted Edwards curves [6]. However, unlike the original Schnorr scheme, EdDSA uses a double-size hash function (to help alleviate concerns regarding hash-function security) and generates the per-message secret nonces in a deterministic fashion by hashing each message together with a long-term secret. Thus, EdDSA does not consume fresh randomness for each message to be signed, which makes the scheme attractive for constrained environments (e.g. embedded systems) where the generation of random numbers is very costly due to the absence of reliable sources of entropy. In ECDSA, on the other hand, a unique and unpredictable random number is required for each computation of a signature, whereby even a small weakness in the random-number generation can have fatal consequences and may, in the worst case, leak the signer's secret key. Thus, the deterministic nonce generation method of EdDSA is not only a performance feature but also a security feature. To verify an EdDSA signature, one has to check whether an equation of the form $R = kP - lQ$ holds or not. This is normally accomplished by computing $kP - lQ$ and then comparing the obtained result with R [8].

A common problem of both ECDSA and EdDSA is that the verification is significantly slower and also consumes much more memory than the generation of a signature. The high computational complexity of the verification operation of curve-based signature schemes is widely recognized in the literature and has initiated a body of research on techniques to speed up double-scalar multiplication [19]. When using a simultaneous approach to compute $R = kP \pm lQ$, this can be achieved by representing the two scalars k and l in such a way that the number of required point arithmetic operations is reduced, or by reducing the individual cost of the point arithmetic operations, or through the combination of both (as in e.g. [7]). While the massive computational burden of verification affects basically any implementation, the problem of high memory consumption is mainly relevant for embedded software that runs on resource-limited devices with little memory, such as smart cards or wireless sensor nodes. Recently, Liu et al. [25] presented a lightweight elliptic curve software for embedded platforms and reported that, on a 16-bit MSP430 microcontroller, the verification operation of their signature scheme consumes about 5 kB of stack memory, while the signature generation needs a stack space of merely 1.6 kB. In other words, the verification is roughly three times more "memory hungry" than the generation of a signature. In the past, there was relatively little awareness of this problem because resource-constrained devices like smart cards were exclusively used to generate signatures, but not for verification. However, the recent growth of the Internet of things has created a demand to support advanced security protocols (involving verifications) on restricted devices, and in such settings the memory consumption is indeed a serious problem, as was recently pointed out in [3].

In this paper, we present an approach to make the double-scalar multiplication required for the verification of an EdDSA signature more "lightweight" in terms of RAM footprint. Our basic idea is to exploit the birational equivalence between twisted Edwards curves and Montgomery curves in order to combine their individual arithmetic benefits. More concretely, we split the computation of $kP - lQ$ into two separate steps, namely the fixed-base scalar multiplication kP carried out with a fixed-base comb method using the twisted Edwards form of the curve, and the variable-base scalar multiplication lQ, which we perform with the straightforward (i.e. "X-coordinate-only") Montgomery ladder on the birationally-equivalent Montgomery curve [29]. At the end of the ladder computation, the (projective) Y coordinate of the result is recovered according to the formulae from [31], and the obtained projective point is then converted to the corresponding projective point on the birationally-equivalent twisted Edwards curve so that it can be subtracted from kP. Intuitively, one would expect this approach to be memory-efficient since the two scalar multiplications are carried out sequentially and both the fixed-base comb method on the twisted Edwards curve and the variable-base Montgomery ladder on the Montgomery curve can be optimized to have a RAM footprint of below 1 kB as shown in [26]. On the other hand, one would also expect the "separated" approach to be slower than a simultaneous double-scalar multiplication since it requires more point additions and doublings. The experimental results we report in this paper allow one to analyze the trade-offs between execution time and RAM footprint these two approaches provide. We also discuss some corner cases in the point conversion and the recovery of the Y coordinate that require special attention.

2   Preliminaries

In this section, we first describe the EdDSA signature scheme and then give an overview of the arithmetic properties of (twisted) Edwards curves.

EdDSA. The Edwards-curve Digital Signature Algorithm (EdDSA) is a state-of-the-art signature scheme that provides high speed in software (especially on 64-bit platforms) and high security [8,9]. EdDSA was obviously inspired by the classical Schnorr signature algorithm [36], which, in its original form, uses $\mathbb{Z}_p$ as underlying algebraic structure, but can be straightforwardly adapted for elliptic curve groups; see e.g. [10, Sect. 4.2.3] for a formal description of a curve-based variant. However, EdDSA comes with a number of enhancements compared to [10] that were developed with the goal to improve the real-world security of the scheme. The major differences between EdDSA and the EC-Schnorr signature algorithm described in [10] are as follows.

- EdDSA is a deterministic signature scheme since it employs a deterministic process to generate the secret scalar r (called "session key" in [8]) needed to sign a message M. Concretely, EdDSA generates r by hashing a long-term secret together with M. In this way, the signing operation does not require any fresh randomness and it is also guaranteed that a value r is never used for different messages. On the other hand, the classical EC-Schnorr scheme from [10] has to produce a fresh random value r for each message M to be signed. This r must be unique for every M and chosen uniformly from the set $\{1, 2, \ldots, \ell - 1\}$, where ℓ is the order of the base point. Even marginal deviations from randomness or a slight non-uniformity of the distribution from which r is taken can enable an attack against the EC-Schnorr scheme that may allow an adversary to get the signer's private key. EdDSA avoids such problems and is, therefore, particularly suited for environments where accessing a source of high-quality randomness is not easily possible.

- A distinguishing characteristic of curve-based Schnorr signature schemes is that they hash the message M together with $R = rB$, i.e. the result of the scalar multiplication between the secret scalar r and the base point B. The EC-Schnorr variant specified in [10] actually computes $\text{HASH}(M, x_R)$ where x_R is the x-coordinate of R. EdDSA, on the other hand, also includes the signer's public key A in the hash computation; more precisely, it computes $\text{HASH}(R, A, M)$ as part of the signature generation. The purpose of this so-called key-prefixing is to provide an "inexpensive way to alleviate concerns that several public keys could be attacked simultaneously" [8]. Indeed, as recently proven by Bernstein [5], single-user security for Schnorr signatures tightly implies multi-user security for key-prefixed Schnorr signatures in the standard model. Shortly after the publication of [5], Kiltz et al. [22] found that key-prefixing is not needed to ensure multi-user security and provided a reduction showing that "strong" single-user unforgeability tightly implies "strong" multi-user unforgeability in the random oracle model. However, to date, proving multi-user security using standard unforgeability assumptions without key-prefixing remains being an open problem.

- EdDSA supports fast verification of (large) batches of signatures, which is not (efficiently) possible when using the EC-Schnorr scheme from [10]. The saving in execution time that can be achieved through a batch verification of 64 signatures (versus an individual verification of 64 signatures) is more than 52% according to the experimental results reported in [8]. To achieve this speed-up, the designers of EdDSA modified the signature generation to output the (compressed) point $R = rB$ as first component of the signature instead of $\text{HASH}(M, x_R)$ as in EC-Schnorr. This tweak does not impact the security compared to EC-Schnorr since, given an EC-Schorr signature and the signer's public key, one can always recover R as in [10, Sect. 4.2.3.2].

- When designing an elliptic curve signature scheme, it is common practice to choose a hash function with an output length matching the bit-length of the order ℓ of the base point B. Choosing the hash function in this way is also recommended for the EC-Schnorr algorithm in [10]. However, the designers of EdDSA were more conservative and recommend to employ a double-size hash function, claiming it "helps alleviate concerns regarding hash-function security" [8]. Specifically, they recommend to use SHA-512 when EdDSA is instantiated with a twisted Edwards curve that is birationally equivalent to Curve25519 and a base point B whose order ℓ has a bit-length of 253.

Algorithm 1. EdDSA signature generation (sketch)

Input: Domain parameters $(\mathbb{F}_q, E, B, \ell)$, signer's key pair (a, A), signer's long-term secret n for session-key generation, and message M.
Output: Signature (R, s) of M.
1: $r \leftarrow \text{HASH}(n, M) \bmod \ell$
2: $R \leftarrow rB$
3: $h \leftarrow \text{HASH}(R, A, M) \bmod \ell$
4: $s \leftarrow r + ha \bmod \ell$
5: return (R, s)

Algorithm 1 specifies a (slightly) simplified version of the EdDSA signature generation as described in [8]. We left out some details that are not relevant in the context of the present paper. One such detail concerns the long-term secrets a and n, which are generated by hashing a secret "master key." In addition, the points R and A in line 3 and 5 are actually compressed, i.e. represented by the y-coordinate and one bit of the x-coordinate (see [8] for further details). When using the curve promoted by the EdDSA designers, which is a twisted Edwards curve birationally equivalent to Curve25519 [4], then a compressed point fits in 32 bytes and the complete signature has a size of 64 bytes. As shown in Algorithm 1, the message M is actually hashed twice, whereby one of the inputs to the second hash computation in line 3, namely the point $R = rB$, depends on the result of the first hash computation in line 1. This dependency may require the signer to buffer the complete message M, which could exceed the available memory capacity when M is large. Furthermore, this "double hashing" is also computationally expensive for large messages[1]. On the other hand, when M is relatively small, then the overall execution time of the signature generation is primarily determined by the scalar multiplication $R = rB$ in line 2, which is, in fact, a fixed-base scalar multiplication since B is a pre-defined point.

Algorithm 2. EdDSA signature verification (sketch)

Input: Domain parameters $(\mathbb{F}_q, E, B, \ell)$, signer's public key A, message M, and alleged signature (R, s).
Output: Acceptance or rejection of signature.
1: $h \leftarrow \text{HASH}(R, A, M) \bmod \ell$
2: return *Accept* if $R = sB - hA$ and *Reject* otherwise

Algorithm 2 describes the operations that need to be performed in order to verify an EdDSA signature. In particular, for short messages, one can assume

---

[1] RFC 8032 [21] specifies besides the original EdDSA scheme also a pre-hash version that replaces the message M in Algorithm 1 by its hash value $m = \text{HASH}(M)$. This pre-hashing potentially reduces the execution time and RAM requirements for large messages, but loses the collision-resilience feature of the original EdDSA.

that the hash computation in line 1 is relatively inexpensive, which means the overall execution time will be mainly determined by checking whether R equals $sB - hA$ or not. This check can be carried out in a few different ways, but the most common approach is to compute $sB - hA$ using an algorithm optimized for double-scalar multiplication (i.e. an algorithm that computes sB and hA in an interleaved or simultaneous fashion with "joint" doublings) and compare the result with R. The performance can be further improved by pre-computation of multiples of the points B and A (and possibly also combinations thereof) as well as by using a special representation of the two scalars s and h to minimize their joint weight; see e.g. [7,12,19] for a more detailed treatment. However, on memory-restricted devices, it generally makes sense to represent the scalars in Joint-Sparse Form (JSF) [37] since in this case the verifier has to pre-compute and store just two points, namely $B - A$ and $B + A$. An alternative technique to verify an EdDSA signature consists of computing $R + hA$ and sB, and then checking whether they are equal or not, which can be efficiently done using the projective representations of the points (i.e. no projective-to-affine conversions are required). However, a drawback of this approach is that the verifier has to carry out a costly decompression of R.

Twisted Edwards Curves. EdDSA uses a special class of elliptic curves, the so-called *twisted Edwards (TE)* curves, which were first described by Bernstein et al. in 2008 [6]. A TE curve over a non-binary finite field $\mathbb{F}_q$ is defined by an equation of the form

$$E_T : ax^2 + y^2 = 1 + dx^2y^2 \qquad (1)$$

where a and d are distinct and non-zero. The order of a TE curve is a multiple of four, and every TE curve contains a point of order two, which is $(0, -1)$. An interesting feature of TE curves is the existence of a neutral element $\mathcal{O} = (0, 1)$ that is an affine point on the curve. The formula for point addition

$$\underbrace{(x_3, y_3)}_{P_3} = \underbrace{(x_1, y_1)}_{P_1} + \underbrace{(x_2, y_2)}_{P_2} = \left(\frac{x_1y_2 + y_1x_2}{1 + dx_1x_2y_1y_2}, \frac{y_1y_2 - ax_1x_2}{1 - dx_1x_2y_1y_2} \right)$$

is *unified* and can, therefore, also be used for point doubling, i.e. it yields the correct result when $P_1 = P_2$. Further, it is *complete* when a is a square and d is a non-square in $\mathbb{F}_q$, so that the correct sum is computed for any pair of points (including special cases like $P_1 = \mathcal{O}$, $P_2 = \mathcal{O}$, $P_2 = -P_1$). The additive inverse of a point (x, y) is the point $(-x, y)$. Any TE curve is birationally-equivalent to a Montgomery curve [29] (i.e. a curve defined by $By^2 = x^3 + Ax^2 + x$ over $\mathbb{F}_p$) and vice versa. The specific TE curve recommended by the EdDSA designers is birationally-equivalent to Curve25519 [4] and has the parameters $a = -1$ and $d = -121665/121166 \in \mathbb{F}_p$ with $p = 2^{255} - 19$. The group $E_T(\mathbb{F}_p)$ is isomorphic to $\mathbb{Z}_\ell \times \mathbb{Z}_8$ where ℓ is a 253-bit prime (see [8,9] for more details).

When $a = -1$, the *extended TE coordinates* introduced in [20] allow one to perform a "mixed" point addition with only seven multiplications (7M) in the underlying field [26]. Doubling a point in extended projective coordinates costs three multiplications (3M) and four squarings (4S).

3   Implementation Options for EdDSA Verification

In this section we will have a closer look at different ways the verification of an EdDSA signature can be implemented, whereby we pay special attention to the double-scalar multiplication $sB - hA$. The straightforward approach, which is used by most (lightweight) cryptographic libraries, is to compute sB and hA in a combined fashion (i.e. with "joint" doublings) following e.g. the simultaneous or interleaving strategy [19]. An alternative approach is to completely separate these two scalar multiplications and exploit the birational equivalence between the TE form and the Montgomery form.

3.1   Simultaneous Double-Scalar Multiplication

There are two main approaches for performing the double-scalar multiplication $sB - hA$ in a combined fashion, namely the simultaneous method [19] and the interleaving technique [28], which have their origin in corresponding algorithms for multi-exponentiation. Both methods reduce the number of point doublings by half (compared to the separate computation of sB and hA) at the expense of increased RAM consumption for storing a pre-computed table that contains multiples (and possibly also linear combinations[2]) of the two base points A and B. Furthermore, both methods can utilize a "low-weight" representation of the scalars, e.g. *Non-Adjacent Form (NAF)* or *Joint-Sparse Form (JSF)* [19], which determines the actual execution time (i.e. the number of point additions) and the size of the pre-computed table. However, when RAM is limited, it makes generally sense to restrict the size of the table to a few points, e.g. four points including A and B. In this case, the simultaneous double-scalar multiplication with a JSF representation of the scalars s and h executes, on average, the same number of point additions in the evaluation phase as the interleaving technique with width-3 NAFs (see [19, Table 3.6] for a more detailed analysis). Since the width-3 NAFs of s and h require more RAM than their JSF representation, we decided to implement the simultaneous method.

The JSF utilizes a binary (i.e. radix-2) signed-digit number system with the digit set $D = \{-1, 0, 1\}$ to represent a pair of integers a, b such that they have minimal joint Hamming weight, which means the number of non-$(0, 0)$ columns is as small as possible. Solinas gave in [37] a formal definition of the JSF based on three properties and also proved both its uniqueness and optimality. More concretely, he showed that any pair of integers has a unique JSF and that this JSF has the least density of non-$(0, 0)$ columns among all joint expansions. The number of digits of the JSF representation of two positive integers exceeds the bitlength of the larger of these two integers by at most one digit. However, since each digit is from D and requires two bits for its representation, the JSF of the scalars s and h needed for EdDSA verification occupies 128 bytes in RAM.

---

[2] The main difference between the simultaneous method and the interleaving method is that, in the latter case, the table entries are disjoint with respect to the two base points A and B (i.e. each pre-computed value involves only a single base point).

Algorithm 3. Simultaneous method for double-scalar multiplication.

Input: Twisted Edwards curve E_T over $\mathbb{F}_q$ of cardinality $h\ell$ where ℓ is prime, rational
  points $A \in E_T(\mathbb{F}_q)$ and $B \in E_T(\mathbb{F}_q)$, scalars $h \in [0, \ell-1]$ and $s \in [0, \ell-1]$.
Output: Point $R = sB - hA$ in affine coordinates.
  1: $(s', h') \leftarrow$ JOINTSPARSEFORM(s, h)
  2: $T \leftarrow [-A, B + A, B, B - A]$ {table with 2 affine and 2 proj. points}
  3: $T \leftarrow$ PROTOEXTAFF(T) {table with 4 extended affine points}
  4: $Q \leftarrow \mathcal{O}$
  5: **for** i from LENGTH$(s', h') - 1$ down to 0 **do**
  6:     $Q \leftarrow 2Q$
  7:     $d_i \leftarrow 3s'_i + h'_i$
  8:     **if** $(d_i > 0)$ **then** $Q \leftarrow Q + T[d_i - 1]$ **end if**
  9:     **if** $(d_i < 0)$ **then** $Q \leftarrow Q - T[\text{ABS}(d_i) - 1]$ **end if**
 10: **end for**
 11: $R \leftarrow$ PROTOAFF(Q)
 12: **return** R

Algorithm 3 shows a simplified implementation of the simultaneous method for the double-scalar multiplication $sB - hA$ using the JSF for the scalars. The computation of the JSF of the scalars s and h in line 1 is relatively inexpensive and can be done as specified in e.g. [37] or [19, Algorithm 3.50]. Thereafter, the entries of the table T are generated, starting with the sum $S = B + A$ and the difference $D = B - A$, which we obtain using the projective addition formulae from [6, Sect. 6]. We convert these two (projective) points to affine coordinates by taking advantage of the simultaneous inversion technique, i.e. we invert the product $Z_S Z_D$ and then obtain $1/Z_S$ and $1/Z_D$ by multiplying the result of the inversion by Z_D and Z_S, respectively [19, Algorithm 2.26]. Next, the four affine points $-A$, B, S, and D have to be represented in extended affine coordinates of the form (u, v, w) where $u = (x + y)/2$, $v = (y - x)/2$, $w = dxy$ [9,24] and stored in table T. The bulk of the computation, in particular the doubling and addition/subtraction of points, is carried out in a relatively simple loop whose number of iterations corresponds to the length of the JSF expansion of the two scalars (approximately the bitlength of ℓ). In each iteration, a point doubling is performed (line 6) and an index d_i to access the table T is calculated based on the digits s'_i and h'_i (line 7). This index d_i is in the range $[-4, 4]$; depending on its value and sign, an entry of table T may be added or subtracted as specified in line 8 and 9. Since the negation of a point is cheap, it suffices to have a table with only four pre-computed points. The point Q (represented with extended projective coordinates) is initialized to the neutral element $\mathcal{O}$ and updated in each iteration of the loop until it eventually holds the result $sB - hA$, which is finally converted to standard affine coordinates (line 11).

Since, on average, roughly half of the columns of the JSF expansion of s and h are not $(0, 0)$ [37], the probability that $d_i \neq 0$ is roughly 50%. Thus, it can be expected that only in roughly half of the iterations of the loop a point addition (or subtraction) is actually performed. On the other hand, a point doubling is carried out in each iteration. Using the basic cost models for a mixed addition (7M) and projective doubling (3M + 4S) mentioned in Sect. 2, we can estimate that, on average, $0.5 \cdot 7 + 3 = 6.5$ multiplications and four squarings in $\mathbb{F}_p$ are executed per iteration. Consequently, the complete cost of the loop amounts to about $6.5n$ multiplications and $4n$ squarings in $\mathbb{F}_p$ (where n is the length of the JSF expansion), i.e. roughly 6.5M + 4S per scalar bit. The pre-computed table T contains four points in extended affine coordinates, which means in our case the table occupies 384 bytes in RAM (96 bytes per point).

3.2 Two Separate Scalar Multiplications

An obvious alternative to the simultaneous method for obtaining $sB - hA$ is to split the computation into two completely separate parts, namely a fixed-base scalar multiplication sB, and a variable-base scalar multiplication hA. Intuitively, one expects this separated approach to be slower than the simultaneous method since significantly more point doublings have to be performed, which is likely the reason why this approach has, to our knowledge, never been analyzed in the literature. However, this disadvantage can be mitigated by exploiting the birational equivalence between TE curves and Montgomery curves, enabling us to take advantage of the highly-efficient Montgomery ladder to implement the variable-base scalar multiplication hA. The primary advantage of the separated approach is low memory consumption (in relation to the simultaneous method) since it requires neither a table with pre-computed points nor additional space for a JSF representation of the two scalars.

Algorithm 4. Scalar multiplication on TE curve using Montgomery ladder

---

Input: Twisted Edwards curve E_T over $\mathbb{F}_q$ of cardinality $h\ell$ where ℓ is prime, rational
    point $P = (x, y) \in E_T(\mathbb{F}_q)$ with $\mathrm{ord}(P) \geq \ell$, scalar $k \in [0, \ell - 1]$.
Output: Point $Q = kP$ in projective coordinates.
1: if $k = 0$ then return $(0 : 1 : 1)$
2: if $k = \ell - 1$ then return $(-x : y : 1)$
3: $P_m \leftarrow \mathrm{TEDToMON}(P)$
4: $(Q_1, Q_2) \leftarrow \mathrm{MONLADDER}(P_m)$
5: $Q_r \leftarrow \mathrm{RECOVERY}(Q_1, Q_2, P_m)$
6: $Q \leftarrow \mathrm{MONToTED}(Q_r)$
7: return Q

Algorithm 4 explains how one can perform a variable-base scalar multiplication kP (where P is a public key, i.e. a rational point on a TE curve) using the Montgomery ladder on the birationally-equivalent Montgomery curve, which is in the case of Ed25519 a curve[3] that is isomorphic to Curve25519. At first, the

---

[3] The specific Montgomery curve that is birationally-equivalent to the TE curve used by Ed25519 has the same parameter A as Curve25519 (i.e. $A = 48662$ [4]), but the parameter B differs since $B = -(A + 2) = -48664$ instead of $B = 1$.

point P on the TE curve is mapped to the Montgomery curve with help of the formulae given in [6]. This mapping involves a costly inversion, since to achieve maximum performance, the input point for the Montgomery ladder needs to be represented in affine coordinates. Thereafter, the Montgomery ladder is carried out in a similar fashion as in X25519 key exchange [4] (i.e. the point arithmetic involves only the projective X and Z coordinate) and, thus, achieves the same efficiency. However, there are two deviations from the X25519 ladder, namely (i) the Y coordinate of the resulting point has to be recovered, and (ii) the main loop of the ladder (as specified in e.g. [17]) needs to be modified because, unlike X25519, it can not be taken for granted that the most significant "1" bit of the scalar is always at the same position. Finally, the resulting point in projective $(X : Y : Z)$ coordinates has to be converted to the corresponding point on the TE curve. This TE point can be in projective coordinates since it is added to the result of the fixed-base scalar multiplication sB, which is usually also given in projective coordinates. Only at the very end, a single inversion is necessary to get the final result (i.e. the sum of the results of the two scalar multiplications) in affine coordinates. Although the basic principle of performing the variable-base scalar multiplication hA on the birationally-equivalent Montgomery curve is fairly straightforward, there are a couple of corner cases that require special attention. Such corner cases can occur in (i) the point conversions between the TE form and the Montgomery form, and (ii) the recovery of the Y coordinate at the end of the Montgomery ladder.

Corner Cases of Point Conversion. An affine point (x_t, y_t) on a TE-form elliptic curve E_T can be converted to the corresponding point (x_m, y_m) on the birationally-equivalent Montgomery curve E_M using the following map [6].

$$\phi : (x_t, y_t) \mapsto (x_m, y_m) = \left(\frac{1 + y_t}{1 - y_t}, \frac{1 + y_t}{(1 - y_t)x_t} \right) \tag{2}$$

Obviously, the map ϕ is not defined for $x_t = 0$ or $y_t = 1$. Since the parameters a and d of a TE curve E_T must be distinct and nonzero, there exists only one point with $y_t = 1$, namely the neutral element $(0, 1)$, which corresponds to the point at infinity $\mathcal{O}$ on the birationally-equivalent Montgomery curve. There are two points on E_T with $x_t = 0$; one is the neutral element $(0, 1)$ and the other is the point $(0, -1)$. This point has order 2 and corresponds to the point $(0, 0)$ on the Montgomery curve, which also has order 2 [6].

Given an affine point (x_m, y_m) on a Montgomery curve E_M governed by the equation $By^2 = x^3 + Ax^2 + x$, one can compute the corresponding point on the birationally-equivalent TE curve E_T using the map

$$\psi : (x_m, y_m) \mapsto (x_t, y_t) = \left(\frac{x_m}{y_m}, \frac{x_m - 1}{x_m + 1} \right). \tag{3}$$

The map ψ is not regular at points with $x_m = -1$ or $y_m = 0$; in particular ψ is undefined at the affine point $(0, 0)$ on E_M. Another special case for which ψ is irregular are the points with $x_m = -1$. By setting x_m to -1, we can write the Montgomery-curve equation as $By_m^2 = A - 2$ to make it clear that such points only exist when $(A - 2)/B$ is a square in $\mathbb{F}_p$, which obviously does not apply to our curve. Hence, in summary, corner cases in the conversion of points between the TE model and the birationally-equivalent Montgomery model can only be caused by points of low order. However, since the input point for the variable-base scalar multiplication hA is the signer's public key A, it should never have low order, provided the signer generated his/her key pair in a proper fashion as specified in [8]. We will discuss low-order points further in the next subsection and describe how our implementation deals with them.

Corner Cases of Y-Coordinate Recovery. Situations that require special attention can also emerge during the recovery of the Y coordinate as described in [31]. According to Algorithm 4, the Montgomery ladder actually returns two points, namely $Q_1 = kP_m$ and $Q_2 = Q_1 + P_m = kP_m + P_m = (k+1)P_m$ (see [13] for details). The X and Z coordinates of these two points, along with the affine x and y coordinates of the input point P_m, allow one to re-compute the projective Y-coordinate of Q_1, which is relatively inexpensive since it requires only ten multiplications and six additions/subtractions in $\mathbb{F}_p$. Given the points $Q_1 = (X_1 : Z_1)$, $Q_2 = (X_2 : Z_2)$, $P_m = (x_m, y_m)$, a full projective representation of Q_1 (including Y coordinate) can be obtained as follows [31]:

$$X_r = 2By_m Z_1 Z_2 X_1$$
$$Y_r = Z_2[(X_1 + x_m Z_1 + 2AZ_1)(X_1 x_m + Z_1) - 2AZ_1^2] - (X_1 - x_m Z_1)^2 X_2$$
$$Z_r = 2By_m Z_1 Z_2 Z_1$$

The coordinate Z_r of this new representation of Q_1 is a product of y_m, Z_1^2, and Z_2, but this does normally not change the value of the affine x coordinate since $x_r = X_r/Z_r = X_1/Z_1$. However, the equation for Z_r shows that recovering the affine y coordinate $y_r = Y_r/Z_r$ does not work when (i) the y coordinate of the ladder-input P_m is 0, or (ii) the projective Z coordinate of one of the output-points of the ladder (i.e. Z_1 or Z_2) is 0. The former case is only possible when P_m has order 2 [13], which means $P_m = (0, 0)$ since there are no other points in the 2-torsion group of our Montgomery curve. A pragmatic approach to deal with this corner case is to simply reject a public key if it has low order (as we will discuss in detail in the next subsection). Preventing low-order points from entering the ladder also simplifies the analysis of the second corner case, i.e. the case $Z_1 = 0$ or $Z_2 = 0$. Namely, when we exclude low-order points as input to the ladder and insist that k is in the range $[0, \ell - 1]$, then $Z_1 = 0$ (i.e. $Q_1 = \mathcal{O}$) is only possible when $k = 0$. On the other hand, $Z_2 = 0$ (i.e. $Q_2 = \mathcal{O}$) implies $Q_1 = -P_m$ since $Q_2 = Q_1 + P_m$, which can only occur when $k = \ell - 1$.

So, in summary, when the order of the ladder input P_m is at least ℓ, there remain only two corner cases that require special attention when recovering the Y coordinate at the end of the ladder, namely $k = 0$ and $k = \ell - 1$. As shown in Algorithm 4, our implementation handles these special cases through if-then clauses (line 1 and 2) without actually executing the ladder.

Single Ladder for X25519 and Ed25519. The Montgomery ladder can be used to implement not only EdDSA verification, but also ECDH key exchange as described in [4]. This naturally raises the question whether one and the same ladder implementation can serve both cryptosystems and, in this way, reduce the code size of an ECC library. As already mentioned before, there are some subtle differences between a conventional X25519 ladder (see e.g. [17]) and the ladder we use to compute hA as part of EdDSA verification. In particular, due to the so-called "clamping" of scalars according to [4], the highest "1" bit of an X22519 scalar is always at the same position, which is not guaranteed for the scalar h computed during EdDSA verification (line 1 of Algorithm 2) since it is a hash value reduced modulo ℓ. Furthermore, a ladder for X25519 key exchange has to be resistant to timings attacks, whereas a ladder for EdDSA verification does not. Nonetheless, it is possible to implement a "unified" ladder that suits both X25519 and Ed25519 by adopting one of the following two strategies. The first is to initialize the ladder as usual (i.e. $Q_1 = (x_m : 1)$ and $Q_2 = 2Q_1$), then scan for the most-significant "1" bit in the scalar, and start the iteration of the ladder loop from the next-lower bit. This scanning for the highest "1" bit does not introduce a vulnerability to timing attacks, even when it is implemented in a naive way, since X25519 scalars are always "clamped" as specified in [4]. An alternative way is to initialize the ladder with $Q_1 = (0 : 1)$ and $Q_2 = (x_m : 1)$ to make it work correctly with leading "0" bits in a scalar. More precisely, this initialization allows one to fix the number of ladder iterations for X25519 and Ed25519 to e.g. 256 because the processing of leading "0" bits does not change Q_1 and also not the quotient X_2/Z_2 [13]. We implemented the first method as it enables slightly better performance for EdDSA verification.

Computation of $R = sB - hA$. Besides the variable-base scalar multiplication hA, we also have compute sB, where $s \in [0, \ell - 1]$ is extracted from the signature to be verified and $B \in E_T(\mathbb{F}_p)$ is the generator of the cyclic sub-group specified by the parameter set for EdDSA [8]. This computation is a fixed-base scalar multiplication and can be carried out much faster than the variable-base scalar multiplication hA. Our software implementation executes this fixed-base scalar multiplication via a *fixed-base comb method* [19] with a radix-2^4 signed-digit representation for the scalar s, which means four bits of s are processed at once. The implementation uses a look-up table of eight pre-computed points that are stored in flash memory (and not in RAM) since B is fixed and known a priori. Our implementation of the fixed-base comb method is, in essence, the same as in [26], where a detailed description can be found. After computation of the two points sB and hA, which are obtained in projective coordinates, the latter has to be subtracted from the former. We use the (projective) addition formulae provided in [6] for this subtraction. Finally, the point $R = sB - hA$ is converted to standard affine coordinates and then compressed so that it can be compared with the compressed point contained in the signature.

Thanks to the extended projective coordinates introduced in [20], a mixed point addition (i.e. an addition where one point is given in extended projective coordinates and the other point in extended affine coordinates) costs just seven multiplications (7M) in $\mathbb{F}_p$ [26]. Furthermore, the doubling of a point in extend projective coordinates requires four multiplications (4M) and three squarings (3M). Our fixed-base comb method (with eight pre-computed points) executes $n/4$ point doublings the same number of point additions, where n refers to the bitlength of the scalar. The overall cost of the fixed-base scalar multiplication sB amounts to $(7n + 3n)/4 = 2.5n$ multiplications and $4n/4 = 1n$ squarings in $\mathbb{F}_p$, i.e. 2.5M + 1S per bit of the scalar. Thanks to the Montgomery ladder, the variable-base scalar multiplication hA takes only 5M + 4S per scalar bit [4]. In summary, the overall cost of the separated approach to compute sB and hA is 7.5M + 5S per bit, which is only slightly (i.e. 1M + 1S) worse than the average number of multiplications/squarings for the simultaneous technique. Both the simultaneous technique and the separated method also involve two inversions in $\mathbb{F}_p$, one at the beginning and one at the end of the scalar multiplications.

3.3   Compatibility with Other ECC Libraries

The initial Ed25519 specification from [8,9] does not mandate much validation of input data and is also relatively vague when it comes to dealing with certain "corner cases." In particular, Ed25519 as specified in [8,9] does not validate the signer's public key A; it does not even carry out a *partial* public-key validation (by checking $cA \neq \mathcal{O}$ [1], where c is the cofactor, i.e. $c = \#E(\mathbb{F}_p)/\ell$) to ensure that A does not have low order. However, due to the lack of key validation, the Ed25519 signature scheme can not guarantee non-repudiation or resilience to key-substitution attacks (see [11, Sect. A] for an example). Another problem is the omission of clear guidance on how to handle corner cases, which has led to a number of Ed25519 variants, as well as inconsistencies and incompatibilities between implementations. As analyzed in e.g. [11,16], existing implementations of variants or tweaks of Ed25519 differ with respect to the following aspects.

- whether a non-canonically encoded scalar s is accepted as valid input,
- whether non-canonically encoded points A, R are accepted as valid input,
- whether the points A, R are allowed to have low order,
- whether the verification procedure uses the cofactored ("batched") equation $8R = 8(sB - hA)$ or the more strict cofactorless equation $R = sB - hA$.

The specific way how an Ed25519 implementation deals with corner cases does not affect the verification of honestly-generated signatures, but can cause divergence when the signer (or an attacker) crafts a signature so that it is accepted by some implementations and rejected by others. This is especially problematic when an Ed25519 signature is verified by many entities seeking for a consensus (e.g. contract signing, electronic voting, blockchain transactions [11]).

Our software is compatible with the widely-used LibSodium library (version 1.0.16 or newer), which means it rejects an alleged signature when s, A or R is non-canonically encoded, or when A or R has low order. Any alleged signature passing these input checks is then verified using the cofactorless equation.

4   Experimental Results

The target platform of our performance assessment of the two implementation options for EdDSA verification described in the last section is the well-known and widely-used 16-bit MSP430 architecture from Texas Instruments. MSP430 microcontrollers were designed for extremely low power dissipation; this covers not only the active processing power, but also standby and memory read/write power, respectively [14]. Regarding the latter it should be noted that MSP430 devices were among the first to be equipped with Ferro-electric Random Access Memory (FRAM), which has similar attributes like SRAM (e.g. fast read and write operations, low power dissipation, high reliability and endurance), but is non-volatile, like EEPROM or flash memory, and can hold data even after it is powered off. This feature makes it relatively easy to switch from active mode to standby or sleep mode, thereby enabling energy savings even for short periods of inactivity, since data can simply remain in FRAM. For these reasons, Texas Instruments markets the MSP430 family as "ultra-low-power" microcontrollers to emphasize their suitability for the Internet of Things (IoT) [14].

The MSP430 uses the von-Neumann memory model, which means code and data share a unified address space, and there is a single address bus and single data bus that connects the CPU core with RAM, flash/ROM, and peripheral modules. Twelve out of a total of 16 registers (each 16 bits wide) are available for general use; the remaining four serve a special purpose. The MSP430 architecture has a reduced instruction set consisting of 27 core instructions that can be split into three categories: double-operand instructions (which overwrite one of the operands with the result), single-operand instructions, and jumps. This minimalist instruction set is orthogonal and supports seven addressing modes altogether, including modes for direct memory-to-memory transfers without an intermediate register holding [38]. The used addressing mode(s) determine the latency of double-operand instructions, which can vary between one clock cycle (when both source and destination operand are held in registers) and six clock cycles (operands are in RAM or in flash). Some MSP430 models, including the MSP430F1611 we use for our benchmarking, have a memory-mapped hardware multiplier capable to carry out (16×16)-bit multiply and multiply-accumulate operations [38]. Since this multiplier is a memory-mapped peripheral, it has to be accessed by writing the two operands to specific locations in memory. The MSP430F1611 is equipped with 10 kB RAM and 48 kB flash.

Our implementation of the field-arithmetic operations is a slightly modified and improved version of the ECC software for MSP430(X) devices introduced in [24]. This library is written in Assembly language and provides all low-level operations needed to perform point addition and doubling on Montgomery and TE curves, respectively. Since our target device is a 16-bit microcontroller, the elements of $\mathbb{F}_p$ are represented as arrays of (unsigned) 16-bit words, i.e. arrays of type uint16_t. Except for inversion, the arithmetic functions do not execute operand-dependent conditional jumps or branches (i.e. their execution time is constant), which contributes to preventing timing attacks against the signature generation. Although the verification of an EdDSA signature does not involve

Table 1. Execution time and binary code size of 255-bit field-arithmetic operations on an MSP430F1611 microcontroller.

Operation	Exec. time (cycles)	Code size (bytes)
Addition	322	100
Subtraction	332	140
Multiplication (incl. red.)	5388	352
Squaring (incl. red.)	3826	388
Mul. by 32-bit constant	1040	240
Inversion (incl. masking)	197102	942

any secret information, it still makes sense to use a constant-time $\mathbb{F}_p$-arithmetic library since it can be shared between the signature generation and verification functions. The $\mathbb{F}_p$-inversion of our library is based on the Extended Euclidean Algorithm (EEA), but uses a "multiplicative masking" technique to randomize the execution time and thwart timing attacks (see [24] for details).

Table 1 specifies the execution time (including function-call overhead) and code size of the most important operations of our $\mathbb{F}_p$-arithmetic library on an MSP430F161 microcontroller. These timings are slightly better than the ones reported in [24], which is due to a couple of further Assembly optimizations we added to the source code. The code size of the full library for $\mathbb{F}_p$-arithmetic is just slightly more than 2.2 kB, which is very small compared to other MSP430 implementations, e.g. [2,18,23,27,32,33]. This small code size became possible because our arithmetic library is not purely optimized for high performance (as most other libraries) but aims for a trade-off between size and speed.

Table 2. Execution time, RAM footprint, and binary code size (excluding the field arithmetic) of point-arithmetic operations on an MSP430F1611 microcontroller.

Operation	Exec. time (cycles)	RAM footpr. (bytes)	Code size (bytes)
Point addition (TE curve)	39718	72	272
Point doubling (TE curve)	33451	68	268
Point addition (Mon curve)	25811	132	220
Point doubling (Mon curve)	20776	128	184
Recovery Y coord. (Mon curve)	56117	96	302
Conversion Mon to TE	22519	124	116
Conversion TE to Mon	22521	124	112

Table 2 summarizes the execution time, RAM footprint, and (binary) code size of some point-arithmetic operations. Point addition and point doubling on

Table 3. Execution time, RAM footprint, and binary code size of scalar multiplication and full EdDSA verification on an MSP430F1611 microcontroller.

Operation	Exec. time (cycles)	RAM footpr. (bytes)	Code size (bytes)
Table pre-computation (TE curve)	261926	612	288
Double-scalar mul. (TE curve)	14126254	878	674 + 2230
EdDSA verification (simultaneous)	14206712	980	6143
Fixed-base scalar mul. (TE curve)	4682599	596	602 + 2230
Variable-base scalar mul. (Mon curve)	12138929	478	1356 + 2230
EdDSA verification (separated)	17516534	596	7850

a Montgomery curve is significantly faster than on a TE curve, which is little surprising since the projective point arithmetic on the former involves only the X and Z coordinate. The recovery of the projective Y coordinate is a bit more costly, but this operation is performed only once. The results for the code size in the right column cover only the size of the function itself and do not include sub-functions like the field-arithmetic operations (this makes sense because the field arithmetic is shared across all higher-level operations).

Finally, Table 3 compares the execution time, RAM footprint, and code size of the simultaneous method and the separated technique for double-scalar multiplication and full EdDSA signature verification, respectively. As expected, the separated technique is slower than the simultaneous method, but the difference (with respect to overall verification time) is relatively small, namely about 3.3 million clock cycles, which is approximately 24% of the verification time of the simultaneous method. On the other hand, the simultaneous method consumes almost 1 kB RAM, which is 394 bytes more than the amount of RAM needed for the separated technique. This significant difference can be explained by the fact that the separated method (i) does not need to store table with four precomputed points in RAM, and (ii) also does not occupy RAM for storing the JSF representation of two scalars. The execution time of EdDSA verification is mainly dominated by the double-base scalar multiplication, which contributes more than 98% to the overall execution time when the message to be verified is small. The execution times for the entire EdDSA verification listed in Table 3 were determined with a message of a length of only a few bytes, which means the compression function of the SHA-512 hash function was executed only once to obtain the 512-bit digest. Our assembler implementation of the compression function has an execution time of about 38500 clock cycles, which is negligible compared to the double-scalar multiplication.

5   Conclusions

All major elliptic-curve signature schemes have in common that the verification of a signature requires much more computation time than its generation.

Even worse, most existing implementation results reported in the literature indicate that verifying an EdDSA signature consumes significantly more RAM than the signing operation, which poses a serious problem for resource-restricted devices like sensor nodes that often have only a few kilobytes of RAM. The enormous computational cost and large RAM footprint of the verification is mainly due to the double-scalar multiplication $R = sB - hA$, which is normally implemented using the simultaneous method with joint doublings. In this paper we proposed an alternative approach that splits the computation of $sB - hA$ up into two separate operations: a fixed-base scalar multiplication sB and a variable-base scalar multiplication hA. By exploiting the birational equivalence between the twisted Edwards model and the Montgomery model, we compute the variable-base scalar multiplication with the fast Montgomery ladder. Our experiments show that, on a 16-bit MSP430F1611 microcontroller, the separated method is only 24% slower than the simultaneous method, but consumes about 40% less RAM, mainly because it does not need to store a table of precomputed points and also does not require a JSF-representation of the scalars. This makes the separated approach an attractive alternative to the simultaneous technique whenever RAM is a scarce resource.

Acknowledgements. Zhe Liu is supported by the National Key R&D Program of China (Grant No. 2020AAA0107703), the National Natural Science Foundation of China (Grants No. 62132008, 61802180), the Natural Science Foundation of Jiangsu Province (Grant No. BK20180421), and the National Cryptography Development Fund (Grant No. MMJJ20180105).

References

1. Antipa, A., Brown, D., Menezes, A., Struik, R., Vanstone, S.: Validation of elliptic curve public keys. In: Desmedt, Y.G. (ed.) PKC 2003. LNCS, vol. 2567, pp. 211–223. Springer, Heidelberg (2003). https://doi.org/10.1007/3-540-36288-6_16
2. Ateniese, G., Bianchi, G., Capossele, A.T., Petrioli, C.: Low-cost standard signatures in wireless sensor networks: a case for reviving pre-computation techniques? In: Proceedings of the 20th Annual Network and Distributed System Security Symposium (NDSS 2013). The Internet Society (2013)
3. Bauer, J., Staudemeyer, R.C., Pöhls, H.C., Fragkiadakis, A.: ECDSA on things: IoT integrity protection in practise. In: Lam, K.-Y., Chi, C.-H., Qing, S. (eds.) ICICS 2016. LNCS, vol. 9977, pp. 3–17. Springer, Cham (2016). https://doi.org/10.1007/978-3-319-50011-9_1
4. Bernstein, D.J.: Curve25519: new Diffie-Hellman speed records. In: Yung, M., Dodis, Y., Kiayias, A., Malkin, T. (eds.) PKC 2006. LNCS, vol. 3958, pp. 207–228. Springer, Heidelberg (2006). https://doi.org/10.1007/11745853_14
5. Bernstein, D.J.: Multi-user Schnorr security, revisited. Cryptology ePrint Archive, Report 2015/996 (2015). http://eprint.iacr.org/2015/996
6. Bernstein, D.J., Birkner, P., Joye, M., Lange, T., Peters, C.: Twisted Edwards curves. In: Vaudenay, S. (ed.) AFRICACRYPT 2008. LNCS, vol. 5023, pp. 389–405. Springer, Heidelberg (2008). https://doi.org/10.1007/978-3-540-68164-9_26

7. Bernstein, D.J., Chuengsatiansup, C., Lange, T.: Double-base scalar multiplication revisited. Cryptology ePrint Archive, Report 2017/037 (2017). http://eprint.iacr.org/2017/037

8. Bernstein, D.J., Duif, N., Lange, T., Schwabe, P., Yang, B.-Y.: High-speed high-security signatures. In: Preneel, B., Takagi, T. (eds.) CHES 2011. LNCS, vol. 6917, pp. 124–142. Springer, Heidelberg (2011). https://doi.org/10.1007/978-3-642-23951-9_9

9. Bernstein, D.J., Duif, N., Lange, T., Schwabe, P., Yang, B.Y.: High-speed high-security signatures. J. Cryptogr. Eng. 2(2), 77–89 (2012)

10. Bundesamt für Sicherheit in der Informationstechnik (BSI): Elliptic Curve Cryptography. Technical Guideline TR-03111 (2012). http://www.bsi.bund.de/SharedDocs/Downloads/EN/BSI/Publications/TechGuidelines/TR03111/BSI-TR-03111_pdf.html

11. Chalkias, K., Garillot, F., Nikolaenko, V.: Taming the many EdDSAs. In: van der Merwe, T., Mitchell, C., Mehrnezhad, M. (eds.) SSR 2020. LNCS, vol. 12529, pp. 67–90. Springer, Cham (2020). https://doi.org/10.1007/978-3-030-64357-7_4

12. Cohen, H., Frey, G.: Handbook of Elliptic and Hyperelliptic Curve Cryptography, Discrete Mathematics and Its Applications, vol. 34. Chapmann & Hall/CRC, Sydney (2006)

13. Costello, C., Smith, B.: Montgomery curves and their arithmetic. J. Cryptogr. Eng. 8(3), 227–240 (2017). https://doi.org/10.1007/s13389-017-0157-6

14. Dang, D., Plant, M., Poole, M.: Wireless connectivity for the Internet of Things (IoT) with MSP430 microcontrollers (MCUs). Texas Instruments white paper, March 2014. http://www.ti.com/lit/wp/slay028/slay028.pdf

15. de Meulenaer, G., Gosset, F., Standaert, F.X., Pereira, O.: On the energy cost of communication and cryptography in wireless sensor networks. In: Proceedings of the 4th IEEE International Conference on Wireless and Mobile Computing, Networking and Communications (WIMOB 2008), pp. 580–585. IEEE Computer Society Press (2008)

16. de Valence, H.: It's 255:19AM. Do you know what your validation criteria are? Blog post (2020). http://hdevalence.ca/blog/2020-10-04-its-25519am

17. Düll, M., et al.: High-speed Curve25519 on 8-bit, 16-bit and 32-bit microcontrollers. Des. Codes Crypt. 77(2–3), 493–514 (2015)

18. Gouvêa, C.P., Oliveira, L.B., López, J.: Efficient software implementation of public-key cryptography on sensor networks using the MSP430X microcontroller. J. Cryptogr. Eng. 2(1), 19–29 (2012)

19. Hankerson, D.R., Menezes, A.J., Vanstone, S.A.: Guide to Elliptic Curve Cryptography. Springer, New York (2004). https://doi.org/10.1007/b97644

20. Hisil, H., Wong, K.K.-H., Carter, G., Dawson, E.: Twisted Edwards curves revisited. In: Pieprzyk, J. (ed.) ASIACRYPT 2008. LNCS, vol. 5350, pp. 326–343. Springer, Heidelberg (2008). https://doi.org/10.1007/978-3-540-89255-7_20

21. Josefsson, S., Liusvaara, I.: Edwards-Curve Digital Signature Algorithm (EdDSA). Internet Research Task Force, Crypto Forum Research Group, RFC 8032, January 2017

22. Kiltz, E., Masny, D., Pan, J.: Optimal security proofs for signatures from identification schemes. In: Robshaw, M., Katz, J. (eds.) CRYPTO 2016. LNCS, vol. 9815, pp. 33–61. Springer, Heidelberg (2016). https://doi.org/10.1007/978-3-662-53008-5_2

23. Liu, A., Ning, P.: TinyECC: a configurable library for elliptic curve cryptography in wireless sensor networks. In: Proceedings of the 7th International Conference on Information Processing in Sensor Networks (IPSN 2008), pp. 245–256. IEEE Computer Society Press (2008)

24. Liu, Z., Großschädl, J., Li, L., Xu, Q.: Energy-efficient elliptic curve cryptography for MSP430-based wireless sensor nodes. In: Liu, J.K., Steinfeld, R. (eds.) ACISP 2016. LNCS, vol. 9722, pp. 94–112. Springer, Cham (2016). https://doi.org/10. 1007/978-3-319-40253-6_6

25. Liu, Z., Longa, P., Pereira, G.C.C.F., Reparaz, O., Seo, H.: FourQ on embedded devices with strong countermeasures against side-channel attacks. In: Fischer, W., Homma, N. (eds.) CHES 2017. LNCS, vol. 10529, pp. 665–686. Springer, Cham (2017). https://doi.org/10.1007/978-3-319-66787-4_32

26. Liu, Z., Wenger, E., Großschädl, J.: MoTE-ECC: energy-scalable elliptic curve cryptography for wireless sensor networks. In: Boureanu, I., Owesarski, P., Vaudenay, S. (eds.) ACNS 2014. LNCS, vol. 8479, pp. 361–379. Springer, Cham (2014). https://doi.org/10.1007/978-3-319-07536-5_22

27. Marín, L., Pawlowski, M.P., Jara, A.J.: Optimized ECC implementation for secure communication between heterogeneous IoT devices. Sensors 15(9), 21478–21499 (2015)

28. Möller, B.: Algorithms for multi-exponentiation. In: Vaudenay, S., Youssef, A.M. (eds.) SAC 2001. LNCS, vol. 2259, pp. 165–180. Springer, Heidelberg (2001). https://doi.org/10.1007/3-540-45537-X_13

29. Montgomery, P.L.: Speeding the Pollard and elliptic curve methods of factorization. Math. Comput. 48(177), 243–264 (1987)

30. National Institute of Standards and Technology (NIST): Digital Signature Standard (DSS). FIPS Publication 186-4, July 2013. http://nvlpubs.nist.gov/nistpubs/FIPS/NIST.FIPS.186-4.pdf

31. Okeya, K., Sakurai, K.: Efficient elliptic curve cryptosystems from a scalar multiplication algorithm with recovery of the y-coordinate on a montgomery-form elliptic curve. In: Koç, Ç.K., Naccache, D., Paar, C. (eds.) CHES 2001. LNCS, vol. 2162, pp. 126–141. Springer, Heidelberg (2001). https://doi.org/10.1007/3-540-44709-1_12

32. Pabbuleti, K., Mane, D., Schaumont, P.: Energy budget analysis for signature protocols on a self-powered wireless sensor node. In: Saxena, N., Sadeghi, A.-R. (eds.) RFIDSec 2014. LNCS, vol. 8651, pp. 123–136. Springer, Cham (2014). https://doi.org/10.1007/978-3-319-13066-8_8

33. Pendl, C., Pelnar, M., Hutter, M.: Elliptic curve cryptography on the WISP UHF RFID tag. In: Juels, A., Paar, C. (eds.) RFIDSec 2011. LNCS, vol. 7055, pp. 32–47. Springer, Heidelberg (2012). https://doi.org/10.1007/978-3-642-25286-0_3

34. Rescorla, E.K.: The Transport Layer Security (TLS) Protocol Version 1.3. Internet Engineering Task Force, Network Working Group, RFC 8446, August 2018

35. Rivest, R.L., Shamir, A., Adleman, L.M.: A method for obtaining digital signatures and public key cryptosystems. Commun. ACM 21(2), 120–126 (1978)

36. Schnorr, C.P.: Efficient identification and signatures for smart cards. In: Brassard, G. (ed.) CRYPTO 1989. LNCS, vol. 435, pp. 239–252. Springer, New York (1990). https://doi.org/10.1007/0-387-34805-0_22

37. Solinas, J.A.: Low-weight binary representations for pairs of integers. Technical report, CORR 2001-41, Centre for Applied Cryptographic Research (CACR), University of Waterloo, Waterloo, Canada (2001)

38. Texas Instruments Inc: MSP430x1xx Family User's Guide (Rev. F). Manual, February 2006. http://www.ti.com/lit/ug/slau049f/slau049f.pdf

A Dummy Location Selection Algorithm Based on Location Semantics and Physical Distance

Dongdong Yang[1,2], Baopeng Ye[3], Yuling Chen[1,2(✉)], Huiyu Zhou[4],
and Xiaobin Qian[5]

[1] State Key Laboratory of Public Big Data, College of Computer Science
and Technology, Guizhou University, Guiyang, China
ylchen3@gzu.edu.cn
[2] Guangxi Key Laboratory of Cryptography and Information Security,
Guilin University of Electronic Technology, Guilin, China
[3] Information Technology Innovation Service Center of Guizhou Province,
Guiyang, China
[4] School of Informatics, University of Leicester, Leicester, UK
[5] Guizhou CoVision Science and Technology Co., Ltd., Guiyang, China

Abstract. With the development of smart devices and mobile positioning technologies, location-based services (LBS) has become more and more popular. While enjoying the convenience and entertainments provided by LBS, users are vulnerable to the increased privacy leakages of locations as another kind of quasidentifiers. Most existing location privacy preservation algorithms are based on region cloaking which blurs the exact position into a region, and hence prone to inaccuracies of query results. Dummy-based approaches for location privacy preservation proposed recently overcome the above problem, but did not consider the problem of location semantic homogeneity, query probability and physical dispersion of locations simultaneously. In this paper, we propose a dummy location selection algorithm based on location semantics and physical distance ($SPDDS$) that takes into account both side information, semantic diversity and physical dispersion of locations. $SPDDS$ solves a simplified problem of single objective optimization by uniting the three objectives (location semantic diversity, query probability and physical dispersion of locations) together. The efficiency and effectiveness of the proposed algorithms have been validated by a set of carefully designed experiments. The experimental results also show that our algorithms significantly improve the privacy level, compared to other dummy-based solutions.

Keywords: Location privacy · Dummy selection · Semantic diversity · Query probability · Physical dispersion

© Springer Nature Switzerland AG 2021
R. Deng et al. (Eds.): ISPEC 2021, LNCS 13107, pp. 283–295, 2021.
https://doi.org/10.1007/978-3-030-93206-0_17

1 Introduction

With the rapid developments of positioning capabilities and the widespread use of wireless networks technology, the location-based service (LBS) has come into our daily life. More and more location-based applications have emerged providing various services for people's work and daily life needs. For example, visitors can send Point of Interest query to the LBS servers. Game players can share their game positions and scores with others nearby.

However, despite the great convenience supplied by LBS, it introduces serious challenges of personal privacy. When a user sends a query to the LBS servers, the untrusted servers may collect the users' personal details surreptitiously including location information and queried interests. Then the untrusted servers can track the user or release the user's personal information to others, which may cause potential damage to the user. Thus, we need to take appropriate measures to protect users' location privacy.

Many approaches have been taken to address such privacy problems, where the $k-$anonymity (e.g. [1,8]) and location obfuscation are commonly used. The $k-$anonymity model, which has been widely used in data privacy preservation, makes the target user's information indistinguishable from that of at least $k-1$ other users, so that the probability of location leakage is therefore at most $\frac{1}{k}$. The location obfuscation is to blur the user's exact location into a cloaked region, so that adversaries cannot figure out the accurate location of the target user. In fact, the location obfuscation and $k-$anonymity are often combined together to generate a region which contains k users including the target user. However, there are some limitations in the privacy protection model above. First, it mostly relys on a trusted proxy, called Anonymizer, to anonymize the user's accurate location into a cloaked region when issued a query and refine the result according to the exact user information finally. Once the Anonymizer is attacked by the adversary, the privacy of all users would leak out. Second, it is difficult to balance the service availability with location privacy. If the size of cloaked region is too big, it will impair the Quality of Service (QoS), otherwise it will cause location leakage.

Thus the another representative approach for location privacy protection is to deploy dummy but exact locations instead of cloaking regions which probably provides more precise and effective service. If $k-1$ dummy locations have been selected based on certain algorithms for every query, then we say that it also follows the $k-$anonymity model. But how to select $k-1$ appropriate locations is still a challenge. For example, if these dummy locations are all too close to the true location, the adversary can infer that the user probably is in this small region. Besides, if location query probability distribution in the result set is not uniform, the adversary can easily filter out some locations with low probability such as lake, volcano and the likes. Finally, it is possible that the whole street or area making the same business with the popularity of industrial congregation. A lot of times 'where are you stay' exposes the privacy of 'what are you doing'. To an extreme case, the adversary infers what the user is doing with a big chance when all locations including dummies and the real one are of the same type.

Some algorithms have noticed one or two of the three phenomena above and put forward some selection strategies for generating dummy locations. But none have consider the problem of location semantic homogeneity, query probability and location physical dispersion simultaneously. Actually, through the analysis above, we know that all the three factors mater when generating dummy locations. Consequently, dummy-based schemes should consider these three factors simultaneously, otherwise some of the user's privacy may be leaked.

Therefore, we propose a dummy selection mechanism considering both semantic diversity, physical dispersion and query probability to make the query probability of locations in the result set as close as possible while locations spread as far as possible both semantically and physically. The major contributions of this paper are as follows:

(1) To protect users' location privacy against adversary with additional context information, we propose a new dummy selection algorithms called $SPDDS$ that takes into account both location semantic diversity, physical dispersion and query probability.

(2) We conduct a set of simulation experiments based on a WiFi access point to evaluate the performance of our algorithm. Experimental results show that our algorithm is efficient when the adversary has additional context information such as map information and side information in comparison with other dummy-based algorithms.

The rest of the paper is organized as follows. We discuss the related work in Sect. 2. Section 3 presents some preliminaries of this paper. We present the $SPDDS$ algorithm in Sect. 4. Section 5 shows the evaluation results. We conclude the paper in Sect. 6.

2   Related Work

Location privacy preservation as a popular problem has been well studied in the literature. In this section, we review major existing techniques for preventing location privacy leakage including spatial obfuscation and deployment of location dummies in Sects. 2.1 to 2.2, respectively.

2.1   Spatial Obfuscation

Spatial obfuscation is the most commonly location privacy approaches and its fundamental principle is to blur an exact position into a cloaked region so that the adversary can not find out the accurate location of the target user, thereby unable to infer the information of the target user. It is often used together with $k-$anonymity model, making that the cloaked region is sharing with at least k users [7]. Gedik et al. [7] proposed a personalized $k-$anonymity algorithm called Clique-Cloak in which it transformed the problem of finding the cloaking user set into Maximum Clique Problem (MCP) and allowed users to adjust their level of anonymity as needed. Mokbel et al. [12] proposed a Quad-tree-like algorithm to making region cloaking. Ghinita et al. [9] employed the Hibert curve to approximate the spatial proximity between queries. Bamba et al. [2] applied both $k-$anonymity and $l-$diversity algorithms while making region cloaking.

Spatial obfuscation might still lead to privacy issues when the user sends continuous location queries along his/her way. An experienced adversary (e.g. the Service Provider) which enables to collect user's historical cloaked regions and some side information like the user's mobility patterns (e.g. speed limit) can link these cloaked regions and infer the user's location privacy [17]. Cheng et al. [5] presented two approaches, namely patching and delaying respectively, to prevent the user's location from being deduced. Then Xu and Cai [18] proposed a novel technique to deal with this problem within polynomial time complexity. Pan et al. [15] proposed a new incremental clique-based cloaking algorithm, called IClique- Cloak, to defend against such attacks. It extended the edge of current cloaked region so that the last cloaked region can be fully covered by the new maximum arrival boundary (MAB). Taking a region for an exact position, spatial obfuscation hides the exact position of the user ensuring privacy preservation, but impairs the quality-of-service (QoS) of each query.

2.2 Location Dummies

Location dummies are aimed to secure users' accurate location by sending $k-1$ false locations ("dummies") together with the true location so that the probability of location leakage is reduced to $\frac{1}{k}$. Compared to the spatial obfuscation, this approach sends exact positions instead of cloaked regions to a Service Provider, which can return a more precise query result. However, the crux of this problem is how to deploy dummies which cannot be distinguished from the true location.

Kido et al. [10] first put forward a dummy selection algorithm in consideration of ubiquity and congestion, but the algorithm did not consider factors such as query probability. Subsequently, although Zhao Dapeng et al. [6] proposed the ABR algorithm based on query probability, which is lack of considering the physical dispersion and location semantic diversity. The $UPHIF$ algorithm proposed by Li Chang et al. [3] protected location privacy to a certain extent, but did not consider the location semantic diversity. Niu et al. [13] selected dummy locations based on entropy metrics, and proposed a dummy location selection (DLS) algorithm and its improved algorithm ($enhanced-DLS$). Although the $enhanced-DLS$ scheme consider both query probability and physical dispersion but lacking of considering the location semantic diversity. Although [4,19] fully considered the location semantic diversity and physical dispersion, but they did not consider the query probability.

3   Preliminaries

We first introduce some relative definitions used in this paper, and then introduce the system architecture based on WiFi Access Points (APs).

3.1   Relative Definitions of Location Privacy Protection Algorithm

Definition 1. According to [4], location semantic tree (LST), a tree structure used to represent the semantic relations between two locations within the range of a Wi-Fi Access Points (Wi-Fi AP), which satisfies the following requirements:

a) each non-leaf node stands for the category of its children nodes and each leaf node for a real location l.
b) the depth of LST, denoted as h, is equal to the maximum number of layers of categories plus 1.
c) the semantic distance $d_{sem}(l_i, l_j)$ $(i \neq j)$ is the number of hops from leaf node n_i to leaf node n_j.

Definition 2. User's privacy requirements S, represented by two-tuple (k, u) that has the following meanings:

a) k denotes the anonymous degree of our location privacy preservation model. More specifically, each query is sent with at least $k - 1$ dummy locations and its offset location (we use offset location instead of the real location), making that the probability of offset location leakage is therefore $\frac{1}{k}$.
b) u represents the minimum acceptable value of semantic distance between two locations in dummy location set (DLS). In other words, it satisfies the inequality:

$$\min [d_{sem}(l_i, l_j)] \geq u \tag{1}$$

Definition 3. Location map distance. If we let Map_{cur} represent the map information within the range of the current Wi-Fi AP. For any two locations l_i, l_j $(i \neq j)$, the location map distance is the physical distance between the two locations on Map_{cur}, the value of which ranges from tens of meters to hundreds.

Definition 4. Location query probability (LQP). As shown in Fig. 1, in a map divided into $m \times m$ cells with equal size. Each cell has a query probability based on the previous query history, which is denoted as

$$p_i = \frac{number\ of\ queries\ in\ cell\ i}{number\ of\ queries\ in\ whole\ map} \tag{2}$$

Where $i = 1, 2, \cdots, m^2$, $\sum_{i=1}^{m^2} p_i = 1$. The depth of the color in the figure indicates LQP (the darker the color, the greater the LQP), and the white area indicates that the location has never had a location service request, so these locations may be rivers, barren mountains and other places that are easily filtered by the adversary.

For any two locations $l_i, l_j (i \neq j)$, location query probability distance, denoted as $d_{que}(l_i, l_j)$, is the difference between query probability of two locations.

Definition 5. Location physical dispersion (PD), which has been used to measure the effectiveness of the algorithm against location homogeneity attacks, is

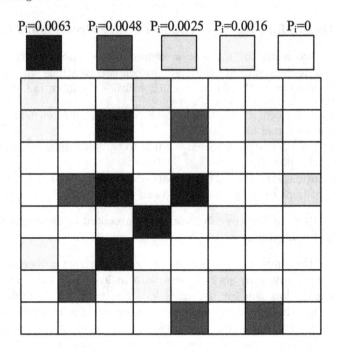

Fig. 1. Location query probability diagram

obtained by computing the minimum physical distance between any two locations in a DLS. The specific process is shown in (4):

$$PD = Min\left[d_{phy}\left(l_i, l_j\right)\right] \tag{3}$$

Where $i, j = 1, 2, \cdots, k, i \neq j$. The greater the minimum distance between any two locations in the DLS, the greater the PD and the greater the coverage of the DLS, the better the algorithm's resistance to location homogeneity attacks.

Definition 6. θ−Secure Set of Dummy Locations. Dummy location set (DLS) consisting of $k - 1$ dummy locations and the offset location, where the semantic distance between l_i and l_j satisfies:

$$1 - \frac{|SEM|}{C_k^2} \geq \theta \tag{4}$$

where $SEM = \{d_{sem} \,|\, d_{sem}\left(l_i, l_j\right) < u\}$, $k = |DLS|$ and C_k^2 is a combination formulas, we call DLS a $\theta-$ secure set. We use θ as a privacy protection index of location semantics in our experimental analysis in Sect. 5. Our aim is to achieve the maximum θ, i.e. to make it equal to 1, such that two locations in DLS belong to different categories.

Definition 7. Entropy (H). We use H to measure the query probability between two locations in DLS, which is defined as:

$$H = -\sum_{i=1}^{k} p_i \cdot \log_2 p_i \tag{5}$$

where p_i is the query probability of each location in the DLS, and $\sum_{i=1}^{k} p_i = 1$. The more similar the query probability between two locations in DLS are, the greater the H. The maximum entropy is achieved when all the k possible locations have the same probability $\frac{1}{k}$, where the maximum entropy will be $H_{\max} = \log_2 k$.

3.2 System Structure

The system architecture in our paper is shown in Fig. 2. We implement our idea by using WiFi Access Points (APs), which has been widely used in mobile environments [11,13,14,16]. As one of the most widely used wireless communication technologies, WiFi technology has getting more and more focus. Governments have started offering ubiquitous WiFi for public use which has much stronger signal, larger covered range and more computing power and storage compared to the home WiFi. In our architecture, APs not only offer the network support but also provide data for selecting dummy location by saving and maintaining the local location semantic tree.

In our approach, the WiFi APs collect the location semantic information within its radio range and save it as a location semantic tree. Since the utilities of a location is not often change, the local location semantic tree in an AP is relative stable and not update frequently and hence put little impact on the function of AP. Before forwarding a query, the mobile user first requests the local location semantic tree from the WiFi AP which he is connecting with and then selects $k-1$ dummy locations meeting its own privacy requirements according to the dummy selection mechanism. Next, the user sends its queries with the real location as well as the dummies to the Service Provider. Then the Service Provider returns a candidate results based on the locations sent by the mobile user. And the user refines the result and get the target one of current query.

4 The Algorithm

Based on the analysis above, the final dummy location set not only needs to make locations in the result set spread as far as possible both semantically and physically but also to make ones query probability as close as possible. In other words, the final dummy location set needs to simultaneously satisfy (6), (7) and (8):

$$DLS = \arg\min \left\{ \max [d_{que}(l_i, l_j)] \right\} \tag{6}$$

$$DLS = \arg\max \left\{ \min [d_{sem}(l_i, l_j)] \right\} \tag{7}$$

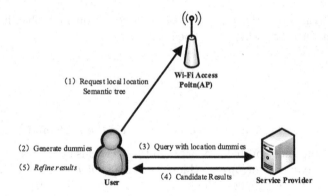

Fig. 2. System structure

$$DLS = \arg\max\{\min[d_{phy}(l_i, l_j)]\} \tag{8}$$

Where $l_i, l_j \in DLS, i \neq j$. It can be formulated as a Multi-Objective Optimization Problem (MOP) since three factors are considered simultaneously. However, we put forward a simpler objective formulae considering the complexity of MOP. In each dummy location set we would like to make sure that (9) can be satisfied. Consequently, we propose a dummy location selection algorithm based on location semantics and physical distance ($SPDDS$).

$$DLS = \arg\max\left\{\frac{\min[d_{sem}(l_i, l_j) + r \cdot d_{phy}(l_i, l_j)]}{\max[d_{que}(l_i, l_j) + 1]}\right\} \tag{9}$$

Where $l_i, l_j \in DLS, i \neq j$. $d_{que}(l_i, l_j) + 1$ is to avoid the situation where the two locations have the same probability, that is, the difference between the query probability of the two locations is 0. Here r is a controllable factor for balancing the share of semantic distance, physical distance and query probability distance since $d_{sem}(l_i, l_j) \leq 2 \cdot (h - 1)$, where h is the depth of LST, and hence is usually less than 10 while $d_{phy}(l_i, l_j)$, as Wi-Fi transmission distance, ranges from hundreds of meters to thousands, whereas the query probability distance is always less than 1. Consequently, we set $r = 0.03$.

The main purpose of this algorithm is to generate a set of dummy locations, in which the query probability of locations as close as possible while locations spread as far as possible both semantically and physically. Generally speaking, our $SPDDS$ algorithm needs to search a big database to find an optimal set of dummy locations, in which all locations satisfy (9). Given a user's privacy requirement S, besides the real location, we need to determine the other k-1 cells to assign the dummy locations. The following shows how the $SPDDS$ algorithm addresses this problem.

(1) As the first step, a particular user needs to determine a proper privacy requirement S, where the degree of anonymity k is closely related to the user's location privacy and the system overhead. Specifically, a bigger k

leads to higher degree of anonymity but also higher overhead due to the cost incurred by the selected dummy locations.

(2) Formula (9) is satisfied when any two locations in the submitted k locations both have the smallest location query probability distance $d_{que}(.)$, the biggest location map distance $d_{phy}(.)$ and location semantic distance $d_{sem}(.)$. At the beginning of our $SPDDS$ algorithm, the user divides the Map_{cur} as the sample space into $m \times m$ grids and generates a dummy location candidate set $(DLCS)$ for all $p_i > 0$ locations in the whole grid space. Next, the user generates semantic distance matric $(\boldsymbol{SDM})$ according to the LST, geographic distance matrix $(\boldsymbol{GDM})$ according to the Map_{cur} and probability distance matric $(\boldsymbol{PDM})$ according to the LQP respectively. And then the user filters out such locations in $DLCS$ whose semantic distance with newly added locations in DLS are all less than or equal to u according to $\boldsymbol{SDM}$. Later the user chooses $Loc \in DLCS$ as $BestLoc$ in such a way that Loc is chosen with the biggest value of m which is computed by Formula (10) according to $\boldsymbol{SDM}$, $\boldsymbol{GDM}$ and $\boldsymbol{PDM}$.

$$m = \frac{d_{sem}(Loc, DLS.last) + r \cdot [d_{phy}(Loc, DLS.last)]}{d_{que}(Loc, DLS.last)} \tag{10}$$

(3) Finally, a set consisting of the user's real location and $k-1$ dummy locations is generated. Algorithm 1 shows the formal description of the $SPDDS$ algorithm.

5   Experimental Evaluation

In this section, we compare the performance of our proposed $SPDDS$ algorithm with serval existed dummy-based algorithms from three assessment metrics as follows: 1) PD. It means the minimum physical distance of all locations in DLS indicating the level of locations' physical dispersion. The greater PD is, the more dispersed the dummy locations in the DLS. 2) θ. As shown in Definition 6, it refers to the level of semantic diversity in the result set. The greater θ is, the higher level of semantic diversity is. 3) H. As shown in Definition 7, it reflects the query probability distribution in DLS. The greater H is, the more similar the query probability of two locations in DLS is.

5.1   Experimental Setup

Our algorithm is implemented in MATLAB and performed on a Windows 10 PC with an Intel Core i5-8500 CPU, a 3.00 GHz processor and a 8.00 GB main memory. We use a real road map of Guangzhou from Google Maps, since Guangzhou as a provincial capital in southern China is a big city with enough users in LBS and its central urban area has been covered by Wi-Fi APs in 2016. The coverage area of each Wi-Fi AP is about 700–800 m, the sample space is divided into 13×13 cells with equal size, and a total of 13559 sample trajectories are

Algorithm 1. A dummy location selection algorithm based on location semantic and physical distance $(SPDDS)$

Input: l: user's real location; S: user's privacy requirement; Map_{cur}: map information in current Wi-Fi AP; LST: location semantic tree; LQP: location query probability;

Output: DLS: dummy location set;

1: divide the Map_{cur} as the sample space into $m \times m$ grids;
2: generate a dummy location candidate set $(DLCS)$ for all $p_i > 0$ locations in the whole grid space;
3: generate semantic distance matric $(\boldsymbol{SDM})$ according to the LST, geographic distance matrix$(\boldsymbol{GDM})$ according to the Map_{cur} and probability distance matric $(\boldsymbol{PDM})$ according to the LQP respectively;
4: $DLS = \{l\}$;
5: remove l from $DLCS$;
6: **while** $|DLS| < k$ **do**
7:    **if** $DLCS = \phi$ **then**
8:       anonymity failed;
9:    **else**
10:       $max = 0; BestLoc = \phi$;
11:       **for** each Loc in $DLCS$ **do**
12:          **if** $d_{sem}(Loc, DLS.last) \leq u$ **then**
13:             remove Loc from $DLCS$;
14:             **continue;**
15:          **else**
16:             $m = \frac{d_{sem}(Loc,DLS.last)+r \cdot [d_{phy}(Loc,DLS.last)]}{d_{que}(Loc,DLS.last)}$;
17:             compute the maximum value of m according to $\boldsymbol{SDM}, \boldsymbol{GDM}$ and $\boldsymbol{PDM}$, which is recorded with max, and then assign the corresponding Loc to $BestLoc$;
18:          **end if**
19:       **end for**
20:       $DLS = DLS \cup \{BestLoc\}$;
21:       remove $BestLoc$ from $DLCS$;
22:    **end if**
23: **end while**
24: **return** DLS

used as historical data to calculate the historical query probability of each cell. Besides, all locations in our experiments are divided into 6 categories semantically as follows: Education and Science, Administration and Housing, Medical care, Shopping malls, Public places, Catering and Entertainment. The value ranges of the main parameters u and k of the experiment are $3 \leq u \leq 7$ and $2 \leq k \leq 30$ respectively.

5.2   Experimental Results

Figure 3(a) shows the PD comparison chart of $SPDDS$, $MaxMinDistDS$ [4], $SimpMaxMinDistDS$ [4], and $enhanced-DLS$ [13] algorithms. As we can see, the PD of $SPDDS$, $enhanced-DLS$, and $MaxMinDistDS$ are close when $k \leq 4$; at $k \geq 5$, the PD of $MaxMinDistDS$ is slightly larger than that of $SPDDS$ and $enhanced-DLS$. Under the same value of k, the PD of $SPDDS$ and $enhanced-DLS$ is slightly larger than that of $SimpMaxMinDistDS$. In additional, with the increase of k, the PD of the four algorithms are both reduced gradually. The reason for this is obvious: it becomes harder to maintain a high level of dispersion with more and more dummies. In summary, $MaxMinDistDS$ has the largest PD, $SPDDS$, $enhanced-DLS$, and $SimpMaxMinDistDS$ decrease in order, which means that the $MaxMinDistDS$ behaves better in keeping physical dispersion than the other three algorithms, but the $SPDDS$ algorithm is also acceptable.

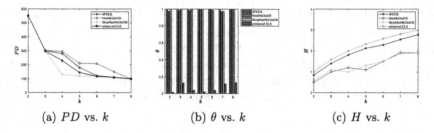

(a) PD vs. k (b) θ vs. k (c) H vs. k

Fig. 3. $SPDDS$'s performance evaluation

In Fig. 3(b), we compare the value of θ between $SPDDS$, $MaxMinDistDS$ [4], $SimpMaxMinDistDS$ [4], and $enhanced-DLS$ [13] algorithms. As shown in the Figure, with the increases of k, the value of θ of $SPDDS$, $MaxMinDistDS$ and $SimpMaxMinDistDS$ algorithms hardly change and close to the maximum value 1. However, that of $enhanced-DLS$ algorithms is always at a relative low. The reason is that the $SPDDS$, $MaxMinDistDS$, and $SimpMaxMinDistDS$ algorithms all consider the semantic information of the location when selecting dummy locations, thereby ensuring semantic diversity, while the $enhanced-DLS$ algorithms only consider the query probability of each location point instead of considering the situation that each location point may have the same semantic information. Moreover, the location points with higher query probability are often in hotspot areas, between which the semantic information is very similar and therefore not satisfying the semantic diversity. Consequently, the $enhanced-DLS$ behaves badly in the semantic diversity. In summary, the $KLPPS$ scheme can effectively resist location similarity attacks.

We compare the value of entropy H between $SPDDS$, $MaxMinDistDS$ [4], $SimpMaxMinDistDS$ [4], and $enhanced-DLS$ [13] algorithms in Fig. 3c. As we can see, H increases with k. Among these algorithms, the $enhanced-$

DLS has the biggest value of H ($\log_2 k$) since all the k locations in DLS have the same probability to be treated as the real user; while the $SPDSS$ is the second since the query probabilities of the k locations in DLS are as close as possible but not the same. Both $MaxMinDistDS$ and $SimpMaxMinDistDS$ are the worst since they only consider location semantic diversity and location physical dispersion instead of location query probability when generating dummy locations. Comparing our $SPDDS$ with $enhanced - DLS$, we can see that the entropy of $enhanced - DLS$ is a little bit better than $SPDDS$, which results from that $SPDDS$ sacrifices some entropy to maximize PD and θ.

6   Conclusion

In this paper, we proposed a dummy location selection algorithm called $SPDDS$. First, we select all locations that satisfy the semantic diversity with the existing locations in the current dummy location set (DLS) as dummy location candidate set ($DLCS$). Second, we select an optimal location in the $DLCS$ as $BestLoc$, which is added in the DLS. Finally, a set consisting of the user's real location and $k-1$ dummy locations is generated, and the query probability of locations in the result set as close as possible while locations spread as far as possible both semantically and physically. A series of experiments have been conducted to evaluate our algorithm and the results show that our proposed algorithm behave well in incorporating map information and compare favorably with the existing methods.

Acknowledgements. This study is supported by Foundation of National Natural Science Foundation of China (Grant Number: 61962009); Major Scientific and Technological Special Project of Guizhou Province (20183001); Science and Technology Support Plan of Guizhou Province ([2020]2Y011); Foundation of Guangxi Key Laboratory of Cryptography and Information Security (GCIS202118).

References

1. Atallah, M.J., Frikken, K.B.: Privacy-preserving location-dependent query processing. In: The IEEE/ACS International Conference on Pervasive Services, 2004. ICPS 2004. Proceedings, pp. 9–17. IEEE (2004)
2. Bamba, B., Liu, L., Pesti, P., Wang, T.: Supporting anonymous location queries in mobile environments with privacygrid. In: Proceedings of the 17th International Conference on World Wide Web, pp. 237–246 (2008)
3. Chang, L., Xing, Z., Fei, Y., Wanjie, L., Shuai, L.: Fake location generation scheme based on user preference selection. Comput. Eng. Des. **40**(4), 914–919 (2019)
4. Chen, S., Shen, H.: Semantic-aware dummy selection for location privacy preservation. In: 2016 IEEE Trustcom/BigDataSE/ISPA, pp. 752–759. IEEE (2016)
5. Cheng, R., Zhang, Yu., Bertino, E., Prabhakar, S.: Preserving user location privacy in mobile data management infrastructures. In: Danezis, G., Golle, P. (eds.) PET 2006. LNCS, vol. 4258, pp. 393–412. Springer, Heidelberg (2006). https://doi.org/10.1007/11957454_23

6. Dapeng, Z., Guangxuan, S., Yuanyuan, J., Xiaoling, W.: Query probability-based location privacy protection approach. J. Comput. Appl. **37**(2), 347–351 (2017)
7. Gedik, B., Liu, L.: Location privacy in mobile systems: a personalized anonymization model. In: 25th IEEE International Conference on Distributed Computing Systems (ICDCS 2005), pp. 620–629. IEEE (2005)
8. Ghinita, G., Kalnis, P., Khoshgozaran, A., Shahabi, C., Tan, K.L.: Private queries in location based services: anonymizers are not necessary. In: Proceedings of the 2008 ACM SIGMOD International Conference on Management of Data, pp. 121–132 (2008)
9. Ghinita, G., Kalnis, P., Skiadopoulos, S.: Prive: anonymous location-based queries in distributed mobile systems. In: Proceedings of the 16th International Conference on World Wide Web, pp. 371–380 (2007)
10. Kido, H., Yanagisawa, Y., Satoh, T.: An anonymous communication technique using dummies for location-based services. In: ICPS 2005. Proceedings. International Conference on Pervasive Services, 2005, pp. 88–97. IEEE (2005)
11. Luo, W., Hengartner, U.: Veriplace: a privacy-aware location proof architecture. In: Proceedings of the 18th SIGSPATIAL International Conference on Advances in Geographic Information Systems, pp. 23–32 (2010)
12. Mokbel, M.F., Chow, C.Y., Aref, W.G.: The New Casper: query processing for location services without compromising privacy. In: Proceedings of the 32nd International Conference on Very Large Data Bases, pp. 763–774 (2006)
13. Niu, B., Li, Q., Zhu, X., Cao, G., Li, H.: Achieving k-anonymity in privacy-aware location-based services. In: IEEE INFOCOM 2014-IEEE Conference on Computer Communications, pp. 754–762. IEEE (2014)
14. Niu, B., Li, Q., Zhu, X., Cao, G., Li, H.: Enhancing privacy through caching in location-based services. In: 2015 IEEE Conference on Computer Communications (INFOCOM), pp. 1017–1025. IEEE (2015)
15. Pan, X., Xu, J., Meng, X.: Protecting location privacy against location-dependent attacks in mobile services. IEEE Trans. Knowl. Data Eng. **24**(8), 1506–1519 (2011)
16. Saroiu, S., Wolman, A.: Enabling new mobile applications with location proofs. In: Proceedings of the 10th Workshop on Mobile Computing Systems and Applications, pp. 1–6 (2009)
17. Xu, J., Tang, X., Hu, H., Du, J.: Privacy-conscious location-based queries in mobile environments. IEEE Trans. Parall. Distrib. Syst. **21**(3), 313–326 (2009)
18. Xu, T., Cai, Y.: Location anonymity in continuous location-based services. In: Proceedings of the 15th Annual ACM International Symposium on Advances in Geographic Information Systems, pp. 1–8 (2007)
19. Yongbing, Z., Qiuyu, Z., Zongyi, L., Hongxiang, D., Moyi, Z.: A k-anonymous location privacy protection method of dummy based on approximate matching. Control Decision **35**(1), 55–64 (2020)

DenseGAN: A Password Guessing Model Based on DenseNet and PassGAN

Chaohui Fu[1], Ming Duan[1,2]([⊠]), Xunhai Dai[1], Qiang Wei[1], Qianqiong Wu[1],
and Rui Zhou[1]

[1] Information Engineering University, Zhengzhou 450001, China
mdscience@sina.com
[2] Henan Key Laboratory of Network Cryptography, Zhengzhou 450001, China

Abstract. Password authentication has become one of the most significant authentication methods because of low cost and convenience, and its security is getting more and more attention. The vulnerability of password security mainly lies in the password construction method which inevitably has many human characteristics. With the development of deep learning, these human characteristics are more and more explored, which bring new challenges to password security. In 2019, a PassGAN password guessing model was proposed, and its performance is remarkable when the maximum training password length is 10. However, when the length is extended to 15, the performance gets worse.

To address this issue, in this paper an approach is proposed to innovate the structure of PassGAN by using DenseNet, and two novel password guessing DenseGAN models are proposed, which both can generate high-quality password guesses. With the first DenseGAN model, when the maximum training password length is 15, the generated passwords were able to match 2.7–4.8% of the passwords in the testing datasets more than PassGAN. Specifically, with the second DenseGAN model, when the maximum training password length is 10, the generated passwords were able to match 0.5% of the passwords in the testing datasets more than PassGAN, when the maximum training password length is 15, the match is 6.2% to 12.5% of the passwords more than PassGAN.

Keywords: Password guessing · DenseNet · PassGAN

1 Introduction

As an important means of identity authentication, password is widely used. Specifically, with the development of the Internet of Things, more and more network entities use passwords for interconnection because of the convenience. Therefore, password authentication is still one of the most important authentication methods in the foreseeable future, and its security is getting more and more attention. The vulnerability of password security mainly lies in the password construction method which inevitably has many human characteristics, for example easy-to-remember, short length, reuse, personal information correlation, natural language correlation and so on.

R. Deng et al. (Eds.): ISPEC 2021, LNCS 13107, pp. 296–305, 2021.
https://doi.org/10.1007/978-3-030-93206-0_18

Traditional password guesses generally use key search and word list dictionary [1]. There also have been probability attack methods based on the password relevant characteristics, for example n-grams Markov [2] and PCFG [3], and password distribution methods based on Zipf [4], and a parameterized by desired success rate method [5].

In recent years, the ability of deep learning has been greatly developed in natural language processing. Similarly, it has also been developed in password guessing. A method using long-short term memory (LSTM) model [6] is proposed in 2016 by William Melicher. The model's performance is better than Markov and other traditional algorithm models.

The framework of Generative Adversarial Nets [7] is proposed in 2017 by Ian Goodfellow, then it was used in PassGAN [8] model for password guessing. Its performance is remarkable when the maximum training password length is 10. However, when the length is extended to 15, the performance gets worse.

In December 2017, Teng Nanjun proposed a PG-RNN [9] model based on RNN. The performance of this model is about 1.2% better than PassGAN. In 2019, Sungyup Nam proposed a Recurrent Neural Network GAN password Cracker on the basis of PassGAN [10]. Two approaches were developed to improve the performance of PassGAN. The first is to change the generative and discriminative network based on CNN into RNN. The second is to use the dual-discriminator GAN. The performance of the improved PassGAN base on RNN is 10–15% better than PassGAN base on CNN. However, in practice the computational complexity of the model training is far more than PassGAN base on CNN.

To improve the PassGAN's performance and avoid the huge computational complexity, in this paper an approach is proposed to innovate the structure of PassGAN model by using DenseNet, and two novel password guessing DenseGAN model are proposed, which can generate high-quality password guesses. With the first DenseGAN model, when the maximum training password length is 15, the generated passwords were able to match 2.7–4.8% of the passwords in the testing datasets more than PassGAN. Specifically, with the second DenseGAN model, when the maximum training password length is 10, the generated passwords were able to match 0.5% of the passwords in the testing datasets more than PassGAN, when the maximum training password length is 15, the match is 6.2% to 12.5% of the passwords more than PassGAN.

2 Background

2.1 Generative Adversarial Nets

Generative Adversarial Nets (GAN) [7] is a neural network proposed by Ian Goodfellow in 2014. It's the basis of PassGAN and our models. GAN is composed of a generative model and a discriminative model. In our model the generative model is used to capture the distribution of real training passwords, and the discriminative model is used to estimate the probability that a password sample comes from real training dataset. The generative model G and discriminative model D can be various neural models, such as CNN, RNN, etc.

The goal of GANs is to train the generative model to make a fake sample without being detected and to train the discriminative network to detect the fake sample. During the training, first fix the generative model parameters and train the discriminative model. After that training, fix the parameters of the discriminative model, then train the generative model and repeat the above process until the generative model can cheat the discriminative model. In the constant confrontation between the two, a Nash equilibrium will be reached in the end.

2.2 PassGAN

PassGAN is a password guessing model based on GAN developed by Stevens Institute of technology in 2017. Unlike the traditional password generation method, PassGAN can learn the distribution characteristics and statistical character rules of password set, and use the obtained characteristics to generate passwords. PassGAN have been proved that it can generate high-quality artificial passwords. Taking some RockYou datasets as the training set, the passwords generated by the trained model can match 21.9% of the LinkedIn testing set with the size of 40593596 and 34.6% of the RockYou testing set with the size of 1978367. The Generative Adversarial Nets used in PassGAN is IWGAN [11], which can better solve the problems of training instability and failing to converge of WGAN [12].

2.3 DenseNet

DenseNet [13] was proposed by Gao Huang in 2016. The main idea of DenseNet is to make each layer of the deep learning network to be connected to the other layer in a feed-forward fashion. We use DenseNet to improve our model by choosing and connecting some layers together. The DenseNet model has some advantages in solving the vanishing-gradient problem, strengthening feature propagation, encouraging feature reuse and reducing the number of parameters. And in the benchmark tests it is proved that DensNet model has a high performance.

3   DenseGAN

We call the PassGAN model improved by DenseNet as DenseGAN. The original purpose of this improvement is to improve the utilization of features in each layer, so the layers of residual block are connected as shown in Figs. 1, 2, 3 and 4.

Connected layers with different depths in the network allow information flow across many layers unimpededly, and forms a highway network [14], can obtain more features and solve the gradient disappearance problem, which have been proved to be effective. This point is further supported by DenseNet and ResNets [15]. In DenseNet each layer is connected to the other layers, while in ResNets identity mapping is used in the residual block. Inspired by the ideas we add some outputs of the upper layers in the deep learning network to the next layers. In order to avoid disorder and weakening characteristics, we reduce the number of the layers to be added. Crucially, this approach is different from DenseNet. Firstly, the basic block of DenseNet is convolutional block, and the basic block of our model is residual block. Secondly, the features are combined by concatenating them in Densenet model, while they are combined through summation before being passed into a next layer. The summation is used in the residual block too. Therefore, although the model draws on the idea of DenseNet connecting some layers to enhance feature extraction, it is more like an enhanced residual network.

In order to demonstrate the idea's effectiveness, we constructed two DenseGAN models, selected several datasets, and carried out the deep learning network training, password generation, password match and so on. In addition, the parameters of the network model are reset, the batch size is set to 1024, and the number of training iterations is adjusted for different sizes of training sets. Adam optimizer's coefficients β^1 and β^2 is set to 0.5 and 0.9, and the learning rate is set to 10^{-4}.

The following figures show the two DenseGAN models' network topology, and the two models are named DenseGAN1 and DenseGAN2. In the figures, the blocks represent layers of the network, the lines with arrow indicates the flow of the layers' states, and the lines without arrow indicate that the output state of the previous layer is added to the input state of the next block.

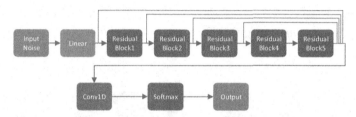

Fig. 1. Generator architecture of DenseGAN1.

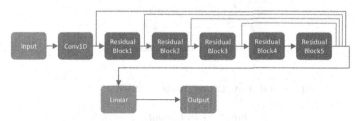

Fig. 2. Discriminator architecture of DenseGAN1

Let's write rb_i ($i = 1, 2, ..., 5$) for Residual Block1, Residual Block2, ..., Residual Block5. The input of the Conv1D layer in Fig. 1 and the input of the Linear layer in Fig. 2 can be separately represented as:

$$Input_{Conv1d} = Output_{Linear} + \sum_{i=1}^{3} 0.3 * Output_{rb\_i} + Output_{rb\_5}$$

$$Input_{Linear} = Output_{Conv1d} + \sum_{i=1}^{3} 0.3 * Output_{rb\_i} + Output_{rb\_5}$$

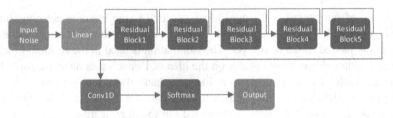

Fig. 3. Generator architecture of DenseGAN2.

Some layers' inputs in this figure can be represented as:

$$Input_{rb\_1} = Output_{Linear}$$

$$Input_{rb\_2} = Output_{rb\_1} + 0.3 * Output_{Linear}$$

$$Input_{rb\_i} = 0.3 * Output_{rb\_(i-1)} + Input_{rb\_(i-1)} \quad (i = 3, 4, 5)$$

$$Input_{Conv1D} = 0.3 * Output_{rb\_5} + Input_{rb\_5}$$

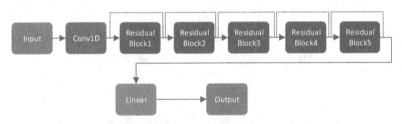

Fig. 4. Discriminator architecture of DenseGAN2.

Some layers' inputs in this figure can be represented as:

$$Input_{rb\_1} = Output_{Conv1D}$$

$$Input_{rb\_2} = Output_{rb\_1} + 0.3 * Output_{Conv1D}$$

$$Input_{rb\_i} = 0.3 * Output_{rb\_(i-1)} + Input_{rb\_(i-1)} \quad (i = 3, 4, 5)$$

$$Input_{Linear} = 0.3 * Output_{rb\_5} + Input_{rb\_5}$$

Table 1. Training and testing datasets.

Dataset	Password number	Filtered password number	Training password number	Testing password number
CSDN	6428632	6428280	5142624	1285656
RockYou	32584881	32584847	26067878	6516969
Yahoo	442811	442808	354246	88562
RenRen	4768600	4739010	3791209	947802

4 Datasets

During the password match, the datasets used are mainly public datasets collected from the network, for example CSDN, RockYou, Yahoo and RenRen. In practice we removed the Unicode passwords from the datasets. The training set and testing set account for 80% and 20% of the total dataset respectively, which are not intersecting. The following two tables gives the details of the datasets.

Table 1 shows the numbers of the datasets. Table 2 shows the password length distribution. The distribution shows that passwords with 1–15 lengths account for more than 98.9% of the total passwords, and those with 11–15 lengths account for more than 8%, especially in the CSDN dataset, passwords with 11–15 lengths account for 21.72% of the total passwords. Therefore, it is necessary to expand the password guessing length to 15 lengths. And some interesting things can be seen from this table, for example, passwords of length 6 in the CSDN dataset account for only 1.29%, while passwords of the same length in the RockYou dataset account for 26.06%, indicating that CSDN users who are mostly related to the IT industry are more security conscious than RockYou users.

Table 2. Password length distribution.

Password length	6	1–5	1–10	1–15	11–15
CSDN	1.29%	0.63%	77.19%	98.91%	21.72%
RockYou	26.06%	4.32%	90.86%	99.22%	8.36%
Yahoo	17.98%	1.93%	88.90%	99.71%	10.82%
RenRen	25.40%	6.82%	89.98%	99.71%	9.72%

5 Experiments

In this section, the password match performances between DenseGAN and PassGAN will be evaluated. Firstly, the DenseGAN models is to be trained with the training datasets. Secondly, the trained model is used to generate 1 billion passwords, which is called generative set. Thirdly, count the number of the same passwords in the testing dataset and in the generative set, named match num. Fourthly, the match number is divided by the number of the passwords in testing set, and the result is named match rate. Fifthly, calculate the PassGAN's match rate similarly. Finally, compare the match rates of the two model. To get a superior match rate, a single DenseGAN or PassGAN model must be trained and saved with various training epochs, correspondingly the passwords must be generated.

5.1 Experiments on DenseGAN1

In order to compare the performance, two PassGAN and two DenseGAN models were trained by CSDN and RockYou datasets respectively. The training password length corresponding to the model is 1–15. The following Table 3 gives the details of the match rate of DenseGAN1 and PassGAN.

Table 3. Match rate of DenseGAN1 and PassGAN.

Model	Training set	Testing set	Password length	Match rate
PassGAN	CSDN	CSDN	1–15	33.55%
DenseGAN1	CSDN	CSDN	1–15	38.36%
PassGAN	RockYou	RockYou	1–15	38.54%
DenseGAN1	RockYou	RockYou	1–15	41.29%

The table shows the DenseGAN1's match rate is about 4.8% higher than PassGAN's with the CSDN dataset, and is about 2.7% higher with the RockYou dataset.

5.2 Experiments on DenseGAN2

In order to compare the performance of DenseGAN2 and PassGAN model, the corresponding PassGAN and DenseGAN2 models are trained with CSDN and RockYou datasets respectively. The training password length corresponding to the models are 1–10 and 1–15.

Match in the Same Datasets. In this experiment, the training set and the testing set comes from the same dataset. Eight models were trained, and 8 match rates were calculated. The following Table 4 gives the details of the match rates of DenseGAN2 and PassGAN with the same datasets.

The table shows that when the maximum training password length is 10, the DenseGAN2's match rate is 0.5% higher than PassGAN's, when the maximum length is 15, the DenseGAN2's match rate is 6.2–12.5% higher than PassGAN's.

Match in the Different Datasets. In order to test the generalization ability of the two models, the testing dataset is set different from the training dataset. The following Table 5 gives the details of the match Rate of DenseGAN2 and PassGAN with different datasets.

Table 4. Match rate of DenseGAN2 and PassGAN with same datasets.

Network type	Training set	Testing set	Password length	Match rate
PassGAN	CSDN	CSDN	1–10	40.43%
DenseGAN2	CSDN	CSDN	1–10	40.92%
PassGAN	RockYou	RockYou	1–10	49.46%
DenseGAN2	RockYou	RockYou	1–10	49.92%
PassGAN	CSDN	CSDN	1–15	33.47%
DenseGAN2	CSDN	CSDN	1–15	39.61%
PassGAN	RockYou	RockYou	1–15	38.54%
DenseGAN2	RockYou	RockYou	1–15	51.04%

Table 5. Match rate of DenseGAN2 and PassGAN with different datasets.

Network type	Training set	Testing set	Password length	Match rate
PassGAN	CSDN	RenRen	1–10	56.06%
DenseGAN2	CSDN	RenRen	1–10	56.50%
PassGAN	RockYou	Yahoo	1–10	34.53%
DenseGAN2	RockYou	Yahoo	1–10	34.53%
PassGAN	CSDN	RenRen	1–15	42.57%
DenseGAN2	CSDN	RenRen	1–15	43.65%
PassGAN	RockYou	Yahoo	1–15	25.50%
DenseGAN2	RockYou	Yahoo	1–15	35.84%

The table shows that when the testing dataset and training dataset come from different dataset the DenseGAN2's match rate is higher than that of PassGAN's. That is, DenseGAN has a slightly better generalization ability.

From the comparison of the results, when the training password length is 1–10 or 1–15, DenseGAN2's match rate is slightly better than PassGAN's. Specially, when the training password length is 1–15 and the training set is RockYou and the testing set is Yahoo, DenseGAN2's match rate is about 10% higher than PassGAN's.

5.3 Comparison Between DenseGAN1 and DenseGAN2

Although DenseGAN1 performs well when the password length is 1–15, when the password length is 1–10, the match rate of DenseGAN1 is slightly lower than that of PassGAN and DenseGAN2, and the performance of DenseGAN1 in other aspects is also lower than that of DenseGAN2.

In the first model, when the blocks are connected together, a kind of Cascade-Correlation [16] structure is established. The connected block becomes a complex feature detector in the network, which enhances the ability of feature acquisition. At the same time, too many addition operations destroy some features of password distribution and distort some features, so the performance of DenseGAN1 decreases.

In a residual block, the underlying mapping $H(x)$ [15] can be represented by the stacked nonlinear layers $F(x)$ and the identity mapping x as $H(x) = F(x) + x$. Because of the identity mapping, the degradation problem was solved, and the accuracy can be gained from greatly increased depth. In our second model, the underlying mapping is $H(x) = F(x) + x + 0.3x$, and the features can be magnified without being destroyed and transferred to the deeper layers, so the performance of DenseGAN2 is better.

6 Conclusion

In 2019, a PassGAN password guessing model was proposed, and its performance is remarkable when the training maximum password length is 10. However, when the length is extended to 15, the performance gets worse. To address this issue, in this paper an approach is proposed to innovate the structure of PassGAN model by using DenseNet, and two novel password guessing DenseGAN models are proposed, and three experiments are performed. With the first DenseGAN model, when the maximum training password length is 15, the generated passwords were able to match 2.7–4.8% of passwords more than PassGAN in the testing datasets. Specifically, with the second DenseGAN model, when the maximum training length of training passwords is 10, the generated passwords were able to match 0.5% of passwords more than PassGAN in the testing datasets, when the maximum length is 15, the match is 6.2% to 12.5% of passwords more than PassGAN. When the testing dataset and training dataset come from different datasets the DenseGAN2's match rate is higher than that of PassGAN, which shows DenseGAN has a slightly better generalization ability. The comprehensive experimental results show that the performance of the improved DenseGAN is better than PassGAN, and the approach to improve PassGAN inspired by DenseNet is useful. We predict the approach is also available to other password guessing models. At the end, because the hyperparameter and the connections between the layers are set empirically and subjectively we believe a better performance DenseGAN model can be obtained by more detailed tuning of hyperparameters.

References

1. Morris, R., Thomson, K.: Password security: a case history. Commun. ACM **22**(11), 594–597 (1979)
2. Ma, J., Yang, W., Luo, M., Li, N.: A study of probabilistic password models. In: 2014 IEEE Symposium on Security and Privacy, pp. 689–704. IEEE, Berkeley (2014)
3. Weir, M., Aggarwal, S., De Medeiros, B., Glodek, B.: Password cracking using probabilistic context-free grammars. In: 2009 30th IEEE Symposium on Security and Privacy, pp. 391–405. IEEE, Oakland (2009)
4. Wang, D., Cheng, H., Wang, P., Huang, X., Jian, G.: Zipf's law in passwords. IEEE Trans. Inf. Forensics Secur. **12**(11), 2776–2791 (2017)

5. Bonneau, J.: The science of guessing: analyzing an anonymized corpus of 70 million passwords. In: 2012 IEEE Symposium on Security and Privacy, pp. 538–552. IEEE, San Francisco (2012)
6. Melicher, W., et al.: Fast, lean, and accurate: modeling password guessability using neural networks. In: Proceedings of the 25th USENIX Security Symposium, pp. 175–191. Austin, TX, USA (2016)
7. Goodfellow, I.J., et al.: Generative adversarial nets. In: Proceedings of the 27th International Conference on Neural Information Processing Systems, pp. 2672–2680. Montreal, QC, Canada (2014)
8. Hitaj, B., Gasti, P., Ateniese, G., Perez-Cruz, F.: PassGAN: a deep learning approach for password guessing. In: Deng, R.H., Gauthier-Umaña, V., Ochoa, M., Yung, M. (eds.) ACNS 2019. LNCS, vol. 11464, pp. 217–237. Springer, Cham (2019). https://doi.org/10.1007/978-3-030-21568-2_11
9. Teng, N., Huaxiang, L.U., Jin, M., Junbin, Y.E., Zhiyuan, L.I.: PG-RNN: a password-guessing model based on recurrent neural networks. CAAI Trans. Intell. Syst. **13**(6), 889–896 (2018)
10. Nam, S., Jeon, S., Moon, J.: Recurrent GANs password cracker for IoT password security enhancement. In: Proceedings of the International Workshop on Information Security Applications, pp. 247–258. Jeju Island, Korea (2019)
11. Gulrajani, I., Ahmed, F., Arjovsky, M., Dumoulin, V., Courville, A.: Improved training of Wasserstein GANs. In: Proceedings of the 31st International Conference on Neural Information Processing Systems, pp. 5769–5779. Curran Associates Inc., Long Beach (2017)
12. Arjovsky, M., Chintala, S., Bottou, L.: Wasserstein generative adversarial networks. In: Proceedings of the 34th International Conference on Machine Learning, pp. 214–223. JMLR.org, Sydney (2017)
13. Huang, G., Liu, Z., Van Der Maaten, L., Weinberger, K.: Densely connected convolutional networks. In: 2017 IEEE Conference on Computer Vision and Pattern Recognition (CVPR), pp. 2261–2269. IEEE, Honolulu (2017)
14. Srivastava, R.K., Greff, K., Schmidhuber, J.: Training very deep networks. In: NIPS2015, Curran Associates, Inc. (2015)
15. He, K., Zhang, X., Ren, S., Sun, J.: Deep residual learning for image recognition. In: CVPR, pp. 770–778. IEEE, Las Vegas (2016)
16. Fahlman, S.E., Lebiere, C.: The cascade-correlation learning architecture. In: NIPS, pp. 524–532. MIT Press, Cambridge (1989)

Impossible Differential Cryptanalysis and Integral Cryptanalysis of the ACE-Class Permutation

Tao Ye[1], Yongzhuang Wei[1(✉)], Lingcheng Li[1], and Enes Pasalic[2]

[1] Guilin University of Electronic Technology, Guilin 541004, China
walker_wyz@guet.edu.cn
[2] FAMNIT & IAM, University of Primorska, Koper, Slovenia

Abstract. ACE is a block cipher proposal that entered the 2nd round of the NIST Lightweight Cryptography Standardization process. So far, not much cryptanalysis has been devoted to the ACE permutation and specifically impossible differential distinguishers covering more than 10-steps have not been specified yet. In this article, a MILP (Mixed Integer Linear Programming) model that describes the propagation of word-oriented trails is employed (also considered in [15]), which serves as a basis for a new automatic cryptanalytic tool for finding impossible differential distinguishers. As an application, the cryptographic security of the ACE permutation can be evaluated using this new tool. Specifically, we show that impossible differential distinguishers for the ACE permutation can be built for up to 12 steps, essentially covering the largest number of steps so far by an impossible differential distinguisher. Due to the high efficiency of our method, we can explore all possible linear permutations to modify the original one. The security of these modified ACE permutations against integral and impossible differential attacks can then be evaluated by using our MILP model of word-oriented trails. In particular, the modified ACE that uses a linear permutation (4, 2, 3, 0, 1) instead of its original version offers better security against integral and impossible differential cryptanalysis. At the same time, ACE with the modified linear permutation preserves the same resistance against differential and linear cryptanalysis.

Keywords: Impossible differential distinguishers · Integral distinguishers · MILP · Automatic cryptanalytic tool · ACE permutation

1 Introduction

With the development of the Internet of Things, information security has become even more essential research discipline. Block ciphers constitute an important family of cryptographic primitives, primarily used for establishing the secrecy

R. Deng et al. (Eds.): ISPEC 2021, LNCS 13107, pp. 306–326, 2021.
https://doi.org/10.1007/978-3-030-93206-0_19

of communication. From the security aspects, their ability to withstand various cryptanalytic attacks is of crucial importance. These attacks include differential cryptanalysis [4], linear cryptanalysis [10], impossible differential cryptanalysis [3,7], integral cryptanalysis [8] and many other methods that evolved during the last thirty years. Recently, using MILP-like techniques, some new automated search tools for evaluating the security of block ciphers against linear or differential attacks [18–20] have been proposed. Apart from these standard techniques, impossible differential and integral cryptanalysis have also been efficiently applied in cryptanalysis of many block ciphers [5,11–13]. Thus, devising an efficient automatic method/algorithm aimed at searching for impossible and integral distinguishers is a quite important research task.

Impossible differential cryptanalysis was independently introduced by Knudsen [7] and Biham [3]. In order to obtain an impossible differential distinguisher, two (truncated) differentials with probability one need to be constructed by the cryptanalyst, which are applied in the forward (encryption) and backward (decryption) direction, respectively. Having the situation that these two differentials are mismatched in the middle stage of the cipher, essentially leads to the specification of an impossible differential distinguisher. Then, using such a distinguisher, a key-recovery attack can be mounted by prepending and/or appending additional rounds. Those encryption (secret) keys that give rise to an impossible differential are the wrong ones and therefore can be excluded from the set of candidate keys. Recently, some automated methods that employ MILP-based techniques for finding impossible differential distinguishers were proposed in [5,11].

Integral cryptanalysis [8] was proposed by Knudsen in 2002. The first step is to obtain an integral distinguisher. Let P be a set of plaintext blocks, where certain parts of plaintexts are active whereas the remaining words are kept fixed (commonly set to zero). After the r-th encryption round, it is required that the sum of the corresponding ciphertexts over the entire values of C is zero in some output bits. In this case, an r-round integral distinguisher of the considered block cipher is obtained. We also mention the so-called *division property* [12] introduced by Todo which is an efficient method to construct integral distinguishers. Especially, based on the MILP model of the division property proposed by Xiang et al. [13], some automatic cryptanalytic tools have been designed to evaluate the security of various ciphers [6,17]. However, for relatively large block sizes (e.g. dealing with blocks of more than 256 bits), the MILP model that describes the division property (through linear inequalities whose number grows exponentially) becomes infeasible to handle computationally when the number of rounds gets large.

The Related Work. The ACE cipher has successfully entered the 2nd round stage in the NIST LWC (Light Weight Cryptography) competition. In [2], the designers of ACE provided 8-step integral distinguishers, and additionally they made a claim that any distinguisher obtained by using the miss/meet-in-the-middle technique cannot cover more than 10 steps. In [9], based on the use of characteristic matrices, the authors constructed two 8-step impossible differential distinguishers and also claimed that impossible differential distinguishers of the ACE permutation can not cover more than 8 steps. However, these claims have become questionable especially with the development of some new cryptanalytic methods.

A new method for finding impossible differential and integral distinguishers, implicitly using the concept of word oriented trails, was proposed by Zhang et al. [16] in FSE 2020. The main idea is that the expression of the internal state can be represented by the words of plaintexts or ciphertexts. By counting the number of times that each word appears in the state expression, the resistance against the impossible differential and integral cryptanalysis can be evaluated. Nevertheless, in order to acquire the internal state expression, a lot of man-made work is necessary. For decreasing this workload, a method that describes the propagation of every word of plaintexts or ciphertexts was needed. To solve this problem a new automatic tool for finding integral distinguishers was proposed in [15] and it was successfully used in the specification of a 12-step integral distinguisher of the ACE permutation. This result further compromises the security claims made by the designers regarding the strength of the ACE permutation. Since the security of AEC also heavily relies on the choice of its linear layer, an important question is the existence of other linear permutations that may provide better security than the original choice. This is also the main research motivation of this work.

Our Contributions. In this paper, using a MILP-model of word-oriented trails, an automatic search tool for finding impossible differential distinguishers is designed. To show the efficiency of our method, related to the security of ACE [2] and in particular its permutation, we first demonstrate the existence of an impossible differential distinguisher (in difference to 12-step integral distinguisher in [15]) that covers up to 12 steps. Therefore, to strengthen its design, we investigate other linear permutations than the one used in ACE and estimate the security of these tweaked designs against impossible differential and integral cryptanalysis. The main conclusion is that replacing the original linear permutation by $(4, 2, 3, 0, 1)$ induces better security margins of the tweaked ACE cipher, thus having a better resistance against integral and impossible differential cryptanalysis than the original version. At the same time, the modified ACE cipher has the same resistance against differential and linear cryptanalysis compared to its original version. The summary on the cryptanalysis of ACE and its tweaked version is listed in Table 1 and 2, respectively.

Organization of This Paper. The rest of this paper is organized as follows. In Sect. 2, a brief description of the ACE permutation and similar kind of permutations is given. In Sect. 3, the concept of word-oriented trails is defined, and additionally we describe a method of constructing the MILP model for word-oriented trails. In Sect. 4, a new automatic search technique for integral distinguishers is presented. We also estimate the security of the ACE-class permutations (including different linear permutations) with respect to the existence of integral distinguishers (covering maximum number of steps). Similarly, based on the MILP model for word-oriented trails, we also propose an automatized search for impossible differential distinguishers. To demonstrate the efficiency of our approach, some impossible differential distinguishers for the original ACE permutation are given in Sect. 5. Thereafter, we estimate the security of the ACE-class permutations against impossible differential attacks for different linear permutations and conclude that there exist better choices. Some concluding remarks are given in Sect. 6.

Table 1. Summary of attacks on the ACE cipher

Steps	Distinguishers	Resource
8	ID	[2]
12	ID	[15]
8	IDD	[9]
12	IDD	New

Table 2. Summary of attacks on the ACE-class cipher

Linear permutation ρ in ACE	The maximum number of steps of ID	The maximum number of steps for IDD	The minimum number of active S-boxes in 16-step encryption
(2, 4, 1, 0, 3) (original)	12	12	21
(4, 2, 3, 0, 1) (new)	10	11	21

ID: Integral distinguisher; IDD: Impossible differential distinguisher.

2 Preliminaries

2.1 Integral Property

The integral property [8] was first considered by Knudsen et al. in [8]. An integral distinguisher can be specified by using the following properties related to a multiset of ciphertexts after a certain number of encryption rounds:

(a) If the elements in the multiset are taking all possible values and each value is equally frequent, such a multiset is called *active*; the symbol a is used to represent this set.

(b) If the XOR of all elements in the multiset is zero, then the multiset is called *balanced*; the symbol b is used to represent this set.

(c) If the value of each element in the multiset is the same, then the multiset is called *constant*; the symbol c is used to represent this set.

(u) If the multiset cannot be distinguished from a random set, then the multiset is called the *unknown* set; the symbol u is used to represent this set.

The above types of multisets have the following propagation properties.

Property 1. If the input of a bijective component (commonly S-box) is an active or constant set, then the output is also an active or constant set [8].

Property 2. The sum of two active sets is a balanced set (the XOR sum of all elements in the multiset is zero), the sum of two balanced sets is also a balanced set [8].

2.2 The ACE Permutation

The ACE-AEAD (Authenticated Encryption with Associated Data) algorithm, which entered the 2nd round of the lightweight crypto standardization process [1], was proposed by Mark Aagaard et al. [2]. The ACE permutation is a core component of ACE-AEAD, thus having an enormous impact on the security of ACE-AEAD.

The ACE permutation uses 16 steps/rounds and acts on the 320-bit state. The input to the ACE permutation is processed through the step/round function. More specifically, the nonlinear operation in each round is achieved using the unkeyed reduced-round Simeck [14] block cipher (with block size of 64 bits and 8 encryption rounds), whereas the linear operation is based on the XOR operation on 64-bit blocks.

In the r-th step, the input data X^{r-1} of the ACE permutation, consisting of 320 bits, is split into five 64-bit data blocks ($X^{r-1}[0]$, $X^{r-1}[1]$, $X^{r-1}[2]$, $X^{r-1}[3]$, $X^{r-1}[4]$), where $X^{r-1}[k] \in F_2^{64}$ for $0 \leq k \leq 4$. The output of the r-th step is X^r and the use of three different S-boxes in the r-th round is denoted by SB_j^r, where $1 \leq r \leq 16$, $0 \leq j \leq 2$. The S-boxes SB_0^r, SB_1^r and SB_2^r are applied to $X^{r-1}[0]$, $X^{r-1}[2]$ and $X^{r-1}[4]$, respectively. The ACE permutation has two types of constants, the round constants RC_j^r are used in the Simeck S-boxes SB_j^r, and the step constants SC_j^r are used in each round to XOR the words $X_1^{r-1}, X_3^{r-1}, X_4^{r-1}$. We refer to [2] for more details about the constants used in the ACE permutation. Figure 1 visualizes the structure of ACE.

The linear permutation in ACE is quite simple and the notation ACE_ρ refers to the (permuting) action of ρ on the set of five 64-bit elements $X[i]$, for $i = 0, \ldots, 4$. For example, the action of $\rho = (3, 2, 0, 4, 1)$ on the state ($X[0]$, $X[1]$, $X[2]$, $X[3]$, $X[4]$) results in a new state ($X[2]$, $X[4]$, $X[1]$, $X[0]$, $X[3]$), thus $X[i]$ is moved to the ρ_i-th position. These permutations, specified by the action of ρ, are called ACE-class permutations.

2.3 Permutation Functions in Cryptosystems

Definition 1 *(Permutation Function).* *Let $Y = f(X)$, where X and Y are elements of $\mathbb{F}_2^n$ (a vector space of binary vectors of length n). If Y is taking all possible values in $\mathbb{F}_2^n$ when X ranges through $\mathbb{F}_2^n$, then f is a permutation function of X.*

Now, considering the ACE permutation and referring to Fig. 1, assuming the absence of the step constants, we can derive the relationship between the input X^{r-1} and output X^r of the ACE step function as follows:

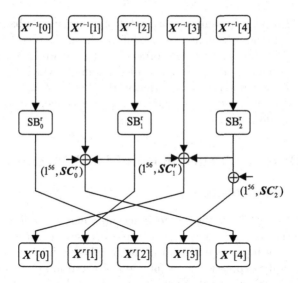

Fig. 1. Structure of the ACE permutation

$$X^r[0] = X^{r-1}[3] \oplus SB_2^r(X^{r-1}[4])$$
$$X^r[1] = SB_1^r(X^{r-1}[2])$$
$$X^r[2] = SB_0^r(X^{r-1}[0]) \qquad (1)$$
$$X^r[3] = SB_2^r(X^{r-1}[4])$$
$$X^r[4] = X^{r-1}[1] \oplus SB_1^r(X^{r-1}[2])$$

Now, referring to the first two rounds of the ACE permutation, again neglecting the step constants, the expression for $X^2[0]$ becomes $SB_2^1(X^0[4]) \oplus SB_2^2(X^0[1] \oplus SB_1^1(X^0[2]))$. From this expression, we deduce that $X^0[4]$ only appears once in the expression for $X^2[0]$. Assuming that $X^0[4]$ is taking all possible of values in F_2^{64} (keeping the other words fixed), then since the S-box of the ACE permutation is bijective we conclude that $X^2[0]$ is also taking all possible values in F_2^{64}. Therefore, $X^2[0]$ is a permutation function of $X^0[4]$. In accordance to this conclusion, we can specify the following property related to the permutation function.

Property 3. Consider a word-based block cipher whose round function is $f : F_2^{n \times m} \to F_2^{n \times m}$ and its S-box is a bijection. Let the initial state be $X^0 = (X^0[0], X^0[1], \ldots, X^0[m-1])$, where $X^0[i] \in F_2^n$, $0 \le i \le m-1$, and denote the internal state after r encryption rounds by $X^r = (X^r[0], X^r[1], \ldots, X^r[m-1])$, where $X^r[j] \in F_2^n$, $0 \le j \le m-1$. If $X^0[i_1]$ appears once in the algebraic representation of $X^r[j_1]$, when the other words of X^0 are fixed, then $X^r[j_1]$ is a permutation of $X^0[i_1]$, where $0 \le i_1, j_1 \le m-1$.

Notice that Property 3, using the permutation function as a basis, implies the possibility of specifying certain impossible differential and integral distinguishers, as demonstrated in [16]. However, in order to get a permutation function, the internal state expression needs to be specified manually which becomes tedious when the number of rounds increases. Hence, the design of an automatic search method for finding distinguishers that employ the concept of a permutation function is highly desirable.

3   Word-Oriented Trails and Its MILP Model

3.1   Word-Oriented Trails

Let $f : F_2^{n \times m} \rightarrow F_2^{n \times m}$ be the round function, where m and n represent the number of words and bits in each word, respectively. In order to count the number of words of input plaintexts that appear in the internal state, we have to provide the state expression as a function of these input words. Neglecting the internal structure of a nonlinear transformation, the main goal is to obtain the output expression after r encryption rounds by iterating the expression of a single round function.

For instance, considering the ACE permutation, based on the Eq. (1) we can get the expression of any internal state. Then, using these expressions, one can determine the exact number of appearances of any input word in these expressions. For example, without considering the elimination of identical words in XOR operations, the upper bound on the number of times that the word $X^0[0]$ appears in the internal expression of different blocks $X^r[i]$ of any round r and $0 \le i \le 4$, denoted by N_0^r, is listed as follows.

$$N_0^0 = (1,0,0,0,0) \stackrel{f_{ACE}}{\rightarrow} N_0^1 = (0,0,1,0,0) \stackrel{f_{ACE}}{\rightarrow} N_0^2 = (0,1,0,0,1)$$

$$\stackrel{f_{ACE}}{\rightarrow} N_0^3 = (1,0,0,1,1) \stackrel{f_{ACE}}{\rightarrow} N_0^4 = (2,0,1,1,0) \cdots \stackrel{f_{ACE}}{\rightarrow} N_0^7 = (4,1,1,3,3). \tag{2}$$

For every word, the number of times it appears in the state expression is fixed. Based on this property, the notion of word-oriented trails, originally introduced in [15], is defined as follows.

Definition 2 (Word-oriented trails). *Let $f : F_2^{n \times m} \rightarrow F_2^{n \times m}$ be the round function in encryption direction, the initial input state be $X^0 = (X^0[0], X^0[1], \ldots, X^0[m-1]) \in F_2^{n \times m}$, the input state expression in r-th round is X^{r-1}, and denote the corresponding output by X^r. Let $N_j^r = (N_j^r[0], \ldots, N_j^r[m-1])$, $0 \le j \le m - 1$, denote the upper bound on the number of times that $X^0[j]$ appears in the expression of each element of X^r. The following trail is called the word-oriented trail of $X^0[j]$:*

$$N_j^0 \stackrel{f}{\rightarrow} N_j^1 \stackrel{f}{\rightarrow} N_j^2 \stackrel{f}{\rightarrow} \cdots. \tag{3}$$

This definition immediately implies the following property of word-oriented trails.

Property 4. Let $f : F_2^{n \times m} \to F_2^{n \times m}$ denote the round function of a specific block cipher. If $N_j^r[k] = 0$ or $N_j^r[k] = 1$, then $N_j^r[k]$ is the number of times that $X^0[j]$ appears in the expression of $X^r[k]$. When $N_j^r[k] \geq 2$, then $N_j^r[k]$ is the upper bound on the number of times that $X^0[j]$ appears in the expression of $X^r[k]$, $0 \leq j, k \leq m - 1$.

Proof. In word-oriented trails, the cancellation of identical words due to the XOR operation is not considered. If $N_j^r[k] = 0$ or $N_j^r[k] = 1$, we can therefore deduce that $N_j^r[k]$ is the actual number of times that $X^0[j]$ occurs in the expression of $X^r[k]$. When $N_j^r[k] \geq 2$, we cannot determine whether there is a cancellation of the same words (XOR operation does not act directly on these words), and $N_j^r[k]$ is the upper bound on the number of appearances of $X^0[j]$ in the expression for $X^r[k]$.

In the decryption direction, one considers the inverse round function $(f)^{-1}$: $F_2^{n \times m} \to F_2^{n \times m}$. The definition of word-oriented trails in this (backward) direction is similar to Definition 2, the difference is that the input state expression of the r-th round is Y^{r-1}, and the upper bound on the number of times of $Y^0[j]$ appears in each element of Y^r is denoted by $W_j^r = (W_j^r[0], \cdots, W_j^r[m-1])$, $0 \leq j \leq m - 1$. Notice that in this direction the ciphertext corresponds to $Y^0 = (Y^0[0], \ldots, Y^0[m-1])$ and the state after r decryption rounds is denoted by $Y^r = (Y^r[0], \ldots, Y^r[m-1])$.

3.2   The MILP Model of Word-Oriented Trails

In order to obtain the word-oriented trails, we have to efficiently derive the internal state expression (in an automatized manner) that depends on the input words. For this purpose, a linear inequality system which describes the word-oriented trails is introduced.

The number of occurrences of each word in the input and output expression of a bijective S-box is the same, thus the S-box operation has no effect on word-oriented trails. Therefore, we only need to make the linear inequality system (describing the word-oriented trails) which is affected by the linear operations used. For a specific word-based block cipher, the basic linear operations are XOR operation and linear permutation. Hence, we only need to describe the word-oriented trails with respect to these operations by using linear inequalities.

Property 5. **Modelling word-oriented trails w.r.t a linear permutation:** Let the round function $f : F_2^{n \times m} \to F_2^{n \times m}$ be applied in the r-th round. If there is a swapping operation $X^r[k] \to X^r[k_1]$ (two words of the internal state changing their position), based on the definition of word-oriented trails, we can use the following equation to describe the trail of the j-th word.

$$N_j^r[k] - N_j^r[k_1] = 0, \qquad 0 \leq j, k, k_1 \leq m - 1 \qquad (4)$$

Property 6. **Modelling word-oriented trails w.r.t. XOR operation:** Let the round function $f : F_2^{n \times m} \to F_2^{n \times m}$ be applied in the r-th round. If there is a relationship (XOR) $\boldsymbol{X}^r[k_1] \oplus \boldsymbol{X}^r[k_2] \oplus \cdots \oplus \boldsymbol{X}^r[k_l] = \boldsymbol{X}^{r+1}[k]$, we can use the following equation to describe the trail of the j-th word.

$$\boldsymbol{N}_j^r[k_1] + \boldsymbol{N}_j^r[k_2] + \cdots + \boldsymbol{N}_j^r[k_l] = \boldsymbol{N}_j^{r+1}[k] \qquad 0 \leq j, k, \ldots, k_l \leq m - 1 \quad (5)$$

In a word-based block cipher, its linear layer operates simultaneously on every word. Therefore, in order to obtain its word-oriented trails, these linear operations should be split into XOR and linear permutations and then using Property 4–6 we can construct the model of word-oriented trails based on these basic operations. Finally, the MILP model of the round function can be constructed by employing the structure of these word-oriented trails. In what follows, the model of word-oriented trails for an r-round encryption or decryption is denoted by M_e^r or M_d^r, respectively.

4   Automated Search for Integral Distinguishers of Word-Based Block Ciphers and Its Applications

4.1   Searching for Integral Distinguishers in the Encryption Direction

For a block cipher whose round function is $f : F_2^{n \times m} \to F_2^{n \times m}$, in order to construct its model of word-oriented trails, the initial input of the word trail needs to be assigned. According to the definition of word-oriented trails, if we want to determine word-oriented trails of the j-th word in the input plaintext block, we assume that the word $\boldsymbol{X}^0[j]$ appears only in the expression for the j-th word of the plaintext and not in the remaining words. Therefore, we can use the following equations to describe the initial word-oriented trails of the constituent words in the plaintext.

$$\begin{cases} \boldsymbol{N}_j^0[k] = 1, \text{ if } j = k, 0 \leq k, j \leq m - 1, \\ \boldsymbol{N}_j^0[k] = 0, k \neq j. \end{cases} \quad (6)$$

According to Property 3, if $\boldsymbol{X}^0[j]$ appears exactly once in the algebraic expression of $\boldsymbol{X}^r[k]$ and the other words in $\boldsymbol{X}^0$ are fixed, then $\boldsymbol{X}^r[k]$ is a permutation function of $\boldsymbol{X}^0[j]$. Furthermore, if $\boldsymbol{X}^0[j]$ is taking all possible values in $\mathbb{F}_2^n$ and the other words in $\boldsymbol{X}^0$ are fixed to a constant in $\mathbb{F}_2^n$, then the sum of $\boldsymbol{X}^r[k]$ must be equal to 0^n (where 0^n denotes the all-zero vector of length n).

Therefore, if in a word-oriented trail (considering the j-th word say) $\boldsymbol{N}_j^0 \xrightarrow{f} \boldsymbol{N}_j^1 \xrightarrow{f} \boldsymbol{N}_j^2 \xrightarrow{f} \cdots \xrightarrow{f} \boldsymbol{N}_j^r$ there exists some elements in $\boldsymbol{N}_j^r$ which are equal to 1, then we can conclude that there exists an r-round integral distinguisher. Based on the above discussion, the following property can be stated.

Property 7. Let $\boldsymbol{N}_j^r = (\boldsymbol{N}_j^r[0], \boldsymbol{N}_j^r[1], \ldots, \boldsymbol{N}_j^r[m-1])$ be the upper bound on the number of times that the j-th word of plaintext occurs in the expression for each element in $\boldsymbol{X}^r$, where $0 \leq j \leq m - 1$. If $min(\boldsymbol{N}_j^r) = 1$, then we can determine that there is an r-round integral distinguisher.

In order to determine whether there exists an r-round integral distinguisher, we need to construct the model M_e^r which describes r-round word-oriented trails. Then, the Eq. (6) and $min(N_j^r) = 1$ need to be added into this model M_e^r. At this point, we have transformed the problem of searching for integral distinguisher into a MILP problem. If the model M_e^r has feasible solutions, then there is an r-round integral distinguisher for the considered block cipher.

For convenience of the reader, we specify the details of the M_e^r model which is entered into Algorithm 1. For simplicity, we consider the example mentioned in (2) and provide the constraints used in Algorithm 1.

$$
M_e^7 = \begin{cases}
Objective \quad function : None \\
N_0^0[0] = 1 \\
N_0^0[k] = 0, 1 \le k \le 4 \\
N_0^{r-1}[3] + N_0^{r-1}[4] - N_0^r[0] = 0 \\
N_0^{r-1}[2] - N_0^r[1] = 0 \\
N_0^{r-1}[0] - N_0^r[2] = 0 \\
N_0^{r-1}[4] - N_0^r[3] = 0 \\
N_0^{r-1}[1] + N_0^{r-1}[2] - N_0^r[4] = 0 \\
1 \le r \le 7 \\
min(N_0^7) = 1
\end{cases}
\tag{7}
$$

To reduce the time complexity, we use a binary search to decrease the number of calls to the MILP solver. For a cipher whose total number of rounds is R, let the maximal number of rounds for which an integral distinguisher can be obtained (using j-th word-oriented trails) be denoted by r_j^e. Also, let the upper and lower bound on r_j^e (with $0 \le j \le m-1$) be denoted by r_u and r_l, respectively. Furthermore, the initial value of $r = \lfloor (r_u + r_l)/2 \rfloor = \lfloor (R+0)/2 \rfloor$ is $R/2$. Taking into account the structure of a cipher, we need to construct the MILP model M_e^r which describes the r-round word-oriented trails. After that, we add the constraint $min(N_j^r) = 1$ into M_e^r. If the model is feasible, the lower bound on r_j^e is $R/2$, i.e. $r_l = R/2$; if the model is infeasible the upper bound on r_j^e is $R/2$, i.e. $r_u = R/2$. Then, we repeat the above process iteratively. The iteration is stopped as soon as $r_u - r_l \le 1$. In this way, the number of iteration used to determine the value of r_j^e is at most $\lceil \log_2(R) \rceil$.

Algorithm 1 in the appendix is used to describe the above process. The first returned value in Algorithm 1, denoted by r_j^e, is the number of rounds when the j-th word of initial state is first diffused to each word of the output. The second returned value of Algorithm 1 is a vector whose entries indicate balanced words in the output after r_j^e encryption rounds, assuming that the j-th word of initial state is taking all possible values in $\mathbb{F}_2^n$ and the other words are fixed. The function $(\alpha, \beta) = check\_min(X)$ in Algorithm 1 determines the minimum value α in X and returns the corresponding index β, where X is a set, each element of this set is a positive integer.

4.2   Extending the Integral Distinguisher in Decryption Direction

In this section, we consider how to extend the integral distinguisher discussed above in the opposite (decryption) direction. Let the inverse round function be denoted by $f^{-1} : F_2^{n \times m} \rightarrow F_2^{n \times m}$ and the r-round decryption be given by $(f^{-1})^r : F_2^{n \times m} \rightarrow F_2^{n \times m}$. In the decryption direction, let the ciphertext be $\boldsymbol{Y}^0 = (\boldsymbol{Y}^0[0], \ldots, \boldsymbol{Y}^0[m-1])$ so that the intermediate state (after r rounds of the decryption process) can be represented by $\boldsymbol{Y}^r = (\boldsymbol{Y}^r[0], \ldots, \boldsymbol{Y}^r[m-1])$, where each word in $\boldsymbol{Y}^0$ and $\boldsymbol{Y}^r$ is a block of n bits.

If $\boldsymbol{Y}^0[k]$ does not appear in the expression of $\boldsymbol{Y}^r[k']$, where $0 \leq k, k' \leq m-1$, then $\boldsymbol{Y}^0[k]$ does not effect the value of $\boldsymbol{Y}^r[k']$ in the decryption direction. Consequently, we can use the following equation to represent this relationship

$$\boldsymbol{Y}^r[k'] = (f^{-1})^r(\boldsymbol{Y}^0 \backslash \boldsymbol{Y}^0[k]), \tag{8}$$

where $\boldsymbol{Y}^0 \backslash \boldsymbol{Y}^0[k]$ is a vector with $\boldsymbol{Y}^0[k]$ removed. If $\boldsymbol{Y}^r[k']$ is fixed to a constant δ in $\mathbb{F}_2^n$, then the corresponding solutions of (8) constitute the set $\boldsymbol{v}_\delta$, whose cardinality is $2^{n \times (m-2)}$.

On the other hand, in the case that $\boldsymbol{Y}^r \backslash \boldsymbol{Y}^r[k']$ takes all possible values in $F_2^{n \times (m-1)}$ and $\boldsymbol{Y}^r[k']$ is fixed to a constant δ in F_2^n, then after performing r encryption rounds the state of $\boldsymbol{Y}^0$ constitutes the set $\boldsymbol{V}$. The set $\boldsymbol{V}$ is composed of $2^{n \times (m-2)}$ subsets $\boldsymbol{V}_i$, $0 \leq i < 2^{n \times (m-2)}$. The subset $\boldsymbol{V}_i$ is obtained by letting the word $\boldsymbol{Y}^0[k]$ take all possible values in F_2^n, when the state of $\boldsymbol{Y}^0 \backslash \boldsymbol{Y}^0[k]$ is fixed to the i-th element of the set $\boldsymbol{v}_\delta$.

In order to extend the integral distinguisher in the decryption direction, let $\boldsymbol{Y}^0 = \boldsymbol{X}^0$, where $\boldsymbol{Y}^0[k]$ does not appear in the expression of $\boldsymbol{Y}^r[k']$ in the decryption direction and $\boldsymbol{X}^{r'}[k'']$ is a permutation function on $\boldsymbol{X}^0[k]$ in the encryption direction, $0 \leq k, k', k'' \leq m-1$. Figure 2 further explains the relationship between these elements. Since $\boldsymbol{Y}^r \backslash \boldsymbol{Y}^r[k']$ is taking on all possible values in $F_2^{n \times (m-1)}$, then after r encryption rounds the corresponding output set is composed of $2^{n \times (m-2)}$ subsets $\boldsymbol{V}_i$. For each such subset, there is the following relationship

$$\bigoplus_{\boldsymbol{X}^0 \text{ is taking on all values in } \boldsymbol{V}_i} \boldsymbol{X}^{r'}[k''] = 0^n, \tag{9}$$

and then

$$\bigoplus_{i=0}^{2^{n \times (m-2)} > i} \bigoplus_{\boldsymbol{X}^0 \text{ is taking on all elements in } \boldsymbol{V}_i} \boldsymbol{X}^{r'}[k''] = 0^n. \tag{10}$$

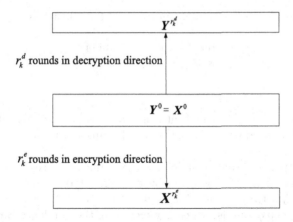

Fig. 2. $r_k^d + r_k^e$ rounds integral distinguisher

Therefore, if we want to extend our integral distinguisher in the decryption direction, we need to determine the maximum integer r_k^d so that the k-th word in $\boldsymbol{Y}^0$ is not fully diffused in $\boldsymbol{Y}^{r_k^d}$. Using the definition of word-oriented trails, we can use the following constraint to determine whether the k-th word in $\boldsymbol{Y}^0$ is fully diffused after r rounds of decryption, thus checking if

$$min(\boldsymbol{W}_k^r) = 0, \tag{11}$$

where $\boldsymbol{W}_k^r$ denotes the upper bound on the number of times the k-th word in $\boldsymbol{Y}^0$ occurs in the expression of each element in $\boldsymbol{Y}^r$, $0 \le k \le m-1$.

To efficiently determine the value of r_k^d, we again use a binary search as discussed before. This procedure is described in Algorithm 2 in the appendix.

4.3   An Integral Distinguisher for the ACE-Class Permutation

For a specific cipher whose round function is $f : F_2^{n \times m} \to F_2^{n \times m}$, by using the following steps (in the specified order), we can obtain integral distinguishers of maximal length (w.r.t. the number of rounds covered) by using the word-oriented trails.

(1) Construct a MILP model using word-oriented trails for the round function in the encryption and decryption direction.
(2) By using Algorithm 1 and Algorithm 2, the values of r_j^e, ω_j, r_j^d, ϕ_j can be determined, $0 \le j \le m-1$.
(3) Calculate the value of $\{r_{in}, \varphi\} = \boldsymbol{check\_max}(r_0^e + r_0^d, r_1^e + r_1^d, \ldots, r_{m-1}^e + r_{m-1}^d)$, where the function $\boldsymbol{check\_max}(\boldsymbol{X})$ is used to obtain the maximum value α in the set $\boldsymbol{X}$ and to return the corresponding index φ.

By applying the above steps, we can show that (using word-oriented trails) the original ACE permutation admits integral distinguishers covering at most 12 steps. The form of this integral distinguishers is listed in Table 3 [15].

Table 3. The 12-step integral distinguisher of the original ACE permutation

The form of input	The form of output
$c^{64}a^{64}a^{64}a^{64}a^{64}$	$u^{64}b^{64}u^{64}u^{64}u^{64}$

In the above table, c^{64} is a 64-bit constant word, a^{64} is a 64-bit active word, b^{64} is a 64-bit balanced word, and u^{64} is a 64 bit unknown word, see Preliminaries for these notions.

The linear permutation ρ in ACE largely affects its security. The original linear permutation in ACE is given by $\rho = (2, 4, 1, 0, 3)$ (acting on words). It can be shown that this permutation induces 21 active S-boxes when designed for 16 encryption steps/rounds, which is affected by the employed Simeck S-boxes. Furthermore, the ACE permutation (again considering 16 rounds) is resistant to both differential and linear cryptanalysis. Nevertheless, there might exist better choices of linear permutations, for instance offering better protection against integral distinguishers whereas at the same time having the same (or even better) resistance against differential and linear cryptanalysis. In order to address this problem, the security of the ACE-class (linear) permutation against integral attacks is therefore evaluated.

Thus, replacing the original linear ACE permutation with a linear permutation ρ, the model of word-oriented trails in the r-th step is given below for the encryption direction:

$$
\begin{cases}
\boldsymbol{N}_j^{r-1}[0] - \boldsymbol{N}_j^r[\rho[0]] = 0 \\
\boldsymbol{N}_j^{r-1}[1] + \boldsymbol{N}_j^{r-1}[2] - \boldsymbol{N}_j^r[\rho[1]] = 0 \\
\boldsymbol{N}_j^{r-1}[2] - \boldsymbol{N}_j^r[\rho[2]] = 0 \\
\boldsymbol{N}_j^{r-1}[3] + \boldsymbol{N}_j^{r-1}[4] - \boldsymbol{N}_j^r[\rho[3]] = 0 \\
\boldsymbol{N}_j^{r-1}[4] - \boldsymbol{N}_j^r[\rho[4]] = 0 \\
j \in [0, 5).
\end{cases}
\tag{12}
$$

Similarly, the same model in the decryption direction is given as:

$$
\begin{cases}
\boldsymbol{W}_j^r[\rho[0]] - \boldsymbol{W}_j^{r-1}[0] = 0 \\
\boldsymbol{W}_j^r[\rho[1]] + \boldsymbol{W}_j^r[\rho[2]] - \boldsymbol{W}_j^{r-1}[1] = 0 \\
\boldsymbol{W}_j^r[\rho[2]] - \boldsymbol{W}_j^{r-1}[2] = 0 \\
\boldsymbol{W}_j^r[\rho[3]] + \boldsymbol{W}_j^r[\rho[4]] - \boldsymbol{W}_j^{r-1}[3] = 0 \\
\boldsymbol{W}_j^r[\rho[4]] - \boldsymbol{W}_j^{r-1}[4] = 0 \\
j \in [0, 5).
\end{cases}
\tag{13}
$$

After applying r iterations (steps) of the Eqs. (12) and (13), we can specify the MILP models M_e^r and M_d^r of r-step word-oriented trails in the encryption and decryption direction for ACE_ρ. Then, an integral distinguisher can be specified by using Algorithm 1 and 2.

Due to the high efficiency of our method, we were able to examine all possible linear permutations ρ on five 64 bits words that might possibly have better properties than the original linear permutation used in ACE. Most notably, we managed to find good linear permutations which only admit integral distinguishers covering at most 10 steps. These results are listed in Table 4, where the third column is the corresponding minimum number of active S-boxes during the 16-step encryption process.

Table 4. Linear permutations ACE_ρ having at most 10-step integral distinguishers

ρ	The number of steps for integral distinguishers	Minimum number of active S-boxes in 16 steps ACE-class permutation
(2, 0, 3, 4, 1)	10	17
(2, 3, 1, 4, 0)	10	19
(4, 2, 0, 1, 3)	10	16
(4, 2, 3, 0, 1)	10	21

To accommodate for the number of active S-boxes of the original linear permutation, thus ensuring the same resistance to differential and linear cryptanalysis, we only consider ρ given by (4, 2, 3, 0, 1). The specification of the integral distinguisher (covering 10 steps only) is given in Table 5, where the same notation is used as previously.

Table 5. The form of integral distinguisher of $ACE_{(4,2,3,0,1)}$

The form of input	The form of output
$c^{64}a^{64}c^{64}a^{64}a^{64}$	$u^{64}b^{64}u^{64}u^{64}u^{64}$

5 A Novel Search for Impossible Differential Distinguishers for Word-Based Block Ciphers

5.1 A Search for Impossible Differential Distinguishers

The notion of impossible differential distinguishers greatly relies on the concept of miss-in-the-middle. For a specific pair of input and output differences $(\triangle_{input}^{i}, \triangle_{output}^{j})$, $0 \leq i, j \leq m - 1$, where $\triangle_{input}^{i}$ represents the difference having only its i-th word active, we first need to determine whether the corresponding word of the internal state is active, inactive, or unknown. This needs to be done both in the encryption and decryption direction. Then, having ensured that meeting in the middle is impossible, one can deduce that $(\triangle^i_{input}, \triangle^j_{output})$ is an impossible differential.

According to the definition of word-oriented trails, we can find the impossible differential distinguisher by checking the number of times that each word appears in the internal state expression. Let again $f : F_2^{n \times m} \to F_2^{n \times m}$ denote the round function, $\triangle^i_{input}$ be the input difference, and let the output difference be $\triangle^j_{output}$. If we want to determine whether there is an r_{id}-round impossible differential distinguisher, where $r_{id} = r_1 + r_2$ and r_1 and r_2 denote the number of rounds in the encryption and decryption direction, respectively, the following constraints need to be added into the MILP model M_{id}:

$$\boldsymbol{N}^{r_1}_i[k'] + \boldsymbol{W}^{r_2}_j[k'] = 1, \tag{14}$$

where $r_1 + r_2 = r_{id}$, $0 < r_1 < r_{id}$, and $0 \le i, j, k' \le m - 1$.

Furthermore, the existence of an r_{id}-round impossible differential distinguisher implies that we need to perform the same task when the variables in $\{r_1, r_2, i, j, k'\}$ take on all possible values. For some specific choice of these variables, denoting by M_{id} an initially empty model, we need to construct an r_1-round MILP model of word-oriented trails in the encryption direction and similarly an r_2-round MILP model in the decryption direction. Then, we update the model M_{id} (originally empty) by adding these two models in the encryption/decryption direction. Also, the equation (14) needs to be added into the updated model M_{id}. At this point, we have transformed the problem of searching for impossible differential distinguisher into a MILP instance. If the particular model M_{id} has feasible solutions, we can deduce that there is an r_{id}-round impossible differential distinguisher and return the values of i, j, k' and r_1. Taking into account the results returned from the solver, we can determine the form of impossible differential distinguishers, specify the input difference $\triangle^i_{input}$ and the impossible output difference $\triangle^i_{output}$.

According to the above discussion, the method of searching for impossible differential distinguishers for word-based block ciphers is described by Algorithm 3 in the appendix. To reduce the number of times the solver is used, binary search is used to determine impossible differential distinguishers that cover the maximal number of rounds. The purpose of lines 4 to 33 in Algorithm 3 is exactly to determine impossible differential distinguishers of maximal length. The line 34 in Algorithm 3 is used to determine the form of input difference, the form of impossible output difference, and the words causing a contradiction in the middle state; all the values being entries of a vector in this specific order. These vectors are also added into the set D as the second return value of Algorithm 3. The first return value of Algorithm 3 is the maximal number of rounds that the specified impossible differential distinguisher can cover.

5.2   Impossible Differential Distinguisher of ACE-Class Permutation

By using Algorithm 3, the security of the original ACE permutation against impossible differential cryptanalysis can be evaluated. This algorithm returns the values of r_{id} and D. The returned value of r_{id} is 12, and the set D is given by $D = \{(3, 2, 4, 5), (3, 2, 3, 6), (3, 2, 0, 7), (3, 2, 2, 8), (3, 2, 1, 9)\}$.

Moreover, we can consider all possible linear permutations ρ on five words, for the purpose of modifying the original linear permutation in ACE. Then, applying Algorithm 3 to these (linear) permutations instead, we can evaluate the security of the variants of ACE against impossible differential cryptanalysis. We were able to find linear permutations for which impossible differential distinguishers (using word-oriented trails) of the tweaked ACE algorithm exist only up to 10 encryption rounds. These linear permutations are listed in Table 6.

Table 6. Linear permutations ρ in ACE_ρ admitting impossible differential distinguishers for at most 10 steps

ρ	Minimum number of active sboxes for 16-step ACE_ρ
(1, 2, 4, 0, 3)	19
(3, 0, 1, 4, 2)	17

However, the minimum number of active S-boxes is not equal to 21 (as for the original linear permutation) for the 16-step encryption process and consequently the linear permutations listed in Table 6 do not provide the same resistance against differential and linear cryptanalysis.

On the other hand, if the linear permutation $(4, 2, 3, 0, 1)$ specified in Sect. 4.3 is used to replace the linear permutation of ACE, by using Algorithm 3, it turns out that this particular permutation will result in impossible differential distinguishers covering at most 11 steps. The results are listed in Table 7.

Table 7. The impossible differential distinguisher of $ACE_{\{4,2,3,0,1\}}$

Step	The index of word that has nonzero difference in plaintext	The index of word that has nonzero difference in ciphertext	The contradiction word in the middle	The number of steps in encryption direction
11	3	4	0	4
11	3	4	4	5
11	3	4	1	6

Compared to the original linear permutation used in ACE which allows for specifying integral and impossible differential distinguishers that cover 12 steps, the use of linear permutation $(4, 2, 3, 0, 1)$ only induces integral distinguisher for at most 10 rounds and impossible differential distinguishers (both using word-oriented trails) covering at most 11 rounds. Moreover, the original linear permutation of ACE and the above mentioned one induce the same security against differential and linear cryptanalysis. Therefore, we can conclude that the security of ACE that uses the linear permutation $(4, 2, 3, 0, 1)$ is stronger than its original version.

6   Conclusions

In this article, the automatic cryptanalytic tool, based on a MILP model of word-oriented trails, to search for impossible differential and integral distinguishers is proposed. Using this approach, we could specify an impossible differential distinguisher of the ACE permutation covering 12 encryption rounds. Moreover, to improve the security of this design, we have found a linear permutation $(4, 2, 3, 0, 1)$ which (replacing the original permutation of ACE) admits at most 11-round impossible differential distinguishers and 10-round integral distinguishers using our MILP model of word-oriented trails. This permutation also ensures the same resistance against the differential and linear cryptanalysis as the original one. Although the proposed distinguishers of ACE do not threat the security of ACE-AEAD, we believe that modelling word-oriented trails as an MILP instance is useful in both cryptanalysis and design of word-based block ciphers.

Acknowledgement. Yongzhuang Wei and Tao Ye are supported in part by the National Natural Science Foundation of China (No. 61872103), and in part by The Innovation Research Team Project of Guangxi Natural Science Foundation (2019GXNS-FGA245004).

Lingcheng Li is supported in part by the National Natural Science Foundation of China (No. 62162016), and in part by the Guangxi Science Foundation for Youths (No. 2020GXNSFBA297076).

A   Appendix 1

Algorithm 1. Determine r_j^e by using word trails

1: **input:** The total number of rounds is R, the index of active word is j, $0 \le j \le m-1$
2: **output:** r_j^e and ω_j
3: Let $r_u = R$, $r_l = 0$, $r_j^e = 0$, $r = 0$, $flag = 0$
4: **while** r_u - $r_l > 1$ **do**
5: $\quad r = \lfloor (r_u + r_l)/2 \rfloor$
6: $\quad$ Construct model M_e^r by using Property 5 and 6
7: $\quad M_e^r.con \leftarrow \boldsymbol{N}_j^0[j] = 1$, $\boldsymbol{N}_j^0[j'] = 0$, $min(\boldsymbol{N}_j^r) = 1$ $j' \ne j$, $0 \le j, j' \le m-1$
8: $\quad$ **if** M_e^r is feasible **then**
9: $\quad\quad r_l = r$, $flag = 1$
10: $\quad$ **else**
11: $\quad\quad r_u = r$, $flag = 0$
12: $\quad$ **end if**
13: **end while**
14: **if** $flag == 1$ **then**
15: $\quad r_j^e = r$
16: **else**
17: $\quad r_j^e = r - 1$
18: **end if**
19: $(1, \omega_j) = \boldsymbol{check\_min}(\boldsymbol{N}_j^{r_j^e})$

Algorithm 2. Determine r_k^d by using word-oriented trails

1: **input:** The number of total rounds is R, the index of active word is k, $0 \le k \le m-1$
2: **output:** r_k^d and ϕ_k
3: Let $r_u = R$, $r_l = 0$, $r_k^d = 0$, $r = 0$, $flag = 0$
4: **while** r_u - $r_l > 1$ **do**
5: $\quad r = \lfloor (r_u + r_l)/2 \rfloor$
6: $\quad$ Construct model M_d^r by using Property 5 and 6
7: $\quad M_d^r.con \leftarrow \boldsymbol{W}_k^0[k] = 1$, $\boldsymbol{W}_k^0[k'] = 0$, $min(\boldsymbol{W}_k^r) = 0$ $0 \le k, k' \le m-1, k' \ne k$
8: $\quad$ **if** M_d^r is feasible **then**
9: $\quad\quad r_l = r$, $flag = 1$
10: $\quad$ **else**
11: $\quad\quad r_u = r$, $flag = 0$
12: $\quad$ **end if**
13: **end while**
14: **if** $flag == 1$ **then**
15: $\quad r_k^d = r$
16: **else**
17: $\quad r_k^d = r - 1$
18: **end if**
19: $(0, \phi_k) = \boldsymbol{check\_min}(\boldsymbol{W}_k^{r_k^d})$

Algorithm 3. Search for impossible differential distinguishers by using word-oriented trails

---

1: **input:** The total number of rounds is R
2: **output:** r_{id}, the set D
3: Let $r_u = R, r_l = 0, r = 0, flag = 0, M_{id} = \emptyset, D = \emptyset$
4: **while** r_u - $r_l > 1$ **do**
5:     flag = 0
6:     $r = \lfloor (r_u + r_l)/2 \rfloor$
7:     **for** $0 < r_1 < r$ **do**
8:         **for** $0 \leq i \leq m - 1$ **do**
9:             **for** $0 \leq j \leq m - 1$ **do**
10:                **for** $0 \leq k' \leq m - 1$ **do**
11:                    Construct the model $M_e^{r_1}$ and $M_d^{r_2}$ by using Property 5 and 6
12:                    $M_{id}.con \leftarrow M_e^{r_1}, M_{id}.con \leftarrow M_d^{r_2}$
13:                    $M_{id}.con \leftarrow \boldsymbol{N}_i^0[i] = 1, \boldsymbol{N}_i^0[i'] = 0, i' \neq i, 0 \leq i' \leq m - 1$
14:                    $M_{id}.con \leftarrow \boldsymbol{W}_j^0[j] = 1, \boldsymbol{W}_j^0[j'] = 0, j' \neq j, 0 \leq j' \leq m - 1$
15:                    $M_{id}.con \leftarrow \boldsymbol{N}_i^{r_1}[k'] + \boldsymbol{W}_j^{r_2}[k'] = 1$
16:                    Solve the MILP model M_{id}
17:                    **if** The model M_{id} is feasible **then**
18:                        $r_l = r$, flag = 1
19:                        The program jumps to line 5
20:                    **end if**
21:                **end for**
22:            **end for**
23:        **end for**
24:    **end for**
25:    **if** flag $== 0$ **then**
26:        $r_u = r$
27:    **end if**
28: **end while**
29: **if** flag $== 1$ **then**
30:    $r_{id} = r$
31: **else**
32:    $r_{id} = r - 1$
33: **end if**
34: Let $r = r_{id}$, and execute lines 7 to 24 of this procedure. If the model M_{id} is feasible, then the vector $[i, j, k', r_1]$ is saved in D
35: **return** r_{id} and D

References

1. https://csrc.nist.gov/projects/lightweight-cryptography (2020)
2. Aagaard, M., AlTawy, R., Gong, G., Mandal, K., Rohit, R.: ACE: an authenticated encryption and hash algorithm. Submission to the NIST LWC Competition (2021). https://uwaterloo.ca/communications-security-lab/lwc/ace

3. Biham, E., Biryukov, A., Shamir, A.: Cryptanalysis of skipjack reduced to 31 rounds using impossible differentials. In: Stern, J. (ed.) EUROCRYPT 1999. LNCS, vol. 1592, pp. 12–23. Springer, Heidelberg (1999). https://doi.org/10.1007/3-540-48910-X_2

4. Biham, E., Shamir, A.: Differential cryptanalysis of DES-like cryptosystems. J. Cryptol. **4**(1), 3–72 (1991). https://doi.org/10.1007/BF00630563

5. Cui, T., Jia, K., Fu, K., Chen, S., Wang, M.: New automatic search tool for impossible differentials and zero-correlation linear approximations. IACR Cryptology ePrint Archive 2016/689 (2016). http://eprint.iacr.org/2016/689

6. ElSheikh, M., Tolba, M., Youssef, A.M.: Integral attacks on round-reduced Bel-T-256. In: Cid, C., Jacobson, M., Jr. (eds.) SAC 2018. LNCS, vol. 11349, pp. 73–91. Springer, Cham (2018). https://doi.org/10.1007/978-3-030-10970-7_4

7. Knudsen, L.R.: DEAL - a 128-bit block cipher. Technical report no. 151. Department of Informatics, University of Bergen, Norway (1998)

8. Knudsen, L., Wagner, D.: Integral cryptanalysis. In: Daemen, J., Rijmen, V. (eds.) FSE 2002. LNCS, vol. 2365, pp. 112–127. Springer, Heidelberg (2002). https://doi.org/10.1007/3-540-45661-9_9

9. Liu, J., Liu, G., Qu, L.: A new automatic tool searching for impossible differential of NIST candidate ACE. Mathematics **8**(9), 1576 (2020). https://doi.org/10.3390/math8091576

10. Matsui, M.: Linear cryptanalysis method for DES cipher. In: Helleseth, T. (ed.) EUROCRYPT 1993. LNCS, vol. 765, pp. 386–397. Springer, Heidelberg (1994). https://doi.org/10.1007/3-540-48285-7_33

11. Sasaki, Yu., Todo, Y.: New impossible differential search tool from design and cryptanalysis aspects. In: Coron, J.-S., Nielsen, J.B. (eds.) EUROCRYPT 2017. LNCS, vol. 10212, pp. 185–215. Springer, Cham (2017). https://doi.org/10.1007/978-3-319-56617-7_7

12. Todo, Y.: Structural evaluation by generalized integral property. In: Oswald, E., Fischlin, M. (eds.) EUROCRYPT 2015. LNCS, vol. 9056, pp. 287–314. Springer, Heidelberg (2015). https://doi.org/10.1007/978-3-662-46800-5_12

13. Xiang, Z., Zhang, W., Bao, Z., Lin, D.: Applying MILP method to searching integral distinguishers based on division property for 6 lightweight block ciphers. In: Cheon, J.H., Takagi, T. (eds.) ASIACRYPT 2016. LNCS, vol. 10031, pp. 648–678. Springer, Heidelberg (2016). https://doi.org/10.1007/978-3-662-53887-6_24

14. Yang, G., Zhu, B., Suder, V., Aagaard, M.D., Gong, G.: The Simeck family of lightweight block ciphers. In: Güneysu, T., Handschuh, H. (eds.) CHES 2015. LNCS, vol. 9293, pp. 307–329. Springer, Heidelberg (2015). https://doi.org/10.1007/978-3-662-48324-4_16

15. Ye, T., Wei, Y., Li, L.: Integral cryptanalysis of ACE encryption algorithm. J. Electron. Inf. Technol. **43**(4), 908–914 (2021). https://doi.org/10.11999/JEIT200234

16. Zhang, W., Cao, M., Guo, J., Pasalic, E.: Improved security evaluation of SPN block ciphers and its applications in the single-key attack on SKINNY. IACR Trans. Symmetric Cryptol. **2019**(4), 171–191 (2019). https://doi.org/10.13154/tosc.v2019.i4.171-191

17. Zhang, W., Rijmen, V.: Division cryptanalysis of block ciphers with a binary diffusion layer. IET Inf. Secur. **13**(2), 87–95 (2019). https://doi.org/10.1049/iet-ifs.2018.5151

18. Zhang, Y., Sun, S., Cai, J., Hu, L.: Speeding up MILP aided differential characteristic search with Matsui's strategy. In: Chen, L., Manulis, M., Schneider, S. (eds.) ISC 2018. LNCS, vol. 11060, pp. 101–115. Springer, Cham (2018). https://doi.org/10.1007/978-3-319-99136-8_6

19. Zhou, C., Zhang, W., Ding, T., Xiang, Z.: Improving the MILP-based security evaluation algorithm against differential/linear cryptanalysis using a divide-and-conquer approach. IACR Trans. Symmetric Cryptol. **2019**(4), 438–469 (2019). https://doi.org/10.13154/tosc.v2019.i4.438-469
20. Zhu, B., Dong, X., Yu, H.: MILP-based differential attack on round-reduced GIFT. In: Matsui, M. (ed.) CT-RSA 2019. LNCS, vol. 11405, pp. 372–390. Springer, Cham (2019). https://doi.org/10.1007/978-3-030-12612-4_19

Privacy-Preserving Contact Tracing Protocol for Mobile Devices: A Zero-Knowledge Proof Approach

Joseph K. Liu[1]([envelope]), Man Ho Au[2], Tsz Hon Yuen[2], Cong Zuo[4], Jiawei Wang[1], Amin Sakzad[1], Xiapu Luo[3], Li Li[1], and Kim-Kwang Raymond Choo[5]

[1] Department of Software Systems and Cybersecurity, Faculty of Information Technology, Monash University, Melbourne, Australia
joseph.liu@monash.edu
[2] The University of Hong Kong, Pok Fu Lam, Hong Kong
[3] The Hong Kong Polytechnic University, Hung Hom, Hong Kong
[4] Nanyang Technological University, Singapore, Singapore
[5] The University of Texas at San Antonio, San Antonio, USA

Abstract. In this paper, we propose a privacy-preserving contact tracing protocol for smart phones, and more specifically Android and iOS phones. The protocol allows users to be notified, if they have been a close contact of a confirmed patient. The protocol is designed to strike a balance between privacy, security, and scalability. Specifically, the app allows all users to hide their past location(s) and contact history from the Government, without affecting their ability to determine whether they have close contact with a confirmed patient whose identity will not be revealed. A zero-knowledge protocol is used to achieve such a user privacy functionality. In terms of security, no user can send fake messages to the system to launch a false positive attack. We present a security model and formally prove the security of the protocol. To demonstrate scalability, we evaluate an Android and an iOS implementation of our protocol. A comparative summary shows that our protocol is the most comprehensive and balanced privacy-preserving contact tracing solution to-date.

1 Introduction

The COVID-19 pandemic has significantly changed many aspects of our society, with both short-term impacts (e.g., temporary lockdowns, and social and physical distancing) and long-term impacts (e.g., economic [9]). In recent times, a number of cities, states, and countries are re-opening, where some businesses and activities are allowed to operate and proceed with certain limitations (e.g., wearing of personal protection equipment, and practising social/physical distancing). However, there is also the possibility of individuals, and in some instances large number of individuals, coming in close proximity with another person with undetected COVID-19 infection (e.g., the individual is asymptomatic or display

© Springer Nature Switzerland AG 2021
R. Deng et al. (Eds.): ISPEC 2021, LNCS 13107, pp. 327–344, 2021.
https://doi.org/10.1007/978-3-030-93206-0_20

mild symptoms) unknowingly. A recent high profile example is the recent incident involving the sitting U.S. president [11,25]. This highlights the importance of contact tracing [17,22], particularly in the current climate where there is the potential of a subsequent wave of COVID-19 affecting the public. The U.S. Centers for Disease Control and Prevention (CDC), for example, has released resources, such as contact tracing communications toolkit and guidelines for various stakeholder groups. The effectiveness of contact tracing, particularly digital contact tracing, has also been the focus of recent studies. For example, in a recent *Science* article, Ferretti et al. [12] reported that *"Improved sensitivity of testing in early infection could also speed up the algorithm and achieve rapid epidemic control"*.

Contact tracing allows relevant stakeholders, such as healthcare authorities, to identify and reach out to potentially infected individuals, so that appropriate measures can be taken (e.g., further testing, self-quarantine, and/or hospitalization). However, there are limitations in contact tracing. For example, how can we ensure that individuals who have unknowingly come into contact with a person with undetected COVID-19 infection be identified and subsequently contacted? This reinforces the importance of leveraging technologies, such as smart devices with built-in features such as Bluetooth communication and geolocation (e.g., mobile and wearable devices), to facilitate contact tracing.

A number of automated contact tracing protocols and applications (apps) have been developed, and examples include those designed by Apple Inc. and Google Inc. (GAEN) [1,2], the decentralized privacy-preserving proximity tracing (DP-3T) app [23], and those reported in [7,21]. A security analysis is provided in [10] for some of these schemes, such as GAEN, DP-3T, etc. The approaches in [7,21] rely on the use of smart devices to learn and possibly share the device user's location and associated timestamp with other users. However, such approaches may reveal certain metadata about the user's device (e.g., make and model) and contact information. Hence, there have been studies on the security of these approaches [15]. For example, it was revealed that DP-3T is vulnerable to relay and replay attacks, and an interactive scheme designed to prevent relay and replay attacks without affecting the existing features was presented [24]. In addition, a non-interactive scheme to counter relay and replay attacks in DP-3T [23] and the approaches of [7,21] was introduced in [20], using 'delayed authentication'. This is a novel message authentication code (MAC) in which the verification step is done in two phases, where the key is not required in one phase and the message is not in the other phase. A fake exposure notification attack on GAEN-based schemes is described in [4].

Similar to other healthcare frameworks [3,8,16,18], there are also privacy considerations in the use of such contact tracing apps. Individual citizens may not wish to be traced, particularly when they are participating in sensitive events (e.g., political demonstrations). As recent as January 2021, the Singapore Government reportedly contact tracing data will be made available to the law enforcement agency to facilitate the investigation of serious criminal cases[1]. This clearly has privacy implications. This reinforces the importance of having a privacy-preserving contact tracing system. However, designing secure, privacy-preserving, and scalable contact tracing apps remains a challenge, and this is the challenge we seek to address in this proposal.

Our Contributions. In this paper, we will design a privacy-preserving COVID-19 contact tracing protocol for Bluetooth-enabled smartphone users. The protocol allows users to record their close contacts in a privacy-preserving yet authenticated manner (i.e., prevents the sending of fabricated identification information). The 'closeness' can be customized based on existing medical advice, say within 6 ft. The zero-knowledge proof allows the user to preserve his/her *privacy*, in the sense that users can hide their prior locations and contact histories, for example from unauthorized entities. For example, when a user has been determined to be infected, (s)he proves using the zero-knowledge protocol to the medical doctor all his/her previous close contacts. Without gaining direct access to the contacts, information required to notify the related individuals is published, without the public learning the identity of the patient. Hence, the medical doctor does not learn the patient's contacts, including the location, name or any identification information. However, the individual been notified can be assured that (s)he is a close contact of an infected person. The probability of this particularly individual of correctly guessing the infected person among a list of close contacts is not better than a wild guess. The zero-knowledge protocol also ensures that no one is able to send any fabricated message, in the sense that if a user is not determined by a medical doctor to be infected, (s)he will not be able to convince others using the app. In addition, a confirmed infected patient will not be capable of convincing anyone who is not a close contact to be a close contact. As the notification does not include any link to any website or contain any attachment, this reduces the risk of malware/ransomware infection.

The layout of this paper is as follows. We present the system and threat models in Sect. 2. The cryptographic primitives that underpin our proposed system are presented in Sect. 3. We then present our proposed system in Sect. 4, and describe the implementation and evaluation findings in Sects. 5 and 6 respectively. The last two sections present our discussion and conclusion. The recent literature will be reviewed in the full version [19]. *Remark:* We also want to remind readers that the references on preprints posted on arXiv or IACR eprint are not peer-reviewed by arXiv or IACR; they should not be relied upon without context to guide clinical practice or health-related behavior and should not be reported in news media as established information without consulting multiple experts in the field.

---

[1] https://www.technologyreview.com/2021/01/05/1015734/singapore-contact-tracing-police-data-covid/, last accessed January 13, 2021.

2   System and Threat Models

2.1   System Model

Our system comprises the following entities:

- Bulletin board $\mathcal{BB}$: Once information has been posted on the BB, it cannot be erased. The BB can be instantiated by using a blockchain system.
- User: User refers to an individual who has our contact tracing app installed on their smartphone. In the rest of this paper, we will use Alice and Bob to denote two individual users who have come into close contact.
- Medical doctor $\mathcal{D}$: Individuals can be only be confirmed to be positive by a practising D, who is also affiliated with a medical institution (e.g., medical practice or hospital).
- Government $\mathcal{GV}$: $\mathcal{GV}$ is responsible for the registration of users and their app. This is not an unreasonable requirement, since users need to provide proof of identification when signing up for their smartphones. $\mathcal{GV}$'s public/private key pair is $(PK_{\mathcal{GV}}, SK_{\mathcal{GV}})$, and clearly $PK_{\mathcal{GV}}$ is known to the public.

In our system model, we assume that no one is able to modify the app, and the owner can read all data generated, stored and communicated via the app installed on an Internet-connected and Bluetooth-enabled smartphone (e.g., WiFi). We also assume that users will not reveal their infection status publicly (e.g., social media posts) or share their own secret keys.

2.2   Threat Model

The adversary is assumed to be honest-but-curious, in the sense that they follow the defined algorithms but are sufficiently curious to learn more information. Also in our threat model, we only include *cryptographic attack*. In other words, network attacks (e.g. distributed denial of service), software attacks (e.g. modifying the app and uploading the modified app to a third-party app store), physical attacks (e.g. stealing the smartphone), etc., are out of scope. Under these conditions, we define the following threat model to our system (see also Fig. 1):

1. [**Traceability Completeness**] All close contacts of a confirmed infected individual (hereafter referred to as patient) will be notified of the contact date(s). All honest-but-curious *cryptographic* adversaries should not be able to prevent any close contact of the patient from being notified. In Fig. 1, Bob and John are the close contacts of Alice, and both Bob and John should be notified as a close contact of a patient (without learning that the patient is Alice).
2. [**False Positive (case 1)**] Anyone who is not a patient cannot impersonate as one and send out messages to their close contacts (e.g., ask them to self-quarantine). In Fig. 1, Andy cannot send any "close contact message" to Ben and Bob. Peter also cannot send any "close contact message" to Bob.

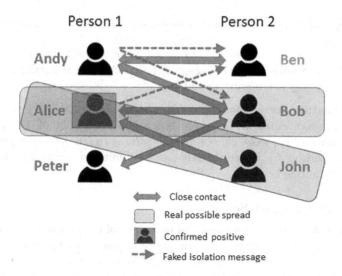

Person 1   **Person 2**

Andy   Ben

Alice   Bob

Peter   John

Close contact

Real possible spread

Confirmed positive

Faked isolation message

Fig. 1. Threat model

3. [**False Positive (case 2)**] Patients can only send messages to their close contacts (e.g. ask them to self-isolate). For example, as shown in Fig. 1, Alice is not able to send any "close contact message" to Ben, who is not her close contact. Here, we do not consider the medical doctor as an adversary in both cases (2) and (3).

4. [**Patient Privacy**] Other than the medical doctor who certified that the user is infected, no one else should not be able to find out the identity of the patient (in the sense not better than a wild guess). For example, as shown in Fig. 1, Ben does not know any information about the patient. Bob, a close contact of Alice, who had met both Andy and Peter, can correctly guess Alice as the patient with a probability of 1/3. John, another close contact of Alice, will know Alice is the patient.

5. [**Contact Privacy**] No one, except the owner of the app, should be able to find out the identity or location of the close contact of a patient, as shown in Fig. 1. An *cryptographic* adversary may attempt to (unsuccessfully) locate information about the close contact of a patient.

3 Cryptographic Primitives

3.1 Signature Scheme

A signature scheme consists of three algorithms, which are defined as follow:

- $(SK, PK) \leftarrow \mathsf{KeyGen}(\lambda)$ as a PPT algorithm that on input a security parameter $\lambda \in \mathbb{N}$ outputs a secret/public key pair (SK, PK).

- $\sigma \leftarrow \mathsf{Sign}(SK, M)$ that on input a secret key SK and a message M produces a signature σ.
- accept/reject $\leftarrow \mathsf{Verify}(PK, \sigma, M)$ that on input a public key PK, a message M and a signature σ returns accept or reject. An accept output implies that the message-signature pair is *valid*.

A secure signature scheme should provide existential unforgeability against adaptive chosen-message attacks, based on the standard definition of [14]. *Existential unforgeability under a weak chosen message attack (a.k.a. weakly unforgeable)* is a weaker definition [6], where the adversary submits all signature queries prior to seeing the public key.

3.2 Group Signature Scheme

A group signature allows a user to sign on behalf of the group, while the verifier only knows that the signer is one of the users of this group without knowing the signer's identity. In this setting, there is a group manager tasked with setting up of the group (e.g., publication of the group public key) and issuing of individual user's secret key. The group manager may also have the ability to open the signature, that is, to find out who the actual signer is.

There are several algorithms in a group signature scheme. For simplicity, we only state the algorithms related to our system here:

- $\sigma \leftarrow \mathsf{GSign}(USK, GPK, M)$ that on input a user secret key USK (issued by the group manager), group public key GPK (generated by the group manager) and a message M produces a signature σ.
- accept/reject $\leftarrow \mathsf{GVerify}(GPK, \sigma, M)$ that on input a group public key GPK, a message M and a signature σ, returns accept or reject. An accept output implies that the message-signature pair is *valid*.

We follow the standard security definition of group signature in [5], including anonymity and traceability which also implies unforgeability.

3.3 Mathematical Assumptions

Bilinear Pairings. Let $\mathbb{G}_1$, $\mathbb{G}_2$ and $\mathbb{G}_T$ be cyclic groups of prime order q. u is a generator of $\mathbb{G}_1$ and g denotes a generator of $\mathbb{G}_2$. A function $e : \mathbb{G}_1 \times \mathbb{G}_2 \rightarrow \mathbb{G}_T$ is a bilinear map if the following properties hold:

- Bilinearity: $e(A^x, B^y) = e(A, B)^{xy}$ for all $A \in \mathbb{G}_1$, $B \in \mathbb{G}_2$ and $x, y \in \mathbb{Z}_q$;
- Non-degeneracy: $e(u, g) \neq 1$, where 1 is the identity of $\mathbb{G}_T$;
- Efficient computability: there exists an algorithm that can efficiently compute $e(A, B)$ for all $A \in \mathbb{G}_1$ and $B \in \mathbb{G}_2$.

Assumption 1 underpins our contact privacy (see Sect. 2.2), which is similar to the truncated decision $(q' + 2)$-ABDHE problem [13].

Definition 1 (Assumption 1). *Suppose that $\tilde{u} \in_R \mathbb{G}_1$, $g \in_R \mathbb{G}_2$, $b \in_R \mathbb{Z}_q$, $Z_0 \in_R \mathbb{G}_T$ and $Z_1 = e(\tilde{u}, g)^{b^{q'+2}}$. When given $(\tilde{u}, \tilde{u}^b, \ldots, \tilde{u}^{b^{q'}}) \in \mathbb{G}_1$ and $g, g^b \in \mathbb{G}_2$, no PPT adversary can distinguish Z_0 and Z_1 with non-negligible probability.*

3.4 Zero-Knowledge Proof

A zero-knowledge proof is a two-party protocol that allows one party to convince the other party that the topic presented is true without revealing anything else. In this paper, we are interested in zero-knowledge proof for NP language. Specifically, let R be a polynomial time decidable binary relation and L_R be the NP language defined by R, i.e., $L_R = \{x | \exists w \ s.t. (x, w) \in R\}$. We say w is a witness for statement x. The zero-knowledge proof protocol we considered in this paper is known as Σ-Protocol, which is a 3-move protocol between prover P and verifier V such that the second message (from V to P) is just the random coins of V. A Σ-protocol between P and V satisfies the following properties.

- *Completeness*: If $x \in L_R$, prover P with auxiliary input w convinces V with overwhelming probability.
- *Special Soundness*: Given two transcripts (t, c, z) and (t, c', z') for statement x, there exists an algorithm that outputs w s.t. $(x, w) \in R$.
- *Honest Verifier Zero-Knowledge (HVZK)*: Given x and c, there exists an algorithm that outputs (t, z) such that (t, c, z) is indistinguishable to the real transcript between P with auxiliary input w and V.

Σ-Protocol can be converted to full zero-knowledge in the common reference string model using standard techniques. Also, it can be converted to non-interactive zero-knowledge argument in the random oracle model by replacing the random coins of the verifier with the output of a cryptographic hash function on the first message of the prover.

4 Our Proposed System

There are four phases in our system. In the **Registration Phase**, each user chooses his/her secret key and public key, and uploads the public key to the Government website for registration. This allows the Government to link the public key with the user's name or identity. This is to provide accountability and prevent double or multiple registration of the same user. This process will repeat each day with a new key pair registered. A medical doctor gets an additional individual secret key issued by his/her affiliated organization (e.g., hospital), which is used to generate a group signature on behalf of the affiliated organization.

In the **Meeting Phase**, each user's app will use Bluetooth to broadcast a package to other users' smartphones (and the apps) at a regular time interval (e.g., a minute). Upon receiving a threshold number of the same package within a certain timeframe (e.g., 15 min), the app will confirm the relevant user as a close contact. After a mutual validation (of package) process, the two apps will jointly generate two different credentials to be stored on each smartphone. The credential will be used later to prove to the medical doctor (in zero-knowledge) that the other person is a close contact, if one party is medically confirmed to be infected.

In the **Medical Treatment Phase**, the patient executes the zero-knowledge proof protocol with the medical doctor, to prove (s)he has close contact with other individuals. However, the doctor is not able to learn the identities, public keys, or location of the close contact(s). The doctor signs the zero-knowledge proof using the group signature user secret key (on behalf of his/her affiliated organization), and posts the signature together with the proof to the bulletin board for public awareness (e.g., statistics about the number of infected individuals).

In the **Tracing Phase**, each user checks whether the new entry in the bulletin board is related to them, based on computations using their own secret key. This can be performed either manually (e.g., pull) or automatically (i.e., having the checks pushed to apps).

Next, we will present the detailed description of each phases.

4.1   The Phases

Setup Phase: In this phase, $\mathcal{GV}$ first generates the parameters and the users register with $\mathcal{GV}$. Users also need to update the key with $\mathcal{GV}$ daily, unless they are medically confirmed as infected. The detailed steps are outlined below:

1. **(Parameter Generation)** The input $1^\lambda \in \mathbb{N}$ is a security parameter, and let $\mathbb{G}_1$, $\mathbb{G}_2$ and $\mathbb{G}_T$ be cyclic groups of prime order q such that q is a λ-bit prime. Also, let $e : \mathbb{G}_1 \times \mathbb{G}_2 \to \mathbb{G}_T$ be a bilinear map. $\mathcal{GV}$ selects generators $u, u_1, u_2 \in \mathbb{G}_1$ and $g, g_1, g_2 \in \mathbb{G}_2$. Let $H : \{0,1\}^* \to \mathbb{Z}_q$ be a cryptographic hash function. $\mathcal{GV}$ also selects its secret and public key pair $(SK_G, PK_G) \leftarrow$ KeyGen(λ). $\mathcal{GV}$ publishes public parameters $(\lambda, H, PK_G, u, u_1, u_2, g, g_1, g_2)$. In practice, these parameters can also be embedded into the user's app which can be downloaded from the official app stores.

2. **(User Registration)** On each day, non-infected user (e.g., Alice) chooses a secret key SK_A as $a \in \mathbb{Z}_q$ and computes the public key PK_A as $A = g^a$. The user, say Alice, registers with $\mathcal{GV}$ by uploading her personal information and PK_A[2]. $\mathcal{GV}$ also randomly generates an identifier $\text{ID}_A \in \mathbb{Z}_q$ for Alice. $\mathcal{GV}$ generates a signature $\sigma_A \leftarrow \text{Sign}(SK_G, \{\text{``-VE''}, PK_A, \text{ID}_A, \text{DATE}\})$ and sends $\sigma_A$ and $\text{ID}_A$ back to Alice, where DATE is the current date. Alice checks the signature by running $\text{Verify}(PK_G, \sigma_A, \{\text{``-VE''}, PK_A, \text{ID}_A, \text{DATE}\})$. If this is valid, Alice stores σ_A and ID_A in her app. Otherwise, she aborts.

   NOTE: $\mathcal{GV}$ will give a signature with $\{\text{``+VE''}, PK_A, \text{ID}_A, \text{DATE}\}$ (instead of the typical ``-VE'' message) to confirmed infected user. This is to distinguish a confirmed case from others. The infected user's public key will also not be updated.

3. **(Additional step taken by the medical doctor)** Each medical doctor $\mathcal{D}$ gets an additional group signature user secret key GSK from the hospital manager (who acts as the group manager of the group signature) in the app. Each hospital also publishes the group signature group public key GPK.

---

[2] $\mathcal{GV}$ may record the related identification information (e.g., name, phone, email) of the user if this is a first-time registration.

Meeting Phase: In this phase, each non-confirmed user (e.g. Alice) will use bluetooth to broadcast the hash $h_A = H(\text{``-VE''}, \text{ID}_A, PK_A, \sigma_A)$ to the surrounding people periodically (e.g. every minute). For any confirmed user, a ``+VE'' package (e.g. *without hashing* (``+VE'', $\text{ID}_P, PK_P, \sigma_P$) denoting the owner of the app who has been confirmed by the medical doctor as positive) will be broadcasted instead. If it has been received, other users should report to $\mathcal{GV}$ immediately after verifying the signature σ_P. Otherwise once another user (e.g. Bob) has received a number of the same hash broadcast within a certain time (e.g. receive 15 packages in 15 min), they (Alice and Bob) are considered as close contact. In below, we describe a protocol executed between Alice and Bob so that Alice will record Bob's information as her close contact. Bob will also Alice's information as his close contact at the end of the protocol.

1. **(Package Validation)** After receiving (a threshold number of) Alice's hash h_A, Bob('s smartphone) pairs with Alice('s smartphone) and Bob needs to validate Alice's package. Bob first asks Alice to send him the tuples $(\text{ID}_A, PK_A, \sigma_A)$. Then, Bob computes $h'_A = H(\text{``-VE''}, \text{ID}_A, PK_A, \sigma_A)$ and checks if $h_A = h'_A$. Bob aborts if it is not equal; otherwise, he continues and randomly generates a challenge number $r_B \in_R \mathbb{Z}$ and sends r_B to Alice. Alice uses her SK_A ($a \in \mathbb{Z}_q$) to generate a Schnorr signature on the message r_B, as follow:

   (a) Randomly chooses $k \in_R \mathbb{Z}_q$.
   (b) Computes $t = H(g^k, r_B)$.
   (c) Computes $s = k - at \bmod q$.
   (d) Outputs the signature $\sigma'_A = (s, t)$ for message r_B.

   Alice sends σ'_A to Bob for verification. Bob first verifies PK_A ($A \in \mathbb{G}_2$) by running

   $$\texttt{Verify}(PK_G, \sigma_A, \{PK_A, \text{ID}_A, \texttt{DATE}\}). \tag{1}$$

   If it is valid, Bob verifies Alice's Schnorr's signature $\sigma'_A = (s, t)$ by checking if

   $$t = H(g^s A^t, r_B)$$

   If it is equal, Bob stores Alice's package $(\text{ID}_A, A, \sigma_A)$ in his app. Otherwise, aborts the protocol.
   Similarly for Alice, Bob's package $(\text{ID}_B, B, \sigma_B)$ will be stored in Alice's app if the verification is successful.

2. **(Identity Mutual Commitment)** Alice and Bob need to store each other's identification information and subsequently generate a zero-knowledge proof to $\mathcal{D}$ as a close contact to a patient (if either of them is confirmed). In order to ensure the correct generation of the proof, we need to have an additional mutual commitment in this phase.
   Bob uses his secret key $b \in \mathbb{Z}_q$ and Alice's identifier ID_A to generate

   $$\sigma''_B = u^{\frac{1}{H(\text{ID}_A)+b}}$$

and sends σ_B'' to Alice. Alice checks if

$$e(\sigma_B'', g^{H(\text{ID}_A)}B) = e(u, g)$$

If it is equal, Alice stores $(B, \text{ID}_B, \sigma_B'', \text{DATE})$ in her app.
Alice uses her secret key $a \in \mathbb{Z}_q$ and Bob's identifier $\text{ID}_A \in \mathbb{Z}_q$ to generate

$$\sigma_A'' = u^{\frac{1}{H(\text{ID}_B)+a}}$$

and sends σ_A'' to Bob. Bob checks if

$$e(\sigma_A'', g^{H(\text{ID}_B)}A) = e(u, g)$$

If it is equal, Bob stores $(A, \text{ID}_A, \sigma_A'', \text{DATE})$ in his app.

The meeting phase is illustrated in Fig. 2.

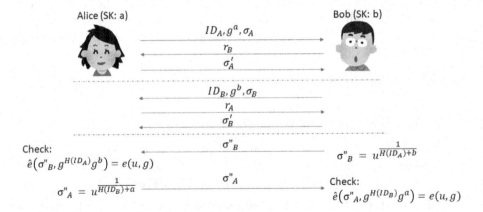

Fig. 2. Meeting phase

Medical Treatment Phase: In this phase, we assume Alice is determined to be infected by the medical doctor $\mathcal{D}$. Alice also informs $\mathcal{D}$ of her close contacts during the dates required, without revealing their identifiers or public keys. Instead, she (Alice's app) will generate a pseudo-public key of each of her close contacts (e.g., Bob) together with a zero-knowledge proof from the mutual commitment generated in the **Meeting Phase** – see Step (2) to prove that she has contacted with the people. $\mathcal{D}$ then publishes the pseudo-public key to $\mathcal{BB}$ and the public can check whether this pseudo-public key is associated with them.

$\mathcal{D}$ and Alice execute the following protocol:

1. **(Authentication of Alice)** $\mathcal{D}$ authenticates Alice by executing **Meeting Phase** Step (1) (Package Validation) and obtains her identifier ID_A.

2. **(Contact Retrieval)** Alice retrieves her contacts that she came into contact with during the incubation period, say DATE_i. Suppose Alice was in contact with Bob on May 13, then Alice retrieves $(\text{ID}_B, B, \sigma_B'', 13\text{th May})$ from her app.

3. **(Pseudo-Public Key)** Alice generates the pseudo-public key for Bob, by first randomly choosing $x \in_R \mathbb{Z}_q$ and computing:

$$h = e(u, g)^x, \qquad \widehat{B} = e(u, B)^x = e(u, g^b)^x = h^b \qquad (2)$$

Then, $(h, \widehat{B})$ is sent to $\mathcal{D}$.

4. **(Zero-Knowledge Proof)** Alice needs to prove to $\mathcal{D}$ that $(h, \widehat{B})$ is correctly formed. *Correct* means Alice has received a valid signature σ_B'' under the public key $B = g^b$ and $\widehat{B} = h^b, h = e(u, g)^x$. Note that $\mathcal{D}$ also knows Alice's identifier ID_A. Conceptually, Alice needs to prove in zero-knowledge that

$$PK\{(\sigma_B'', B, x) :$$
$$h = e(u, g)^x, \widehat{B} = e(u, B)^x, e(\sigma_B'', g^{H(\text{ID}_A)}B) = e(u, g)\}. \qquad (3)$$

In order to instantiate this proof, Alice first randomly generates $s_1, s_2, t \in_R \mathbb{Z}_q$ and computes

$$A_1 = g_1^{s_1} g_2^{s_2}, \qquad A_2 = Bg_1^{s_2}, \qquad C = \sigma_B'' u_1^t$$

Alice sends A_1, A_2, C to $\mathcal{D}$ and proves that

$$PK\{(s_1, s_2, t, \alpha_1, \alpha_2, \beta_1, \beta_2, x) :$$
$$A_1 = g_1^{s_1} g_2^{s_2} \wedge A_1^x = g_1^{\alpha_1} g_2^{\alpha_2} \wedge$$
$$A_1^t = g_1^{\beta_1} g_2^{\beta_2} \wedge h = e(u, g)^x \wedge \widehat{B} = e(u, A_2^x g_1^{-\alpha_2}) \wedge$$
$$e(Cu_1^{-t}, g^{H(\text{ID}_A)} A_2 g_1^{-s_2}) = e(u, g)\} \qquad (4)$$

This can be turned into a non-interactive zero-knowledge proof, using the following algorithm:

[Proof Generation]
(a) Randomly chooses $r_1, r_2, r_3, r_4, r_5, r_6, r_7, r_8 \in_R \mathbb{Z}_q$.
(b) Computes

$$T_1 = g_1^{r_1} g_2^{r_2}, \qquad T_2 = A_1^{-r_6} g_1^{r_4} g_2^{r_5}, \qquad T_3 = A_1^{-r_3} g_1^{r_7} g_2^{r_8},$$

$$T_4 = e(u, g)^{r_6}, \qquad T_5 = e(u, A_2^{r_6} g_1^{-r_5}),$$

$$T_6 = e(u_1^{r_3}, g^{H(\text{ID}_A)} A_2) e(C^{r_2} u_1^{-r_8}, g_1)$$

(c) Computes the hash

$$c = H(T_1, T_2, T_3, T_4, T_5, T_6, \widehat{B}, h, A_1, A_2, C, \text{DATE})$$

where DATE is the current date.

(d) Computes

$$z_1 = r_1 - cs_1 \bmod q$$
$$z_2 = r_2 - cs_2 \bmod q$$
$$z_3 = r_3 - ct \bmod q$$
$$z_4 = r_4 - cs_1 x \bmod q$$
$$z_5 = r_5 - cs_2 x \bmod q$$
$$z_6 = r_6 - cx \bmod q$$
$$z_7 = r_7 - cs_1 t \bmod q$$
$$z_8 = r_8 - cs_2 t \bmod q$$

(e) Outputs the proof $\pi : (c, z_1, z_2, z_3, z_4, z_5, z_6, z_7, z_8)$.

[Proof Verification] Computes

$$T_1' = A_1^c g_1^{z_1} g_2^{z_2}$$
$$T_2' = A_1^{-z_6} g_1^{z_4} g_2^{z_5}$$
$$T_3' = A_1^{-z_3} g_1^{z_7} g_2^{z_8}$$
$$T_4' = h^c e(u, g)^{z_6}$$
$$T_5' = \widehat{B}^c e(u, A_2^{z_6} g_1^{-z_5})$$
$$T_6' = \left(\frac{e(C, g^{H(\mathrm{ID}_A)} A_2)}{e(u, g)} \right)^c e(u_1^{z_3}, g^{H(\mathrm{ID}_A)} A_2) e(C^{z_2} u_1^{-z_8}, g_1)$$

Accepts the proof if, and only if,

$$c = H(T_1', T_2', T_3', T_4', T_5', T_6', \widehat{B}, h, A_1, A_2, C, \mathtt{DATE})$$

5. **(Publish Pseudo-Public Key)** If the proof is correct, $\mathcal{D}$ generates a group signature $\sigma_D \leftarrow \mathsf{GSign}(USK, GPK, M)$ on message $M = (h, \widehat{B}, \mathtt{DATE})$ and publishes $(\sigma_D, h, \widehat{B}, \mathtt{DATE})$ into $\mathcal{BB}$. $\mathcal{D}$ also informs $\mathcal{GV}$ that Alice (with identifier ID_A and public key A) has been confirmed as positive. $\mathcal{GV}$ will update its entry on Alice: $\{$''+VE'', $PK_A, \mathrm{ID}_A, \mathtt{DATE}\}$ and sign this entry every date (update $\mathtt{DATE}$ only) until Alice has deemed to be fully recovered (and no longer infectious).

Tracing Phase: At the end of each day (e.g., 23:59:59 h), each non-infected user, say Bob, executes the following step:

Bob scans through $\mathcal{BB}$ for all new entries. For each entry

$$(\sigma_D, h, \widehat{B}, \mathtt{DATE})$$

Bob first retrieves his secret key SK_B $(b \in \mathbb{Z}_q)$ corresponding to that $\mathtt{DATE}$ and checks if:

$$\widehat{B} = h^b. \tag{5}$$

If yes, Bob then verifies the signature by running $\mathsf{GVerify}(\sigma_D, GPK, \{h, \widehat{B}, \mathtt{DATE}\})$. If it is valid, he has been in close contact with a confirmed patient on $\mathtt{DATE}$.

4.2   Security Discussion

We first state our lemmas in the context of the threat model outlined in Sect. 2.2, while the detailed analysis of each lemma will be presented in the full version [19].

1. [Traceability Completeness]

Lemma 1. *Our system provides Traceability Completeness if our protocol is correct.*

2. [False Positive (case 1)]

Lemma 2. *Our system does not have Case 1 False Positive error if the underlying group signature scheme (Sect. 3.2) is unforgeable.*

3. [False Positive (case 2)]

Lemma 3. *Our system does not have Case 2 False Positive error if the zero-knowledge proof in Eq. (3) is sound and the Boneh-Boyen signature [6] is weakly unforgeable.*

4. [Patient Privacy]

Lemma 4. *Our system provides Patient Privacy from the public unconditionally, and from the patient's close contacts if the underlying signature scheme (Sect. 3.1) is unforgeable.*

5. [Contact Privacy]

Lemma 5. *Our system provides Patient Privacy if the zero-knowledge proof in Eq. (3) and its instantiations are zero-knowledge and Assumption 1 (on page 6) holds in the random oracle model.*

5   Implementation

We have launched the contact tracing app for both Android and iOS platforms. We tested the Android version on Android 8.0 and 10.0, while the iOS version on iOS 13.7. Figure 3 illustrates its architecture. The contact tracing app consists of four main modules, namely Bluetooth service, device discovery service, Crypto manager, and utility module. When the app is installed for the first time, the Crypto manager will be initialised with a set of operations such as key generation, downloading public keys or parameters from other parties, etc. Then, the app will start two background services which will interact with other components:

- Crypto manager module encapsulates most of aforementioned operations of Crypto algorithms, such as signing, verification, and etc. The module also helps the user generate key pairs $((SK_A, PK_A))$ on a daily basis. Then, it will upload the user's personal information and PK_A to $\mathcal{GV}$ for finishing the registration, and will wait for the identifier ID_A and the signature σ_A from $\mathcal{GV}$, which will be stored in the storage module along with SK_A, PK_A and other user information.

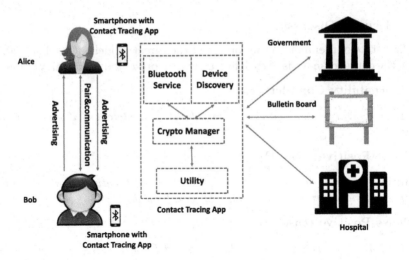

Fig. 3. A diagram of the workflow and architecture of our implementation.

- The device discovering service is a background service listening to nearby Bluetooth advertising packets and filtering out irrelevant packets. When the number of packets received from other devices running our contact tracing app exceeds a predefined threshold, which is set to 15 packets within 15 min from the same sender by default, it will pair with that device for further communication.
- The Bluetooth service is another background service listening to nearby Bluetooth pair and connection requests. It also advertises the user's own hash of message periodically to nearby devices.
- The Utility component handles regular tasks such as user interface activities, Network IO, to support other components of this app. For example, user may need to download information from Bulletin Board, which is running on the servers maintained by governments or hospitals.

6 Evaluation

We have conducted experiments to carefully evaluate the performance of our contact tracing system. We install the app in a Google Pixel 4 and a Google Pixel 2 smartphones for emulating the interactions of two people, and execute the tool for doctor in a PC (Macbook Pro, Core i7, 16 GB RAM). As to run the test for the iOS version, we use an iPhone 11 and an iPhone SE2 as test machines.

To characterize the latency required by our solution, we measure the three phases in the contract tracing app, including meeting, medical treatment and tracing phase. We execute the process including advertising data, receiving and processing packets, for 100 times and compute the latency of each phase. In the Android tests, the mean delay and the standard deviation for them are 94 ms (49), 144 ms (19), 5 ms (0.3), respectively, When it comes to the iOS tests, the latency of these three phases is 136 ms (48), 187 ms (11), 5 ms (0.2).

Moreover, we evaluate the time required by the tool for a doctor to finish the verification. By running the tool to conduct the verification for 100 times, we observe the mean elapsed time is 515 ms and standard deviation is 224.

Note that the mean time for tracing phase includes 1 checking on Eq. (5) plus one verification of a group signature. In reality, there should be a very large number of checking on Eq. (5) (e.g., 10000) which represents the number of new contacts made by the overall number of new patients. Therefore we also separately evaluate the time of executing this equation. The mean time is only 72 ms. The running of the verification of a group signature should be only a few (e.g., 2 or 3). We can argue that even if there are 100 new patients confirmed each day, and each patient has around 20 to 30 close contacts (and overall a few hundred contacts over the past two weeks), the running time for the tracing phase is still acceptable, and can be completed within a few hours in this extreme case. We have also addressed a practical consideration for this case in the next section.

7   Discussion

In addition to the findings presented in the preceding section, we will discuss a few practical issues for privacy-preserving contact tracing.

7.1   Cluster Identification and Formation

Cluster formation is essential to the analysis of how diseases spread in the community. For example, the identification of clusters can inform government mitigation strategy as observed in the responses in Singapore and Hong Kong. Specifically, once clusters in Singapore (e.g., foreign workers' dormitories) were identified, individuals in these clusters were quarantined. Similarly, in Hong Kong, the identification of a cluster (in the same residential building) facilitated the scientists in narrowing the specific cause of the spread (in this context, leaking toilet pipes).

In our privacy-preserving contact tracing app, the meeting location for users is hidden from the Government and the medical doctor. We propose that cluster identification and formation should be performed after the contact tracing phase. Suppose that Alice is infected and she has contact with Bob and John. If John is not infected, the meeting location of Alice and John should be kept private. If Bob is infected, then the Government can perform normal cluster identification and formation between Alice and Bob (e.g., to determine if they worked in the same organization, visited the same venues, or lived in the same building), based on information provided by the patients or their devices.

7.2 Privacy Leakage

In our proposal, we also consider privacy leakage that stems from the medical doctor. For example, if the medical doctor is a pediatrician, then it is likely that the patient is a child. Therefore, we use the anonymity property of group signature to ensure that such information is not leaked through the doctor's signature on the bulletin board.

On the other hand, it is also possible for the Government to host COVID-19 information website with an appropriate access control policy, rather than relying on the bulletin board. Only authorized medical doctors can post on this website and the identity of the medical doctor is hidden. Then, we can replace the group signature and the bulletin board with a standard signature (from the doctor) and the COVID-19 information website. All users should trust the validity of the information posted on this website.

7.3 Improving System Performance

The number of computation required in the tracing phase is directly proportional to the number of newly confirmed patients each day. In other to improve the system performance in a country with a large number of new confirmed cases each day, we suggest that our protocol can be parameterized to the state, city, or county level. This can be easily achieved by adjusting the group signature so that the state, city, or county forms a group (instead of a hospital) and users from the state, city, or county only needs to check those entries signed by the medical doctors in the state, city, or county. In this case, the checks can be significantly simplified.

8 Conclusion

In this paper, we proposed a privacy-preserving COVID-19 contact tracing app. Using zero knowledge proof, our apps allows the notification of close contacts, without revealing the location and identification of these close contacts (to governments). We formally proved the security of our approach, and the findings from our evaluation of the Android and iOS prototype demonstrated the utility of the app in a real-world setting. Future research includes extending the evaluation to a broader population, such as the students and staff members of the authors' institutions.

References

1. Apple Inc and Google Inc., Contact tracing Bluetooth specification v1.1 (2020). https://www.blog.google/documents/58/Contact_Tracing_-_Bluetooth_Specification_v1.1_RYGZbKW.pdf. Accessed 30 Apr 2020

2. Apple Inc and Google Inc., Contact tracing cryptography specification (2020). https://www.blog.google/documents/56/Contact_Tracing_-_Cryptography_ Specification.pdf. Accessed 30 Apr 2020
3. Au, M.H., et al.: A general framework for secure sharing of personal health records in cloud system. J. Comput. Syst. Sci. **90**, 46–62 (2017)
4. Avitabile, G., Friolo, D., Visconti, I.: TEnK-U: terrorist attacks for fake exposure notifications in contact tracing systems. Cryptology ePrint Archive, Report 2020/1150 (2020). https://eprint.iacr.org/2020/1150
5. Bellare, M., Micciancio, D., Warinschi, B.: Foundations of group signatures: formal definitions, simplified requirements, and a construction based on general assumptions. In: Biham, E. (ed.) EUROCRYPT 2003. LNCS, vol. 2656, pp. 614–629. Springer, Heidelberg (2003). https://doi.org/10.1007/3-540-39200-9_38
6. Boneh, D., Boyen, X.: Short signatures without random oracles. In: Cachin, C., Camenisch, J.L. (eds.) EUROCRYPT 2004. LNCS, vol. 3027, pp. 56–73. Springer, Heidelberg (2004). https://doi.org/10.1007/978-3-540-24676-3_4
7. Chan, J., et al.: PACT: privacy sensitive protocols and mechanisms for mobile contact tracing (2020)
8. Chen, Z., et al.: Verifiable keyword search for secure big data-based mobile healthcare networks with fine-grained authorization control. Future Gener. Comput. Syst. **87**, 712–724 (2018)
9. Chetty, R., Friedman, J.N., Hendren, N., Stepner, M., et al.: How did COVID-19 and stabilization policies affect spending and employment? A new real-time economic tracker based on private sector data. Technical report, National Bureau of Economic Research (2020)
10. Danz, N., Derwisch, O., Lehmann, A., Puenter, W., Stolle, M., Ziemann, J.: Security and privacy of decentralized cryptographic contact tracing. Cryptology ePrint Archive, Report 2020/1309 (2020). https://eprint.iacr.org/2020/1309
11. Dawsey, J., Dawsey, J., Abutaleb, Y., Stanley-Becker, I., Achenbach, J.: Little evidence that White House has offered contact tracing, guidance to hundreds potentially exposed (2020). https://www.washingtonpost.com/health/white-house-covid-contact-tracing/2020/10/03/2a6b8e2a-05a1-11eb-897d-3a6201d6643f_story. html. Accessed 5 Oct 2020
12. Ferretti, L., et al.: Quantifying SARS-CoV-2 transmission suggests epidemic control with digital contact tracing. Science **368**(6491) (2020)
13. Gentry, C.: Practical identity-based encryption without random oracles. In: Vaudenay, S. (ed.) EUROCRYPT 2006. LNCS, vol. 4004, pp. 445–464. Springer, Heidelberg (2006). https://doi.org/10.1007/11761679_27
14. Goldwasser, S., Micali, S., Rivest, R.L.: A digital signature scheme secure against adaptive chosen-message attacks. SIAM J. Comput. **17**(2), 281–308 (1988)
15. Gvili, Y.: Security analysis of the COVID-19 contact tracing specifications by Apple Inc. and Google Inc. Cryptology ePrint Archive, Report 2020/428 (2020). https:// eprint.iacr.org/2020/428
16. He, K., Weng, J., Liu, J.K., Zhou, W., Liu, J.-N.: Efficient fine-grained access control for secure personal health records in cloud computing. In: Chen, J., Piuri, V., Su, C., Yung, M. (eds.) NSS 2016. LNCS, vol. 9955, pp. 65–79. Springer, Cham (2016). https://doi.org/10.1007/978-3-319-46298-1_5
17. Hellewell, J., et al.: Feasibility of controlling COVID-19 outbreaks by isolation of cases and contacts. Lancet Glob. Health **8**(4), e488–e496 (2020)
18. Liu, J., Huang, X., Liu, J.K.: Secure sharing of personal health records in cloud computing: ciphertext-policy attribute-based signcryption. Future Gener. Comput. Syst. **52**, 67–76 (2015)

19. Liu, J.K., et al.: Privacy-preserving COVID-19 contact tracing app: a zero-knowledge proof approach. Cryptology ePrint Archive, Report 2020/528 (2020). https://eprint.iacr.org/2020/528
20. Pietrzak, K.: Delayed authentication: preventing replay and relay attacks in private contact tracing. Cryptology ePrint Archive, Report 2020/418 (2020). https://eprint.iacr.org/2020/418
21. Rivest, R., et al.: The pact protocol specification (2020). https://pact.mit.edu/wp-content/uploads/2020/04/The-PACT-protocol-specification-ver-0.1.pdf
22. Salathé, M., et al.: COVID-19 epidemic in Switzerland: on the importance of testing, contact tracing and isolation. Swiss Med. Weekly **150**(11–12), w20225 (2020)
23. Troncoso, C., et al.: Decentralized privacy-preserving proximity tracing (2020). https://github.com/DP-3T/documents/blob/master/DP3T20%White%20Paper.pdf. Accessed 30 Apr 2020
24. Vaudenay, S.: Analysis of DP3T. Cryptology ePrint Archive, Report 2020/399 (2020). https://eprint.iacr.org/2020/399
25. Warren, M., Liptak, K., Shallwani, P.: White House's inept 'contact tracing' effort leaves the work to others (2020). https://www.cnn.com/2020/10/04/politics/white-house-contact-tracing-covid/index.html. Accessed 5 Oct 2020

A Novel Certificateless Multi-signature Scheme over NTRU Lattices

Xinjian Chen[1], Qiong Huang[1,2(✉)], and Jianye Huang[3]

[1] College of Mathematics and Informatics, South China Agricultural University,
Guangzhou 510642, China
`chenxj@stu.scau.edu.cn, qhuang@scau.edu.cn`
[2] Guangzhou Key Lab of Intelligent Agriculture, Guangzhou 510642, China
[3] School of Computing and Information Technology, University of Wollongong,
Wollongong, NSW 2500, Australia
`jh207@uowmail.edu.au`

Abstract. With the help of multi-signature technology, multiple signatures on the same message could be compressed into one compact signature, which is efficient for financial applications such as blockchain for saving storage space and transmission bandwidth costs. Due to the advantage of no certificate and no escrow feature, certificateless signature is widely used in many applications since its introduction in 2003. Unfortunately, traditional signature schemes may face serious security threats with the advent of quantum computers as their underlying security assumptions (RSA or discrete logarithm problems) may no longer hold anymore. Lattice-based cryptography is considered to be quantum secure. Therefore, we propose a novel certificateless multi-signature (CLMS) scheme over NTRU lattices in this paper, which is provably secure in the random oracle model based on the ring version of the short integer solution assumption (Ring-SIS). To the best of our knowledge, our scheme is the first lattice-based CLMS scheme. Compared with closely related works in the literature, our scheme is based on certificateless cryptography, which not only solves the key escrow problem, but also relieves the certificate management problem effectively.

Keywords: Multi-signature · Certificateless multi-signature · NTRU lattices · Ring-SIS

1 Introduction

1.1 Multi-signature

In real world, it is needed that some different individuals or units are required to sign on a common document in order to make the document effective. Multi-signature is a key technology to solve this problem in the era of digital information. In 1983, the notion of *multi-signature* was firstly proposed by Itakura

This work is supported by the Major Program of Guangdong Basic and Applied Research (2019B030302008), National Natural Science Foundation of China (61872152), and Science and Technology Program of Guang-zhou (201902010081).

R. Deng et al. (Eds.): ISPEC 2021, LNCS 13107, pp. 345–362, 2021.
https://doi.org/10.1007/978-3-030-93206-0_21

and Nakamura [26], which requires a group of signers to sign on a common message m and jointly construct a final multi-signature which could be verified with their public keys $\{pk_1, \cdots, pk_n\}$. Obviously, the simplest way to generate a multi-signature is to set $\sigma_m = \{\sigma_1, \cdots, \sigma_n\}$, called trivial multi-signature [15]. However, it is composed of n individual signatures, causing its size to be linear with the number of signers, which is not efficient for applications. Aiming to save storage space and transmission bandwidth costs efficiently, the size of multi-signature is desired to be much smaller than the trivial one, even approximately close to the size of an individual signature. According to [7], in standard multi-signature schemes, security is commonly defined through an experiment with a single honest "target" signer, effectively viewing all other signers as corrupted. Security requires that it be infeasible to forge a multi-signature involving the target signer, after seeing many signatures on messages of its choice. Multi-signature is widely used in modern applications, such as blockchain bitcoin transactions [5], electronic medical record [17], electronic contract signing [18] and so on.

At the beginning, multi-signature schemes mainly work in the public key infrastructure (PKI) [10], in which a user's public key and private key is generated by itself. However, in order to authorize the relationship between a user and the corresponding public key, a trusted third-party called *certificate authority* (CA) should be involved in the system to issue a digital certificate for users. Therefore, it does require more storage space and computing consumption to generate certificates and verify them, respectively. As the number of users increases, the burden of managing certificates becomes huge, causing the certificate management problem.

To deal with the aforementioned problem, Shamir proposed the *identity-based cryptography* (IBC) in 1984 [41]. In such a new cryptosystem, the public keys of users are selected from their system identities like email address, physical IP address and etc. There is no need to issue certificates for users anymore, thereby solving the certificate management problem. Therefore, many identity-based multi-signature schemes have been proposed by researchers. However, the private keys of users are generated by a trusted third-party called *private key generator* (PKG). Since the PKG masters the secret private keys of all the users, identity-based cryptosystems suffer from key escrow problem.

To solve the key escrow problem in IBC, a new notion of *certificateless public key cryptography* (CL-PKC) was introduced by Al-Riyami and Paterson in 2003 [1]. In this new cryptosystem, PKG is still involved in the system, but it only generates partial secret keys for users. Each user chooses another private key component. As a result, the PKG does not know the full private keys of users. Therefore, CL-PKC efficiently solves the key escrow problem in IBC, and also relieves the certificate management problem in PKI effectively. Since the proposal of CL-PKC, it has attracted the interests of many researchers and lots of related works have been presented. Therefore, we mainly study the certificateless multi-signature in this paper.

On the other hand, with the development of quantum computing technology, traditional security assumptions (RSA or discrete logarithm problem) may no longer hold anymore, which makes traditional multi-signature schemes may not be secure as before. Concretely, Shor [42] presented efficient algorithms to solve integer factorization problem and discrete logarithm problem on a quantum computer in 1994. Subsequently, a quantum mechanical search algorithm was introduced by Grover with the advantage that it is polynomially faster than classic algorithms [16]. As a result, traditional signature schemes based on the hardness of these problems are facing huge security challenge. To solve this problem, some new alternatives have been proposed, among which lattice-based cryptography is the most concerned. At present, lattice-based cryptosystems are potential to be quantum secure. There is no known polynomial-time algorithm to solve hard lattice problems even on a quantum computer. Therefore, we aim to construct a lattice-based certificateless multi-signature scheme in this paper in order to resist the quantum attacks, which is very important for financial applications.

1.2 Related Works

The notion of multi-signature was firstly proposed by Itakura and Nakamura in 1983 [26]. Since then, a large number of multi-signature schemes including the works in [29,31] have been presented by researchers. However, most of these schemes could not provide a convincing security proof. As a matter of fact, only works in [37] and [39] provide convincing security models to prove the security of the schemes. The difference among them is that the security model of [37] is stronger than the other one. However, the scheme of [37] has the issue that the group of signers must be known in advance, which is not suitable in practice. Subsequently, Bellare and Neven constructed a six-move multi-signature scheme in 2006, which is provably secure in the plain public key model [7]. The novelty of the model is that it only requires that all users should have a corresponding public key in the system. Note that their signing protocol is interactive. Afterwards, aiming to improve the scheme of [7], Bagherzandi et al. [3] and Ma et al. [35] proposed two-round multi-signature schemes in 2008 and 2010, respectively. In 2016, Syta et al. [44] constructed a new multi-signature scheme which supports highly scalable functionality. Subsequently, Maxwell et al. [36] proposed a multi-signature scheme in 2018, which implements key aggregation in multi-signature. Afterwards, Boneh et al. [8] presented new pairing-based multi-signature schemes supporting key aggregation and batch verification. In order to avoid the certificate management problem in PKI-based schemes, many identity-based multi-signature schemes have been proposed such as the works in [2,4,6,24,46]. Regarding certificateless multi-signature schemes, a lot of works were proposed by the researchers such as the schemes in [22,23,25,45], to solve the key escrow problem on the identity-based schemes.

However, all the above-mentioned multi-signature schemes are mainly based on traditional security assumptions (RSA or discrete logarithm problems) which may no longer hold anymore with the development of quantum computing technology. As a result, these signature schemes may no longer be secure as before. In 2013, Kong et al. [28] proposed two multi-signature schemes. One is a trivial broadcast multi-signature scheme in which the multi-signature size is linear with the number of users. The other is a sequential multi-signature scheme with a constant signature size. Afterwards, Choi and Kim [9] constructed a linear homomorphic multi-signature scheme based on lattice in 2016. Unfortunately, their scheme suffers from a complex reset process when new members join in the system. In 2016, Bansarkhani and Sturm [5] constructed a broadcast multi-signature scheme based on the hard lattice problem, which is provably secure in the plain public key model. Its multi-signature size is approximately close to an individual signature. Based on the work in [5], new lattice-based multi-signature schemes were presented by Ma et al. [34] and Fukumitsu et al. [12] in 2019, respectively. Subsequently, a lattice-based multi-signature scheme was presented by Peng et al. [40] in 2020, in which a multi-signature consists of individual signatures and an NIWI proof [38]. However, its multi-signature size is linear with the number of users. Recently, Kansal et al. [27] proposed a lattice-based multi-signature scheme that is proven to be secure in the plain public key model. The scheme supports public key aggregation. On the other hand, NTRU lattices are popularly used in constructing post-quantum secure cryptosystems, such as [11,19–21,47].

To the best of our knowledge, the existing lattice-based multi-signature schemes are mainly based on the public-key infrastructure, which leads to the complex certificate management problem. There is no quantum-secure certificateless multi-signature scheme up to now.

1.3 Our Contributions

In order to solve the aforementioned problem, we propose a certificateless multi-signature (CLMS) scheme based on the hard lattice problem in this paper. Concretely, we make contributions in this paper as follows.

1. We propose a CLMS scheme over NTRU lattices in this paper. To the best of our knowledge, it is the first lattice-based CLMS scheme in the literature. Our signing algorithm is a six-move interactive protocol among all the signers, while the verification algorithm is non-interactive, which could be operated by each individual verifier.
2. Our CLMS scheme is provably secure in the random oracle model based on the ring version of the *short integer solution* assumption (Ring-SIS) which is widely used to construct lattice-based cryptographic schemes.
3. Compared with the CLS scheme [47] which is a lattice-based certificateless signature (not multi-signature) scheme, our CLMS is a multi-signature scheme and the multi-signature size of our scheme is much smaller than a bundled signature consisting of N individual signatures (of CLS scheme), as we perform

an accumulation operation on N signatures instead of simply concatenating them. Compared with the existing PKI-based multi-signature schemes [5,12,27,34], our CLMS is the first lattice-based multi-signature scheme constructed in the certificateless setting, which could solve key escrow problem and alleviate the certificate management problem effectively.

2 Preliminaries

2.1 Notations

In this paper, n is a positive power-of-two integer and q represents a prime that is convergent to 1 modulo $2n$. $\mathbb{Z}_q$ denotes a integer set, of which the elements are belong to the range $[-(q-1)/2, (q-1)/2]$. $\widetilde{\mathbf{B}} = \{\widetilde{\mathbf{b}}_1, \widetilde{\mathbf{b}}_2, \cdots, \widetilde{\mathbf{b}}_n\}$ defines the Gram-Schmidt orthogonalization form of $\mathbf{B} = \{\mathbf{b}_1, \mathbf{b}_2, \cdots, \mathbf{b}_n\}$. $\mathcal{R}$ denotes the ring $\mathbb{Z}[x]/(x^n+1)$ and $\mathcal{R}_q$ represents the ring $\mathbb{Z}_q[x]/(x^n+1)$. The elements of both rings are polynomials with max degree $n-1$ and coefficients that are belong to $\mathbb{Z}$ and $\mathbb{Z}_q$, respectively. $f = \sum_{i=0}^{n-1} f_i x^i$ is a polynomial in $\mathcal{R}_q$. So is $g = \sum_{i=0}^{n-1} g_i x^i$. Also, we could represent a polynomial f by using a vector $[f_0, f_1, ..., f_{n-1}]$ which consists of its coefficients. Among two polynomials f and g, we define two mathematical operations as shown in Eq. (1). One is addition $f+g$ in $\mathcal{R}_q$, the other defines multiplication $f \cdot g$ in $\mathcal{R}_q$.

$$f + g = \sum_{i=0}^{n-1} (f_i + g_i)\, x^i \ (\mathrm{mod}\ q)$$

$$f \cdot g = \sum_{k=0}^{n-1} \left(\sum_{i+j=k\ (\mathrm{mod}\ n)} f_i g_j \right) x^k \ (\mathrm{mod}\ q) \tag{1}$$

2.2 Anticirculant Matrices

Definition 1 (Anticirculant matrix). *For a polynomial* $f = \sum_{i=0}^{N-1} f_i x^i$, *we could define an N-dimensional anticirculant matrix as follows.*

$$A_N(f) = \begin{pmatrix} (f) \\ (x \cdot f) \\ \vdots \\ (x^{N-1} \cdot f) \end{pmatrix} = \begin{pmatrix} f_0 & f_1 & \cdots & f_{N-1} \\ -f_{N-1} & f_0 & \cdots & f_{N-2} \\ \vdots & \vdots & \vdots & \vdots \\ -f_1 & -f_2 & \cdots & f_0 \end{pmatrix} \tag{2}$$

In the rest of this paper, we will omit the subscript N and take $A(f)$ to represent the anticirculant matrix.

2.3 NTRU Lattices

Definition 2 (NTRU lattices). *Assume that q is a positive integer, n is a power-of-two integer, and $h = g \cdot f^{-1} \bmod q$ with $f, g \in \mathcal{R}_q$. The NTRU lattice used in this paper is*

$$\Lambda_{h,q} = \left\{ (u, v) \in \mathcal{R}^2 \,\middle|\, u + h \cdot v = 0 \bmod q \right\}. \tag{3}$$

$\Lambda_{h,q}$ *is a full-rank lattice of $\mathbb{Z}^{2n}$, which could be generated by*

$$\mathbf{A}_{h,q} = \begin{pmatrix} -A(h) & I_n \\ qI_n & O_n \end{pmatrix}, \tag{4}$$

where I_n and O_n represent the unit matrix and null matrix, respectively.

However, when h is uniformly distributed in $\mathcal{R}_q$, $\mathbf{A}_{h,q}$ will suffer from a complex Gram-Schmidt orthogonalization process. To deal with this problem, Hoffstein et al. [19] constructed another basis

$$\mathbf{B}_{f,g} = \begin{pmatrix} A(g) & -A(f) \\ A(G) & -A(F) \end{pmatrix}, \tag{5}$$

where $F, G \in \mathcal{R}_q$ and $f \cdot G - g \cdot F = q$. According to [11], $\mathbf{B}_{f,g}$ is a short basis for $\Lambda_{h,q}$. With the help of [11,13], our trapdoor generation algorithm is constructed as follows.

Lemma 1 [11]. *With a power-of-two integer n, a prime q, and $\sigma_f = 1.17\sqrt{\frac{q}{2n}}$ (σ_f chosen such that $\|\tilde{\mathbf{B}}_{f,g}\| \leq 1.17\sqrt{q}$), we could construct a probabilistic polynomial-time (PPT) algorithm $TrapGen(q, n)$, of which the output result is a polynomial $h = g \cdot f^{-1} \bmod q$ statistically close to uniform in $\mathcal{R}_q$ and a short basis $\mathbf{B}_{f,g}$ of $\Lambda_{h,q}$.*

2.4 Gaussian Distribution and Rejection Sampling

Definition 3 (Gaussian Distribution). *Assuming the center $\mathbf{c} \in \mathbb{R}^n$ and the standard deviation $s > 0$, the continuous Gaussian distribution over $\mathbb{R}^n$ could be defined as follows.*

$$\rho_{s,\mathbf{c}}(\mathbf{v}) = \left(\frac{1}{\sqrt{2\pi}s} \right)^n e^{\frac{-\|\mathbf{v} - \mathbf{c}\|^2}{2s^2}}, \tag{6}$$

where $\mathbf{v} \in \mathbb{R}^n$.

Take a symbol $\rho_{s,\mathbf{c}}(\Lambda)$ to represent $\sum_{\mathbf{v} \in \Lambda} \rho_{s,\mathbf{c}}(\mathbf{v})$ for any lattice $\Lambda \in \mathbb{R}^n$. Then the discrete Gaussian distribution over $\mathbb{R}^n$ could be defined as $\mathcal{D}_{\Lambda,s,\mathbf{c}}(\mathbf{v}) = \rho_{s,\mathbf{c}}(\mathbf{v})/\rho_{s,\mathbf{c}}(\Lambda)$, where $\mathbf{v} \in \Lambda$. When $\mathbf{c} = \mathbf{0}$, we will take $\mathcal{D}_{\Lambda,s}$ and ρ_s to represent $\mathcal{D}_{\Lambda,s,\mathbf{0}}$ and $\rho_{s,\mathbf{0}}$, respectively.

In the lattice-based signature scheme, rejection sampling technique [21,32] is used to make sure that the distribution of the output signature is independent of that of the signing key. When a signer signs a message with the signing key S_{ID}, the signature algorithm generally includes the following three steps:

(1) Choose a vector $\mathbf{y} \in \mathcal{D}_{\mathbb{Z}^n, \sigma}$;
(2) Compute a candidate signature $\mathbf{z} = S_{ID} \cdot \mathbf{c} + \mathbf{y}$, where $\mathbf{c}$ represents the hash value associated with the message;
(3) Output the signature $\mathbf{z}$ with probability $\min[\mathscr{F}(\mathbf{z})/M \cdot \mathscr{G}(\mathbf{z}), 1]$, which means it outputs candidate signature $\mathbf{z}$ if $\mathscr{F}(\mathbf{z}) \leq M \cdot \mathscr{G}(\mathbf{z})$ holds and rejects it otherwise.

In the algorithm, $\mathscr{F}$ is the target distribution of the output signature $\mathbf{z}$ (independent of the signing key S_{ID}). If there is a probability distribution $\mathscr{G}$ and a real number $M > 0$, satisfying that for all $\mathbf{v}$, $\mathscr{F}(\mathbf{v}) \leq M \cdot \mathscr{G}(\mathbf{v})$ always holds, then the probability of successfully outputting candidate signature $\mathbf{z}$ is $\mathscr{F}(\mathbf{z})/M \cdot \mathscr{G}(\mathbf{z})$, where M is the expected number of repetitions for successfully outputting a signature.

2.5 Sampling Algorithm

Definition 4 (Sampling Algorithm). *Assuming that q is a prime number, $\mathbf{B}_{f,g}$ is a short basis of NTRU lattice $\Lambda_{h,q}$ and a polynomial $t \in \mathcal{R}_q$. If the Gaussian parameter $s \geq \|\widetilde{\mathbf{B}_{f,g}}\| \omega(\sqrt{\log 2n})$ and $0 < \varepsilon < 1$, then for $\mathbf{u} = (t, 0) \in \mathbb{Z}_q^{2n}$, we could obtain the following conclusions [11,13,30]:*

(1) $\Pr\left[\mathbf{x} \leftarrow \mathcal{D}_{\Lambda_{h,q}, s, \mathbf{u}} : \|\mathbf{x} - \mathbf{u}\| > s \cdot \sqrt{2n}\right] \leq (1 + \varepsilon)/(1 - \varepsilon) \cdot 2^{-2n}$.
(2) There exists a PPT algorithm $SampleGau(\mathbf{B}_{f,g}, s, \mathbf{u})$ that could output $(s_1, s_2) \in \mathcal{R}_q^2$ satisfying $s_1 + h \cdot s_2 = t$ and $\|(s_1, s_2)\| \leq s \cdot \sqrt{2n}$.

2.6 Hardness Assumption

Definition 5 (Ring-SIS$_{m,q,\beta}$ Problem). *Given a vector $\mathbf{a} = (a_1, a_2, \cdots, a_m)^T \in \mathcal{R}_q^m$ consisting of m polynomials chosen uniformly from $\mathcal{R}_q^m$, Ring-SIS$_{m,q,\beta}$ problem is to find a nonzero vector of small polynomials $\mathbf{x} = (x_1, x_2, \cdots, x_m)^T \in \mathcal{R}^m$ satisfying $\mathbf{a}^T \mathbf{x} = \sum_{i=1}^m a_i \cdot x_i = 0 \bmod q$ and $0 < \|\mathbf{x}\| \leq \beta$.*

3 Definition and Security Model of CLMS

3.1 Definition of CLMS

With an identity set $\mathbf{ID} = \{ID_1, ID_2, \cdots, ID_N\}$ and a message m, a certificateless multi-signature scheme (CLMS) includes the following seven algorithms [5,34,47]:

- **Setup**(1^n)**:** Taking as input the security parameter 1^n, the setup algorithm computes private key S_{PKG} of the private key generator (PKG) and system public parameters *params*, and outputs the system public parameters *params*.

- **Extract-Partial-Private-Key**$(ID_i, S_{PKG}, params)$**:** Taking as input an identity ID_i of the signer i, the system master private key S_{PKG} and the system public parameter *params*, this algorithm outputs a partial private key D_i corresponding to the signer i.

- **Set-Secret-Value**$(ID_i, params)$**:** Taking as input an identity ID_i of the signer i and the system public parameter *params*, this algorithm outputs a secret value S_i corresponding to the signer i.

- **Set-Private-Key**$(D_i, S_i, params)$**:** Taking as input the partial private key D_i and the secret value S_i of the signer i and the system public parameter *params*, this algorithm outputs a private key SK_i corresponding to the signer i.

- **Set-Public-Key**$(S_i, params)$**:** Taking as input the secret value S_i of the signer i and the system public parameter *params*, this algorithm outputs a public key PK_i corresponding to the signer i.

- **CL-Sign**$(\mathbf{ID}, m, params)$**:** Taking as input an identity set $\mathbf{ID} = \{ID_1, ID_2, \cdots, ID_N\}$, a message m and the system public parameters *params*, this algorithm outputs a multi-signature θ or a symbol $\perp$ representing failure. In some CLMS schemes, the multi-signature generation algorithm is an interactive protocol that requires all the signers to interact with each other before outputting the final multi-signature. In such a protocol, the private keys of signers are seen as their local input.

- **CL-Verify**$(\mathbf{ID}, m, \mathbf{PK}, \theta, params)$**:** Taking as input the identity set $\mathbf{ID}$ of all the signers, a message m, the public key set $\mathbf{PK}$ of all the signers, a multi-signature θ and the system public parameters *params*, this algorithm outputs 1 ("accept") if the multi-signature θ is valid, otherwise it outputs 0 ("reject").

Correctness: If all signers honestly follow the **CL-Sign** protocol to sign on a common message m, a multi-signature θ will be generated, which satisfies **CL-Verify**$(\mathbf{ID}, m, \mathbf{PK}, \theta, params) = 1$.

3.2   Security Model of CLMS

In this paper, our CLMS scheme considers two types of adversaries according to [47]. One is the external adversary $\mathcal{A}_1$ that can replace user's public key but cannot access the system master secret key. The other is the internal adversary $\mathcal{A}_2$ that controls the PKG and leads the generation of the system master secret key, but cannot replace the user's public key. According to [7], we assume that there is only one honest signer in the signing group with the identity ID^*. The adversary can run the **CL-Sign** algorithm and interact with the honest user by taking as input the signers' identity set $\mathbf{ID} = \{ID_1, ID_2, \cdots, ID_N\}$ and a message m, where $ID^* \in \mathbf{ID}$. Subsequently, we introduce the first game between the adversary $\mathcal{A}_1$ and the challenger $\mathcal{C}$ as follows.

(1) **Setup.** The challenger $\mathcal{C}$ runs the **Setup** algorithm to generate master private key S_{PKG} and system public parameters $params$. It retains S_{PKG} and sends $params$ to the adversary $\mathcal{A}_1$.

(2) **Queries.** The adversary $\mathcal{A}_1$ can adaptively issue polynomially many queries as follows.
   - **Partial-Private-Key-query.** When $\mathcal{A}_1$ queries a signer's partial private key with ID_i, $\mathcal{C}$ runs the **Extract-Partial-Private-Key** algorithm to generate D_i, and returns D_i to the adversary $\mathcal{A}_1$.
   - **Create-User-query.** When $\mathcal{A}_1$ issues a query with ID_i, $\mathcal{C}$ generates the user's secret value S_i, private key SK_i and public key PK_i, and returns $\{PK_i, SK_i\}$ to the adversary $\mathcal{A}_1$.
   - **Replace-Public-Key-query.** When $\mathcal{A}_1$ issues a query with ID_i and PK_i', $\mathcal{C}$ replaces the user's public key PK_i with PK_i'.
   - **Sign-query.** When $\mathcal{A}_1$ queries a multi-signature with the identity set $\mathbf{ID} = \{ID_1, ID_2, \cdots, ID_N\}$ and message m, $\mathcal{C}$ runs the **CL-Sign** algorithm to generate a multi-signature θ, and returns θ to the adversary $\mathcal{A}_1$.

(3) **Forgery.** $\mathcal{A}_1$ outputs a multi-signature tuple $(m', ID^*, \mathbf{ID}', \mathbf{PK}', \theta')$. If the following conditions are met, the adversary $\mathcal{A}_1$ wins the game.
   (a) $\mathbf{CL\text{-}Verify}(\mathbf{ID}', m', \mathbf{PK}', \theta', params) = 1$;
   (b) $ID^* \in \mathbf{ID}'$, and ID^* has not been issued during the **Partial-Private-Key-query** phase; and
   (c) $(\mathbf{ID}', m')$ has not been issued during the **Sign-query** phase.

Next, we introduce the second game between the adversary $\mathcal{A}_2$ and the challenger $\mathcal{C}$ as follows.

(1) **Setup.** The challenger $\mathcal{C}$ runs the **Setup** algorithm to generate master private key S_{PKG} and system public parameters $params$, and sends them to the adversary $\mathcal{A}_2$.

(2) **Queries.** The adversary $\mathcal{A}_2$ can adaptively issue polynomially many queries as follows.
   - **Create-User-query.** The same as that in the first game.
   - **Public-Key-query.** When $\mathcal{A}_2$ queries a signer's public key with ID_i, $\mathcal{C}$ returns the public key PK_i to the adversary $\mathcal{A}_2$.
   - **Sign-query.** The same as that in the first game.

(3) **Forgery.** $\mathcal{A}_2$ outputs a multi-signature tuple $(m', ID^*, \mathbf{ID}', \mathbf{PK}', \theta')$. If the following conditions are met, the adversary $\mathcal{A}_2$ wins the game.
   (a) $\mathbf{CL\text{-}Verify}(\mathbf{ID}', m', \mathbf{PK}', \theta', params) = 1$;
   (b) $ID^* \in \mathbf{ID}'$, and ID^* has not been issued during the **Create-User-query** phase; and
   (c) $(\mathbf{ID}', m')$ has not been issued during the **Sign-query** phase.

Definition 6 (EUF-ID-CMA). *For any PPT adversary $\mathcal{A}_1$ and $\mathcal{A}_2$, if both probabilities of $\mathcal{A}_1$ winning the first game and $\mathcal{A}_2$ winning the second game are negligible, the CLMS scheme is existentially unforgeable under adaptive chosen-identity and chosen-message attacks.*

Besides, if adversaries are required to submit the challenge identity ID^* before seeing any system public parameter, the CLMS scheme is existentially unforgeable under *selective*-identity and chosen-message attacks (*EUF-SID-CMA* secure).

4   Our CLMS Scheme over NTRU Lattices

Our CLMS scheme is constructed as follows.

- **Setup.** Given the system security parameter 1^n, the PKG selects two real numbers $s, \sigma > 0$ and a prime number q, and then runs the $TrapGen(q, n)$ algorithm to generate a polynomial $h = g \cdot f^{-1} \bmod q$ and a short basis $\mathbf{B}_{f,g}$, where $\|f\| \leq s\sqrt{n}$, $\|g\| \leq s\sqrt{n}$ and

$$\mathbf{B}_{f,g} = \begin{pmatrix} A(g) & -A(f) \\ A(G) & -A(F) \end{pmatrix} \in \mathbb{Z}_q^{2n \times 2n}. \tag{7}$$

  Next, the PKG chooses three hash functions $H_0 : \{0, 1\}^* \rightarrow \mathbb{Z}_q^n$, $H_1 : \mathbb{Z}_q^n \rightarrow \mathbb{Z}_q^n$, and $H_2 : \{0, 1\}^* \rightarrow \{\mathbf{e} | \mathbf{e} \in \{-1, 0, 1\}^n, \|\mathbf{e}\|_1 \leq \lambda\}$. Subsequently, the PKG sets the system master private key $S_{PKG} = \mathbf{B}_{f,g}$ and the system public parameters $params = \langle h, H_0, H_1, H_2 \rangle$, where h represents the system master public key. Finally, the PKG secretly keeps S_{PKG} and outputs the system public parameters $params$.
- **Extract-Partial-Private-Key.** Given an identity $ID_i \in \{0, 1\}^*$, the PKG runs the $SampleGau(\mathbf{B}_{f,g}, s, (H_0(ID_i), 0))$ algorithm to generate $(s_{i,1}, s_{i,2})$ satisfying $s_{i,1} + h \cdot s_{i,2} = H_0(ID_i)$ and $\|(s_{i,1}, s_{i,2})\| \leq s \cdot \sqrt{2n}$. Finally, the PKG sends the partial private key $D_i = (s_{i,1}, s_{i,2})$ to signer i through a secure channel. According to [33], it is hard to recover D_i when given h and $H_0(ID_i)$.
- **Set-Secret-Value.** Given an identity $ID_i \in \{0, 1\}^*$, the signer i randomly selects two secret values $s'_{i,1}, s'_{i,2} \in \mathcal{D}_{\mathbb{Z}^n, s}$ and $\|(s'_{i,1}, s'_{i,2})\| \leq s \cdot \sqrt{2n}$, and sets the secret value $S_i = (s'_{i,1}, s'_{i,2})$.
- **Set-Private-Key.** Given a user's partial private key D_i and secret value S_i, this algorithm sets the user's private key $SK_i = (D_i, S_i)$.
- **Set-Public-Key.** Given a user's secret value S_i, it sets the public key $PK_i = s'_{i,1} + h \cdot s'_{i,2}$.
- **CL-Sign.** Given an identity set $\mathbf{ID} = \{ID_1, ID_2, \cdots, ID_N\}$ and a message m, the **CL-Sign** algorithm works as follows (see Fig. 1). At first, each signer i selects $Y_i = (y_{i,1}, y_{i,2})$, $Y'_i = (y'_{i,1}, y'_{i,2})$ and computes $r_i = y_{i,1} + h \cdot y_{i,2}$, $r'_i = y'_{i,1} + h \cdot y'_{i,2}$, respectively. The signer then obtains $d_i = H_1(r_i)$ and $d'_i = H_1(r'_i)$. Note that d_i and d'_i could be seen as commitments for r_i and r'_i to ensure the correct transmission of r_i and r'_i. Subsequently, the signer i

broadcasts (d_i, d_i') to other signers and obtains all (d_j, d_j') from them. The signer then broadcasts (r_i, r_i') to other signers and receives all (r_j, r_j') from them. Afterwards, every signer could check the validity of (r_j, r_j') and compute $r = \sum_{j=1}^{N} r_j \bmod q$ and $r' = \sum_{j=1}^{N} r_j' \bmod q$. Subsequently, the signer i computes $c_i = H_2(ID_i, r, r', \mathbf{ID}, m)$, generates a signature $sig_i = SK_i \cdot c_i + (Y_i, Y_i')$ with probability $\min[\mathcal{D}_{\mathbb{Z}^n, \sigma}(sig_i)/M\mathcal{D}_{\mathbb{Z}^n, \sigma, SK_i \cdot c_i}(sig_i), 1]$ where $M = O(1)$, and broadcasts it to other signers. After receiving all sig_j from other signers, the signer i computes $sig = \sum_{j=1}^{N} sig_j$ and outputs the final multi-signature (sig, r, r').

CL-Sign

Signer i Cosigners $j, j \neq i$

(1) $Y_i = (y_{i,1}, y_{i,2}) \leftarrow \mathcal{D}_{\mathbb{Z}^n, \sigma} \times \mathcal{D}_{\mathbb{Z}^n, \sigma}$
$Y_i' = (y_{i,1}', y_{i,2}') \leftarrow \mathcal{D}_{\mathbb{Z}^n, \sigma} \times \mathcal{D}_{\mathbb{Z}^n, \sigma}$

(2) $r_i = y_{i,1} + h \cdot y_{i,2}, \, r_i' = y_{i,1}' + h \cdot y_{i,2}'$

(3) $d_i = H_1(r_i), \, d_i' = H_1(r_i')$

(4) $\xrightarrow{\quad (d_i, d_i') \quad}$

(5) $\xleftarrow{\quad (d_j, d_j') \quad}$

(6) $\xrightarrow{\quad (r_i, r_i') \quad}$

(7) $\xleftarrow{\quad (r_j, r_j') \quad}$

(8) Check $d_j \overset{?}{=} H_1(r_j)$ and $d_j' \overset{?}{=} H_1(r_j')$ for all $j \neq i$

(9) $r = \sum_{j=1}^{N} r_j \bmod q, \, r' = \sum_{j=1}^{N} r_j' \bmod q$

(10) $c_i = H_2(ID_i, r, r', \mathbf{ID}, m)$

(11) $sig_i = \begin{pmatrix} z_i \\ z_i' \end{pmatrix} = \begin{pmatrix} z_{i,1} \\ z_{i,2} \\ z_{i,1}' \\ z_{i,2}' \end{pmatrix} \leftarrow SK_i \cdot c_i + \begin{pmatrix} Y_i \\ Y_i' \end{pmatrix} = \begin{pmatrix} s_{i,1} \\ s_{i,2} \\ s_{i,1}' \\ s_{i,2}' \end{pmatrix} \cdot c_i + \begin{pmatrix} y_{i,1} \\ y_{i,2} \\ y_{i,1}' \\ y_{i,2}' \end{pmatrix}$
with probability $\min[\mathcal{D}_{\mathbb{Z}^n, \sigma}(sig_i)/M\mathcal{D}_{\mathbb{Z}^n, \sigma, SK_i \cdot c_i}(sig_i), 1], \, M = O(1)$

(12) $\xrightarrow{\quad sig_i \quad}$

(13) $\xleftarrow{\quad sig_j \quad}$

(14) $sig = (z, z') = \sum_{j=1}^{N} sig_j$

(15) Output(sig, r, r')

Fig. 1. Concrete **CL-Sign** algorithm

- **CL-Verify.** Given a multi-signature (sig, r, r') on message m with the identity set $\mathbf{ID} = \{ID_1, ID_2, \cdots, ID_N\}$ and public key set $\mathbf{PK}$, it computes $c_i = H_2(ID_i, r, r', \mathbf{ID}, m)$, and outputs 1 ("accept") if $\|z\|, \|z'\| \leq 2N \cdot \sigma \sqrt{2n}$, $z^{(1)} + h \cdot z^{(2)} = r + \sum_{i=1}^{N}(H_0(ID_i) \cdot c_i)$ and $z'^{(1)} + h \cdot z'^{(2)} = r' + \sum_{i=1}^{N}(PK_i \cdot c_i)$, and 0 ("reject") otherwise.

5 Security Analysis

Theorem 1. *If the* Ring-SIS$_{2,q,\beta}$ *problem on NTRU lattice* $\Lambda_{h,q}$ *is intractable, the* CLMS *scheme is EUF-SID-CMA secure against any PPT external adversary* $\mathcal{A}_1$ *in the random oracle model.*

Proof. Assuming that there is a PPT forger $\mathcal{A}_1$, who can query the random oracles (including H_0, H_1, H_2) at most ℓ_H times, invoke the signing algorithm with the honest signer at most ℓ_S times, and successfully provide a forgery with non-negligible probability δ. Then we could construct an algorithm $\mathcal{B}$ to solve the Ring-SIS$_{2,q,\beta}$ problem on NTRU lattice $\Lambda_{h,q}$. On input $h_1, h_2, \cdots, h_{\ell_H + \ell_S} \in \{\mathbf{e} | \mathbf{e} \in \{-1, 0, 1\}^n, \|\mathbf{e}\|_1 \leq \lambda\}$, algorithm $\mathcal{B}$ runs the forger $\mathcal{A}_1$ as follows.

(1) **Initialization.** $\mathcal{A}_1$ sends the identity ID^* of the honest signer to $\mathcal{B}$.

(2) **Setup.** Given the system parameter 1^n, $\mathcal{B}$ randomly chooses a polynomial $h \in \mathcal{R}_q$, sets the system public parameter $params = \langle h, H_0, H_1, H_2 \rangle$ and returns $params$ to $\mathcal{A}_1$, where H_0, H_1, and H_2 are random oracles controlled by $\mathcal{B}$.

(3) **Queries.** $\mathcal{B}$ initializes two counters $ctr1$, $ctr2$ to zero, and defines five initially empty lists $L_0[\cdot]$, $L_1[\cdot]$, $L_2[\cdot, \cdot]$, $L_3[\cdot]$ and $L_C[\cdot]$. Concretely, L_0, L_1 and L_2 are used to simulate the random oracles H_0, H_1 and H_2. L_3 assigns a unique index $1 \leq j \leq \ell_H + N \cdot \ell_S$ to each ID_i that is either a signer's identity in a signing query or the first parameter of H_2 query. L_C stores the results of **Create-User-query** phase. Besides, $\mathcal{B}$ sets $L_3[ID^*] \leftarrow 0$ for the target identity, randomly chooses $s_1, s_2 \in \mathcal{D}_{\mathbb{Z}^n, s}$ satisfying $\|(s_1, s_2)\| \leq s\sqrt{2n}$ and sets $D^* = (s_1, s_2)$. It then computes $P^* = s_1 + h \cdot s_2$ and sets $L_0[ID^*] \leftarrow (P^*, D^*)$. Finally, $\mathcal{B}$ responds to the queries issued by $\mathcal{A}_1$ as follows.

  (a) **H_0-query.** When $\mathcal{A}_1$ queries the oracle H_0 with ID_i, $\mathcal{B}$ converts $L_0[ID_i]$ into (P_i, D_i) and responds P_i to $\mathcal{A}_1$, if $L_0[ID_i]$ has been defined. Otherwise, $\mathcal{B}$ randomly selects $s_{i,1}, s_{i,2} \in \mathcal{D}_{\mathbb{Z}^n, s}$ satisfying $\|(s_{i,1}, s_{i,2})\| \leq s\sqrt{2n}$, computes $P_i = s_{i,1} + h \cdot s_{i,2}$ and sets $L_0[ID_i] \leftarrow (P_i, D_i = (s_{i,1}, s_{i,2}))$. Finally, $\mathcal{B}$ returns P_i to $\mathcal{A}_1$.

  (b) **H_1-query.** When $\mathcal{A}_1$ queries the oracle H_1 with r_i, $\mathcal{B}$ responds $L_1[r_i]$ to $\mathcal{A}_1$ if $L_1[r_i]$ has been defined. Otherwise, $\mathcal{B}$ chooses $d_i \in \mathbb{Z}_q^n$ at random and sets $L_1[r_i] \leftarrow d_i$. Finally, $\mathcal{B}$ returns d_i to $\mathcal{A}_1$.

  (c) **H_2-query.** When $\mathcal{A}_1$ queries the oracle H_2 with (ID_i, Q) where $Q = (r, r', \mathbf{ID}, m)$, $\mathcal{B}$ increases $ctr2$ and sets $L_3[ID_i] = ctr2$, if $L_3[ID_i]$ has not been defined. $\mathcal{B}$ sets $index = L_3[ID_i]$. If $L_2[index, Q]$ has been defined, $\mathcal{B}$ responds $L_2[index, Q]$ to $\mathcal{A}_1$. Otherwise, $\mathcal{B}$ selects c_j from $\{\mathbf{e} | \mathbf{e} \in$

$\{-1, 0, 1\}^n$, $\|\mathbf{e}\|_1 \leq \lambda\}$ and sets $L_2[j, Q] \leftarrow c_j$ for $1 \leq j \leq \ell_H + N \cdot \ell_S$. $\mathcal{B}$ increases $ctr1$ and assigns $L_2[0, Q] = h_{ctr1}$. Finally, $\mathcal{B}$ returns $L_2[index, Q]$ to $\mathcal{A}_1$.

(d) **Partial-Private-Key-query.** When $\mathcal{A}_1$ queries a signer's partial private key with ID_i, $\mathcal{B}$ first checks whether D_i has already been in L_0. If so, $\mathcal{B}$ responds to $\mathcal{A}_1$ with D_i. Otherwise, $\mathcal{B}$ issues the $H_0(ID_i)$ query to generate D_i and returns it to $\mathcal{A}_1$.

(e) **Create-User-query.** When $\mathcal{A}_1$ issues a query with ID_i, $\mathcal{B}$ first checks whether $L_C[ID_i]$ has been defined. If so, $\mathcal{B}$ returns the user's key pair $\{PK_i, SK_i\}$ to $\mathcal{A}_1$. Otherwise, $\mathcal{B}$ issues the **Partial-Private-Key-query** with ID_i to generate D_i when $ID_i \neq ID^*$. If $ID_i = ID^*$, $\mathcal{B}$ sets $D_i = \perp$. Subsequently, $\mathcal{B}$ performs the **Set-Secret-Value** algorithm, **Set-Private-Key** algorithm, and **Set-Public-Key** algorithm to generate the user's S_i, SK_i and PK_i. $\mathcal{B}$ then assigns $L_C[ID_i] \leftarrow \{D_i, S_i, SK_i, PK_i\}$. Finally, $\mathcal{B}$ returns $\{PK_i, SK_i\}$ to $\mathcal{A}_1$.

(f) **Replace-Public-Key-query.** When $\mathcal{A}_1$ issues a query with ID_i and PK_i', $\mathcal{B}$ replaces the user's public key PK_i with PK_i'.

(g) **Sign-query.** When $\mathcal{A}_1$ queries a multi-signature with identity set $\mathbf{ID} = \{ID_1, ID_2, \cdots, ID_N\}$ and message m, $\mathcal{B}$ responds to $\mathcal{A}_1$ as follows.

  (i) $\mathcal{B}$ first checks whether $ID^* \in \mathbf{ID}$. If not, it stops the protocol and outputs $\perp$. If $ID_1 \neq ID^*$, $\mathcal{B}$ then swaps the positions of ID_1 and ID^* and reassigns $\mathbf{ID} = \{ID_1 = ID^*, ID_2, \cdots, ID_N\}$. Subsequently, $\mathcal{B}$ checks whether $L_3[ID_k]$ has been defined for $2 \leq k \leq N$. If not, it increases $ctr2$ and sets $L_3[ID_k] = ctr2$. $\mathcal{B}$ then increases $ctr1$ and assigns $c_1 = h_{ctr1}$. Subsequently, $\mathcal{B}$ randomly selects $z_{i,1}, z_{i,2}, z_{i,1}', z_{i,2}' \in \mathcal{D}_{\mathbb{Z}^n, \sigma}$ and computes $r_1 = \mathbf{A}z_1 - H_0(ID_1) \cdot c_1$, $r_1' = \mathbf{A}z_1' - PK_1 \cdot c_1$. $\mathcal{B}$ then queries $d_1 = H_1(r_1)$ and $d_1' = H_1(r_1')$. Finally, $\mathcal{B}$ broadcasts (d_1, d_1') to other signers.

  (ii) After receiving (d_k, d_k') from $\mathcal{A}_1$ (playing the role of other signers) for $2 \leq k \leq N$, $\mathcal{B}$ checks whether $L_1[r_k] = d_k$ holds for each d_k. If not, $\mathcal{B}$ aborts the protocol and outputs $\perp$. In the same way, $\mathcal{B}$ checks the validity of each d_k'. Subsequently, $\mathcal{B}$ computes $r = \sum_{k=1}^N r_k \bmod q$ and $r' = \sum_{k=1}^N r_k' \bmod q$. $\mathcal{B}$ then sets $L_2[0, r, r', \mathbf{ID}, m] = c_1$, randomly chooses values from the set $\{\mathbf{e}|\mathbf{e} \in \{-1, 0, 1\}^n, \|\mathbf{e}\|_1 \leq \lambda\}$ and saves to $L_2[j, r, r', \mathbf{ID}, m]$ for $1 \leq j \leq \ell_H + N \cdot \ell_S$. Finally, $\mathcal{B}$ broadcasts (r_1, r_1') to other signers.

  (iii) After receiving (r_k, r_k') from $\mathcal{A}_1$ for $2 \leq k \leq N$, $\mathcal{B}$ checks whether $d_k = H_1(r_k)$ holds for each r_k. If not, $\mathcal{B}$ ceases the protocol and outputs $\perp$. In the same way, $\mathcal{B}$ checks the validity of each r_k'. Subsequently, $\mathcal{B}$ broadcasts (z_1, z_1') to other signers.

  (iv) After receiving (z_k, z_k') from $\mathcal{A}_1$ for $2 \leq k \leq N$, $\mathcal{B}$ computes $z = \sum_{k=1}^N z_k$ and $z' = \sum_{k=1}^N z_k'$. Finally, $\mathcal{B}$ returns the multi-signature $\theta = (z, z', r, r')$ to $\mathcal{A}_1$.

(4) **Forgery.** $\mathcal{A}_1$ forges a valid multi-signature $(\overline{z}, \overline{z}', \overline{r}, \overline{r}')$ on message $\overline{m}$ and identity set $\overline{\mathbf{ID}}$ with non-negligible probability δ. Note that $ID^* \in \overline{\mathbf{ID}}$, ID^* has not been issued during the **Partial-Private-Key-query** phase and $(\overline{\mathbf{ID}}, \overline{m})$ has not been issued during the **Sign-query** phase.

Assume that the index J satisfies $1 \leq J \leq \ell_H + \ell_S$. According to the successful forgery provided by $\mathcal{A}_1$, we obtain the first tuple $(\overline{z}, \overline{z}', \overline{r}, \overline{r}', \overline{h_J})$, and we could possess another tuple $(\hat{z}, \hat{z}', \hat{r}, \hat{r}', \widehat{h_J})$ using the forking lemma [7]. According to the forking lemma, the interactive environments are identical before the first query $H_2(ID^*, \overline{r}, \overline{r}', \overline{\mathbf{ID}}, \overline{m})$ or $H_2(ID^*, \hat{r}, \hat{r}', \widehat{\mathbf{ID}}, \hat{m})$. So we could obtain $L_2[0, \overline{r}, \overline{r}', \overline{\mathbf{ID}}, \overline{m}] = \overline{h_J}$ and $L_2[0, \hat{r}, \hat{r}', \widehat{\mathbf{ID}}, \hat{m}] = \widehat{h_J}$, where $\overline{m} = \hat{m}$, $\overline{\mathbf{ID}} = \widehat{\mathbf{ID}}$, $\overline{r} = \hat{r}$ and $\overline{r}' = \hat{r}'$. Besides, all entries $L_3[\overline{ID}_i]$ and $\overline{c_i} = L_2[L_3[\overline{ID}_i], \overline{r}, \overline{r}', \overline{\mathbf{ID}}, \overline{m}]$ are assigned before the setting $L_2[0, \overline{r}, \overline{r}', \overline{\mathbf{ID}}, \overline{m}] = \overline{h_J}$. Consequently, we could obtain $\overline{c_i} = \widehat{c_i}$ in both performances for $\overline{ID}_i \neq ID^*$. On the contrary, we possess $\overline{c}^* = \overline{h_J}$ and $\hat{c}^* = \widehat{h_J}$ for ID^* where $\overline{h_J} \neq \widehat{h_J}$. Subsequently, assume that I^* represents the number of occurrences of ID^* in $\overline{\mathbf{ID}}$. According to $\mathbf{A}\overline{z} - \sum_{i=1}^{N} H_0(\overline{ID}_i)\overline{c_i} = \overline{r} = \hat{r} = \mathbf{A}\hat{z} - \sum_{i=1}^{N} H_0(\overline{ID}_i)\widehat{c_i}$, the following equation could be obtained:

$$\mathbf{A}(\overline{z} - \hat{z} + |I^*| \cdot D^*(\hat{c}^* - \overline{c}^*)) = 0. \tag{8}$$

Owing to $\|\overline{z}\|, \|\hat{z}\| \leq 2N \cdot \sigma\sqrt{2n}$ and $\|D^*\overline{c}^*\|, \|D^*\hat{c}^*\| \leq \lambda \cdot s\sqrt{2n}$, we could obtain $\|\overline{z} - \hat{z} + |I^*| \cdot D^*(\hat{c}^* - \overline{c}^*)\| \leq 4N \cdot \sigma\sqrt{2n} + 2|I^*| \cdot \lambda s\sqrt{2n}$. According to the preimage min-entropy property [13], we could obtain $D' = (s_1', s_2')$ satisfying $s_1' + h \cdot s_2' = H_0(ID^*)$ and $D' \neq D^*$. As a result, $(\overline{z} - \hat{z} + |I^*| \cdot D^*(\hat{c}^* - \overline{c}^*)) - (\overline{z} - \hat{z} + |I^*| \cdot D'(\hat{c}^* - \overline{c}^*)) = |I^*| \cdot (D^* - D')(\hat{c}^* - \overline{c}^*) \neq 0$. If $(\overline{z} - \hat{z} + |I^*| \cdot D^*(\hat{c}^* - \overline{c}^*)) = 0$, then $(\overline{z} - \hat{z} + |I^*| \cdot D'(\hat{c}^* - \overline{c}^*)) \neq 0$. So $(\overline{z} - \hat{z} + |I^*| \cdot D^*(\hat{c}^* - \overline{c}^*)) \neq 0$ with non-negligible probability. With $\mathbf{A} = (1, h)$ and $D^* = (s_1, s_2)$ we possess the following equation.

$$(\overline{z}^{(1)} - \hat{z}^{(1)} + |I^*| \cdot s_1(\hat{c}^* - \overline{c}^*)) + h \cdot (\overline{z}^{(2)} - \hat{z}^{(2)} + |I^*| \cdot s_2(\hat{c}^* - \overline{c}^*)) = 0 \tag{9}$$

According to Eq. (9) and [14,32], we could obtain two polynomials $\mathbf{u}_1$ and $\mathbf{u}_2$ with small (nonzero) coefficients to satisfy $\mathbf{u}_1 + h \cdot \mathbf{u}_2 = 0$. Therefore, we could solve Ring-SIS$_{2,q,\beta}$ for $\beta \leq 4N \cdot \sigma\sqrt{2n} + 2|I^*| \cdot \lambda s\sqrt{2n}$, which is believed to be hard [43].

Finally, $\mathcal{B}$ can solve Ring-SIS$_{2,q,\beta}$ with probability sol at least

$$\left(\frac{1}{2} - 2^{-100}\right) \cdot \delta \cdot \left(\frac{\delta}{\ell_H + \ell_S} - \frac{1}{|D_{H_2}|}\right) \approx \frac{\delta^2}{2(\ell_H + \ell_S)}, \tag{10}$$

where D_{H_2} denotes the range of random oracle H_2. If δ is non-negligible, so is sol. Therefore, our CLMS scheme is existentially unforgeable against any PPT external adversary $\mathcal{A}_1$ in the random oracle model. □

Theorem 2. *If the* Ring-SIS$_{2,q,\beta}$ *problem on NTRU lattice* $\Lambda_{h,q}$ *is intractable, the CLMS scheme is EUF-SID-CMA secure against any PPT internal adversary* $\mathcal{A}_2$ *in the random oracle model.*

Due to the page limit, we leave the proof of Theorem 2 to the full version.

According to Theorem 1 and Theorem 2, our CLMS scheme is *EUF-SID-CMA* secure against any PPT adversary in the random oracle model.

6   Comparison

As shown in Table 1, we make a comparison between CLS scheme [47] and our CLMS scheme in terms of the number of signers, the sizes of signing key and signature, and security property.

Table 1. Comparison CLS scheme [47] and our CLMS scheme

Schemes	Signers' number	Signing key size	Signature size	Security
CLS [47]	1	$\leq 4n \log (s\sqrt{n})$	$4n \log 12\sigma + \lambda(\log n + 1)$	EUF-ID-CMA
CLMS	N	$\leq 4n \log (s\sqrt{n})$	$4n \log (N \cdot 12\sigma) + 2n \log q$	EUF-SID-CMA

Legends: n: the system parameter; λ: positive integers; N: signers' number; $s = \left\| \widetilde{\mathbf{B}_{f,g}} \right\| \omega(\sqrt{\log 2n})$; $\sigma = 12\lambda s\sqrt{n}$.

Compared with the CLS scheme [47] which is a lattice-based certificateless signature (not multi-signature) scheme, our CLMS is a multi-signature scheme and the multi-signature size of our scheme is much smaller than a bundled signature consisting of N individual signatures (of CLS scheme) as we perform an accumulation operation on N signatures instead of simply concatenating them. To the best of our knowledge, the existing lattice-based multi-signature schemes are mainly based on the public-key infrastructure such as [5,12,27,34], which leads to the complex certificate management problem. Our CLMS is the first lattice-based multi-signature scheme constructed in the certificateless setting, which could solve key escrow problem and alleviate the certificate management problem effectively.

7   Conclusion

In this paper we proposed a certificateless multi-signature (CLMS) scheme over NTRU lattices which is provably secure in the random oracle model based on Ring-SIS assumption. To the best of our knowledge, it is the first lattice-based CLMS scheme in the literature. Compared with the CLS scheme [47], our CLMS is a multi-signature scheme and the multi-signature size of our scheme is much smaller compared to a bundled signature using N individual signatures (of CLS) as we perform an accumulation operation on N signatures instead of simply concatenating them. Compared with the existing PKI-based multi-signature schemes [5,12,27,34], our CLMS is the first lattice-based certificateless multi-signature scheme, which could solve key escrow problem and alleviate the certificate management problem effectively. Finally, we leave the problem of constructing a CLMS scheme with stronger security as one of our future research directions.

References

1. Al-Riyami, S.S., Paterson, K.G.: Certificateless public key cryptography. In: Laih, C.-S. (ed.) ASIACRYPT 2003. LNCS, vol. 2894, pp. 452–473. Springer, Heidelberg (2003). https://doi.org/10.1007/978-3-540-40061-5_29
2. Babu, A.R., Gayathri, N.B., Reddy, P.V.: Efficient ID-based key-insulated multi signature scheme without pairings. In: 2019 Innovations in Power and Advanced Computing Technologies (i-PACT). IEEE, March 2019
3. Bagherzandi, A., Cheon, J.H., Jarecki, S.: Multisignatures secure under the discrete logarithm assumption and a generalized forking lemma. In: Proceedings of the 15th ACM Conference on Computer and Communications Security - CCS 2008, pp. 449–458. ACM Press (2008)
4. Bagherzandi, A., Jarecki, S.: Identity-based aggregate and multi-signature schemes based on RSA. In: Nguyen, P.Q., Pointcheval, D. (eds.) PKC 2010. LNCS, vol. 6056, pp. 480–498. Springer, Heidelberg (2010). https://doi.org/10.1007/978-3-642-13013-7_28
5. El Bansarkhani, R., Sturm, J.: An efficient lattice-based multisignature scheme with applications to bitcoins. In: Foresti, S., Persiano, G. (eds.) CANS 2016. LNCS, vol. 10052, pp. 140–155. Springer, Cham (2016). https://doi.org/10.1007/978-3-319-48965-0_9
6. Bellare, M., Neven, G.: Identity-based multi-signatures from RSA. In: Abe, M. (ed.) CT-RSA 2007. LNCS, vol. 4377, pp. 145–162. Springer, Heidelberg (2006). https://doi.org/10.1007/11967668_10
7. Bellare, M., Neven, G.: Multi-signatures in the plain public-key model and a general forking lemma. In: Proceedings of the 13th ACM Conference on Computer and Communications Security - CCS 2006, pp. 390–399. ACM Press (2006)
8. Boneh, D., Drijvers, M., Neven, G.: Compact multi-signatures for smaller blockchains. In: Peyrin, T., Galbraith, S. (eds.) ASIACRYPT 2018. LNCS, vol. 11273, pp. 435–464. Springer, Cham (2018). https://doi.org/10.1007/978-3-030-03329-3_15
9. Choi, R., Kim, K.: Lattice-based multi-signature with linear homomorphism. In: 2016 Symposium on Cryptography and Information Security. The Institute of Electronics, Information and Communication Engineers, Tokyo (2016)
10. Diffie, W., Hellman, M.: New directions in cryptography. IEEE Trans. Inf. Theory **22**(6), 644–654 (1976)
11. Ducas, L., Lyubashevsky, V., Prest, T.: Efficient identity-based encryption over NTRU lattices. In: Sarkar, P., Iwata, T. (eds.) ASIACRYPT 2014. LNCS, vol. 8874, pp. 22–41. Springer, Heidelberg (2014). https://doi.org/10.1007/978-3-662-45608-8_2
12. Fukumitsu, M., Hasegawa, S.: A tightly-secure lattice-based multisignature. In: Proceedings of the 6th on ASIA Public-Key Cryptography Workshop - APKC 2019, pp. 3–11. ACM Press (2019)
13. Gentry, C., Peikert, C., Vaikuntanathan, V.: Trapdoors for hard lattices and new cryptographic constructions. In: Proceedings of the Fourtieth Annual ACM Symposium on Theory of Computing - STOC 2008, pp. 197–206. ACM Press (2008)
14. Güneysu, T., Lyubashevsky, V., Pöppelmann, T.: Practical lattice-based cryptography: a signature scheme for embedded systems. In: Prouff, E., Schaumont, P. (eds.) CHES 2012. LNCS, vol. 7428, pp. 530–547. Springer, Heidelberg (2012). https://doi.org/10.1007/978-3-642-33027-8_31

15. Goldwasser, S., Micali, S., Rivest, R.L.: A digital signature scheme secure against adaptive chosen-message attacks. SIAM J. Comput. **17**(2), 281–308 (1988)
16. Grover, L.K.: Quantum mechanics helps in searching for a needle in a haystack. Phys. Rev. Lett. **79**(2), 325–328 (1997)
17. Guo, H., Li, W., Meamari, E., Shen, C.C., Nejad, M.: Attribute-based multi-signature and encryption for EHR management: a blockchain-based solution. In: 2020 IEEE International Conference on Blockchain and Cryptocurrency (ICBC). IEEE, May 2020
18. Harn, L., Lin, C.H.: Contract signature in e-commerce. Comput. Electr. Eng. **37**(2), 169–173 (2011)
19. Hoffstein, J., Howgrave-Graham, N., Pipher, J., Silverman, J.H., Whyte, W.: NTRUSign: digital signatures using the NTRU lattice. In: Joye, M. (ed.) CT-RSA 2003. LNCS, vol. 2612, pp. 122–140. Springer, Heidelberg (2003). https://doi.org/10.1007/3-540-36563-X_9
20. Hoffstein, J., Pipher, J., Silverman, J.H.: NTRU: a ring-based public key cryptosystem. In: Buhler, J.P. (ed.) ANTS 1998. LNCS, vol. 1423, pp. 267–288. Springer, Heidelberg (1998). https://doi.org/10.1007/BFb0054868
21. Hung, Y.H., Tseng, Y.M., Huang, S.S.: Revocable ID-based signature with short size over lattices. Secur. Commun. Netw. **2017**, 1–9 (2017)
22. Islam, S.H., Biswas, G.P.: Certificateless strong designated verifier multisignature scheme using bilinear pairings. In: Proceedings of the International Conference on Advances in Computing, Communications and Informatics - ICACCI 2012. ACM Press (2012)
23. Islam, S.H., Biswas, G.: Certificateless short sequential and broadcast multisignature schemes using elliptic curve bilinear pairings. J. King Saud Univ. Comput. Inf. Sci. **26**(1), 89–97 (2014)
24. Islam, S.H., Das, A.K., Khan, M.K.: Design of a provably secure identity-based digital multi-signature scheme using biometrics and fuzzy extractor. Secur. Commun. Netw. **9**(16), 3229–3238 (2016)
25. Islam, S.H., Farash, M.S., Biswas, G., Khan, M.K., Obaidat, M.S.: A pairing-free certificateless digital multisignature scheme using elliptic curve cryptography. Int. J. Comput. Math. **94**(1), 39–55 (2015)
26. Itakura, K., Nakamura, K.: A public-key cryptosystem suitable for digital multisignatures. NEC Res. Dev. **71**, 1–8 (1983)
27. Kansal, M., Singh, A.K., Dutta, R.: Efficient multi-signature scheme using lattice. Comput. J. (2021). https://doi.org/10.1093/comjnl/bxab077
28. Kong, F.Y., Diao, L.H., Yu, J., Jiang, Y.L., Zhou, D.S.: Lattice-based multi-signature schemes. Appl. Mech. Mater. **411–414**, 3–6 (2013)
29. Li, C.-M., Hwang, T., Lee, N.-Y.: Threshold-multisignature schemes where suspected forgery implies traceability of adversarial shareholders. In: De Santis, A. (ed.) EUROCRYPT 1994. LNCS, vol. 950, pp. 194–204. Springer, Heidelberg (1995). https://doi.org/10.1007/BFb0053435
30. Lu, X., Yin, W., Wen, Q., Jin, Z., Li, W.: A lattice-based unordered aggregate signature scheme based on the intersection method. IEEE Access **6**, 33986–33994 (2018)
31. Lysyanskaya, A.: Unique signatures and verifiable random functions from the DH-DDH separation. In: Yung, M. (ed.) CRYPTO 2002. LNCS, vol. 2442, pp. 597–612. Springer, Heidelberg (2002). https://doi.org/10.1007/3-540-45708-9_38
32. Lyubashevsky, V.: Lattice signatures without trapdoors. In: Pointcheval, D., Johansson, T. (eds.) EUROCRYPT 2012. LNCS, vol. 7237, pp. 738–755. Springer, Heidelberg (2012). https://doi.org/10.1007/978-3-642-29011-4_43

33. Lyubashevsky, V., Peikert, C., Regev, O.: On ideal lattices and learning with errors over rings. In: Gilbert, H. (ed.) EUROCRYPT 2010. LNCS, vol. 6110, pp. 1–23. Springer, Heidelberg (2010). https://doi.org/10.1007/978-3-642-13190-5_1
34. Ma, C., Jiang, M.: Practical lattice-based multisignature schemes for blockchains. IEEE Access **7**, 179765–179778 (2019)
35. Ma, C., Weng, J., Li, Y., Deng, R.: Efficient discrete logarithm based multi-signature scheme in the plain public key model. Des. Codes Cryptogr. **54**(2), 121–133 (2010). https://doi.org/10.1007/s10623-009-9313-z
36. Maxwell, G., Poelstra, A., Seurin, Y., Wuille, P.: Simple Schnorr multi-signatures with applications to bitcoin. Des. Codes Cryptogr. **87**(9), 2139–2164 (2019). https://doi.org/10.1007/s10623-019-00608-x
37. Micali, S., Ohta, K., Reyzin, L.: Accountable-subgroup multisignatures. In: Proceedings of the 8th ACM Conference on Computer and Communications Security - CCS 2001, pp. 245–254. ACM Press (2001)
38. Micciancio, D., Vadhan, S.P.: Statistical zero-knowledge proofs with efficient provers: lattice problems and more. In: Boneh, D. (ed.) CRYPTO 2003. LNCS, vol. 2729, pp. 282–298. Springer, Heidelberg (2003). https://doi.org/10.1007/978-3-540-45146-4_17
39. Ohta, K., Okamoto, T.: Multi-signature schemes secure against active insider attacks. IEICE Trans. Fundam. Electron. Commun. Comput. Sci. **82**, 21–31 (1999)
40. Peng, C., Du, X.: New lattice-based digital multi-signature scheme. In: Qin, P., Wang, H., Sun, G., Lu, Z. (eds.) ICPCSEE 2020. CCIS, vol. 1258, pp. 129–137. Springer, Singapore (2020). https://doi.org/10.1007/978-981-15-7984-4_10
41. Shamir, A.: Identity-based cryptosystems and signature schemes. In: Blakley, G.R., Chaum, D. (eds.) CRYPTO 1984. LNCS, vol. 196, pp. 47–53. Springer, Heidelberg (1985). https://doi.org/10.1007/3-540-39568-7_5
42. Shor, P.: Algorithms for quantum computation: discrete logarithms and factoring. In: Proceedings of the 35th Annual Symposium on Foundations of Computer Science, pp. 124–134. IEEE Computer Society Press (1994)
43. Stehlé, D., Steinfeld, R.: Making NTRU as secure as worst-case problems over ideal lattices. In: Paterson, K.G. (ed.) EUROCRYPT 2011. LNCS, vol. 6632, pp. 27–47. Springer, Heidelberg (2011). https://doi.org/10.1007/978-3-642-20465-4_4
44. Syta, E., et al.: Keeping authorities "honest or bust" with decentralized witness cosigning. In: 2016 IEEE Symposium on Security and Privacy (SP), pp. 526–545. IEEE, May 2016
45. Tanwar, S., Kumar, A.: An efficient multi-receiver certificate less digital multisignature scheme with anonymity. CSI Trans. ICT **8**(3), 311–318 (2020). https://doi.org/10.1007/s40012-020-00274-8
46. Wei, L., Zhang, L., Huang, D., Zhang, K., Dai, L., Wu, G.: PSDAAP: provably secure data authenticated aggregation protocols using identity-based multisignature in marine WSNs. Sensors **17**(9), 2117 (2017)
47. Xie, J., Hu, Y., Gao, J., Gao, W., Jiang, M.: Efficient certificateless signature scheme on NTRU lattice. KSII Trans. Internet Inf. Syst. (TIIS) **10**(10), 5190–5208 (2016)

StrGAN for Generating Enhanced Samples

Junfeng Wu[1], Jinwei Wang[1(✉)], Junjie Zhao[1], and Xiangyang Luo[2]

[1] Nanjing University of Information Science and Technology, Nanjing 210044, China
[2] State Key Laboratory of Mathematical Engineering and Advanced Computing,
Zhengzhou 450003, China

Abstract. Most studies use the negative effect of perturbation to mislead the neural network, such as adversarial examples, while ignoring the positive effect of improving neural networks' performance. In this work, we use enhanced samples with positive perturbation to improve target classifiers' performance and propose an algorithm of strong generative adversarial networks (StrGAN) to generate enhanced samples. StrGAN directly generates enhanced samples of unlabeled data. Since StrGAN and the target classifier are independent of each other, it can effectively reduce the classifier's computing resources and training time while improving the performance. The experiment shows that the enhanced samples generated by StrGAN have higher accuracy than original samples, and its accuracy can increase by up to 28.6%.

Keywords: Adversarial examples · Enhanced samples · Generative adversarial networks

1 Introduction

With the rapid development of artificial intelligence technology, machine learning and deep learning algorithms have been widely used in many complex fields, such as target detection [8,21,25], face recognition [1,9,23], natural language processing [4,20,22], and image classification [12,13,18]. However, some studies find that deep neural networks are susceptible to tiny perturbations which can cause changes in the network judgment. Adversarial examples [19] use the negative effect of perturbation to make the network produce wrong judgments. We consider using the positive effect to enhance the network judgment and call these kinds of samples with positive perturbations as enhanced samples. By using the enhanced samples can effectively improve the performance of the target network. Therefore, the study of enhanced samples is of great significance for improving the performance of the neural network.

However, the current methods of generating adversarial examples are mainly divided into traditional and generative adversarial networks based. Goodfellow et al. [6] proposed FGSM, which generates adversarial examples by adding a small perturbation in the gradient direction. Moosavi-Dezfooli et al. [15]

© Springer Nature Switzerland AG 2021
R. Deng et al. (Eds.): ISPEC 2021, LNCS 13107, pp. 363–373, 2021.
https://doi.org/10.1007/978-3-030-93206-0_22

proposed Deepfool, which uses iterative calculations to generate adversarial perturbations. Carlini and Wagner [2] proposed the C&W method, limiting the L_∞, L_2, and L_0 norms to generate invisible adversarial perturbations. These traditional methods can generate adversarial perturbation effectively, but their adversarial characteristics are hardly robust. Goodfellow et al. [5] proposed Generative Adversarial Networks (GAN), which brings new directions for the research of adversarial examples. Chaowei Xiao et al. [24] proposed the Adv-GAN, which adds a classifier to the original GAN architecture to make the prediction label close to the target label. On this basis, Mangla et al. [14] proposed an improved method AdvGAN++, which introduces the hidden layer of the classifier as a feature extractor to directly enable the generator to learn the transition from the latent feature space to the adversarial example.

These methods are all designed based on the idea that negative perturbations in adversarial examples can mislead the network. As far as we know, there are no related works that use positive perturbations to improve classification performance. In this paper, we consider adding positive perturbations to the sample to convey useful information that enhances judgment instead of causing misjudgment. This work is to make the target classifier maintain the original correct judgment of the sample and change the original wrong judgment. Based on the in-depth study of various methods of generating adversarial examples, inspired by the ideas of AdvGAN [24] and AdvGAN++ [14], we proposed StrGAN to generate enhanced samples. First, train different target classifiers so that they can identify each class relatively accurately. Then, re-divide the datasets to make the training set and test set maintain a low accuracy and use them for training StrGAN to generate enhanced samples. Finally, the accuracy of the enhanced samples generated by StrGAN is improved compared with the original samples.

Section 2 introduces the specific design of this scheme in detail. Section 3 will compare and analyze the experimental results. Section 4 summarizes the advantages and disadvantages of StrGAN and looks forward to future work.

2   Proposed Method

2.1   Overall Architecture

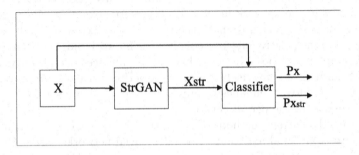

Fig. 1. Evaluation process of the proposed method.

Figure 1 shows the evaluation process of the proposed method, in which the StrGAN we proposed is used to generate enhanced samples. The classifiers used in this work respectively are AlexNet [11], VGG16 [17], and ResNet18 [7].

As shown in Fig. 1, by inputting the original sample X of unknown label into the trained StrGAN to directly get the corresponding enhanced sample X_{str}, then respectively send X and the corresponding X_{str} into the target classifier to get their respective accuracy P_X and $P_{X_{str}}$. Comparing $P_{X_{str}}$ with P_X can directly observe the effectiveness of this algorithm.

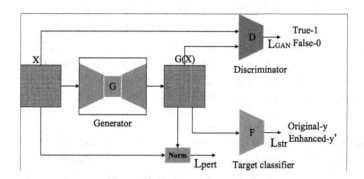

Fig. 2. StrGAN architecture.

Figure 2 illustrates the overall architecture of StrGAN. The core idea of Str-GAN is to directly map the input samples into enhanced samples through the generator. The discriminator is used to constrain the generated enhanced samples to appear similar to the original samples. The target classifier is used to constrain the predicted labels to be close to the original labels. After training, the generator can instantly produce enhanced samples for any input samples without requiring access to the target classifier.

As shown in Fig. 2, StrGAN is composed of three parts: a generator G, a discriminator D, and the target classifier F. The generator G takes the original sample x as its input and generates the corresponding enhanced sample $G(x)$. The discriminator D takes x and $G(x)$ as input and outputs the result of one neuron for judging whether the input is an original sample. The purpose of D is to make the generated sample indistinguishable from the original sample.

In order to improve the performance of the target classifier F, F takes $G(x)$ as its input and outputs the corresponding predicted label y'. By calculating the difference between the original label y and the predicted label y' to constrain the label y' equal to the label y. To bound the magnitude of the perturbation, we use l_2 norm to calculate the distance between $G(x)$ and x. During the training, the parameters of the target classifier are fixed. By solving the min-max game to get the optimal parameters of the generator and the discriminator, thereby obtain the final enhanced sample $G(x)$. Among them, L_{GAN}, L_{str}, and L_{pert} are part of the optimized loss function, and their specific implementation details will be introduced in Sect. 2.4.

2.2 Generator Designment

The generator is the most important part of StrGAN, and its architecture is shown in Fig. 3. It can be seen from Fig. 3 that the original samples are processed first before being input into the generator for convolution. Here use the method of converting RGB to YCbCr [10] to process the original sample, and the conversion formula is shown in Eq. (1).

$$\begin{cases} Y = 0.299 * R + 0.587 * G + 0.114 * B \\ Cb = -0.1687 * R - 0.3313 * G + 0.5 * B + 128 \\ Cr = 0.5 * R - 0.4187 * G - 0.0813 * B + 128 \end{cases} \tag{1}$$

YCbCr is widely used in computer systems, where Y refers to the brightness component, Cb refers to the blue chroma component, and Cr refers to the red chroma component. Processing the sample into YCbCr format may make the generator only learn its transformation matrix. In order to better learn the sample features, we remove the red chroma component Cr (remove Cb is also possible), which has no effect on the image quality, so the channels are changed from three to two. Although the Cr channel is removed, the generator can roughly guess the information of the Cr channel from the information of the Y and Cb channels, and learn how to add positive perturbations on the Cr channel to improve the classification performance.

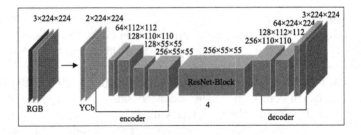

Fig. 3. Generator architecture.

The generator consists of one encoder, one decoder, and four residual blocks (ResNet-Block). The first two are responsible for the encoding and decoding of the sample, and the residual blocks are used for identity mapping. The generator has sixteen layers, in which the encoder and the decoder each have four layers, and the rest layers are residual blocks. The encoder uses down-sampling to convolve the input samples from $2 \times 224 \times 224$ to $256 \times 55 \times 55$, during which the number of channels increases exponentially. As the network depth increases, the sample size and the number of channels remain unchanged in the residual blocks. The decoder uses up-sampling and takes the output of the residual block as its input for deconvolution. Samples are deconvolved from $256 \times 55 \times 55$ to $3 \times 224 \times 224$ which is the same size as original samples, and the number of channels decreases exponentially during this period.

2.3   Discriminator Designment

The discriminator uses a five-layers network, including four convolutional layers and one fully-connected layer. The overall architecture of the discriminator is shown in Fig. 4.

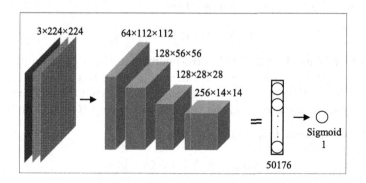

Fig. 4. Discriminator architecture.

Convolutional layers in discriminator are similar to the encoder in the generator, and they use down-sampling to convolve the input sample from $3 \times 224 \times 224$ to $256 \times 14 \times 14$. The fully-connected layer takes the output of convolutional layers as its input and outputs one neuron. In the process of downsampling, the size of the convolution kernel is 4, the step size is 2, and the padding is 1. After each convolution, the sample becomes half the size of the previous sample, and the number of channels is doubled. In the final output layer, only one neuron is included to represent the two classifications, and the sigmoid function is used to compress the output result to between 0 and 1.

2.4   Loss Functions

The objective loss function is formulated with adversarial loss, classification loss, and perturbation loss as:

$$L = L_{GAN} + \alpha L_{str} + \beta L_{pert} \tag{2}$$

where α and β are hyperparameters, which are used to balance the L_{str} and L_{pert}.

Adversarial Loss. L_{GAN} is defined as:

$$L_{GAN} = E_x l_{BCE} \left[D(x), 1 \right] + E_x l_{BCE} \left[D(G(x)), 0 \right] \tag{3}$$

where E_x refers to calculate the expected value about original sample x, which represents the same meaning in all functions used in this paper. $D(\cdot)$ and $G(\cdot)$ denote the output of discriminator and generator. l_{BCE} refers to the binary cross-entropy loss calculation. Here we use 1 for true and 0 for false. For the generator, the purpose is to make the value of $D(G(x))$ close to 1, while the discriminator is to make the value of $D(x)$ close to 1, and the value of $D(G(x))$ close to 0. By solving the min-max game between generator and discriminator to achieve the optimal value of the adversarial loss.

Classification Loss. L_{str} is expressed as:

$$L_{str} = E_x l_{CE}[F(G(x)), y] \tag{4}$$

where y represents the real label corresponding to the original sample x, $F(\cdot)$ denotes the output of the target classifier. l_{CE} refers to the cross-entropy loss calculation. By minimizing the cross-entropy loss between the predicted label of the generated sample $G(x)$ and the real label to make $F(G(x))$ close to y.

Perturbation Loss. L_{pert} is presented as:

$$L_{pert} = E_x \|x - G(x)\|_2 \tag{5}$$

where $\| \cdot \|_2$ refers to L_2 norm calculation. By minimizing the L_2 norm of the difference between the original sample x and the generated sample $G(x)$ to make $G(x)$ be close to x.

2.5   Implementation Details

The learning rate of the target classifier and StrGAN are all set to 0.0001, and the optimizer is Adam. When training StrGAN, we set the epoch to 120 and the image batch size to 20. In the process of optimizing the loss function (as shown in Eq. 2), we set $\alpha = 100$ and $\beta = 0.01$, which is to make the generator pay more attention to the change of image labels instead of image visual quality.

3   Experiments

3.1   Datasets

We perform experiments on ImageNet [3] and the cats&dogs [16] datasets. Two-class, three-class, and five-class datasets are designed corresponding to 25000, 30000, and 50000 samples. The target classifier's classification accuracy is trained at about 80% to ensure its normal performance so that it can identify each class relatively accurately. Then further divide the datasets into lower accuracy to train StrGAN so that it can better reflect the improved performance of Str-GAN. The redivided two-class, three-class, and five-class datasets correspond to 10000, 15000, and 25000 samples. We train StrGAN on the training set and do evaluations on the test set.

3.2   Performance Evaluation

StrGAN Based on AlexNet. When using AlexNet as the target classifier, the results of enhanced samples generated by StrGAN are shown in Table 1. The first column is the dataset class. The second and third columns are the accuracy of the original sample and the corresponding enhanced sample. The fourth column shows the best accuracy during the test. As shown in the table, the accuracy of the enhanced sample is higher than that of the original sample. The improved accuracy of the two-class sample is highest at 18.4%.

Table 1. Enhanced samples generated for AlexNet (YCbCr)

Class	Original-acc	Enhanced-acc	Best-acc
Two	53.8%	69.9%	**72.2%**
Three	63.3%	78.3%	79.1%
Five	60.9%	69.2%	69.7%

StrGAN Based on VGG16. When taking VGG16 as the target classifier, the results of enhanced samples generated by StrGAN are shown in Table 2. The table is the same as Table 1. From the table, we can see the improved accuracy of the three-class sample is the highest at 17.5%.

Table 2. Enhanced samples generated for VGG16 (YCbCr)

Class	Original-acc	Enhanced-acc	Best-acc
Two	63.1%	72.2%	74.1%
Three	61.4%	75.9%	**78.9%**
Five	59.0%	64.3%	65.9%

StrGAN Based on ResNet18. The results of enhanced samples generated by StrGAN for ResNet18 are shown in Table 3. This table is the same as Table 1 and Table 2. As shown in the table, we can see the improved accuracy of the three-class sample is the most obvious, which is 28.6%.

Table 3. Enhanced samples generated for ResNet18 (YCbCr)

Class	Original-acc	Enhanced-acc	Best-acc
Two	58.8%	77.6%	77.7%
Three	59.5%	87.2%	**88.1%**
Five	65.0%	78.6%	78.6%

The YCbCr at the end of the title of Table 1, 2 and Table 3 means that the original samples are processed into YCbCr format before generating enhanced samples. From Table 1, 2 and Table 3, it can be seen that the accuracy of the enhanced samples is generally higher than that of the original samples. Among them, the improvement effect based on ResNet18 is the most obvious. Experimental results show that the enhanced samples generated by StrGAN effectively improves the performance of the target classifier.

3.3   Comparison and Analysis

To further confirm the correctness of the idea in this paper, we changed the method of sample processing. Instead of converting the sample to YCbCr, we directly add random gaussian noise to the original sample. We compare the improved accuracy of different classifiers after YCbCr and noise processing, and the comparison results are shown in Table 4.

Table 4. Comparison of improved accuracy with different processing on different classifiers

Class	Classifiers	Improved (YCbCr)	Improved (Noise)
Two	AlexNet	18.4%	**21.1%**
	VGG16	11.0%	14.0%
	ResNet18	**18.9%**	17.8%
Three	AlexNet	15.8%	16.0%
	VGG16	17.5%	16.6%
	ResNet18	**28.6%**	**25.3%**
Five	AlexNet	8.8%	7.6%
	VGG16	6.9%	7.0%
	ResNet18	**13.6%**	**13.1%**

As shown in Table 4, the first column is the class, the second column is the classifier, and the third and fourth columns respectively represent the improved accuracy of the enhanced samples generated after different processing. Among them, YCbCr means that the original sample is processed into YCbCr format before input into the generator of our StrGAN, and Noise means that the original sample is added with a random noise before input into the generator of our StrGAN.

Table 4 shows that the improved accuracy of enhanced samples generated after noise processing is similar to the YCbCr processing, indicating that the generation of enhanced samples does not focus on the samples' processing but the algorithms' realization. Among the three target classifiers, the improvement effect based on ResNet18 is the most obvious. The improved accuracy of the three-class samples is 28.6%, which is significantly higher than the other two. Because of the simple architecture of the AlexNet, its training time is the shortest.

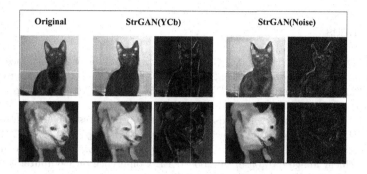

Fig. 5. Comparison of enhanced samples and original samples

Figure 5 shows the comparison of enhanced samples and original samples. The first column represents the original sample, the second and third columns are the enhanced samples generated after YCbCr preprocessing and its absolute difference with the original sample, and the fourth and fifth columns correspond to the results after noise preprocessing. In our experiment, all YCbCr preprocessing represents YCb format with the Cr component removed. It can be seen from Fig. 5 that the visual quality of the enhanced samples generated after the two preprocessing methods is somewhat different from the original image, but the overall layout is similar. From their absolute difference images, we can see that the samples after YCb processing are smoother than that of noise processing and the edge effect is more obvious.

Overall, the experiment shows that the enhanced sample can improve the performance of the target classifier, and the improvement effect is significant. However, there are still some problems. When the classes of samples increase, the improvement effect decreases or even becomes negative. The overall visual quality of the enhanced samples is not high, and some even affect human eye recognition. It is believed that the improvement of these problems can further promote the development of enhanced samples.

4 Conclusion

This paper proposes enhanced sample to improve the performance of neural networks. The so-called enhanced samples refer to those samples with positive perturbations. To generate enhanced samples, we proposes an algorithm StrGAN. StrGAN can directly map the input samples into enhanced samples to achieve the purpose of enhancing the network. Since StrGAN and the target classifier in the model are independent of each other, it can effectively reduce the classifier's computing resources and training time. But StrGAN has some overfitting problems, and the perturbation in enhanced samples is quite apparent. In future work, we plan to reduce the over-fitting problem while focusing on enhancing the samples' visual quality to generate high-quality enhanced samples.

References

1. Cao, D., Zhu, X., Huang, X., Guo, J., Lei, Z.: Domain balancing: face recognition on long-tailed domains. In: 2020 IEEE/CVF Conference on Computer Vision and Pattern Recognition (CVPR), pp. 5670–5678 (2020). https://doi.org/10.1109/CVPR42600.2020.00571
2. Carlini, N., Wagner, D.: Towards evaluating the robustness of neural networks. In: 2017 IEEE Symposium on Security and Privacy (SP), pp. 39–57. IEEE (2017)
3. Deng, J., Dong, W., Socher, R., Li, L.J., Li, K., Fei-Fei, L.: ImageNet: a large-scale hierarchical image database. In: 2009 IEEE Conference on Computer Vision and Pattern Recognition, pp. 248–255. IEEE (2009)
4. Gogineni, A.K., Swayamjyoti, S., Sahoo, D., Sahu, K.K., Kishore, R.: Multiclass classification of vulnerabilities in Smart Contracts using AWD-LSTM, with pre-trained encoder inspired from natural language processing. arXiv preprint arXiv:2004.00362 (2020)
5. Goodfellow, I., et al.: Generative adversarial nets. In: Advances in Neural Information Processing Systems, pp. 2672–2680 (2014)
6. Goodfellow, I.J., Shlens, J., Szegedy, C.: Explaining and harnessing adversarial examples. arXiv preprint arXiv:1412.6572 (2014)
7. He, K., Zhang, X., Ren, S., Sun, J.: Deep residual learning for image recognition. In: Proceedings of the IEEE Conference on Computer Vision and Pattern Recognition, pp. 770–778 (2016)
8. Huang, S., Cornelis, B., Devolder, B., Martens, M., Pizurica, A.: Multimodal target detection by sparse coding: application to paint loss detection in paintings. IEEE Trans. Image Process. **29**, 7681–7696 (2020)
9. Huang, Y., et al.: CurricularFace: adaptive curriculum learning loss for deep face recognition. In: 2020 IEEE/CVF Conference on Computer Vision and Pattern Recognition (CVPR), pp. 5900–5909 (2020). https://doi.org/10.1109/CVPR42600.2020.00594
10. Jin, X., Chang, Q.: RGB to YCbCr color space transform based on FPGA. Modern Electron. Tech. **18**, 73–75 (2009)
11. Krizhevsky, A., Sutskever, I., Hinton, G.E.: ImageNet classification with deep convolutional neural networks. Commun. ACM **60**(6), 84–90 (2017)
12. Li, Q., Shen, L., Guo, S., Lai, Z.: Wavelet integrated CNNs for noise-robust image classification. In: 2020 IEEE/CVF Conference on Computer Vision and Pattern Recognition (CVPR), pp. 7243–7252 (2020)
13. Li, X., Wu, J., Sun, Z., Ma, Z., Cao, J., Xue, J.H.: BSNet: Bi-similarity network for few-shot fine-grained image classification. IEEE Trans. Image Process. **30**, 1318–1331 (2021)
14. Mangla, P., Jandial, S., Varshney, S., Balasubramanian, V.N.: AdvGAN++: harnessing latent layers for adversary generation. arXiv preprint arXiv:1908.00706 (2019)
15. Moosavi-Dezfooli, S.M., Fawzi, A., Frossard, P.: DeepFool: a simple and accurate method to fool deep neural networks. In: Proceedings of the IEEE Conference on Computer Vision and Pattern Recognition, pp. 2574–2582 (2016)

16. Parkhi, O.M., Vedaldi, A., Zisserman, A., Jawahar, C.: Cats and dogs. In: 2012 IEEE Conference on Computer Vision and Pattern Recognition, pp. 3498–3505. IEEE (2012)
17. Simonyan, K., Zisserman, A.: Very deep convolutional networks for large-scale image recognition. arXiv preprint arXiv:1409.1556 (2014)
18. Sun, H., Zheng, X., Lu, X.: A supervised segmentation network for hyperspectral image classification. IEEE Trans. Image Process. **30**, 2810–2825 (2021)
19. Szegedy, C., et al.: Intriguing properties of neural networks. arXiv preprint arXiv:1312.6199 (2013)
20. Torfi, A., Shirvani, R.A., Keneshloo, Y., Tavaf, N., Fox, E.A.: Natural language processing advancements by deep learning: a survey. arXiv preprint arXiv:2003.01200 (2021)
21. Uzair, M., Brinkworth, R.S., Finn, A.: Bio-inspired video enhancement for small moving target detection. IEEE Trans. Image Process. **30**, 1232–1244 (2021)
22. Wang, H., et al.: HAT: hardware-aware transformers for efficient natural language processing. arXiv preprint arXiv:2005.14187 (2020)
23. Wang, Q., Wu, T., Zheng, H., Guo, G.: Hierarchical pyramid diverse attention networks for face recognition. In: 2020 IEEE/CVF Conference on Computer Vision and Pattern Recognition (CVPR), pp. 8323–8332 (2020). https://doi.org/10.1109/CVPR42600.2020.00835
24. Xiao, C., Li, B., Zhu, J.Y., He, W., Liu, M., Song, D.: Generating adversarial examples with adversarial networks. arXiv preprint arXiv:1801.02610 (2018)
25. Zhu, H., Ni, H., Liu, S., Xu, G., Deng, L.: TNLRS: target-aware non-local low-rank modeling with saliency filtering regularization for infrared small target detection. IEEE Trans. Image Process. **29**, 9546–9558 (2020). https://doi.org/10.1109/TIP.2020.3028457

A Secure and Privacy-Preserving Data Transmission Scheme in the Healthcare Framework

Huijie Yang[1(✉)], Tianqi Zhou[1], Chen Wang[1], and Debiao He[2(✉)]

[1] School of Computer and Software, Nanjing University of Information Science and Technology, Nanjing, China
[2] School of Mathematics and Statistics, Wuhan University, Wuhan, China
hedebiao@whu.edu.cn

Abstract. With the continuous development of the Internet of Things (IoT) and people's demand for telemedicine, smart healthcare technology is developing rapidly. Wearable sensors, the basic components in smart healthcare, contain patients' sensitive data such as physiological data and personal health information. Meantime, during the transmission and interaction of those sensitive data, patients' privacy may leak which causes harm to them. Therefore, data security for wearable sensors is essential to protect patient's privacy. In our paper, a secure and privacy-preserving data transmission scheme in the healthcare framework is proposed. In particular, the k-out-of-n OT technology is introduced, and a lightweight $(OT)_k^n$ protocol is designed to ensure the two-way privacy of the communication parties and reduce the communication overhead during transmission. In addition, theoretical and experimental analyses indicate that the proposed scheme is practical for data transmission with high security and efficiency.

Keywords: Data transmission · Privacy-preserving · Oblivious transfer · Wearable sensor

1 Introduction

Currently, the smart healthcare framework is composed of sensor technology and healthcare infrastructure, which can employ wearable sensors to remotely monitor the physiological parameters of patients [17]. Generally, three layers compose a smart healthcare framework, that is, the data collection layer, the data processing layer and the medical service layer [14]. The data collection layer mainly includes patient physiological data (heart rate, body temperature, blood oxygen, etc.), exercise data, environmental data, etc. collected by various wearable sensors, and then are transmitted to the phone. At the data processing layer, the server stores data, and performs calculation and analysis on the data. The medical service layer allows doctors and nurses to interact with the server to ensure that they can access patient data and provide timely diagnosis or advice for patients. This framework effectively assist doctors in understanding the health

© Springer Nature Switzerland AG 2021
R. Deng et al. (Eds.): ISPEC 2021, LNCS 13107, pp. 374–391, 2021.
https://doi.org/10.1007/978-3-030-93206-0_23

status of patients, predict the health status or disease of patients, and play an early warning role. However, it involves the problem of easy leakage of sensitive data regardless of the stages of collection, transmission, and interaction [16].

Consider the following situation: nowadays, the COVID-19 is still continuing. Once the certain area is classified as an epidemic area, the treatment of basic diseases will be postponed, except for emergency diseases. At this time, how to establish a secure and privacy-preserving Internet of Medical Things, which employs the patients' wearable devices to diagnose in a timely manner, is particularly important. And, the wearable sensor includes physiological data, exercise data and environmental data, etc., which involve the user's private information. This requires the confidentiality of sensor data. To meet the mentioned goal, a higher level of security algorithm to encrypt the data is applied in some protocols, sacrificing the efficiency of those. In addition, if the data is monitored or stolen by malicious users during transmission, the user's disease, behavior and lifestyle habits will be leaked. Worse, malicious users can analyze group living habits and laws via monitoring multi-person sensor data, such as understanding people suffering from diseases through big data, and people taking the subway at 8 o'clock every day, and so on. Thus, how to ensure that the user's privacy is not leaked during the sensors data transmission phase is one of the main contents of our scheme. Moreover, doctors only have the privilege to access the data of patients under his charge, but do not realize the others. In case the patient's physiological data is leaked, malicious users may understand the data, learn about and spread the patient's condition, which may cause discrimination against him by others.

The oblivious transfer (OT) algorithm is a good method to solve the problem mentioned above. Various OT protocols have been put forward, including 1-out-of-2 OT, 1-out-of-k OT and k-out-of-n OT. These OT protocols have been employed to ensure the privacy-preserving of data in various environments, such as medical record system [11], VANETs [19] and so on.

Motivation of This Paper: As it is mentioned above, some data transmission protocols are not suitable for the healthcare framework with the wearable sensors. Therefore, a secure data transmission scheme is proposed in our paper, which protects the privacy of wearable sensors and users in the data transmission phase based on oblivious transfer and ciphertext-policy attribute-based encryption (CP-ABE) technologies. The OT algorithm is used to ensure the privacy-preserving of patients. The OT algorithm can ensure that the servers are unable to figure out that which medical records the doctors select, so as to prevent the servers from investigating the health status of patients. And CP-ABE scheme is used to encrypt the medical records. To accomplish this goal, the following three crucial issues should be considered for us. First, the confidentiality of data of wearable sensors should be guaranteed in the transmission phase. The security of sensor data is the basis of our protocol. If there is a problem with the data, the subsequent phases are directly terminated. Sensor data mainly includes the patient's physiological data, medical data, etc., which are related to the patient's life safety. If the data is tampered with, it will affect the diagnosis. Second, ensure privacy among wearable sensors, devices, servers and users under the healthcare framework. On the one hand, doctors only learn the data of users managed by them during the $(OT)_k^n$ phase, but have no right to obtain the others. On the other hand, the server cannot realize which data is accessed by the doctor. In addition, the storage traces of data are hidden from malicious persons. Malicious persons cannot infer the user's area by analyzing which server the data comes from.

1.1 Main Contributions

We design a secure and privacy-preserving data transmission scheme in the healthcare framework that is to resolve the above issues. The main contributions are as follows.

- **A secure and privacy-preserving healthcare framework with wearable sensors is designed, which assures the security of data during transmission.** Assuming that a patient u_1 has many wearable sensors s_i, and their data is transmitted to servers via the gateway or mobile phone. Then, doctors d_1 access the patient data according to the authority. In the above process, sensors, gateways, and servers all contain u_1's private data. There is also a risk of privacy leakage or data tampering by malicious users during the data transmission phase between entities. Through applying the proposed healthcare framework, u_1's medical data can not be obtained, and the privacy of each entity will be protected. Figure 1 shows the healthcare framework with wearable sensors.
- **A lightweight $(OT)_k^n$ protocol that protect the privacy between servers and users is proposed.** Normally, doctors d_1 employ the stored keys to decrypt data of servers. It is worth noting that d_1 should store a large number of keys, and the cost of key update is high. To solve the above security breaches, we integrate CP-ABE technology into OT protocol and design a lightweight $(OT)_k^n$ protocol. The server can only find data based on u_{id} and category provided by d_1, but it does not learn those data which d_1 looks forward to accessing. Moreover, d_1 can not gain the other data, expect for the required data, which effectively protects the two-way privacy between servers and doctors.
- **Data confidentiality is efficiently ensured and the computation of our scheme is effectively reduced.** Through analysis and proof, the security of our protocol satisfies the definition in the security model. Besides, the computation and storage resources of sensors are limited. The protocol we designed for data encryption and transmission is lightweight. We compare our protocol with similar protocols from different phases through theoretical performance analysis and experiment analysis.

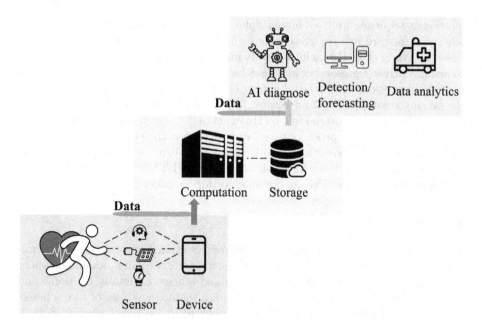

Fig. 1. The healthcare framework with wearable sensors

1.2   Related Work

In order to facilitate the timely treatment of patients, smart healthcare system continues to develop [12,13]. It can quickly collect the physiological data of patients and provide it to doctors, then doctors can analyze and diagnose the patient's symptoms in a timely manner. Following this, the healthcare framework was gradually established to standardize the various stages of smart medical care. In 2009, three forms of healthcare system transformation are determined by Wendt et al. [20], which also address the need to establish a comprehensive conceptual framework for analyzing healthcare systems and their transformations. As wearable sensors continue to improve, the amount of data that can be collected is increasing exponentially. A patient-centered framework which brings big data to personalized healthcare is proposed via Chalwa et al. [3], which demonstrates its applicability to patient-centered outcomes, meaningful use, and reducing re-admission rates. Then, in 2021, a novel healthcare monitoring framework based on the cloud environment and a big data analytics engine is proposed by Ali et al. [1], which can precisely store and analyze healthcare data, and to improve the classification accuracy.

In addition, healthcare data are sensitive data involving patients. Once privacy is leaked, it will cause harm to patients. In order to protect the privacy, in 2018, Sharma et al. have proposed a privacy preservation scheme for WSN based healthcare application employing the concepts of secret sharing and hashing function [15]. Then, an efficient and privacy-preserving disease risk prediction scheme for e-healthcare is proposed by Yang et al. [21], which unitizes a super-increasing sequence and a homomorphic cryptographic algorithm. In 2021, a scheme of forward privacy preserving for IoT-enabled healthcare systems is proposed by Wang et al. [18], which mainly includes a searchable encryption scheme to achieve privacy preserving and searchable function.

Moreover, k-out-of-n OT technology is combined with our scheme to protect the privacy among doctors and servers. In 2020, an accountable and efficient data sharing scheme for industrial IoT by Huang et al. [9], which decentralizes a k-out-of-n oblivious transfer protocol together with a zero-knowledge proof technique to enable the data receiver's private key. In 2021, Wang et al. propose a scheme to protect the users' privacy in the situation of VANET's feature matching based on a k-out-of-n OT and Private Set Intersection protocol [19].

1.3   Organization

The rest of this paper is organized as follows. Section 2 presents some preliminaries in cryptographic. Section 3 describes the system model, design goals and threat model. Section 4 introduce the proposed scheme in details. Section 5 and 6 demonstrate the security analysis and performance analysis of our scheme, respectively. Finally, conclusions of this paper and our work are given in Sect. 7.

2   Preliminaries

2.1   Notations

Some frequently used notations and corresponding meanings are given in Table 1.

Table 1. Notations in our scheme

Symbol	Description
$\mathbb{G}, \mathbb{G}_T$	Cyclic multiplicative groups
g	Generator of $\mathbb{G}$
h_1, h_2	One-way hash function
(sk_i, pk_i)	The private and public key pair of sensors in registration
(sk_s, pk_s)	The private and public key pair of sensors in authentication
sek	The symmetric key to encrypt data
k_t	The encrypted sek
w_y	The y-th number of data m_y to be required
M_d	The encrypted data via sek
$\mathbb{D}$	The set of doctor attributes
$\mathbb{P}$	The set of patient attributes
$\mathbb{A}$	The attributes set

2.2   Smooth Projective Hashing

The definition of smooth projective hashing (SPH) is proposed by Cramer et al. [6,10]. There are two keys in VSPH, sk_v is the private hash key, pk_v is the public hash key. The tuple of SPH is denoted as $\mathbb{H} = (H, K, X, L, B, \beta, \alpha)$. The set of hash functions with $K(\xi)$ as the key is $\{H_k : X \to B\}_{k \in K}$, where X is the data set, B is the set of hash values and K is the set of hash function's key. Then, defines the projective hashing function $\beta : k \to \alpha$, that is, $\alpha = \beta(k)$ holds, where α is the set of projective key. The difficult subset membership problem illustrates two finite non-empty sets $X, W \subseteq 0, 1^{ploy|k|}$ and a relationship $R \subset X \times W$ for each instance ξ. In other words, $\xi = (X, W, R)$ makes the corresponding $L = \{x : \exists w.s.t(x, w) \in R\}$ non-empty.

Definition 2.1 Smooth Projective Hashing: (H, K, B, β, α) is the projective hashing function of difficult subset membership problem M. Each instance $\xi \in M$ exists a function f which $f(x; \beta(k), w) = H_k(x)$ holds, where $x \in L(\xi)$, $k \in K(\xi)$ and $\alpha = \beta(k)$ establish.

2.3   Ciphertext Policy Attribute Based Encryption

Our protocol uses the ciphertext policy attribute based encryption algorithm (CP-ABE) proposed by Fuchun Guo et al. [7] It is mainly divided into four steps, which is described as follows.

- Setup: Input a security parameter s and a set of attributes $\mathbb{A} = \{A_1, A_2, \cdots, A_n\}$, the public parameters pk_m and a master secret key msk are output via the setup algorithm.
- Encrypt: Input the public parameters pk_m, a access policy $\mathbb{P}$ and a data d, the encrypt algorithm $Enc(\mathbb{P}, d)$ is performed to output the ciphertext CT.
- KeyGen: Input the public parameter pk_m and a master secret key msk and a subset of attributes $\mathbb{A}$, the decryption key of $sk_{\mathbb{A}}$ is output via the key generation algorithm.
- Decrypt: Input a ciphertext CT which is constructed by a access policy $\mathbb{P}$, the public parameter pk_m and the key $sk_{\mathbb{A}}$, the data d is computed by the decryption algorithm. Otherwise, aborts the scheme.

2.4   k-out-of-n Oblivious Transfer Protocol

This k-out-of-n OT protocol is proposed by Chu et al. [5], which supports to choose k message by a receiver. The OT protocol not only protect the privacy of a receiver, but also a sender.

Input: parameters $g, h_1, h_2, \mathbb{G}_q$, where $\mathbb{G}_q$ is the subgroup of $\mathbb{Z}_q^*$, h_1, h_2 are hash functions and $g \in \mathbb{G}_q$ holds. The sender has data $\{m_1, m_2, \cdots, m_n\}$ and a receiver selects the number of data $\{\delta_1, \delta_2, \cdots, \delta_k\}$.

Output: $m_{\delta_1}, m_{\delta_2}, \cdots, m_{\delta_k}$.

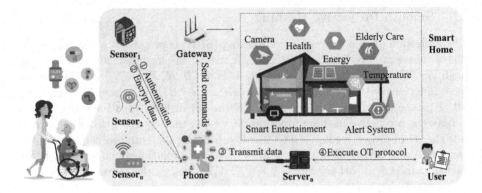

Fig. 2. System model

1. A receiver computes $w_{\delta_j} = h_1(\delta_j)$ and $A_j = w_{\delta_j} g^{a_j}$, where $a_j \in \mathbb{Z}_q^*$ and $j = 1, 2, \cdots, k$ hold. Then, he sends $A_1, A_2, \cdots, A_k$ to the sender.
2. A sender constructs $y = g^x$, $D_j = (A_j)^x$, $w_i = h_1(i)$ and $c_i = m_i \oplus h_2(w_i^x)$, where $x \in \mathbb{Z}_q^*$, $i = 1, 2, \cdots, n$ and $j = 1, 2, \cdots, k$ establish.
3. A sender sends $y, D_1, D_2, \cdots, D_k$ and $c_1, c_2, \cdots, c_n$ to the receiver.
4. A receiver computes $K_j = D_j/y^{a_j}$ and $m_{\delta_j} \oplus h_2(K_j)$. Finally, the receiver obtains the required data $m_{\delta_1}, m_{\delta_2}, \cdots, m_{\delta_k}$.

3   Problem Statement

3.1   System Model

A healthcare framework with wearable sensors is proposed to transfer secure data, while it also protect the privacy of all entities. On the one hand, the privacy of sensitive data in the sensor is protected. The data is encrypted to store in sensor, and malicious users cannot obtain the data directly. Meantime, even if a malicious user steals k sensor keys sk_s and the input value c_i which has been used to generate the key, he also could not understand the physical unclonable function by guessing. On the other hand, protect the privacy of servers. The doctor can only learn the requested data, and other data in the server cannot be learned. In addition, the dynamic joining or exit of groups are supported by this protocol, and it can also resist collusion attacks by revoked or malicious users. The system model contains four entities, wearable sensors, phone/devices, servers and doctors. Figure 2 shows a system model of the proposed scheme.

Patients wear a variety of sensors, including hospital-specific sensors for certain diseases. These sensors can facilitate a determined doctor to know the patient's condition in time. Meantime, it is also convenient for doctors to conduct multidisciplinary medical consultations in the cloud. Therefore, the sensor mainly includes the patient's physiological data, movement data, etc., those involves the patient's privacy. In addition, patients will move at any time, and data will be stored in the cloud to ensure that doctors in different hospitals can obtain the data. A many-to-many secure transmission model between users (doctors and patients) and servers is constructed by our scheme. First, the sensor/phone completes the registration phase, and employs zero-knowledge proof to prove that the sensor has generated a key for a phone. Then, a set of attributes of users such as doctors and patients is generated. Secondly, two-way authentication is performed between the sensor and the mobile phone to prevent a certain device from forging its identity. Only the sensor that has been authenticated, its ID will be stored by the phone. Then, the sensor encrypts data and transmits it to the phone. Also apply a symmetric key to re-encrypt the private key so that a phone decrypt the sensor data. Third, the OT protocol is employed between doctors and sensors for secure data transmission, which also protects the privacy of both parties. The doctor sends k request to servers via data serial numbers. They perform OT protocol to transfer data. Consequently, severs return k accessed data. Finally, the doctor executes the CP-ABE algorithm to decrypt the re-encrypted key, then applies this key to decrypt ciphertext.

3.2 Security Model

The $(OT)_k^n$ protocol can be utilize to ensure the privacy preserving during the data transmission. A secure $(OT)_k^n$ protocol should satisfy the following security requirements.

Reviewer's Security. We assume that $\mathcal{A}$ is the adversary who can conspire with the data sender. We can say that the protocol ensures the reviewer's security if the adversary $\mathcal{A}$ is not able to figure out what data the receiver has selected. The game between the challenger $\mathcal{C}$ and the adversary $\mathcal{A}$ is presented as follows.

- Setup: The challenger $\mathcal{C}$ selects secret keys and generates system parameters of $(OT)_k^n$ protocol. And it sends secret keys and system parameters to the adversary $\mathcal{A}$. Besides, $\mathcal{C}$ sets u_y for data m_y, where $1 \leq y \leq n$.
- Query I: The adversary $\mathcal{A}$ can query about M_{A_j} adaptively in this phase. $\mathcal{A}$ inputs the reviewer's choice j and the challenger $\mathcal{C}$ returns M_{A_j} and add it into the Q list;
- Challenge: The adversary $\mathcal{A}$ inputs his/her target (j_0, j_1). The challenger $\mathcal{C}$ selects $b \in \{0,1\}$ and computes M_{A_b}. If $M_{A_b} \in Q$, the game aborts. Otherwise, $\mathcal{C}$ sends M_{A_b} to the adversary $\mathcal{A}$.
- Query II: This phase is the same as Query I, expect that the adversary $\mathcal{A}$ can not query about j_0 or j_1 in this phase.
- Guess: The adversary $\mathcal{A}$ outputs his/her guess b^*. If $b^* = b$, $\mathcal{A}$ wins. Otherwise, $\mathcal{A}$ fails.

Sender's Security. We assume that $\mathcal{A}$ is the adversary who can conspire with the data reviewer. We can say that the protocol ensures the sender's security if the adversary $\mathcal{A}$ is not able to obtain data other than the data he/she has selected. The game between the challenger $\mathcal{C}$ and the adversary $\mathcal{A}$ is presented as follows.

- Setup: The challenger $\mathcal{C}$ selects secret keys and generates system parameters of $(OT)_k^n$ protocol. And it sends system parameters to the adversary $\mathcal{A}$. Besides, $\mathcal{C}$ sets u_y for data m_y, where $1 \leq y \leq n$.
- Query I: The adversary $\mathcal{A}$ can query about θ_j adaptively in this phase. $\mathcal{A}$ inputs his/her choice j. The challenger $\mathcal{C}$ returns θ_j to $\mathcal{A}$ and adds the j into the $\hat{Q}$ list;
- Challenge: The adversary $\mathcal{A}$ onputs his/her target j^*. If $j^* \in Q$, the game aborts.
- Query II: This phase is the same as Query I, expect that the adversary $\mathcal{A}$ can not query about j^* in this phase.
- Test: The adversary $\mathcal{A}$ outputs θ_{j^*}. If θ_{j^*}, $\mathcal{A}$ wins. Then $\mathcal{A}$ can compute Y_{j^*} via $f(g^{Tw_{j^*}}, \theta_{j^*}, w_{j^*})$ and obtain $m_{j^*} = p_{j^*} \oplus Y_{j^*}$. Otherwise, $\mathcal{A}$ fails.

4   Our Proposed Scheme

The proposed scheme is described in details in this section. Our scheme are divided into four parts, in which initialization phase is introduced in section A, registration phase is presented in section B, mutual authentication phase is stated in section C, k-out-of-n OT $(OT)_k^n$-data transmission phase and decryption phase are illustrated in section D and section E, respectively.

4.1   Initialization Phase

Assume that there are j wearable sensors (WS_1, WS_2, $\cdots$, WS_j), a phones/devices (P_a), b servers ($S_1, S_2, \cdots, S_b$) which each server has n stored data.

Set two multiplicative cyclic groups $\mathbb{G}$ and $\mathbb{G}_T$, bilinear mapping $e : \mathbb{G} \times \mathbb{G} \to \mathbb{G}_T$, and denote the generator of $\mathbb{G}$ as g. Set the hash functions $h_1 : \mathbb{G} \times \mathbb{G} \times \{0,1\}^n \times \mathbb{Z}_p^* \to \mathbb{Z}_p^*$ and $h_2 : \mathbb{Z}_p^* \to \mathbb{G}$, where n is the fixed value. And then, the phone inputs a security parameter s, computes its public key pk_p and private key sk_p, and sets a value v. Besides, the setup algorithm in CP-ABE scheme is executed to generate pubic-private keys pair (p_t, p_s), set a universe of attributes $\{A_1, A_2, \cdots, A_n\}$ and form a access policy $\mathbb{P}$ with the security parameter λ as input.

Key generation center (KGC) generates keys for doctors via the KeyGen algorithm in the CP-ABE scheme. The doctor inputs his attributes $\mathbb{A}$ and the KGC outputs the private key $sk_d = KeyGen_{ABE}(\mathbb{A}, p_t, p_s)$.

4.2   Registration Phase

We employ physical unclonable function (PUF) to assistant wearable sensors to generate the key. Sensors compute and send the zero-knowledge proofs to the phone, which proves to phone the key which has been generated, to accomplish the registration. When the phone successfully verifies proofs, it can store ID and other necessary information of sensors. The registration phase of our scheme includes three steps, they are described briefly below.

- Step 1: For $1 \leq i \leq v$, the sensor selects $c_i \xleftarrow{R} \mathbb{Z}_p^*$ as the input of the PUF. Then, it computes private key $sk_i = PUF(c_i)$ and public key $pk_i = g^{sk_i}$. Meantime, it applies the public key pk_p of phone to calculate $T_i = e(pk_p, h_2(c_i))$.
- Step 2: The sensor selects $r_i \xleftarrow{R} \mathbb{Z}_p^*$, constructs the commitment value $M_i = g^{r_i}$, challenge value $H_i = h_1(M_i||pk_i||c_i||ID)$, and response value $R_i = r_i - H_i \times sk_i$. Finally, it sends the proof π_i to the phone.

$$\pi_i = (c_i, M_i, pk_i, H_i, R_i) \quad (1 \leq i \leq v)$$

- Step 3: The phone generates $H_i' = h_1(M_i||pk_i||c_i||ID)$ and checks whether the following formulas $H_i' \overset{?}{=} H_i$ and $M_i \overset{?}{=} g^{R_i}pk_i^{H_i'}$ hold. If those formulas do not hold, the scheme aborts. Otherwise, the phone stores a list $(c_i, pk_i)(1 \leq i \leq v)$ for the sensor ID.

4.3 Mutual Authentication Phase

In the healthcare framework, only after sensors and phones are mutually authenticated to ensure that the device is in a trusted state, can data be transmitted. In this phase, sensors and the phone perform the following steps.

- Setp 1 - Connection Request
    1. Case 1: Sensor actively sends an authentication request to the phone. Sensor send its ID to the phone. The phone randomly picks pair (c', pk') from the list $(c_i, pk_i)(1 \leq i \leq v)$ of sensor ID, and then computes BLS signature $\sigma(c') = h_2(c')^{sk_p}$. At last, it sends c' and $\sigma(c')$to the sensor.
    2. Case 2: The phone actively sends an authentication request to sensors. It confirms the identity ID of sensor which requests authentication. Then, it randomly picks pair (c', pk') from the list (c_i, pk_i) $(1 \leq i \leq v)$ of sensor ID, and then computes BLS signature $\sigma(c') = h_2(c')^{sk_p}$. At the end, it sends c' and $\sigma(c')$to the sensor.
- Step 2 - Sensor $\rightarrow$ Phone Authentication
    1. According to values c', the sensor figures out T' to check whether $T' \overset{?}{=} e(g, \sigma(c'))$. If the equation is true, the phone has been certified by sensors. Otherwise, the algorithm aborts since the value c' has been tempered with.
    2. The sensor inputs c' into the PUF and computes private key $sk' = PUF(c')$ and public key $pk_s' = g^{sk'}$. Then, it selects $r' \xleftarrow{R} \mathbb{Z}_p^*$, generates the commitment value $M' = g^{r'}$, challenge value $H' = h_1(M'||pk_s'||c_s'||ID)$, and respond value $R' = r' - H' \times sk_s'$. Finally, it generates the proof π' as follows.

$$\pi' = (c', M', pk_s', H', R')$$

3. The sensors randomly selects a symmetric key sek to encrypt its data $M_d = Enc_s(sek, d)$. Then, it performs ELGammal algorithm to encrypt the above symmetric key sek by utilizing the public key of the phone (i.e. $CT = Enc(pk_p, sek)$), so that the ciphertext can be decrypted by the phone. Finally, the sensor sends (π', M_d, CT) to the phone.

- Step 3 - Phone $\to$ Sensor Authentication

1. The phone extracts pk'_s from π' and checks $pk' \overset{?}{=} pk'_s$. If it is not true, the protocol aborts. Then, the phone verifies whether the following equations $H' \overset{?}{=} h_1(M'||pk'||c'||ID)$ and $M' \overset{?}{=} g^{R'} pk'^{H'}$ hold. If they are true, the mutual authentication is completed. Otherwise, the scheme aborts.

2. Then, the phone decrypts CT to obtain the symmetric key $sek = Dec(CT, sk')$. After that, the phone employ sek to decrypt M_d, which $d = Dec'(sek', M_d)$ holds.

4.4 Data Transmission Phase

The data can be transmitted in the channel after it is encrypted. To solve the problem of exposing server location privacy, this phase encrypt data via the CPABE algorithm. That is, only authorized doctors can get the private key. This prevents doctors from storing a large number of server private keys and reduces the waste of resources. When the encrypted data has stored in servers, the doctor can access the authorized user. Then, he performs OT protocol to obtain Fig. 3. The specific steps are as follows.

The Doctor	The Server
	Choose numbers $x, f_y \in \mathbb{Z}_p^*$
	Compute $T = 2^{\lceil \log p \rceil}$
	Generate $\xi = g^x \; u_y = g^{T f_y}$
	Compute $Y_y = H_{f_y x}(g^{2 w_y})$
	$p_y = m_y \oplus Y_y$
(u_y, p_y, w_y, CT_y)	

Selects k data according to the tag w_j
Choose numbers $\alpha_j \overset{R}{\leftarrow} \mathbb{Z}_p^*$
Compute $M_{A_j} = u_j^{\alpha_j}$ k parameters M_{A_j}

    η_j Compute k parameters
                 $\eta_j = M_{A_j}^x$
Compute k parameters $\theta_j = \eta_j^{\frac{1}{\alpha_j}}$
$T = 2^{\lceil \log p \rceil}$
$f(g^{T w_j}, \theta_j, w_j) = Y_j'$
$m_j = p_j \oplus Y_j'$

Fig. 3. The steps of $(OT)_k^n$ algorithm

- Step 1: $CT \leftarrow Encrypt(\mathbb{P}, sek)$

  The phone sets the access policy $\mathbb{P}$ for the data, executes CP-ABE algorithm to encrypt sek, and uploads the ciphertext CT to cloud, which $CT = Enc_{ABE}(\mathbb{P}, sek)$ holds. Meanwhile, it sets tag w for the data M_d and uploads (w, M_d) to cloud.

- Step 2: $k - out - of - n$ OT protocol $((OT)_k^n)$

  Hypothesis that the cloud has n ciphertext m_y, where $1 \leq y \leq n$ constructs. Data m_y corresponding to tag w_y.

  1. The cloud randomly chooses numbers $x, f_y \in \mathbb{Z}_p^*$, computes $T = 2^{\lceil \log p \rceil}$ and generates $\xi = g^x$ and $u_y = g^{T f_y}$. Then, it utilizes the VSPH algorithm to calculate $Y_y = H_{f_y x}(g^{2w_y})$ and $p_y = m_y \oplus Y_y$. Finally, the cloud publics $(u_y, p_y, w_y, CT_y)(1 \leq y \leq n)$.

  2. The doctor selects k data according to the tag w_j, where $1 \leq j \leq k$ holds. Then, he randomly chooses number $\alpha_j \overset{R}{\leftarrow} \mathbb{Z}_p^*$, and computes $M_{A_j} = u_j^{\alpha_j}$. At last, he sends k parameters M_{A_j} to the cloud.

  3. The server computes and sends k parameters $\eta_j = M_{A_j}^x$ to the doctor.

  4. The doctor computes k parameters $\theta_j = \eta_j^{\frac{1}{\alpha_j}}$, $T = 2^{\lceil \log p \rceil}$, $f(g^{T w_j}, \theta_j, w_j) = Y_j'$, and $m_j = p_j \oplus Y_j'$ finally.

4.5 Decryption Phase

When the doctors obtain the ciphertext to perform the following steps to decrypt.

The doctor utilizes his private key to decrypt the ciphertext CT_j to obtain the symmetric key sek_j.

$$sek_j = DEC_{ABE}(CT_j, sk_d, p_t)$$

Then, the doctor utilizes the symmetric key sek_j to decrypt m_j to obtaining the data.

5   Security Analysis

In this section, the formal security proofs are presented to illuminate that the proposed $(OT)_k^n$ protocol satisfies reviewer's security and sender's security. Besides, the security analysis are given to prove the data transmission protocol is secure and privacy preserving.

Theorem 1: The proposed $(OT)_k^n$ protocol satisfies reviewer's security when the decisional Diffie-Hellman (DDH) assumption holds.

$$Adv_{\mathcal{A}} \leq n \times \epsilon_{DDH}$$

Proof: The game between the challenger $\mathcal{C}$ and the adversary $\mathcal{A}$ has been described in security model. To prove Theorem 1, we need to prove that $\mathcal{A}'s$ advantage of breaking reviewer's security is a negligible function. We expand and improve the game to reduce the above problem to DDH problem.

Table 2. Computational cost comparison

Entities	Authentication phase	Transmission phase	Decryption phase	$(OT)_k^n$ protocol
Sensors	$4T_p + T_e + T_{h_1} + ENC$	/	/	/
Phones	$4T_p + T_{h_1} + T_{h_2} + DEC$	$ENC - CP - ABE$	/	/
Cloud	/	$[offline](3n+1)T_p + [online]kT_p$	/	$[offline]3(n+1)T_p + [online]kT_p$
Doctors	/	$[offline]kT_p + [online]3kT_p$	$DEC + DEC - CP - ABE$	$[offline]kT_p + [online]3kT_p$

[a]T_x: XOR Operation; T_e: Weil Operation; T_{h_1}: Hash Operation in h_1; T_{h_2}: Hash Operation in h_2; and T_E: Power Operation.

[b]n: The number of data; ENC: The symmetric encryption; DEC: The symmetric decryption.

- Setup: The challenger $\mathcal{C}$ is the solver of DDH problem. $\mathcal{C}$ will obtain a DDH tuple $(\mathbb{G}, g, g^a, g^b, Z)$, where $Z = g^{ab}$ (the probability is $\frac{1}{2}$) or $Z \xleftarrow{R} \mathbb{G}$ (the probability is $\frac{1}{2}$). The Setup phase is the same as that in the security model expect that the challenger guess $\mathcal{A}'s$ target j' and set $u_{j'} = g^a$ $\mathcal{C}$ when he/she sets u_y for data m_y.
- Query I: The adversary $\mathcal{A}$ inputs the choice j. The challenger $\mathcal{C}$ chooses $\alpha_j \xleftarrow{R} \mathbb{Z}_p^*$, computes $M_{A_j} = u_j^{\alpha_j}$ and returns it to $\mathcal{A}$.
- Challenge: The adversary $\mathcal{A}$ outputs his/her targets (j_0, j_1). If $j_0 \neq j' \wedge j_1 \neq j'$, the game aborts. Otherwise, the challenger $\mathcal{C}$ sets $j_b = j'$, $\alpha_{j_b} = b$, $M_{A_b} = Z$ and sends M_{A_b} to $\mathcal{A}$.
- Query II: The adversary $\mathcal{A}$ inputs the choice j. If $j = j_0$ or $j = j_1$, the game aborts. Otherwise, $\mathcal{C}$ chooses $\alpha_j \xleftarrow{R} \mathbb{Z}_p^*$, computes $M_{A_j} = u_j^{\alpha_j}$ and returns it to $\mathcal{A}$.
- Guess: The adversary $\mathcal{A}$ outputs his/her guess b^*. If $b^* = b$, the challenger $\mathcal{C}$ outputs $Z = g^{ab}$. Otherwise, $\mathcal{C}$ outputs $Z \xleftarrow{R} \mathbb{G}$.

Now, we consider $\mathcal{C}'s$ advantage of solving the DDH problem. We assume that $\mathcal{A}'s$ advantage of breaking reviewer's security is ϵ. We denote $p = 1$ and $p = 0$ as the events that the value Z $\mathcal{C}$ achieved is g^{ab} or the random value from $\mathbb{Z}_p^*$. And we denote $p*$ as $\mathcal{C}'s$ guess. Besides, we denote E as the event that the game aborts. We can easily obtain that $\Pr[p = p^*|E] = \frac{1}{2}$, $\Pr[p^* = p|\neg E \wedge p = 0] = \frac{1}{2}$ and $\Pr[p^* = p|\neg E \wedge p = 1] = \frac{1}{2} + \epsilon$.

$$Adv_{\mathcal{C}} = \Pr[p = p^*] - \frac{1}{2}$$

$$= \Pr[p = p^*|E] \times \Pr[E] + \Pr[p = p^*|\neg E] \times \Pr[\neg E] - \frac{1}{2}$$

$$= \frac{1}{2}\Pr[E] + \Pr[p = p^*|\neg E \wedge p = 0] \times \Pr[\neg E] \times \Pr[p = 0]$$

$$+ \Pr[p = p^*|\neg E \wedge p = 1] \times \Pr[\neg E] \times \Pr[p = 1] - \frac{1}{2}$$

$$= \frac{1}{2}(1 - \Pr[\neg E]) + \frac{1}{4} \times \Pr[\neg E] + (\frac{1}{4} + \frac{\epsilon}{2}) \times \Pr[\neg E] - \frac{1}{2}$$

$$= \frac{\epsilon}{2} \times \Pr[\neg E]$$

Since $\Pr[\neg E] = \frac{2}{n}$, where n is the number of data, $Adv_{\mathcal{C}} = \frac{\epsilon}{2} \times \frac{2}{n} = \frac{\epsilon}{n}$. Therefore, $Adv_{\mathcal{A}} = \epsilon = n \times Adv_{\mathcal{C}} = n \times \epsilon_{DDH}$.

Theorem 2: The proposed $(OT)_k^n$ protocol satisfies sender's security when the computational Diffie-Hellman (CDH) assumption holds.

$$Adv_{\mathcal{A}} \leq n \times \epsilon_{CDH} - \frac{n-1}{p}.$$

Proof: The game between the challenger $\mathcal{C}$ and the adversary $\mathcal{A}$ has been described in security model. To prove Theorem 2, we need to prove that $\mathcal{A}'s$ advantage of breaking sender's security is a negligible function. We expand and improve the game to reduce the above problem to CDH problem.

- Setup: The challenger $\mathcal{C}$ is the solver of CDH problem. $\mathcal{C}$ will obtain a CDH tuple $(\mathbb{G}, g, g^a, g^b)$. $\mathcal{C}$ sets $x = a$, $\xi = g^a$ and generates other system parameters. Then $\mathcal{C}$ sends ξ and system parameters to $\mathcal{A}$. When $\mathcal{C}$ sets u_y for data m_y, he/she guesses $\mathcal{A}'s$ target j' and sets $f_{j'} = \frac{b}{T}$, $u_{j'} = g^b$.
- Query I: The adversary $\mathcal{A}$ his/her choice j. The challenger computes $\theta_j = \xi^{Tf_j}$ and sends ξ, $u_j = g^{Tf_j}$, θ_j to the adversary $\mathcal{A}$. Besides, $\mathcal{C}$ adds j into $\hat{Q}$ list.
- Challenge: The adversary $\mathcal{A}$ outputs his/her target j^*. If $j' \neq j^*$ or $j^* \in \hat{Q}$, the game aborts.
- Query II: It is the same as Query I expect that the adversary should not query about j^*.
- Test: The adversary $\mathcal{A}$ outputs his/her result θ_{j^*} and $\mathcal{C}$ takes θ_{j^*} as the solution of CDH problem.

Assume that the $\mathcal{A}'s$ advantage of outputting right θ_{j^*} is ϵ. E is denoted as the event that the game aborts. Therefore, we can get that $Adv_{\mathcal{C}} = \Pr[\mathcal{A} \rightarrow \theta_{j^*}|E] \times \Pr[E] + \Pr[\mathcal{A} \rightarrow \theta_{j^*}|\neg E] \times \Pr[\neg E] = \frac{1}{p}(1 - \Pr[\neg E]) + \epsilon \times \Pr[\neg E]$. Since $\Pr[\neg E] = \frac{1}{n}$, $Adv_{\mathcal{C}} = \frac{n-1}{np} + \frac{\epsilon}{n}$. Thus, $Adv_{\mathcal{A}} = \epsilon = n \times Adv_{\mathcal{C}} - \frac{n-1}{p} = n \times \epsilon_{CDH} - \frac{n-1}{p}$.

Theorem 3: The proposed data transmission protocol is secure and privacy-preserving.

Proof: The proposed $(OT)_k^n$ protocol has been proved to satisfy reviewer's security and sender's security. The CP-ABE proposed by Guo et al. has been proved to be secure under aMSE-DDH assumption in [7]. Besides, the smooth projective hashing adopted in this paper is secure under the Nth residuosity assumption [8]. Thus, the proposed data transmission protocol is secure and privacy-preserving under DDH, CDH, aMSE-DDH and Nth residuosity assumptions.

6   Performance

In this section, we first analyse the proposed scheme and provide a simplified comparison in Table 2. And then, we conduct a comparative in OT algorithm analysis with POT and BP-OT. POT scheme was proposed by Biesmans et al. [2] to ensure the privacy of users and the security of providers in the mobile pay-TV. There are many comments and knowledge proofs that are needed to be generated in POT scheme. Thus, it's time cost is large. And BP-OT was proposed by Chen et al. [4]. Chen et al. utilized bilinear pair, which costs a lot, to put forward a k-out-of-n OT protocol.

6.1   Performance Analysis

Most of computation cost come from the hash operation in h_1, hash operation in h_2, power operation, weil operation and XOR operation, which are described as T_{h_1}, T_{h_2}, T_p, T_e and T_x. Normally, the overhead of the XOR operation T_x is ignored. In Table 2, n presents the number of data, ENC describes the symmetric encryption, DEC is the symmetric decryption.

In mutual authentication phase, a phone verifies signatures from sensors and sensors determined the identity of the phone via proof, which cost computation overhead $8T_p + T_e + 2T_{h_1} + T_{h_2} + ENC + DEC$. The encryption and decryption algorithms are employed to hide private key and assist transmission phase to transfer the data. In the data transmission phase, servers and cloud perform k-out-of-n OT protocol to deliver the required data, which cost $4kT_p + ENC - CP - ABE$ computation overhead. In particular, in k-out-of-n OT protocol, the initial processing of data and the calculation of some parameters by the cloud can be calculated offline, and those calculation overhead is ignored. In addition, at this phase, the phone applies CP-ABE algorithm to re-encrypt the key, but note that the data has been encrypted in the authentication stage. Meantime, both the doctor and server privacy are ensured via this phase. At decryption phase, the doctor decrypts the re-encrypted key to obtain *sek* after passing the access policy. Then, he uses the key *sek* to decrypt the ciphertext, which costs the computation overhead $DEC + DEC - CP - ABE$. This method effectively guarantees the confidentiality of the data. And, group users can also dynamically join and exit.

6.2   Performance Evaluation

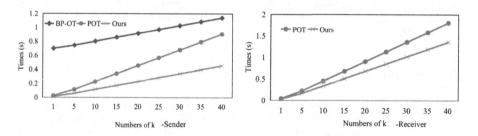

Fig. 4. The comparison of our scheme and other schemes

The C language with PBC library (pbc-0.5.14) and GMP library (GMP-6.1.2) are employed for simulating our proposed $(OT)_k^n$ protocol, BP-OT protocol and POT protocol. All simulations on a desktop with features as follows: 1) CPU: Intel(R) Core(TM) i5-9500 CPU @ 3.00 GHz 3.00 GHz; 2) ROM: 6.0 GB; 3) Storage: 20G; 4) system type: 64-bit. It's worth noting that we perform experiments on a virtual machine. So only four of the CPU's six cores are used.

The computational comparison of three protocols on the sender is provide in Fig. 4-sender. n describes the number of data, which is supposed as 50. k presents the numbers of required data. The X-axis introduced the parameter k. The Y-axis represents the time cost to perform k-out-of-n OT protocol about sender-side. As described in Fig. 4-sender, the least overhead is cost by our protocol. In particular, we only considered k-out-of-n OT protocol in POT protocol, and none of the other technologies used for verification calculate the overhead, such as signatures and zero-knowledge proofs.

The computational comparison of two protocols on the receiver is provide in Fig. 4-receiver. The X-axis and Y-axis have the same meaning with the above. As the computation overhead of BP-OT increases with the value of k, the time will reach 30 s, which does not match the actual situation, so it is not included in the Fig. 4-receiver.

7   Conclusion

In this paper, a data transmission scheme in the healthcare framework is proposed to protect the privacy of entities and ensure the confidentiality of data. Based on the CP-ABE technology, the proposed secure transmission protocol realizes the secure access of authorized users and also protects the security of key *sek*. Meantime, the two-way privacy of servers and doctors is protected through k-out-of-n OT protocol. In addition, the protocol of authentication and transmission phase is lightweight, which reduces a lot of computational overhead and makes our protocol more realistic. After analyzing the security of our scheme, it is proved that our scheme protects data confidentiality, and is also secure.

Acknowledgment. This work is supported by the National Natural Science Foundation of China under Grants No. U1836115, No. 61922045, No. 61672290, No.61877034, the Natural Science Foundation of Jiangsu Province under Grant No. BK20181408, the Peng Cheng Laboratory Project of Guangdong Province PCL2018KP004, the CICAEET fund.

References

1. Ali, F., et al.: An intelligent healthcare monitoring framework using wearable sensors and social networking data. Future Gener. Comput. Syst. **114**, 23–43 (2021)
2. Biesmans, W., Balasch, J., Rial, A., Preneel, B., Verbauwhede, I.: Private mobile pay-TV from priced oblivious transfer. IEEE Trans. Inf. Forensics Secur. **13**(2), 280–291 (2017)
3. Chawla, N.V., Davis, D.A.: Bringing big data to personalized healthcare: a patient-centered framework. J. Gen. Intern. Med. **28**(3), 660–665 (2013). https://doi.org/10.1007/s11606-013-2455-8
4. Chen, Y., Chou, J.S., Hou, X.W.: A novel k-out-of-n oblivious transfer protocols based on bilinear pairings. IACR Cryptology ePrint Archive 2010/27 (2010)
5. Chu, C.-K., Tzeng, W.-G.: Efficient k-out-of-n oblivious transfer schemes with adaptive and non-adaptive queries. In: Vaudenay, S. (ed.) PKC 2005. LNCS, vol. 3386, pp. 172–183. Springer, Heidelberg (2005). https://doi.org/10.1007/978-3-540-30580-4_12
6. Cramer, R., Shoup, V.: Universal hash proofs and a paradigm for adaptive chosen ciphertext secure public-key encryption. In: Knudsen, L.R. (ed.) EUROCRYPT 2002. LNCS, vol. 2332, pp. 45–64. Springer, Heidelberg (2002). https://doi.org/10.1007/3-540-46035-7_4
7. Guo, F., Mu, Y., Susilo, W., Wong, D.S., Varadharajan, V.: CP-ABE with constant-size keys for lightweight devices. IEEE Trans. Inf. Forensics Secur. **9**(5), 763–771 (2014)
8. Halevi, S., Kalai, Y.T.: Smooth projective hashing and two-message oblivious transfer. J. Cryptol. **25**(1), 158–193 (2012). https://doi.org/10.1007/s00145-010-9092-8
9. Huang, C., Liu, D., Ni, J., Lu, R., Shen, X.: Achieving accountable and efficient data sharing in industrial Internet of Things. IEEE Trans. Ind. Inf. **17**(2), 1416–1427 (2020)
10. Kalai, Y.T.: Smooth projective hashing and two-message oblivious transfer. In: Cramer, R. (ed.) EUROCRYPT 2005. LNCS, vol. 3494, pp. 78–95. Springer, Heidelberg (2005). https://doi.org/10.1007/11426639_5
11. Liu, Y.N., Wang, Y.P.: An improved electronic medical record system (IEMRS) using oblivious transfer. J. Chin. Inst. Eng. **42**(1), 48–53 (2019)
12. Lu, R., Lin, X., Shen, X.: SPOC: a secure and privacy-preserving opportunistic computing framework for mobile-healthcare emergency. IEEE Trans. Parallel Distrib. Syst. **24**(3), 614–624 (2012)
13. Omachonu, V.K., Einspruch, N.G.: Innovation in healthcare delivery systems: a conceptual framework. Innov. J. Public Sect. Innov. J. **15**(1), 1–20 (2010)
14. Pramanik, M.I., Lau, R.Y., Demirkan, H., Azad, M.A.K.: Smart health: big data enabled health paradigm within smart cities. Expert Syst. Appl. **87**, 370–383 (2017)
15. Sharma, N., Bhatt, R.: Privacy preservation in WSN for healthcare application. Procedia Comput. Sci. **132**, 1243–1252 (2018)

16. Shen, J., Gui, Z., Chen, X., Zhang, J., Xiang, Y.: Lightweight and certificateless multi-receiver secure data transmission protocol for wireless body area networks. IEEE Trans. Dependable Secure Comput. (2020). https://doi.org/10.1109/TDSC.2020.3025288

17. Sundaravadivel, P., Kougianos, E., Mohanty, S.P., Ganapathiraju, M.K.: Everything you wanted to know about smart health care: evaluating the different technologies and components of the Internet of Things for better health. IEEE Consum. Electron. Mag. **7**(1), 18–28 (2017)

18. Wang, K., Chen, C.M., Tie, Z., Shojafar, M., Kumar, S., Kumari, S.: Forward privacy preservation in IoT enabled healthcare systems. IEEE Trans. Ind. Inform. (2021). https://doi.org/10.1109/TII.2021.3064691

19. Wang, X., Kuang, X., Li, J., Li, J., Chen, X., Liu, Z.: Oblivious transfer for privacy-preserving in VANET's feature matching. IEEE Trans. Intell. Transp. Syst. **22**(7), 4359–4366 (2021)

20. Wendt, C., Frisina, L., Rothgang, H.: Healthcare system types: a conceptual framework for comparison. Soc. Policy Adm. **43**(1), 70–90 (2009)

21. Yang, X., Lu, R., Shao, J., Tang, X., Yang, H.: An efficient and privacy-preserving disease risk prediction scheme for e-healthcare. IEEE Internet Things J. **6**(2), 3284–3297 (2018)

Correction to: Information Security Practice and Experience

Robert Deng⬤, Feng Bao, Guilin Wang, Jian Shen, Mark Ryan, Weizhi Meng, and Ding Wang

Correction to:
R. Deng et al. (Eds.): *Information Security Practice and Experience*, LNCS 13107,
https://doi.org/10.1007/978-3-030-93206-0

The original version of this chapter "Out of Non-linearity: Search Impossible Differentials by the Bitwise Characteristic Matrix" contained the following errors which have been now corrected:

(1) In section 2.2, a missing closing parenthesis has been included.
(2) In section 3.1, a sentence was missing.
(3) In section 3.2, an extra dot has been removed from first display equation.
(4) In appendix A, the first 3 matrices which has been written in {\scriptsize}, due to the changes of the pages, we have changed the {\scriptsize} to {\small} for the first 3 matrices, and the other remain the same.

The original version of this chapter "Automatic Key Recovery of Feistel Ciphers: Application to SIMON and SIMECK" contained the following error which has been now corrected:

In the introduction part, "Crypto 2020" should be "Eurocrypt 2020".

The updated version of these chapters can be found at
https://doi.org/10.1007/978-3-030-93206-0_6
https://doi.org/10.1007/978-3-030-93206-0_10

© Springer Nature Switzerland AG 2022
R. Deng et al. (Eds.): ISPEC 2021, LNCS 13107, p. C1, 2022.
https://doi.org/10.1007/978-3-030-93206-0_24

Author Index

Printed in the United States
by Baker & Taylor Publisher Services